Exercise and Sport Sciences Reviews

VOLUME 1

Exercise and Sport Sciences Reviews

VOLUME 1

EDITED BY

Jack H. Wilmore

Department of Physical Education
University of California, Davis
Davis, California

ACADEMIC PRESS   New York   San Francisco   London   1973

A Subsidiary of Harcourt Brace Jovanovich, Publishers

ACADEMIC PRESS, INC.
111 Fifth Avenue, New York, New York 10003

United Kingdom Edition published by
ACADEMIC PRESS, INC. (LONDON) LTD.
24/28 Oval Road, London NW1

LIBRARY OF CONGRESS CATALOG CARD NUMBER: 72-12187

PRINTED IN THE UNITED STATES OF AMERICA

80 81 82 83   9 8 7 6 5 4 3

Dedication

Although *Exercise and Sport Sciences Reviews* (*ESSR*), by nature of the topics and/or subjects investigated, encompasses the concerns of the scientific community at large, no field of knowledge has a greater central focus in this area than that of Physical Education and the mutual concerns of international coaching and training programs. It is to these fields and their participants—researchers, teachers, coaches, trainers, athletes, and students—that this *ESSR* series is dedicated. Furthermore, on behalf of the scientific community, the Editorial Advisory Board and contributing authors are dedicating Volume 1 of this serial publication to the memory of the eleven colleagues and students of the Sports Sciences who tragically lost their lives during the course of Olympiad **XX**:

David Berger, **28**, weight lifter and law graduate of Columbia University

Ze'ev Friedman, **28**, weight lifter and physical educator at Haifa

Yosef Gottfreund, **40**, wrestling referee

Eliezer Halfin, **24**, wrestler

Joseph Romano, **32**, weight lifter

Amitzur Shapiro, **40**, track and field coach and physical educator at Wingate Institute

Kehat Shorr, **53**, marksmanship coach

Mark Slavin, **18**, wrestler

Andre Spitzer, **27**, fencing coach at the Orde Wingate Institute for Physical Education and Sport

Ya'acov Springer, **52**, weight-lifting referee and high school physical educator at Bat-Yam

Moshe Weinberg, **32**, wrestling coach and physical educator at Wingate Institute

Contents

Biochemical Adaptations to Exercise: Anaerobic Metabolism

Philip D. Gollnick and Lars Hermansen

Biochemical Adaptations to Exercise: Aerobic Metabolism

John O. Holloszy

Adaptations in Strength and Muscular Endurance Resulting from Exercise

David H. Clarke

The Role of Exercise in Weight Control

Lawrence B. Oscai

Physiological Responses of Women to Exercise

Barbara L. Drinkwater

The Quantification of Endurance Training Programs

Michael L. Pollock

Biomechanical and Neuromuscular Aspects of Running

Stanley L. James and Clifford E. Brubaker

Cinematographic Analyses of Human Movement

Anne E. Atwater

Electromyographic Analyses of Basic Movement Patterns

John V. Basmajian

Technological Advances in Sports Medicine and in the Reduction of Sports Injuries

Allan J. Ryan

Physiological Assessment of Maximal Performance

Francis J. Nagle

Cinematographic, Electromyographic, and Electrogoniometric Techniques for Analyzing Human Movements

Marlene Adrian

Sampling Theory and Procedures

Robert W. Schutz

Analysis of Change

Charles O. Dotson

List of Contributors

Numbers in parentheses indicate the pages on which the authors' contributions begin.

MARLENE ADRIAN (339), *Department of Physical Education, Washington State University, Pullman, Washington*

ANNE E. ATWATER (217), *Department of Physical Education for Women, The University of Arizona, Tucson, Arizona*

JOHN V. BASMAJIAN (259), *Regional Rehabilitation Research and Training Center, Emory University, Atlanta, Georgia*

CLIFFORD E. BRUBAKER (189), *Center of Research for Human Performance, School of Health, Physical Education and Recreation, University of Oregon, Eugene, Oregon*

DAVID H. CLARKE (73), *Department of Physical Education, University of Maryland, College Park, Maryland*

CHARLES O. DOTSON (393), *Department of Physical Education, University of Maryland, College Park, Maryland*

BARBARA L. DRINKWATER (125), *Institute of Environmental Stress, University of California at Santa Barbara, Santa Barbara, California*

PHILIP D. GOLLNICK (1), *Department of Physical Education for Men, Washington State University, Pullman, Washington*

LARS HERMANSEN (1), *Institute of Work Physiology, Oslo, Norway*

JOHN O. HOLLOSZY (45), *Department of Preventive Medicine, Washington University School of Medicine, St. Louis, Missouri*

STANLEY L. JAMES (189),* *Center of Research for Human Performance and Department of Athletics, University of Oregon, Eugene, Oregon, and University of Oregon Medical School, Portland, Oregon*

FRANCIS J. NAGLE (313), *Department of Physiology and Physical Education, University of Wisconsin, Madison, Wisconsin*

* Present address: Orthopedic and Fracture Clinic, P. C., 750 East 11th Avenue, Eugene, Oregon 97401.

xi

LAWRENCE B. OSCAI (103), *Department of Physical Education, University of Illinois at Chicago Circle, Chicago, Illinois*

MICHAEL L. POLLOCK (155), *Department of Physical Education, Wake Forest University, and Department of Medicine, Bowman Gray School of Medicine, Winston-Salem, North Carolina*

ALLAN J. RYAN (285), *Department of Physical Education and Rehabilitation Medicine, University of Wisconsin–Madison, Madison, Wisconsin*

ROBERT W. SCHUTZ (365), *School of Physical Education and Recreation, The University of British Columbia, Vancouver, Canada*

Preface

Exercise and Sport Sciences Reviews is a serial publication, the purpose of which is to promote professional and interdisciplinary communication in the sciences concerning biological, behavioral, kinesiological, historical, and philosophical aspects of movement, activity, and performance.

Categorically, the first volume includes reviews on the biological and kinesiological sciences, while it is planned that Volume 2 will encompass review articles in the behavioral, historical, and philosophical fields. Related reviews in the area of methodology and instrumentation will also appear in each volume. This categorical format will be maintained for subsequent volumes, i.e., a replication of general categories will appear in alternate years.

Contributors for all volumes are selected by the Editor-in-Chief and a six-member Editorial Advisory Board. Topics for review are selected on the basis of professional relevance, need, and the extent of information available in the contemporary literature. The Editorial Advisory Board is receptive to suggestions concerning future selections of potential contributors and topics worthy of review.

EDITORIAL ADVISORY BOARD
EXERCISE AND SPORT SCIENCES REVIEWS

Acknowledgments

Exercise and Sport Sciences Reviews was initiated by Perry B. Johnson (University of Toledo), Past Chairman of the Research Council of the American Association for Health, Physical Education, and Recreation (AAHPER) when he appointed an Annual Review Committee during the Fall of 1970. It is fair to say that his foresight provided the important first step. Dorothy Mohr (Sacramento State University) and J. Grove Wolf (University of Wisconsin) succeeded Dr. Johnson as Chairpersons of the AAHPER Research Council, and their continued support and encouragement throughout the project's young history has been most valuable.

The Scholarly Directions Committee (SDC) of AAPHER, consisting of Robert Morford (University of Washington), Waneen Wyrick (University of Texas), and Lawrence Locke (University of New Mexico), funded an initial "Conceptualization Conference" which facilitated the growth and development of this review series. Also, a grant from the College of Education, Temple University, made possible a second conference at an extremely critical point in time.

EDITORIAL ADVISORY BOARD
EXERCISE AND SPORT SCIENCES REVIEWS

Biochemical Adaptations to Exercise: Anaerobic Metabolism

Philip D. Gollnick

DEPARTMENT OF PHYSICAL EDUCATION FOR MEN,
WASHINGTON STATE UNIVERSITY, PULLMAN, WASHINGTON

and

Lars Hermansen

INSTITUTE OF WORK PHYSIOLOGY, OSLO, NORWAY

I. Introduction

The contraction of skeletal muscle is powered by the breakdown of adenosine triphosphate (ATP). For muscular contraction to continue for more than a few seconds the level of ATP in the muscle must continually

1

be restored. Replenishment of ATP can take place via the oxidative (aerobic) or glycolytic (anaerobic) pathways. Oxidative metabolism and the influence of exercise and training on it are reviewed in this volume by Holloszy (p. 45). The purpose of this paper is to consider the importance and regulation of anaerobic metabolism during exercise and any adaptations in this system that result from training.

In this discussion anaerobic metabolism will be considered as any metabolic process by which energy is delivered to the contractile apparatus of skeletal muscle that does not depend upon an immediate consumption of oxygen.

II. Anaerobic Energy Reserves of Muscle

A. Anaerobic Potential of Different Fiber Types

Mammalian skeletal muscle is composed of fibers possessing different contractile and metabolic properties. These properties suggest that each fiber type may play a dominant role in a specific type of muscular work. Most investigators have identified two distinct fiber types in human muscle. These have been called red and white fibers on the basis of oxidative capacity determined from the histochemical estimation of mitochondria or mitochondrial oxidative enzymes (37). They have also been identified as type I or type II on the basis of the myofibrillar ATPase activity (17). Type I fibers have low, and type II high, myosin ATPase activity. Recently Gollnick and associates (51) have adopted the nomenclature of slow twitch (ST) and fast twitch (FT) fibers, since it has been demonstrated in animals that a low and high myosin ATPase activity is associated with fibers that have slow and fast contractile characteristics, respectively (11).

The ST fiber of human skeletal muscle is further characterized as having higher overall oxidative capacity than the FT fibers. However, it is apparent that a spectrum of oxidative capacities exists in both fiber types, with some overlap in the center of the continuum. It is also clear that the oxidative potential of both fiber types can be significantly increased by training (8,51). This latter fact makes fiber classification based solely on oxidative capacity difficult to interpret. The glycolytic capacity of the FT fibers in human muscle, as judged from α-glycerophosphate dehydrogenase activity, is clearly higher than that of the ST fibers. Based on histochemical methods there does not appear to be any major difference in the glycogen reserves of the two fiber types (51,52,54).

In most animal muscle a third fiber type has been identified. This fiber has high myosin ATPase and high oxidative and glycolytic capacity. This has been called a fast-twitch red fiber (11). Barnard et al. (11) have called the other two fiber types in rat and guinea pig muscle fast-twitch white and slow-twitch intermediate. The fast-twitch white fiber has low oxidative and high glycolytic capacity and thus is somewhat similar to the FT fiber of human muscle. The slow-twitch intermediate fiber has low glycolytic capacity and an oxidative capacity that appears to be intermediate, as viewed histochemically, between the fast-twitch white and fast-twitch red fibers. The glycogen content of the slow-twitch intermediate fiber of rats and guinea pigs also is less than that of the other two fiber types (105).

The anaerobic potential of skeletal muscle fibers is also related to the quantity, intracellular localization, and isoenzyme of lactate dehydrogenase (LDH). In rat and guinea pig muscle the fast-twitch white fibers have the highest total LDH activity (55,105). This is predominately the muscle isoenzyme (M-LDH) that is localized in the sarcoplasmic reticulum (7,43,55). Slow-twitch intermediate fibers have the lowest total LDH activity (55,105). This is the heart isoenzyme (H-LDH) and it is found in the mitochondrion (7,53,55,91,105). The total LDH activity of fast-twitch red fibers is intermediate to the other two fibers (55,105). These fibers possess both the M- and H-LDH isoenzymes (55,105). In human skeletal muscle (vastus lateralis) the ST fibers have H-LDH and FT fibers M-LDH (55). There are no fibers in human skeletal muscle that contain both isoenzymes in concentrations comparable to the fast-twitch red fibers in rat or guinea pig skeletal muscle. The kinetics of the LDH isoenzymes are such that the muscle form of the enzyme favors the formation of lactate from pyruvate, whereas the heart type catalyzes the opposite reaction. These properties plus the subcellular localization of the isoenzymes would aid the production of lactate by FT fibers and its oxidation by ST fibers. This could also result in an uptake of lactate by the ST fibers during exercise.

In man the two fiber types are distributed in a mosaic pattern throughout the muscle (37,76). No muscle has yet been identified that is composed of only one fiber type. However, the relative proportion of the two fiber types does vary from individual to individual (37,51). However, in animals such as the rat and guinea pig, some muscles, such as the soleus, or parts of muscles, such as the medial head of the gastrocnemius, do exist that are composed almost entirely of one fiber type (11,36).

Biochemically the ST fiber of human muscle appears suited for prolonged endurance type work, where its oxidative potential can be used to its fullest. Conversely, FT fibers appear suited to high speed intense work of short duration. Recent studies (53), in which the glycogen depletion patterns of the two fiber types were followed, have demonstrated that in prolonged exercise of up to 3 hr duration, requiring about 65% of the max $\dot{V}_{O_2}$ of the subject, the first fibers to become depleted of their glycogen were the ST fibers. There was a progressive depletion of the glycogen in the FT fibers as the work continued. FT fibers were the first to become depleted of their glycogen reserves during high intensity work (*54*). In the first experiment, blood lactate did not exceed an average of 4 mM. In the latter experiment, where six exercise bouts at a work load equivalent to 150% max $\dot{V}_{O_2}$ were performed for 1 min with 10 min rest periods interspersed, the final blood lactate was above 16 mM. These data support the thesis that the two fiber types are recruited somewhat differently in response to different intensities of work.

From the metabolic properties of the two fiber types of human muscle it could be assumed that lactate was formed preferentially in FT fibers. However, very high muscle lactates have been reported with heavy exercise. This suggests that both fiber types are capable of high anaerobic metabolism or that extremely high lactate concentrations exist in the FT fibers. At present it is impossible to localize the lactate within the muscle in order to determine whether or not one or the other fiber type is primarily responsible for its production.

In contrast to human muscle, the fast-twitch red fibers of rats and guinea pigs are the first to become depleted of their glycogen reserves during spontaneous exercise (*35*). During intense muscular contraction produced by electrical stimulation the fast-twitch white fibers are the first to consume their glycogen stores (*34,46,89*). With high intensity running all three fiber types of rat skeletal muscle become depleted of their glycogen reserves (*2*). The rate of depletion of fast-twitch white fibers is dependent upon running speed and is closely related to the level of lactate in the blood after the exercise (*2*).

B. ATP, CP, and Glycogen. Quantities and Potential for Use

Energy can be supplied to the contractile elements of skeletal muscle anaerobically from ATP and creatinephosphate (CP) and from the degradation of glycogen to lactate. The average concentrations of ATP and CP in human skeletal muscle are about 4 and 16 mmole kg^{-1} wet muscle, respectively (*74,81,82,85*). These compounds are collectively referred to as the phosphagens. They are reduced during exercise and may serve as anaerobic energy sources. The magnitude of their reductions has been the subject of several investigations.

The first studies on the effects of exercise on phosphagen depletion in human muscle were probably those of Hultman and co-workers (*74*). They observed a linear relationship between work intensity and the reduction in muscular CP. ATP declined with moderate work and little further change was noted thereafter.

Karlsson, Diamant, and Saltin (81) subsequently followed the ATP and CP levels in muscle over work intensities ranging from 60 to 100% of the aerobic power of trained and untrained subjects. In both groups they observed a small decline in ATP and a nearly linear decline in CP. Final CP concentration in the muscle was only about 25% that of the resting value. There was no difference in the CP depletion pattern of the trained as compared to the untrained subjects.

Piper et al. (107) observed depletion patterns for ATP and CP in the electrically stimulated gastrocnemius muscle of anesthetized dogs similar to those described above.

Knuttgen and Saltin (85) also followed the phosphagen concentrations in the muscles of man during 4 min bouts of exercise that required $\dot{V}_{O_2}$'s ranging from 19 to 95% of the subjects' maximal aerobic power. They did not find the linear relationship between work intensity and CP depletion as described above. At work intensities below 60% max $\dot{V}_{O_2}$ they reported only small declines in ATP and CP. A small additional decline in ATP occurred at work loads representing 75 to 95% max $\dot{V}_{O_2}$. On the other hand, CP was approximately 80% depleted after working at 75% of aerobic power, with only a slight additional decline occurring at the highest work load.

Karlsson and Saltin (82) also investigated the depletion of muscular ATP and CP during work that could be sustained 2–3 min, 5–7 min, or 15–20 min. During the lighter loads the work was interrupted after 2 min, and after 6 min, respectively, to obtain muscle samples at times corresponding to the points of exhaustion in the heavier loads. After 2 min of exercise the reduction in ATP was similar for all work loads. No further decline was noted when the work was continued. The same pattern existed for CP with the exception that a slightly lower concentration remained in the muscle after the heaviest work load. They found that the oxygen deficit was almost identical for all three work loads and was closely related to the phosphagen depletion.

The maximum ATP depletion observed in skeletal muscle following exercise is about 40% that of the resting level. This suggests that not all the ATP contained in muscle is available for utilization by the contractile apparatus. In contrast, the CP stores can be nearly depleted by exercise. This suggests that the major role for this compound is to reload the ATP for muscular contraction.

The rate and magnitude of the degradation of muscle glycogen for anaerobic metabolism are governed by the intensity of the exercise. Only that portion of the glycogen which is degraded to lactate as a result of a lack of adequate energy production for the aerobic metabolism can be considered as an anaerobic energy source. During very heavy exercise glycogen depletion is rapid and muscle lactate concentrations may exceed 20 mM (see below). Under these conditions the degradation of glycogen represents a significant source of energy for the muscle. Exercise of this intensity produces exhaustion long before the glycogen stores of the muscle are depleted. From these experiments it must be concluded that factors other than the glycogen reserves of the muscle limit work capacity at these intensities and duration. These are discussed below. It is also obvious that any augmentation of the glycogen stores of the muscle will have little or no effect on the ability to sustain this type of exercise.

III. Anaerobic Energy Release

A. BIOCHEMICAL PROCESS

The initial anaerobic event at the onset of exercise is the splitting of ATP during muscular contraction. Although suspected for many years, this was first demonstrated in 1962 by Davies and co-workers (19,75). These experiments were technically difficult because of the rapid resynthesis of ATP by the transfer of the phosphate of CP to ADP. This was overcome by poisoning frog muscle with 1-fluoro-2,4-dinitrobenzene to inhibit the enzyme creatine phosphoryltransferase. When these muscles were stimulated in an anaerobic environment the ATP content of muscle declined, with ADP and AMP increasing proportionally. The reduction in ATP was related to the number of contractions. Subsequent studies with human (74,81,82,85), insect (113), dog (107), and rat (72) muscle also demonstrated a reduction in ATP during muscular contraction. In these latter studies it has not been possible to relate the reduction in ATP to the time or intensity of the work since the ATP is rapidly replenished by the metabolic systems of the muscle.

ATP can be replenished anaerobically by the transfer of the phosphate group from CP to ADP as described above. This probably is the second anaerobic mechanism during exercise. This reaction occurs so rapidly that it made the demonstration of a breakdown in ATP difficult. In fact, it was believed by several investigators that the splitting of CP provided the energy for contraction (see Ref. 20, for example).

A second method for restoring the ATP in muscle is the condensation of 2 ADPs to 1 ATP and 1 AMP. This is catalyzed by the enzyme myokinase and is often referred to simply as the myokinase reaction. Davies and co-workers found some evidence for this reaction in stimulated frog muscle that was poisoned with 1-fluoro-2,4-dinitrobenzene (19,75). How significant this reaction is in exercising man or animals is unknown.

The anaerobic breakdown of glycogen or glucose to lactate can also supply energy to the contracting muscle. This mechanism is perhaps more important quantitatively than the phosphagen (ATP + CP) stores. Glycolysis occurs in the sarcoplasm of the muscle. This pathway is described in most elementary textbooks of biochemistry. Although the enzymes are often referred to as "soluble enzymes," they are bound to structures in the cell and should not be thought of as floating around in the sarcoplasm in an unorganized manner (*3,118*).

The anaerobic degradation of 1 mole of glucose or glycogen (180 gm) to lactate results in the net gain of 2 and 3 moles of ATP, respectively. This does represent a significant amount of energy, enabling the muscle to perform work beyond the aerobic capacity of the body. In this context the production of lactate should not be viewed as a detrimental consequence of exercise but rather as a useful mechanism enabling the body to perform exceptionally fast or heavy work.

B. INTRACELLULAR REGULATION OF GLYCOGENOLYSIS AND GLYCOLYSIS

The lactate level in skeletal muscle is low at rest and increases dramatically during the first seconds of heavy exercise (see, e.g., Fig. 3). This demonstrates that the flow of substrate through the glycolytic pathway is tightly coupled to the energy needs of the muscle. Glycolysis may be regulated by several enzymes. However, it is most frequently assumed that the activation of the enzymes phosphorylase and phosphofructokinase controls the rate of glycolysis.

Since glycolysis is most dependent upon the glycogen stores of the muscle, its phosphorolysis into glucose 1-phosphate (G 1-P) units is the first regulatory step. This reaction is catalyzed by the enzyme phosphorylase, which has been shown to be bound to glycogen particles isolated from skeletal muscle (*96*). Phosphorylase exists in a form that is inactive except in the presence of 5'-AMP, phosphorylase *b*, and a form active in the absence of 5'-AMP, phosphorylase *a*. Phosphorylase *b* can be converted to phosphorylase *a* by the mechanisms presented in Fig. 1. One mode of activation is via the adrenergic hormones. These activate the adenyl cyclase system and increase the level of 3',5'-cyclic AMP in the tissue. This results in the conversion of an inactive phosphorylase *b* kinase to the active form. The activation of phosphorylase involves the dimerization of two phosphorylase *b* units into a single phosphorylase *a* moiety and requires the consumption of two ATPs. However, it has been demonstrated that the conversion of phosphorylase *b* to phosphorylase *a* occurs in skeletal muscle in response to electrical stimulation without an increase in 3',5'-cyclic AMP or the conversion of phosphorylase *b* kinase from the inactive to the active form (*33,122*). This apparently is the re-

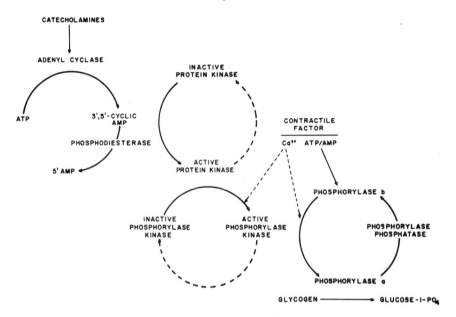

Fig. 1. Diagram for the activation of glycogenolysis via the enzyme phosphorylase. A hormonal control by the catecholamines and a contraction-coupled control via Ca^{2+} is shown.

sult of the affinity of the inactive phosphorylase *b* kinase for phosphorylase *b* being greatly increased in response to elevations in calcium ion concentration (*18*). The concentrations of calcium producing this effect are of the magnitude released from the sarcoplasmic reticulum during muscular contraction (*18*). This second method for activating phosphorylase is referred to as a contractile factor. It is apparent that such a system would be tightly coupled to the contractile process and thus to the metabolic needs of the muscle. Following termination of the muscular activity, phosphorylase *a* is cleaved back to two units of phosphorylase *b* by the enzyme phosphorylase phosphatase. This process has been studied in frog muscle. A sharp decline in phosphorylase occurs, with resting values reached in about 1 min (*28*).

As stated above, phosphorylase *b* is active in the presence of high AMP concentrations. There are also indications that the level of AMP in muscle may increase during exercise. The role of the phosphorylase *b* activity in controlling glycogenolysis is not clear. The rapid conversion of phosphorylase *b* to the *a* form at the onset of muscular contraction would seem to preclude an important role for phosphorylase *b*. A strain of mice does exist in which the skeletal muscle contains no phosphorylase *b* kinase. Danforth and Lyon [(*30*); Danforth and Helmreich (*29*)] have compared the glycogenolytic response in the muscle of these and normal mice to electrical stimulation. During 6 sec of tetanic stimulation, 70% of the total phosphorylase appeared in the a form in normal mice, whereas all remained in the b form in the kinase-deficient mice. Glycogen was broken down rapidly and lactate was formed in the muscle of both groups of mice. However, the rate of increase and the maximal level attained was twice as great in the normal as compared to the kinase-deficient mice. Furthermore, Helmreich and Cori (61) have shown from measurements *in vivo* that the change in the ATP:AMP ratio during muscular contraction can account for only about a twofold increase in phosphorylase activity, whereas a 60-fold increase was actually observed. These data suggest that the activation of phosphorylase b resulting from increases in AMP concentration is of minor importance in regulating glycogenolysis at the onset of exercise.

There have been suggestions that phosphorylase b is important in initiating glycolysis during anoxia (99,100,104). However, Mayer and co-workers (95) have demonstrated a nearly complete conversion of phosphorylase b to phosphorylase a in the anoxic rat heart. This occurred in the beta-blocked and catecholamine-depleted heart as well as in the normal heart. This even casts doubt on the role of phosphorylase b in anoxia.

At the present time all the information concerning the regulation of phosphorylase activation during muscular work has been derived from experiments with electrical stimulation of animal muscles. Direct experimentation with voluntary activity of differing intensities and durations is needed. These experiments could produce data concerning the relative importance of the hormonal activation of phosphorylase as compared to the contractile factor.

The second major regulatory enzyme in glycolysis appears to be phosphofructokinase (PFK). This enzyme is present in the lowest concentration and thus may be a key regulator in the flow of substrate to subsequent steps. The increased concentration of the hexose monophosphates in human muscle during work as compared to that of fructose 1,6-diphosphate is also consistent with PFK exerting a major regulatory role in glycolysis. In addition, it is known that PFK exists both in an active and inactive form and that some of the changes that occur from rest to activity could influence these activity states.

Studies have revealed that PFK is allosterically inhibited by ATP, CP, and citrate. Conversely, the inhibited enzyme can be activated by 5'-AMP, 3',5'-cyclic AMP, and inorganic phosphate (P_i). The exact method by which PFK is regulated in mammalian muscle is unknown. The importance of 3',5'-cyclic AMP has been extensively investigated (92) but as mentioned above, glycolysis has been shown to be activated in skeletal muscle under conditions where there is no change in its concentration. Furthermore, when PFK is prepared from or assayed in freshly isolated tissue it is always in the fully activated form. This may, however, be the result of some degree of anoxia activating the enzyme during the preparation.

Some of the changes that occur during exercise could also activate the enzyme. For example, it is known that the levels of ATP and CP decrease, whereas glucose 6-phosphate (G 6-P), fructose 6-phosphate, and, perhaps, AMP, ADP, and P_i increase. The hexose monophosphates are known to activate PFK, as do increases in ADP and AMP. The decline in ATP in conjunction with a rise in the other adenyl nucleotides may exert a key role in the regulation of PFK activity. Atkinson (*6,117*) has referred to the energy balance made up of ATP, ADP, and AMP as the adenylate charge of the cell and related it to enzyme regulation and to the PFK system. He has defined the energy charge of the cell by the following equation:

$$\text{Energy charge} = \frac{(\text{ATP}) + \frac{1}{2}(\text{ADP})}{(\text{ATP}) + (\text{ADP}) + (\text{AMP})}.$$

When only ATP is present the charge is 1.0, and when only AMP is present the charge is 0. Atkinson has shown that a small decline in the adenylate charge (from 1.0 to 0.9) results in an insignificant change in ATP but a large change in AMP. This could be as much as 100 μM of AMP if the total adenylate pool is 4 mM. Such a change produces a large increase in the activity of PFK (*117*). These changes in AMP and adenylate charge were also modified by citrate.

Whether or not regulation of PFK is via the adenylate energy charge remains unanswered. This has been discussed in a recent paper by Purich and Fromm (*108*). They have concluded that although the adenylate energy charge, as conceived by Atkinson, may exert a regulatory role in controlling metabolic rate and enzyme activities, other factors in the cell may also contribute. The complexity of the intact cells makes these studies extremely difficult and *in vitro* results may not reflect *in vivo* conditions.

C. HORMONAL VERSUS CONTRACTILE FACTOR IN THE REGULATION OF GLYCOLYSIS

Several experiments have been reported in which the importance of the adrenergic system in controlling glycogenolysis and glycolysis was evaluated. Gollnick and co-workers (*48*) found no difference in the glycogen depletion in liver and skeletal muscle of adrenodemedullectomized, beta-blocked rats as compared to normal animals. In additional studies

(*116*), it was also shown that destruction of the sympathetic nerve endings by the injection of 6-hydroxydopamine and adrenodemedullectomy did not reduce the magnitude of the exercise-induced reduction of glycogen in the liver and skeletal muscle of rats. Harris, Bergström, and Hultman (*59*) have also studied the effect of beta blockade on the glycolytic response of human muscle to exercise. They found no difference in the magnitude of the glycogen, CP, or ATP reduction or the increase in lactate or pyruvate after beta blockade. These experiments support the concept that the hormonal regulation of glycogenolysis and glycolysis plays a minor role in the exercising man or animal. In contrast to these studies, Cronin reported a sharp depression in blood lactate of exercising dogs after beta blockade (*27*), and in exercising dogs, Barnard and Foss (*12*) found that beta blockade reduced the blood lactate level by about 35%.

D. SUMMARY

Both phosphorylase and phosphofructokinase are regulatory enzymes in glycolysis. However, both appear to be activated synchronously and proportionately during muscular contraction (*30*). On this basis Danforth and Lyon (*30*) concluded that the rate of glycogen degradation is limited by the phosphorylase reaction.

IV. Anaerobic Processes and Muscular Exercise

A. ANAEROBIC PROCESSES OPERATING AT THE ONSET OF EXERCISE

Several methods exist for supplying energy to the contractile apparatus without an immediate consumption of oxygen. One question that arises is how these anaerobic mechanisms are interrelated. Margaria *et al.* (*93*) have suggested that the principle energy source at the onset of heavy exercise comes from splitting of the phosphagen stores. In this hypothesis, the activation of the anaerobic breakdown of glycogen and the production of lactate would be delayed until a substantial depletion of the phosphagen had occurred. These conclusions were based upon experiments in which blood lactate was measured after short (5–30 sec) bouts of treadmill running.

Saltin and co-workers (*115*) have conducted experiments in which biopsy samples of the vastus lateralis muscle were taken after 10, 20, 60, and 180 sec of bicycle work, representing from 105 to 110% of the subjects aerobic power. Oxygen consumption was measured for each work bout. Blood samples were taken from the femoral vein and brachial artery. It is known that a considerable lag in the increase in oxygen consumption exists in the early stages of exercise. This is shown in Fig. 2, for one subject. Thus, a considerable oxygen deficit occurs

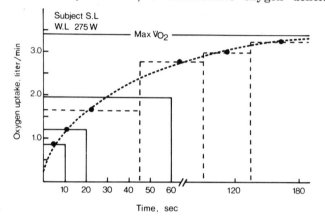

Fig. 2. The increase in oxygen uptake as a function of time during heavy exercise (*115*).

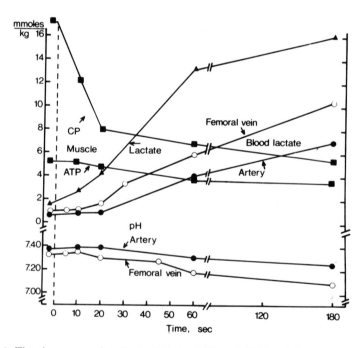

Fig. 3. The time course for the depletion of CP and ATP and the appearance of lactate in the muscle (▲), arterial (●), and femoral venous (○) blood during heavy exercise. Blood pH is also given (*115*).

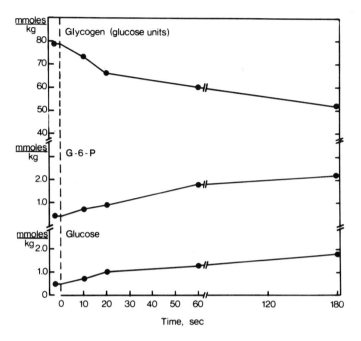

Fig. 4. Reduction in muscle glycogen and the increases in glucose 6-phosphate (G 6-P) and glucose in muscle during exercise (*115*).

early in the exercise. As shown in Fig. 3, the CP content of the muscle was reduced by about 5 mM after 10 sec of work. There was little or no change in ATP. However, the lactate level in the muscle had increased. The production of lactate was accompanied by a reduction in glycogen (Fig. 4) and a rise in the glucose 6-phosphate and free glucose in the muscle. After 20 sec of work these changes were even more apparent.

From the results of Saltin *et al.* (*115*) it appears that glycolysis is initiated in the muscle at the onset of heavy exercise. These data, along with the finding of an almost complete activation of the phosphorylase system in about 3 sec during electrical stimulation, demonstrate that the initiation of glycolysis occurs early in the transition from rest to heavy exercise.

B. LACTATE PRODUCTION DURING EXERCISE

It has been known for many years that lactate is produced during vigorous muscle contractions, both in isolated muscle preparations (*42,69,97*) and in the intact animal or human organism (*10,63,69,70*).

These facts are based on both indirect evidence (i.e., from measurements of the blood lactate concentration) and on direct evidence from measurements of the lactate concentration in the muscle tissue itself. One crucial question that arises is to what extent the concentration of lactate measured in the blood is representative of the lactate concentration in the muscles and the rest of the body.

Lactate is known to be a small and easily diffusible molecule. Furthermore, it is assumed mainly from animal studies that lactate diffuses rapidly from the cells where it is produced to all water compartments of the body. For instance, it was shown by Evans (*42*) that within 30 sec after a short tetanic contraction, the concentration of lactate in the blood was approximately the same as that observed in the muscle. Furthermore, recent studies by Diamant and co-workers (*32*) indicate that there is a rapid distribution of lactate also in the intact human organism. However, in these studies it was shown that the lactate concentration in the skeletal muscle was much higher than in the blood immediately after maximal exercise of about 3 min duration. However, shortly after (i.e., approximately 7 min) the cessation of work, at the time when the peak blood lactate value was reached, the muscle and the blood lactate concentrations were approximately the same. These results indicate that the transportation of lactate from the muscle cells where it is produced to the blood and other tissues is a fairly rapid process.

On the other hand, it should be emphasized that an important time factor is involved, since the equilibrium between the muscle and the blood may take as much as 5–10 min to be reached. Furthermore, measurements of the lactate concentration in the cerebrospinal fluid in human subjects before and after maximal exercise to exhaustion revealed that the lactate is not evenly distributed in all water compartments (*64*). Although the blood lactate concentration increased from 1.2 mM at rest to 14.6 mM 5 min after the maximal work, no change in the lactate concentration in the cerebrospinal fluid was observed. Although these results indicate that the lactate is not evenly distributed, it should be emphasized that the cerebrospinal fluid space (i.e., approximately 150 ml) represents only a small fraction of the total body water.

These results indicate that there is a blood–cerebrospinal fluid barrier for lactate in human subjects. These results are also in agreement with earlier observations of Harris *et al.* (*58*), showing that the concentration of lactate in arterial and venous blood in the brain was the same, indicating a blood–brain barrier.

It can be concluded that the blood lactate concentration may give valuable information not only about the changes taking place in the blood, but about the changes taking place in the muscles and the rest of the body. There are, on the other hand, important exceptions to this general view that should not be overlooked. The blood lactate concentration should, rather, be regarded as an indication of the extent to which the anaerobic processes are activated.

The blood lactate concentration at rest and during exercise is dependent upon the rate of lactate production, the rate of lactate diffusion from the cells to the blood, and of the rate of lactate removal. There are several factors which influence the rate of lactate production as well as the lactate removal. The following factors may be mentioned as being of importance.

During continuous exercise on the bicycle or on the treadmill the blood lactate concentration may or may not increase depending upon the intensity of the word load (Fig. 5). During light to moderately heavy work (i.e., up to approximately 50% of the individual's maximal oxygen uptake) the blood lactate concentration remains almost unchanged during the exercise period, or it may even decrease slightly. During moderately heavy to heavy work loads (i.e., approximately 50 to 85% of maximal oxygen uptake) the blood lactate concentration usually increases fairly rapidly during the first few minutes (5–10 min). If the work load is continued for more than 10 min, the blood lactate may either level off or decrease toward resting values. However, it should be emphasized that a constant elevated value may be maintained for work periods of 30 min or more. During very heavy exercise (i.e., 90% or more of the individual's maximal oxygen uptake) there is a continuous increase in the blood lactate concentration until the subjective feeling of exhaustion or fatigue is incompatible with continuation of the work. Thus, the blood lactate concentration during exercise in relation to time may either be unchanged, show a temporary increase and thereafter a decline, or it may show a continuous increase, depending upon the work load performed (Fig. 5).

In relation to the work load (Fig. 6), blood lactate concentration remains almost unchanged up to a work load representing approximately 50 to 60% of the individual's maximal oxygen uptake. From then on, there is a steep increase in the blood lactate concentration with an increasing work load. Thus, a work load demanding 50 to 60% of the individual's maximal oxygen uptake represents a critical level beyond which the lactate production is markedly enhanced.

It is well known that the blood lactate concentration is lower in well-trained than in untrained subjects exercising at the same absolute work load. This is commonly explained by the higher maximal oxygen uptake in well-trained subjects. However, as shown in Fig. 6, the blood lactate concentration is lower in the well-trained than in the untrained

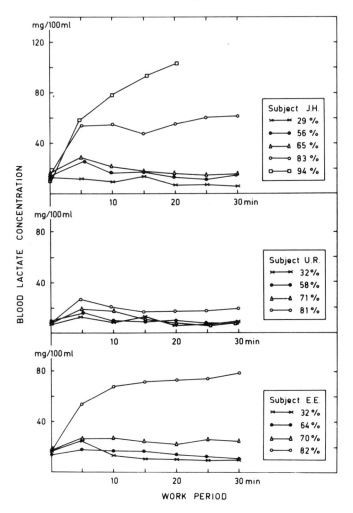

Fig. 5. Individual values for the blood lactate concentration during continuous treadmill running at different speeds for 30 min (*68*).

subjects, even when the work load is expressed in relation to the individual's maximal oxygen uptake. Studies by Ekblom (*39*) have shown that the blood lactate concentration during exercise at a constant work load decreased in the same subject during long-term physical training. This was also the case even when the work loads were expressed as percent of the individual's maximal oxygen uptake. Consequently, it can be concluded that physical training elicits changes not only in the capacity to transport oxygen to the muscles, but also changes in the muscle itself.

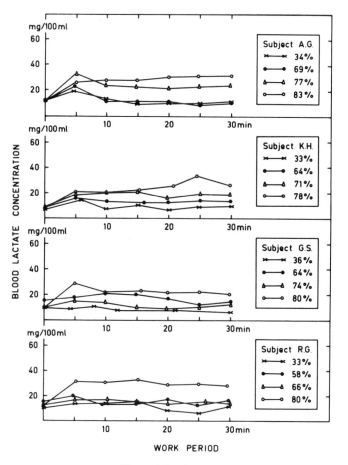

Fig. 5 (Continued).

The oxygen tension in the inspired air is another factor which influences the blood lactate concentration. Figure 7 gives the results of a study in which the blood lactate concentration was measured in one subject during bicycle exercise at sea level and at two simulated altitudes (i.e., 2300 and 4000 m above sea level) in a low pressure chamber (*66*).

It can be seen that the same maximal concentrations of lactate were achieved regardless of altitude. Except for the lowest work loads (i.e., demanding an oxygen uptake of approximately 1 liter/min) the blood lactate concentration increases during submaximal exercise with decreasing oxygen tension in the inspired air (i.e., increasing altitude). However, when blood lactate concentration was related to the relative work load, all values from the different altitudes fell on the same line (Fig. 7,

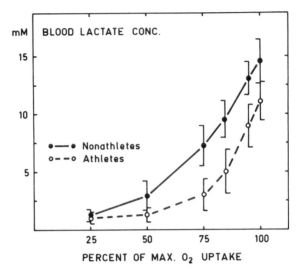

Fig. 6. Average values (and SD) for the blood lactate concentration in relation to relative work (i.e., percentage of the individual's maximal oxygen uptake) during bicycle exercise in six nonathletes and eight athletes, with an average maximal oxygen uptake of 44.0 and 66.8 ml/kg × min, respectively (*64*).

right panel). Thus, if the oxygen tension in the inspired air is decreased, the rate of lactate production during submaximal exercise is increased to the same extent that the maximal oxygen uptake is reduced. It should, however, be remembered that the above results are obtained after acute exposure to each altitude.

Studies by Williams and co-workers (*124*) have shown that the environmental temperature is a factor which influences the rate of lactate production during submaximal exercise. The increase in blood lactate concentration in relation to work load occurred at a significantly lower work intensity during exercise in a warm (i.e., 36°C) than in a comfortable (i.e., 20°C) condition.

Asmussen and Nielsen (*4*) and others (*120,121*) have shown that the blood lactate concentration is higher during exercise with small muscle groups (i.e., arm exercise) than during work with large muscle groups (i.e., leg exercise) at the same oxygen uptake. Furthermore, it was shown by Hermansen and Saltin (*67*) that the blood lactate concentration is lower during submaximal treadmill exercise than during bicycle exercise at the same metabolic rate. Thus, both the amount of the total muscle mass activated in relation to the oxygen uptake, and the type of work are factors that influence the rate of lactate production.

Although it has been known for a long time that the rate of lactate production is increased as a result of muscular work, and that this pro-

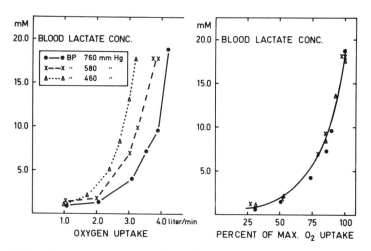

Fig. 7. Blood lactate concentration in relation to absolute (left panel) and relative (right panel) work load during bicycle exercise at sea level (BP 760 mm Hg) and at acute exposure to altitude, i.e., at 2300 m (BP 580 mm Hg) and at 4000 m (BP 462 mm Hg) in a low pressure chamber. Only one subject participated in the study (*66*).

duction is affected by several factors, the significance of the lactate production during submaximal work is still a subject of dispute. According to Margaria and co-workers (*94,114*) no lactate is produced during any submaximal work load once a steady state of oxygen uptake is reached. The increase in blood lactate concentration observed in most studies is, according to these authors, limited to the first phase of the exercise period during which the oxygen debt is contracted. The lactate is produced, therefore, to provide the necessary regeneration of ATP until the aerobic processes can take over. On the other hand, several studies (*82,101*) have shown that the lactate concentration, both in the muscles and in the blood, increases with time during submaximal work load which approaches the maximal level (i.e., 90% or more of the maximal oxygen uptake). Thus, if these observations are correct, it is more proper to regard the lactate production as part of the metabolic processes (aerobic and anaerobic) that regenerate ATP from ADP, not only at the onset of work, but also during the whole exercise period.

However, it is not possible on the basis of these results alone to explain why lactate is produced during submaximal exercise, and there are still several other questions regarding lactate production to be answered. For instance, in what ways are the rate of lactate production increased with decreasing oxygen tension in the inspired air? Why is the lactate production higher when using small muscle groups than during exercise with larger muscle groups? Why is the lactate production higher, at the same oxygen uptake, during bicycle exercise than during treadmill running, although large muscle groups are engaged in both types of exercise? The complete answers to all these questions are still not known. The following results and suggestions may be mentioned as being of importance. The most commonly offered explanation for the lactate production during submaximal and maximal exercise is the lack of adequate oxygen supply to the working muscle cells (*5,10,88*). Results from the studies of Whalen and Nair (*123*) and Bolme and Novotny (*16*) indicate that hypoxia may occur even in resting skeletal muscle.

On the other hand, as shown by Carlson and Pernow (*21*) and by Keul *et al.* (*84*), lactate is produced regardless of a relatively high oxygen content and oxygen tension in the femoral venous blood even during maximal exercise. In the studies of Keul *et al.* (*84*) an oxygen tension of 21.7 mm Hg was observed during maximal exercise. This oxygen tension is higher than the "critical oxygen tension" for the oxidative phosphorylation in the mitochondria (*119*). Thus, according to these authors (*84*), insufficient oxygen supply does not seem acceptable as the cause of lactate production during exercise. These authors suggest that there is an imbalance between the glycolytic and the oxidative capacity of the cell.

Recent studies by Kaijser (*79*) showed that elevated oxygen tension in the arterial blood reduced the lactate production only to a minor extent. The author concluded that the links in the oxygen transport system must be saturated with oxygen, and the main limiting factor in the rate of oxygen utilization would therefore be found at the mitochondrial level.

These results seem to indicate that lactate is produced in spite of a fairly high oxygen tension in the venous blood; thus great care should be taken when making assumptions concerning changes in the cells from measurement of the changes occurring in the blood.

As indicated earlier, mammalian skeletal muscle is composed of different types of fibers, each possessing different contractile and metabolic properties. Furthermore, it is known that the motor neurons in the anterior horn could be divided into two main groups, the large motor neurons (α-cells) and the small motor neurons (γ-cells). The α-cells innervate the extrafusal muscle cells (i.e., the slow and fast twitch muscle cells). Furthermore, the large motor neurons (α-cells) are usually divided into two subgroups, the larger (α_1-cells) and the smaller ones (α_2-cells), although some overlapping seems to exist. Based on evidence from animal studies (*62*) it is reasonable to assume that the slow twitch muscle fibers are innervated by the α_2-motor neurons, and the fast twitch muscle cells are innervated by the α_1-motor neurons. Due to the fact that small motor neurons have a lower threshold for excitation, slow twitch muscle fibers are activated during exercise at low intensities, whereas the contribution of α_1-motor neurons and fast twitch fibers increases with increasing work load. Furthermore, it is reasonable to assume that some motor units are working at a maximal or nearly maximal level, while others are working at a submaximal level. Recent studies by Hoes et al. (71) suggest that even during maximal work (i.e., leading to exhaustion during 4–6 min), not all the motor units are activated. These results and suggestions are of possible importance when trying to explain lactate production, even during submaximal work.

The enzyme lactic dehydrogenase (LDH) catalyzes the reaction as presented in the following equation:

$$\text{Pyruvate} + \text{NADH}^+ + \text{H}^+ \overset{\text{LDH}}{\rightleftharpoons} \text{lactate} + \text{NAD}^+.$$

In the presence of pyruvate and $\text{NADH}^+ + \text{H}^+$, the equilibrium of this reaction strongly favors the lactate production. During resting conditions the concentration of pyruvate in the muscle and in the blood is very low (80). Therefore, if the concentration of pyruvate were increased to very high levels during exercise, this of course could have explained the increased lactate production. However, recent studies (80) have shown that the pyruvate concentration in the muscles increases from 0.06 to 0.14 mM kg^{-1} wet muscle. This twofold increase in the muscle pyruvate concentration, therefore, cannot explain more than a small fraction of the lactate production observed even during submaximal exercise. It was shown by Karlsson (80) that the enzymatic activity of LDH in skeletal muscle of man exceeded the highest observed rate of lactate production by a factor of three to five. In the same studies (80) it was also shown that the LDH activity increased during prolonged exercise. On the other hand, there is evidence (49) which suggests that the LDH activity is not changed during shorter work periods (i.e., less than 30 min).

From these results it follows that, if the pyruvate concentration and the LDH activity are changed only to a minor extent, the regulation of the lactate production is most probably connected to changes in the $\text{NADH}^+ + \text{H}^+/\text{NAD}^+$ relationship. The more work there is to be done, the larger the amount of ATP that is used. When the amount of ATP which can be regenerated by oxidative phosphorylation is less than the amount of ATP which is used during the muscle contractions, intracellular pO_2 decreases and the ratios ADP/ATP and AMP/ATP are increased.

Furthermore, changes in the cytoplasmic adenine nucleotide system are, according to Krebs and Veech (88), linked to the mitochondrial

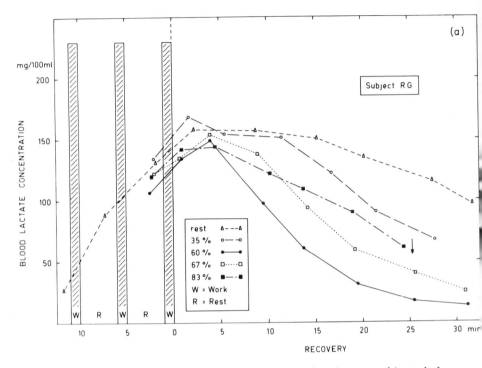

Fig. 8. Blood lactate concentration in relation to time for two subjects, before, during, and after three maximal exercise bouts to exhaustion. The recovery period consisted of rest (i.e., sitting on a chair), or walking or running on the treadmill at different speeds. Part (a) is subject RG and part (b) subject JH.

NAD and NADP couples, which, in turn, are linked to the cytoplasmic NAD and NADP couples. Insufficient oxygen supply therefore tends to increase the mitochondrial and cytoplasmic concentration of $NADH^+ + H^+$. In order to continue regenerating ATP, pyruvate must be converted to lactate. Thus, lactate production is probably caused by the increased cytoplasmic concentration of $NADH^+ + H^+$. The regulation of the flow of substrates in the glycolytic pathway has been discussed earlier.

Finally, it should be emphasized that these metabolic changes which occur in the muscle as a whole cannot be regarded as a single uniform process, but rather as a sum of metabolic changes going on in individual motor units (i.e., muscle cells).

C. Lactate Removal During Exercise

Jervell (*77*) in 1928 was probably one of the first to discover that the blood lactate concentration could be made to fall at a faster rate, com-

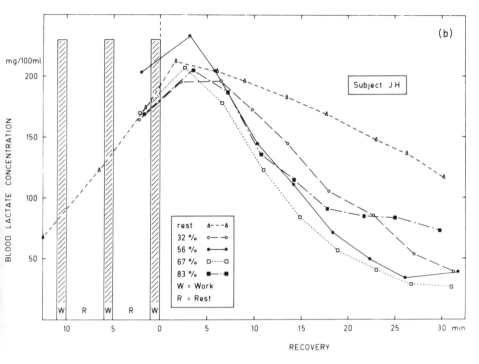

Fig. 8(b)

pared with resting conditions, if moderate exercise was performed in the recovery period. This observation was verified by Bang (*10*) in 1936, and later by several other investigators (*31,47,78,102,111,112*).

However, little attention has been paid to the relationship between the rate of lactate removal and the severity of the work load performed in the recovery period. This problem was studied in a recent investigation of Hermansen and Stensvold (*68*). As shown in Fig. 8, the blood lactate concentration was increased to very high levels by performing an intermittent maximal exercise. The maximal intermittent exercise consisted of three maximal work bouts, each lasting for approximately 60 sec, with a rest period of about 4 min in between. The maximal intermittent exercise program was followed by 30 min of continuous walking or running at different work loads, or resting (i.e., sitting on a chair). The blood lactate concentration was found to increase from about 10 mg/100 ml of blood (9 mg/100 ml = 1 mM) to approximately 150–200 mg/100 ml after the last (third) exercise bout. During the recovery, which consisted of rest or exercise, the blood lactate concentration decreased toward resting values.

As shown in Fig. 8, the blood lactate concentration decreased at a

much faster rate when the subjects performed exercise than when resting
in the recovery period. It should also be noted that the slopes of the
curves were affected by the intensity of the work load performed in the
recovery period. The rate of lactate removal (i.e., the net removal) was
calculated from the slopes of the rectilinear parts of the curves describing the changes in blood lactate concentration with time (i.e., between
approximately the 5th and the 15th min of the recovery period). The
removal rate was expressed as milligrams of lactate per 100 ml of blood
each minute (i.e., mg/100 ml × min). The rate of lactate, calculated
according to this method, was found to be approximately 2–3 mg/100
ml × min at rest. The removal rate increased with increasing intensity
of the work performed in the recovery period, up to a work level demanding approximately 60 to 70% of the individual's maximal oxygen uptake.
The average maximal rate of lactate removal was found to be about
8 mg/100 ml × min at 63% of the individual's maximal oxygen uptake
(Fig. 9). Beyond this critical level, a pronounced decrease in the removal
rate was observed. However, it should be emphasized that the rate of

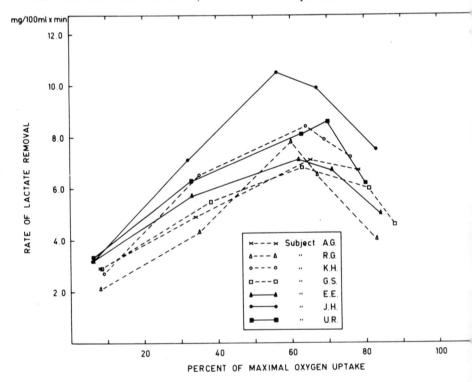

Fig. 9. The rate of lactate removal (i.e., net removal) in relation to work load.

lactate removal was on the average significantly higher at the highest work loads (i.e., approximately 80% of maximal oxygen uptake) than at rest. Thus, a work load demanding about 60 to 70% of the individual's maximal oxygen uptake seems to be critical both for the production and removal of lactate.

In seeking the explanations for the increased rate of lactate removal, several factors must be considered. The importance of the liver in the elimination of lactate during exercise is pointed out by several investigators (10,31,109). In addition to the liver, skeletal muscles (78) and other tissues (86,87) are able to remove lactate even during the course of muscular work. If one supposes that lactate is evenly distributed in the extracellular and intracellular water, it is possible to calculate the approximate amount of lactate produced in the body or removed from it. Using the values given in Fig. 8, it means that the total net production of lactate was about 70 to 100 gm. For the purposes of these calculations it was assumed that the fraction of water was 0.8 for the blood and 0.6 for the rest of the body, as proposed by Margaria et al. (94). With regard to the net removal of lactate in the recovery period, it means that approximately 1 gm of lactate was removed each minute during rest. Correspondingly, during exercise at 63% of the maximal oxygen uptake the rate of removal was about 4 gm/min.

According to the studies of Rowell et al. (109–111), approximately 50% of the total amount of lactate eliminated was removed by the liver, indicating that the liver was the main site of lactate removal during exercise. However, both the blood lactate concentration and the total amount of lactate removed per minute were much lower than in the present study. Using the values for liver blood flow and the highest arteriovenous lactate difference given by Rowell (109), the total amount of lactate removed was approximately 150 mg/min (i.e., about 3 to 4% of the lactate removed in the present study). Thus, if these calculations are correct, the importance of the liver in the elimination of lactate during exercise may be regarded as negligible.

Lactate is to a certain extent eliminated in sweat and urine. [For references, see Knuttgen (86).] Furthermore, it is also known that lactate is metabolized in the myocardium and resting skeletal muscle (22,79). However, the significance of the working skeletal muscles in the removal of lactate during exercise has so far been neglected. The skeletal muscles constitute the largest organ of the body, representing approximately 40% of the body weight (1). Furthermore, it is a well-known fact that the splanchnic blood flow is reduced markedly during exercise (109). A similar reduction in the blood flow is observed in other organs as well (*109*). On the other hand, the blood flow through the working skeletal muscle is increased with increasing work load, and the turnover of different metabolic substrates is high (*79,80*).

Thus, according to the results presented in Fig. 9, it seems reasonable to assume that the oxidation of lactate in the working muscles is the preferred pathway, rather than oxidation or gluconeogenesis in other tissues.

Finally, it should also be emphasized that these results indicate that skeletal muscle, rather than the liver, may be regarded as the main site for lactate removal during exercise.

D. Relative Contribution of Anaerobic and Aerobic Processes to Total Energy Metabolism

The energy needed for muscular work is derived from both anaerobic and aerobic energy processes. The relative importance of these two energy-liberating processes depends upon several factors, i.e., the type of work, the intensity, and the duration of the work. During prolonged work of relatively low intensity, most of the energy is derived from oxidation of carbohydrates and fat, while during short exhaustive exercise the energy needed is derived mostly from anaerobic processes.

Measurements of oxygen uptake at rest and during exercise provide an accurate method for determining the aerobic energy output, since 4.7–5.0 kcal is liberated per liter of oxygen consumed. The individual's maximal oxygen uptake, however, sets an upper limit for the amount of energy which can be liberated per unit time by aerobic processes. During heavy exercise of short duration, energy is also derived from the splitting of energy-rich substances (i.e., ATP, CP, and glycogen). However, at present it is difficult to obtain an accurate and direct measure of the anaerobic energy output. In fact, there are no generally accepted methods by which the anaerobic energy output could be quantitatively determined. The relative contributions of the anaerobic and aerobic processes to total energy output, therefore, could not be exactly determined.

However, it is possible to calculate the amount of energy (kcal) liberated by anaerobic processes by measurements of changes in the concentrations of ATP, CP, and lactate in the muscles during exercise. According to Karlsson (*80*) it is reasonable to assume a total maximal energy output of approximately 30 kcal by anaerobic processes.

Based on the results from this study (*80*) and from others (*15,63,74,82*) and a maximal oxygen uptake of 5 liters/min, the relative contributions of the anaerobic and aerobic processes to total energy metabolism

TABLE I

RELATIVE CONTRIBUTION OF ANAEROBIC AND AEROBIC PROCESSES TO TOTAL
ENERGY OUTPUT DURING MAXIMAL EXERCISE OF DIFFERENT DURATION

Work time, maximal exercise	Energy output (kcal)			Relative contribution (%)	
	Anaerobic processes	Aerobic processes	Total	Anaerobic processes	Aerobic processes
10 sec	20	4	24	83	17
1 min	30	20	50	60	40
2 min	30	45	75	40	60
5 min	30	120	150	20	80
10 min	25	245	270	9	91
30 min	20	675	695	3	97
60 min	15	1200	1215	1	99

during maximal exercise of different durations can be indicated. Such an indication is presented in Table I.

It appears that 10 sec is too short a time to load the anaerobic processes to a maximal extent. There is also evidence (63,64) which suggests that anaerobic processes are not maximally stressed during prolonged maximal exercise (i.e., 10, 30, and 60 min). Furthermore, it is assumed that a work time of 10 sec and 1 min is too short a time to load the oxygen transport system maximally. During prolonged severe exercise it is postulated that 90 and 80% of the individual's maximal oxygen uptake can be maintained during 30 and 60 min, respectively.

V. Anaerobic Processes and Muscular Fatigue

Vigorous strong contractions of a muscle lead to the well-known state of muscle fatigue, i.e., an inability of the muscle to continue supplying the same mechanical work. Unfortunately, the precise explanation for this phenomenon is not yet known.

However, several investigations have been performed to study the mechanical responses and the changes in the metabolic processes of the muscle during maximal work to exhaustion. These results allow one to speculate about the possible chemical basis for this type of fatigue.

It is known that the muscle itself is easily fatigued without any obvious changes in the function of the nervous system. The motor neurons continue to function properly and the nerve impulses pass through the neuromuscular junctions. Furthermore, no change in the action potentials spread along the muscle fiber could be observed. Therefore, this type of muscular fatigue is thought to be associated with changes in the muscle itself. The possible reasons for this fatigue will be further discussed in the following.

A. ATP AND CP LEVELS IN MUSCLE AT THE END OF MAXIMAL WORK

The changes in the concentration of ATP and CP during maximal work are described in Fig. 10. From these results it is obvious that the concentration of CP falls very rapidly during maximal work. If the

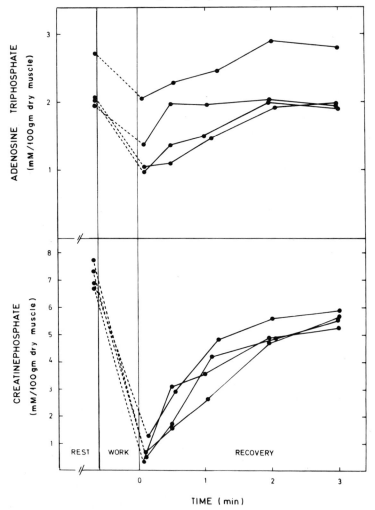

Fig. 10. The concentration of adenosine triphosphate and creatine phosphate in the lateral part of m. vastus lateralis before and at different time intervals after maximal exercise to exhaustion in man (Hermansen and Hultman, unpublished results).

work period lasts for 2–3 min, as in these experiments, the concentration of CP at the end of a maximal exercise to exhaustion approaches zero. This means that the stores of CP are depleted, or almost depleted, during vigorous exercise to exhaustion.

The concentration of ATP also decreases during maximal work. However, the decrease is comparatively small, i.e., average decrease does not comprise more than 30 to 40% of the initial (total) content of the muscle. Thus, even at complete exhaustion the concentration of ATP is approximately 60 to 70% of that in the resting cell.

Although it has been difficult to measure, it is reasonable to believe that ADP also may be used, at least partly, in the processes of ATP resynthesis (i.e., the myokinase reaction).

In conclusion, the concentration of CP is approximately zero, and the concentration of ATP is about 60 to 70% of the resting values in skeletal muscle of man after maximal exercise of short duration to exhaustion.

B. Lactate and pH Levels in Muscle and Blood at the End of Maximal Work

According to the studies of Karlsson and co-workers (*80*), the concentration of lactate in the muscles at the end of maximal work (of different duration) to exhaustion was found to be approximately the same whether the maximal work lasted for 2–3 min or about 7 min. The muscle lactate concentration, however, was lower when the maximal work time was extended to 10–20 min. The highest single values for muscle lactate concentration in the studies of Karlsson (*80*) were 22.0 and 24.8 mM in two subjects. Similar high values for muscle lactate concentration have been reported after short maximal isometric contractions leading to exhaustion within 5 min (*38*).

In a recent study by Hermansen (*64*), the peak blood lactate concentration was measured on the same individual after 13 different maximal work periods (Fig. 11). Each of the 13 maximal runs was continued until the subject was unable to keep the speed set by the treadmill. Although there is a tendency toward somewhat lower blood lactate values at the shortest and the longest work periods, it should be noted that the blood lactate concentration at the time of exhaustion was approximately the same in all experiments. In other words, when the subjective feeling of fatigue or complete exhaustion reached a stage which was incompatible with continuation of the work, the blood lactate concentration had increased to approximately 18 mM for the subject studied. All the results reported in Fig. 11 were measured after con-

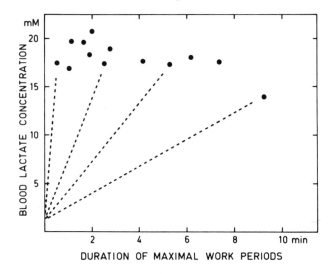

Fig. 11. Peak blood lactate concentration after 13 different maximal exercise bouts on the treadmill in one male subject (*64*).

tinuous exercise, i.e., the subjects ran only once each experimental day. Thus, these results seemed to support the thesis that a high blood lactate concentration might be a limiting factor for work of a short duration.

However, if intermittent maximal exercise of short duration is per-

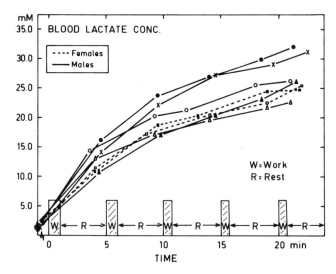

Fig. 12. Blood lactate concentration during intermittent maximal exercise on the treadmill in two female and five male subjects (*64*).

formed (Fig. 12), the blood lactate concentrations were found to be much higher than during continuous exercise. The highest value observed in one male subject was 32.0 mM (or 288 mg/100 ml). Furthermore, as can be seen from Fig. 12, the blood lactate concentration increased after each of the five work periods to very high values in all subjects. In spite of lower blood lactate concentrations in the first than in the second exercise bout, and so on, the subjects were completely exhausted after each of the work periods which lasted for approximately 60 sec. Thus, from these results it was concluded that the blood lactate concentration was not the limiting factor during maximal exercise of short duration. The highest blood lactate concentrations given in Fig. 12 were even higher than the highest values reported by Karlsson (80) for the lactate concentration in the muscles.

However, the studies of Karlsson were performed on the bicycle ergometer, and those reported in Fig. 12 were obtained during treadmill exercise. This fact alone may explain the differences observed. It should further be noted that the differences in the maximal blood lactate values from one subject to another are fairly large. Most of the maximal values observed in this study (Fig. 12) were approximately the same as those observed in the muscles in the studies of Karlsson (80). Thus, the difference between the highest lactate concentrations in the blood and muscle may possibly be explained by differences in the subjects studied (i.e., individual differences).

Accumulation of lactate inside the cell will tend to decrease the intracellular pH. Figure 13 gives the results from measurements of muscle and capillary blood pH after maximal exercise to exhaustion on the bicycle ergometer. The muscle pH was determined by measurements of the pH in homogenates of samples taken from the lateral part of the quadriceps muscle using the biopsy technique described by Bergström (14). The muscle pH decreased from 6.98 (average resting value) to 6.46 immediately after the maximal exercise had stopped. The corresponding fall in blood pH was 7.40 to 7.18 in these experiments. It should also be emphasized that variations in the muscle pH values were larger than in the blood pH values. Thus, it can be concluded that there is a rapid fall in both muscle and blood pH during maximal exercise.

C. CHANGES IN THE ACID–BASE BALANCE DURING MAXIMAL WORK

As indicated above, maximal exercise of short duration gives rise to an increased production of lactic acid in the muscle cells, which in turn diffuses out into the blood where it causes changes in acid–base status of the blood and the rest of the body.

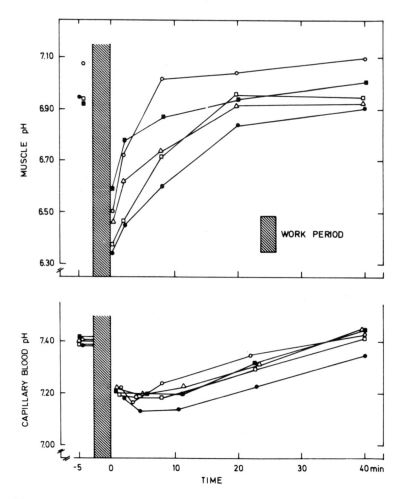

Fig. 13. Muscle pH (upper panel) and capillary blood pH (lower panel) before and at different time intervals after maximal bicycle exercise to exhaustion (*65*).

It is generally believed (*23,57*) that blood pH values lower than 7.0 are incompatible with life. However, in a recent study by Osnes and Hermansen (*103*) it was shown that a large number of the experimental subjects attained blood pH values below this level (Fig. 14). Thus, from these results it is obvious that healthy subjects are able to tolerate changes in blood pH values down to 6.80. However, all subjects reported pain in the muscle groups which had been involved in the exercise (i.e., the gluteal and the quadriceps muscles).

According to the physiological law of pH stability, the pH of blood and most other body compartments may change very little. If the con-

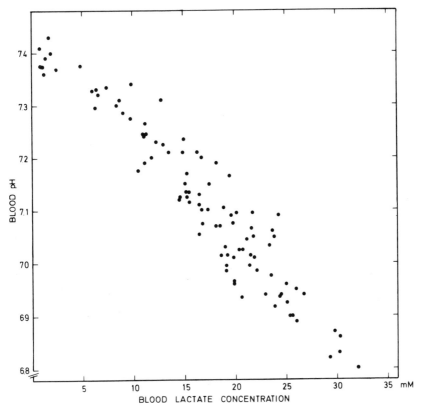

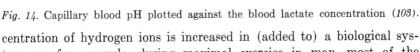

Fig. 14. Capillary blood pH plotted against the blood lactate concentration (*103*).

centration of hydrogen ions is increased in (added to) a biological system, as, for example, during maximal exercise in man, most of the hydrogen ions are absorbed by the buffer systems, i.e., mainly by the bicarbonate and protein buffer systems.

Figure 15 gives the individual values for plasma bicarbonate and blood lactate concentration. It can be seen that there is a gradual decrease in the plasma bicarbonate concentration with increasing concentration of lactate in the blood. It should also be noted that when the blood lactate concentration increases (i.e., up to approximately 15 mM), there is a nearly equivalent decrease in the plasma bicarbonate concentration. Thus, if the increase in lactate concentration in plasma is the same as that for whole blood, almost all lactate which enters the blood is buffered by the CO_2/HCO_3 system. However, when the lactate concentration in the blood increases to higher values, other buffer systems play an increasingly important role. It should also be emphasized that the plasma bicarbonate concentration is approaching zero when the

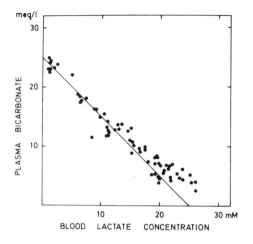

Fig. 15. Plasma bicarbonate concentration plotted against blood lactate concentration. The line represents equivalent changes in bicarbonate and lactate concentrations (*103*).

blood lactate concentration is increased to about 30 m*M* (the highest value obtained in these studies was 32.0 m*M*).

D. LIMITING FACTORS IN MAXIMAL WORK OF SHORT DURATION

It is rather well established that one of the main limiting factors in prolonged severe exercise (i.e., aerobic energy release) is the amount of oxygen which can be transported to the muscle cells per unit of time. However, little is known about the limiting factor(s) in maximal work of short duration (i.e., anaerobic energy release).

In 1967 it was suggested by Cerretelli (*23*) that the blood pH might be the limiting factor. However, from the results presented in Fig. 16, it is evident that the blood pH is *not* the limiting factor in this study. The fact that blood pH after maximal intermittent exercise decreased to lower values than those observed after one (continuous) maximal exercise bout clearly shows that the blood pH did not limit the work performance. Furthermore, in the intermittent exercise (Fig. 16) the blood pH at the start of the third, fourth, and fifth exercise bouts was much lower than at the start of the first or second work period. From the results presented above (Fig. 12) it appears that the blood lactate concentration also is not a limiting factor. On the other hand, as early as 1907 Fletcher and Hopkins (*44*) observed that a high concentration of lactic acid was found at the same time as muscle fatigue appeared. Later studies by Meyerhof (*97*), showing an increased performance of

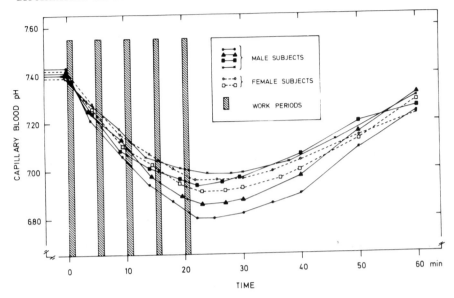

Fig. 16. Capillary blood pH measured at rest and at different time intervals during an intermittent exercise program, i.e., five exercise bouts of approximately 1 min duration with 4 min rest periods in between and during the final recovery period (*65*).

isolated muscles placed in alkaline Ringer's solution, further emphasized the role of lactic acid as a possible factor in muscle fatigue.

In the studies of Asmussen *et al.* (*5*) it was suggested that the limit for maximal work is set by a critical value for lactic acid in the working muscles. More recently, Karlsson (*80*) has measured the concentration of lactate in the muscle tissue during submaximal and maximal work. It is evident from these studies that the highest values for lactate in the muscles were observed during maximal exercise of short duration. High lactate values in the muscles during severe exercise have also been reported by Bergström *et al.* (*15*). According to Karlsson (*80*), a close correlation exists between maximal muscle lactate concentration and the subjective feeling of fatigue. However, it should be pointed out that the causal relationship between muscle fatigue and muscle lactate concentration has not yet been established.

Accumulation of lactate inside the muscle cells will tend to lower the intracellular pH. It is also well known that only minor changes from the normal pH value can produce alterations in the rates of the chemical reactions in the cells, some being depressed and others accelerated. Hill (*69*) observed that the formation of lactic acid in response to stimulation stopped when the internal pH dropped to about 6.3. These observations are substantially in agreement with the results presented in Fig. 17.

Furthermore, it was observed by Hermansen and Osnes (*65*) that the pH of the homogenate from samples of resting muscles showed a pronounced fall during the measuring period (i.e., 60 sec), indicating a rapid production of acid metabolites. However, in the muscle samples obtained immediately after maximal exercise, no change in the pH of the muscle homogenate was observed. In this connection it is interesting to note that decreased pH has been shown to reduce the rate of glycolysis in nervous tissue (*25,26*).

Thus, it is possible that lowered pH in the muscles caused by formation of lactic acid and other acid metabolites might affect the glycolytic processes. If these suggestions are correct, the changes in pH in the

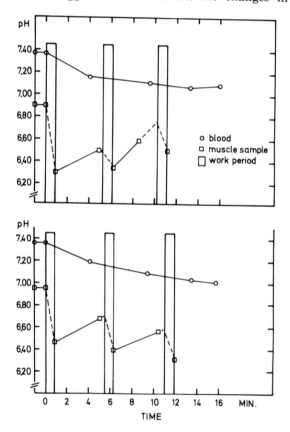

Fig. 17. Capillary blood and muscle pH before and during intermittent maximal exercise on the bicycle ergometer (*65*).

muscles might possibly be a limiting factor by reducing the rate of anaerobic glycolysis and consequently also the rate of ATP synthesis. In fact, Hultman et al. (74) have recently suggested that the limiting factor is the availability of energy-rich phosphates in the muscles. Hence, according to these authors, the lack of metabolic substrate (ATP) is considered to be the limiting factor in maximal work to exhaustion. On the other hand, recent studies on cardiac muscle (83) and on skeletal muscle (45) have provided evidence suggesting that increased hydrogen ion concentration may affect the myosin–actin interaction during the process of contraction. Thus, these results may indicate that accumulation of metabolic end products might act as a limiting factor during maximal work to exhaustion.

Therefore, at the present time it is not possible to explain precisely the state of fatigue. It may be that a decreased pH in the muscle cells may limit the work performance through an inhibition of the glycolytic processes, or it may affect the myosin–actin interaction in the muscles, or a combination of both factors may exist.

In summary, it is still an open question whether or not lack of metabolic substrates or accumulation of metabolic end products or a combination of both is the limiting factor.

VI. Effect of Training on Anaerobic Potential of Skeletal Muscle

Numerous reports have appeared in the literature in which the activities of the enzymes of the glycolytic pathway were examined in the skeletal muscles of trained and untrained animals. Enzymes studied included aldolase (60), lactic dehydrogenase (9,49,50,56,73,98,125,126), phosphorylase (9,56,73,98), hexokinase (9,13,90,98,106,126), α-glycerophosphate dehydrogenase (24), and phosphofructokinase (9,73,98). Although there are some exceptions, most of these studies have not found any difference in enzyme activities between trained and untrained animals. This may have resulted from the use of training programs that did not stress the anaerobic system. In most of the early experiments rather mild swimming programs were used. As Holloszy has shown the intensity of these programs did not even induce adaptations in the oxidative potential of skeletal muscle.

Increases in hexokinase activity of guinea pig and rat skeletal muscle were reported after training consisting of treadmill running (9,13,73,90, 125). Single bouts of running also produced elevation in the activity of this enzyme. The response of this enzyme to acute and chronic exercise was thoroughly investigated by Barnard and Peter (*13*). They found similar increases in hexokinase activity of guinea pig muscle irrespective of the intensity or duration of the exercise program. Furthermore, when the training was prolonged the activity declined progressively. They concluded that the responsiveness of hexokinase to acute and chronic exercise was such that it was not a criterion for evaluating the trained state.

Holloszy *et al.* (*73*) have studied the effects of training on phosphorylase, phosphofructokinase, hexokinase, lactate dehydrogenase, and pyruvate kinase activity in rat skeletal muscle. These enzymes were chosen since each occupies a key position in the control of glycolysis. The training program used was sufficiently intense to elicit significant increases in oxidative capacity in the skeletal muscle. It consisted of endurance running with sprints interspaced at regular intervals. No changes occurred in the activities of the anaerobic enzymes.

Baldwin and co-workers (*9*) have studied the effects of training on several anaerobic enzymes of rat muscles that were composed primarily of fast-twitch white, fast-twitch red, and slow-twitch intermediate fibers. Enzymes assayed included hexokinase, phosphorylase, phosphofructokinase, pyruvate kinase, 3-phosphoglyceraldehyde dehydrogenase, and lactic dehydrogenase. They found that hexokinase activity paralleled the changes in oxidative potential in all three fiber types. Reductions in glycolytic enzyme activities were observed in muscle composed of fast-twitch red muscle. In contrast, there were significant increases in glycolytic potential in the slow-twitch intermediate muscle (soleus).

Fewer studies have been conducted in which the activities of glycolytic enzymes were measured in trained and untrained groups or before and after training. Gollnick *et al.* (*51*) compared the PFK activity in muscle of trained and untrained men. Their sample included a wide age range and athletes participating in several sports. They observed no consistent difference in the PFK activity, although there were marked differences in oxidative capacity as judged from succinic dehydrogenase activity. Based on the histochemical estimation of oxidative potential from the reduced diphosphopyridine nucleotide diaphorase activity, it was apparent that both fiber types were more oxidative in the muscle samples from the trained subjects. This effect of training on the oxidative potential was similar to that reported in the rat by Baldwin *et al.* (*8*).

Eriksson and co-workers (*41*) have studied the effects of training on the PFK activity of biopsy samples from the vastus lateralis muscle of 10- to 11-year-old boys. The training consisted of working on the bicycle ergometer 3 days a week, 20 min each day, for 2 months. Prior to training, the PFK activity of these boys was about half that of normal untrained adults. After training, it had increased by about 40%. Succinic dehydrogenase activity also had increased. It is interesting that in untrained 10- to 11-year-old boys the lactate concentration in the blood and muscle at submaximal and maximal work loads is significantly lower than in adults. After training, significantly higher lactate concentrations were observed at the same relative work loads in 10- and 11-year-old boys. This may have been due to changes in the anaerobic capacity of the muscles. The increase in muscle and blood lactate after training was opposite to the effect seen in adults (see Holloszy, this volume, p. 45).

In another study, Gollnick and associates (52) measured the PFK activity in the samples from the vastus lateralis muscle of subjects before and after a 5-month training program. The training consisted of working on the bicycle ergometer 1 hr 4 days each week at a load requiring from 75 to 90% of their aerobic power. This training program resulted in a doubling of the PFK activity. Succinic dehydrogenase activity also was approximately 100% higher after, as compared to before, training. Histochemical analysis of the muscle samples revealed that oxidative potential of both fiber types had increased by training. However, glycolytic capacity, as judged from α-glycerophosphate dehydrogenase activity, appeared to increase only in the FT fibers.

The ATP concentration is higher in the skeletal muscle of trained, as compared to untrained, subjects (40,81). This small change is probably due to the higher mitochondrial density in trained muscle. The magnitude of this change is too small to represent a significant storage of ATP for use anaerobically.

Increases in CP of muscle have also been reported in skeletal muscle after training (40). It is also doubtful whether these changes markedly alter anaerobic capacity.

References

1. Andres, R., Cader, G., and Zierler, K. L. (1956). J. Clin. Invest. 35, 671–682.
2. Armstrong, R. B., Shepherd, R. E., and Gollnick, P. D. Amer. J. Physiol. (Submitted for publication.)
3. Arnold, H., and Pette, D. (1968). Eur. J. Biochem. 6, 163–171.
4. Asmussen, E., and Nielsen, M. (1946). Acta Physiol. Scand. 12, 171–188.
5. Asmussen, E., von Döbeln, W., and Nielsen, M. (1948). Acta Physiol. Scand. 15, 57–62.
6. Atkinson, D. E. (1968). Biochemistry 7, 4030–4034.
7. Baba, N., and Sharma, H. M. (1971). J. Cell Biol. 51, 621–635.

8. Baldwin, K. M., Klinkerfuss, G. H., Terjung, R. L., Molé, P. A., and Holloszy, J. O. (1972). *Amer. J. Physiol.* **222**, 373–378.
9. Baldwin, K. M., Winder, W. W., Terjung, R. L., and Holloszy, J. O. (1972). *Med. Sci. Sports* **4**, 50.
10. Bang, O. (1936). *Scand. Arch. Physiol.* **74**, Suppl. 10.
11. Barnard, R. J., Edgerton, V. R., Furukawa, T., and Peter, J. B. (1971). *Amer. J. Physiol.* **220**, 410–414.
12. Barnard, R. J., and Foss, M. L. (1969). *J. Appl. Physiol.* **27**, 813–816.
13. Barnard, R. J., and Peter, J. B. (1969). *J. Appl. Physiol.* **27**, 691–695.
14. Bergström, J. (1962). *Scand. J. Clin. Lab. Invest., Suppl.* **68**.
15. Bergström, J., Guarnieri, G., and Hultman, E. (1971). *J. Appl. Physiol.* **30**, 122–125.
16. Bolme, P., and Novotny, J. (1969). *Acta Physiol. Scand.* **77**, 333–343.
17. Brooke, M. H., and Engel, W. K. (1969). *Neurology* **19**, 221–233.
18. Brostrom, C. O., Hunkeler, F. L., and Krebs, E. G. (1971). *J. Biol. Chem.* **246**, 1961–1967.
19. Cain, D. F., and Davies, R. E. (1962). *Biochem. Biophys. Res. Commun.* **8**, 361–366.
20. Carlson, F. D., and Siger, A. (1960). *J. Gen. Physiol.* **44**, 33–60.
21. Carlson, L. A., and Pernow, B. (1961). *Acta Physiol. Scand.* **52**, 328–342.
22. Carlsten, A., Hallgren, B., Jagenburg, R., Svanborg, A., and Werkö, L. (1961). *Scand. J. Clin. Lab. Invest.* **13**, 418–428.
23. Cerretelli, P. (1967). *In* "Exercise at Altitude" (R. Margaria, ed.), pp. 58–64. Excerpta Medica Foundation, Amsterdam.
24. Chepinoga, O. P. (1939). *Ukr. Biokim. Zh.* **14**, 15–26.
25. Graig, F. N. (1943–1944). *J. Gen. Physiol.* **27**, 325–338.
26. Craig, F. N., and Beecher, H. K. (1942–1943). *J. Gen. Physiol.* **26**, 473–478.
27. Cronin, R. F. P. (1967). *J. Appl. Physiol.* **22**, 211–216.
28. Danforth, W. H., Helmreich, E., and Cori, C. F. (1962). *Proc. Nat. Acad. Sci. U. S.* **48**, 1191–1199.
29. Danforth, W. H., and Helmreich, E. (1964). *J. Biol. Chem.* **239**, 3133–3138.
30. Danforth, W. H., and Lyon, J. B., Jr. (1964). *J. Biol. Chem.* **239**, 4047–4050.
31. Davies, C. T. M., Knibbs, A. V., and Musgrove, J. (1970). *Int. Z. Angew. Physiol.* **28**, 155–161.
32. Diamant, B., Karlsson, J., and Saltin, B. (1968). *Acta Physiol. Scand.* **72**, 383–384.
33. Drummond, G. I., Harwood, J. P., and Powell, C. A. (1969). *J. Biol. Chem.* **244**, 4235–4240.
34. Edgerton, V. R., Barnard, R. J., Peter, J. B., Simpson, D. R., and Gillespie, C. A. (1970). *Exp. Neurol.* **27**, 46–56.
35. Edgerton, V. R., Simpson, D. R., Barnard, R. J., and Peter, J. B. (1970). *Nature (London)* **225**, 866–867.
36. Edgerton, V. R., and Simpson, D. R. (1969). *J. Histochem. Cytochem.* **17**, 829–838.
37. Edström, L., and Nyström, B. (1969). *Acta Neurol. Scand.* **45**, 257–269.
38. Edwards, R. H. T., Harris, R. C., Hultman, E., Kaijser, L., Koh, D., and Nordesjö, L.-O. (1972). *J. Physiol. (London)* **220**, 335–352.
39. Ekblom, B. (1969). *Acta Physiol. Scand. Suppl.* **328**.
40. Eriksson, B. O., Gollnick, P. D., and Saltin, B. *Acta Physiol. Scand.* (In press.)

41. Eriksson, B. O., Karlsson, J., and Saltin, B. (1971). *Acta Paediat. Scand. Suppl.* **217,** 154–157.
42. Evans, C. L. (1930). "Recent Advances in Physiology." J. Churchill and A. Churchill, London.
43. Fahimi, H. D., and Amarasingham, C. R. (1964). *J. Cell Biol.* **22,** 29–48.
44. Fletcher, W. M., and Hopkins, F. G. (1906–1907). *J. Physiol. (London)* **35,** 247–250, 296–302.
45. Fuchs, F., Reddy, Y., and Briggs, F. N. (1970). *Acta Biochim. Biophys.* **221,** 407–409.
46. George, J. C., and Neme, R. V. (1965). *J. Anim. Morphol. Physiol.* **12,** 246–248.
47. Gisolfi, C., Robinson, S., and Turrell, E. S. (1966). *J. Appl. Physiol.* **21,** 1767–1772.
48. Gollnick, P. D., Soule, R. G., Taylor, A. W., Williams, C., and Ianuzzo, C. D. (1970). *Amer. J. Physiol.* **219,** 729–733.
49. Gollnick, P. D., Struck, P. J., and Bogyo, T. P. (1967). *J. Appl. Physiol.* **22,** 623–627.
50. Gollnick, P. D., and Hearn, G. R. (1961). *Amer. J. Physiol.* **210,** 694–696.
51. Gollnick, P. D., Armstrong, R. B., Saubert, C. W., IV, Piehl, K., and Saltin, B. (1972). *J. Appl. Physiol.* **33,** 312–319.
52. Gollnick, P. D., Armstrong, R. B., Saltin, B., Saubert, C. W., IV, Sembrowich, W. L., and Shepherd, R. E. (1973). *J. Appl. Physiol.* (Submitted.)
53. Gollnick P. D., Armstrong, R. B., Saubert, C. W., IV, Sembrowich, W. L., Shepherd, R. E., and Saltin, B. *J. Appl. Physiol.* (Submitted for publication.)
54. Gollnick, P. D., Armstrong, R. B., Sembrowich, W. L., Shepherd, R. E., and Saltin, B. *J. Appl. Physiol.* (Submitted for publication.)
55. Gollnick, P. D., and Armstrong, R. B. *J. Appl. Physiol.* (Submitted for publication.)
56. Gould, M. K., and Rawlinson, W. A. (1959). *Biochem. J.* **73,** 41–44.
57. Guyton, A. C. (1966). *In* "Textbook of Medical Physiology," 3rd ed. Saunders, Philadelphia, Pennsylvania.
58. Harris, P., Bateman, M., and Gloster, J. (1962). *Clin. Sci.* **23,** 545–560.
59. Harris, R. C., Bergström, J., and Hultman, E. (1971). *In* "Muscle Metabolism During Exercise" (B. Pernow and B. Saltin, eds.), pp. 301–305. Plenum, New York.
60. Hearn, G. R., and Wainio, W. W. (1957). *Amer. J. Physiol.* **190,** 206–209.
61. Helmreich, E., and Cori, C. F. (1964). *Advan. Enzyme Regul.* **3,** 91–107.
62. Henneman, E., Somjen, G., and Carpenter, D. O. (1965). *J. Neurophysiol.* **28,** 560–580.
63. Hermansen, L. (1969). *Med. Sci. Sports* **1,** 32–38.
64. Hermansen, L. (1971). *In* "Muscle Metabolism During Exercise" (B. Pernow and B. Saltin, eds.), pp. 401–407. Plenum, New York.
65. Hermansen, L., and Osnes, J.-B. (1972). *J. Appl. Physiol.* **32,** 304–308.
66. Hermansen, L., and Saltin, B. (1967). *In* "Exercise at Altitude" (R. Margaria, ed.), pp. 48–53. Excerpta Medica Foundation, Amsterdam.
67. Hermansen, L., and Saltin, B. (1969). *J. Appl. Physiol.* **26,** 31–37.
68. Hermansen, L., and Stensvold, I. (1972). *Acta Physiol. Scand.* **86,** 191–201.
69. Hill, A. V. (1955–1956). *Proc. Roy. Soc., Ser. B* **144,** 1–22.
70. Hill, A. V., and Lupton, H. (1923). *Quart J. Med.* **16,** 135–171.
71. Hoes, M. J. A. J. M., Binkhorst, R. A., Smeekes-Kuyl, A. E. M. C., and Vissers, A. C. A. (1968). *Int. Z. Angew. Physiol.* **26,** 33–42.

72. Hohorst, H. J., Reim, M., and Bartels, H. (1962). *Biochem. Biophys. Res. Commun.* **7**, 142–146.
73. Holloszy, J. O., Oscai, L. B., Molé, P. A., and Don, I. J. (1971). *In* "Muscle Metabolism During Exercise" (B. Pernow and B. Saltin, eds.), pp. 51–61. Plenum, New York.
74. Hultman, E., Bergström, J., and McLennan-Anderson, N. (1967). *Scand. J. Clin. Lab. Invest.* **19**, 56–66.
75. Infante, A. A., and Davies, R. E. (1962). *Biochem. Biophy. Res. Commun.* **9**, 410–415.
76. Jennekens, F. G. I., Tomlinson, B. E., and Walton, J. N. (1971). *J. Neurol. Sci.* **14**, 37–45.
77. Jervell, O. (1929). *Acta Med. Scand. Suppl.* **24**.
78. Jorfeldt, T. (1970). *Acta Physiol. Scand. Suppl.* **338**.
79. Kaijser, L. (1970). *Acta Physiol. Scand. Suppl.* **346**.
80. Karlsson, J. (1971). *Acta Physiol. Scand. Suppl.* **358**.
81. Karlsson, J., Diamant, B., and Saltin, B. (1971). *Scand. J. Clin. Lab. Invest.* **26**, 385–394.
82. Karlsson, J., and Saltin, B. (1970). *J. Appl. Physiol.* **29**, 598–602.
83. Katz, A. M. (1970). *Physiol. Rev.* **50**, 63–158.
84. Keul, J., Doll, E., and Keppler, D. (1969). *In* "Muskelstoffwechsel." Barth, München.
85. Knuttgen, H. G., and Saltin, B. (1972). *J. Appl. Physiol.* **32**, 690–694.
86. Knuttgen, H. G. (1971). *In* "Muscle Metabolism During Exercise" (B. Pernow and B. Saltin, eds.), pp. 361–369. Plenum, New York.
87. Krebs, H. (1964). *Proc. Roy. Soc., Ser. B* **159**, 545–563.
88. Krebs, H. A., and Veech, R. L. (1969). *In* "Mitochondria Structure and Function" (L. Ernster and Z. Drahota, eds.), pp. 101–109. Academic Press, New York.
89. Kugelberg, E., and Edström, L. (1968). *J. Neurol. Neurosurg. Psychiat.* **31**, 415–423.
90. Lamb, D. R., Peter, J. B., Jeffress, R. N., and Wallace, H. A. (1969). *Amer. J. Physiol.* **217**, 1628–1632.
91. McMillian, P. J., and Wittum, R. L. (1971). *J. Histochem. Cytochem.* **19**, 421–425.
92. Mansour, T. E. (1969). *Advan. Enzyme Regul.* **8**, 37–51.
93. Margaria, R., Cerretelli, P., and Mangili, F. (1964). *J. Appl. Physiol.* **19**, 623–628.
94. Margaria, R., Cerretelli, P., di Prampero, P. E., Massari, C., and Torelli, G. (1963). *J. Appl. Physiol.* **18**, 371–377.
95. Mayer, S. E., Williams, B. J., and Smith, J. M. (1967). *Ann. N. Y. Acad. Sci.* **139**, 686–702.
96. Meyer, F., Heilmeyer, L. M. G., Jr., Haschke, R. H., and Fischer, E. H. (1970). *J. Biol. Chem.* **245**, 6642–6648.
97. Meyerhof, O. (1925). *In* "Chemical Dynamic of Life Phenomena." Lippincott, Philadelphia, Pennsylvania.
98. Morgan, T. E., Cobb, L. A., Short, F. A., Ross, R., and Gunn, D. R. (1971). *In* "Muscle Metabolism During Exercise" (B. Pernow and B. Saltin, eds.), pp. 87–95. Plenum, New York.
99. Morgan, H. E., and Parmeggiani, A. (1964). *J. Biol. Chem.* **239**, 2435–2439.
100. Morgan, H. E., and Parmeggiani, A. (1964). *J Biol. Chem.* **239**, 2440–2445.

101. Nagle, F., Robinhold, D., Howley, E., Daniels, J., Baptista, G., and Stoedefalke, K. (1970). *Med. Sci. Sports* **2**, 182–186.
102. Newman, E. V., Dill, D. B., Edwards, H. T., and Webster, F. A. (1937). *Amer. J. Physiol.* **118**, 457–462.
103. Osnes, J.-B., and Hermansen, L. (1972). *J. Appl. Physiol.* **32**, 59–63.
104. Øye, I. (1967). *Acta Physiol. Scand.* **70**, 229–238.
105. Peter, J. B., Sawaki, S., Barnard, R. J., Edgerton, V. R., and Gillespie, C. A. (1971). *Arch. Biochem. Biophys.* **144**, 304–307.
106. Peter, J. B., Jeffress, R. N., and Lamb, D. R. (1968). *Science* **160**, 200–201.
107. Piper, J., di Prampero, P. E., and Cerretelli, P. (1968). *Amer. J. Physiol.* **215**, 523–531.
108. Purich, D. L., and Fromm, H. J. (1972). *J. Biol. Chem.* **247**, 240–265.
109. Rowell, L. B. (1971). *In* "Muscle Metabolism During Exercise" (B. Pernow and B. Saltin, eds.), pp. 127–141. Plenum, New York.
110. Rowell, L. B., Brengelmann, G. L., Blackmon, J. R., Twiss, R. D., and Kusumi, F. (1968). *J. Appl. Physiol.* **24**, 475–484.
111. Rowell, L. B., Karning, K. K., II, Evans, Th. O., Kennedy, J. Ward, Blackmon, J. R., and Kusumi, F. (1966). *J. Appl. Physiol.* **21**, 1773–1783.
112. Rämmal, K., and Ström, G. (1949). *Acta Physiol. Scand.* **17**, 452–456.
113. Sacktor, B., and Hurlburt, E. C. (1966). *J. Biol. Chem.* **241**, 632–634.
114. Saiki, H., Margaria, R., and Cuttica, F. (1967). *Int. Z. Angew. Physiol.* **24**, 57–61.
115. Saltin, B., Gollnick, P. D., Eriksson, B. O., and Piehl, K. (1972). *Onset of Exercise—Symposium, Toulouse*, pp. 63–76.
116. Sembrowich, W. L., Ianuzzo, C. D., Saubert, C. W., IV, Shepherd, R. E., and Gollnick, P. D. (unpublished data).
117. Shin, L. C., Fall, L., Walton, G. M., and Atkinson, D. E. (1968). *Biochemistry* **7**, 4041–4045.
118. Sigel, P., and Pette, D. (1969). *J. Histochem. Cytochem.* **17**, 225–237.
119. Stainsby, W. N., and Welch, H. G. (1966). *Amer. J. Physiol.* **211**, 177–183.
120. Stenberg, J. (1966). *Acta Physiol. Scand. Suppl.* **273**.
121. Stenberg, J., Åstrand, P.-O., Ekblom, B., Royce, J., and Saltin, B. (1967). *J. Appl. Physiol.* **22**, 61–65.
122. Stull, J. T., and Mayer, S. E. (1971). *J. Biol. Chem.* **246**, 5716–5723.
123. Whalen, W. J., and Nair, P. (1969). *Fed. Proc.* **28** (comm. 1442), 519.
124. Williams, C. G., Bredell, G. A. G., Wyndham, C. H., Strydom, N. B., Morrison, J. F., Peter, J., Fleming, P. F., and Ward, J. S. (1962). *J. Appl. Physiol.* **17**, 625–638.
125. Yakovlev, N. N. (1968). *Biochemistry (USSR)* **33**, 602–607.
126. Yampolskaya, L. I. (1952). *Sechenov Physiol. J. USSR* **39**, 91–99.

Biochemical Adaptations to Exercise: Aerobic Metabolism[1]

John O. Holloszy

DEPARTMENT OF PREVENTIVE MEDICINE, WASHINGTON
UNIVERSITY SCHOOL OF MEDICINE, ST. LOUIS, MISSOURI

[1] Work supported by U. S. Public Health Service Research Career Development
Award K4-HD19573 and by PHS Research Grant HDO1613.

I. Introduction

Until quite recently it was generally believed that the improvement in exercise capacity that occurs in response to regularly performed endurance exercise is due to increased delivery of blood and oxygen to the working muscle cells made possible by exercise-induced cardiovascular adaptations. Endurance exercise training was equated with training of the "oxygen transporting system." However, within the past six years, evidence has accumulated which shows that, in addition to the cardiovascular adaptations, major adaptations also occur in the skeletal muscles which result in an increase in the capacity for aerobic metabolism. It is the purpose of this review to describe and evaluate these adaptations in skeletal muscle, both in the context of data from applied physiological studies and in the context of the regulatory mechanisms that control the energy transfer pathways in the muscle cell.

II. Applied Physiological and Clinical Studies of the Adaptation to Endurance Exercise Training

A. MAXIMAL OXYGEN UPTAKE ($\dot{V}_{O_2 max}$)

Physical training of the endurance type, such as prolonged running, results in an increase in maximal oxygen uptake capacity in previously sedentary individuals (*24,25,56,58,88,89,91*). The magnitude of the increase in $\dot{V}_{O_2 max}$ with training depends both on the individual's initial level of training and on the intensity, frequency, and duration of the exercise program. In the majority of studies the increase has been in the range of 10 to 20% for programs of 3–6 months duration. However, much larger increases are possible. In a study on the effects of bed rest and of training, Saltin and co-workers (*91*) demonstrated a 37% increase in $\dot{V}_{O_2 max}$ in three sedentary young men subjected to a strenuous program of running for 55 days following 20 days of bed rest. The value of 37% refers to the increase above initial, pre-bed rest values. $\dot{V}_{O_2 max}$ declined markedly as a result of 20 days of bed rest, and when the values obtained after the bed rest were compared to the values after training, $\dot{V}_{O_2 max}$ increased 100%. The effect of the duration of intensive training is demonstrated in a report by Ekblom (*24*), who trained a group of young men for 16 weeks and found that $\dot{V}_{O_2 max}$ increased approximately 16%. One subject, who showed a 20% increase at the end of 16 weeks, trained intensively for an additional 47 months during which time his $\dot{V}_{O_2 max}$ increased further, to result in a total increase of 44%.

On the average, the increase in $\dot{V}_{O_2 max}$ results equally from an increase in cardiac output, secondary to a higher stroke volume, and an increase in arteriovenous oxygen difference (24,25,89,91). In other words, increased extraction of O_2 by the working muscles appears to play as great a role in the increase in $\dot{V}_{O_2 max}$ with training as does the increase in maximum cardiac output.

B. Muscle Glycogen Depletion During Submaximal Exercise

In addition to the increase in maximal oxygen uptake, major effects of endurance exercise training are also demonstrable during submaximal exercise. In this review, the term submaximal exercise is loosely defined as work requiring less than the $\dot{V}_{O_2 max}$. In recent years, much important information regarding muscle metabolism during exercise has been obtained on humans by means of serial needle biopsies of the quadriceps muscle. Using this technique, Hermansen et al. (38) and Saltin and Karlsson (93) have shown that the rates of muscle glycogen depletion are similar in trained and untrained individuals at the same relative work level (i.e., at the same percentage of their $\dot{V}_{O_2 max}$). Since trained individuals have a higher O_2 uptake at the same relative work level, the rate of muscle glycogen depletion during work at the same absolute, submaximal work level (i.e., at the same rate of O_2 consumption) is lower in the trained state. The data of Saltin and Karlsson (93) are particularly convincing in regard to this point, since they were obtained on the same individuals before and after training.

C. Muscle and Blood Lactate Concentrations During Submaximal Exercise

It is well established that physically trained individuals have lower blood lactate levels than untrained during submaximal exercise (19,25, 38,44,87,93,94). This appears to be true not only at the same absolute work level and oxygen uptake (19,25,44,87,94), but even at the same relative oxygen uptake (38,44,93,94) when the trained individual is exercising at a higher work level than the untrained. It has recently been shown that muscle lactate levels are also lower, both at the same absolute and at the same relative work levels, in well-trained as compared to untrained men, and in the same subject retested after a program of endurance exercise (93,94).

D. Respiratory Quotient (R.Q.)

Individuals who have adapted to endurance exercise derive a greater percentage of their energy from oxidation of fatty acids and less from carbohydrate than do untrained individuals during submaximal exercise (*15,38,48,92,93*). This is reflected in a lower R.Q. (*15,38,92,93*) and an increased rate of conversion of ^{14}C-labeled long-chain fatty acids to $^{14}CO_2$ (*48*). Trained men have lower R.Q.'s than untrained, even during work of the same relative intensity (i.e., at the same percentage of their $\dot{V}_{O_2 max}$) (*38,93*).

E. Concentrations of Creatine Phosphate (CP) and ATP in Skeletal Muscle During Exercise

Using the needle biopsy technique and enzymatic microanalytic methods, two groups of investigators in Sweden have demonstrated that there is a rapid decrease in the concentrations of CP and ATP in the quadriceps muscles of men during bicycle exercise (*45,53*). The steady state level of CP attained appears to be inversely related to the absolute work load (*45*), while the magnitude of the decrease in CP and ATP concentrations appears to be an almost linear function of the relative work load (*53*). As might be expected from the latter finding, the decrease in muscle CP plus ATP concentrations was found to be smaller in a group of men when they were retested at the same absolute work load following a program of endurance exercise training (*94*).

F. Oxygen Uptake During Submaximal Exercise

If there are no differences in skill (i.e., efficiency) in performing the test activity, oxygen utilization is similar in trained and untrained individuals during submaximal exercise of the same intensity. In numerous studies, oxygen uptake was found to be unchanged at various submaximal levels of work following training programs that resulted in significant increases in $\dot{V}_{O_2 max}$ (*17,91–93,103*). Occasionally, oxygen consumption has been slightly lower at the same absolute work level following training (*25,88*) as a result of an increase in skill. In no instance, to this reviewer's knowledge, has an increase in steady state oxygen consumption at the same submaximal exercise level occurred as a result of training.

G. Oxygen Delivery to the Working Muscles

For many years it has been customary among exercise physiologists to attribute lactate production during exercise to "anaerobic glycolysis" secondary to muscle hypoxia, even during relatively mild exercise. In this context it was believed that improved delivery of oxygen to the working muscles was responsible for the lower lactate levels and greater endurance seen in trained individuals. This concept needs revision in light of currently available information.

1. Lactate Production by Well-Oxygenated Muscles

Doll and co-workers (*22*) have reported that oxygen tension in the femoral vein was approximately 21 mm Hg in a group of young men during strenuous exercise when the working muscles were producing large amounts of lactate. Since this value is well above the so-called critical pressure of 7.0 mm Hg reported by Bretschneider (*10*), Doll *et al.* (*22*) interpreted their results to indicate that the increased lactate production was not due to muscle hypoxia. More direct evidence has been provided by Jöbsis and Stainsby (*52*), who found, by means of fluorometric measurements of the steady state oxidation–reduction level of mitochondrial DPN, that dog gastrocnemius muscles were well oxygenated while contracting at a frequency that causes an outpouring of lactate. They felt, therefore, that the lactate production was not caused by hypoxic stimulation of anaerobic glycolysis, but was the result of an imbalance between glycolysis and the rate of pyruvate utilization in the TCA cycle (*52*).

The finding that well-oxygenated skeletal muscle produces lactate at high work rates should not be cause for surprise. There are four possible fates for pyruvate in skeletal muscle. These are (a) conversion to lactate via the reaction catalyzed by lactate dehydrogenase, (b) conversion to alanine by means of the glutamate pyruvate transaminase reaction, (c) oxidation via the citric acid cycle, or (d) conversion to malate by means of the reaction catalyzed by malic enzyme. The DPNH formed in the cytoplasm during glycolysis can be oxidized either by lactate dehydrogenase or by the mitochondria. Since mitochondria are impermeable to DPNH, the latter reaction is an indirect one, with the DPNH first being oxidized in the cytoplasm, followed by transport of the electrons into the mitochondria via various shuttle systems (*102*).

There does not appear to be any mechanism in the skeletal muscle cell for protecting DPNH and pyruvate from lactate dehydrogenase and channeling them directly into the mitochondria. Therefore, the relative rates of conversion of pyruvate to lactate and of oxidation of pyruvate by the mitochondria are largely determined (under aerobic conditions) by the capacity of lactate dehydrogenase to compete with the mitochondria and with glutamate pyruvate transaminase for pyruvate, and with the shuttle systems for DPNH. In view of the high levels of lactate dehydrogenase activity and the relatively low content of mitochondria in skeletal muscle, particularly in the white fibers, it would be most remarkable if well-oxygenated skeletal muscle did not produce considerable lactate during rapid glycolysis.

2. Muscle Hypoxia, Lactate Production, and the Effect of Training

Although there seems little doubt that well-oxygenated muscle can produce lactate during work, the possibility that muscle hypoxia occurs during strenuous submaximal exercise has not been ruled out. However, regardless of whether or not hypoxia occurs, it seems unreasonable to attribute the lower lactate levels found in the trained, as compared to the untrained, state to better oxygenation of the working muscles. If untrained muscles are hypoxic during submaximal exercise, and if a better oxygen supply were responsible for the lower lactate production by trained muscles, then one would expect the trained individual to have a higher oxygen uptake than the untrained at the same submaximal work level. In other words, if a tissue is hypoxic, so that oxygen supply is the factor limiting oxygen consumption, then oxygen uptake will increase if oxygen supply to the tissue is improved. However, as discussed in Section II,F, it is well documented that oxygen consumption at a given absolute work level is not increased by training.

3. Blood Flow to the Working Muscles

Closely related to the belief that lactate production indicates muscle hypoxia is the concept that the lower lactate levels and the greater endurance for submaximal work that result from endurance exercise training are due to increased delivery of blood and oxygen to the working muscles. This does not appear to be correct. It has now been shown by a number of investigators that blood flow per kilogram of working muscle, measured by the ^{133}Xe clearance method, is lower in trained than in sedentary individuals at the same absolute submaximal work level (*17,18,32,98,104*). A lower muscle blood flow following endurance exercise training has been clearly demonstrated both in normal subjects (*32,98*) and in patients with coronary heart disease (*17,18,104*). Further evidence comes from studies using the plethysmographic technique, showing that blood flow in the calf immediately after a submaximal exercise test is lower in the trained than in the untrained state (*26,100*). The working muscles compensate for the lower blood flow in the trained state by extracting more oxygen.

The results of an interesting study by Cobb *et al.* (*20*), in which direct measurements of external iliac vein blood flow were made during exercise, are in keeping with the above findings. Arterial lactate levels and lactate efflux during exercise were directly correlated with exercise blood flow, i.e., the subjects with the greatest blood flow through the exercising limb were also those with the highest lactate levels.

III. Comparative Biochemical Studies on Muscle

In view of the above evidence that oxygen delivery to, and oxygen utilization by, the skeletal muscles during submaximal exercise are not increased by training, it seems likely that other adaptations, probably within the muscles themselves, must be primarily responsible for the lower lactate levels, the slower glycogen depletion, the lower R.Q., and the greater endurance seen in trained individuals. One line of evidence that stimulated the investigation of this possibility came from comparative studies. Paul and Sperling (77) and Lawrie (64) found a good correlation between the function of a muscle and its content of mitochondria. Within the same animal, the most active muscles have the highest respiratory capacity (64,77). A similar relationship is found in comparisons of the same muscle groups in different species (64,77). For example, the breast muscles of mallards and pigeons, which spend long periods in flight, are rich in mitochondria and have ten times as great a respiratory capacity as the breast muscles of domestic chickens which do not fly (77). Similarly, Lawrie has reported that the levels of cytochrome oxidase and succinate dehydrogenase activity in psoas muscle of the sedentary laboratory rabbit are approximately one-third as high as those found in the active wild hare (64). Although these differences may, in part, be genetically determined, it seemed possible that an adaptive response might also be playing a role. This turned out to be the case.

IV. Biochemical Adaptations in Muscle That Result in an Increase in the Capacity for Aerobic Metabolism

A. Skeletal Muscle Myoglobin

The myoglobin content of skeletal muscles generally closely parallels their respiratory capacity (64). In land mammals, skeletal muscles that have a dark red color are rich in both myoglobin and mitochondria, in contrast to white appearing muscles which have a low respiratory capacity and are myoglobin poor (64). Whipple (105) was probably the first to suggest that exercise might increase the concentration of myoglobin in muscle. This suggestion was based on his finding that the muscles of an active hunting dog had a higher content of myglobin than did the muscles of more sedentary dogs (*105*). Further suggestive evidence came from a study by Shenk *et al.* (*96*), who found that cattle grazing in a pasture had a higher concentration of muscle myoglobin than did penned cattle.

The hypothesis that exercise can increase muscle myoglobin concentration was confirmed, under controlled conditions of exercise, diet, and heredity, by the finding that myoglobin increased significantly in leg muscles of rats subjected to programs of treadmill running (*65,76*). The concentration of myoglobin increased approximately 80% in hind limb muscles of rats trained for 12 weeks by means of a program of treadmill running (*76*). Only the muscles directly involved in the exercise have an increased myoglobin content (*76*). It has been shown in *in vitro* studies that myoglobin increases the rate of oxygen transport through a fluid layer (*37,95,107*). It seems likely that myoglobin may also facilitate oxygen utilization in muscle *in vivo* by increasing the rate of oxygen diffusion through the cytoplasm to the mitochondria.

B. INCREASE IN CAPACITY OF SKELETAL MUSCLE TO OXIDIZE CARBOHYDRATE

In 1967 it was reported that when young male rats are subjected to a program of treadmill running, a twofold increase occurs in the capacity of the mitochondrial fraction from their gastrocnemius muscles to oxidize pyruvate (*39*). In the exercise program responsible for this increase, the treadmill speed and duration of the run were progressively increased over a 3 month period until the animals were running continuously, up an 8 deg incline, at 31 m/min, for 2 hr, with 12 intervals of running at 42 m/min, each lasting 30 sec, interspersed at 10 min intervals through the exercise session. They were exercised 5 days per week. This program results in a large increase in endurance (*29,39,76*); it does not cause hypertrophy of the leg muscles (*39,76*).

The mitochondria obtained from the muscles of the exercised animals exhibit a high level of respiratory control and tightly coupled oxidative phosphorylation (*39,67*). This finding indicates that the increase in mitochondrial electron transport capacity is associated with an increase in the ability to regenerate ATP via oxidative phosphorylation.

To avoid possible differences in the percentage yield of mitochondria from muscles of trained and sedentary animals, subsequent studies were performed on whole homogenates of leg muscles. Under conditions of uncontrolled respiration (i.e., in the presence of nonlimiting amounts of P_i, ADP, and substrate), whole homogenates of hind limb muscles from the trained animals have twice as high a rate of oxygen consumption, with pyruvate plus malate as substrate (29,40), and generate $^{14}CO_2$ from pyruvate-2-^{14}C twice as rapidly (3), expressed per gram of fresh muscle, as comparable homogenates from sedentary animals.

There is an approximately 60% increase in the protein content of the mitochondrial fraction of skeletal muscle in response to the running program (39). As a result, the twofold increase in the capacity of the runner's hind limb muscles to oxidize pyruvate is largely obscured when oxygen consumption is expressed per milligram of mitochondrial protein.

That exercise can induce an increase in the capacity of skeletal muscle to oxidize pyruvate has been confirmed in guinea pigs (5) and in humans (68), providing evidence that this is a general rather than a species specific phenomenon. Barnard et al. (5) reported a 65% increase in mitochondrial oxygen uptake per gram skeletal muscle in two guinea pigs subjected to a running program. Morgan and co-workers (68) conducted a study on ten men who exercised 2 hr daily for 1 month. Each subject pedaled a bicycle with one leg while the other leg remained at rest. The exercise load was progressively increased from 300 to 900 kg m/min. The nonexercised extremity served as a control for the exercised. An increase of approximately 45% in the capacity of quadriceps muscle of the exercised extremity to oxidize pyruvate occurred in response to the exercise.

C. Increase in Capacity of Skeletal Muscle to Oxidize Fat

Fat can serve as the major energy source for skeletal muscle during prolonged exercise (15,35,79,109). The relative amounts of fat and carbohydrate utilized during submaximal exercise vary with the level of physical training. Measurements of R.Q. and of the rate of conversion of ^{14}C-labeled fatty acids to $^{14}CO_2$ show that physically trained individuals oxidize more fat and less carbohydrate than untrained individuals during submaximal exercise (15,38,48,92,93). This finding led to an examination of the effect of endurance exercise training on the capacity of skeletal muscle to oxidize fatty acids. The mitochondrial fraction of gastrocnemius and quadriceps muscles from rats subjected to the exercise program described in Section IV,B, utilized approximately twice as much O_2 (expressed as μl O_2/hr/gm fresh muscle) as that of the sedentary group, with either palmitate, oleate, linoleate, palmityl CoA, or palmityl carnitine as substrate (67). Measurements were made under conditions of uncontrolled respiration. Since the protein content of the mitochondrial fraction increases approximately 60%

in the exercised animals, the increase in the capacity to oxidize fatty acids is partly obscured when O_2 consumption is expressed per milligram of mitochondrial protein. The increase in the capacity to oxidize fatty acids is demonstrable over a wide physiologic range of concentrations (Fig. 1).

This effect of training is also demonstrable in whole homogenates of muscle. The rate of $^{14}CO_2$ production by homogenates of hind limb muscles with palmitate-1-^{14}C as substrate is significantly greater in trained than in sedentary rats (*40,66,67*). The running program also results in an approximately twofold increase in the capacity of muscle to oxidize palmitate-U-^{14}C, oleic-1-^{14}C, and palmityl-1-^{14}C CoA (*67*). Since endurance exercise induces an increase of similar magnitude in the capacity of skeletal muscle to oxidize carbohydrate, it seems reasonable to ask why the trained individual derives a greater percentage of his energy from fatty acid oxidation during submaximal exercise than does his untrained counterpart.

The answer probably lies in certain of the control mechanisms that regulate carbohydrate catabolism. Among these is the rate of fatty acid oxidation; high rates of fat oxidation inhibit glycolysis and pyruvate oxidation (*69,74,80*). At a given metabolic rate, the rate of oxidation

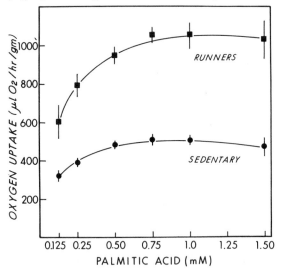

Fig. 1. Relationship between palmitic acid concentration and rate of O_2 utilization by the mitochondrial fraction from muscles of exercised and sedentary animals. Each flask contained 1 mM L-carnitine and 0.025 mM CoA. Each point is the mean for four to six animals. The vertical bars represent twice the SE. O_2 uptake is expressed as microliters of O_2 utilized per hour by the mitochondrial fraction from 1 gm of fresh muscle. [From Molé *et al.* (*67*).]

of fatty acids by a tissue appears to be determined by two factors. These are the concentration of fatty acids (i.e., substrate availability), and the capacity of the tissue for oxidation of fat. When the metabolic rate is held constant, at rest or during steady state exercise, the rate of fat oxidation increases linearly with fatty acid concentration (9,78,79). Saturating concentrations of free fatty acids do not appear to have been reached in the *in vivo* experiments reported in the literature. Thus, the availability of fatty acids to the mitochondria is most likely the rate limiting factor for fatty acid oxidation at any given respiratory rate, *in vivo* (9). However, at any given concentration of fatty acids, the rate of fatty acid oxidation will be highest in the tissues with the greatest capacity for oxidation of fat. For example, at comparable concentrations of fatty acids, the heart will oxidize fatty acids more rapidly than will skeletal muscle, and red muscle will oxidize fat more rapidly than will white. Similarly, the muscles of trained individuals, with their greater capacity for fat oxidation, could be expected to oxidize more fat, at the same fatty acid concentration, than those of untrained individuals. The reason for this is that the rate at which a substrate is utilized is a function of the level of enzyme activity, regardless of whether or not substrate concentration is at a saturating level (cf. Fig. 1).

In addition to its effect on muscle, endurance exercise training appears to induce adaptive changes which result in a greater release of fatty acids from adipose tissue, and higher levels of plasma-free fatty acids, during submaximal exercise (34,47). It seems likely that the increase in the capacity of muscle to oxidize fatty acids, and the greater mobilization of fatty acids, act synergistically to account for the trained individual's greater utilization of fat as an energy source during exercise.

D. Increases in Levels of Specific Enzymes

Underlying the increase in the capacity to oxidize carbohydrates and fatty acids, and to generate ATP via oxidative phosphorylation, is a rise in the levels of activity of the mitochondrial enzymes responsible for these processes. In general, these enzymes increase in parallel. However, there are some exceptions to this pattern.

1. Citric Acid Cycle and Related Enzymes

The levels of activity of citrate synthase (3,43), aconitase (40), DPN-specific isocitrate dehydrogenase (43), and succinate dehydrogenase (29,39,43), increase twofold in hindlimb muscles of rats subjected to the program of running described in Section IV,B. In contrast, the levels of α-ketoglutarate dehydrogenase and mitochondrial malate dehydrogenase

increase only about 50% (43) while the citrate-cycle-related enzyme glutamate dehydrogenase increases approximately 35% (43). These findings
provide evidence that the mitochondrial citrate cycle and citrate-cycle-
related enzymes do not increase in parallel during the adaptation of
skeletal muscle to exercise. As a result there is a change in mitochondrial
composition.

2. Enzymes of the Mitochondrial Cristae

An approximately twofold increase occurs in the levels of the components of the mitochondrial respiratory chain involved in the oxidation of DPNH and succinate in the hind-limb muscles of rats subjected
to the program of running described in Section IV,B. These include
DPNH dehydrogenase (39), succinate dehydrogenase (29,39,43), DPNH
cytochrome c reductase (39), succinate oxidase (29,39,71), cytochrome c
(29,39,41,43,67,70,71), and cytochrome oxidase (29,39,41,71). Mitochondrial coupling factor one catalyzes the oxidative phosphorylation of
ADP to ATP, coupled to electron transport (84). This enzyme, which
is closely associated with the respiratory chain in the mitochondrial
cristae, increases to the same extent as the components of the respiratory chain (70). In contrast to the respiratory chain enzymes that link
the oxidation of DPNH and succinate to oxygen, mitochondrial α-glycero-
phosphate dehydrogenase does not increase in mixed skeletal muscle in response to the running program (41).

A number of investigators, working with both rodents (7,61) and
humans (68,104), have confirmed the finding that the constituents of
the mitochondrial respiratory chain increase in skeletal muscle in response to endurance exercise.

Kraus and co-workers (61) have reported two-fold increases in succinate dehydrogenase and cytochromes b, c, and a in leg muscles of
rats subjected to programs of running or swimming. In contrast to the
finding of Holloszy and Oscai (41), Kraus et al. (61) reported a twofold increase in α-glycerophosphate dehydrogenase in skeletal muscle.
The reason for this discrepancy is, at present, unexplained.

Barnard and Peter (7) reported increases in the concentrations of
cytochromes c and a in gastrocnemius muscles in guinea pigs subjected
to a 10 week program of treadmill running and sprinting at the end of
which they were running for 50 min per day at various speeds. In adult
guinea pigs this program resulted in a 68% increase in cytochrome c
concentration, while in young guinea pigs cytochrome c increased 87%.

In the study by Morgan and co-workers (68) mentioned in Section
IV,B, in which ten men performed bicycle exercise for 2 hr per day for
1 month, DPNH dehydrogenase, succinate dehydrogenase, and cyto-

chrome oxidase all increased significantly in the exercised as compared to the nonexercised muscles.

In another study on humans, Varnauskas *et al.* (*104*) observed a 44% increase in succinate oxidase activity in vastus lateralis muscles of seven medical students subjected to training on a bicycle ergometer for 6 weeks.

3. Enzymes Involved in Fatty Acid Catabolism

The effect of training on ATP-dependent palmityl CoA synthetase, carnitine palmityl transferase, and palmityl CoA dehydrogenase activities in skeletal muscle has been studied in rats subjected to the program of running described in Section IV,B. The levels of activity, expressed per gram wet weight of muscle, of these enzymes involved in the activation, transport, and catabolism of long chain fatty acids increased approximately twofold in gastrocnemius and quadriceps muscles of the runners (*3,40,67*).

In the presence of optimal concentrations of cofactors, skeletal muscle mitochondria oxidize palmitate and palmityl carnitine at approximately the same rates (*67*). This suggests that neither ATP-dependent palmityl CoA synthetase nor carnitine palmityl transferase is rate limiting for fatty acid oxidation in skeletal muscle. It also seems unlikely that the level of activity of palmityl CoA dehydrogenase is rate limiting, since it is approximately five to six times higher than that of carnitine palmityl transferase. As mentioned earlier in Section IV,C, it appears that the rate limiting factor for the oxidation of fatty acids in muscle is the availability of substrate. However, the rate of an enzymatic reaction will increase with the level of enzyme activity (i.e., with the concentration of active enzyme) even though substrate concentration is considerably below saturating (i.e., rate limiting). Thus, even when substrate concentration is rate limiting, an increase in the level of an enzyme or series of enzymes can result in an increase in the rate of utilization of the substrate (cf. Fig. 1).

4. Changes in Mitochondrial Composition

As described above, the levels of activity of a variety of mitochondrial enzymes involved in the oxidation of carbohydrate and fat increase twofold in hind-limb muscles of rats in response to a program of running. Yet mitochondrial protein increases only 55 to 60% (*39,41,67,70*). This appears to be due to a change in mitochondrial composition, with some enzymes increasing twofold, others increasing only 35 to 50%, while some do not increase at all. Among the enzymes that do not increase are mitochondrial creatine phosphokinase and adenylate kinase (70), and mitochondrial α-glycerophosphate dehydrogenase (41). The activities of these enzymes are unchanged when expressed per gram of muscle. However, because of the increase in mitochondrial protein, the specific activities of these enzymes are significantly decreased when expressed per milligram of mitochondrial protein (41,70).

The finding that α-glycerophosphate dehydrogenase, adenylate kinase, and creatine phosphokinase do not increase seems consistent with what is known regarding the adaptation of muscle to endurance exercise. This adaptation has as its major feature an increase in the capacity for aerobic metabolism. In contrast, glycolytic activity does not increase (42), and may even decrease (4). It has been shown that the capacity of a muscle to oxidize α-glycerophosphate parallels its glycolytic capacity and is inversely related to its capacity for aerobic metabolism (81). White muscle, which has a high capacity for glycolysis and a low capacity for aerobic metabolism, has high levels of α-glycerophosphate dehydrogenase, adenylate kinase, and creatine phosphokinase, relative to cardiac muscle, which has a very high capacity for oxidative metabolism and a relatively low glycolytic capacity (21,81,90,97). In this context, it appears that when skeletal muscle adapts to endurance exercise, it becomes more like cardiac muscle in that its content of mitochondria and its capacity to generate ATP from oxidation of pyruvate and fatty acids increase. As a result of the decrease in the specific activities of creatine phosphokinase, adenylate kinase, and α-glycerophosphate dehydrogenase, expressed per milligram of mitochondrial protein, skeletal muscle mitochondria also become more like heart mitochondria in their enzyme pattern.

Barnard and Peter (7) have reported that the concentration of cytochrome c increases more than that of cytochrome a in gastrocnemius muscles of guinea pigs subjected to a running program. They interpreted this difference as further evidence that different mitochondrial components respond differently to exercise training. This finding must be viewed with considerable caution, as the cytochromes of the mitochondrial electron transport chain generally occur in fixed molar ratios to each other in tissues of animals. The results of studies on rats subjected to the program of running described in Section IV,B are in conflict with the report of Barnard and Peter (7), and provide evidence that cytochrome c and cytochrome a do increase in parallel (3,39,41,71). In all these studies the concentration of cytochrome c and the level of activity of cytochrome oxidase (which is a measure of cytochrome a activity) were found to increase to approximately the same extent. This discrepancy may relate to the use of whole homogenates for spectrophotometric measurements of cytochrome a (7); it will require spectrophotometric measurements on more purified preparations with less nonspecific background absorbance to resolve this question.

E. ELECTRON MICROSCOPIC AND HISTOCHEMICAL STUDIES

The results of the biochemical studies described above clearly show that endurance exercise can bring about an adaptive increase in skeletal muscle mitochondria. They do not, however, provide any information as to whether this is due to an increase in the size and/or the number of mitochondria. To answer this question, a number of investigators have compared electron micrographs of trained and untrained muscle. Gollnick and King (31) have reported an increase in both the size and number of mitochondria in skeletal muscles of rats subjected to a 10 week long program of running, during the last week of which they ran for 1 hr per day.

There is currently some disagreement regarding the nature of the response of mitochondria in human skeletal muscle. Morgan and co-workers (68) have reported a large increase in mitochondrial volume, with a minimal increase in number, in quadriceps muscles of men subjected to 2 hr of bicycling per day for 1 month. In contrast, Kiessling et al. (55) reported that a program of running resulted in a large increase in the number of mitochondria in vastus lateralis muscle, but no increase in size. However, they did find that highly trained endurance athletes have significantly hypertrophied mitochondria.

A number of investigators have also performed histochemical studies of the response of the different skeletal muscle fiber types to endurance exercise. A system of nomenclature for the histochemical characteristics of the different fiber types in rodent skeletal muscle, which will be used here, employs the terms white (low oxidative, high myosin ATPase), red (high oxidative, high myosin ATPase), and intermediate (intermediate oxidative capacity, low myosin ATPase) (6,30,73). (It is possible that this system of classification may not be applicable to human skeletal muscle.) Using the staining intensity of succinate dehydrogenase (23, 27,59), DPNH diaphorase (5,23), or malate dehydrogenase (23) as the criterion for distinguishing the fiber types, it was found that the percentage of fibers with the staining characteristics of white muscle decreased, while the percentage of red appearing fibers increased in mixed skeletal muscles, such as the quadriceps, plantaris, and gastrocnemius, of rodents. In contrast, no changes in the staining intensity of these enzymes was seen in the soleus (23), which consists almost entirely of intermediate fibers (3,23). These findings were interpreted as indicating that white muscle fibers are converted to red, and that this change in fiber type is responsible for the increase in respiratory capacity of mixed skeletal muscle that occurs in response to endurance exercise training (*5,23,49*). This interpretation turns out to be incorrect.

F. BIOCHEMICAL RESPONSES OF SPECIFIC MUSCLE TYPES

The capacity for oxidative metabolism of white muscle, which makes up approximately 50% of the mass of gastrocnemius and quadriceps muscles in the rat, is approximately one-fifth as great as that of red muscle (*3*). If, as has been suggested on the basis of the histochemical findings (*5,23,49*), the adaptation of skeletal muscles to endurance exercise consisted of a conversion of white to red fibers, with no change in the red or the intermediate fibers, then the respiratory capacity of the white fibers would have to rise sevenfold to bring about the twofold increase seen in whole gastrocnemius and quadriceps muscles of trained rats.

This interpretation seemed unlikely. In the first place, leg muscles of highly trained animals still have a large white appearing component on gross inspection. A sevenfold increase in respiratory capacity of the white fibers should result in a uniformly red appearing muscle, since myoglobin content roughly parallels respiratory capacity (*64*). In the second place, it had been shown, prior to the histochemical studies, that soleus muscle undergoes an adaptive increase in the levels of activity of cytochrome oxidase and succinate oxidase in response to endurance exercise (*39*).

In a study designed to resolve this question, it was found that the capacity to oxidize pyruvate and fatty acids increased approximately twofold in the superficial, white and the deep, red portions of the quadriceps, as well as in the soleus muscles of rats subjected to a program of running (*3*). Similar increases occurred in the levels of a number of mitochondrial marker enzymes. Since exercise induced an approximately twofold increase in the capacity for aerobic metabolism of all three muscle types, their relationship to each other with respect to respiratory capacity was unchanged. Thus, white fibers still had only approximately one-fifth as great a capacity for oxidative metabolism as red fibers in the muscles of the runners. This finding is not compatible with the concept that white muscle fibers are converted to red in response to exercise. Another explanation is therefore needed for the histochemical observation that, using the criterion of staining intensity of respiratory enzymes, the percentage of "red" appearing fibers in mixed muscle increases, and the percentage of "white" appearing fibers decreases, while no changes are evident in the soleus in response to endurance exercise (*3,5,23,27,59*).

The explanation for this apparent discrepancy probably lies in the relative insensitivity of the histochemical staining techniques, which are qualitative rather than quantitative in nature. As they are generally used, the stains for the respiratory enzymes serve to distinguish fibers with an oxidative capacity above some critical level which makes them appear "red," from "white" fibers with an oxidative capacity below this level. Endurance exercise apparently increases respiratory enzyme levels sufficiently in certain white fibers, perhaps those with highest initial respiratory capacity, to reach the critical staining intensity needed to give a "red" appearance. As a result, the number of white appearing fibers decreases. On the other hand, the initial staining intensity of the respiratory enzymes in the red and intermediate fibers is probably already so dark that any further darkening of the stain due to the exercise-induced increase in respiratory enzyme levels is not readily detectable.

A number of studies have been conducted to determine whether an increase in respiratory capacity also occurs in the heart in response to endurance exercise. Arcos *et al.* (*2*) and Kraus and Kirsten (*60*) have reported increases in the respiratory capacity (per gram of myocardium) in the hearts of rats subjected to programs of swimming. Subsequent studies employing the same program of swimming used by Arcos and co-workers, as well as the program of running described in Section IV,B, have demonstrated that this is not the case (*71,72*). Although respiratory capacity per gram of cardiac muscle is unchanged, the total respiratory enzyme content of the heart increases in proportion to the degree of exercise-induced cardiac hypertrophy (*72*).

G. Effect of the Intensity of the Exercise Stress

As a result of the work of Hearn and Wainio (*36*) and of Gould and Rawlinson (*33*), it was generally believed for a number of years that major enzymatic adaptations do not occur in skeletal muscle in response to endurance exercise. These investigators subjected rats to 30 min of swimming per day for 5 to 8 weeks. No increase in succinate dehydrogenase (*36*), lactate dehydrogenase (*33*), malate dehydrogenase (*33*), or phosphorylase (*33*) occurred in hind-limb muscles of the swimmers. These findings effectively discredited the earlier reports of some Russian workers who claimed that a program of swimming, starting with 1 min per day and increasing by 1 min per day to 30 min, resulted in increases in phosphagen, "phosphorolytic activity," lactate dehydrogenase activity, and succinate dehydrogenase activity.

The finding of Hearn and Wainio (*36*) that 30 min of daily swimming does not induce an increase in succinate dehydrogenase in rat skeletal muscle, which has since been confirmed (*39*), should not come as a surprise. It is generally true that a stimulus must be sufficiently intense to tax an organism's capacity to maintain homeostasis if it is to bring about an adaptive response. Thirty min of swimming is well within the capacity of untrained rats, which can swim for hours if water temperature is maintained between 32°and 36°C. More prolonged swimming can, however, induce adaptive changes in skeletal muscles of rats. For example, cytochrome c concentration increased 44% in gastrocnemius muscles of rats that swam in groups of five or six in containers 47 cm in diameter for 6 hr, 6 days per week (*40*). As might be expected, the adaptive increase in mitochondrial enzymes and respiratory capacity also varies with the duration and speed of treadmill running; however, this relationship has not been studied in detail.

V. Theoretical Implications of the Increased Respiratory Capacity of Trained Muscle

A. BACKGROUND INFORMATION REGARDING THE MECHANISMS BY WHICH OXYGEN CONSUMPTION IS GEARED TO WORK RATE

Because of the difficulties involved in studying respiration during work in single muscle cells, most of the available information regarding the regulation of O_2 consumption and oxidative phosphorylation in muscle cells comes from studies on whole muscles stimulated to contract either *in situ* or *in vitro*. In this type of study all the cells in a muscle are stimulated to contract together by means of supramaximal shocks. As a result, the response of the whole muscle reflects the behavior of all its constituent cells. This is quite different from the graded responses seen during normal exercise, in which varying numbers of motor units are recruited.

When load is held constant, the rate of O_2 consumption by muscle cells is a function of the frequency of contraction (*14,28*). For example, in cat soleus muscles stimulated to contract *in situ*, the increase in O_2 consumption (expressed as ml/min/100 mg) is four times as great at 240 contractions per minute as it is at 60 contractions per minute (*28*). Thus, the oxygen uptake of muscle cells can be varied over a wide range by varying the work rate. The mechanisms by which O_2 consumption is geared so closely to work rate relate to the tight coupling of oxidative phosphorylation to electron transport in intact mitochondria. Unless ADP and P_i are available for the synthesis of ATP via oxidative phosphorylation, electron transport and O_2 utilization do not occur. If the supplies of O_2 and of substrate are not limiting, the rate of O_2 consumption is largely determined by the intramitochondrial concentrations of ADP and P_i (11,57,63). The levels of ADP and P_i and the rate of O_2 consumption are low in resting muscle. With the onset of exercise, ATP and creatine phosphate are split, and the intramitochondrial levels of ADP and P_i rise.

It has been shown in frog muscles in which creatine phosphokinase was poisoned with dinitrofluorobenzene that approximately 0.3–0.4 mmole of ATP is hydrolyzed per kilogram of muscle per twitch (46). If a proportional increase occurred in the concentration of ADP in muscle mitochondria, electron transport and O_2 consumption would be stimulated maximally. However, this does not happen in muscles in which creatine phosphokinase has not been poisoned. Spectrophotometric and fluorometric studies on intact frog and toad sartorius muscles have demonstrated that the amount of ADP reaching the mitochondria is only a very small portion of that which is formed per twitch (11–13, 50,51). It has been calculated that the ADP concentration increases approximately 5–7 μmoles per twitch per kilogram of muscle during the first few twitches of a series (50,51). This is approximately 2% of the value expected on the basis of ATP hydrolysis, and is in rather close agreement with values calculated on the basis of the kinetics of the creatine phosphokinase reaction (50,51). Thus, most of the ADP formed during a muscle contraction is rephosphorylated by the creatine phosphokinase–creatine phosphate system before reaching the mitochondria.

The increase in mitochondrial ADP concentration produced by a series of contractions follows a saturation curve, with a plateau or steady state being attained after about 30 twitches in toad sartorius muscle (50,51). The magnitude of the steady state concentration of ADP and, therefore, also of O_2 consumption, is a function of the stimulation frequency (51).

Once a steady state, submaximal level of O_2 consumption is attained in a muscle cell, the rate of ATP formation via oxidative phosphorylation during and between muscle contractions must be sufficiently great to balance the amounts of ATP and CP split during the contraction. In the period between the onset of muscle contractions and the attainment of the steady state, before ATP hydrolysis is balanced by oxidative phosphorylation, the concentrations of CP and ATP fall until the steady state is attained (*45,53,54,82*). During this interval, ADP and P_i levels in the mitochondria must rise to the steady state levels determined by the work rate, at which point they turn on electron transport and oxidative phosphorylation sufficiently to balance ATP hydrolysis.

The presence of high levels of adenylate kinase activity in the cytoplasm results in the conversion of some of the ADP that is formed to AMP. The steady state concentration of AMP in skeletal muscle during exercise is maintained at a relatively low level, probably in the range of two to four times the resting value, by the action of adenylate deaminase. This enzyme is responsible for the formation of ammonia in muscle during exercise (*99*).

B. Effect of the Adaptive Increase in Respiratory Capacity on the Response of Muscle to Submaximal Exercise

As reviewed in Section II,F, O_2 consumption is the same in the trained and untrained states during submaximal exercise of a given intensity. Skeletal muscle that has adapted to endurance exercise has up to twice as many mitochondrial cristae per gram as untrained muscle. Therefore, to attain a given submaximal level of O_2 consumption, the concentrations of ADP and P_i must increase less and attain lower steady state levels in muscles of trained as compared to untrained individuals, because, with more mitochondria, each mitochondrion has to be "turned on" to a lesser extent to balance a given rate of ATP hydrolysis by the myofibrils. In other words, the greater the number of mitochondria per gram of muscle, the lower must be the O_2 uptake per mitochondrion at a given submaximal level of O_2 consumption (expressed per gram of muscle). It follows from this line of reasoning that in the process of attaining a given steady state level of O_2 uptake, the concentrations of CP and ATP must decrease to a lesser extent, and stabilize at higher levels, in muscles of trained as compared to untrained individuals. A smaller drop in CP and ATP levels with a smaller increase in ADP and P_i concentrations should also result in lower steady state concentrations of AMP and, possibly, of ammonia.

The intracellular concentrations of ATP, CP, P_i, ADP, AMP, and NH_4^+ to a large extent control the rate of glycolysis in muscle (*62,75, 101,106,108*). ATP and CP inhibit phosphofructokinase, and this inhibition is counteracted by P_i, ADP, AMP, and NH_4^+ (*62,75,101,106,108*). Therefore, because of higher steady state concentrations of ATP and CP, and lower levels of AMP, P_i, ADP, and, possibly, of NH_4^+ in muscle that has adapted to endurance exercise, glycolysis should occur at a slower rate in the trained than in the untrained state at a given submaximal level of work and O_2 utilization. This should result in slower rates of muscle glycogen depletion and lactate formation in trained individuals during submaximal exercise.

Experimental evidence supporting this line of reasoning comes from a study by Saltin and Karlsson (94). Using serial muscle biopsies, these investigators found that, in the same individual tested at the same submaximal level of work and O_2 consumption before and after adapting to a program of endurance exercise, the fall in CP and ATP concentrations, the rate of glycogen depletion, and the concentration of lactate in quadriceps muscle were all lower in the trained state (94).

As reviewed in Section II,D, individuals who have adapted to endurance exercise derive a greater percentage of their energy from oxidation of fatty acids and less from carbohydrate than do untrained individuals during submaximal exercise. This is reflected in a lower R.Q. This shift in the carbon source for the citric acid cycle likely plays an important role (in addition to the Pasteur effect discussed above) in accounting for the slower rates of glycogen depletion and the lower lactate concentrations seen in trained individuals during submaximal exercise. An increase in the oxidation of fatty acids results in a decrease in carbohydrate utilization (80), brought about, in part, by a reduction in the rate of glycolysis (69,86). This appears to be mediated by an increase in the concentration of citrate which is an inhibitor of phosphofructokinase (74). In addition, the formation of acetyl CoA during oxidation of fatty acids inhibits pyruvate dehydrogenase and, by this means, carbohydrate oxidation (85).

One factor that has been implicated in the development of muscle fatigue, that forces an individual performing prolonged exercise to stop or slow his pace, is depletion of muscle glycogen stores (1,8). Clearly, the glycogen-sparing effects, mediated by the mechanisms outlined above, of the adaptations induced in skeletal muscle by endurance exercise could postpone depletion of muscle glycogen, and the fatigue associated with it, during prolonged exercise.

Another factor which may limit endurance during prolonged exercise is the development of hypoglycemia (16,83). Increased oxidation of fatty acids appears to decrease glucose uptake by muscle (86) and could, through this mechanism, protect physically trained individuals against hypoglycemia during prolonged exercise.

C. $\dot{V}_{O_2 max}$ AND THE ADAPTIVE RESPONSE OF MUSCLE TO ENDURANCE EXERCISE

When an individual adapts to endurance exercise, both his $\dot{V}_{O_2 max}$ and the concentration of mitochondria in his skeletal muscles increase. Since the mitochondria are responsible for O_2 utilization, an obvious ques-

John O. Holloszy

tion raised by these findings is whether the increase in muscle mitochondria plays a role in the increase in $\dot{V}_{O_2\,max}$. Although it is difficult
for this reviewer to visualize conditions under which the increase in
mitochondria would not play a role in the increase in $\dot{V}_{O_2\,max}$ with training, insufficient experimental information is available at present to
give this question a categorical answer. Therefore, to put the question
in perspective, the first part of this section will be devoted to a review
of data relating to the contributions of the cardiovascular system, and
of factors within the muscles, to the increase in $\dot{V}_{O_2\,max}$ induced by
exercise.

When an individual responds to endurance exercise training with an
increase in $\dot{V}_{O_2\,max}$, his maximum cardiac output is usually also increased
(*24,25,89,91*). A rise in maximum cardiac output implies an increase in
the capacity to supply O_2 to the working muscles. However, it must be
remembered that studies using the ^{133}Xe clearance method have shown
that maximum blood flow to the working muscles, expressed as milliliters
per minute per gram, is not increased in the trained state (*32*). If these
results obtained with the ^{133}Xe clearance method are valid and generally applicable, it would appear that an increase in $\dot{V}_{O_2\,max}$ brought about
by an increase in maximum cardiac output is due to delivery of O_2 to
a larger mass of working muscle rather than to delivery of more O_2 to
the individual muscle cells. On the average, an increase in maximal
cardiac output appears to account for approximately 50% of the rise
in $\dot{V}_{O_2\,max}$ that occurs with training (*24,25,89,91*). The other 50% of the
increase in $\dot{V}_{O_2\,max}$ appears to result from an increase in O_2 extraction
by the muscles, reflected in an increase in the arteriovenous O_2 difference
(*24,25,89,91*). Thus, any increase in O_2 utilization by the individual
muscle cells appears to be due to extraction of a greater percentage of
the O_2 from the blood rather than to increased delivery of O_2. As a
result of the increased extraction, the O_2 tension in venous blood, and,
therefore, also the mean O_2 tension in the muscle capillaries, is lower in
the trained than in the untrained state during work requiring the $\dot{V}_{O_2\,max}$.
No experimental information is available relative to the mechanisms
by which trained muscle cells extract greater amounts of O_2 from the
blood. However, it does seem reasonable that the lower mean O_2 tension
in capillary blood reflects a lower O_2 tension in skeletal muscle cells.
Actually, it seems inevitable that O_2 tension in muscle cells and, secon-
darily, in the capillaries, must be lower in the trained state if, as discussed above, O_2 delivery to the working muscle cells is unchanged,
while the concentration of mitochondria in muscle, and the work rate
required to attain $\dot{V}_{O_2\,max}$ are increased.

It has been argued that O_2 availability in the working muscles is the factor that limits $\dot{V}_{O_2 max}$, and that the increase in muscle mitochondria cannot, therefore, be responsible for an increase in $\dot{V}_{O_2 max}$. Another argument that has been raised is that the increase in mitochondria that occurs with training is proportionally greater than the increase in $\dot{V}_{O_2 max}$, and that the increase in mitochondria cannot, therefore, be responsible for the rise in $\dot{V}_{O_2 max}$.

These overly simplistic arguments are based on two assumptions: (a) if O_2 supply is limiting, then an increase in mitochondria cannot result in an increase in $\dot{V}_{O_2 max}$; and (b) an increase in $\dot{V}_{O_2 max}$ secondary to an increase in muscle mitochondria must be directly proportional to the increase in mitochondria. The purpose of the remainder of this section is to show that these assumptions are fallacious.

Any discussion of the factors limiting $\dot{V}_{O_2 max}$ is hampered by lack of information regarding the O_2 tension in the working muscle cells. No useful purpose would be served here by a review of the literature on the controversial subject of whether or not O_2 supply is the factor limiting $\dot{V}_{O_2 max}$, since the published experimental results are not sufficiently clear cut to resolve this question. However, since a major argument against a role for the increase in muscle mitochondria in the increase in $\dot{V}_{O_2 max}$ with training depends on the premise that the muscles are hypoxic, it will be assumed for the purpose of this discussion (and it may quite possibly be correct) that O_2 supply to the mitochondria is the factor limiting $\dot{V}_{O_2 max}$.

Following the line of reasoning developed earlier in this section, if skeletal muscle is hypoxic in the untrained state at $\dot{V}_{O_2 max}$, then skeletal muscle hypoxia should be more marked in the trained state during work requiring the $\dot{V}_{O_2 max}$. Recapitulating, an increase in muscle mitochondria, together with an increase in the work rate required to attain $\dot{V}_{O_2 max}$, in the face of an unchanged maximum blood flow, should result in a lower O_2 tension in the muscle cells.

How can an increase in the relative degree of hypoxia in the muscles be compatible with an increase in $\dot{V}_{O_2 max}$? This question can be answered most readily by means of a hypothetical example. Let us suppose that O_2 tension in a working muscle cell falls to a level at which the mitochondrial respiratory chain can function at only 98% of its maximum capacity, in an untrained individual exercising at his $\dot{V}_{O_2 max}$. Let us further suppose that following a program of endurance exercise the concentration if mitochondria in this skeletal muscle cell was increased 50%. As a result of the increase in mitochondria and in the work rate required to attain $\dot{V}_{O_2 max}$, O_2 tension falls to a level which permits the mitochondria in this muscle cell to respire at only 75% of their maximum capacity in the trained individual exercising at $\dot{V}_{O_2 max}$. It can be calculated that, with this degree of hypoxia, a 50% increase in mitochondria would account for a 14.8% increase in oxygen consumption. If maximum respiratory capacity of the untrained skeletal muscle cell is 100, then O_2 consumption in the working muscle cell during exercise at $\dot{V}_{O_2 max}$ is $100 \times 0.98 = 98$. If maximum respiratory capacity of the muscle cell after training is 150, then O_2 utilization by the working muscle cell during exercise at $\dot{V}_{O_2 max}$ is $150 \times 0.75 = 112.5$; $112.5 - 98 = 14.5$; $14.5 \div 98 = a$ 14.8% increase in $\dot{V}_{O_2 max}$ attributable to the 50% increase in muscle mitochondria.

The only purpose of this hypothetical example is to demonstrate that (a) an increase in muscle mitochondria can result in an increase in $\dot{V}_{O_2 max}$ even if O_2 supply is limiting, and that (b) the increase in $\dot{V}_{O_2 max}$ does not have to be proportional to the increase in mitochondria. It represents only one of a number of possibilities, and no claim is being made here either for or against the hypothesis that the working muscle cells are hypoxic during work requiring the $\dot{V}_{O_2 max}$. The answer to this question awaits the development of methods that will permit measurement of O_2 tension in the muscle cells during strenuous exercise.

References

1. Ahlborg, B., Bergström, J., Ekelund, L.-G., and Hultman, E. (1967). *Acta Physiol. Scand.* **70**, 129–142.
2. Arcos, J. C., Sohal, R. S., Sun, S. C., Argus, M. F., and Burch, G. E. (1968). *Exp. Mol. Pathol.* **8**, 49–65.
3. Baldwin, K. M., Klinkerfuss, G. H., Terjung, R. L., Molé, P. A., and Holloszy, J. O. (1972). *Amer. J. Physiol.* **222**, 373–378.
4. Baldwin, K. M., Terjung, R. L., Winder, W. W., and Holloszy, J. O. In preparation.
5. Barnard, R. J., Edgerton, V. R., and Peter, J. B. (1970). *J. Appl. Physiol.* **28**, 762–766.
6. Barnard, R. J., Edgerton, V. R., Furukawa, T., and Peter, J. B. (1971). *Amer. J. Physiol.* **220**, 410–414.
7. Barnard, R. J., and Peter, J. B. (1971). *J. Appl. Physiol.* **31**, 904–908.
8. Bergström, J., Hermansen, L., Hultman, E., and Saltin, B. (1967). *Acta Physiol. Scand.* **71**, 140–150.
9. Bremer, J. (1967). *In* "Cellular Compartmentalization and Control of Fatty Acid Metabolism" (J. Bremer and F. C. Gran, eds.), pp. 65–88. Academic Press, New York.
10. Bretschneider, H. J. (1961). *Verhl. Deut. Ges. Kreislaufforsch.* **27**, 32–59.
11. Chance, B. (1959). *Ann. N. Y. Acad. Sci.* **81**, 477–489.
12. Chance, B., and Connelly, C. M. (1957). *Nature (London)* **179**, 1235–1237.
13. Chance, B., and Jöbsis, F. F. (1959). *Nature (London)* **184**, 195–196.
14. Chapler, C. K., and Stainsby, W. N. (1968). *Amer. J. Physiol.* **215**, 995–1004.
15. Christensen, E. H., and Hansen, O. (1939). *Skand. Arch. Physiol.* **81**, 160–171.

16. Christensen, E. H., and Hansen, O. (1939). *Skand. Arch. Physiol.* **81**, 172–179.
17. Clausen, J. P., Larsen, O. A., and Trap-Jensen, J. (1969). *Circulation* **40**, 143–154.
18. Clausen, J. P., and Trap-Jensen, J. (1970). *Circulation* **42**, 611–624.
19. Cobb, L. A., and Johnson, W. P. (1963). *J. Clin. Invest.* **42**, 800–810.
20. Cobb, L. A., Smith, P. H., Lwai, S., and Short, F. A. (1969). *J. Appl. Physiol.* **26**, 606–610.
21. Dart, C. H., and Holloszy, J. O. (1969). *Circulation Res.* **25**, 245–253.
22. Doll, E., Keul, J., and Maiwald, C. (1968). *Amer. J. Physiol.* **215**, 23–29.
23. Edgerton, V. R., Gerchman, L., and Carrow, R. (1969). *Exp. Neurol.* **24**, 110–123.
24. Ekblom, B. (1969). *Acta Physiol. Scand. Suppl.* **328**, 1–45.
25. Ekblom, B., Åstrand, P.-O., Saltin, B., Stenberg, J., and Wallström, B. (1968). *J. Appl. Physiol.* **24**, 518–528.
26. Elsner, R. W., and Carlson, L. D. (1962). *J. Appl. Physiol.* **17**, 436–440.
27. Faulkner, J. A., Maxwell, L. C., Brook, D. A., and Lieberman, D. A. (1971). *Amer. J. Physiol.* **221**, 291–297.
28. Folkow, B., and Halicka, H. D. (1968). *Microvascular Res.* **1**, 1–14.
29. Fuge, K. W., Crews, E. L., Jr., Pattengale, P. K., Holloszy, J. O., and Shank, R. E. (1968). *Amer. J. Physiol.* **215**, 660–663.
30. Gauthier, G. F. (1970). *In* "The Physiology and Biochemistry of Muscle as a Food" (E. J. Briskey, R. G. Cassens, and B. B. Marsh, eds.), pp. 103–130. Univ. of Wisconsin Press, Madison, Wisconsin.
31. Gollnick, P. D., and King, D. W. (1969). *Amer. J. Physiol.* **216**, 1502–1509.
32. Grimby, G., Häggendal. E., and Saltin, B. (1967). *J. Appl. Physiol.* **22**, 305–310.
33. Gould, M. K., and Rawlinson, W. A. (1959). *Biochem. J.* **73**, 41–44.
34. Havel, R. J., Carlson, L. A., Ekelund, L.-G., and Holmgren, A. (1964). *J. Appl. Physiol.* **19**, 613–618.
35. Havel, R. J., Naimark, A., and Borchgrevink, C. F. (1963). *J. Clin. Invest.* **42**, 1054–1063.
36. Hearn, G. R., and Wainio, W. W. (1956). *Amer. J. Physiol.* **185**, 348–350.
37. Hemmingsen, E. A. (1963). *Comp. Biochem. Physiol.* **10**, 239–244.
38. Hermansen, L., Hultman, E., and Saltin, B. (1967). *Acta Physiol. Scand.* **71**, 129–139.
39. Holloszy, J. O. (1967). *J. Biol. Chem.* **242**, 2278–2282.
40. Holloszy, J. O., Molé, P. A., Baldwin, K. M., and Terjung, R. L. (1973). *In* "Factors Limiting Performance Capacity" (J. Keul, ed.), pp. 63–77. Thiem, Stuttgart.
41. Holloszy, J. O., and Oscai, L. B. (1969). *Arch. Biochem. Biophys.* **130**, 653–656.
42. Holloszy, J. O., Oscai, L. B., Molé, P. A., and Don, I. J. (1971). *In* "Muscle Metabolism During Exercise" (B. Pernow and B. Saltin, eds.), pp. 51–61. Plenum, New York.
43. Holloszy, J. O., Oscai, L. B., Don, I. J., and Molé, P. A. (1970). *Biochem. Biophys. Res. Commun.* **40**, 1368–1373.
44. Holmgren, A., and Ström, G. (1959). *Acta Med. Scand.* **163**, 185–193.
45. Hultman, E., Bergström, J., and McLennan-Anderson, N. (1967). *Scand. J. Clin. Lab. Invest.* **19**, 56–66.
46. Infante, A. A., and Davies, R. E. (1962). *Biochem. Biophys. Res. Commun.* **9**, 410–415.
47. Issekutz, B., Jr., Miller, H. I., Paul, P., and Rodahl, K. (1965). *J. Appl. Physiol.* **20**, 293–296.
48. Issekutz, B., Jr., Miller, H. I., and Rodahl, K. (1966). *Fed. Proc.* **25**, 1415–1420.

49. Jeffress, R. N., and Peter, J. B. (1970). *Bull. Los Angeles Neurol. Soc.* **35,** 134–144.

50. Jöbsis, F. F. (1963). *J. Gen. Physiol.* **46,** 929–969.

51. Jöbsis, F. F., and Duffield, J. C. (1967). *J. Gen. Physiol.* **50,** 1009–1047.

52. Jöbsis, F. F., and Stainsby, W. N. (1968). *Resp. Physiol.* **4,** 292–300.

53. Karlsson, J., Diamant, B., and Saltin, B. (1970). *Scand. J. Clin. Lab. Invest.* **26,** 385–394.

54. Karlsson, J., and Saltin, B. (1970). *J. Appl. Physiol.* **29,** 598–602.

55. Kiessling, K. H., Piehl, K., and Lundquist, C.-G. (1971). *In* "Muscle Metabolism During Exercise" (B. Pernow and B. Saltin, eds.), pp. 97–101. Plenum, New York.

56. Kilbom, A. (1971). *Scand. J. Clin. Lab. Invest.* **28,** Suppl. 119, 1–34.

57. Klingenberg, M., and Von Hafen, H. (1963). *Biochem. Z.* **337,** 120–145.

58. Knehr, C. A., Dill, D. B., and Neufeld, W. (1942). *Amer. J. Physiol.* **136,** 148–156.

59. Kowalski, K., Gordon, E. E., Martinez, A., and Adamek, J. A. (1969). *J. Histochem. Cytochem.* **17,** 601–607.

60. Kraus, H.. and Kirsten, R. (1970). *Pfluegers Arch.* **320,** 334–347.

61. Kraus, H., Kirsten, R., and Wolff, J. R. (1969). *Pfluegers Arch.* **308,** 57–79.

62. Krzanowski, J., and Matschinsky, F. M. (1969). *Biochem. Biophys. Res. Commun.* **34,** 816–823.

63. Lardy, H. A., and Wellman, H. (1953). *J. Biol. Chem.* **201,** 357–370.

64. Lawrie, R. A. (1953). *Biochem. J.* **55,** 298–305.

65. Lawrie, R. A. (1953). *Nature (London)* **171,** 1069–1070.

66. Molé, P. A., and Holloszy, J. O. (1970). *Proc. Soc. Exp. Biol. Med.* **134,** 789–792.

67. Molé, P. A., Oscai, L. B., and Holloszy, J. O. (1971). *J. Clin. Invest.* **50,** 2323–2330.

68. Morgan, T. E., Cobb, L. A., Short, F. A., Ross, R., and Gunn, D. R. (1971). *In* "Muscle Metabolism During Exercise" (B. Pernow and B. Saltin, eds.), pp. 87–95. Plenum, New York.

69. Newsholme, E. A., and Randle, P. J. (1964). *Biochem. J.* **93,** 641–651.

70. Oscai, L. B., and Holloszy, J. O. (1971). *J. Biol. Chem.* **246,** 6968–6972.

71. Oscai, L. B., Molé, P. A., Brei, B., and Holloszy, J. O. (1971). *Amer. J. Physiol.* **220,** 1238–1241.

72. Oscai, L. B., Molé, P. A., and Holloszy, J. O. (1971). *Amer. J. Physiol.* **220,** 1944–1948.

73. Padykula, H. A., and Gauthier, G. F. (1967). *In* "Exploratory Concepts in Muscular Dystrophy and Related Disorders" (A. T. Milhorat, ed.), pp. 117–128. Excerpta Med. Found., Amsterdam.

74. Parmeggiani, A., and Bowman, R. H. (1963). *Biochem. Biophys. Res. Commun.* **12,** 268–273.

75. Passonneau, J. V., and Lowry, O. H. (1963). *Biochem. Biophys. Res. Commun.* **13,** 372–379.

76. Pattengale, P. K., and Holloszy, J. O. (1967). *Amer. J. Physiol.* **213,** 783–785.

77. Paul, M. H., and Sperling, E. (1952). *Proc. Soc. Exp. Biol. Med.* **79,** 352–354.

78. Paul, P. (1970). *J. Appl. Physiol.* **28,** 127–132.

79. Paul, P., and Issekutz, B., Jr. (1967). *J. Appl. Physiol.* **22,** 615–622.

80. Paul, P., Issekutz, B., Jr., and Miller, H. I. (1966). *Amer. J. Physiol.* **211,** 1313–1320.

81. Pette, D. (1966). *In* "Regulation of Metabolic Processes in Mitochondria" (J. M. Tager, S. Papa, E. Quagliariello, and E. C. Slater, eds.), pp. 28–49. Elsevier, Amsterdam.
82. Piiper, J., di Prampero, P. E., and Cerretelli, P. (1968). *Amer. J. Physiol.* **215**, 523–531.
83. Pruett, E. D. R. (1970). *J. Appl. Physiol.* **28**, 199–208.
84. Racker, E., and Horstman, L. L. (1967). *J. Biol. Chem.* **242**, 2547–2551.
85. Randle, P. J., Garland, P. B., Hales, C. N., Newsholme, E. A., Denton, R. M., and Pogson, C. I. (1966). *Recent Progr. Horm. Res.* **22**, 1–48.
86. Randle, P. J., Newsholme, E. A., and Garland, P. B. (1964). *Biochem. J.* **93**, 652–665.
87. Robinson, S., and Harmon, P. M. (1941). *Amer. J. Physiol.* **132**, 757–769.
88. Robinson, S., and Harmon, P. M. (1941). *Amer. J. Physiol.* **133**, 161–169.
89. Rowell, L. B. (1971). *In* "Physiology of Work Capacity and Fatigue" (E. Simonson, ed.), pp. 143–144. Thomas, Springfield, Illinois.
90. Sacktor, B., and Cochran, D. G. (1958). *Arch. Biochem. Biophys.* **74**, 266–276.
91. Saltin, B., Blomqvist, G., Mitchell, J. H., Johnson, R. L., Jr., Wildenthal, K., and Chapman, C. B. (1968). *Circulation* **38**, Suppl. 7, 1–78.
92. Saltin, B., Hartley, L. H., Kilbom, A., and Åstrand, I. (1969). *Scand. J. Clin. Lab. Invest.* **24**, 323–334.
93. Saltin, B., and Karlsson, J. (1971). *In* "Muscle Metabolism During Exercise" (B. Pernow and B. Saltin, eds.), pp. 289–299. Plenum, New York.
94. Saltin, B., and Karlsson, J. (1971). *In* "Muscle Metabolism During Exercise" (B. Pernow and B. Saltin, eds.), pp. 395–399. Plenum, New York.
95. Scholander, P. F. (1960). *Science* **131**, 585–590.
96. Shenk, J. H., Hall, J. L., and King, H. H. (1934). *J. Biol. Chem.* **105**, 741–752.
97. Shonk, C. E., and Boxer, G. E. (1964). *Cancer Res.* **24**, 709–721.
98. Stenberg, J. (1971). *In* "Coronary Heart Disease and Physical Fitness" (O. A. Larsen and R. O. Malmborg, eds.), pp. 80–83. Munksgaard, Copenhagen.
99. Tornheim, K., and Lowenstein, J. M. (1972). *J. Biol. Chem.* **247**, 162–169.
100. Treumann, F., and Schroeder, W. (1968). *Z. Kreislaufforsch.* **57**, 1024–1033.
101. Uyeda, K., and Racker, E. (1965). *J. Biol. Chem.* **240**, 4682–4688.
102. Van Dam, K., and Meyer, A. J. (1971). *Annu. Rev. Biochem.* **40**, 115–160.
103. Varnauskas, E., Bergman, H., Houk, P., and Björntorp, P. (1966). *Lancet* **2**, 8–12.
104. Varnauskas, E., Björntorp, P., Fahlen, M., Prerovsky, I., and Stenberg, J. (1970). *Cardiovasc. Res.* **4**, 418–422.
105. Whipple, G. H. (1926). *Amer. J. Physiol.* **76**, 693–707.
106. Williamson, J. R. (1966). *J. Biol. Chem.* **241**, 5026–5036.
107. Wittenberg, J. B. (1966). *J. Biol. Chem.* **241**, 104–114.
108. Wu, R., and Racker, E. (1959). *J. Biol. Chem.* **234**, 1029–1035.
109. Zierler, K. L., Maseri, A., Klassen, G., Rabinowitz, D., and Burgess, J. (1968). *Trans. Ass. Amer. Physicians* **81**, 266–272.

Adaptations in Strength and Muscular Endurance Resulting from Exercise

David H. Clarke

DEPARTMENT OF PHYSICAL EDUCATION, UNIVERSITY OF MARYLAND,
COLLEGE PARK, MARYLAND

Man's interest in strength development extends beyond published record; primitive man depended upon physical strength and prowess for the satisfaction of his personal needs and protection. History reveals ample evidence that the well-developed body was important in the emergence of athletics, for both combative and noncombative events, and has served as an expression of man's personality and general health as well.

The modern era in the science of strength development received its impetus during World War II in response to the demands created by the orthopedically handicapped soldier. The increased emphasis on rehabilitation and the creation of physical reconditioning specialists to augment already existing personnel in physical and occupational therapy resulted in newer techniques for the measurement of muscular strength. It was during this time, for example, that the cable tensiometer was adapted from the aircraft industry for use in human strength testing (*32–34*).

I. Isotonic Training

The first major attempt to systematize the procedures for isotonic training is generally accredited to the work of DeLorme and Watkins (48), who presented a protocol for load-resisting exercises. Commonly referred to under the rubric of progressive resistance exercises (PRE), they involve three sets of exercise, each one based on the amount of load that can be raised against gravity no more than ten times, i.e., ten repetitions maximum (10 RM). The first set requires the use of one-half of the 10 RM, to be lifted ten times, the second set utilizes three-fourths of the 10 RM, also lifted ten times, and the final set is the 10 RM. Since the program is designed to be progressive, the amount of weight to be utilized for the 10 RM must be adjusted periodically as strength increases. Thus, when the 10 RM becomes 15 RM, a new assessment is made, a process which may be repeated weekly, as required.

In addition to proving effective with normal muscles, these procedures have resulted in increased strength and work capacity for those muscles weakened by poliomyelitis (47) and other orthopedic conditions (45). DeLorme (44) made a clear distinction between the relationship of repetitions to resistance, stating that low repetition, high resistance exercises produce power, whereas high repetition, low resistance exercises result in endurance, and claiming them to be mutually exclusive, each type of exercise being incapable of producing both results.

Progressive resistance exercises in one form or another are ordinarily employed by those individuals desirous of applying force through a full range of motion in order to achieve gains in strength. An alternative procedure was developed by Zinovieff (147) in response to what he considered a difficulty in employing the original DeLorme procedures to patients, namely, that the final 10 RM reduced the quality of contraction. Frequently, fatigue impaired the ability to perform a full range of motion, and the load itself often resulted in pain to involved joints. Therefore, he proposed what is known as the Oxford technique, a total of 100 contractions which began after a brief warm-up, with the first set consisting of 10 RM. Each succeeding bout of ten repetitions was done with the weight reduced, so that, as fatigue increased, the performer was still lifting 10 RM, and thereby exercising to maximum capacity.

Application of PRE to adolescent boys in both elbow flexion and knee extension for 4 months by DeLorme and associates (46) resulted in an average increase in strength of 59% and 49%, respectively, as measured by 1 RM. When Houtz et al. (79) applied PRE to female subjects, exercising the quadriceps and those muscles involved in hand curls, it was found that strength more than doubled in 4 weeks. The authors felt that the most important element in daily performance was the will to perform a maximum physiological effort. McMorris and Elkins (97) employed both the DeLorme and Oxford training techniques to the right triceps in two groups of subjects and found little difference in the two training methods, both causing significant strength gains.

The question of which of the possible procedures of PRE is most effective in producing strength increases has been the subject of several investigations. For example, Berger has employed the technique of 1 RM as the criterion measure of strength, and in one study (9), placed subjects into six groups which trained in the bench press exercise. The groups used resistances of 2, 4, 6, 8, 10, and 12 RM. Those that trained with 4, 6, and 8 repetitions had significantly greater gains in strength than the other groups, suggesting that the optimum range for training was somewhere between 3 and 9 repetitions, at least when the training regimen involved only one set. When the training included one, two, and three sets, each one employing 2, 6, and 10 RM, he found (7) that all combinations resulted in significant strength increases, but that no advantage was gained by exercising with heavier loads for 2 RM than with lighter loads at 10 RM. In fact, the optimum number of repetitions per set seemed to be 6 RM for three sets. Further (12), when groups employed 2 RM for six sets, 6 RM for three sets, and 10 RM for three sets, all groups gained significantly in strength, but yet no difference existed between groups.

An alternate procedure was compared to the usual 10 RM training technique by Berger and Hardage (15), in which one of their two groups performed ten repetitions for one set, but each repetition was adjusted in such a manner that it required maximum effort. This was accomplished by beginning with 1 RM and gradually reducing the load for each subsequent repetition. Both groups improved significantly in the 1 RM bench press after 8 weeks of training, but the 1 RM group improved significantly more than the regular 10 RM group, revealing that the intensity of each effort was an important consideration in training. Thus, when a group of subjects who trained at 90% of the 10 RM twice a week, and the 10 RM once a week, were compared with a group that worked with the 10 RM procedures each of the 3 days (10), both groups improved significantly in strength, but no difference was found between them. This finding was emphasized further (14), when the 1 RM deep knee bend was utilized as a criterion of isotonic strength. Seven groups of subjects, including a control group, trained for 6 weeks, including 1 RM performed only once a week, 66, 80, and

90% of the 1 RM performed twice a week, and 1 RM and 66% of the 1 RM employed three times a week. Most of the experimental groups increased significantly in strength, but the group that trained with only one repetition at 66% of the 1 RM a total of 3 times a week had mean strength scores significantly less than the other groups.

When comparing various programs for arms and legs, Capen (*24*) found that three sets of 1 RM were better than one set of 8–15 RM for the development of strength, but apparently little advantage was gained when both the resistance and the number of repetitions were increased, as compared with a system that increased the number of repetitions, but retained the original 5 RM weight. However, when three groups of subjects were compared by O'Shea (*107*), using training programs that involved three sets of 9–10 RM, 5–6 RM, or 2–3 RM, although all groups improved significantly in strength, no significant difference was observed among them.

The application of progressive resistance exercises can be expected to increase strength of various muscle groups when applied over some 6 weeks or longer (*5,30,63,68,84,92,125*), even when 60% of the 1 RM is employed as the training resistance (*18,65*). The use of weight training principles is generally more effective than conditioning exercises that employ non-weight training activities for increasing strength (*23,91*).

II. Isometric Training

The use of isometric exercises for purposes of strength development received an important stimulus from the reports of Hettinger and Müller (*74*) in 1953, who had subjects train at various percentages of strength by exerting isometric tension. They found that maximum strength increased an average of 5% of the original value per week when the tension was held for 6 sec at two-thirds of maximum strength. Very little difference existed when the tension was increased to 100% or when repeated exercises totalling 45 sec were given.

Confirmation of the size of the gain to be expected from isometric exercises has not been found in subsequent experimentation (*105*); Müller and Rohmert (*106*) summed up the more recent evidence by pointing out that the closer one was to his theoretical maximum trained strength (termed "Endkraft"), the smaller the gains were likely to be. Thus, the sedentary person with greater relative muscle atrophy would be expected to achieve the largest gains through isometric training. Crakes (*39*), in fact, in employing young men in a research design similar to that of Hettinger and Müller, could only find an average strength gain of 2% a week, after an initial period was permitted while the subjects learned to take strength tests.

Josenhans (81), employing isometric procedures on grip strength and the flexor and extensor muscles of the index finger, the elbow, and the knee, found that the 40% increase in muscle force was significantly related to the number of contractions given. Rose et al. (116) applied an overload principle to 5 sec isometric contractions of the quadriceps muscles, finding final strength changes to vary between 80% and 400% over initial values.

In a study in which trained subjects were separated into high, middle, and low strength groups, Morehouse (101) employed either 1, 3, 5, or 10 maximum isometric contractions performed at each session. After 5 weeks subjects had improved significantly in strength; in fact, similar amounts and rates of improvement were made by all groups regardless of the amount of initial strength.

The use of various percentages of maximum strength in isometric training has been the subject of some interest. Rarick and Larsen employed the prescribed procedure of Hettinger and Müller of 2/3 maximum for one 6-sec period each day, compared with a technique involving 80% maximum, using five periods of 6 sec each, testing prepubescent (112) and postpubescent (111) males on wrist flexion. Gains for all groups were significant after 4 weeks of training, although the two groups were not significantly different from each other, showing that one 6-sec bout of isometric exercise per day was about as effective for developing strength as bouts given more frequently and at higher levels of tension. Mayberry (95) could not confirm this finding when men and women subjects were subdivided into experimental and control groups matched on isometric wrist flexor strength. One experimental group trained with one maximal isometric contraction, and the other experimental group performed one isometric contraction of 50% maximum. No significant increase in strength was found in either group. Cotten (38), on the other hand, employed high school boys and girls, dividing them into four groups which trained for one contraction per day at 25, 50, 75, and 100% of maximum isometric elbow flexion strength. All groups, with the single exception of the subjects who trained with 25% resistance, increased significantly in strength.

The test of whether maximum contractions given in multiple bouts are more beneficial than the usual procedures for gaining strength was undertaken by Meyers (98), who utilized the elbow flexor muscles in a program of 6 weeks duration. The subjects in one experimental group held three maximum isometric contractions, each for 6 sec, at an angle of 170 deg flexion, while subjects in the second group performed twenty

6-sec maximal contractions employing the same angle. Maximum strength was assessed before and after the training period at elbow flexion angles of 90 and 170 deg. The protracted exercise resulted in significant gains at both angles, while the shorter exercise was more specific, causing increased strength only at the training angle of 170 deg. Thus, the longer period of work was more beneficial for strength development at an angle of 90 deg than the shorter work period during training. Such large gains were not found by Hansen (*62,64*), who used female subjects in whom sustained and repeated isometric contractions were employed. Isometric strength increases ranged from approximately 4% to 11%.

The use of isometric training procedures to effect gains in a battery of strength tests was undertaken by Wolbers and Sills (*146*). Subjects performed a series of exercises for 8 weeks that required isometric contractions; significant gains over a control group in back lift, leg lift, and right and left grip were found. No improvement occurred in the vertical jump, however.

III. Isotonic versus Isometric Training

Several attempts have been made to compare the effectiveness of isometric techniques with those of isotonic in producing changes due to training. It should be pointed out that certain difficulties have been encountered by investigators in equalizing the intensity of training, because of obvious difficulties in equating work loads. While the physical work done in an isometric situation may lack quantification, it is still true that such contractions require considerable energy expenditure (*28*). Nevertheless, there has been an interest in knowing whether one form of training is equivalent to the other.

The literature reveals rather wide differences in the selection of training procedures, and since the body of published research fails to reveal clear-cut methodology for increased strength development, the various training protocols have also differed. In an early study, Rasch and Morehouse (*113*) employed the 5 RM method of PRE involving three sets of arm presses and curls which took 15 sec to perform. A second group of subjects trained isometrically at $\frac{2}{3}$ maximum also performing the exercise for 15 sec. At the end of a 6 week period, substantial increases were obtained for isotonic exercise in elbow flexion and arm elevation, and for isometric exercise in arm elevation alone. No significant gain was made from isometric training of the elbow flexor muscles. In general, then, subjects who performed the isotonic exercise gained greater strength than did subjects who employed isometric exercise, and, further, all subjects tended to do better in familiar exercises than when unfamiliar procedures were employed, suggesting the possibility that much of observed strength development may come from the acquisition of skill. There may also be some specificity involved when muscle groups are tested for strength at various joint angles. Boileau (16) employed isometric and isotonic contractions, each utilizing the elbow flexor muscles loaded at ⅔ maximum for 6 sec, and tested at joint angles of 173, 115, and 65 deg. At 173 deg, both groups improved significantly, with the isotonic group improving significantly more than the isometric group, but at 115 deg the isometric group was not significantly improved. At 65 deg, only the isotonic and isometric groups improved significantly, but at 115 and 65 deg, only the isotonic group was better than a control group employed. The finding of joint angle specificity has also been reported for wrist flexor training (6).

The use of the larger muscles of the back in isometric and isotonic exercise by Berger (8) resulted in significant improvement by both groups, but the isometric group gained significantly more in isometric strength, and the isotonic group was better in the test of isotonic strength (1 RM), revealing additional specificity. Using a bench press task, the isometrically trained subjects were at a distinct disadvantage, failing to achieve significant strength gains in seven of the nine groups employed (7,11). Meyers and Ohnmacht (99) had three groups of subjects perform either (a) light resistive exercises, including push-ups, (b) PRE, or (c) isometric elbow extension exercise at 165 deg. After 8 weeks of training, there were no significant differences among the three groups on isometric and isotonic tasks, except on an isometric elbow extension test given at a joint angle of 125 deg.

Combining a training program of 9 weeks duration so that all major muscle groups were exercised either isotonically (PRE), isometrically (5–10 sec maximal contractions), or with a concentration on dynamic speed, McCraw and Burnham (96) found little difference in arm strength. For the measure of leg strength, the isotonic and isometric programs were better than the speed exercises, especially for subjects high in initial scores. Both arm and leg endurance seemed to be facilitated by performance of speed exercises, once again favoring the individuals having considerable initial strength. Coleman (36), working with the elbow flexor muscles for 12 weeks in isometric (two 10-sec contractions) and isotonic (5 RM) exercise, while attempting to equate the load, duration, and range of motion, found no significant difference in the effectiveness between the two methods, even though both produced significant increases in strength. Ward and Fisk (*141*), on the other hand, found a more rapid rate of increase with isometric training.

The effect that training with rapid and slow contractions would have on muscular strength was studied by Salter (*119*), employing supination of the left hand. Subjects in the isotonic groups lifted a load equal to 75% of maximum at a rate of two per minute or 15 per minute. The isometric groups exerted maximum tension, also performing 2 or 15 per minute, and a control group did not exercise. All training procedures were effective in causing significant improvement in muscular strength, but no significant difference was found between the groups. Similar results were obtained by Chui (*27*), who used two groups training with rapid and slow isotonic contractions, and compared them with isometric procedures. The slow isotonic contractions were administered at a cadence requiring 2 sec for movement and 2 sec for recovery. The isometric contractions were held for 6 sec, all groups employing a weight equal to a 10 RM resistance. Each group gained significantly in strength, but no advantage was found for any procedure. Apparently it makes little difference if the rate of movement is changed in isotonic contractions, since the group that employed rapid contractions was not significantly more improved than those using slow movements, although undoubtedly there are some optimal limits of speed for various severities of exercise, as pointed out by Hellebrandt and Houtz (*69*). In fact, in their study of pacing, involving the systematic increase in rate of movement, they found this procedure to be as effective a method of training as PRE. When the isometric contractions during quadriceps training are lengthened to 30 sec, Lawrence, Meyer, and Matthews (*85*) found the development of strength to be less than by isotonic methods by about 14%, even though the overall gains ranged from 66% to 77%. Brodin (*20*) found fairly large differences in strength increase when maximum 6 sec isometric exercise was compared with a 10 RM program involving the abductor digiti quinti muscle of the hand. After 8 weeks the isotonic training produced an increase of 65%, while the isometric training brought about only a 20% change. The author attributed the difference in results to the assumption that the isometric method was less stimulating than the usual isotonic procedures.

The question of whether total body conditioning programs involving the two types of exercise will result in muscular endurance changes was examined by Howell and others (*80*). They administered a series of isometric exercises (the Commander Set) and isotonic exercises (weight lifting) to two groups, and after 8 weeks compared their ability to that of a control group on an all-out bicycle ride. Both experimental groups were found to improve significantly on the work task, but the control group did not. Further, there was no significant improvement between the groups that trained either isotonically or isometrically.

Mathews and Kruse (93) employed the Kelso–Hellebrandt elbow flexion ergometer, loaded with a weight equivalent to 3/16 of the subject's strength, in isotonic training, each bout of which was carried to exhaustion at a cadence of 30 per minute. The isometric group employed three 6-sec maximum contractions, and both groups were further subdivided so that frequency of training could range from a low of two to a high of five times per week. No common regression line was found in the eight groups thus formed, indicating the high specificity of strength changes, regardless of exercise frequency. A reasonably comparable number of subjects gained strength from both forms of training, but the average time involved in the actual training bouts was 18 sec for isometric and 120 sec for isotonic. Similar findings were reported by Baer et al. (2) who exercised wrist flexors isotonically at fast and slow rates, and isometrically at a slow rate. The isotonic exercise was at 75% of maximum and continued to exhaustion. A maximum increase in strength was produced by isometric exercise when performed at a rate of ten 5-sec contractions per minute, although this was nearly matched by the isotonic exercise when the same rate (ten per minute) was employed. Extending the rate of exercise to 30 per minute did not increase the strength gain.

The use of one maximum isometric contraction, or a fraction of maximum, has been of interest to several investigators. Bonde Peterson (17) employed one daily maximum isometric contraction, ten daily maximum isometric contractions, as well as 15 min of heavy ergometic work for four groups of subjects, in addition to a control group, in exercise involving elbow flexion and knee extension. Neither of the two isometric procedures significantly increased isometric strength, although the heavy dynamic work was effective when both the right and left knee extensors were treated as a single group. Walters et al. (140) had one group of subjects hold full isometric elbow flexion tension daily and a second group hold two-thirds of full tension. Both methods employed were effective in developing strength, although the full isometric tension was superior. Utilizing both arms, Morgan (102) studied the effectiveness of a maximum isometric contraction and isotonic exercise on elbow flexion strength at angles of 75, 90, 115, and 180 deg. No significant strength changes were found in either arm for isometric training, or for the left arm in isotonic exercise. However, a significant strength increase was found in the right arm for the isotonic group, when measured at the 115 deg angle.

Darcus and Salter (41) designed training procedures so that no fatigue curve was produced, giving 30 contractions at 1 min intervals, involving pronation, supination, and elbow flexion, in both isotonic and isometric forms of exercise. Both types of training were effective in increasing strength, but isotonic training was superior. Isometric training was carried out in only one position of the joint, but resulted in an increase in a variety of positions tested, and it was found that a reciprocal arrangement existed between flexion and supination, i.e., isometric training in flexion caused an increase in the strength of supination.

IV. Eccentric Training

The use of eccentric contractions has been of limited interest as a mechanism for training, although exercise physiologists and kinesiologists have expressed academic concern, differentiating between the so-called positive and negative aspects of muscle activity. Most of the studies previously cited that employed the typical isotonic movements usually did not separate the concentric and eccentric components, thus leaving some ambiguity in interpreting the results. Which phase of the repetition might be the major contributor to strength development could not be known with assurance. The answer may remain somewhat elusive, since the results of studies using eccentric contractions appear somewhat contradictory.

In his study involving isometric and isotonic training, Bonde Peterson (17) included a group that performed ten daily maximum eccentric contractions of the elbow flexor and knee extensor muscles. No measurable effect on isometric muscular strength was found. In a similar study involving the right knee extensor muscles, Laycoe and Marteniuk (86) had one group of subjects engage in three maximal eccentric contractions of 6 sec duration per day, while a second group performed a similar routine of isometric contractions. Both groups improved significantly over a control group, but neither differed from the other. Similar results were obtained by Seliger et al. (123), who found that the gain in strength from weight lifting was approximately the same as the gain found in weight lowering. Boileau (16) employed three groups of experimental subjects who trained for 7 week, three times a week. Isometric, concentric, and eccentric groups all performed 6-sec contractions at ⅔ maximum and were tested for elbow flexion strength at angles of 173, 115, and 65 deg. Some specificity was observed in the results of this study. For example, at 173 deg, a significant increase was observed in all three experimental groups, with concentric exercise better than static. At 115 deg, a significant increase occurred only in concentric training, but at 65 deg both static and concentric were significantly improved. Thus, the eccentric training group improved only when measured at an angle of 173 deg.

Singh and Karpovich (128) determined the effect of eccentric training on a muscle group and its antagonist. The forearm extensors were given 20 maximum eccentric contractions four times a week for 8 weeks, and the forearm flexors were tested for maximum strength during concentric, eccentric, and isometric contractions before and after the training period. Concentric and isometric strength of the exercised muscles increased approximately 40%, whereas the eccentric strength increased only 23%. The corresponding increases in strength of the antagonists were: 31% for concentric, 26% for isometric, and 17% for eccentric strength. Thus, eccentric training produced rather considerable strength gains, not only in the agonistic muscle, but in the antagonists as well.

V. Isokinetic Exercise

One of the newest developments in the field of strength and endurance development has been the inauguration of what has been called isokinetic exercise, or accommodating resistance exercise (77,110). The isokinetic contraction resembles the isotonic contraction, since the joint moves through a range of motion, but the speed of movement may be held constant by a special device. Thus, the rate of limb motion may be preset and any effort applied encounters an equal counteracting force. This increased force fails to produce increased acceleration, but simply increased resistance throughout the full range of movement.

The use of such a concept has received some clinical application (37), but its use in training studies is somewhat limited. In 1966, Thistle and colleagues (134) compared isokinetic training with isotonic and isometric procedures, and found that, after 8 weeks, the isokinetic group gained 35% in total work, while the isotonic and isometric groups gained 27.5% and 9.4%, respectively. Moffroid et al. (100) performed a similar experiment with quadriceps and hamstring muscles. At the end of 4 weeks, significant increases in isometric strength of the quadriceps occurred for the three groups, with the single exception of the isotonic group when tested at 90 deg. Using the same angle for the hamstring muscles, only the isometric group gained significantly in isometric strength, although both the isokinetic and isometric groups were significantly improved when tested at an angle of 45 deg. When tested for isokinetic work, none of the groups improved significantly in the quadriceps, but the isokinetic group was significantly better when the hamstrings were tested.

VI. Muscle Training and Motor Performance

For many, the value inherent in physical training is to try to augment performance in some other area, or to improve one's ability in an activity requiring a coordinated response. Untold numbers of athletes and nonathletes apparently subscribe to the dictum that other things being equal the one with the greatest strength will achieve the greatest results. When applied as a supplement to the normal conditioning program, weight training has been shown to be effective in producing greater gains in physical fitness than a normal conditioning program alone for participants in football, basketball, and track and field (*22, 26*). The primary interest in this area, however, seems to have been to identify the specific elements that may be expected to undergo modification as a result of isotonic training. A few have even employed isometric procedures, and some investigators have looked at both.

Kusinitz and Keeney (*84*) employed adolescent boys in 8 weeks of general resistance exercises, providing two groups matched on age, strength, ponderal index, and Harvard step test results, with one group serving as control. The experimental group improved significantly in some anthropometric measures, as well as in strength and endurance of the arm and shoulder girdle, while both groups improved significantly in the burpee and dodge run. The experimental group, however, gained twice as much as the control group in the dodge run, and in no case did the control group exceed the performance of the experimental group. Working with slightly older subjects, Schultz (*121*) employed six groups that participated in weight training, direct practice, repetitive sprinting, and all possible combinations of the three. After 9 weeks the direct practice group was significantly better in a zigzag run, but no change in any group had occurred in the shotput test. Examining specifically the question of agility, Hilsendager *et al.* (*75*) divided subjects into four experimental groups and a control group, administering exercises to improve (a) agility, (b) speed, (c) strength, and (d) speed and strength. The group assigned to participate in agility demonstrated significant improvement in a majority of the agility tests; strength training failed to modify this aspect of motor performance.

The motor coordination of boys in basketball and baseball skills and manipulative tasks was studied by Calvin (*21*). An experimental group trained with weights for 4 months, and was compared with a control group matched on age, height, weight, and selected anthropometric and strength measures. Both groups gained significantly in the anthropometric and strength tests, although the experimental group improved more than the control group in half of the anthropometric items. However, the only item of coordination that was significantly better for the experimental group was a basketball wall bounce test. Weight training failed to differentiate subjects in rate of manipulation, or in baseball accuracy. A similar result was obtained by Masley et al. (92), when a control group involved in non-weight training activity (volleyball) was compared with a group engaged in specific weight training exercise. Both groups gained significantly in a task involving fencing foil target coordination, but an additional group that participated in very little activity failed to improve significantly.

Vertical jumping has come under rather specific scrutiny, as has the standing broad jump, and various attempts have been made to determine if changing the strength component will improve the performance ability. In a comprehensive study involving isotonic training, both with a 10 RM regime and 50 to 60% of the jumping squats 10 RM, isometric training, and vertical jumping practice itself, Berger (13) found that those groups engaged in isotonic training were the only ones to improve significantly. Moreover, isotonic training was more effective than isometric exercise for increasing vertical jumping ability. Ball and associates (3) also failed to find that isometric exercise was effective in improving performance in the vertical jump, while Campbell (22) and Chui (26) have reported positive effects when employing weight training of an isotonic nature. Chui also found that systematic weight training was effective in increasing the standing broad jump, as did Schultz (121) when the weight training was combined with direct practice of the skill itself.

The effectiveness of weight training on sprint running ability has been of concern to some investigators. For example, Dintiman (51) divided 145 subjects into groups that engaged for 8 weeks in either a flexibility training program, a weight training program, or a combination of both, and examined their performance ability in the 50-yard dash. Flexibility training was not helpful in improving running ability, nor was weight training alone, but a combination of both was more effective in decreasing running times than just sprint training alone. On the other hand, none of the training groups used by Schultz (121), which included weight training, as well as repetitive sprinting, showed any differential effect on 60-yard dash times. Similar attempts have been made to examine the effect of weight training on swimming performance, and the results have been mixed. Davis (*42*) found that participation in an intensive and comprehensive weight training program significantly decreased the time required to swim the 25- and 50-yard crawl stroke, whereas Thompson and Stull (*135*) failed to find changes in the 30-yard sprint swim due to weight training alone. Weight training combined with swimming was effective, but the largest change occurred in the group that concentrated on sprint swimming without use of any weight training.

Speed of movement may be said to result from some physical force acting on a mass (*30*), and the result of any muscular effort must be increased movement of the body itself or of one of its limbs. It has been well established that individual differences in strength are highly task specific, and that an individual's limb strength has little or no correlation with his ability to move that limb at maximal speed (*29,73, 131*). The question remains, however, as to whether or not increasing one's strength will increase the speed of movement. Zorbas and Karpovich (*148*) raised the issue of whether increasing the amount of muscle bulk might even bind the individual, causing decreased performance. Therefore, they obtained a large group of weight lifters ($N = 300$) and compared their ability to perform a movement involving clockwise rotation of the arm, 24 revolutions for time, with nonlifters. The weight lifters were found to be significantly faster in this task. Certainly, there was no evidence that weight training produced a slowing of movement time, a position established also by DeLorme *et al.* (*46*).

Masley and associates (*92*) employed a device similar to that of Zorbas and Karpovich, and trained one group of subjects with weights, while another group played volleyball, and a third received very little activity, and served as a control. The weight training group was significantly improved in strength as well as movement time; however, the volleyball group also gained in strength but failed to change movement time, leading to a rejection of the hypothesis that an increase in strength is associated with an increase in speed. A similar conclusion was reached by Wilkin (*144*), but on somewhat different evidence. He employed three groups, one that participated in weight training for 2 months, another that was composed of chronic weight lifters, and a control group. The experimental task involved a hand crank similar to a bicycle pedal arrangement that was turned at maximum speed for 75 sec. All three groups improved significantly in movement time in the first 15-sec period, the weight training group continued to increase up to 45 sec, and the weight lifters improved significantly throughout the 75-sec task; however, when the amounts of increase were compared, no group improved significantly more than the control at any time.

The relationship between changes in strength and changes in speed of movement was examined by Clarke and Henry (*30*) using a horizontal adductive arm swing. A group of subjects participated in weight training exercises and were compared with a control group. The experimental subjects gained significantly in strength and movement time, whereas the control group declined. The correlation between individual differences in the amount of change in the strength/mass ratio and movement time change was $r = 0.405$, leading to the interpretation that changes in strength cannot predict very closely changes that will occur in speed of movement.

The use of both isotonic and isometric strength training procedures and their influence on speed of movement has also been investigated. Chui (*27*) employed an isometric training group and isotonic groups that performed (a) rapid contractions and (b) slow contractions, together with a control group. Speed of movement was examined with no resistance and with varying amounts of resistance. Each experimental group gained significantly in movement time, but improvements made by use of isometric contractions were not significantly greater than gains made by isotonic methods. It also made no real difference if isotonic exercises were performed rapidly or slowly. Whitley and Smith (*143*) used a combination isometric–isotonic exercise program, another involving isotonic overload, plus a program of free swinging arm movement, and a control group. Both the isometric–isotonic and isotonic overloads increased significantly in strength and in speed of movement, although no differences in movement time occurred between them. Speed was not increased by the control group, nor by the subjects who engaged in the free swinging movements.

VII. Muscle Training and Muscular Endurance

Differentiation between the effects of training on strength and endurance is often confused, since the literature frequently fails to take note of the difference between a test of strength and one of endurance. Without doubt, much more attention has been paid to the changes that take place in strength, judging from the plethora of studies that have employed tests of maximum tension. Yet, ample justification can be found to support the contention that the functional capacity of muscle, i.e., its endurance, is as important as the strength of that muscle.

The literature in this area reveals a lack of any standardization in tests of endurance, and the investigator has been free to devise his own procedures. Thus, the range of techniques may go from tests of push-ups or sit-ups to the use of various ergographic devices, and may employ tests that are isotonic in nature or are predominately isometric, although the former is more typical.

The use of isotonic training procedures is exemplified in a study by Capen (23), who had two groups of subjects, one of which was given weight training exercises and the other general conditioning exercises. The muscular endurance items included were chins, push-ups, sit-ups, and squat jumps. No significant differences in improvement were obtained between the two groups in any of these tests, suggesting that weight training is as effective as conditioning exercises in the development of muscular endurance. Bonde Peterson (18) found that training with varying numbers of contractions of the elbow flexors resulted in an increase in muscular endurance.

Employing the left elbow flexors, Hansen (63) had subjects perform isotonic exercise with a 1-RM load ten times a day for 5 weeks. Before and after training the isometric and isotonic endurances were tested, but Hansen felt that the changes found here were not important. In a later study, Hansen (65) had subjects lift a load equal to 60% of 1 RM 28 times a minute for 6 weeks. A rather large increase in isotonic endurance (630%) was found, as measured by the total work output achieved in flexing the elbow joint to exhaustion, but no increase was obtained in isometric endurance. He felt that the main causes of this great increase in working capacity obtained by isotonic endurance training were improved neuromuscular coordination, along with an increased vascularization. After 6 weeks of elbow flexion PRE, Shaver (125) tested relative endurance on an arm lever ergometer loaded at 20, 25, 30, and 35% of maximum strength. There was a significant increase over a control group in muscular endurance as evidenced by work capacity at all relative loads.

Several investigators have employed various types of exercise in their training procedures. For example, Walters et al. (140) had groups (a) hold full isometric tension 15 sec each day, (b) hold ⅔ of full isometric tension for 15 sec, and (c) lift isotonic loads at ⅓ of 1 RM as fast as possible within 15 sec. Endurance was improved. Bonde Peterson (17), on the other hand, failed to find endurance changes to sustained isometric contraction in training programs that included a single daily maximum isometric contraction, ten daily isometric contractions, ten daily eccentric contractions, or heavy bicycle ergometer work. In another study, subjects exposed either to a program of isometric exercises or one involving isotonic exercises (49) improved significantly in muscular endurance as measured by Rogers' Arm Strength Test. No differences existed between the two groups, however.

When the muscular endurance is expressed in terms of net oxygen consumption, as measured during sustained elbow flexion, Cotten (38) found that exercising isometrically at 25% of maximum was more beneficial than employing loads of 50 or 75% during the training period. However, it should be pointed out that the group that trained at a load equal to 100% of maximum strength was also tested at the three contraction loads of 25, 50, and 75%, where it was found that significant improvement occurred in contraction duration at these other loads, but changed the oxygen consumption at only the 75% condition. This may indicate that the type of training beyond 25% causes changes more in strength than in endurance.

A similar conclusion may be reached in a rather different way, when one examines the protection that resistance exercise provides to reduce the amount of fatigue experienced in muscular performance. Clarke and Stull (31) invoked a routine of endurance exercises in one study, and the usual PRE program in another (132), and found rather similar results when examining the fatigue curves produced from a 5-min bout of elbow flexion exercise. Significant gains were made in initial and final strength, and in total work, but the relative work done (defined as fatigable work) was not changed. The resultant fatigue curves after the training periods were quite similar to those obtained initially, except for the finding that they were consistently higher. The conclusion appears warranted that the primary effect of "strength" and "endurance" training is the enhancement of muscular strength.

VIII. Cross Transfer

The phenomenon of the cross transfer of strength from the exercised ipsilateral muscles to the unexercised contralateral muscles has been the subject of research since before the turn of the century. Scripture and co-workers (122) have generally been acknowledged as the pioneers in published works of this sort, since they reported that after a period of exercise involving the right hand, concomitant improvement was experienced in the left hand. They attributed this cross transfer to "indirect practice." In continuing experimentation from the same laboratory, Davis (43) employed the term "cross education" to the effects that he observed, postulating that some central mechanism must be operating in addition to those peripheral factors associated with increased muscular nutrition. At about the same time, Wissler and Richardson (145) also found evidence of cross transfer when training two subjects, suggesting that there was a diffusion of motor impulses to the contralateral arm.

The revival of interest in matters of cross transfer followed soon after the publication by DeLorme (44) of his procedures for the development of strength. One of the earlier studies designed to examine this issue was undertaken by Hellebrandt et al. (72), who employed female subjects who exercised the knee extensors and the elbow flexors and other muscles of the arm. The finding of a concurrent training effect of the contralateral musculature led to a reflection on the possible connection between the isometric co-contraction of these muscles and the severity of the effort put forth by the subject in order to preserve balance and to counteract the shifting of the center of gravity. Later, Hellebrandt et al. (70) had subjects perform maximal volitional wrist extension, and found that the contractile power and endurance of the nonexercised hand were increased. Hellebrandt and associates (67,71) have reported further evidence in support of the cross transfer effect both for normal and for therapeutic applications.

Slater-Hammel (129) administered 3 weeks of right arm flexions, and found that the subjects gained significantly over a control group in the contralateral, or left arm. He suggested some caution in interpreting the results, feeling it possible that the bilateral effects could result from raising the subject's tolerance to fatigue, or perhaps from a transfer of motor coordination. At any rate, he also urged use of cross transfer by therapists engaged in rehabilitation of patients with joint immobilization (130). Similar recommendations were made by Klein (82,83) for the reconditioning of knee injuries.

Maximum contractions of the quadriceps during training produced cross transfer of strength in all normal subjects examined by Rose et al. (116), and Logan and Lockhart (89) found gains in the contralateral knee extensors following PRE at all joint angles tested, which included 95, 115, 135, 155, and 175 deg. Shaver (124) administered a 6-week PRE program to the elbow flexors of the ipsilateral (exercised) arm and tested both arms on a cable tensiometer for strength changes, and on an arm lever ergometer loaded at 20, 25, 30, and 35% of maximum strength for endurance changes. Significant improvement in both strength and endurance in both arms was found, the latter occurring at all treatment levels. No significant differences were found in a control group. The change in strength for the contralateral elbow flexors was in agreement with Mathews et al. (94), but the finding of muscular endurance transfer was not.

It should be mentioned that certain histological evidence favors the concept of cross transfer from isotonic exercise. Reitsma (115) performed procedures on three groups of white rats so that in the first group, the rectus femoris was made the only knee extensor, in the second group, the plantaris was made the only plantar flexor, and, in the third group, the soleus was made the only plantar flexor. As a result of 3 weeks of running for a maximum of 12 hr per day, 5½ days per week, there was evidence of muscle fiber regeneration in the same muscle of the nonoperated side.

Some effort has been made to determine the appropriateness of isometric exercise as a means for producing cross transfer effects. Meyers (98) divided subjects in such a way that one group performed three 6-sec maximum isometric contractions of the elbow flexor muscles three times per week for 6 weeks, and the second group was given 20 6-sec maximal contractions three times per week for 6 weeks. The first exercise group gained significantly in strength of the contralateral limb when tested specifically at the training angle (170 deg), but did not improve in muscular endurance. On the other hand, Gardner (54), following the Hettinger and Müller (74) prescription of a ⅔ maximal contraction held for 6 sec, had subjects in groups assigned to exercise the knee extensors of the preferred limb at angles of 115, 135, and 145 deg three times per week for 6 weeks. No significant improvement in strength was found in any of the groups in the nonexercised limb when compared with a control group. A similar finding was reported by Mayberry (95) for exercise involving maximal and submaximal isometric training of the wrist flexors, in which no significant increases in strength of the contralateral extremity were found.

Rasch et al. (114) approached the problem in a different manner; they trained the elbow flexors by maximum isometric contractions for 6 weeks, and then assessed the strength changes of their antagonists, the elbow extensors. At all angles tested (45, 90, and 135 deg), significant improvement occurred in the strength of the antagonistic muscles. Singh and Karpovich (128) reversed the process by training elbow extensors to examine the effect on their more powerful antagonists, the flexors. In addition, they employed maximum eccentric contractions four times a week for 8 weeks, and then tested the muscles for concentric, eccentric, and isometric strength. The corresponding gains in strength of the antagonists were 30.9, 16.7, and 26.4%. The authors explained this rather sizable improvement by noting both by palpation and by electromyographic evidence that during maximum contraction of the agonists the antagonistic muscle also contracted. Darcus and Salter (41) also found cross transfer to occur in the antagonistic muscles of the arm following training, with evidence of concomitant changes occurring in corresponding muscles of the opposite side. It was their feeling that it is unnecessary to exercise to fatigue in order to achieve such a result.

A few studies have employed both isotonic and isometric training procedures to determine their effect on cross transfer. Rasch and Morehouse (*113*) found that a 11.6 lb gain in the nonexercised elbow flexor muscles resulted from isotonic training, as compared with 14.4 lb in the exercised arm. No changes resulted from isometric training. For arm elevation, approximately 25 lb were gained in both the exercised and nonexercised muscles after isotonic training, but, again, no significant changes occurred as a result of isometric exercise. Lawrence and associates (*85*) found that when isotonic exercise was performed, a higher percentage of strength was developed in the contralateral quadriceps muscle than when isometric exercises were employed. The increase in strength of the nonexercised muscles ranged between 65 and 100% of that gained by the exercised muscles. Coleman (*36*) attempted to set up isotonic and isometric contractions of equal load and duration, and after 12 weeks of training in elbow flexion found that both methods of exercise produced a significant increase in strength of the unexercised limb. Moreover, no significant difference existed between the effectiveness of the exercise methods. Wellock (*142*) found that some cross transfer occurred from right knee flexors to left knee flexors, although the transfer was not as great as from the right knee flexors to the contralateral extensors, as a result of either isotonic or isometric exercise. One observation by Brodin (*20*) in the isotonic training of subjects was a clear cross transfer of strength to the abductor digiti quinti muscle in the untrained hand.

Several investigators have made reference to the occurrence of action potentials in contralateral musculature (*19,60,72,127*), bringing into focus the irradiation of nerve impulses to extremities other than the ones directly engaged in physical activity.

IX. Retention of Muscular Strength and Endurance

There has been sporadic interest in the question of how long newly acquired strength or endurance might persist, but not until recent years has the matter been approached systematically. The primary form of exercise in studies of retention has been isotonic, but a few investigators have employed isometric contractions, and occasionally both have been used. The amount of time lapse between the end of training and the retention testing has varied rather widely, ranging from a few days to approximately a year.

The effectiveness of isotonic training procedures in causing the retention of muscular strength has been noted by McMorris and Elkins (*97*), who employed both the DeLorme procedure and the Oxford technique (see Section I). One year after the end of the 12-week training period, the subjects still retained 45% of their gain in elbow flexion strength. Berger (14) observed that isotonic strength will not be reduced after 6 weeks posttraining following 3 weeks of training. High retention of muscular endurance has been noted as well. An early study, employing heavy resistance isotonic exercise, by Houtz and associates (79) found no evidence of significant loss in muscular work capacity after a 65 day lay-off, an amount of time which actually exceeded in duration the initial period of training. Following a 4-week elbow flexion training program, Clarke et al. (35) found only a slight loss in newly gained muscular endurance 4 weeks later, and Egolinskii (52) revealed that following rest intervals of 6, 12, and 18 months, a significant amount of newly developed muscular endurance was retained. Motor performance items may also be retained, as Schultz (121) observed; only a test of zigzag run was adversely affected by a 13 day absence from training.

Waldman and Stull (137) devised an arm-lever ergometer as an elbow flexion training apparatus and for 8 weeks subjects engaged in an endurance exercise program. After this period, they were randomly assigned to groups that ceased training for either 8, 10, or 12 weeks. It was found that a significant loss of endurance existed among all groups at the end of these periods of inactivity. In order to determine more precisely where the limits of inactivity reside, Sysler and Stull (133) employed periods of 1, 3, and 5 weeks after training and found that the groups which stopped training for 3 and 5 weeks lost more muscular endurance than did the group which remained inactive for only 1 week. An interesting observation by Waldman and Stull was that retraining of the muscles following inactivity was achieved in approximately one-fourth the number of training sessions required initially. Rose et al. (116) found that, once the plateau of muscular strength had been obtained, it could be maintained by exercise as infrequent as once a month.

A few investigators have studied strength retention following isometric training. Müller (104) found that the loss of strength after training by daily contractions was at the rate at which it was gained, finding that inactivity lowered strength by about 30% per week. Hislop (76), on the other hand, found no drop-off in strength 11 months after isometric training. Working with both prepubescent and postpubescent males, Rarick and Larsen (111,112) found that a significant loss in strength occurred 4 weeks after isometric training, even though in most cases the strength was still substantially higher than pretraining means. In his study involving the isometric training of subjects with diverse initial strengths, Morehouse (101) found that significant strength losses occurred 8 weeks after training, but that strength could be maintained when at least one contraction of 100% maximum was performed every 2 weeks or less. Apparently, intensity of effort is more important than the frequency at which contractions are performed.

Rasch and Morehouse (113) employed both isotonic and isometric training procedures, and studied retention after a 6-week lay-off. In arm elevation, where significant increases occurred during training, no decrease occurred in the isotonic group, but a significant decrease was found in the isometric group. Walters et al. (140) and Ward and Fisk (141) found significant retention to occur up to 2½ months.

X. Hypertrophy of Skeletal Muscle

Evidence for the efficacy of various training methods has come primarily from the results of selected performance parameters, such as those provided by tests of strength and endurance. The search for histological and structural evidence of changes taking place within muscle has been of concern to exercise physiologists and others, and while the evidence for performance changes is abundant, relatively few studies have investigated the more difficult questions of internal adaptations to prolonged physical effort.

Muscular hypertrophy, in the pure sense, signifies an increase in the number or in the size of constituent fibers (1), but which of these two alternatives is responsible for the obvious gross change in size that occurs through training has been the subject of inquiry since the classical work of Morpurgo (103) in 1897. He removed the left sartorius muscle of two dogs and subjected them to a 2-month treadmill running program, after which the right sartorius was examined. Training resulted in some 53% increase in cross-sectional hypertrophy, but no increase was found in the number of fibers. This latter finding was later corroborated by Siebert (126) and MacCallum (90).

The ability of the muscle to grow in response to the demands placed on it depends primarily upon the capacity to multiply the so-called functional unit of the organism, which, as defined by Goss (59), is the smallest irreducible structure still capable of carrying out the organ's physiological activities. Thus, since the myofibrils, or rather the sarcomeres, are the functional units of striated muscle, one of the questions that should be answered is whether or not the myofibrillar portion of muscle increases as a result of training, and whether this is accompanied by weight or size changes.

Goldspink (57) conditioned mice through an exercise consisting of pulling on a weight to retrieve food, and reported a 30% increase in the average fiber cross-sectional area, attributing this increase to the conversion of so-called "small phase" fibers into "large phase" fibers. He also found a three- or fourfold increase in the number of myofibrils per fiber. Denny-Brown (50) found a twofold increase in the myofibrillar portion of muscle, and Rowe (117) reported significantly higher weight and cross-sectional area of mouse soleus muscle, accompanied by a 140% increase in total myofibril cross-sectional area. Goldberg (55) presented histological evidence that the weight increase was correlated with the increased diameter of the muscle cells. Penman (108,109) observed a significant increase in myosin filament fiber diameter and concentration in human striated muscle, along with a smaller distance between myosin filaments and a smaller number of actin filaments in orbit around a myosin filament. It would appear, therefore, that there is an increased packing density of contractile elements within a cell, as well as a change in the ratio of actin to myosin. In fact, Schreiber and associates (120) suggested that one of the early responses to overload was the increased synthesis of myosin.

In working with guinea pigs, Helander (66), found a rise of approximately 15% in the nitrogen component (actomyosin) of the myofilament as a result of training, but Holmes and Rasch (78) failed to find significant changes in the number of myofibrils per fiber at seven different cross-sectional levels of the rat sartorius, although the pattern of distribution suggested increases at the ends of the muscle rather than at the center. Decreased myofibrillar protein concentration was found by Goldberg (56), Hamish et al. (61), and by Gordon et al. (58) in rats, although in the latter study, subjects doing forceful exercise showed a tendency to increase in the myofibrillar protein concentration, even though there was no appreciable muscle weight gain.

A hypothesis that would favor hyperplasia, i.e., the formation of new muscle fibers, received some support in a study by van Linge (136), who surgically implanted the plantaris muscle of female rats into the calcaneus after denervation of the triceps surae and resection of the calcaneal tendon. The formation of new muscle fibers was observed after prolonged heavy training. Rowe and Goldspink (118) performed gastrocnemius tenotomy on laboratory mice to observe the effect of training on the soleus alone. There was a significant increase in the number of muscle fibers in the female mice, but not in the male mice; the overall average diameter increase was 32%. Employing three groups of rats, Reitsma (115) surgically made (a) the rectus femoris the only knee extensor, (b) the plantaris the only plantar flexor, and (c) the soleus the only plantar flexor. Following a vigorous training program, the rectus femoris showed 28% hypertrophy, the plantaris gained 104% hypertrophy with rare instances of fiber splitting, and in the soleus muscle 151% hypertrophy was found, with considerable evidence of pathology, such as necrosis, fiber splitting, and branching. Lesch and co-workers (*87*) concluded that rapid hypertrophy brought about by such an acute work load is actually accompanied by a reduction in muscle contractility, as indicated by a decreased maximal velocity of shortening and tetanic tension, suggesting that a delay may exist between the formation of new muscle mass and its ability to generate tension.

Additional experiments performed on laboratory animals emphasize the hypertrophy of skeletal muscle. For example, Walker (*138,139*) employed mice and found after extended training that there was a significant increase in mean fiber diameter, as well as an increase in tension. Carrow *et al.* (*25*) found that with forced and voluntary exercise of male rats there was a greater increase in the cross-sectional area of red gastrocnemius fibers than of white, although there was a greater increase in the number of capillaries per fiber for white than red fibers. Utilizing young rabbits, Crawford (*40*) attained a greater girth and weight of the tibialis anterior when it was forced to accept a greater load in exercise by elimination of the synergistic action of the extensor digitorum longus. Barnard *et al.* (*4*), on the other hand, reported no significant hypertrophy or changes in contractile properties of muscle with trained guinea pigs, although they were able to maintain a higher level of isometric muscular endurance.

There is a paucity of available material on human muscle on this topic, although Etemadi and Hosseini (*53*) performed an individual postmorten fiber count on the biceps muscle of a 66-year-old lumberjack. Two other subjects, both nonathletes of approximately the same age, were used as controls. Not only was the cross-sectional area of the lumberjack's biceps muscle approximately twice as large as both other subjects, but the total number of muscle fibers was higher by nearly one-third.

The literature concerning human intact muscular hypertrophy has derived primarily from limb circumferential measurements, and quite often as a matter of secondary interest to the assessment of strength changes from training. Some of the studies reviewed previously (Section I) that involved isotonic training procedures also reported on changes in hypertrophy. For example, in the early work of DeLorme (*44,46*), both normal and weakened muscles were found to respond to PRE training by increasing in size. McMorris and Elkins (*97*) found significant gains in arm circumference when both PRE and the Oxford technique were used, with very little difference noted between the two procedures. On the other hand, the 10 RM procedure employed by Barney and Bangerter

(5) resulted in a significant increase in thigh circumference, but their bulk and "power" programs did not. Even though strength gains were found, the selected PRE programs used by O'Shea (107), which ranged from 9–10 RM to 2–3 RM, showed an overall increase in thigh girth (3 to 6%), but no significant difference between the groups.

A few studies have dealt with changes in size as a result of isometric training programs, although the evidence here is not very supportive of the case for hypertrophy. Neither Rose et al. (116) nor Hislop (76), for example, were able to find limb circumference changes, but Meyers (98), employing short term and protracted isometric training, found that both procedures resulted in a significant increase in relaxed arm girth.

Some data are available on the comparison of girth changes between isotonic and isometric training. Rasch and Morehouse (113) found significant increases in girth of the upper arm in both conditions, although greater gains were found in strength and hypertrophy in the isotonic exercise group. Liberson and Asa (88) and Ward and Fisk (141) found no significant hypertrophy in their comparative studies of the two types of training, and Morgan (102) was able to find a significant increase in girth in only one of the two groups trained by isometric procedures but not at all as a result of isotonic training. Boileau (16), on the other hand, reported significant dominant arm girth changes as a result of both isometric and isotonic training, as well as from eccentric procedures.

XI. Summary

The use of progressive isotonic exercise in nearly any form can be expected to result in an increase in muscular strength. Regimens that range from 2 RM for one set to 10 RM for three sets all seem to result in significant gains, although an optimal combination may be to train at 6 RM for three sets, three times a week.

Isometric exercise has been found to result in strength gains, but the amount of this gain may not be predictable. The amount of tension applied to be effective may vary from 50% to maximum, and the duration of contraction may be 5 sec, given as frequently as one contraction per day, or in various combinations.

Studies that have compared the relative effectiveness of isotonic and isometric training provide mixed results. It has been typical to find strength increases from both types of exercise, but very often no significant difference occurs between them, especially when some attempt is made to equate the intensity of training.

The use of eccentric contractions in training does not result in greater gains in strength than procedures that employ isotonic or isometric contractions. Their use in training appears to be limited.

Isokinetic exercise, which is an isotonic form of exercise, except that the rate of movement is controlled, may provide a training that is comparable or even better than isotonic exercise alone.

Prediction of the effects of training on various items of motor performance is not presently possible, as the results of research are rather thoroughly mixed. Isotonic exercise has proven more successful than isometric, but practice of the task itself seems more beneficial, especially if the element of skill is high. Weight training has been found effective in improving the speed of isolated movements, although there is very little predictability regarding the amount of this change.

Muscular endurance changes may be expected to result from a program of training, although the literature is not clear as to which type of exercise program is more beneficial. Muscular strength may be enhanced by either strength or endurance training.

Cross transfer of strength occurs in muscles of the contralateral extremity as a result of exercising ipsilateral muscles, although the effect may not be found when isometric exercise is employed. Studies that have compared the effectiveness of both isotonic and isometric training programs favor the former as a means of inducing the cross transfer phenomenon.

Muscular strength, once gained, will persist for some time before it gradually returns to pretraining levels. Reports have noted that some strength has been retained for several months, although a significant loss will occur after 3 to 4 weeks. The pattern of retention is very similar whether the exercise program has involved isotonic or isometric contractions.

The increase in strength associated with training is accompanied by gross changes in the size of the muscle. This hypertrophy has been found to result from an increase in the myofibrillar protein concentration of muscle, as well as from an increased packing density of contractile elements within the cell. Limb girth changes usually accompany isotonic exercise, but may not result from isometric activity.

References

1. Adams, R. D., Denny-Brown, D., and Pearson, C. M. (1953). "Diseases of Muscle." Hoeber, New York.
2. Baer, A. D., Gersten, J. W., Robertson, B. M., and Dinken, H. (1955). *Arch. Phys. Med. Rehabil.* **36**, 495–502.

3. Ball, J. R., Rich, G. Q., and Wallis, E. L. (1964). *Res. Quart.* **35**, 231–235.
4. Barnard, R. J., Edgerton, V. R., and Peter, J. B. (1970). *J. Appl. Physiol.* **28**, 767–770.
5. Barney, V. S., and Bangerter, B. L. (1961). *Res. Quart.* **32**, 138–146.
6. Belka, D. E. (1968). *Res. Quart.* **39**, 244–250.
7. Berger, R. A. (1962). *Res. Quart.* **33**, 168–181.
8. Berger, R. A. (1962). *Res. Quart.* **33**, 329–333.
9. Berger, R. A. (1962). *Res. Quart.* **33**, 334–338.
10. Berger, R. A. (1962). *Res. Quart.* **33**, 637.
11. Berger, R. A. (1963). *Res. Quart.* **34**, 131–135.
12. Berger, R. A. (1963). *Res. Quart.* **34**, 396–398.
13. Berger, R. A. (1963). *Res. Quart.* **34**, 419–424.
14. Berger, R. A. (1965). *Res. Quart.* **36**, 141–146.
15. Berger, R. A., and Hardage, B. (1967). *Res. Quart.* **38**, 715–718.
16. Boileau, R. A. (1962). Master's Thesis, Univ. of Maryland, College Park, Maryland.
17. Bonde Peterson, F. (1960). *Acta Physiol. Scand.* **48**, 406–416.
18. Bonde Peterson, F., Graudal, H., Hansen, J. W., and Hvid, N. (1961). *Int. Z. Angew. Physiol.* **18**, 468–473.
19. Bowers, L. (1966). *Res. Quart.* **37**, 302–312.
20. Brodin, H. (1963). *Acta Orthop. Scand.* **33**, 208–219.
21. Calvin, S. (1959). *Res. Quart.* **30**, 387–398.
22. Campbell, R. L. (1962). *Res. Quart.* **33**, 343–348.
23. Capen, E. K. (1950). *Res. Quart.* **21**, 83–93.
24. Capen, E. K. (1956). *Res. Quart.* **27**, 132–142.
25. Carrow, R. E., Brown, R. E., and Van Huss, W. D. (1967). *Anat. Rec.* **159**, 33–39.
26. Chui, E. (1950). *Res. Quart.* **21**, 188–194.
27. Chui, E. F. (1964). *Res. Quart.* **35**, 246–257.
28. Clarke, D. H. (1960). *Res. Quart.* **31**, 3–6.
29. Clarke, D. H. (1960). *Res. Quart.* **31**, 570–574.
30. Clarke, D. H., and Henry, F. M. (1961). *Res. Quart.* **32**, 315–325.
31. Clarke, D. H., and Stull, G. A. (1970). *Res. Quart.* **41**, 19–26.
32. Clarke, H. H. (1948). *Res. Quart.* **19**, 118–147.
33. Clarke, H. H. (1950). *Res. Quart.* **21**, 399–419.
34. Clarke, H. H., Bailey, T. L., and Shay, C. T. (1952). *Res. Quart.* **23**, 136–148.
35. Clarke, H. H., Shay, C. T., and Mathews, D. K. (1954). *J. Ass. Phys. Ment. Rehabil.* **8**, 184–188.
36. Coleman, A. E. (1969). *Res. Quart.* **40**, 490–495.
37. Coplin, T. H. (1971). *J. NATA* **6**, 110–114.
38. Cotten, D. (1967). *Res. Quart.* **38**, 366–374.
39. Crakes, J. G. (1957). Master's Thesis, Univ. of Oregon, Eugene, Oregon.
40. Crawford, G. N. C. (1961). *Proc. Roy. Soc. Ser. B* **154**, 130–138.
41. Darcus, H. D., and Salter, N. (1955). *J. Physiol. (London)* **129**, 325–336.
42. Davis, J. F. (1955). *Phys. Educator* **12**, 28–29.
43. Davis, W. W. (1898). *Studies Yale Psychol. Lab.* **6**, 6–50.
44. DeLorme, T. L. (1945). *J. Bone Joint Surg.* **27**, 645–667.
45. DeLorme, T. L. (1946). *Arch. Phys. Med.* **27**, 607–630.
46. DeLorme, T. L., Ferris, B. J., and Gallagher, J. R. (1952). *Arch. Phys. Med.* **33**, 86–92.

47. DeLorme, T. L., Schwab, R. S., and Watkins, A. L. (1948). *J. Bone Joint Surg., Amer. Vol.* **30-A,** 834–847.
48. DeLorme, T. L., and Watkins, A. L. (1948). *Arch. Phys. Med.* **29,** 263–273.
49. Dennison, J. D., Howell, M. L., and Morford, W. R. (1961). *Res. Quart.* **32,** 348–352.
50. Denny-Brown, D. (1960). *In* "Neuromuscular Disorders," Proc. Ass. Res. Nerv. Ment. Dis. (R. D. Adams, L. M. Eaton, and G. M. Shy, eds.), pp. 147–196. Williams & Wilkins, Baltimore, Maryland.
51. Dintiman, G. B. (1964). *Res. Quart.* **35,** 456–463.
52. Egolinskii, Y. A. (1961). *Fiziol. Zh. SSSR im. I. M. Sechenova* **47,** 38–47.
53. Etemadi, A. A., and Hosseini, F. (1968). *Anat. Rec.* **162,** 269–274.
54. Gardner, G. W. (1963). *Res. Quart.* **34,** 98–101.
55. Goldberg, A. L. (1967). *Amer. J. Physiol.* **213,** 1193–1198.
56. Goldberg, A. L. (1969). *J. Biol. Chem.* **244,** 3217–3222.
57. Goldspink, G. (1964). *J. Cell. Comp. Physiol.* **63,** 209–216.
58. Gordon, E. E., Kowalski, K., and Fritts, M. (1967). *J. Amer. Med. Ass.* **199,** 103–108.
59. Goss, R. J. (1966). *Science* **153,** 1615–1620.
60. Gregg, R. A., Mastellone, A. F., and Gersten, J. W. (1957). *Amer. J. Phys. Med.* **36,** 269–280.
61. Hamish, M., Lesch, M., Baron, J., and Kaufman, S. (1967). *Science* **157,** 935–937.
62. Hansen, J. W. (1961). *Int. Z. Angew. Physiol.* **18,** 474–477.
63. Hansen, J. W. (1963). *Int. Z. Angew. Physiol.* **19,** 420–424.
64. Hansen, J. W. (1963). *Int. Z. Angew. Physiol.* **19,** 430–434.
65. Hansen, J. W. (1967). *Int. Z. Angew. Physiol.* **23,** 367–370.
66. Helander, E. A. S. (1961). *Biochem. J.* **78,** 478–482.
67. Hellebrandt, F. A. (1951). *J. Appl. Physiol.* **4,** 136–144.
68. Hellebrandt, F. A., and Houtz, S. J. (1956). *Phys. Ther. Rev.* **36,** 371–383.
69. Hellebrandt, F. A., and Houtz, S. J. (1958). *Phys. Ther. Rev.* **38,** 319–322.
70. Hellebrandt, F. A., Houtz, S. J., and Krikorian, A. M. (1950). *J. Appl. Physiol.* **2,** 446–452.
71. Hellebrandt, F. A., Houtz, S. J., and Partridge, M. J. (1957). *Amer. J. Phys. Med.* **36,** 196–211.
72. Hellebrandt, F. A., Parrish, A. M., and Houtz, S. J. (1947). *Arch. Phys. Med.* **28,** 76–85.
73. Henry, F. M., and Whitley, J. D. (1960). *Res. Quart.* **31,** 24–33.
74. Hettinger, T. L., and Müller, E. A. (1953). *Arbeitsphysiologie* **15,** 111–126.
75. Hilsendager, D. R., Strow, M. H., and Ackerman, K. J. (1969). *Res. Quart.* **40,** 71–75.
76. Hislop, H. J. (1963). *J. Amer. Phys. Therapy Ass.* **43,** 21–38.
77. Hislop, H. J., and Perrine, J. J. (1967). *Phys. Therapy* **47,** 114–117.
78. Holmes, R., and Rasch, P. J. (1958). *Amer. J. Physiol.* **195,** 50–52.
79. Houtz, S. J., Parrish, A. M., and Hellebrandt, F. A. (1946). *Physiotherapy Rev.* **26,** 299–304.
80. Howell, M. L., Kimoto, R., and Morford, W. R. (1962). *Res. Quart.* **33,** 536–540.
81. Josenhans, W. K. T. (1962). *Rev. Can. Biol.* **21,** 315–323.
82. Klein, K. K. (1955). *J. Ass. Phys. Ment. Rehabil.* **9,** 159–161.
83. Klein, K. K., and Williams, H. E. (1954). *J. Ass. Phys. Ment. Rehabil.* **8,** 52–53.
84. Kusinitz, I., and Keeney, C. E. (1958). *Res. Quart.* **21,** 294–301.

85. Lawrence, M. S., Meyer, H. R., and Matthews, N. L. (1962). *J. Amer. Phys. Therapy Ass.* **42**, 15–20.
86. Laycoe, R. R., and Marteniuk, R. G. (1971). *Res. Quart.* **42**, 299–306.
87. Lesch, M., Parmley, W. W., Hamish, M. T., Kaufman, S., and Sonnenblick, E. H. (1968). *Amer. J. Physiol.* **214**, 685–690.
88. Liberson, W. T., and Asa, M. M. (1959). *Arch. Phys. Med. Rehabil.* **40**, 330–336.
89. Logan, G. A., and Lockhart, A. (1962). *J. Amer. Phys. Therapy Ass.* **42**, 658–660
90. MacCallum, J. B. (1898). *Bull. Johns Hopkins Hosp.* **9**, 208–215.
91. MacQueen, I. J. (1954). *Brit. Med. J.* **2**, 1193–1198.
92. Masley, J. W., Hairabedian, A., and Donaldson, D. N. (1953). *Res. Quart.* **24**, 308–315.
93. Mathews, D. K., and Kruse, R. (1957). *Res. Quart.* **28**, 26–37.
94. Mathews, D. K., Shay, C. T., Godin, F., and Hogdon, R. (1956). *Res. Quart.* **27**, 206–212.
95. Mayberry, R. P. (1959). *Proc. Coll. Phys. Educ. Ass.* **62**, 155–158.
96. McCraw, L. W., and Burnham, S. (1966). *Res. Quart.* **37**, 79–88.
97. McMorris, R. O., and Elkins, E. C. (1954). *Arch. Phys. Med. Rehabil.* **35**, 420–426.
98. Meyers, C. R. (1967). *Res. Quart.* **38**, 430–440.
99. Meyers, C. R., and Ohnmacht, F. W. (1963). *Proc. Coll. Phys. Educ. Ass.* **66**, 113–117.
100. Moffroid, M., Whipple, R., Hofkosh, J., Lowman, E., and Thistle, H. (1969). *Phys. Therapy* **49**, 735–746.
101. Morehouse, C. A. (1967). *Res. Quart.* **38**, 449–456.
102. Morgan, W. P. (1960). Master's Thesis, Univ. of Maryland, College Park, Maryland.
103. Morpurgo, B. (1897). *Virchows Arch. Pathol. Anat. Physiol.* **150**, 522–544.
104. Müller, E. A. (1959). *Ergonomics* **2**, 216–222.
105. Müller, E. A. (1962). *Rev. Can. Biol.* **21**, 303–313.
106. Müller, E. A., and Rohmert, W. (1963). *Int. Z. Angew. Physiol.* **19**, 403–419.
107. O'Shea, P. (1966). *Res. Quart.* **37**, 95–102.
108. Penman, K. A. (1969). *Res. Quart.* **40**, 764–772.
109. Penman, K. A. (1970). *Res. Quart.* **41**, 418–424.
110. Perrine, J. J. (1968). *J. Health, Phys. Educ. Rec.* **39**, 40–44.
111. Rarick, G. L., and Larsen, G. L. (1958). *Res. Quart.* **29**, 333–341.
112. Rarick, G. L., and Larsen, G. L. (1959). *Int. Z. Angew. Physiol.* **18**, 13–21.
113. Rasch, P. J., and Morehouse, L. E. (1957). *J. Appl. Physiol.* **11**, 29–34.
114. Rasch, P. J., Pierson, W. R., and Logan, G. A. (1961). *Int. Z. Angew. Physiol.* **19**, 18–22.
115. Reitsma, W. (1969). *Amer. J. Phys. Med.* **48**, 237–258.
116. Rose, D. L., Radzyminski, S. F., and Beatty, R. R. (1957). *Arch. Phys. Med. Rehabil.* **38**, 157–164.
117. Rowe, R. W. D. (1969). *Comp. Biochem. Physiol.* **28**, 1449–1453.
118. Rowe, R. W. D., and Goldspink, G. (1968). *Anat. Rec.* **161**, 69–76.
119. Salter, N. (1955). *J. Physiol. (London)* **130**, 109–113.
120. Schreiber, S. S., Oratz, M., Evans, C. D., Gueyikian, I., and Rothschild, M. A. (1970). *Amer. J. Physiol.* **219**, 481–486.
121. Schultz, G. W. (1967). *Res. Quart.* **38**, 108–118.
122. Scripture, E. W., Smith, T. L., and Brown, E. M. (1894). *Studies Yale Psychol.* **2**, 114–119.

123. Seliger, V., Dolejs, L., Karas, V., and Pachlopnikova, I. (1968). *Int. Z. Angew. Physiol.* **26,** 227–234.
124. Shaver, L. G. (1970). *Med. Sci. Sports* **2,** 165–171.
125. Shaver, L. G. (1971). *Res. Quart.* **42,** 194–202.
126. Siebert, W. W. (1960). *J. Ass. Phys. Ment. Rehabil.* **14,** 153–157.
127. Sills, F. D., and Olson, A. L. (1958). *Res. Quart.* **29,** 213–221.
128. Singh, M., and Karpovich, P. V. (1967). *J. Appl. Physiol.* **23,** 742–745.
129. Slater-Hammel, A. T. (1950). *Res. Quart.* **21,** 203–209.
130. Slater-Hammel, A. T. (1951). *J. Ass. Phys. Ment. Rehabil.* **4,** 24–26.
131. Smith, L. E. (1961). *Res. Quart.* **32,** 208–220.
132. Stull, G. A., and Clarke, D. H. (1970). *Res. Quart.* **41,** 189–193.
133. Sysler, B. L., and Stull, G. A. (1970). *Res. Quart.* **41,** 105–109.
134. Thistle, H. G., Hislop, H. J., Moffroid, M., and Lowman, E. W. (1967). *Arch. Phys. Med. Rehabil.* **48,** 279–282.
135. Thompson, H. L., and Stull, G. A. (1959). *Res. Quart.* **30,** 479–485.
136. van Linge, B. (1962). *J. Bone Joint Surg., Brit. Vol.* **44-B,** 711–721.
137. Waldman, R., and Stull, G. A. (1969). *Res. Quart.* **40,** 396–401.
138. Walker, M. G. (1966). *Comp. Biochem. Physiol.* **19,** 791–797.
139. Walker, M. G. (1968). *Experientia* **24,** 360.
140. Walters, C. E., Stewart, C. L., and LeClaire, J. F. (1960). *Amer. J. Phys. Med.* **39,** 131–141.
141. Ward, J., and Fisk, G. H. (1964). *Arch. Phys. Med. Rehabil.* **45,** 614–620.
142. Wellock, L. M. (1958). *Phys. Therapy Rev.* **38,** 671–675.
143. Whitley, J. D., and Smith, L. E. (1966). *Res. Quart.* **37,** 132–142.
144. Wilkin, B. M. (1952). *Res. Quart.* **23,** 361–369.
145. Wissler, C., and Richardson, W. W. (1900). *Psychol. Rev.* **7,** 29–38.
146. Wolbers, C. P., and Sills, F. D. (1956). *Res. Quart.* **27,** 446–450.
147. Zinovieff, A. N. (1951). *Brit. J. Phys. Med.* **14,** 129–132.
148. Zorbas, W. S., and Karpovich, P. V. (1951). *Res. Quart.* **22,** 145–148.

The Role of Exercise in Weight Control

Lawrence B. Oscai

DEPARTMENT OF PHYSICAL EDUCATION, UNIVERSITY OF ILLINOIS
AT CHICAGO CIRCLE, CHICAGO, ILLINOIS

I. Introduction

Controlling body weight is a problem faced by many people in our society today. Statistics published by the United States Public Health

Service show that a large segment of the American population over 30 years of age is at least 20% overweight (68). The medical implications of this condition are clear; overweight individuals are plagued with a number of abnormalities including an increased risk of coronary heart disease (54), impaired carbohydrate metabolism (88,100), hypertension (11), and a variety of endocrine disturbances (88,100).

As pointed out by Mayer (62), the use of exercise in the control of body weight has often been minimized in the minds of many as a result of claims that the amount of exercise needed to change caloric balance is too great to be practical and that an increase in caloric expenditure associated with exercise is always accompanied by a corresponding rise in appetite and food intake which can impair weight reduction. Mayer (62), in a careful examination of the former claim, presented evidence to show that a practical approach to exercise can result in an increase in caloric expenditure sufficient to produce a marked change in caloric balance. The latter claim, that exercise consistently stimulates the appetite, is not based on documented experimental or clinical evidence. Results from recent studies, considered in detail in this review, show that exercise does not always stimulate appetite and may even suppress the voluntary intake of food.

When attempts are made to control weight, serious consideration must be given to body growth and composition, especially to the total-body content of fat. Special emphasis is always given to body fat because of its significant contribution to the total amount of weight added during periods of positive caloric balance. It will become quite apparent in this review that fat is the body component most markedly affected by regularly performed endurance exercise. As a result, consideration will be given to the various factors in operation during the development of adipose mass and to how these factors are affected by exercise.

In the final analysis, to control body weight by means of exercise, it must be shown that exercise can maintain body weight at ideal levels and can produce a negative caloric balance sufficient to produce a substantial weight loss in conditions of obesity. Many of the available studies indicating that exercise can play a major role in this area are presented.

II. Effects of Exercise on Appetite, Body Growth, and Composition

A. Effect of Exercise on Appetite of Humans

The general feeling among many people regarding exercise and appetite is that exercise performed on a regular basis increases appetite and food intake sufficiently to counterbalance the increased energy expenditure associated with work. The belief that exercise consistently stimulates the appetite is not compatible with a number of carefully controlled studies conducted on humans and experimental animals. Some confusion arises, most likely, because people make no distinction between long hours of physical labor and shorter bouts of more strenuous exercise. There is little doubt that physical labor such as that performed by lumberjacks and farm laborers for eight or more hours per day results in a marked increase in appetite and food intake. Karvonen et al. (55) obtained information on the diet of lumberjacks actively engaged in forest work in eastern Finland. These investigators reported that the mean energy value of the daily diet in five lumberjacks' camps was 4763 kcal (55). This daily intake of calories is approximately double that (2500 kcal/day) which is normally consumed by a sedentary individual of normal body weight in isocaloric balance. Consuming 2500 kcal/day allows for the following daily activities: 8 hr sleeping (1.17 kcal/min), 1 hr standing, light activity (2.60 kcal/min), 8 hr in a sedentary occupation (2.20 kcal/min), 1 hr walking (3.11 kcal/min), 2 hr conversing (1.83 kcal/min), 2 hr reading (1.29 kcal/min), and 2 hr sitting (1.29 kcal/min) (20).

In contrast to long hours of manual labor, more vigorous exercise of shorter duration does not appear to stimulate the appetite. Dempsey (26) subjected a group of obese and nonobese young men to an 8 week program of daily exercise, strenuous enough to cause a marked decrease in the weights of both groups. A daily record of food intake showed that 1 hr of exercise per day had no effect on appetite. A program of endurance exercise consisting of 45 min of jogging and light calisthenics, 3 days per week, which significantly increased the exercise tolerance of a group of middle-aged men, had no effect on appetite and food intake (48,89).

B. EFFECT OF EXERCISE ON APPETITE OF MALE ANIMALS

Perhaps a clearer idea of the effect of exercise on appetite can be gained from studies conducted on laboratory animals. Stevenson et al. (91) reported that 4 hr of swimming, 4 days per week, had no effect on appetite and food intake of male rats. Similar results were found in two other studies in which male rats were subjected to 6 hr of daily swimming, representing light exercise of extended duration (71,73). The male swimmers in one study took in an average of 86 ± 2 cal/day compared to 84 ± 3 cal/day for the freely eating sedentary males (71).

In contrast to light work of extended duration, heavy work of shorter duration suppresses the appetite of male rats. Crews *et al.* (*23*) were able to show that a 12 week program of vigorous treadmill running, 2 hr per day, significantly decreased the food intake of male rats. Exercising animals in this study took in a total of 6090 ± 261 cal over the 3 month period, compared to 7638 ± 224 cal for the sedentary, freely eating animals. Stevenson *et al.* (*91*) reported that 60 to 120 min of strenuous swimming, 4 days per week, for 4 weeks, reduced the voluntary intake of food in their male animals. Oscai and Holloszy (*69*) exercised grossly overweight male rats vigorously enough to produce a marked reduction in body weight over an 18 week period. Swimming, 2 hr per day, 6 days per week, with weights attached to the animals' tails, significantly decreased the appetite of these male rats, as evidenced by the finding that swimmers took in a total of 8935 cal compared to 9985 cal for the sedentary, freely eating animals. In a more recently completed study, Ahrens *et al.* (*1*) subjected both young and mature male rats to 30 min of daily treadmill running for 8 weeks. Results from this study reveal that both exercising groups experienced significant reductions in appetite and food intake.

The above findings suggest that the appetite suppression effect of exercise is related more to the severity of the work than to the duration. Thus, light exercise of extended duration does not suppress the appetite while a more severe exercise stress of shorter duration does. It appears likely that appetite suppression induced by exercise is mediated by the increased levels of catecholamines associated with the stress of exercise (*86,97*). In this context, it is of interest that epinephrine and norepinephrine are extremely low or close to resting levels in the blood during light and moderate exercise but increase markedly in response to heavy work (*37,38*).

C. EFFECT OF EXERCISE ON APPETITE OF FEMALE ANIMALS

Appetites of female animals respond differently to regularly performed endurance exercise than those of male animals. Mayer *et al.* (*63*) were perhaps the first investigators to report that exercise stimulates the appetite of female animals. This work was followed by the study of Crews and Aldinger (*24*), indicating that female rats subjected to 6 hr of daily swimming had an approximate 26% increase in food intake. More recently, the responses of both male and female rats to the same swimming program were compared (*71*). In this study, female rats, permitted unrestricted access to food, took in an average of 75 ± 1 cal/day, which was significantly greater than the value of 61 ± 2 cal/

day for the sedentary female animals. In contrast, exercise had no effect on the voluntary intake of food of the male animals.

The foregoing results indicate that strenuous exercise either suppresses or has no effect on the appetite of male animals but stimulates the appetite of female rats. Until recently, no one was aware that appetites of male and female animals respond differently to strenuous exercise. The realization that they do respond differently has been of considerable help in clearing up a number of apparent discrepancies and controversies regarding exercise and food intake. The physiological basis for this interesting sex difference in the effect of exercise on appetite in rats remains to be elucidated.

D. COMMONLY USED METHODS TO DETERMINE BODY COMPOSITION IN HUMANS AND EXPERIMENTAL ANIMALS

Before beginning a discussion regarding the influence of exercise on body growth and composition, it might be of some value to briefly mention the methods which are currently used to assess body composition. Obviously, a direct chemical analysis of the living human body cannot be performed. However, it is possible to estimate percentages and total amounts of body fat and lean tissue. Although a number of methods are available (33,58), most investigators studying the effect of exercise on body composition in humans have relied mainly on the underwater weighing and skinfold techniques to estimate composition. The underwater weighing technique, which is based on Archimedes' principle (9), involves calculating body fat, using an appropriate formula (82), from a measurement of density of the whole body. Body density is determined by the ratio of body weight to the difference between body weight in air and in water after making appropriate corrections for lung and gastrointestinal gases (101). Skinfold thickness measurements are obtained with calipers at a number of sites on the body following recommendations of the Committee on Nutritional Anthropometry of the Food and Nutrition Board of the National Research Council (56). Multiple regression equations are available to derive body density (102). It is possible then to convert body density values into body fat percentages (8,102).

Body composition in animals is determined directly by employing chemical and gravimetric techniques. It is possible to obtain percentages and total amounts of protein, fat, minerals, and water. Exercise-induced changes in body composition are usually obtained by comparing exercising animals with comparable sedentary controls.

E. Effects of Exercise on Body Growth and Composition
of Young Humans

Information regarding the effect of exercise on body growth during
the period from childhood through young adulthood is scarce. This is
true because, as Rarick (*81*) has pointed out, difficulties arise when
attempts are made to exercise human subjects on a regular basis for
a number of years. Furthermore, it is extremely difficult in a long term
study involving humans to sort out the effects of other variables such
as diet and heredity which markedly affect body size.

Some evidence is available, however, to show that regularly performed
exercise can have a favorable effect on body composition of both male
and female children.

Wells *et al.* (*99*) reported that after 4 weeks of intensive physical
training, adolescent girls showed an increase in specific gravity (from
approximately 1.053 to 1.058), a decrease in the sum of 10 skinfold
thicknesses (from approximately 102 mm to 85 mm), and a slight increase in body weight. These changes reflect an increase in lean tissue
and a decrease in the total-body content of fat. Jokl (*51*) reported
similar changes in fat and lean tissue in adolescent boys and girls in
response to five months of physical training.

Parizkova (*76*) estimated body fat and lean tissue (hydrostatic
weighing) in 15 boys, 11 years of age. The boys were followed closely
over the next 4 years and reexamined at 15 years of age. During this
four year period, they exercised regularly by participating in activities
organized by sport clubs and in unorganized sport activities. Although
exercise did not produce a reduction in the total-body content of fat,
it did prevent a rise which usually accompanies a weight gain of approximately 25 kg over a 4 year period. The initial value for body fat of
5.7 kg for the active boys was very close to the value of 6.0 kg obtained
4 years later. In contrast, body fat, in a group of sedentary boys of the
same age and of approximately the same height and weight, increased
from 6.9 kg to 9.7 kg over the 4 year period. An increase in lean body
mass was observed in both groups, but the rise was greater in the active
boys. In another study, Parizkova (*75*) measured subcutaneous fat in
female gymnasts, aged 13 to 14 years, who trained regularly for 2 years,
and found a marked reduction in the layer of subcutaneous fat in a
comparison between these athletes and a group of sedentary girls of the
same age, height, and weight. Novak (*67*) determined body density
using the underwater weighing method in 18 adolescent boys who participated regularly in sport and in 20 nonparticipants of approximately

the same age, height, and weight. Body fat in the athletes amounted to 7.2% of the body weight compared to 14.9% for the nonparticipants.

Collectively, the above findings show that exercise can affect body composition of young, growing humans by lowering or preventing an increase in body fat and by increasing lean tissue.

F. Effect of Exercise on Body Composition of Adult Humans

Exercise-induced changes in body composition in adults similar to those observed in youth would appear to be desirable in view of the fact that the increase in body fat with age accounts for the gains in body weight (16); fat-free weight remains unchanged or decreases slightly with advancing years (14). Studies have been conducted on adult humans to show that exercise does have a favorable effect on body composition either with or without a change in body weight.

Welham and Behnke (98) compared a group of professional football players with a group of age-matched naval personnel and reported that even though the athletes were heavier, a majority of them had higher specific gravities, reflecting a greater amount of lean tissue and less fat. In another study by Keys and Brozek (57), measurements of skinfolds over the triceps muscle and the tip of the scapula were made to obtain estimates of body fat in men who held jobs requiring heavy physical labor, such as steel workers and miners, and in men who occupied sedentary positions, such as office work. They reported that men in the physically demanding positions were considerably leaner than those in the less active jobs.

Few would question that competitive marathon running is currently one of the most physically demanding athletic endeavors in our society. Marathon runners, during training, expend as much as 5000 to 6000 kcal/day (22). Costill et al. (21) obtained skinfold measurements from six sites on a group of competitive marathon runners and on a group of age-matched college professors who were roughly of the same weight. Using these data to estimate body density and fat, these investigators were able to show that the bodies of the sedentary faculty men contained approximately twice as much fat (16.3%) as those of the athletes (7.5%). Moore and Buskirk (65) reported similar results in a comparison between a group of habitually sedentary individuals and age-matched varsity athletes (wrestlers, football players, and gymnasts).

In addition to comparative studies, a number of longitudinal studies have been conducted to examine the effects of exercise on body composition. In these longitudinal studies, estimates of body composition were made prior to and immediately following a number of months of regularly performed exercise. Thompson *et al.* (*93*), using skinfold measurements, estimated body fat in college basketball and hockey players during a season of varsity competition. Body weight of the athletes remained constant but they lost subcutaneous fat in the three sites measured; chest, abdomen, and over the triceps. Similar changes were reported by Thompson (*92*) in a group of college football players during a season of competition.

Skinner *et al.* (*89*) found that exercising a minimum of three times per week, approximately 40 min per session, for a period of 6 months, was effective in significantly increasing specific gravity from 1.058 to 1.063 (determined by underwater weighing) and significantly decreasing the sum of six skinfold measurements from 107.7 mm to 99.3 mm in 15 previously sedentary middle-aged men. Oscai and Williams (*74*) reported that jogging at least 3 miles per session, three times per week, for 16 weeks, resulted in a mild but consistent reduction in body weight in moderately overweight middle-aged males. The weight reduction was primarily the result of loss of fat (estimated from skinfold measurements obtained over the triceps, chest, and mid-axilla), as this body component decreased from a value of 23.7 kg to 20.0 kg; fat-free weight remained essentially unchanged (*74*). Pollock *et al.* (*80*), Ribisl (*83*), Wilmore *et al.* (*103*), and Boileau *et al.* (*13*) reported similar changes in body weight and in the total-body content of fat in adult males in response to 9 to 20 week long programs of jogging. Fat-free weight remained essentially unchanged in three of these studies (*80,83,103*). However, Boileau *et al.* (*13*) reported increments in fat-free weight in lean and in obese male college students on the basis of anthropometric, densitometric, and hydrometric analyses of body composition in response to exercise. Carter and Phillips (*19*) followed exercise-induced changes in body composition in seven middle-aged men over a 2 year period. Jogging approximately 30 min per session, 2 or 3 days per week for 24 months, was effective in reducing body weight by 6% and body fat by 20%.

In addition to the investigations conducted on adult males, Moody *et al.* (*64*) studied the effect of exercise on body weight and composition in overweight college women. Eleven females were subjected to a walk–jog program requiring an expenditure of approximately 500 kcal/day, 6 days per week for 8 weeks. In response to the exercise, body weight and the mean of 10 skinfold thickness measurements decreased significantly from 67.1 kg to 64.7 kg and from 20.2 mm to 12.7 mm, respectively. On the basis of weight and skinfold thickness measurements, it was estimated that total-body content of fat had decreased an average of 5.3 kg, which was approximately double the reduction in total body weight; fat-free weight increased from 49.0 kg to 51.9 kg.

G. EFFECTS OF EXERCISE ON BODY GROWTH AND COMPOSITION OF MALE ANIMALS

It is well documented that male animals subjected to programs of regularly performed treadmill running or swimming gain weight more slowly and have lower final body weights than comparable freely eating sedentary controls (*5,6,23,25,31,35,47,70,71,73,94,96*). The slower rate of weight gain is due to an increase in caloric expediture associated with exercise and in some cases, to a significant reduction in food intake (*23,69,91*).

Studies have been performed to identify the components of the body which are reduced in weight to account for the lower total body weights of the exercisers. Jones *et al.* (*52*) reported that the difference between the final body weights of exercising and sedentary, freely eating, male animals, of approximately 60 gm, could be explained almost entirely by the lower fat content of the carcasses of the exercising animals. Crews *et al.* (*23*), Oscai *et al.* (*73*), and Pitts (*79*) also found fat to be the body constituent most markedly affected by exercise. In these studies, total lean body mass was also lower in the exercising than in the sedentary freely eating male rats.

H. EFFECTS OF EXERCISE ON BODY GROWTH AND COMPOSITION OF FEMALE ANIMALS

In contrast to male animals, female rats that exercise regularly gain weight at approximately the same rate as sedentary, freely eating controls (*24,71*). This is made possible by a rise in food intake which apparently balances the increase in caloric expenditure associated with exercise (*24,63,71*).

The carcasses of exercising female animals may contain as little as one-half as much fat as those of freely eating sedentary controls of similar body weight (*72*). Fat-free weight in female animals is significantly increased in response to exercise (*72*).

Surprisingly, the increase in lean tissue in response to endurance exercise occurs in the absence of an increase in the size of limb and girdle muscles directly involved with exercise (*3,47,72,78*). These observations provided the motivation for a study to determine which components of the lean body mass account for the greater lean tissue mass in the carcasses of animals subjected to endurance exercise (*72*).

Female animals which exercised 6 hr daily for 21 weeks had body weights similar to those of a group of comparable freely eating sedentary controls, but their carcasses contained significantly more lean tissue (72). A detailed analysis of body composition showed that the tissue group making the greatest contribution to the increase in lean body mass was the eviscerated carcass, consisting of the head and neck, spine, rib cage, clavicles, pelvis, and remaining attached musculature, after removal of the front and hind limbs with attached shoulder and pelvic girdle muscles. Other tissue groups making contributions were: (a) the skin and subcutaneous tissue; (b) the heart, lungs, liver, kidneys, and blood; (c) the intestinal tract, pancreas, uterus, ovaries, mesentery, omentum, and retroperitoneal adipose tissue; and (d) the tail. There was no hypertrophy of the limb and girdle muscles directly involved with the exercise. These muscles are also the weight-bearing or antigravity muscles normally involved in supporting the animals body weight. Perhaps the rats' everyday activities in their cages provided a great enough anabolic stimulus to the weight-bearing muscles so that the repetitive, weak muscle contractions associated with prolonged running or swimming did not have an additional effect. On the other hand, contractions sufficiently forceful to provide a stimulus to protein synthesis may occur only rarely in the non-weight-bearing muscles of sedentary rats confined in individual cages. As a result, the isometric contractions involved in stabilizing the head, spine, scapula, and tail during exercise may provide a sufficient stimulus above usual cage activity to result in hypertrophy.

III. Factors Which Control Body Fat

A. Recent Advances in Sizing and Counting Fat Cells

It is commonly known that fat is stored in adipose tissue cells which form depots located at various sites in the body. The amount of fat stored in each depot is dependent upon the size and number of its constituent cells. Until recently, little attention was given to the cellular character of an adipose depot in normal and abnormal conditions. This situation existed primarily because of a realization among many investigators working in this area that older available methods, a few of which are still being used in research laboratories, for counting and sizing fat cells have serious limitations. Many complain that the microscopic determination of cell size and number in adipose tissue is too time consuming since it involves the measurement and counting of a large number of cells. Criticism regarding the deoxyribonucleic acid

(DNA) method to reflect cell number is more serious. Uncertainty exists as to whether or not it is possible to completely separate fat cells from other contaminating cellular elements (stromal-vascular elements). A complete isolation of fat cells appears necessary in view of the observations of Rodbell (85) and of Hollenberg and Vost (46) that DNA content of nuclei of contaminating elements in adipose tissue can exceed that of the fat cells.

Over the past few years, primarily as a result of the efforts of Hirsch and Gallian (42), relatively simple and reliable techniques for sizing and counting fat cells have been developed. It is now possible to isolate fixed fat cells from small fragments of adipose tissue and then size and count them with a high degree of precision using an automatic cell counter (42). The use of these new techniques now makes it possible to perform studies of the cellular development of an adipose depot in humans and animals.

B. Development of Adipose Cellularity in Animals

In rats, it has been clearly shown that both cell number and size increase in epididymal and retroperitoneal depots until approximately 15 weeks of age (43,50). At that point, cell number becomes fixed and only the size of the cell changes with further increases in adiposity. Cellularity in the subcutaneous depot exhibits a different pattern; cell division in this depot does not cease until 26 weeks of age in a rat (50).

C. Development of Adipose Cellularity in Humans

In humans, fat cells accumulate very rapidly in early life. The work of Hirsch and Knittle (44) indicated that in the first year of life, a roughly threefold increase can occur in the number of fat cells found in the body. Available data suggest that this period of rapid growth is followed by a much slower but continuous increase in adipose tissue cellularity which extends into early adult life (44). The precise point in life, however, when it is no longer possible to detect a change in the total number of cells in humans remains to be elucidated. Although the time is not precisely known, cell division appears to cease at some point between puberty and early adulthood. Hirsch and Knittle (44), for example, have clearly shown that human adipose cells are still increasing in number at 13 years of age, at which time adult number has not yet been reached. On the other hand, when individuals 20 years of age and older were studied (87), it was found that fat cell number had stabilized and that these cells were not capable of further proliferation even though the subjects under observation gained an average of

16.2 kg of body weight, of which 10.4 kg was determined to be fat, as a result of prolonged high caloric intake. In this study, determinations of adipose cell size and number were made before and after weight gain. In contrast to hyperplasia, fat cell enlargement occurs much more slowly in early life. Evidence for this comes from recent work showing that it takes approximately 6 years from the time of birth for fat cells to triple in size (*44*). Under conditions of normal growth (i.e., in the absence of obesity), fat cells appear to continue to enlarge at a slow rate throughout adolescence and into adulthood, where adult size is reached.

D. EFFECT OF WEIGHT LOSS ON ADIPOSE CELL SIZE AND NUMBER

It is becoming increasingly clear that, once formed, fat cells are not easily destroyed. To date, no known clinical procedure, outside of surgical removal, is effective in reducing the total number of cells in an adipose depot. Even in the face of a substantial weight loss produced by means of caloric restriction, the size of adipose cells of rats were greatly reduced but cell number remained unaffected (*43*). Similar results have been reported by Salans *et al.* (*87*) in humans. A weight loss of 15.6 kg, of which 11.2 kg was determined to be fat, was associated with a reduction in adipose cell size but no change in total number.

IV. The Role of Exercise in the Possible Prevention
and Therapy of Obesity

A. THE ROLE OF EXERCISE IN THE POSSIBLE PREVENTION OF OBESITY

The finding that adipose cell number can be changed only in the first 15 to 26 weeks of life in rats (*43,50*) has focused interest on physical activity and nutritional patterns early in life. To curb the potential for obesity, it appears necessary to limit the total number of fat cells in the body since a marked increase in number, rather than in size, is primarily responsible for massive obesity (*45*).

As discussed previously in this review (Sections II,G and II,H), regularly performed endurance exercise results in a marked decrease in the total-body content of fat in young, growing animals (*23,40,52, 73,79*). Recently, the cellular character of epididymal fat pads of exercised rats, at least 15 weeks of age, was studied to determine if the reduction in fat was due to a decrease in cell number, size, or both (*73*). This fat depot was found to contain fewer (35%) and significantly smaller cells in the exercisers than in sedentary, freely eating controls. If this reduction is a permanent effect of exercise on adipose tissue cellularity, as the work of Hirsch and Han (*43*), and Johnson *et al.* (*50*) suggests, it would have interesting implications with respect to the development of severe obesity. Further studies will be necessary before a broader understanding of the role of exercise in this area is achieved.

B. WEIGHT CHANGES PRODUCED BY EXERCISE ALONE

Under normal conditions, obesity results when caloric intake exceeds caloric needs. Thus, obesity can be reversed either by reducing caloric intake below expenditure, or by raising caloric expenditure above intake. Exercise would appear to be a logical approach to increasing caloric expenditure and thus reducing body weight. Recently, evidence was presented to show that it is possible to increase caloric expenditure sufficiently by means of regularly performed exercise to produce a marked decrease in body weight. Obese male rats were subjected to 2 hr of daily swimming for 18 weeks (*69*). The weight loss, which amounted to approximately 25% of the animals' initial weight, resulted from both a suppression of appetite and an increase in caloric expenditure, with the latter contributing roughly three times as much as the former to the negative energy balance. The major portion (78%) of the weight loss that occurred in the exercising animals was due to a loss of fat. As discussed in the preceding section (Section III,D), a reduction in body fat of older animals is characterized by a decrease in adipose cell size without a change in cell number (*43*). On the basis of these observations, it is reasonable to assume that the marked reduction in the total-body content of fat of the adult, obese rats in response to exercise was due solely to a decrease in adipose cell size.

It would be interesting to see if a comparable weight change could be produced in obese humans by means of exercise alone. Future studies will be necessary to determine whether or not this is possible.

Large amounts of lean tissue, in addition to fat, are lost when the weight of an obese individual is reduced by means of caloric restriction (*15,30,58,104*). Estimates of the contribution of the lean component of the tissue lost to the total weight loss in response to caloric restriction are variable but have amounted to as much as 35 to 45% (*15,30,58,104*). One advantage of exercise over caloric restriction is that it provides considerable protection against the loss of protein and fat-free weight associated with a negative caloric balance. Evidence for this comes from a study in which the effects of weight changes produced by exercise and by food restriction on body composition were compared (*69*). Table I shows that both weight reducing groups lost approximately

TABLE I

Effects of Weight Changes Produced by Exercise or Food Restriction on Body Composition Over a Period of 18 Weeks

Group	Carcass weight[a] (gm)	Protein (gm)	Fat (gm)	Ash (gm)	Water (gm)
Exercising rats (8)	496 ± 23	84.2 ± 3.5	105.2 ± 14.6	12.2 ± 0.7	295.2 ± 7.0
Sedentary, food-restricted rats (8)	498 ± 20	73.0 ± 2.7	135.4 ± 14.9	12.3 ± 0.1	278.1 ± 5.8
Baseline rats (7)[b]	676 ± 39	93.0 ± 2.4	245.0 ± 30.4	13.9 ± 0.6	324.8 ± 14.5

Values are means ± SEM. The number of rats per group is given in parentheses.

[a] After removal of hair and feces.

[b] The baseline group was sacrificed at the beginning of the study.

180 gm. However, although the weight loss of the exercising and of the sedentary, caloric restricted animals was the same, the exercisers lost significantly more fat and less than one-half as much protein (Table I). The finding that the exercising animals were leaner than the sedentary controls of the same weight points to a lipid-mobilizing effect of exercise. It has been shown that during prolonged exercise, fatty acid mobilization does increase markedly (7,41,84). This effect appears to be mediated, in part, by increased activity of the sympathetic nervous system (66,97). It appears that the cumulative effects of daily, exercise-induced bouts of lipolysis could be responsible for the greater fat loss of the exercised animals. Furthermore, this fat-mobilizing effect, which persists for a considerable time after the cessation of exercise (41,84), could play a role in the conservation of lean tissue by making available to muscle and organ cells more of the energy stored as fat. The greater lean body mass of the exercising animals, as compared with the sedentary, food restricted controls, could also reflect stimuli for amino acid conservation and protein synthesis, such as a direct effect of exercise on muscle (39) and the anabolic effects of increased levels of growth hormone secretion secondary to the exercise (34).

C. Weight Changes Produced by Exercise Combined with Mild to Severe Food Restriction

In contrast to using exercise alone, exercise can be used simultaneously with food restriction to produce a negative caloric balance in obese patients. An advantage of using this type of regimen to produce a negative caloric balance is that it accelerates the rate of weight loss over that produced by exercise alone or food restriction alone. Buskirk et al. (18) simultaneously exercised and food-restricted a group of obese men and women to produce a negative caloric balance. These investigators (18) reported that the subjects lost weight and body fat at a faster rate on this regimen than when placed in negative energy balance without exercise. Passmore et al. (77) reported that a 6 week program of physical exercise combined with caloric restriction (400 kcal/day) also resulted in a rapid rate of weight loss in a group of obese patients. The subjects lost an average of 15.3 kg over a period of 40 to 45 days. The subjects under investigation remained in good health during the weight reducing program and it did not interfere in any way with their sense of well-being or activities. Sprynarova and Parizkova (90) examined seven obese boys (mean age, 11 years) just before and immediately following 7 weeks' stay in a recreation camp where they undertook a program of daily physical exercise and mild food restriction (1700

kcal/day). Body weight decreased significantly from 57.3 to 50.7 kg (*90*).
Exercise combined with food restriction may be a sensible approach
to weight reduction for obese individuals who desire to lose weight at
a fairly rapid rate but cannot tolerate severe caloric restriction or prolonged, strenuous exercise.

D. Weight Changes Produced by Exercise Combined
   with Total Fasting

Total fasting as a treatment of the grossly overweight condition was
introduced by Bloom in 1959 (*12*). Since then, this approach has been
used fairly extensively but restricted to cases of severe obesity. Treatment is usually carried out on a hospital metabolic ward under the
supervision of a physician, since total fasting does put considerable
strain on the body and metabolic complications can result. The advantage of total fasting in the management of obesity is mainly psychological in nature in that grossly overweight subjects lose weight at a
very rapid rate. Numerous reports indicate that obese individuals subjected to total fasting can lose between approximately 500 to 1000 gm/
day (*4,10*). The contribution of increased caloric expenditure to the
negative caloric balance is often negligible since physical activity for
fasting obese individuals is usually restricted to a minimum. It seems
logical that, if a program of regularly performed endurance exercise
could be incorporated into a program of weight reduction involving total
fasting, then an even faster rate of weight reduction could be achieved.
This possibility was tested. Two groups of obese male rats were
matched for weight at the beginning of the study and then weight-
reduced to approximately one-half of their initial body weights (*2*).
The group weight-reduced by means of total fasting alone lost 353 ±
5 gm in 41 days, while the group which was exercised without receiving
any food lost approximately the same amount (341 ± 30 gm) in 27
days. Throughout the study, both groups appeared healthy and alert.

V. The Role of Exercise in Maintaining Normal Body Weight

A. Exercise in Maintaining Body Weight at Reduced Levels
   to Prevent the Mildly Overweight Condition

Most individuals who have a weight problem are only mildly overweight. This condition develops gradually over a number of years,
usually after formal education has ended. A lack of physical activity
is commonly implicated as an important factor leading to the develop-

ment of mild obesity. Greene (*36*) reported that in 236 out of 350 cases of adult obesity, the beginning of this condition could be traced directly to a sudden decrease in physical activity.

The above observations suggest that, in the absence of a decrease in physical activity, body weight could be maintained close to normal levels. Previously in this review (Sections II,E and II,F), numerous studies (*13,19,48,51,74,80,83,89,103*) were presented to show that it is clearly possible to fit 2 to 5 days of exercise, 30 to 60 min per session, into the schedules of busy humans. This amount of time devoted to an exercise program apparently does not inconvenience the subjects and appears to be well within their exercise tolerance. More importantly, body weight tends to remain stable and may even drop slightly in response to the exercise. Body weights were slightly but significantly reduced in a group of middle-aged males, of initially normal body weight, who exercised regularly over a 2 year period (*19*). Body weight in a group of sedentary control subjects in this study increased significantly. These results provide evidence that exercise is effective in preventing a rise in body weight which leads to the overweight condition and is all too often associated with a sedentary existence. Furthermore, it is reasonable to assume that with continued exercise, over a longer period of time, exercise could effectively control body weight indefinitely.

B. Exercise in Maintaining Body Weight at Reduced Levels to Prevent the Grossly Overweight Condition

Mild obesity can lead to severe obesity. As in the case of mild obesity, a decrease in exercise appears to be an important factor in weight gains leading to the grossly overweight condition. It has been demonstrated in animals (*59–61*) and observed in human beings (*17,49,53,95*) that the grossly obese are considerably less active than the nonobese. Furthermore, although caloric intake is often greater in a grossly obese person than in a normal person (*53*), obesity often can be traced directly to physical inactivity without an abnormal increase in food intake (*49*).

It has been demonstrated on a number of occasions that it is possible to treat the symptoms of obesity, resulting in a weight reduction to normal body weight or close to normal (*12,15,28-30,36,58,69,87,104*). However, results showing that it is possible to keep body weight at reduced levels after treatment are very discouraging. One hundred and six obese patients were weight-reduced to varying degrees by means of food restriction (*32*). Follow-up data on these subjects indicate that a vast majority of them gain back all of the lost weight within a few years after treatment (*27*). One difficulty confronting obese individuals who have experienced substantial weight losses is that it seems necessary for them to exist on a diet lower in total number of calories to maintain their body weights at reduced levels than that for normal individuals without a chronic history of a weight problem (*27*).

Although it seems reasonable that exercise could help to prevent the regain of body weight, the role of exercise in this area remains undefined. In view of the magnitude of the health problem presented by obesity, considerable future work regarding the role of exercise in this area is obviously needed.

Acknowledgment

The author expresses appreciation to Mrs. Ellen M. Marx for assistance in the preparation of this manuscript.

References

1. Ahrens, R. A., Bishop, C. L., and Berdanier, C. D. (1972). *J. Nutr.* **102**, 241–248.
2. Babirak, S. P., Dowell, R. T., and Oscai, L. B. (In preparation.)
3. Baldwin, K. M., Klinkerfuss, G. H., Terjung, R. L., Molé, P. A., and Holloszy, J. O. (1972). *Amer. J. Physiol.* **222**, 373–378.
4. Ball, M. F., Canary, J. J., and Kyle, L. H. (1967). *Ann. Intern. Med.* **67**, 60–67.
5. Banister, E. W., Tomanek, R. J., and Cvorkov, N. (1971). *Amer. J. Physiol.* **220**, 1935–1940.
6. Barnard, R. J., Edgerton, V. R., and Peter, J. B. (1970). *J. Appl. Physiol.* **28**, 762–766.
7. Basu, A., Passmore, R., and Strong, J. A. (1960). *Quart. J. Exp. Physiol.* **45**, 312–317.
8. Behnke, A. R. (1961). *In* "Techniques for Measuring Body Composition" (J. Brozek, ed.), pp. 118–133. Headquarters Quartermaster Research and Engineering Command, Natick, Massachusetts.
9. Behnke, A. R., Feen, B. G., and Welham, W. C. (1942). *J. Amer. Med. Ass.* **118**, 495–498.
10. Benoit, F. L., Martin, R. L., and Watten, R. H. (1965). *Ann. Intern. Med.* **63**, 604–612.
11. Bjerkedal, T. (1957). *Acta Med. Scand.* **159**, 13–26.
12. Bloom, W. L. (1959). *Metabolism, Clin. Exp.* **8**, 214–220.
13. Boileau, R. A., Buskirk, E. R., Horstman, D. H., Mendez, J., and Nicholas, W. C. (1971). *Med. Sci. Sports* **3**, 183–189.
14. Brozek, J. (1952). *Fed. Proc.* **11**, 784–793.
15. Brozek, J., Grande, F., Anderson, J. T., and Keys, A. (1963). *Ann. N. Y. Acad. Sci.* **110**, 113–140.

16. Brozek, J., and Keys, A. (1953). *Geriatrics* **8**, 70–75.
17. Bruch, H. (1940). *Amer. J. Dis. Child.* **60**, 1082–1109.
18. Buskirk, E. R., Thompson, R. H., Lutwak, L., and Whedon, G. D. (1963). *Ann. N. Y. Acad. Sci.* **110**, 918–940.
19. Carter, J. E. L., and Phillips, W. H. (1969). *J. Appl. Physiol.* **27**, 787–794.
20. Consolazio, C. F., Johnson, R. E., and Pecora, L. J. (1963). "Physiological Measurements of Metabolic Functions in Man." McGraw-Hill, New York.
21. Costill, D. L., Bowers, R., and Kammer, W. F. (1970). *Med. Sci. Sports* **2**, 93–95.
22. Costill, D. L., and Fox, E. L. (1969). *Med. Sci. Sports* **1**, 81–86.
23. Crews, E. L., Fuge, K. W., Oscai, L. B., Holloszy, J. O., and Shank, R. E. (1969). *Amer. J. Physiol.* **216**, 359–363.
24. Crews, J., and Aldinger, E. E. (1967). *Amer. Heart J.* **74**, 536–542.
25. Dawson, C. A., and Horvath, S. M. (1970). *Med. Sci. Sports* **2**, 51–78.
26. Dempsey, J. A. (1964). *Res. Quart.* **35**, 275–287.
27. Dole, V. P. (1972). Personal communication.
28. Drenick, E. J., Swendseid, M. E., Blahd, W. H., and Tuttle, S. G. (1963). *J. Amer. Med. Ass.* **187**, 100–105.
29. Duncan, G. G., Jenson, W. K., Fraser, R. I., and Cristofori, F. C. (1962). *J. Amer. Med. Ass.* **181**, 309–312.
30. Entenman, C., Goldwater, W. H., Ayres, N. S., and Behnke, A. R. (1958). *J. Appl. Physiol.* **13**, 129–134.
31. Faulkner, J. A., Maxwell, L. C., Brook, D. A., and Lieberman, D. A. (1971). *Amer. J. Physiol.* **221**, 291–297.
32. Feinstein, A. R., Dole, V. P., and Schwartz, I. L. (1958). *Ann. Intern. Med.* **48**, 330–343.
33. Forbes, G. B. (1962). *Pediatrics* **29**, 477–494.
34. Glick, S. M., Roth, J., Yalow, R. S., and Berson, S. A. (1965). *Recent Progr. Horm. Res.* **21**, 241–283.
35. Gollnick, P. D., and Taylor, A. W. (1969). *Int. Z. Angew. Physiol.* **27**, 144–153.
36. Greene, J. A. (1939). *Ann. Intern. Med.* **12**, 1797–1803.
37. Haggendal, J. (1971). *In* "Muscle Metabolism During Exercise" (B. Pernow and B. Saltin, eds.), pp. 119–125. Plenum, New York.
38. Haggendal, J., Hartley, L. H., and Saltin, B. (1970). *Scand. J. Clin. Lab. Invest.* **26**, 337–342.
39. Hamish, M. T., Lesch, M., Baron, J., and Kaufman, S. (1967). *Science* **157**, 935–937.
40. Hanson, D. L., Lorenzen, J. A., Morris, A. E., Ahrens, R. A., and Wilson, J. E., Jr. (1967). *Amer. J. Physiol.* **213**, 347–352.
41. Havel, R. J., Naimark, A., and Borchgrevink, C. F. (1963). *J. Clin. Invest.* **42**, 1054–1063.
42. Hirsch, J., and Gallian, E. (1968). *J. Lipid Res.* **9**, 110–119.
43. Hirsch, J., and Han, P. W. (1969). *J. Lipid Res.* **10**, 77–82.
44. Hirsch, J., and Knittle, J. L. (1970). *Fed. Proc.* **29**, 1516–1521.
45. Hirsch, J., Knittle, J. L., and Salans, L. B. (1966). *J. Clin. Invest.* **45**, 1023. (Abstr.)
46. Hollenberg, C. H., and Vost, A. (1968). *J. Clin. Invest.* **47**, 2485–2498.
47. Holloszy, J. O. (1967). *J. Biol. Chem.* **242**, 2278–2282.
48. Holloszy, J. O., Skinner, J. S., Toro, G., and Cureton, T. K. (1964). *Amer. J. Cardiol.* **14**, 753–760.
49. Johnson, M. L., Burke, B. S., and Mayer, J. (1956). *J. Clin. Nutr.* **4**, 37–44.

50. Johnson, P. R., Zucker, L. M., Cruce, J. A. F., and Hirsch, J. (1971). *J. Lipid Res.* **12**, 706–714.
51. Jokl, E. (1963). *Ann. N. Y. Acad. Sci.* **110**, 778–794.
52. Jones, E. M., Montoye, H. J., Johnson, P. B., Martin, S. M. J. M., Van Huss, W. D., and Cederquist, D. C. (1964). *Amer. J. Physiol.* **207**, 460–466.
53. Juel-Nielsen, N. (1953). *Acta Paediat.* **42**, 130–145.
54. Kannel, W. B., LeBauer, E. J., Dawber, T. R., and McNamara, P. M. (1967). *Circulation* **35**, 734–744.
55. Karvonen, M. J., Pekkarinen, M., Metsala, P., and Rautanen, Y. (1961). *Brit. J. Nutr.* **15**, 157–164.
56. Keys, A. (1956). *Hum. Biol.* **28**, 111–123.
57. Keys, A., and Brozek, J. (1957). *Metabolism, Clin. Exp.* **6**, 425–434.
58. Keys, A., and Brozek, J. (1953). *Physiol. Rev.* **33**, 245–325.
59. Marshall, N. B., and Mayer, J. (1954). *Amer. J. Physiol.* **178**, 271–274.
60. Mayer, J. (1953). *Science* **117**, 504–505.
61. Mayer, J., French, R. G., Zighera, C. F., and Barrnett, R. J. (1955). *Amer. J. Physiol.* **182**, 75–82.
62. Mayer, J. (1960). *In* "Science and Medicine of Exercise and Sports" (W. R. Johnson, ed.), pp. 301–310. Harper, New York.
63. Mayer, J., Marshall, N. B., Vitale, J. J., Christensen, J. H., Mashayekhi, M. B., and Stare, F. J. (1954). *Amer. J. Physiol.* **177**, 544–548.
64. Moody, D. L., Kollias, J., and Buskirk, E. R. (1969). *Med. Sci. Sports* **1**, 75–80.
65. Moore, R., and Buskirk, E. R. (1960). *In* "Science and Medicine of Exercise and Sports" (W. R. Johnson, ed.), pp. 207–235. Harper, New York.
66. Muir, G. G., Chamberlain, D. A., and Pedoe, D. T. (1964). *Lancet* **2**, 930–932.
67. Novak, L. P. (1966). *J. Amer. Med. Ass.* **197**, 891–893.
68. Obesity and Health. (1966). U. S. Dept. of Health, Education, and Welfare, Public Health Service, Washington, D. C.
69. Oscai, L. B., and Holloszy, J. O. (1969). *J. Clin. Invest.* **48**, 2124–2128.
70. Oscai, L. B., Molé, P. A., Brei, B., Holloszy, J. O. (1971). *Amer. J. Physiol.* **220**, 1238–1241.
71. Oscai, L. B., Molé, P. A., and Holloszy, J. O. (1971). *Amer. J. Physiol.* **220**, 1944–1948.
72. Oscai, L. B., Molé, P. A., Krusack, L. M., and Holloszy, J. O. (1973). *J. Nutr.* (In press.)
73. Oscai, L. B., Spirakis, C. N., Wolff, C. A., and Beck, R. J. (1972). *J. Lipid Res.* **13**, 588–592.
74. Oscai, L. B., and Williams, B. T. (1968). *J. Amer. Geriat. Soc.* **16**, 794–797.
75. Parizkova, J. (1959). *Physiol. Bohemoslov.* **8**, 112–117.
76. Parizkova, J. (1968). *Hum. Biol.* **40**, 212–225.
77. Passmore, R., Strong, J. A., and Ritchie, F. J. (1958). *Brit. J. Nutr.* **12**, 113–122.
78. Pattengale, P. K., and Holloszy, J. O. (1967). *Amer. J. Physiol.* **213**, 783–785.
79. Pitts, G. C. (1956). *Amer. J. Physiol.* **185**, 41–48.
80. Pollock, M. L., Cureton, T. K., and Greninger, L. (1969). *Med. Sci. Sports* **1**, 70–74.
81. Rarick, G. L. (1960). *In* "Science and Medicine of Exercise and Sports" (W. R. Johnson, ed.), pp. 440–465. Harper, New York.
82. Rathbun, E. N., and Pace, N. (1945). *J. Biol. Chem.* **158**, 667–676.
83. Ribisl, P. M. (1969). *Int. Z. Angew. Physiol.* **27**, 154–160.
84. Rodahl, K., Miller, H. I., and Issekutz, B., Jr. (1964). *J. Appl. Physiol.* **19**, 489–492.

85. Rodbell, M. (1964). *J. Biol. Chem.* **239**, 753–755.
86. Russek, M., and Pina, S. (1962). *Nature (London)* **193**, 1296–1297.
87. Salans, L. B., Horton, E. S., and Sims, E. A. H. (1971). *J. Clin. Invest.* **50**, 1005–1011.
88. Sims, E. A. H., Goldman, R. F., Gluck, C. M., Horton, E. S., Kelleher, P. C., and Rowe, D. W. (1968). *Trans. Ass. Amer. Physicians* **81**, 153–170.
89. Skinner, J. S., Holloszy, J. O., and Cureton, T. K. (1964). *Amer. J. Cardiol.* **14**, 747–752.
90. Sprynarova, S., and Parizkova, J. (1965). *J. Appl. Physiol.* **20**, 934–937.
91. Stevenson, J. A. F., Box, B. M., Feleki, V., and Beaton, J. R. (1966). *J. Appl. Physiol.* **21**, 118–122.
92. Thompson, C. W. (1959). *Res. Quart.* **30**, 87–93.
93. Thompson, C. W., Buskirk, E. R., and Goldman, R. F. (1956). *Res. Quart.* **27**, 418–430.
94. Tipton, C. M., Terjung, R. L., and Barnard, R. J. (1968). *Amer. J. Physiol.* **215**, 1137–1142.
95. Tolstrup, K. (1953). *Acta Paediat.* **42**, 289–303.
96. Van Huss, W. D., Heusner, W. W., and Mickelsen, O. (1969). *In* "Exercise and Fitness" (B. D. Franks, ed.), pp. 201–214. Athletic Inst., Chicago, Illinois.
97. Vendsalu, A. (1960). *Acta Physiol. Scand.* **49** (Suppl. 173), 57–69.
98. Welham, W. C., and Behnke, A. R. (1942). *J. Amer. Med. Ass.* **118**, 498–501.
99. Wells, J. B., Parizkova, J., and Jokl, E. (1962). *J. Ass. Phys. Ment. Rehabil.* **16**, 35–40.
100. Williams, R. H. (1968). "Textbook of Endocrinology." Saunders, Philadelphia, Pennsylvania.
101. Wilmore, J. H. (1969). *J. Appl. Physiol.* **27**, 96–100.
102. Wilmore, J. H., Girandola, R. N., and Moody, D. L. (1970). *J. Appl. Physiol.* **29**, 313–317.
103. Wilmore, J. H., Royce, J., Girandola, R. N., Katch, F. I., and Katch, V. L. (1970). *Med. Sci. Sports* **2**, 113–117.
104. Young, C. M., and DiGiacomo, M. M. (1965). *Metabolism, Clin. Exp.* **14**, 1084–1094.

Physiological Responses of Women to Exercise

Barbara L. Drinkwater

INSTITUTE OF ENVIRONMENTAL STRESS, UNIVERSITY OF CALIFORNIA
AT SANTA BARBARA, SANTA BARBARA, CALIFORNIA

As more and more women take advantage of opportunities to participate in physically demanding activities, interest in how they respond physiologically to these activities has increased. The development of age group programs in endurance sports such as swimming and track, new emphasis on interscholastic and intercollegiate sports programs for girls, and the increasing popularity of fitness programs for older women have added impetus to the need to know more about the physiological effects of physical activity on females. This concern is not only directed toward the sportswoman. The extension of civil rights legislation to encompass equality of the sexes has made available to women a number of jobs which require considerable physical exertion. Regardless of the unpopularity of the notion that physiological differences between these sexes affect job performance, there is little scientific evidence to support any position on this controversial subject. For example, do the standards set for the safety of men who work in a hot environment apply equally to women? How does age affect the ability of women to perform physical tasks? Does the menstrual cycle affect the physical work capacity of women? Formerly, the answers to questions such as these were largely a matter of theoretical interest and were too frequently based on the subjective impressions of the observer. Today, answers are needed to resolve questions of immediate and practical significance. A solution to some of these problems has been sought by investigators through the determination of the quantitative and qualitative differences between the sexes in their physiological responses to activity.

I. Sex Differences

A. MAXIMAL AEROBIC CAPACITY

Whether or not there is a female response to exercise which is mediated solely by the factor of sex has not been determined. Since the classical study by Åstrand (6) in 1952 of children and young adults of both sexes, considerable energy has been expended in an effort to determine the qualitative and quantitative differences between males and females in their physiological responses to maximal and submaximal work (2,4,23, 25,40,43,48,51,69). While there is no doubt that the maximal aerobic capacity of the average woman is less than that of the average man (6,8, 23,40,48,51,71), there is also evidence that differences between male and female aerobic capacities are influenced by factors other than sex. Hermansen and Andersen (40) have reported data from a study of young Norwegian men and women, which suggest that the level of physical fitness of a subject overrides the effect of sex. Female cross-country skiers had maximal oxygen uptake values averaging 55 ml O_2/kg·min^{-1}, as compared to a mean of 44 ml O_2/kg·min^{-1} for normally active male students. Such findings are not unique to the sport of skiing or to Norway. In Canada and the United States, young female swimmers and track athletes also have maximal aerobic capacities equal to or better than those of males of the same age who are not athletes (26,49). The maximal ventilatory volumes and oxygen pulse, usually high for males, are also greater for the female athlete than for the nonathletic male.

Even among the so-called normal population there is considerable variability within the sexes and an overlap of $\dot{V}_{O_2 max}$ values for the more fit women and the less fit men. In the Norwegian study (40), 76% of the female students overlapped 47% of the male students. For the athletes the overlap was much less, 22% of the women falling within the same range as 7% of the men. A group of Canadian physical education students whose $\dot{V}_{O_2 max}$ was less than the Norwegian athletes but greater than the Norwegian students had an overlap area equally occupied by 32% of the males and 32% of the females (51). Obviously, the broad spectrum of maximal aerobic values cannot be dichotomized on the basis of sex.

However, when a male athlete is compared to a female athlete in aerobic capacity, the male has a decided advantage. On the average, he will exceed the woman's maximal oxygen uptake by 20 to 25% when

$\dot{V}_{O_2 max}$ is expressed as ml $O_2/kg \cdot min^{-1}$ (26,40,49), a wider difference than the 15 to 20% differential found between mean values in normal populations (6,40). Why men have the ability to attain higher oxygen uptake values than women has been a subject for conjecture. Some authors have reported that this difference disappears when $\dot{V}_{O_2 max}$ is expressed in relationship to fat-free body weight or active muscle mass (27,77). There are also reports to the contrary. MacNab et al. (51) tested the aerobic capacity of male and female physical education students on the treadmill and a bicycle ergometer and monitored their responses to submaximal work using both the bicycle and a progressive step test. Regardless of how oxygen uptake was expressed, as a ratio to body weight or lean body mass, the men had significantly higher values on the maximal test and accomplished significantly greater work during the submaximal tests. Although this work was intended to substantiate Von Döbeln's (77) findings of no significant differences between sexes when $V_{O_2 max}$ was related to fat-free weight, the methods of calculating fat-free weight were different for the two studies. Von Döbeln (77) calculated the amount of adipose tissue from the weight of body fat using the formula, adipose tissue = (kilograms of fat/0.62)$^{2/3}$, and determined fat-free weight as body weight (kg) − adipose tissue (kg); MacNab et al. (51) used the formula, body weight (kg) − fat (kg) to arrive at lean body mass. There was also a difference in relative physical fitness between the male and female subjects in the two samples. The $\dot{V}_{O_2 max}$ of the males in the MacNab et al. (51) study was 5% less and the females 25% less than Von Döbeln's subjects. An attempt to equate aerobic capacity between the sexes on the basis of lean body mass requires that other variables such as levels of physical fitness do not act as confounding factors.

A recent report by Davies (27) suggests that there may indeed be some validity to the assertion that differences in male and female response to exercise are related to the factors of body composition. When $\dot{V}_{O_2 max}$ of 116 boys and girls were measured on a bicycle ergometer and related to weight or to lean body mass calculated from skinfold thicknesses, a definite sex difference was observed. However, when maximum aerobic power was related to the volume of the leg (thigh and calf), the sex difference disappeared. Davies concluded that $\dot{V}_{O_2 max}$ was directly related to the active tissue involved in the exercise, in this case the leg muscles, and that aerobic capacity should be standardized by expressing it as a ratio to active muscle mass before considering further aspects of cardiorespiratory performance. While this discussion is of considerable theoretical interest to physiologists, it may be a moot point as far as women are concerned, for in most types of physical work a woman's weight, active and adipose tissue alike, is part of her workload. This point was noted by

TABLE I

Maximal Physiological Responses of Females According to Age and Nationality[a]

Age	Ref.	n	Height (cm)	Weight (kg)	$\dot{V}_{O_2}$ (ml/kg·min^{-1})	Heart rate (beats/min)	$\dot{V}_E$ BTPS	Method[b]	Nationality
4–6	6	7	111.6 ± 1.1	18.4 ± 0.7	47.9 ± 1.5	204 ± 5.0	33.9 ± 1.1	T	Swedish
7–9	6	14	132.0 ± 1.5	27.2 ± 1.5	55.1 ± 0.9	211 ± 2.0	57.3 ± 1.6	T	Swedish
8.5 ± 0.2	82	20	134.0 ± 1.6	30.3 ± 0.9	53.5 ± 1.5	195 ± 2.3	52.7 ± 2.8	B	American
10–11	6	13	140.6 ± 1.4	32.5 ± 0.8	52.4 ± 0.8	209 ± 2.5	61.1 ± 2.7	T	Swedish
10.5 ± 0.1	82	20	143.0 ± 1.7	37.0 ± 1.7	50.7 ± 1.3	196 ± 1.9	59.5 ± 3.5	B	American
12–13	6	13	158.5 ± 1.8	46.7 ± 1.8	49.8 ± 0.7	207 ± 2.8	79.9 ± 3.8	T	Swedish
12–13	59	10	150.0 ± 0.7	41.3 ± 1.0	34.9 ± 1.3			B	Japanese
12	54	18	150.9 ± 0.7	42.7 ± 0.7	39.6 ± 1.6			T	Japanese
12	53	10						T	Japanese
12.4 ± 0.1	82	20	159.0 ± 1.2	49.0 ± 1.1	48.7 ± 1.9	213 ± 2.3	68.2 ± 2.9	B	American
14–15	6	11	164.9 ± 1.4	56.0 ± 2.2	46.0 ± 1.0	194 ± 2.4	70.1 ± 2.3	T	Swedish
14–15	59	10	154.0 ± 0.5	47.9 ± 0.7	28.9 ± 2.2	202 ± .	87.9 ± 3.0	B	Japanese
16–17	6	10	167.7 ± 1.3	57.3 ± 1.5	47.2 ± 0.9	206 ± 2.5	93.8 ± 3.9	B	Swedish
16–17	59	10	154.8 ± 0.2	51.0 ± 0.7	26.7 ± 2.8			B	Japanese
16	54	43	155.4 ± 0.4	51.4 ± 0.8	38.5 ± 0.9			T	Japanese
16	53	12				198 ± 2.0	72.1 ± 3.5	B	Japanese
16.7	48	95	161.9	56.9	33.6	193.5	84.5	B	American
17	54	44	155.0 ± 0.3	50.4 ± 0.7	35.5 ± 0.9			T	Japanese
17	53	16				198 ± 2.1	66.5 ± 2.4	T	Japanese
18	54	15	156.5 ± 0.8	48.7 ± 1.0	39.6 ± 1.2			T	Japanese
18	53	7				195 ± 2.3	61.7 ± 4.1	T	Japanese
18.6	51	24	165.8 ± 1.1	59.2 ± 1.2	39.0 ± 1.1			T	Canadian

19.4	*56*	30	165.5 ± 0.8	57.9 ± 0.9	29.8	184	48	B	American
19.9	*44*	12	162.5 ± 1.6	58.4 ± 1.5	44.3 ± 1.1	191 ± 2.4	79.6 ± 2.5	T	American
19.9	*44*	12	162.5 ± 1.6	58.4 ± 1.5	41.2 ± 1.2	188 ± 1.8	80.8 ± 3.0	B	American
20.3 ± 0.3	*55*	6	164.1 ± 1.6	57.2 ± 2.9	33.6 ± 1.6	189 ± 3.5		T	American
21.3 ± 0.1	*39*	9	162.1 ± 0.3	59.1 ± 0.9	33.5 ± 1.8	193 ± 4.0		ST	Czech.
21.4	*39*	9	158.7 ± 0.6	55.9 ± 0.7	32.1 ± 2.1	181 ± 8.7	71.0 ± 2.3	ST	Algerian
22.6	*40*	12	168.2 ± 1.3	61.1 ± 1.9	38.0 ± 0.8	203 ± 2.8	79.5	B	Norwegian
23.7	*23*	20	162.0	55.0	39.2	193	71.2 ± 6.7	B	English
24.2	*29*	6	167.8 ± 2.7	65.2 ± 3.4	33.8 ± 1.5	194.0 ± 2.1	76.2 ± 5.7	T	American
25.0	*5*	8	166.0 ± 1.9	56.2 ± 2.2	39.9 ± 1.7	187.0 ± 3.4	89.8 ± 1.6	B	Swedish
20.25	*6*	44	165.8 ± 0.8	60.3 ± 0.9	48.4 ± 0.5	198.0 ± 1.5		T	Swedish
19-31	*46*	11			36.8 ± 0.7	194.0 ± 2.0	75.0 ± 4.4	B	Swedish
34.5	*5*	12	165.0 ± 1.5	57.5 ± 1.9	37.3 ± 1.5	185.0 ± 2.0	67.2 ± 4.6	B	Swedish
35.5	*29*	11	164.9 ± 1.3	63.5 ± 3.2	31.1 ± 2.1	180.2 ± 3.6		T	American
34-48	*46*	7			31.0 ± 1.7	177.0 ± 2.0	64.4 ± 4.9	B	Swedish
43.9	*5*	8	164.0 ± 2.0	61.9 ± 1.5	32.5 ± 1.0	178.0 ± 3.0	70.8 ± 3.6	B	Swedish
44.2 ± 1.2	*29*	9	166.2 ± 2.7	63.9 ± 1.6	32.5 ± 2.4	181.9 ± 3.2		T	American
40-49	*17*	18	161.6 ± 1.4	63.8 ± 2.4	28.2 ± 1.2[c]		56.8 ± 3.5	ST	Canadian
52.8 ± 1.1	*29*	7	163.3 ± 2.5	67.0 ± 5.2	25.1 ± 1.9	177.8 ± 5.1	60.5 ± 1.3	T	American
55.6	*5*	16	160.0 ± 0.7	65.4 ± 2.2	28.4 ± 0.7	170.0 ± 2.1		B	Swedish
50-59	*17*	15	160.0 ± 1.8	59.5 ± 2.3	29.6 ± 1.9[c]		30.9 ± 1.5	ST	Canadian
65.5 ± 1.3	*11*	14	162.1 ± 1.6	65.3 ± 1.4	16.8 ± 0.7	140.0 ± 5.0		B	American
60-69	*17*	11			22.9 ± 1.5[c]			ST	Canadian
51-64	*46*	7	157.3 ± 2.3	61.2 ± 3.5	26.9 ± 1.1	173.0 ± 2.0		B	Swedish

[a] Values are means ± SE.
[b] Method: B = bicycle ergometer, T = treadmill, ST = step test.
[c] Predicted maximal values.

Buskirk and Taylor (*19*), who made the reasonable suggestion that the method of expressing oxygen uptake should be related to the purpose of the investigation. When primary interest is in the ability to perform exhausting work, $\dot{V}_{O_2}$ should be expressed as milliliters of O_2 per kilogram. When interest is centered on the performance of the respiratory–cardiovascular systems, the ratio ml O_2/kg-LBW is more pertinent.

In 1966 Shephard (*69*) summarized the work of 70 authors who had previously reported maximal oxygen uptake values for males and females across a wide range of ages. While data for the males could be grouped according to age, national origin, and athletic activity, there was not enough information for active or athletic females to warrant division of the female data on the basis of activity. The higher aerobic capacities noted for males and females from the Scandinavian countries were attributed to a more active life style rather than to a genetic or nutritional effect or a sampling bias. It is interesting to note that in a more recent study (*46*), Swedish women, considered by the author to be representative of the Swedish female population, have maximal values quite similar to those of women in other countries.

An examination of Tables I and II shows no clearly defined pattern of maximal physiological responses related to national origin. More important are the factors of age and physical conditioning. For the non-athlete, maximal aerobic capacity and maximal heart rate decline with age, regardless of nationality. For the athlete, the aerobic requirement of her sport outweighs cultural factors in determining her $\dot{V}_{O_2 max}$. There are not enough data for older female athletes or ex-athletes to indicate how aging affects the woman who is or has been active in competitive sports.

B. SUBMAXIMAL WORK

At the same submaximal load, women are usually working at a higher percentage of their maximal aerobic capacity than men. As a result, their heart rates are higher and, if the workload is high enough, their lactate levels will exceed those of males (*7,23,40*). Although oxygen uptake has been reported as lower for a woman at the same submaximal load as a man, the difference usually disappears when $\dot{V}_{O_2}$ is expressed as ml/kg·min^{-1} rather than as liters/min (*23,40*). It should also be noted that physical fitness again seems to exert a strong influence on the differences between sexes. In the Hermansen and Andersen study (*40*) the heart rates of women athletes were equal to or lower than the rates of male students at all submaximal work loads. However, in most instances a given workload will be a greater strain on the female cardiorespiratory system than on the male.

TABLE II

MAXIMAL PHYSIOLOGICAL RESPONSES OF FEMALE ATHLETES ACCORDING TO SPORT AND NATIONALITY[a]

Age	Ref.	n	Height (cm)	Weight (kg)	$\dot{V}_{O_2}$ (ml/ kg·min^{-1})	Heart rate (beats/min)	$\dot{V}_B$ BTPS	Method[b]	Sport	Nationality
10–11	16	5	148.6	35.5	56.1	194.8	62.5	T	Track	American
12–13	16	5	152.4	41.2	55.4	195.8	78.5	T	Track	American
12.7	79	6	157.5	42.6	52.5	194.0	84.2 (STPD)	T	Track	Canadian
12–14	34	20	155.0 ± 1.3	48.1 ± 1.2	40.9 ± 1.5		62.4 ± 1.9	T	Swimming	Japanese
14–15	30	11	162.2 ± 1.8	52.2 ± 1.6	48.5 ± 1.4	194.7 ± 2.7	80.2 ± 3.6	B	Track	American
14–15	49	6	165.9 ± 2.1	61.1 ± 2.3	49.5 ± 2.4	197.0 ± 2.7	84.1 ± 2.1	T	Swimming	American
13–18	54	20	162.7 ± 1.0	57.5 ± 1.0	49.6 ± 1.0		76.8 ± 1.8	T	Swimming	Japanese
15.8	57	17	163.0	57.4	50.4 ± 0.8		77.1 (STPD)	T	Swimming	Japanese
15–17	54	13	157.0 ± 1.5	52.8 ± 1.1	40.6 ± 1.6		61.3 ± 3.5	T	Swimming	Japanese
16.5	79	6	158.8	52.8	50.2		84.8 (STPD)	T	Skiing	Canadian
17.2	76	10	162.3 ± 0.4	56.5 ± 1.0	42.5 ± 1.2	182.0 ± 2.8	84.9 ± 1.7	T	Gymnastics	Czech.
19.0	35	3		57.6	47.9	189.0	79.7	B	Figure skating	Canadian
19.5	76	10	166.2	63.6	45.9	191.0	100.7	T	Swimming	Czech.
20.0 ± 0.3	55	6	165.3 ± 3.8	61.0 ± 1.4	35.7 ± 2.5	191.0 ± 3.5		T	Basketball	American
20.0	73	7	166.4	61.3	38.7 ± 1.7	184.6 ± 2.6	87.5 ± 9.1	B	Basketball	American
21.5	52	13	164.5	60.8	46.1 ± 1.8	191.4 ± 2.9	96.5 ± 3.8	T	Speed skating	American
25.1 ± 2.6	40	5	169.0 ± 2.6	61.6 ± 2.8	55.0 ± 1.4	186.0 ± 3.6	99.0 ± 6.1	B	Skiing	Norwegian

[a] Values are means ± SE.
[b] Method: B = bicycle ergometer, T = treadmill.

Similar results have been reported for children, ages 6 to 14. At submaximal workloads ranging from 1 to 2.5 W/kg of body weight, Mácek
and Vávra (*50*) found no significant differences in the oxygen uptake
(ml O_2/kg·min^{-1}) of boys ($n = 47$) and girls ($n = 52$). There were a
number of indications, however, that the workload was a more severe
stress on the cardiorespiratory system of the girls. Once the load was
increased beyond 1 W/kg of body weight, the coefficients for the regression of CO_2 production, the respiratory exchange ratio, and lactate on
body weight were all significantly higher for girls. Ventilation and heart
rate coefficients for females were greater at all workloads. When the oxygen uptakes for this group of children were expressed as a percentage of
the $\dot{V}_{O_2 max}$ determined for a similar group of youngsters, girls were found
to be working at greater than 60% of their assumed aerobic capacity at
2 and 2.5 W/kg; boys did not reach this percentage of $\dot{V}_{O_2 max}$ at any workload. Differences between the sexes were small or nonexistent at the lower
body weights and increased at the higher weights. The authors believed
this to be a result of an increasing aerobic power for boys with age, while
the girls' capacity failed to keep pace. The differences might also have
been influenced by determining the workload per unit of body weight,
since at the older ages a smaller proportion of a girl's weight is active
muscle tissue as compared to a boy's.

According to Åstrand *et al.* (*8*), during submaximal work women com-
pensate for the smaller amount of oxygen in their arterial blood due to
smaller blood volumes and lower hemoglobin levels by increasing their
cardiac output ($\dot{Q}$). At maximal levels of exercise, further compensation
is impossible because $\dot{Q}$ is limited by the heart volume, blood volume,
and the venous return. Women, whose heart volumes are usually less than
men's, are thus limited to a relatively low maximal oxygen uptake as a
result of their lower hemoglobin concentrations and smaller hearts (*8,22*).
Åstrand *et al.* (*8*) cite as evidence a comparison of male and female
cardiovascular responses to maximal and submaximal work. At 600 kpm/
min, cardiac output and oxygen uptake were approximately the same for
men and women, but the women compensated for a lower stroke volume
(SV) with a heart rate of 151 beats/min compared to a rate of 106 for the
males. At a maximal load the women's heart rates were still higher than
the men's, but could not compensate for a much lower SV, with the result
that their maximal cardiac output was approximately 6 liters/min less
than the men's maximum of 24.1 liters/min. When all responses were expressed in relation to a hypothetical workload equalling 50% of $\dot{V}_{O_2 max}$,
cardiac output, stroke volume, and oxygen uptake were less and heart rate
was slightly higher for women than for men. However, the ratio of cardiac
output to oxygen uptake ($\dot{Q}/\dot{V}_{O_2}$) was significantly higher for women at

all levels of work. It is evident that the circulatory adjustments of women to exercise do differ from those of men. How these adjustments affect the ability of women to do maximal or submaximal work is still not completely understood.

A study of a younger age group, 10 to 13 years of age, by Bar-Or et al. (10), revealed a similar pattern, higher heart rates and lower stroke volumes for the girls and no differences between the sexes in cardiac output or oxygen uptake at submaximal workloads. However, on the basis of the regression of $\dot{Q}$ (liters/min) on $\dot{V}_{O_2}$ (liters/min), the authors concluded that girls have a higher cardiac output than boys at the same level of oxygen uptake. The apparent contradiction in these two statements may be due to a visual rather than statistical comparison of the two regression lines. It appears from the plot of the points around the regression line that there is considerable intermixing of the boys and girls at the lower end of the $\dot{V}_{O_2}$ continuum and that the differences between the sexes become more apparent at the higher levels of oxygen uptake. In this respect, it should be noted again that a specific $\dot{V}_{O_2}$, expressed as liters/min, represents a different percentage of maximal aerobic capacity for the two sexes. In the case of these subjects, $\dot{V}_{O_2 max}$ was approximately 20% higher for the boys (70), so that at any given level of oxygen uptake the girls were working closer to their maximal level.

Differences in cardiac output between the sexes across an age range of 20 to 85 years were investigated by Becklake et al. (12). Measurements were taken during steady state conditions at work loads of 150, 350, and 550 kg·m/min on the bicycle ergometer. From plots of cardiac output, heart rate, stroke volume, and arteriovenous O_2 difference against $\dot{V}_{O_2}$ liters/min, the authors concluded that differences between the sexes were limited to the younger age groups, 20 to 39 years. In that age bracket, $\dot{Q}$ was higher for women as a result of higher heart rates and stroke volumes, while their arteriovenous O_2 differences were lower than male values. In the older age brackets, heart rates were also higher for women, but stroke volumes were less and cardiac outputs not noticeably different than those of the men. Only six of 60 possible comparisons were found to be significant through the use of multiple t tests. The probability that some of the conclusions were based on differences due to chance cannot be disregarded.

II. Aging Effects

During the early years of her life the maximal working capacity (kgm/min) of the female increases with age, more than doubling between the ages of 5 and 14 (*2,13*). Accompanying this increased working capacity is an almost threefold increase in maximal oxygen intake (liters/min). The importance of physical growth during this period rather than age per se has been noted by Adams *et al.* (*2*) and Bengtsson (*13*), who found larger correlations of working capacity with body size than with age. The direction of the changes which take place depends largely on the method of expressing the response. When $\dot{V}_{O_2 max}$ is expressed as ml O_2/kg·min⁻¹, there is actually a decrement in aerobic capacity from the seventh to the fifteenth year (*6,54,66,67,82*). Maximum ventilatory volumes which increase with age when given as liters/min also show a decrease when expressed as liters/kg·min⁻¹.

Even though younger girls do not achieve the same work capacity as older girls, the strain on the cardiovascular system is approximately equal in relation to their size. In discussing aging effects, distinction must be made between the ability to perform physical work and the response of the cardiorespiratory system to that workload. Wilmore and Sigerseth (*82*) presented data of 62 girls, ages 7 to 13, which demonstrate this point very nicely. Although the younger girls could not do as much physical work as the older girls, the strain on their cardiorespiratory systems was equal to or greater than for the older group. At the same submaximal workloads, younger females had higher heart rates and oxygen uptakes than older girls and were working closer to their maximal loads (*82*). There has been no evidence in any of these studies that prolonged strenuous exercise is physically damaging to a young girl. However, Åstrand (*6*) appears to have some reservations about the suitability of this type of activity for young children of either sex and emphasizes the need for a carefully planned training regimen before endurance events are attempted. This point is considered in more detail in a later section devoted to female athletes.

Many of the changes in physiological responses to exericse which occur during the pubescent period in females have been attributed to the increase in adipose tissue that accompanies sexual maturity. The addition of this body fat and resultant lowering of maximal aerobic capacity, when given as milliliters of O_2 per kilogram, has probably been responsible for the old canard that girls reach their physical peak in the early teen years. As can be seen in Table II, this was an inaccurate conclusion based on too few facts. Now that data on female athletes have become available, it is obvious that puberty need not mark the start of a physical decline for females.

Not a great deal has been added to our knowledge of how aging affects an adult woman's response to exercise since the work of I. Åstrand (*5*) in 1960. Her 44 subjects, primarily housewives who were regular participants in organized calisthenics, were divided into age groups and tested on a bicycle ergometer at increasing submaximal loads until a maximal level was reached. With each successive decade there was a decrease in all physiological variables, except ventilatory efficiency, at the maximal level. Not all differences between successive decades were significant, but the trend across age was consistently downward. However, Åstrand (5) was very careful to point out that there was a large variability within each age group and that some women in the oldest group had a $\dot{V}_{O_2 max}$ higher than some in the 20–29 group. She specifically warns that one must be careful in drawing conclusions from average values and that ". . . when selecting individuals for certain jobs or vice versa, it is certainly very important to test the capacity of the individual" (5, p. 81). At submaximal workloads women of all ages had approximately the same values for $\dot{V}_{O_2}$ (liters/min), heart rate, ventilatory volume, ventilatory efficiency, and blood lactates. However, all of these values represented higher proportions of the maximal capacities of the older women.

One of the reasons suggested by Åstrand (5) for the large variability within age groups was the difference in physical fitness among individuals. Wessel and Van Huss (81) attempted to delineate the role physical activity plays in aging by observing the physiological effects of submaximal treadmill walks on 47 women, ages 20 to 69. Exercise and recovery data were correlated with age and with an "activity score" for all women. The authors concluded that oxygen uptake, oxygen pulse, and ventilation for submaximal work were positively correlated with age and negatively related to physical activity. However, the significant correlation for $\dot{V}_{O_2}$ with age and activity disappeared when oxygen uptake was expressed as ml $O_2/kg \cdot min^{-1}$. Ventilation expressed as ml/kg was not related to age and only barely to activity ($r = 0.26$). The authors recognized the problem caused by the significant intercorrelation of age, weight, and physical activity, but did not statistically remove this effect in their analysis. Another confounding factor was the effect of body weight on a standard treadmill walk. Since the heavier woman was working at a higher level than the lighter one, it should not be surprising if her physiological responses reflected this heavier workload. Because of the positive relationship of body weight to age and the negative relationship of weight to activity, it is difficult to determine with precision which variable was responsible for the observed responses. The same problems were apparent when the women were divided into three groups on the basis of their activity scores. The high negative correlation of weight with activity ($r = -0.80$) makes it difficult to interpret the results, since the least active group was more than 20 lb heavier than the most active group. Only oxygen pulse and oxygen extraction differentiated between groups once the factor of weight difference was removed from $\dot{V}_{O_2}$ and $\dot{V}_E$. A similar study by Wessel *et al.* *(80)*, using an even lighter workload, reported essentially the same results. When oxygen uptake was expressed per unit of body weight, the relationship to age disappeared.

III. Female Athletes

Recently, more attention has been given to the effects of strenuous physical activity on the female athlete. Most of the studies have been descriptive in nature, a comparison of the female athlete with her less active peers, with male athletes, or with female athletes in other sports. Comparisons of this type may provide information about the immediate effects of sports participation on the athlete's physiological response to maximal and submaximal exercise; more difficult to assess are the long term effects. Are there physiological or physical problems associated with strenuous conditioning programs for women, or do these programs have beneficial results for the participants? The only longitudinal data available on women athletes have been provided by a group of Swedish investigators who followed 30 female swimmers across a period of years *(9,33)*. At the time this study was initiated in 1961 by Åstrand *et al.* *(9)*, a survey was made of ex-swimmers who had competed during the period 1946 to 1955 in order to get their subjective reactions to their experiences and to compile objective data of any physical problems which had resulted from their participation. No serious disabilities were reported to be associated with swimming, although about 15% reported menstrual irregularities to have occurred during training. However, when asked if they wanted their own children to participate in competitive swimming, only 24% indicated they were willing to have their girls train according to current practices.

In the main portion of the study, physiological, sociological, and psychological data were gathered for 30 girls who were actively competing in club swimming programs. As a group the girls were significantly taller than untrained girls and had a higher functional capacity which was related to a greater heart volume, total hemoglobin, and vital capacity. Since differences between athletes and nonathletes were correlated with the amount of training, it was concluded that the differences were most likely a result of swimming training rather than an inherent constitutional difference between the two groups.

When the same girls were examined again in 1968 and 1969, a period averaging five years had elapsed since they had last trained regularly *(33)*. Heart and lung volumes had not changed significantly, although the fact that some of the girls were still growing throughout this period was evident in the figures. The most striking changes were a decrease from 52 to 37 ml O_2/kg·min^{-1} in maximal aerobic capacity and a 13% drop in total hemoglobin. This decrement in $\dot{V}_{O_2max}$ is very similar to that found in a group of young American track girls after only a 3 month detraining period (28).

Studies specifically designed to investigate training effects on the physiological response of female athletes are scarce. Sinning and Adrian (73) examined seven members of a women's collegiate basketball team before and after a 2 month period of practice and competition to determine if there were changes in cardiorespiratory response as a result of their participation. Although they found a significant increase in $\dot{V}_{O_2max}$ from 34.4 to 38.7 ml O_2/kg·min, no concomitant changes were found for other cardiovascular or pulmonary function data. They concluded that the training program for this intercollegiate team was not strenuous enough to push the women to their optimum level of physical conditioning. An assumption that basketball as played by women does not require a maximal effort is negated by the data of McArdle et al. (55), who reported telemetered heart rates during games at or near the maximum for their subjects. Finding no improvement in aerobic capacity over the season, they reached the same conclusion as Sinning and Adrian (73), that the most likely reason for the lack of improvement was the moderate intensity of the practice sessions. That women can train to high levels of aerobic capacity can be seen in Table II. The relatively low values for basketball players may improve as coaches gain more experience in preparing their teams for the still new five-player, full-court style of play.

The highest levels of oxygen uptake in Table II are for those endurance sports where the aerobic rather than the anaerobic component of oxygen utilization plays the more important role in the success of athlete. To reach these levels of aerobic capacity requires a training regimen which only a few years ago would have been considered extremely severe for a female. Knowlton and Weber (47) collected data on a young woman during a 17 month period in which she was training for the mile and 2-mile events. Her training schedule emphasized overdistance and interval training and frequently resulted in practice runs totaling more than 5 miles. None of the data collected suggested that this level of physical stress had deleterious effects on the young woman. There were noticeable improvements in her cardiovascular response to a submaximal bicycle test and a maximal treadmill run and in the mechanical performance of her heart as measured by a ballistocardiogram. Resting values, other than the usual bradycardia, showed no consistent trends during the period of training. However, in the final maximal test there was a greater increase in hemoglobin concentration from pre- to post-test measurements. The authors were unable to determine if this change in hemoglobin was a training effect or the result of the girl being able to perform more work during the final test session.

The effect of a strenuous cross-country training program and competition on very young girls, ages 8 to 13, has been reported by Brown *et al.* (*16*). These girls, along with eight controls, were tested before the season and after 6 and 12 weeks of training and competition (Table II, post-training values). The most striking change was the increase of $\dot{V}_{O_2max}$ of the runners, 18% at six weeks and 26% at 12 weeks. Maximum ventilatory volumes remained unchanged and the slight decrease in heart rate attained during maximal and submaximal work was matched by a similar decrease in the control group. Other than a slight unexplained weight loss in two of the younger girls, no detrimental effects of the program were observed. The authors concluded that preadolescent girls responded to endurance training in the same manner as older athletes, perhaps to an even greater degree.

A reversal of this pattern was observed by Drinkwater and Horvath (*28*) in a study of detraining effects on a slightly older group of female track athletes. These girls did not achieve as high a $\dot{V}_{O_2max}$ (47.8 ml O_2/kg·min^{-1}) during the trained state, perhaps because their training was for middle distance rather than the longer events, but they were at a high level of cardiovascular fitness. Three months following cessation of training, their mean maximal oxygen uptake had decreased by 18% to a level only slightly above that expected for nonathletic girls of the same age (40.4 ml O_2/kg·min^{-1}). Maximal heart rate and posttest lactate values did not change significantly, but ventilatory volumes, oxygen pulse, and oxygen debt all decreased in the detrained state. No work has been reported which would indicate how long and how strenuous a training program would have to be in order to return young girls to the trained condition or to maintain them at peak condition.

The physiological cost of an average track practice for a group of high school girls was determined indirectly by Drinkwater and Horvath (*30*) by simulating the practice events on a treadmill. For these girls a track practice was the equivalent of a daily test for maximal aerobic capacity. There were no significant differences in the maximal physiological values attained in the practice session and those reached during a standard test for maximal aerobic capacity. During most of the practice events the girls were working above 80% of their $\dot{V}_{O_2max}$.

The success of the American women in the speed skating events of the 1972 Winter Olympics adds interest to a report by Maksud *et al.* (*52*) of the physiological responses to a maximal treadmill test of 13 candidates for the women's team. The mean $\dot{V}_{O_2 max}$ attained by the female skaters (Table II) was well above that reported for normal populations but less than that reported for the Swedish swimmers and the American track girls. The authors suggested that the training technique of the American team, a submaximal effort during most of the race and a final sprint, challenges the anaerobic rather than the aerobic capacity of the girls and forecasted greater success for these skaters in the sprint events than in the endurance races. Whether it was coincidence or scientific marksmanship, this was exactly what happened in Sapporo as American girls took medals in three of the sprint events.

There is some evidence that the circulatory changes resulting from training do depend on the relative emphasis on sprint or overdistance work during practice sessions. Raven *et al.* (*63*) measured cardiac outputs of young female track athletes during near-maximal exercise and compared their results to those obtained for younger (*10*) and older (*8*) females. Values for both runners and sprinters fell on the regression line of cardiac output on oxygen uptake for older Swedish girls at work levels below 70% of $\dot{V}_{O_2 max}$. Above this point the slope for the Swedish subjects and the sprinters decreased, while the slope for the runners remained the same. At maximal levels of work, cardiac output and stroke volume of the runners were greater than those of the Swedish women, and heart rate was less. The values obtained for the sprinters were all less than those of the older women, but greater than those of the younger age group. Since the runners and sprinters were the same age and body type, the authors concluded that the higher values for the runners were a result of their endurance training.

IV. Training Effects

There is ample evidence in the literature to indicate that men of all ages benefit from physical training programs. Very little is known about the nonathletic woman's response to training. As Brown and Shephard (*17*) point out, many women who have relatively strenuous jobs would benefit from conditioning programs to raise their fitness levels, since physical work exceeding 50% of the maximal aerobic capacity cannot be sustained for an 8-hr day without undue fatigue. What duration and intensity of exercise is required to increase a woman's $\dot{V}_{O_2 max}$ and what effect age has on her ability to improve her capacity has not received much attention in this country.

A recent study by Kilbom (*46*) has provided data on the effects of short term training of Swedish females across a wide range of ages. The women were divided into three age groups, 19 to 31, 34 to 48, and 51 to 64 years of age. For 7 weeks they trained on a bicycle ergometer at 70% of their maximal aerobic capacity, alternating 3 min of work and 2 min of rest for a period of 30 min. As the effect of training was noted in a decreasing heart rate, the intensity of work was increased to keep the rate constant. A second group of 16 women worked at 50% of $\dot{V}_{O_2 max}$ either on a bicycle ergometer or by walking in a park at a predetermined speed. A comparison of responses to the same submaximal workloads before and after training revealed significantly lower heart rates and blood lactates following training for all groups except one, the walkers. Oxygen uptake at a given load did not change significantly as a result of training except for the youngest groups at a 600 kpm/min workload. This last difference may be more apparent than real because of the liberal use of the t test for all comparisons.

Increases in maximal oxygen uptakes and blood lactates following training were significant for all age groups. These increases in $\dot{V}_{O_2 max}$ were inversely related to age and were greater for women who had lower aerobic capacities prior to training and for those who trained at 70% of their maximal ability. According to Kilbom, there do not appear to be any sex differences in the ability to profit from physical training. There were, however, large inter-individual differences which were independent of age, initial capacity, or training intensity. For example, several of the oldest subjects did not respond to the training program, yet the oldest woman increased her aerobic capacity by 15%. Kilbom (*46*) hypothesizes that these individual variations in reaction to training may be due to childhood patterns of activity, the individual's state of training at the start of the study, or the degree of physiological aging.

Thirteen of the same women participated in a study of the changes in cardiac output as a result of the training program. Because there were no differences in the responses of young and middle-aged women, their data were grouped (21 to 48 years, $n = 9$) and compared with that of the older women (53 to 61 years, $n = 4$). At rest and submaximal workloads there were no changes in cardiac output following training. However, for the younger groups a decrease in heart rate was accompanied by a significant increase in stroke volume. An increase of similar magnitude for the older groups was not significant, presumably because of the smaller sample size. There was no change in the arteriovenous oxygen differences for either group. At all workloads, the cardiac output of the older women was less than that of the younger group, a result of their lower heart rate and smaller stroke volume. Systolic, diastolic, and mean pressure were lower after training regardless of age. At maximal workloads the significant increase in $\dot{V}_{O_2}$ was matched by a 10 to 11% increase in cardiac output for the older and younger groups, respectively. Since there was no change in the arteriovenous O_2 differences, the author concluded that the larger stroke volume was responsible for the increase in maximal oxygen uptakes following training.

V. Energy Expenditure

The caloric cost of a physical task is measured by the rate at which an individual expends energy in the performance of that task. Knowledge of these costs has a special importance for those women who attempt to balance their food intake against their daily expenditure of energy, and thus avoid the physical and aesthetic problems associated with obesity. It is also important to those who bear the responsibility for setting activity standards for women in industry and in sports. The energy costs of some ordinary daily and light occupational activities for women have been summarized by Durnin and Passmore (31). However, a precise estimate of the energy expended by women during various sports activities is more difficult to obtain. The necessity of adding bulky equipment to the performer to measure oxygen uptake directly makes such measurements impractical except during simulated competitions. Even then the equipment may well affect performance by interfering with the natural movements and coordination of the athlete. For these reasons, a number of investigators have chosen to predict oxygen uptake from telemetered heart rates using equations based on relationships determined in the laboratory between $\dot{V}_{O_2}$ and heart rate during treadmill or other forms of exercise. These predictions are subject to considerable error (30,68) and should be used as gross estimates only.

Available data for the energy expenditure of women participating in a number of team and individual sports are listed in Table III. To make comparisons between sports possible, original data which were not expressed as kcal/hr or as kcal/kg·hr were converted where possible. Where the number of subjects is small and the caloric cost was predicted rather than measured directly, the estimates of caloric cost should be used cautiously. Although some authors (74,75) have reported significant differences in energy expenditure between various activities, the use of multiple t tests with a sample size of two makes such con-

TABLE III

ESTIMATES OF ENERGY EXPENDITURE DURING SPORTS ACTIVITIES

Activity	Ref.	n	Method	kcal/hr	kcal/ kg·hr[a]	Classi- fication[b]
Team sports						
Basketball	55	6	Predict from heart rate	540.0	8.8	Heavy
Basketball	75	2	Predict from heart rate	538.8	10.5	Heavy
Field hockey	75	2	Predict from heart rate	517.8	10.1	Heavy
Softball	75	2	Predict from heart rate	259.2	5.1	Moderate
Volleyball	75	2	Predict from heart rate	253.8	5.0	Moderate
Individual sports						
Archery	74	2	Predict from heart rate	165.3	2.9	Light
Badminton	74	2	Predict from heart rate	428.5	7.8	Heavy
Bowling	74	2	Predict from heart rate	95.7	1.7	Sedentary
Golf	74	2	Predict from heart rate	235.1	4.2	Moderate
Tennis	74	2	Predict from heart rate	404.4	7.3	Heavy
Track practice	30	9	Direct measurement	480.7	6.2	Heavy
Swimming	9	30	Direct measurement	780.0	14.4	Heavy
Figure skating	65	9	Direct measurement		11.4	Heavy
Figure skating	35	3	Direct measurement	584	11.2	Heavy
Kayak paddling	65	13	Direct measurement		16.2	Heavy
Gymnastics	65	15				
Parallel bars			Direct measurement		8.4	Heavy
Balance beam			Direct measurement		6.6	Heavy
Horse			Direct measurement		9.0	Heavy

[a] Data originally expressed as kcal/min have been computed as kcal/hr and kcal/ kg·hr^{-1}.

[b] Classification has been changed from original articles to conform to Durnin and Passmore's grading system.

clusions suspect. It should also be noted that the rate of energy expended depends on a number of factors which may vary from game to game and person to person. The skill of the player and her opponent, the environmental conditions, and the maximal aerobic capacity of the individual all influence the physiological cost of the activity. Whether a sport can be considered strenuous for a woman must be considered in relation to the percentage of her maximal capabilities involved. The girl whose $\dot{V}_{O_2 max}$ is 50 ml/kg·min^{-1} is capable of expending more energy with less fatigue than a girl whose $\dot{V}_{O_2 max}$ is 30 ml/kg·min^{-1}. Data such as those tabulated in Table III can be used as an indication of the degree of physical conditioning required prior to the sports season to permit a woman to compete without undue strain on her cardiorespiratory system.

There is some question as to whether the energy cost of an activity is the same for men and women. Durnin and Passmore (*31*) have found that the energy cost of walking can be predicted equally well for either sex, using the regression equation $E_w = 0.047W + 0.02$, where E_w is energy in kcal/min, and W is the body weight in kg. Other investigators (*14*) have reported significantly less expenditure of energy by women than men per unit of body weight. Adams (*3*) compared the effects of age, sex, and body weight and composition on the energy requirements of riding a bicycle on a level grade, using indirect calorimetry to measure caloric cost. Significant differences in gross energy expenditure (kcal/min) were apparent between men and women of all ages; but, when expressed in relation to body weight, the differences in energy cost disappeared. Of particular interest is the close agreement between the regression of energy expenditure on body weight computed by Adams (*3*) for bicycling (kcal/min = $0.0467\ WT$ (kg) + 2.34) with the regression equation reported by Durnin and Passmore for walking. Weight was the dominant factor in determining energy requirements for the bicycle ride; neither age nor body composition materially affect the results.

Because evidence is contradictory, it is probably premature to state that there is no difference in energy expenditure by men and women for the same workload, even when the cost is expressed in relation to body weight. A point to be remembered is that for the average woman an expenditure of energy equal to that of the average man represents a larger proportion of her maximal capabilities.

VI. Exercise in the Heat

When a woman exercises in a hot environment, all of her normal responses to physical work are magnified. Core and skin temperatures rise, metabolic heat production and sweat rate increase, and pulse rate and systolic blood pressure rise. The extent of the change depends on many factors, both individual and environmental. Much of the recent research has been devoted to determining the quantitative effect of these factors and whether they elicit the same responses to the same degree in males and females alike.

The results suggest that these questions are more complex than might appear. For example, women's heart rates have been reported as higher (*34,83*), lower (*78*), and no different (*58*) than men's under the same experimental conditions. Similar contradictions can be found for other physiological parameters as well. Although women have a larger number of active sweat glands than men do (*45*), under most circumstances they have a lower total body sweat rate when working in a hot environment (*15,34,83*). This difference in response may be a reflection of the severity of the heat stress resulting from different dry and wet bulb temperatures in the environment. Morimoto *et al.* (*58*) found no differences in sweat rate between the sexes during a 2-hr rest–work exposure to dry bulb temperatures of 36 to 49C at a relative humidity (RH) of 30%. When RH was increased to 80%, the total body sweat rate of the women was significantly less than the men's even though ambient temperature was lower, 34 to 38C. Since rectal and mean skin temperatures of the two groups were approximately the same, he concluded that the females' thermoregulatory mechanisms differed quantitatively from those of the males. In some manner, not completely understood, the women were able to achieve regulation with a lower sweat rate, even though the increase in their metabolic heat production over control values was greater than that of the men. Under similar ambient conditions and the same workload, a treadmill walk at 5.6 km/hr at zero grade, Weinman *et al.* (*78*) found total body sweat rates significantly higher in the males but lower heart rates and less increase in rectal temperatures in the females. They only notable difference between these two studies was in the initial physical condition of the subjects. In the Weinman study the women had lower resting pulse rates than the men did and were considered by the investigators to be the more physically fit group. The reverse situation was reported by Wyndham *et al.* (*83*). In an unacclimatized exposure to work in hot, moist (93F DB, 90F WB) ambient conditions, the female subjects had a much more severe reaction to the heat stress than the males. Ninety-two percent of the women were unable to complete the initial 4-hr experimental session, as compared to 50% of the males. The rectal temperatures and heart rates of the females increased faster and reached higher levels than did those of the males, although, when men did withdraw from a work session, their heart rates and temperature values were approximately the same as those of the women who ceased work. As in other studies, women were found to sweat less than men, although the difference in rates decreased with time and were most marked during the first hour of work.

Much of the difficulty some women and men experience while exercising in a hot environment can be alleviated by the process of acclimatization. Repeated exposures to work under a heat stress will result in lower core and mean skin temperatures, a decrease in heart rate, and an increase in the length of time the woman can withstand the stress (*41,42,78,83*). The increased efficiency of the thermoregulatory mechanisms following acclimatization of males has been attributed to a greater dissipation of excess heat as a result of marked increases in total body sweat (32). There is no conclusive evidence that the same explanation can be advanced for the acclimatization of women. Hertig et al. (41) did note a slight increase in sweat rate following acclimatization of two groups of women (n_1 = 4, n_2 = 5) at two different ambient conditions. Their conclusion that this increase was a major factor in acclimatization was not supported by statistical evidence. In a later paper from the same laboratory, no significant increases in the total body sweat rate of females were observed after eight exposures to moist heat (78). In spite of this, the women were able to complete the same amount of work as the men and at lower pulse rates and rectal temperatures. These investigators suggested (78) that women might be more efficient regulators of body temperature than men, since they achieved the same results with less water loss. Wyndham et al. (83, p. 364) had previously expressed a similar opinion, ". . . that the male . . . is a prolific, wasteful sweater, whereas the female adjusts her sweat rate better to the required heat loss."

While Wyndham's (83) female subjects were able to acclimatize as well as men, the process was more difficult for them physiologically and psychologically. Several of the women became extremely irritable or emotionally disturbed during the sessions and eventually refused to continue with the study. Interestingly, Weinman et al. (78) reported similar symptoms in their male subjects instead of the females and offered the conjecture that the superior physical fitness of the women might account for this change in roles. That physical fitness can play an important role in how subjects respond to acclimatization has been reported by Piwonka and Robinson (61) and Piwonka et al. (62) in studies involving male distance runners. A well-trained male acclimatizes much more easily to heat stress than his untrained counterpart. No comparable studies on highly trained women athletes have been reported, although Cleland et al. (21) did attempt to separate the effects of training from those of acclimatization for a small group of female subjects. After a preliminary training period in a normal environment, the usual increase in working metabolism noted when women are acutely exposed to heat stress did not occur in these subjects. It may be that decreases in metabolism found during acclimatization in previous studies have been a training effect (58,83).

VII. The Menstrual Cycle

Since the menstrual cycle is an obvious physiological difference between the two sexes, it is strange to note how infrequently it is included as an experimental variable in comparative studies of male and female

response to exercise. Most studies of the relationship of physical activity
and the menstrual cycle have attempted to determine how the cycle
phase affects performance or how participation in sports affects the
menstrual function. Very little recent work has been done on the relationship of cycle phases to other physiological effects of exercise.
Phillips (*60*) summarized a number of contradictory results from previous studies of the effect of the menstrual cycle on pulse rate and
blood pressure and concluded, on the basis of her own work, that
there was no phase effect on these variables.

During the Tokyo Olympics a survey of 66 sportswomen was made
to determine if there were any menstrual difficulties as a result of training and competition and what effect the cycle or period of flow had on
performance (*84*). Approximately 41% of the women reported some
disturbance of the menstrual flow during training or competition, but
only 17% felt their performance was adversely affected. An interesting
observation of the athletes who had had children prior to participating
in the Olympics was that they ". . . became stronger, had greater
stamina, and were more balanced in every way after having a child"
(*84*, p. 218). The author concluded that the menstrual cycle and period
were normal for this group of superior women athletes and that any
difficulties reported fell within normal limits. It was noted that some
responses varied according to the sport. Swimmers, for example, were
less confident of their performance during menses, and 33% of them
never trained during their monthly periods. According to Åstrand *et al.*
(*9*), this may be a wise precaution. A gynecological examination of 30
young swimmers disclosed pathogenic organisms in the vaginas of one-
third of the girls. Approximately half of the group reported poorer
performance during menses, and one-third had pain in the lower abdomen while swimming. The combination of bacteriological findings and
subjective reports led Åstrand *et al.* (*9*) to conclude that it was in-
advisable to swim, either in training or competition, during menstruation.

A number of studies of how the menstrual cycle influences the temperature regulatory mechanisms of women were precipitated by Kawahata's (*45*) report in 1960 of the effect of the sex hormones on sweating response. By injecting old men with testosterone and younger males
with estradiol, he demonstrated that the female hormone had an inhibitory effect on sweating, while the male hormone had a sudorific effect.
Additional evidence for this effect was found in the differences in the
onset of sweating observed in adult male and female Japanese, but not
observed in infants or older persons where sex hormones would be less
of a factor. He also reported that the onset of sweating occurred earlier
during the menstrual flow than during other phases of the cycle. Because

of the importance of sweating to the regulation of body temperature during work in hot environments, this finding could have important implications for women. However, other investigators (64) were unable to duplicate Kawahata's results. No change in the latent period of sweating as a result of the menstrual cycle was observed. Since the procedures and environments were comparable, Sargent and Weinman (64) concluded that differences in results were due to large individual differences within small sample groups.

A more recent study by Chapman and Horvath (20) exposed four young women to a hot environment each weekday during a complete menstrual cycle. Their data confirm Kawahata's findings of earlier onset of sweating during the menstrual period. Core temperatures and evaporative sweat rates were both higher during the luteal phase, when progesterone levels are high. Haslag and Hertzman (38) also observed higher core temperatures during the postovulatory phase but no difference in the latent period of sweating, except that it occurred at a higher core temperature during postovulation.

VIII. Altitude Effects

How high altitudes affect the physical performance of women has not received much attention from physiologists. The current state of knowledge has been summed up by Buskirk (18): "Little information exists about the performance of women at altitude except that obtained in Mexico City during the competition in the Pan American and Olympic games. In general, the proportional reduction in performance was the same for women as for men." There appears to be a feeling among some physiologists that women adapt to altitude better than men do, but, except for some early work in 1913 and 1920, there are few data to support that premise. How women cope with exercise at altitude and to what degree their adjustments differ from those of men are not known.

Recent studies by Hannon and his colleagues (36,37) of eight young Missouri women spending a summer at Colorado's Pike's Peak provided some interesting descriptive data for females, but offered no clues as to why women are less adversely affected by altitude than men—if, in fact, they are. Incidences of mountain sickness appeared to be less intense for females than for males and to subside more quickly. Many of the physiological parameters, such as resting heart rate, weight, blood volume, electrocardiograms, and blood chemistries, shifted in the same direction as for men, but to a lesser degree. There were no striking differences between the sexes. A more complete report of the pulmonary function variables showed essentially the same pattern (72). Except for maximum breathing capacity, in which the women's 10% increase at altitude was considerably below the 40 to 50% increment reported for men, changes were approximately the same for women as for men. According to Shields *et al.* (72), there was no evidence to suggest that respiratory difficulties would prevent an adequate adjustment of women to altitude.

IX. Summary

The amount of information available in determining women's physiological response to exercise is relatively small in comparison to that available for men. Yet enough contradictions are already apparent in the literature to make it difficult, if not impossible, to generalize about a female's response to physical activity. Two major problems in determining if there is a response mediated by the factor of sex are the lack of a standard method for presenting the data and the variation in experimental design from one study to the next. For example, should the responses of men and women be compared at a given oxygen uptake, at the same workload, or at the same percentage of their maximal aerobic capacities? Should the physiological variables be expressed relative to body weight, body surface area, lean body mass, active muscle tissue, or as gross quantities? Choice of these factors determines not only the quantitative differences between groups but can even alter the direction of the differences. Perhaps the point made by Buskirk and Taylor (*19*) should be reemphasized, that the purpose of the investigation should determine how the data are expressed. When practical questions need to be answered, such as the ability of men and women to accomplish a specific task, comparisons at the same workload are meaningful. At the same time, it would be misleading to report that oxygen uptake or cardiac output are the same for both sexes without also noting how these values relate to the maximal capabilities of each group. If physiological mechanisms are of primary interest, equating workloads at a specific percentage of each individual's $\dot{V}_{O_2 max}$ may be the best method of comparing the functioning of the physiological systems. The cardiovascular adjustments of an obese female to exercise may not differ from those of a lean woman provided she is not forced to carry the extra burden imposed by her excess weight in addition to the standard workload. It is also important in comparative studies to equate the groups on those factors which are significantly correlated with the variable under investigation or to statistically control the effects of this relationship. Differences between age groups to work in the heat can be completely confounded if the young women represent a physically fit population of females and the older subjects are selected from a group of sedentary overweight women. Because of the close relationship of body size to oxygen uptake, it has been common practice to express $\dot{V}_{O_2}$ as ml/kg·min^{-1}. It is uncommon to find other variables, such as oxygen debt, ventilatory volumes, or maximum breathing capacity, which are also related to size, expressed in the same manner. Yet it has little physiological meaning to conclude that young girls have lower oxygen debts than adult women or that women have smaller ventilatory volumes than men without noting whether these differences disappear when the variables are expressed as a ratio to body size or some other meaningful representation of active protoplasmic mass.

Probably one of the most common causes of contradictory information in the articles reviewed for this chapter has been the tendency of some investigators to ignore the results of their statistical tests in reporting results. While not everyone has equal confidence in statistical procedures, the misuse of statistical results can only lead to confusion. For example, it was not unusual to find nonsignificant differences between groups reported in a results section and then to read later in the same paper an analysis of why the differences between groups existed. In several instances, the abstract and summary of a paper pointed to differences between sexes or age groups when, in fact, the observed differences were no greater than those to be expected by chance.

It is encouraging to note the increasing number of studies devoted to the physiological responses of women to exercise. A considerable amount of data is being accumulated which describes the functional responses of a female while she is exercising. Perhaps some of the emphasis may now turn to the physiological mechanisms which control these responses. Still unresolved is the basic question of the extent to which the factor of sex mediates the physiological response to exercise. Is the woman limited in her maximal aerobic power by her cardiovascular system (8) or are the quantitative differences in $\dot{V}_{O_2 max}$ between the sexes merely a function of how the data are reported (77)? The hypotheses of von Döbeln (77) and Davies (27), that sex differences in $\dot{V}_{O_2 max}$ are nonexistent when related to lean body mass or active muscle tissue, are intriguing enough to warrant further investigation.

Very little attention has been given to other variables which may impose a ceiling on women's ability to perform physical work. What are the effects, if any, of her smaller pulmonary capacities and muscular strength? Do hormonal factors play a role? Is there any difference in the ability of the male and female to mobilize high energy phosphates? The whole area of aging effects on the physiological functioning of females needs to be explored in depth. While cross-sectional studies can provide answers to some of the questions related to aging, there is an even greater need for the more costly and difficult longitudinal studies. Very little work has been done to determine how environmental stressors affect a woman during physical activity. Women have been studied while working in the heat but not in the cold or at high altitude, and the element of age under these conditions has been almost completely neglected. From the very young to the very old, a great deal remains to be learned about how a woman adapts physiologically to exercise.

References

1. Adams, F. H., and Duffie, E. R. (1961). *J. Lancet* **81**, 493.
2. Adams, F. H., Linde, L. M., and Miyake, H. (1961). *Pediatrics* **28**, 55–64.
3. Adams, W. C. (1967). *J. Appl. Physiol.* **22**, 539–549.
4. Andersen, K. L. (1964). *In* "International Research in Sport and Physical Education" (E. Jokl and E. Simon, eds.), pp. 489–500. Thomas, Springfield, Illinois.
5. Åstrand, I. (1960). *Acta Physiol. Scand. Suppl.* **49**, 1–92.
6. Åstrand, P-O. (1952). "Experimental Studies of Physical Working Capacity in Relation to Sex and Age." Munksgaard, Copenhagen.
7. Åstrand, P-O. (1956). *Physiol. Rev.* **36**, 307–335.
8. Åstrand, P-O., Cuddy, T. E., Saltin, B., and Stenberg, J. (1964). *J. Appl. Physiol.* **19**, 268–274.
9. Åstrand, P-O., Engström, L., Eriksson, B., Karlberg, P., Nylander, I., Saltin, B., and Thorén, C. (1963). *Acta Paediat. Suppl.* **147**, 1–76.
10. Bar-Or, O., Shephard, R. J., and Allen, C. L. (1971). *J. Appl. Physiol.* **30**, 219–223.
11. Barry, A. J., Webster, G. W., and Daly, J. W. (1969). *J. Gerontol.* **24**, 284–291.
12. Becklake, M. R., Frank, H., Dagenais, G. R., Ostiguy, G. L., and Guzman, C. A. (1965). *J. Appl. Physiol.* **20**, 938–947.
13. Bengtsson, E. (1955). *Acta Med. Scand.* **154**, 91–109.
14. Booyens, J., and Keatinge, W. R. (1957). *J. Physiol.* **139**, 165–171.
15. Brouha, L., Smith, P. E., Delanne, R., and Maxfield, M. E. (1960). *J. Appl. Physiol.* **16**, 133–140.
16. Brown, C. H., Harrower, J. R., and Deeter, M. F. (1972). *Med. Sci. Sports* **41**, 1–5.
17. Brown, J. R., and Shephard, R. J. (1967). *Can. Med. Ass. J.* **97**, 1208–1213.
18. Buskirk, E. R. (1971). *In* "Physiology of Work Capacity and Fatigue" (E. Simonson, ed.), pp. 312–324. Thomas, Springfield, Illinois.
19. Buskirk, E. R., and Taylor, H. L. (1957). *J. Appl. Physiol.* **11**, 72–78.

20. Chapman, E. C., and Horvath, S. M. (In preparation.)
21. Cleland, T., Horvath, S. M., and Phillips, M. (1969). *Int. Z. Angew. Physiol.* **27**, 15–24.
22. Cotes, J. E., and Davies, C. T. M. (1969). *Proc. Roy. Soc. Med.* **62**, 620–624.
23. Cotes, J. E., Davies, C. T. M., Edholm, O. G., Healy, M. J. R., and Tanner, J. M. (1969). *Proc. Roy. Soc. Ser. B* **174**, 91–114.
24. Cotes, J. E., Dobbs, J. M., Elwood, P. C., Hall, A. M., McDonald, A., and Saunders, M. J. (1969). *J. Physiol. (London)* **203**, 79P–80P.
25. Cumming, G. R. (1967). *Can. Med. Ass. J.* **96**, 868–877.
26. Cumming, G. R., Goodwin, A., Baggley, G., and Antel, J. (1967). *Can. J. Physiol. Pharmacol.* **45**, 805–811.
27. Davies, C. T. M. (1971). *In* "Pediatric Work Physiology" (C. Thorén, ed.), pp. 136–137. *Acta Paediat. Scand. Suppl.* **217**, Stockholm.
28. Drinkwater, B. L., and Horvath, S. M. (1972). *Med. Sci. Sports* **4**, 91–95.
29. Drinkwater, B. L., and Horvath, S. M. (In preparation.)
30. Drinkwater, B. L., and Horvath, S. M. (1971). *Med. Sci. Sports* **3**, 56–62.
31. Durnin, J. V. G. A., and Passmore, R. (1967). "Energy, Work and Leisure." Heineman Educational Books Ltd., London.
32. Eichna, L. W., Park, C. R., Nelson, N., Horvath, S. M., and Palmes, E. D. (1950). *Amer. J. Physiol.* **163**, 585–597.
33. Eriksson, B. O., Engström, I., Karlberg, P., Saltin, B., and Thorén, C. (1971). *In* "Pediatric Work Physiology" (C. Thorén, ed.), pp. 68–71. *Acta Paediat. Scand. Suppl.* **217**, Stockholm.
34. Fox, R. H., Lofstedt, B. E., Woodward, P. M., Eriksson, E., and Werkstrom, B. (1969). *J. Appl. Physiol.* **26**, 444–453.
35. Gordon, T. I., Banister, E. W., and Gordon, B. P. (1969). *J. Sports Med.* **9**, 98–103.
36. Hannon, J. P., Shields, J. L., and Harris, C. W. (1966). *In* "Proceedings of the Symposium on Arctic Biology and Medicine, VI. The Physiology of Work in Cold and Altitude" (C. Helfferich, ed.), pp. 113–245. F. T. Wainwright, Alaska.
37. Hannon, J. P., Shields, J. L., and Harris, C. W. (1969). *J. Appl. Physiol.* **26**, 540–547.
38. Haslag, W. M., and Hertzman, A. R. (1965). *J. Appl. Physiol.* **20**, 1283–1288.
39. Havel, V., Tidjditi, A., Hert, J., Skranc, O., and Barták, K. (1969). *Int. Z. Angew. Physiol.* **27**, 292–298.
40. Hermansen, L., and Andersen, K. L. (1965). *J. Appl. Physiol.* **20**, 425–431.
41. Hertig, B. A., Belding, H. S., Kraning, K. K., Batterton, D. L., Smith, C. R., and Sargent, F. II. (1963). *J. Appl. Physiol.* **18**, 383–386.
42. Hertig, B. A., and Sargent, F. II. (1963). *Fed. Proc.* **22**, 810–813.
43. Ikai, M., Shindo, M., and Miyamura, M. (1969). *Res. J. Phys. Educ.* **14**, 137–141.
44. Kamon, E., and Pandolf, K. B. (1972). *J. Appl. Physiol.* **32**, 467–473.
45. Kawahata, A. (1960). *In* "Essential Problems in Climatic Physiology" (E. H. Yoshimura, K. Ogata, and S. Itoh, eds.), pp. 169–184. Nakado Publ., Kyoto, Japan.
46. Kilbom, A. (1971). *Scand. J. Clin. Lab. Invest. Suppl.* **119**, 1–34.
47. Knowlton, R. G., and Weber, H. (1968). *J. Sports Med.* **8**, 228–235.
48. Knuttgen, H. G. (1967). *J. Appl. Physiol.* **22**, 655–658.
49. Kramer, J. D., and Lurie, P. R. (1964). *Amer. J. Dis. Child.* **108**, 283–297.

50. Mácek, M., and Vávra, J. (1971). *J. Appl. Physiol.* **30**, 200-204.
51. MacNab, R., Conger, P., and Taylor, P. S. (1969). *J. Appl. Physiol.* **27**, 644-648.
52. Maksud, M. G., Wiley, R. L., Hamilton, L. H., and Lockhart, B. (1970). *J. Appl. Physiol.* **29**, 186-190.
53. Matsui, H., Miyashita, M., Miura, M., Amano, K., Mizutani, S., Hoshikawa, T., Toyoshima, S., and Kamei, S. (1971). *J. Sports Med.* **11**, 28-35.
54. Matsui, H., Miyashita, M., Miura, M., Kobayashi, K., Hoshikawa, T., and Kamei, S. (1972). *Med. Sci. Sports* **4**, 29-32.
55. McArdle, W. D., Magel, J. R., and Kyvallos, L. C. (1971). *Res. Quart.* **42**, 178-186.
56. Michael, E. D., Jr., and Horvath, S. M. (1965). *J. Appl. Physiol.* **20**, 263-266.
57. Miyashita, M., Hayashi, Y., and Furuhashi, H. (1970). *J. Sports Med.* **10**, 211-216.
58. Morimoto, T., Slabochova, Z., Naman, R. K., and Sargent, F., II (1967). *J. Appl. Physiol.* **22**, 526-532.
59. Nakagawa, A., and Iskiko, T. (1970). *Jap. J. Physiol.* **20**, 118-129.
60. Phillips, M. (1968). *Res. Quart.* **39**, 327-333.
61. Piwonka, R. W., and Robinson, S. (1967). *J. Appl. Physiol.* **22**, 9-12.
62. Piwonka, R. W., Robinson, S., Gay, V. L., and Manalis, R. S. (1965). *J. Appl. Physiol.* **20**, 379-384.
63. Raven, P., Drinkwater, B. L., and Horvath, S. M. *Med. Sci. Sports* **4**, 205-209.
64. Sargent, F., II, and Weinman, K. P. (1966). *J. Appl. Physiol.* **21**, 1685-1689.
65. Seliger, V. (1968). *Scripta Med.* **41**, 231-240.
66. Seliger, V., Cernak, V., Handzo, P., Horak, J., Jirka, Z., Mácek, M., Pribil, M., Rous, J., Skranc, O., Ulbrich, J., and Urbanek, J. (1971). *In* "Pediatric Work Physiology" (C. Thorén, ed.), pp. 37-41. *Acta Paediat. Scand. Suppl.* **217**, Stockholm.
67. Seliger, V., and Zelenka, V. (1970). *Acta Univ. Carolinae Gymnica* **5**, 1-178.
68. Sharkey, B. J., McDonald, J. F., and Corbridge, L. G. (1966). *Ergonomics* **9**, 223-227.
69. Shephard, R. J. (1966). *Arch. Environ. Health* **13**, 664-672.
70. Shephard, R. J., Allen, C., Bar-Or, O., Davies, C. T. M., Degre, S., Hedman, R., Ishii, K., Kaneko, M., LaCour, J. R., di Prampero, P. E., and Seliger, V. (1969). *Can. Med. Ass. J.* **100**, 560-566.
71. Shephard, R. J., Allen, C., Bar-Or, O., Davies, C. T. M., Degre, S., Hedman, R., Ishii, K., Kaneko, M., LaCour, J. R., di Prampero, P. E., and Seliger, V. (1969). *Can. Med. Ass. J.* **100**, 705-714.
72. Shields, J. L., Hannon, J. P., Harris, C. W., and Platner, W. S. (1968). *J. Appl. Physiol.* **25**, 606-609.
73. Sinning, W. E., and Adrian, M. J. (1968). *J. Appl. Physiol.* **25**, 720-724.
74. Skubic, V., and Hodgkins, J. (1966). *J. Appl. Physiol.* **21**, 133-137.
75. Skubic, V., and Hodgkins, J. (1967). *Res. Quart.* **38**, 305-313.
76. Sprynarova, S., and Parizkova, J. (1969). *J. Sports Med.* **13**, 165-171.
77. von Döbeln, W. (1956). *Acta Physiol. Scand. Suppl.* **126**, 1-79.
78. Weinman, K. P., Slabochova, Z., Bernauer, E. M., Morimoto, T., and Sargent, F., II (1967). *J. Appl. Physiol.* **22**, 533-538.
79. Wells, C. L., Scrutton, E. W., Archibald, L. D., Cooke, W. P., and de la Mothe, J. W. (Submitted for publication.)
80. Wessel, J. A., Small, D. A., Van Huss, W. D., Heusner, W. W., and Cederquist, D. C. (1966). *J. Gerontol.* **21**, 168-181.

81. Wessel, J. A., and Van Huss, W. D. (1969). *J. Sports Med.* **9,** 3–10.
82. Wilmore, J. H., and Sigerseth, P. O. (1967). *J. Appl. Physiol.* **22,** 923–928.
83. Wyndham, C. H., Morrison, J. F., and Williams, C. G. (1965). *J. Appl. Physiol.* **20,** 357–364.
84. Zaharieva, E. (1965). *J. Sports Med.* **5,** 215–219.

The Quantification of Endurance Training Programs

Michael L. Pollock

DEPARTMENT OF PHYSICAL EDUCATION, WAKE FOREST UNIVERSITY,
AND DEPARTMENT OF MEDICINE, BOWMAN GRAY SCHOOL OF MEDICINE,
WINSTON-SALEM, NORTH CAROLINA

I. Introduction

Studies concerning the etiology of coronary heart disease (CHD) have isolated various factors, such as lack of exercise, obesity, hyperlipemia, hypertension, and excessive cigarette smoking (*63,78,79,87*), which are associated with an increased risk for the premature development of CHD. Graham (*69*) and Cureton (*39*) state that although the development of CHD is a result of the complex interaction of these factors, endurance training[1] appears to have a direct or indirect facilitative effect on several of them, such as the reduction in body weight and fat, blood pressure, and serum lipemia (particularly triglycerides). Evidence points to the

---

[1] For the purpose of this report, endurance training is defined as a mode of exercise involving large muscle masses and is performed continuously for a sufficient duration and intensity to stimulate the cardiopulmonary systems. Further clarification will be offered in the text.

fact that CHD begins early in life with many men suffering heart attacks prior to 40 years of age (*170*). Heredity is also closely related to early development of CHD. As a result of the aforementioned factors, epidemiologists recommend early preventive types of programs to help retard and possibly eradicate the development of atherosclerosis.

In order to safely and adequately prescribe exercise to groups and individuals, one must first have a clear understanding of the product with which he is dealing. That is, what is the individual's current status of health and fitness, age, sex, and general objectives for training and initiating a training regimen. The needs and goals of elementary school children, college athletes, and middle-aged men clearly differ. Oftentimes, the athlete has to get in condition quickly because competition is not far off. In this case, many safeguards concerning intensity and progression of exercise are not closely followed. Although the abrupt approach is used in certain instances, its general use is not recommended. The initial experience one encounters with endurance training should be of a moderate nature, allowing time for gradual adaptation. On the basis of our experience with adult programs, the abrupt approach can result in deterring future motivation for participation in endurance activities. Improper prescription can also lead to undue muscle strain or soreness, orthopedic problems, fatigue, and risk of precipitating an ischemic heart attack. The latter would be associated more with middle-aged and older participants.

Age in itself is not deterrent for participating in endurance work. Dill (*50*), Cureton (*37*), and Grimby and Saltin (*71*) have shown how middle-aged and old athletes can perform at a high level well into their sixth and seventh decades of life. Other reports (*39,91,104,126*) on nonathletes who habitually exercise show similar results.

Although there is much evidence available which describes the effects of training on physical fitness, the term in itself means something different to everyone. In general, training regimens should be prescribed relative to their effects on cardiopulmonary function, physique (body composition), and motor development. A balanced program is recommended (*38,92*). This type of program would include a variety of activities which are basically designed to effect the various fitness components. How a program is specifically emphasized will be dependent upon age, need, and specific goals of the group or person involved.

A prerequisite for exercise prescription is a thorough understanding of both evaluation and quantification of various training regimens. The reviews in this volume by Clarke, Oscai, and Nagle deal more specifically with the principles and methodologies involved in evaluation for estimating muscular strength and endurance, body composition, and cardiovascular function, respectively. A critical concern regarding the evaluation of cardiovascular function evolves around the question: How strenuous should a test be? Many investigators feel a near maximal effort is necessary in most cases (*39,73,92,103*), while others favor a less strenuous submaximal evaluation (*76,101,143,165*). Taylor *et al.* (*158*) provide an excellent review on procedures and concepts of stress testing for cardiovascular diagnosis and functional evaluation. Theoretically, it would be advantageous to be able to stress all participants at an intensity above which they will be training. Maximum stress testing is recommended for athletic or occupational groups involved in near or maximal efforts. This would help to insure that the participant was adapting well physiologically to the training regimen. If proper guidelines for stress testing are followed (*62,76,171,172*), whereby electrocardiographic (ECG) and blood pressure monitoring are included, specific contraindications will guide the tester as to when the safety of the testee may be in question. The problem with using submaximal stress tests and, in particular, ones that bring the heart rate up to only 150 beats/min is that they are subject to gross errors in predicting cardiovascular development (*168*) and would not generally bring the participant's heart rate up to his training level. Our experience has shown that sedentary middle-aged men beginning a jogging program train at heart rates ranging from 80 to 90% of maximum (approximately 160 to 185 beats/min).

II. Quantification of Training

Endurance training and its physiological effects have been quantified as to their intensity, duration, and frequency. These results are also interrelated with age, initial status of fitness, and modes of training, e.g., running, swimming, bicycling, skiing, etc. Although there is an abundance of information available concerning training investigations, the lack of standardization in methodology and reporting make it difficult to synthesize. For example, many investigators have reported their results without quantifying their training procedures, i.e., no mention of energy cost, heart rate intensity, miles covered, etc. This problem has been treated in more depth elsewhere (*124*).

To adequately quantify physical training regimens, one must evaluate a myriad of investigations and systematically appraise and categorize them as to their respective value. Within this framework, a multitude of physiological parameters dealing with both cardiovascular and body composition components should be included. Cardiovascular fitness is evaluated by means of resting, submaximal, and maximal types of tests. Also, a wide variety of tests will give a more comprehensive estimation of how training affects various physiological systems. Cureton (*34,39*) and Saltin *et al.* (*141*) have stressed the importance of using a broad spectrum of tests, and point to the problem of interpreting and comparing their findings with others, because few studies include a comprehensive test battery. For example, many investigations have included only the assessment of maximum oxygen intake ($\dot{V}_{O_2 max}$) in evaluating their training results. Therefore, if a subject did not improve in this variable, it would be concluded that the regimen had no effect. This could be erroneous because one can show no improvement in $\dot{V}_{O_2 max}$ and yet improve significantly in other cardiovascular parameters, e.g., resting heart rate and blood pressure, response to a standard work task, and physical working capacity and maximal performance type tests.

In perusing the literature, the author found $\dot{V}_{O_2 max}$ the most commonly used variable, while maximal cardiac output ($\dot{Q}$), stroke volume (SV), arterial–venous oxygen difference, heart volume (HV), blood volume (BV), etc., were used sparingly. Therefore, findings and interpretations found in this review will be limited to the material available. It is hoped that this review will help future investigators to improve methodology in experimental design, and in the reporting of training investigations.

A. INTENSITY

Two classical studies, one by Karvonen *et al.* (*88*) and the other by Hollman and Venrath (*82*), serve as a practical guide for prescribing exercise for young men. The former trained young men for 30 min, five times per week on a motor-driven treadmill and found no significant improvement in maximum working capacity for the group whose sustained heart rate did not reach 135 beats/min. Subjects whose sustained heart rates were above 153 beats/min improved significantly. Hollman and Venrath, in a similar experiment conducted on a bicycle ergometer, found that heart rate values of 130 beats/min or more were needed to stimulate a training response. The group exercising at a rate lower than 130 beats/ min increased only slightly in $\dot{V}_{O_2 max}$ from 2.90 to 3.07 liters/min, while the group that trained above this rate increased from 3.07 to 3.57 liters/ min. The data suggest that young men must exercise at a heart rate level equal to approximately 60% of the difference between their maximal and resting heart rates. Åstrand (*1*) states that one should train at approximately 50% of his maximal oxygen intake ($\dot{V}_{O_2 max}$), which is in agreement with Karvonen, and Hollman and Venrath. Figure 1 illustrates the relationship of maximal oxygen consumption expressed as a percentage

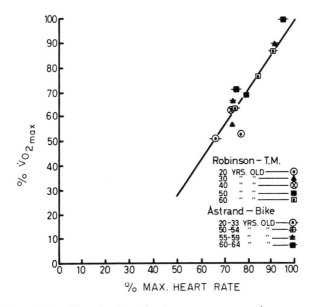

Fig. 1. The relationship of submaximal oxygen consumption expressed as percentage of maximal, and simultaneously measured pulse rate as a percentage of maximal pulse rate, in men of various ages resident in the United States and Sweden [see Taylor *et al.* (*158*)].

of maximal, and simultaneously measured pulse rate as percentage of maximal pulse rate, in men of various ages in the U. S. and Sweden (*158*). As a result of this relationship, heart rate should be considered as one of the standard means for quantifying physical training programs. Techniques and the validation of determining heart rates during training are described elsewhere (*102,120*).

In Fig. 2, Kilbom (*95*) showed a positive relationship between intensity of training and improvement in $\dot{V}_{O_2 max}$. Inconsistencies resulting from age and initial level of fitness will be discussed in Section III,A. Sharkey and Holleman (*145*) walked young men on a motor-driven treadmill three times per week for 6 weeks at 120, 150, and 180 heartbeats/min. They found a direct relationship between improvement in cardiovascular efficiency as measured by $\dot{V}_{O_2 max}$ and the intensity of training.

Shephard (*146*) designed an experiment to systematically look at the training stimulus for improving cardiovascular function. Shephard's design included men training at 96%, 75%, and 39% of $\dot{V}_{O_2 max}$, 5, 3, and 1 day per week, for 20, 10, 5 min per session. Each group trained for ten sessions, with all groups improving in $\dot{V}_{O_2 max}$. He concluded that intensity and duration were the most significant training stimuli, with frequency

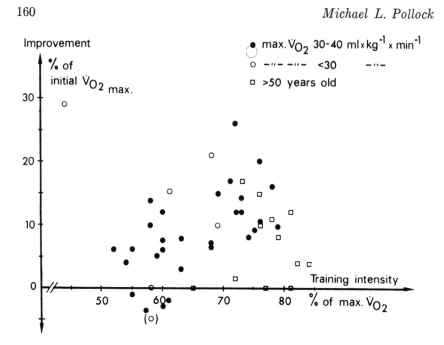

Fig. 2. Individual increase of maximal aerobic power in ml × kg⁻¹ × min⁻¹ in relation to training intensity (expressed in percentage of $\dot{V}_{O_2\,max}$ used during training). See reference for further information concerning the subject shown in parentheses and the one who improved 29% [see Kilbom (*95*)].

being less effective. Improvements ranged from approximately 5 to 10% for the 39% intensity groups to approximately 20% for the highest groups. Shephard found some of his men to improve at training heart rates as low as 120 beats/min. He concluded that the earlier investigations generally included young, moderately active subjects and, thus, a higher intensity of training would be necessary for them to reach a threshold for improvement to occur. He further states that this threshold will be different for varied groups. A lower threshold for possible improvement would be particularly true with sedentary middle-aged and older groups, as well as the less physically active populations found in Canada and the U.S.A. This is in agreement with Durnin *et al.* (*53*), who reported significant training effects in men walking at a low intensity (120 beats/min) approximately 20 km per day. Pollock *et al.* (*125*) found similar improvements with some of their sedentary men, 40 to 55 years of age, who walked for 40 min, four times per week for 20 weeks.

Davies and Knibbs (*47*), in criticizing Shephard's study, said that although Shephard was aware of the problem of habituation, his experimental design did not appear to allow sufficient time for its effect. They said their studies would suggest that at least three occasions of repeated exercise are necessary to overcome the difficulties of habituation (48). Shephard merely discarded his first day's results. Another possible weakness was the fact that he did not actually measure $\dot{V}_{O_2 max}$, but predicted it from cardiac frequency and work output at submaximal levels using the nomogram of Åstrand and Rhyming (8). For these reasons, Davies and Knibbs designed a similar study attempting to avoid these weaknesses. They used 80%, 50%, and 30% of $\dot{V}_{O_2 max}$ as their intensities, and extended the training period to 8 weeks. They also used maximal as well as submaximal tests for their evaluation. In general, their results were in agreement with those of Shephard, except at the lower intensities, i.e., groups working at or below 50% of $\dot{V}_{O_2 max}$ did not improve significantly on the $\dot{V}_{O_2 max}$ test. As shown by their lowest heart rates in response to a standard work test, some efficiency was developed at the lower intensities of training. Faria (58) found no improvement in PWC$_{180}$ with young men bench stepping at HR's up to 120 to 130 beats/min.

In a more recent study, Gledhill and Eynon (67) further substantiated the value of intensity as a stimulus for eliciting a training effect and supported Shephard's findings concerning level of fitness and its relationship to the threshold for attaining a training response. They trained 36 college students for 20 min, 5 days per week, for 5 weeks. The subjects pedalled bicycle ergometers at 120, 135, or 150 beats/min. They found all groups to improve in $\dot{V}_{O_2 max}$, maximal performance, and heart rate at 1500 kpm/min. When groups were subdivided into low and high fitness levels, the high fitness group showed no improvement in $\dot{V}_{O_2 max}$ and end performance time at training heart rates of 120 beats/min, while the low fitness group did improve. This reemphasizes the point that the training stimulus threshold (intensity) has a wide variance.

B. DURATION

As mentioned in Section II,A, duration is an important stimulus for eliciting a training response. Improvements in cardiovascular function have been found after six to ten training sessions which last only 5 to 10 min a day (146). Hollman (81) found increases in maximum O_2 pulse from 14.8 to 17.6 ml/beat in ten subjects who did stationary running 10 min a day for a period of 3 months.

Olree et al. (117) trained young men for either 20, 40, or 60 min and found the longer duration to produce more significant improvements. Their training regimen included a 5 min warm-up period, followed by a training period whereby the resistance on the bicycle ergometer was increased to produce a training heart rate of approximately 180 beats/min. Tooshi (160), using middle-aged men, found similar results when comparing jogging for 15, 30, or 45 min for 20 weeks. Wilmore *et al.* (*166*) conducted a jogging program for middle-aged men three times per week for 10 weeks. Subjects trained either 12 or 24 min per exercise session. Both groups improved significantly in most cardiovascular variables, with the latter group showing an advantage in most items. Wilmore suggested that additional weeks of training could have shown a greater difference between groups. This can be a problem in many training investigations when sedentary subjects are used. It often takes these subjects several weeks to adapt to the initial stress of training; thus, the length of a training experiment can be a critical factor in evaluating them (*106,122,124,128*). Yeager and Brynteson (*169*) trained young women on a bicycle ergometer for 10, 20, and 30 min, 3 days per week, for 6 weeks. Subject's training heart rate averaged 144 beats/min. These authors' results were in agreement with those of Olree, Tooshi, and Wilmore. In these experiments, attempts were made to keep the intensity equal between groups.

Pollock *et al.* (*121*) found jogging for 45 min, 8 miles per week, 2 days per week, for 20 weeks at 80% to 90% of maximal heart rate to show improvements similar to an earlier study (*122*) conducted for 30 min, 2 days per week, at approximately 95% of maximum heart rate (6 miles per week). This helps to illustrate the close interrelationship between intensity and duration of training when prescribing exercise. Recently, Sharkey (*144*) mentioned how previous studies were not designed to separate the effects of intensity from those of duration, and that the sample cells of often only 1 or 2 are limiting; thus, the interaction effects could not be determined. Therefore, he randomly assigned 36 college men to the cells of a 3 × 2 factorial design which included three intensities (training heart rates of 130, 150, and 170 beats/min) and two levels of work (7500 or 15,000 kpm of total work). The 6 week training program was conducted on bicycle ergometers, 3 days per week. He concluded that intensity did not significantly influence the extent of training changes when the total work load was held constant. Also, intensity and duration of training did not interact to produce significantly different training changes. Although more definitive investigations conducted at all ranges of intensity and duration are necessary, the present studies appear to point to the importance of the total amount of work (energy cost) accomplished as the important criterion for cardiovascular improvement. For many years Cureton (*39*) has hypothesized this concept.

C. FREQUENCY

According to Shephard (*146*), and Davies and Knibbs (*47*), frequency is less important a training stimulus than either intensity or duration.

Numerous studies (*47,80,85,146,148*) have sought to evaluate frequency of training by attempting to control the number of total training sessions in various regimens and/or total work output. These investigations generally show no difference in performance with frequency of training. For example, Hill (*80*) trained 24 men, 20 to 44 years of age at 3 or 5 days per week. At the end of 8 weeks, both groups were reevaluated, with both groups improving significantly in $\dot{V}_{O_2 \, max}$. At this stage of the experiment, the 5 day per week group improved significantly more. In an attempt to equalize total training sessions, the 3 day per week group continued to train another 5 weeks. Upon completion of this segment of training, the 3 day group's data equalled that of the 5 day program. In a 4 week training study, Sidney et al. (*148*) found similar results for groups training 2 or 4 days per week when total work was held constant. A group training 1 day per week showed little improvement. These results are not surprising in lieu of the fact that attempts were made to equalize total work output. In prescribing exercise, one should look at frequency of training when duration and intensity are held constant. Also, to evaluate frequency of training sessions per week, without equalizing the total number of training sessions, is an important consideration in exercise prescription. The latter consideration in evaluating frequency of training is more plausible because, in reality, training regimens should not terminate after a few weeks, but continue throughout life. Therefore, the notion of equalizing the number of training sessions can be misleading.

When weeks of training were held constant instead of total number of training sessions, results were generally found with improvements favoring frequency of training (*122,128*). There were some inconsistencies though, with a study by Jackson et al. (*85*) being of particular interest. They conducted a 5 week training experiment with 20 college age men who ran on a treadmill for 10 min either 1, 2, 3, or 5 days per week. The results showed the 5 day group to be superior on the Balke treadmill test (*11*), while the Åstrand–Rhyming submaximal test (*8*) and the Taylor, Buskirk, and Henschel test (*156*) of $\dot{V}_{O_2 \, max}$ favored either the 2 or 3 day groups. The authors concluded that it appeared that training 2 or 3 days per week may be as beneficial as 5 days. The fact that each group was represented by a very small sample size and the subjects were considered low in fitness, coupled with the fact that the program was terminated after just 5 weeks makes interpretation of their results difficult. As mentioned previously, in conducting training experiments with sedentary subjects, it can take several weeks before adaptation to training transpires; thus, a 5 week program would have many limitations in evaluating the effects of endurance regimens. It is certainly possible that the 5 day per week regimen was too frequent for the subjects level of fitness, and, thus, left them partially fatigued during their final test period.

The length of a training experiment appears to be a critical factor in evaluating different training regimens. Pollock *et al.* (*122,128*) conducted two training experiments with middle-aged men (30 to 45 years of age), who trained either 2 or 4 days per week, and found both groups improved in $\dot{V}_{O_2 max}$, heart rate response to a standard work task, and other cardiovascular related variables. Mid-test results of the 16 and 20 week programs showed no differences between groups, but subsequent final testing found the 4 day per week group to have improved significantly more in most variables. Bartels *et al.* (*13*), in a similar study, found no differences between groups after 7 and 13 weeks of interval training. These findings and those of other investigators point to the limitations in interpreting results from investigations conducted over a short time span (*14,166*).

Closely related to frequency of training is the regularity at which one continues or discontinues to participate and its subsequent effect on cardiovascular function. If training is not continued, the improvements gained in a program diminish. Cureton and Phillips (*41*), using equal 8 week periods of training, nontraining, and retraining, found significant improvement, decrement, and improvement, respectively, in cardiovascular efficiency.

Michael and Gallon (*109*) and Fardy (*57*) followed the training of college basketball and soccer players, respectively, over the course of a season, with subsequent periods of detraining. Both groups of athletes showed increases in efficiency during the course of the season, followed by significant reductions during the detraining period. Similar findings were found by Williams and Edwards (*164*), who studied the effect of variant training regimens on cardiovascular efficiency of young college men, and Drinkwater and Horvath (*52*), who studied female high school track athletes. In the latter investigation, the authors concluded that after 3 months of detraining, the cardiovascular efficiency of their subjects decreased to the level of nonathletic girls of similar age.

Bed rest studies have shown decrements in physical working capacity and related cardiovascular parameters (*141,157,159*) Saltin *et al.* (*141*) confined five subjects to bed for 20 days, followed by a 60 day training period. Cardiovascular efficiency measures regressed during bed rest and improved steadily during training. Heart rate response to a submaximal test increased up to 30 beats/min after bed rest and decreased significantly with training. Table I shows the results of selected cardiovascular variables.

In an attempt to determine the effects of different magnitudes of detraining, Kendrick *et al.* (*93*) reevaluated 22 middle-aged men after a 12 week detraining period. Subjects originally trained 8 miles per week, for

TABLE I
EFFECTS OF BED REST AND SUBSEQUENT TRAINING ON CARDIOVASCULAR
FUNCTION OF YOUNG MEN (141)

Variable	Units	Control	Bed rest (20 days)	Training (60 days)
$\dot{V}_{O_2\,max}$	ml/kg/min	43.0	31.8	51.1
$\dot{V}_{E\,max}$	liters/min, BTPS	128.7	98.6	156.4
HR_{max}	beats/min	192.8	196.6	190.8
$\dot{Q}_{max}$	liters/min	20.0	14.8	22.8
SV_{max}	ml	104.0	74.2	119.8
HV	ml	860	770	895

20 weeks, and were subsequently divided into the following three subgroups: group A continued to train 8+ miles per week, group B trained 3 miles per week, and group C was inactive. The results showed group A to maintain and/or improve their level of efficiency, while groups B and C regressed significantly. Group C lost approximately 50% of its original improvement.

Roskamm (134) trained two groups of soldiers 5 days per week for 4 weeks. The results showed both groups improving significantly during this period. A subsequent decrease in working capacity was found within 2 weeks after cessation of training for the group refraining from training.

Siegel et al. (149) trained nine sedentary middle-aged men 12 min, 3 days per week for 15 weeks and found an increase in $\dot{V}_{O_2 max}$ of 19%. After completion of the program, five subjects continued to train once a week for another 14 week period. At this time, $\dot{V}_{O_2 max}$ had decreased to 6% above the initial control level. The remaining four subjects who abstained from training fell below their original control values. Kilbom (94), in a review of how physical fitness can be maintained, recommended that 2 days per week is preferable. It is apparent from this review that training effects are both gained or lost rather quickly, and regular, continual stimulation is necessary in maintaining cardiovascular efficiency.

D. MODES OF TRAINING

There is a multitude of training modes available. They vary from individual to group activities requiring varied levels of skill and being played under varying degrees of competitiveness. The question arises as to the relative value of these activities in producing cardiovascular fitness changes. Previous sections of this review have shown that certain quantities and combinations of intensity, duration, and frequency are necessary to produce and maintain a training effect. The notion of the total amount of work (energy cost) accomplished as an important criterion for fitness development was mentioned in Sections II,B and C and has important implications here. For example, the energy cost of running is generally higher than walking, and yet, many men and women would rather walk than run. When the intensity of walking is less than running, can one get similar training effects by the former if duration and frequency are increased? Questions like this have not been adequately evaluated, but some results look promising. Pollock *et al.* (*121*) trained two groups of middle-aged men at either 80% or 90% of max HR. Distance run per week was held constant (approximately 8 miles), which, in this case, equalized total energy expenditure between the groups. Results from the experiment were similar for both groups.

Theoretically, in lieu of the results from the aforementioned training studies, it would appear that training effects would be independent of mode, if the various combinations of intensity, duration, and frequency are held constant. Little evidence is available comparing the effects of various modes of training. Corbin *et al.* (*28*) compared the effects of running, walking (treadmill), and bicycling (ergometer) training regimens on college men. Each group trained for 20 min, 5 days per week, for 10 weeks, at heart rates approximately 150 to 160 beats/min. In general, they found running and bicycling to be superior training modes when compared to walking. Pollock *et al.* (*123*) in a similar experiment conducted with middle-aged men, found all three modes of training to be equally effective in producing a significant cardiovascular effect. In this study, the subjects trained for 30 min, 3 days per week, for 20 weeks, at 85 to 90% of maximum heart rate (approximately 175 beats/min). These studies agree except for the college age walkers. This discrepancy is not clearly understood, but the facts that the training intensity level was much less for the younger men, and the heart rate training data were not expressed as a percentage of maximum, may be key factors.

Data are also available for highly trained athletes representing a variety of training modes (*17,35,44,59,105,127,140*). In general, endurance athletes all show a high state of cardiovascular fitness. Much evidence is available showing the effects of high energy cost activities, such as running (*26,39,72,84,96,106,113,115,116,118,121,122,130,131,138,142,147, 151,160,161,166*), walking (*53,123,125,145*), bicycling (*13,26,28,42,81,131, 144,149*), swimming (*7,36,59,77,119,154*), and skiing (*24,150*). These regimens show significant increases in cardiovascular efficiency. In contrast, low energy cost activities, such as moderate calisthenics (*19,155*), golf (*66*), and various low organized game activities (*40*) show little or no effect. When intensity was rather low, the latter results were also shown with running, walking, and bicycling training. Although many activities have not been evaluated as to their effects on cardiovascular function, heart rate response and/or energy cost data from such activities exist (12,54,60,99,152). For example, Skubic and Hodgkins (152) studied the heart rate response in women participating in various activities. Tennis and badminton showed moderately high heart rates, but golf, bowling, and archery averaged below 100 beats/min. Based upon these results, the latter three activities would not appear to generate a significant cardiovascular response. Although weight lifting per se is a high energy cost activity, and phases of other sports such as baseball have high energy cost components (running), they are considered to have little or no effect on cardiovascular function (35,78,114,136). This results from high energy cost component being too intermittent; thus, the total energy cost of the activity relative to total time would be considered quite low. Other activities producing significant cardiovascular effects include dancing (43), rope skipping (10,86) tennis (18), soccer (57), basketball (89,109), wrestling (129), football (83), handball (64), and a combination of sports activities and running (137). Cooper (26,27) has emphasized the point concerning the variety of modes of training for eliciting a training response. He devised a point system whereby activities are given point values in respect to their O_2 requirement. Although some discrepancies in point assessments have been found (107), it generally agrees with the aforementioned.

III. Discussion of Quantification of Training

The review of training stimuli shows that training effects are dependent upon intensity, duration, and frequency of training. In general, the lower the intensity, duration, and frequency involved in these training regimens, the lower the magnitude of improvement. Although these trends exist, many inconsistencies were found. As mentioned earlier, the lack of standardized methodologies related to testing, training procedures, and their quantification, and differences in samples as related to weight, age, and initial level of fitness, make interpretation difficult. The length of a training experiment also seems to be a factor. In view of the fact that improvement in many endurance fitness parameters continues over many months of training (1,39,55,84,91,118,122), it is reasonable to believe that short-term studies conducted over a few weeks have certain limitations. This would be particularly true with sedentary middle-aged and older participants, as well as subjects whose possess a low initial level of fitness. It has been suggested that these types of subjects should avoid high intensity work initially and be allowed several weeks for special adaptation (38,39,106,133). A review by Kilbom (94), showed that in two studies where middle-aged men trained by running at high speeds, a high rate (approximately 50%) of orthopedic complications involving the ankles and knees was noted.

A. INITIAL LEVEL OF FITNESS

The concept of the percentage of improvement attained in certain physical fitness parameters being related to one's initial degree of fitness was proposed in the early work of Müller (112). He conducted a series of experiments dealing with the improvement in strength and concluded that the percentage of improvement was directly related to initial strength and its relative distance from a possible endpoint of improvement. This concept has also been true with training studies dealing with cardiovascular parameters (47,53,95,141,142,144, 146). Sharkey (144) noted that the magnitude of change was inversely related to the initial level of fitness ($r = -0.54$). He went on to say that the failure to adequately account for this factor in previous training studies may have resulted in erroneous conclusions. Table II shows improvement in $\dot{V}_{O_2 max}$ from training investigations dealing with boys and men of various ages. In general, it is noted that in the studies which show the largest percentage of improvement, their subjects usually began at a lower initial value. The unusually large improvement found by Cureton and Phillips (41) may have resulted from their subjects not having reached a true $\dot{V}_{O_2 max}$ at initial testing. Saltin (142) plotted the $\dot{V}_{O_2 max}$ data of Rowell (138), Ekblom et al. (56) and Saltin et al. (141) subject at the start of physical conditioning against percentage of improvement, and found a moderate relationship, excluding the older men (Fig. 3). The authors mentioned that the older men did not train as much as the younger men, which would account for some of their lack of improvement.

The data from Table II also suggest an increased percentage of improvement in $\dot{V}_{O_2 max}$ with weeks of training. Not including the results on young boys or old men, the improvement in $\dot{V}_{O_2 max}$ with training approximately 10 weeks was 4 to 14%, and 20+ weeks was 14 to 43%. This helps to illustrate the point that training changes continue to occur over a period of many weeks and months. In contrast to the larger percentage of improvement often found in subjects with low initial levels of fitness, subjects who are already moderately active and/or show high initial values, may bias training results conversely (45,142).

Table III illustrates comparative training results for maximum pulmonary ventilation ($\dot{V}_{E max}$), heart rate (HR), and oxygen pulse (O_2 pulse). Table IV lists comparative data for resting heart rate (RHR), systolic blood pressure (SBP), and diastolic blood pressure (DBP),

TABLE II

COMPARISON OF MAXIMAL OXYGEN INTAKE CHANGES WITH ENDURANCE
TRAINING: MALES

Investigator	Ref.	Age	n	Training (weeks)	Days per week	Activity	$\dot{V}_{O_2 max}$ (ml/kg·min) Pre	Post	Percentage
Ekblom	55	11	6	26	2	Run, games	53.9	59.4	10
Daniels	45	14	14	52	b	Run	60.6	59.6	0
Sherman	147	14	7	15	3	Run	54.0	59.4	10
Larsson[a]	100	17	6	20	c	Run, etc.	38.0	48.8	28
Robinson	133	20	9	12	4	Run	52.8	57.8	9
Knehr	98	20	14	26	3	Run	49.6	51.4	4
Wilmore	166	21	17	10	3	Run	46.5	49.0	5
Ekblom	56	23	8	16	3	Run	45.1	50.7	12
Wilmore	166	30	15	10	3	Run	43.6	46.4	7
Naughton	115	30	15	28	3	Run	31.6	45.3	43
Pollock	122	32	11	20	2	Run	37.7	44.0	17
Pollock	122	33	8	20	4	Run	36.6	49.3	35
Cureton	41	34	6	24	5+	Run	26.5	50.2	93
Oscai	118	37	14	20	3	Run	38.8	47.1	21
Pollock	121	39	22	20	2	Run	37.1	43.3	17
Ismail[d]	84	40	54	32	3	Run, games	46.1	57.0	24
Ribisl	130	40	15	20	3	Run	40.1	45.5	14
Saltin	142	41	42	8–10	2+	Run	37.5	44.3	14
Wilmore	166	41	16	10	3	Run	40.1	44.1	10
Naughton	116	41	18	28	3	Run	31.3	36.8	18
Hartley	74	47	15	8–10	2+	Run	35.5	40.5	14
Kasch	89	47	9	24	3	Run	32.0	36.9	15
Kasch	90	47	30	24	2	Run	29.4	36.0	22
Kasch	90	47	11	24	2	Swim	29.9	36.6	19
Hanson	72	49	7	29	3	Run, games	35.8	42.1	17
Pollock	125	49	15	20	4	Walk	29.9	38.9	30
Wilmore	166	53	7	10	3	Run	40.3	41.8	4
Myhre	113	53	10	24	3	Run, games	29.7	37.0	24
Bjure	142	55	8	8–10	2+	Run	28.0	33.0	19
de Vries[a]	49	69	8	42	3	Run	33.7	36.5	8
Benestad	14	75	13	6	3	Walk	27.0	27.0	0

[a] Predicted $\dot{V}_{O_2 max}$ after Åstrand and Rhyming (8).

[b] Subjects averaged between 336 and 1114 miles per year.

[c] Varied throughout program, but consisted of at least 1 hr weekly of vigorous activities such as swimming, skiing, and running.

[d] Age ranged from 23 to 62 years.

while Table V includes data from highly trained endurance athletes. Corollary to the $\dot{V}_{O_2 max}$ test, $\dot{V}_{E\ max}$, O_2 pulse, and HR are generally determined. In the quantification of training regimens, max O_2 pulse generally follows the pattern of $\dot{V}_{O_2}$, but $\dot{V}_{E\ max}$ and HR do not. $\dot{V}_{E\ max}$ will generally

Michael L. Pollock

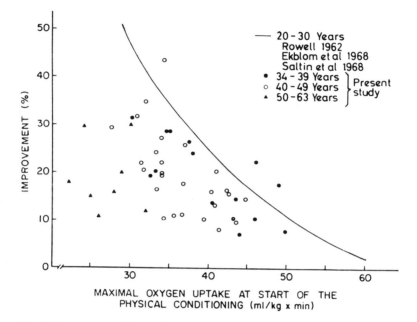

Fig. 3. Improvement in maximal oxygen uptake with 2 to 6 month's physical conditioning in young individuals (the line) and in middle-aged and older subjects in relation to the initial level for their maximal oxygen uptake [see Saltin *et al.* (*142*)].

increase 10 to 20% unless values are rather high to begin with. This increase appears to take place during the first 6 to 10 weeks of training and was not noticeably altered by the varied combinations of frequency, duration, or intensity of training. A few studies showed no change in $\dot{V}_E$, but found substantial changes in $\dot{V}_{O_2 max}$ and O_2 pulse. HR_{max} reductions were found in most studies where the initial values were above 180 beats/min. Except for Wilmore's (*166*) 53 year old group, men whose HR_{max} was lower than this either remained unchanged or increased slightly. The magnitude of change does not appear to be less in the younger groups. The reduction in HR_{max} with training is probably a result of certain adaptations of the heart and nervous system to maintain an optimal cardiac output.

Resting HR is reduced with training, with magnitude of change dependent on the initial level. Most studies show a reduction in HR to the mid to lower 60's. The data for endurance athletes (Table V) average 10 to 15 beats/min lower than the moderately trained groups listed in Table IV, although it is not clear whether this difference is due to genetic factors, training, or both. Resting blood pressure shows mixed results, with little or no change being reported in most investigations. Reductions

TABLE III
Comparison of Maximal Pulmonary Ventilation, Heart Rate, and Oxygen Pulse

Investigator	Ref.	Age (years)	n	Training (weeks)	Days per week	$\dot{V}_E$ [liters/min (BTPS)]		HR (beats/min)		O₂ pulse (ml/beat)	
						Pre	Post	Pre	Post	Pre	Post
Ekblom	55	11	6	26	2	68.0	80.4	204	199	10.5[a]	12.5[a]
Daniels	45	14	14	52	[b]	98.8	105.0	—	—	—	15.5
Sherman	147	14	7	15	3	109.7	116.6	197	194	14.2	20.4
Wilmore	166	21	17	10	3	148.7	153.0	191	184	18.3	18.0
Ekblom	56	23	8	16	3	112.4	147.7	200	198	15.5	21.0
Wilmore	166	30	15	10	3	146.1	145.5	188	182	19.1	19.8
Pollock	122	32	11	20	2	127.2	140.8	186	182	16.6	21.7
Pollock	122	33	8	20	4	128.9	142.6	188	177	16.3	20.2
Oscai	118	37	14	20	3	125.7	128.7	187	179	16.4	19.4
Pollock	121	39	22	20	2	128.0	143.3	188	182	16.3	25.3[a]
Ismail	84	40	54	32	3	—	—	173	179	21.6[a]	20.1
Ribisl	130	40	15	20	3	129.3	143.2	181	179	19.0	18.8[a]
Saltin	142	41	42	8–10	2+	112.1	128.0	190	183	15.2[a]	20.4
Wilmore	166	41	16	10	3	142.7	153.6	179	176	18.6	20.4
Skinner	151	42	14	26	3+	—	—	178	180	—	—
Hartley	74	47	15	8–10	2+	99.7	109.4	182	176	14.7[a]	17.4[a]
Hanson	72	49	7	29	3	70.1	79.2	173	169	15.1[a]	18.2[a]
Pollock	125	49	15	20	4	113.0	133.4	175	174	13.8	17.4
Wilmore	166	53	7	10	3	133.5	137.9	179	169	17.6	19.2
Benestad	14	75	13	6	3	70.0	69.0	153	155	12.6	12.5

[a] Estimated from HR_{max} and $\dot{V}_{O_2\,max}$ (liters/min).
[b] Subjects averaged between 336 and 1114 miles for the year.

TABLE IV

COMPARISON OF RESTING HEART RATE AND BLOOD PRESSURE

Investigator	Ref.	Age (years)	n	Train-ing (weeks)	Days per week	HR (beats/ min) Pre	HR (beats/ min) Post	SBP (mm Hg) Pre	SBP (mm Hg) Post	DBP (mm Hg) Pre	DBP (mm Hg) Post
Casner	22	16.5	26	5	3	77	71	—	—	—	—
Knehr	98	20	14	8	3	67	62	114	113	65	67
Wilmore	166	21	17	10	3	76	63	130	109	69	65
Wilmore	166	30	15	10	3	72	65	134	116	75	71
Pollock	122	32	11	20	2	70	64	—	—	—	—
Pollock	122	33	8	20	4	68	61	—	—	—	—
Pollock	128	36	7	16	4	67	59	120	114	76	73
Oscai	118	37	14	20	3	64	58	—	—	—	—
Pollock	128	37	6	16	2	67	56	118	114	78	76
Pollock	121	39	22	20	2	66	62	118	115	77	79
Ismail	84	40[a]	54	32	3	66	61	120	119	73	70
Ribisl	130	40	15	20	3	72	67	—	—	—	—
Kilbom	96	41	41	8–10	2+	—	—	124	122	83	79
Wilmore	166	41	16	10	3	69	65	137	118	80	70
Naughton	116	41	18	28	3	—	—	134	127	86	82
Skinner	151	42	14	26	3+	82	71	—	—	—	—
Hartley	74	47	15	8–10	2+	66	61[c]	—	—	—	—
Hanson	72	49	7	29	3	77	73	126	124	80	81
Pollock	125	49	15	20	4	65	62	121	118	78	76
Boyer[b]	15	49	23	26	2	—	—	159	146	105	93
Wilmore	166	53	7	10	3	77	68	140	125	81	74
de Vries	49	69	8	42	3	—	—	134	135	76	71

[a] Age of subjects ranged from 23 to 62 years.
[b] Hypertensive subjects.
[c] Supine position.

were less evident when blood pressure was initially considered normal. Boyer and Kasch (*15*) found significant reductions in both SBP and DBP with hypertensive patients after 6 months of training. Both resting SBP and DBP differ little between sedentary and trained normal subjects.

Heart rate response to a standard work task (HR-STD), physical work capacity at a given heart rate (PWC), and a variety of maximal performance tests, e.g., a 1 or 2 mile run for time, have been used to evaluate training regimens. In general, these test variables were considered as significant a discriminator as $\dot{V}_{O_{2}max}$ between the various combinations of regimens discussed in Sections II,A,B, and C. Figure 4 shows the difference in training 2 and 4 days per week on a HR-STD (*122*). The 2 day group (I) reduced their HR's up to 10 beats/min during exercise and 15 beats/min in recovery, while the 4 day group (II) showed 15

TABLE V

PHYSIOLOGICAL MEASURES OF ENDURANCE ATHLETES: MALES

Investigator	Ref.	Age (years)	n	Maximum				Rest		
				$\dot{V}_{O_2}$ (ml/kg·min)	$\dot{V}_E$ (liters/min)	O_2 pulse (ml/beat)	HR (beats/min)	HR (beats/min)	SBP (mm Hg)	DBP (mm Hg)
Daniels	44	21	6	74.7	172.0	—	—	—	—	—
Saltin	140	21–32	20	78.7	156.0	29.8[c]	187	—	—	—
Carter	20	26.6	1	72.3	147.0	28.7[c]	192	46	120	82
Costill	30, 61	21–48	9	70.0	151.6	29.6	185	42	115	75
Pollock	[a]	24	3	68.3	136.2	23.9	182	51	—	—
Costill	29	—	5	—	—	—	189	56	125	81
Pollock	126	38–47	15	48.1	145.8	21.9	178	49	117	76
Pollock	127	40–49	11	57.5	151.0	23.1[c]	178	52	135	83
Grimby	71	42–49	14	55.0	118.5	—	175	—	—	—
Costill	31	45–49	2	64.9	142.1	20.5[c]	184	45[b]	102[b]	62[b]
Dill	50	49	1	59.6	126.0	19.4[c]	188	57	137	81
Grimby	71	50–59	15	49.9	113.7	—	176	52	136	84
Pollock	126	48–57	17	46.7	143.4	21.2	174	42	129	81
Pollock	127	50–59	6	54.5	138.0	19.8[c]	178	60	138	80
Grimby	71	61–68	4	41.1	94.8	—	165	46	122	78
Pollock	127	60–69	6	51.4	140.0	21.0[c]	163	58	126[b]	70[b]
Cureton	37	69	1	58.4	—	—	—	58	—	—
Pollock	127	70–79	3	40.0	98.0	16.1[c]	166	56	141	83

[a] Unpublished data collected by author (August, 1971), on members of the Pan African Track and Field Team.

[b] Supine position.

[c] Estimated from HR_{max} (beats/min) and $\dot{V}_{O_2 \, max}$ (liters/min).

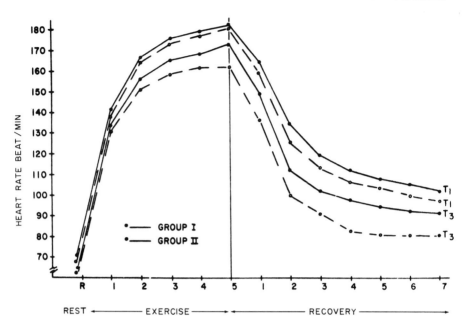

Fig. 4. Effects of training 2 (group I) and 4 (group II) days per week on heart rate response to a standard 5 min treadmill run (6 mph, 5.0% grade). Recovery periods shown on abscissa represent minutes [see Pollock *et al.* (*122*)].

and 25 beats/min reductions for the same time period. The control group remained unchanged.

Changes in cardiac output ($\dot{Q}$), stroke volume (SV), and heart volume are shown in Table VI and heart volume in Fig. 5. Although it is generally agreed that these variables increase significantly with training and that endurance athletes reflect the highest values (*9,135,139*), not many training studies have included these variables. Therefore, further quantification is impossible at this time.

B. AGE

Thus far, the quantification of training as related to age has been mentioned only briefly. Figure 3 illustrates that improvement in $\dot{V}_{O_2 \, max}$ occurs at ages 20 to 63. Saltin (*142*) concluded that although this training effect occurs as readily in middle-aged and old men as in young men, the absolute change is less, i.e., there appears to be an aging effect. This is illustrated in Table II, and is in agreement with Kilbom (*94*).

The small to no improvement reported by de Vries (*49*) and Benestad (*14*) may be somewhat misleading. The latter program was of short duration, and the intensity and duration of training are considered

TABLE VI

COMPARISON OF ATHLETES AND NONATHLETES IN MAXIMUM CARDIAC OUTPUT ($\dot{Q}$), STROKE VOLUME (SV), AND HEART VOLUME (HV)

Investigator	Ref.	Age (years)	n	Status of training[a]	Training (weeks)	$\dot{Q}$ (liters/min)		SV (ml)		HV (ml)	
						Pre	Post	Pre	Post	Pre	Post
Ekblom	55	11	6	MT	26	—	—	—	—	467	490
Ekblom	55	11	7	SC	26	—	—	—	—	431	459
Ekblom	55	11	7	MT	112	—	—	—	—	494	706
Ekblom	55	11	5	SC	112	—	—	—	—	446	574
Saltin	141	20	5	MT	8	20.0	22.8	104.0	119.8	860	895
Ekblom	56	23	8	MT	17	22.4	24.2	112	127	—	—
Hartley	74	23	17	MT	—	21.5	23.2	110	122	—	—
Åstrand	6	25	6	T	—	—	28.9	—	157	—	1073
Hartley	74	47	15	MT	—	18.7	21.1	103	120	—	—
Grimby	70	51	9	T	—	—	26.8	—	158	—	1060
Benestad	14	75	13	MT	6	—	—	—	—	—	832

[a] SC = sedentary control; MT = moderately trained; T = trained.

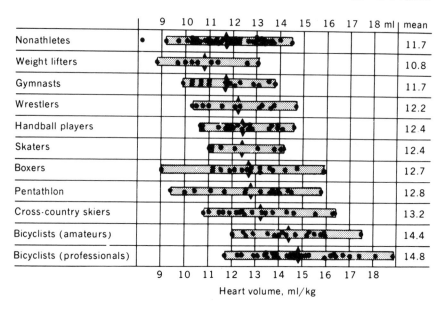

Fig. 5. The heart volume per kilogram body weight for members of different teams of Germany and a group of untrained individuals of the same age. Each dot represents one subject [see Roskamm (*134*)].

minimal in relation to the criteria established in Sections II,A and B. De Vries' regimen was conducted over a much longer period of time, but the training intensity was minimal. The concern for protecting middle-aged and older subjects from overstress is important, and most investigators use much caution in their exercise prescription. As a result of this, sedentary groups need more time to adapt to training. This factor, plus the confounding effects related to the previously discussed training stimuli, make interpretation difficult. The $\dot{V}_{O_2 max}$ data for middle-aged and older endurance athletes reported in Table V show contrasting results. These groups show a markedly superior level of $\dot{V}_{O_2 max}$ in every age category, which is probably the result of both genetic endowment and physical training.

The age decrement mentioned earlier also appears in the trained groups, and becomes particularly evident after age 60. Can this decrement in $\dot{V}_{O_2 max}$ be explained by age itself or are training factors also apparent? The evidence at hand supports both notions. Young endurance runners will train 100 to 200 miles per week (sometimes less if purely interval training is used); whereas the middle-aged and older runners rarely accomplish this. In data collected from the 1971 National Master's AAU track and field meet (July 3 and 4, San Diego, California), and subsequent laboratory evaluations conducted by Pollock, Miller, and Wilmore

(*127*), the average number of miles trained per week was 40, 40, 30, and 20 for the 4th, 5th, 6th, and 7th decades, respectively. Another interesting fact was that most of these men were prior college athletes who had not trained all their lives. Most of the older athletes had been sedentary for many years and had been back in training for only 5 to 10 years. Grimby and Saltin's (*71*) data on middle-aged and older athletes who had trained all their lives are comparable at the 4th decade, but are lower for the 5th and 6th decades. Other data of Pollock *et al.* (*126*), for men who had been training for 5.5 years, are significantly higher than for men completing their first 6 months of training, but are less than for the aforementioned athletic groups. Dill's (*50*) and Costill and Winrow's (*30,31*) data on competitive marathon runners agree. With the onslaught of Master's competition prevailing and the probability of men and women training for competition throughout a lifetime, future data should provide more insight into the aging process and its effects on fitness parameters.

The $\dot{V}_{O_2max}$ improvement with young boys is complicated somewhat by the maturation process, making interpretation more difficult. The data of Ekblom (*55*), Sherman (*147*), and Larsson (*100*) show significant improvements, while Daniels and Oldridge (*45*) do not. Inspection of the results shows Daniels and Oldridge's (*45*) initial values to be much higher than the others; thus, again bringing up the notion concerning initial status of fitness and its relationship to possible improvement. The age-related $\dot{V}_{O_2max}$ values reported by Robinson (*132*) and Cumming (*33*) are in agreement with Ekblom and Sherman, while Larsson *et al.* is lower. The lower values of Larsson *et al.* may be a result of their use of a submaximal bicycle test to predict $\dot{V}_{O_2max}$ (*168*). The 24% improvement found in this study (*168*) shows a consistent relationship with their lower initial values.

C. HEREDITY

The effects of training have been well documented, with clear differences being established between sedentary, moderately trained, and highly trained athletes. Even with these differences, there are broad overlappings between these groups on most physiological parameters. This fact, plus the aging process, makes various standards awkward and somewhat misleading. That is, much of our ability is endowed by heredity (*32,46, 65,97*). Åstrand (*5*) stated that the best way to become a champion athlete is to be selective in the manner in which you pick your parents. Therefore, the fact of having a high $\dot{V}_{O_2max}$, etc. must be interpreted with caution. It is certainly possible to have a high $\dot{V}_{O_2max}$ and be considered in poor condition and to have a low one and be considered fit. The former would be true with a highly trained endurance athlete who has become inactive. Thus, it is recommended that results also be interpreted with respect to the individual's differences and variations.

Longitudinal studies conducted by Ekblom (*55*) and Åstrand *et al.* (*7*) on young boys and girls showed higher than normal improvements in many physiological parameters with endurance regimens, thus suggesting the probability of significant cardiopulmonary and anthropometric modifications occurring during the formative years.

D. BODY COMPOSITION

Although body weight and composition changes resulting from endurance training are not the major concern of this review, there are certain considerations that merit mentioning here (for more detailed information on weight control, see Oscai, this volume, p. 103).

Table VII shows a comparison of body weight and percentage of fat changes resulting from the training of adult men 20 to 60 years of age. These data generally show reductions in body weight from 0 to 3.0 kg

TABLE VII

COMPARISON OF BODY WEIGHT AND COMPOSITION CHANGES WITH TRAINING:
ADULT MEN

Investiga-tor	Ref.	Age (years)	n	Training (weeks)	Days per week	Activity	Total body weight (kg)	Per-centage fat
Golding	68	Young men	4	25	4+	Run, Cal.	−3.0	—
Pollock	122	32	11	20	4	Run	−2.9	−1.0
Pollock	122	33	9	20	2	Run	+0.1	+0.9
Wilmore	166	33	55	10	3	Run	−1.0	−1.1
Pollock	128	36	6	16	4	Run	−0.9	−3.3
Oscai	118	37	14	20	3	Run	−2.4	−2.2
Pollock	128	37	5	16	2	Run	−0.8	+0.4
Pollock	123	38	26	20	3	R, W, B	−1.3	−1.8
Pollock	121	39	22	20	2	Run	−0.7	−0.6
Ribisl	130	40	15	20	3	Run	−2.6	−0.7
Kilbom	96	41	42	8–10	2+	Run	+0.3	—
Naughton	116	41	18	28	3	Run	−2.1	—
Skinner	151	42	15	24	3	Run, Cal.	+0.1	−1.8
Carter	21	47	7	26	2+	Run	−3.0	−3.8
Kasch	a	47	69	24	2+	Run, Swim	−0.7	—
Pollock	125	49	14	20	4	Walk	−1.3	−1.1
Myhre	113	53	10	24	3	Run, Games	−1.4	−3.1

a Unpublished data, San Diego State College.

and percentage of fat from 0 to 3.8%. Although changes of this magnitude are quite reasonable for estimated kilocalorie expenditures encountered during these regimens, direct intergroup comparisons are difficult to make. The lack of dietary control on the one hand, and the quantification and reporting of training on the other, account for this difficulty. Future investigations should attempt to standardize and quantify training protocol, thus helping to facilitate comparisons of this nature.

Since changes in body weight and composition are related to energy expenditure of a program, the regimens with greater combinations of frequency, duration, and/or intensity tend to show greater magnitude of change. These changes tend to manifest themselves with weeks of training, i.e., programs of an 8 to 10 week duration generally result in less change. Keeping in mind the notion mentioned in Section III,B, concerning the initial adaptation period needed for most sedentary men, this does not seem surprising. Carter and Phillips (*21*) found consistent and continual body weight and percentage fat changes during the first year of a 2 year study. The second year, results stabilized.

Pollock *et al.* (*121–123,128*), looking at body weight and composition changes in respect to frequency of training, found no significant reductions in three 2 day per week studies, but did with 3 and 4 days per week programs. This was somewhat perplexing, considering the miles per week trained and estimated kilocalories expended found in one of the studies (*121*). The weekly mileage (8 +) and kilocalorie expenditure (1000 kcal) were equal to the 3 day per week training regimen (*123*), which did show significant reductions. Although the rationale for the phenomenon is not clearly understood, it appears that 2 day per week regimens may not provide the continual stimulation necessary for a pronounced reduction in these variables.

It is interesting to note that the results from fast walking, which was less intense, but of increased frequency and duration, produced significant changes (*125*). This is in agreement with Moody *et al.* (*111*).

E. Training in Females

Treating the quantitative effects of endurance training on females in a separate section should not be interpreted as a minimization, but the fact is that only a limited number of investigations of this type are present in the literature. In fact, only a few training investigations dealing with females have been designed to quantify training regimens as outlined in Sections II,A,B, and C (*95,169*). Several studies have evaluated working capacity (*1,2,7,110,153,163,167*) and anthropometric measurements

(*7,108,111*) of young girls and women. A few investigations have evaluated highly trained women athletes (*7,17,51,108,140*). Others (*5,16,43, 95,111,162,169*) have shown significant cardiovascular function and body composition changes with endurance training. These former data show significant differences between males and females, which become apparent after puberty (*2,4,132*). These differences are discussed more thoroughly by Drinkwater (this volume, p. 125). The results from training investigations show that females adapt to training in the same manner as do males. Therefore, it is concluded that the general findings concerning the quantification of physical training programs summarized in Sections I and II should also apply to women. The need for more investigative endeavors dealing with females is apparent.

F. Continuous versus Intermittent Exercise

The comparison of continuous and intermittent training regimens has been of interest to most exercise physiologists, with the initial efforts of quantification being reported by Åstrand *et al.* (*3*) and Christensen *et al.* (*23,25*). Theoretically, intermittent training would allow runners to train at a faster than competitive pace for a longer period of time, thus eventually improving their actual competitive running time. The increased amount of total work accomplished at a higher intensity by the runners would be a result of the intermittent rest period allowed between bouts of heavy work. The intermittent rest period could be a walk or slow jog, and results in partial recovery prior to the next work bout.

Christensen *et al.* (*23,25*) and Åstrand *et al.* (*3*), in a series of experiments comparing continuous and varying combinations of intermittent work, found several important implications. In one experiment, where subjects ran continuously at 12.4 mph, they became exhausted after approximately 4 min. This phase of the experiment produced high $\dot{V}_{O_2}$, HR, and blood lactate values. Running intermittently at the same speed showed lower $\dot{V}_{O_2}$ and HR values, with only a slight increase in blood lactate. The total exercise period lasted approximately 20 min. While these studies were conducted on young, well-trained subjects, intermittent training may have a definite advantage when working with sedentary, middle-aged and older subjects when beginning training regimens (*1*). The shorter bouts of work with intermittent rest periods can allow them to accomplish more total work with less physiological stress than if they were to run continuously. This is in agreement with factors discussed in Section III,B. Although this approach is recommended for many individuals who are initiating exercise programs, it would not be practical for use with highly trained groups; i.e., the load on the oxygen transport system may not be adequate. In another phase of their experiments, it was found that when intensity was doubled in relation to the intensity of a 1 hr continuous workout, 3 min work to rest bouts resulted in the highest $\dot{V}_{O_2}$, $\dot{V}_E$, HR, and blood lactate values. When the high work rate was performed continuously, the subject could only go for 9 min, with resulting physiological measures being higher than for the intermittent work. Work to rest ratios performed for 2, 1, and ½ min showed a consistent reduction in these variables. The total oxygen used did not vary much between treatments, but the other values, particularly when bouts were performed for 1 and ½ min durations, were significantly lower. In another study (23), it was found that short bouts of high intensity running of up to 30 sec were less demanding when the work to rest ratio was 1:1 or 1:2. In a review of this work, Åstrand and Rodahl (9) summarized by stating that "maximal oxygen uptake (and cardiac output) may be attained in connection with repeated periods of work of very high intensity of as short duration as 10 to 15 sec, providing the rest periods between each burst of activity are very short (of equal or shorter duration than the work periods). In more prolonged work, of several minutes duration, the duration of the rest periods is less critical. In this case it is the intensity of the work that determines the load. If the work periods exceed about 10 min or so, a high level of motivation is required in order to attain maximal oxygen uptakes. In the case of continuous work the high tempo required for the severe taxation of the oxygen-transporting system must alternate with periods of reduced tempo.

"In the case of very short work periods, about 30 sec or shorter, a very severe load may be imposed upon both muscles and oxygen-transporting organs without the engagement of anaerobic processes leading to any significant elevation of the blood lactate. It is thus possible to select the proper work load and work and rest periods in such a manner that the main demand is centered on (1) muscle strength without a major increase in the total oxygen uptake; (2) aerobic processes without significantly mobilizing anaerobic processes; (3) anaerobic processes without maximal taxation of the oxygen-transporting organs; (4) both aerobic and anaerobic processes simultaneously. The alternatives 2 and 4 do not entail maximal taxation of muscle strength; alternative 3 does not necessarily require maximal strength."

The comparison of these training techniques and their effectiveness to increased $\dot{V}_{O_2 max}$ and/or performance is still controversial (75,134). Costill (29), in a review of this subject, is in agreement and states that the present evidence does not favor either continual (over distance) or interval type training for improving distance running. Åstrand and Rodahl (9) and Costill (29) suggest that the type of training used should depend upon the purpose of the training, i.e., aerobic or anaerobic, or a combination thereof. The data point to the need for more inquiry, using various combinations of regimens, larger samples, and including endurance athletes as well as nontrained subjects.

IV. Summary

This paper has dealt with the quantification of endurance training programs, with special emphasis on intensity, duration, frequency, modes of training, and their subsequent effects on cardiovascular and body composition parameters. The review showed that most endurance training regimens elicited significant training effects in most heart rate and metabolic measures. In general, magnitude of change was dependent on intensity, duration, and/or frequency of training, initial level of fitness, and age. Programs involving the most total energy output showed the most improvement. As a result of the lack of sufficient data, many fitness variables, such as cardiac output, stroke volume, heart size, blood volume, etc., could not be quantified as effectively. Some contradictory results were found, but much of this was thought to be a result of differences in methodology related to evaluation and experimental design. The review pointed to the need for better standardization of procedures in conducting training experiments. Within certain limits, it was shown that improvements in physical fitness were independent of mode of training. That is, if intensity, frequency, and duration of training were held constant, a variety of modes of training would produce similar results. The differences between low and high energy cost activities were discussed with respect to their relative value in affecting cardiovascular and body composition parameters. Endurance training improves the physical fitness status of both young and old, with a lesser degree of improvement being found in old age. The latter may be an effect of age, heredity, previous experience, and/or limitation of the prescribed training regimen. Although males and females show basic differences in many physical fitness parameters (a result of basic anatomical and physiological differences), females appear to adapt to endurance training regimens in a manner similar to that of males. The review points to the lack of information regarding the training of females.

References

1. Åstrand, I. (1960). *Acta Physiol. Scand.* **49**, Suppl. 169, 211–217.
2. Åstrand, I. (1967). *Circulation Res.* **20 and 21**, Suppl. 1, 211–217.

3. Åstrand, I., Åstrand, P.-O., Christensen, E. H., and Hedman, R. (1960). *Acta Physiol. Scand.* **48**, 448–453.
4. Åstrand, P.-O. (1952). "Experimental Studies of Physical Working Capacity in Relation to Sex and Age." Munksgaard, Copenhagen.
5. Åstrand, P.-O. (1972). *J. Phys. Educ. Mar-Apr*, 129–136.
6. Åstrand, P.-O., Cuddy, T. E., Saltin, B., and Sternberg, J. (1964). *J. Appl. Physiol.* **19**, 268–274.
7. Åstrand, P.-O., Eriksson, B. O., Nylander, I., Engström, L., Karlberg, P., Saltin, B., and Thorén, C. (1963). *Acta Paediat. Suppl.* **147**, 1–75.
8. Åstrand, P.-O., and Rhyming, I. (1964). *J. Appl. Physiol.* **7**, 218–221.
9. Åstrand, P.-O., and Rodahl, K. (1970). "Textbook of Work Physiology." McGraw-Hill, New York.
10. Baker, J. A. (1968). *Res. Quart.* **39**, 240–243.
11. Balke, B., and Ware, R. W. (1959). *U. S. Armed Forces Med. J.* **10**, 675–688.
12. Banister, E. W., Ribisl, P. M., Porter, G. H., and Cillo, A. R. (1964). *Res. Quart.* **35**, 236–240.
13. Bartels, R., Billings, C. E., Fox, E. L., Mathews, D. K., O'Brien, R., Tanz, D., and Webb, W. (1968). *Abstr. AAHPER Conv.*, p. 13.
14. Benestad, A. M. (1965). *Acta Med. Scand.* **178**, 321–327.
15. Boyer, J., and Kasch, F. (1970). *J. Amer. Med. Ass.* **211**, 1668–1671.
16. Brown, H. C., Harrower, J. R., and Deeter, M. F. (1972). *Med. Sci. Sports* **4**, 1–5.
17. Brown, H. C., and Wilmore, J. H. (1971). Paper presented to the American College of Sports Medicine, Toronto, Canada.
18. Campbell, D. E. (1965). *J. Lipid Res.* **6**, 478–480.
19. Campney, H. K., and Wehr, R. W. (1965). *Res. Quart.* **36**, 393–402.
20. Carter, J. E. L., Kasch, F. W., Boyer, J. L., Phillips, W. H., Ross, W. D., and Sucec, A. (1967). *Res. Quart.* **38**, 355–365.
21. Carter, J. E., and Phillips, W. H. (1969). *J. Appl. Physiol.* **27**, 787–794.
22. Casner, S. W., Campbell, D. E., and Early, R. G. (1968). *J. Sports Med. Phys. Fitness* **8**, 236–240.
23. Christensen, E. H., Hedman, R., and Saltin, B. (1960). *Acta Physiol. Scand.* **50**, 269–286.
24. Christensen, E. H., and Högberg, P. (1950). *Arbeitsphysiologie* **14**, 292–303.
25. Christensen, E. H., and Högberg, P. (1950). *Arbeitsphysiologie* **14**, 249–250.
26. Cooper, K. (1968). "Aerobics." Bantam Books, New York.
27. Cooper, K. (1969). *J. S. S. Med. Ass. Suppl.* **65**, 37–40.
28. Corbin, B., Berryhill, D., and Olree, H. (1968). *Abstr. Res. Papers AAHPER Conv.* p. 33.
29. Costill, D. L. (1968). "What Research Tells the Coach About Distance Running." *AAHPER*, Washington, D. C.
30. Costill, D. L., and Winrow, E. (1970). *Arch. Phys. Med. Rehabil.* **51**, 317–320.
31. Costill, D. L., and Winrow, E. (1970). *Res. Quart.* **41**, 135–139.
32. Cotes, J. E., and Davies, C. T. M. (1969). *Proc. Roy. Soc. Med.* **62**, 620–624.
33. Cumming, G. R. (1967). *Can. Med. Ass. J.* **96**, 868–877.
34. Cureton, T. K. (1947). "Physical Fitness Appraisal and Guidance." Mosby, St. Louis, Missouri.
35. Cureton, T. K. (1951). "Physical Fitness of Champion Athletes," Univ. of Illinois Press, Urbana, Illinois.
36. Cureton, T. K. (1963). *Res. Quart.* **34**, 440–453.

37. Cureton, T. K. (1964). *J. Ass. Phys. Ment. Rehabil.* **18**, 64–72, 80.
38. Cureton, T. K. (1965). "Physical Fitness and Dynamic Health." Dial Press, New York.
39. Cureton, T. K. (1969). "The Physiological Effects of Exercise Programs on Adults." Springfield, Illinois.
40. Cureton, T. K., and Barry, A. J. (1964). "Improving the Physical Fitness of Youth." Antioch Press, Yellow Springs.
41. Cureton, T. K., and Phillips, E. E. (1964). *J. Sports Med. Phys. Fitness* **4**, 1–6.
42. Daley, J. W., Barry, A. J., and Birkhead, N. C. (1968). *J. Geront.* **23**, 134–139.
43. Daniel, S. L., Pollock, M. L., and Startsmen, T. (1969). *Proc. Southern District AAHPER Conv., Columbia, South Carolina,* pp. 98–100.
44. Daniels, J., and Oldridge, N. (1970). *Med. Sci. Sports* **2**, 107–112.
45. Daniels, J., and Oldridge, N. (1971). *Med. Sci. Sports* **3**, 161–165.
46. Davies, C. T. M. (1969). *Proc. Roy. Soc. Med.* **62**, 1171–1174.
47. Davies, C. T. M., and Knibbs, A. V. (1971). *Int. Z. Angew. Physiol.* **29**, 299–305.
48. Davies, C. T. M., Tuxworth, W., and Young, J. M. (1970). *Clin. Sci.* **39**, 247–258.
49. deVries, H. (1970). *J. Gerontol.* **25**, 325–336.
50. Dill, D. B. (1965). *J. Nat. Can. Inst.* **35**, 185–191.
51. Drinkwater, B. L., and Horvath, S. M. (1971). *Med. Sci. Sports* **3**, 56–62.
52. Drinkwater, B. L., and Horvath, S. M. (1972). *Med. Sci. Sports* **4**, 91–95.
53. Durnin, J. V. G. A., Brockway, J. M., and Whitcher, H. W. (1960). *J. Appl. Physiol.* **15**, 161–165.
54. Durnin, J. V. G. A., and Passmore, R. (1967). "Energy, Work, and Leisure." Heinemann Educational Books, London.
55. Ekblom, B. (1969). *J. Appl. Physiol.* **27**, 350–355.
56. Ekblom, B., Åstrand, P.-O., Saltin, B., Stenberg, J., and Wallström, B. (1968). *J. Appl. Physiol.* **24**, 518–528.
57. Fardy, P. S. (1969). *Res. Quart.* **40**, 502–508.
58. Faria, I. E. (1970). *Res. Quart.* **41**, 44–50.
59. Faulkner, J. A. (1967). "What Research Tells the Coach About Swimming," AAHPER, Washington, D. C.
60. Faulkner, J. A., Greey, G., and Hunsicker, P. (1963). *Res. Quart.* **34**, 95–98.
61. Fox, E. L., and Costill, D. L. (1972). *Arch. Environ. Health* **24**, 316–324.
62. Fox, S. M., III, Naughton, J. P., and Haskell, W. L. (1971). *Ann. Clin. Res.* **3**, 404–432.
63. Fox, S. M., III, and Skinner, J. S. (1964). *Amer. J. Cardiol.* **14**, 731–746.
64. Franks, B. D. (1969). *In* "Exercise and Fitness: 1969" (B. D. Franks, ed.), pp. 139–160. Athletic Inst., Chicago, Illinois.
65. Gedda, L. (1961). *In* "Health and Fitness in the Modern World" (L. A. Larson, ed.), pp. 43–64. Athletic Inst., Chicago, Illinois.
66. Getchell, L. (1968). *Arch. Phys. Med. Rehabil.* **49**, 31–35.
67. Gledhill, N., and Eynon, R. (1972). *In* "TRAINING Scientific Basis and Application" (A. W. Taylor, ed.), pp. 97–102. Thomas, Springfield, Illinois.
68. Golding, L. (1958). Ph.D. Thesis, Univ. of Illinois, Urbana, Illinois.
69. Graham, M. (1966). "Prescription for Life." McKay, New York.
70. Grimby, G., Nilsson, N. J., and Saltin, B. (1966). *J. Appl. Physiol.* **21**, 1150–1156.
71. Grimby, G., and Saltin, B. (1966). *Acta Med. Scand.* **179**, 513–526.
72. Hanson, J., Tabakin, B., Levy, A., and Nedde, W. (1968). *Circulation* **38**, 783–799.

73. Harrison, T. R., and Reeves, T. J. (1968). "Principles and Problems of Ischemic Heart Disease." Yearbook, Chicago, Illinois.
74. Hartley, L. H., Grimby, G., Kilbom, A., Nilsson, N. J., Åstrand, I., Bjure, J., Ekblom, B., and Saltin, B. (1969). *Scand. J. Clin. Lab. Invest.* **24**, 335-344.
75. Haskell, W. L. (1965). Ph.D. Thesis, Univ. of Illinois, Urbana, Illinois.
76. Hellerstein, H. K. (1969). *J. S. C. Med. Ass.* **65**, 46-56.
77. Heusner, W. W. (1955). Ph.D. Thesis, Univ. of Illinois, Urbana, Illinois.
78. Heyden, S. (1969). *In* "Atherlosclerosis" (F. G. Schettle and G. S. Boyd, eds.), pp. 245-269. Elsevier, Amsterdam.
79. Heyden, S., Cassel, J. C., Bartel, A., Tyroler, H. A., Hames, C. G., and Cornoni, J. C. (1971). *Arch. Intern. Med.* **128**, 915-919.
80. Hill, J. S. (1969). The Effects of Frequency of Exercise on Cardiorespiratory Fitness of Adult Men. M.S. Thesis, Univ. of Western Ontario, London.
81. Hollmann, W., and Venrath, H. (1963). *Sportarzt.* **9**, 189.
82. Hollmann, W., and Venrath, H. (1962). *In* "Cärl Diem Festschrift" (Körbs, ed.), W. u. a. Frankfurt/Wein.
83. Honet, J. C., Fowler, W. S., Elkins, E. C., and Baker, C. E. (1962). *Arch. Phys. Med. Rehabil.* **43**, 51-56.
84. Ismail, A. H., Corrigan, D., and MacLeod, D. F. (1970). *Proc. 18th World Congr. Sports Med., Oxford, England* (in press).
85. Jackson, J. H., Sharkey, B. J., and Johnson, P. L. (1968). *Res. Quart.* **39**, 295-300.
86. Jones, D. M., Squires, C., and Rodahl, K. (1962). *Res. Quart.* **33**, 236-238.
87. Kannel, W. (1966). *U. S. Pub. Health Serv. Publ.* **1515**.
88. Karvonen, M. J., Kentala, E., and Mustala, O. (1957). *Ann. Med. Exp. Biol. Fenn.* **35**, 307-315.
89. Kasch, F. (1968). Paper presented to American College of Sports Medicine, University Park, Pennsylvania.
90. Kasch, F. (1970). Paper presented to the American College of Sports Medicine, Albuquerque, New Mexico.
91. Kasch, F. (1972). Paper presented Symposium on Exercise and Health, University of North Carolina, Charlotte, North Carolina.
92. Kasch, F., and Boyer, J. L. (1968). "Adult Fitness Principles and Practices." San Diego State College, San Diego, California.
93. Kendrick, Z. B., Pollock, M. L., Hickman, T. N., and Miller, H. S. (1971). *Amer. Corr. Ther. J.* **25**, 79-83.
94. Kilbom, A. (1971). *In* "Coronary Heart Disease and Physical Fitness" (O. A. Larsen and R. O. Malmborg, eds.), pp. 175-179. Univ. Park Press, Baltimore, Maryland.
95. Kilbom, A. (1971). *Scand. J. Lab. Invest. Suppl.* **119**, 1-34.
96. Kilbom, A., Hartley, L., Saltin, B., Bjure, J., Grimby, G., and Åstrand, I. (1969). *Scand. J. Clin. Lab. Invest.* **24**, 315-322.
97. Klissouras, V. (1971). *J. Appl. Physiol.* **31**, 338-344.
98. Knehr, C. A., Dill, D. B., and Neufeld, W. (1942). *Amer. J. Physiol.* **136**, 148-156, 1942.
99. Kozar, A. J., and Hunsicker, P. (1963). *J. Sports Med. Phys. Fitness* **3**, 1-5.
100. Larsson, Y., Persson, B., Sterky, G., and Therén, C. (1964). *J. Appl. Physiol.* **19**, 629-635.
101. Lester, F. M., Sheffield, L. T., and Reeves, T. J. (1967). *Circulation* **36**, 5-14.
102. McArdle, W. D., Zwiren, L., and Magel, J. (1969). *Res. Quart.* **40**, 523-528.
103. McDonough, J. R., and Bruce, R. A. (1969). *J. S. C. Med. Ass.* **65**, 26-33.

104. McDonough, J. R., Kusumi, B. S., and Bruce, R. A. (1970). *Circulation* **41**, 743–751.
105. Magel, J. R., and Faulkner, J. A. (1967). *J. Appl. Physiol.* **22**, 929–938.
106. Mann, G. V., Garrett, L. H., Farhi, A., Murray, H., Billings, T. F., Shute, F., and Schwarten, S. E. (1969). *Amer. J. Med.* **46**, 12–27.
107. Massie, J., Rode, A., Skrien, T., and Shephard, R. J. (1970). *Med. Sci. Sports* **2**, 1–6.
108. Melina, R. M., Harper, A. B., Avent, H. H., Campbell, D. E. (1971). *Med. Sci. Sports* **3**, 32–38.
109. Michael, E. D., Jr., and Gallon, A. (1959). *Res. Quart.* **30**, 303–311.
110. Michael, E. D., Jr., and Horvath, S. M. (1965). *J. Appl. Physiol.* **20**, 263–266.
111. Moody, D. L., Kollias, J., and Buskirk, E. R. (1969). *Med. Sci. Sports* **1**, 75–80.
112. Müller, E. A. (1962). *Rev. Can. Biol.* **21**, 303–313.
113. Myhre, L., Robinson, S., Brown, A., and Pyke, F. (1970). Paper presented to the American College of Sports Medicine, Albuquerque, New Mexico.
114. Nagle, F., and Irwin, L. (1960). *Res. Quart.* **31**, 607–615.
115. Naughton, J., and Balke, B. (1964). *Amer. J. Med. Sci.* **247**, 286–292.
116. Naughton, J., and Nagle, F. (1965). *J. Amer. Med. Ass.* **191**, 102.
117. Olree, H. D., Corbin, B., Penrod, J., and Smith, C. (1969). Final Progress Rep. to NASA, Grant No. NGR-04-002-004.
118. Oscai, L. B., Williams, T., and Hertig, B. (1968). *J. Appl. Physiol.* **24**, 622–624.
119. Pohndorf, R. H. (1958). *Res. Quart.* **29**, 180–192.
120. Pollock, M. L., Broida, J., and Kendrick, Z. (1972). *Res. Quart.* **43**, 77–81.
121. Pollock, M. L., Broida, J., Kendrick, Z., Miller, H., Janeway, R., and Linnerud, A. C. (1972). *Med. Sci. Sports* **4**, 192–197.
122. Pollock, M. L., Cureton, T. K., and Greninger, L. (1969). *Med. Sci. Sports* **1**, 70–74.
123. Pollock, M. L., Dimmick, J., Miller, H. S., Jr., Kendrick, Z., and Linnerud, A. C. (1972). Paper presented to the American College of Sports Medicine, Philadelphia, Pennsylvania.
124. Pollock, M. L., and Franks, B. D. (1972). Paper presented National College Phys. Ed. Ass. Men, New Orleans. (In press.)
125. Pollock, M. L., Miller, H. S., Janeway, R., Linnerud, A. C., Robertson, B., and Valentino, R. (1971). *J. Appl. Physiol.* **30**, 126–130.
126. Pollock, M. L., Miller, H. S., Linnerud, A. C., Royster, C. L., Smith, W. E., and Sonner, W. H. (1970). *Proc. 18th World Congr. Sports Med., Oxford, England.* (In press.)
127. Pollock, M. L., Miller, H. S., and Wilmore, J. H. (1972). *Proc. Sci. Congr. Sports Med. München.* (In press.)
128. Pollock, M. L., Tiffany, J., Gettman, L., Janeway, R., and Lofland, H. (1969). *In* "Exercise and Fitness: 1969" (B. D. Franks, ed.), pp. 161–178. Athletic Inst., Chicago, Illinois.
129. Rasch, P. J., and Kroll, W. (1964). "What Research Tells the Coach About Wrestling." AAHPER, Washington, D. C.
130. Ribisl, P. (1969). *Int. Z. Angew. Physiol.* **27**, 154–160.
131. Roberts, J. A., and Alspaugh, J. W. (1972). *Med. Sci. Sports* **4**, 6–10.
132. Robinson, S. (1938). *Arbeitsphysiologie* **10**, 251–323.
133. Robinson, S., and Harmon, P. M. (1941). *Amer. J. Physiol.* **132**, 757.
134. Roskamm, H. (1967). *Can. Med. Ass. J.* **96**, 895–899.

135. Roskamm, H., and Reindell, H. (1972). *In* "TRAINING Scientific Basis and Application" (A. W. Taylor, ed.), pp. 5-20. Thomas, Springfield, Illinois.
136. Rothermol, B. L. (1969). *In* "Exercise and Fitness: 1969" (B. D. Franks, ed.), pp. 97-106. Athletic Inst., Chicago, Illinois.
137. Rothermol, B. L., Pollock, M. L., and Cureton, T. K. (1968). *Res. Quart.* 39, 1127-1129.
138. Rowell, L. B. (1962). Ph.D. Thesis, Univ. of Minnesota, Minneapolis, Minnesota.
139. Rowell, L. B. (1971). *In* "Physiology of Work Capacity and Fatigue" (E. Simonson, ed.), pp. 132-169. Thomas, Springfield, Illinois.
140. Saltin, B., and Åstrand, P.-O. (1967). *J. Appl. Physiol.* 23, 353-358.
141. Saltin, B., Blomqvist, G., Mitchell, J., Johnson, R. L., Jr., Wildenthal, K., and Chapman, C. B. (1968). *Circulation* 37 and 38, Suppl. 7, 1-78.
142. Saltin, B., Hartley, L., Kilbom, A., and Åstrand, I. (1969). *Scand. J. Clin. Lab. Invest.* 24, 323-334.
143. Scheffield, L. T., Holt, J. H., and Reeves, T. J. (1965). *Circulation* 32, 622-629.
144. Sharkey, B. J. (1970). *Med. Sci. Sports* 2, 197-202.
145. Sharkey, B. J., and Holleman, J. P. (1967). *Res. Quart.* 38, 398-404.
146. Shephard, R. J. (1968). *Int. Z. Angew. Physiol.* 26, 272-278.
147. Sherman, M. (1967). Ph.D. Thesis, Univ. of Illinois, Urbana, Illinois.
148. Sidney, K. H., Eynon, R. B., and Cunningham, D. A. (1972). *In* "TRAINING Scientific Basis and Application" (A. W. Taylor, ed.), pp. 144-148. Thomas, Springfield, Illinois.
149. Siegel, W., Blomqvist, G., and Mitchell, J. H. (1970). *Circulation* 41, 19-29.
150. Sinisalo, U. V., and Juurtola, T. (1957). *Res. Quart.* 28, 288-294.
151. Skinner, J., Holloszy, J. O., and Cureton, T. K. (1964). *Amer. J. Cardiol.* 14, 747-752.
152. Skubic, V., and Hodgkins, J. (1965). *Res. Quart.* 36, 316-326.
153. Sloan, A. (1961). *J. Appl. Physiol.* 16, 167-169.
154. Swenson, E. W., and Zauner, C. W. (1971). *J. Sports Med. Phys. Fitness* 11, 112-117.
155. Taddonio, D. A. (1966). *Res. Quart.* 37, 276-281.
156. Taylor, H. L., Buskirk, E., and Henschel, A. (1958). *J. Appl. Physiol.* 8, 73-80.
157. Taylor, H. L., Erickson, L., Henschel, A., and Keys, A. (1945). *Amer. J. Physiol.* 144, 227-232.
158. Taylor, H. L., Haskell, W., Fox, S. M., III, and Blackburn, H. (1969). *In* "Measurement in Exercise Electrocardiography" (H. Blackburn, ed.), pp. 259-305. Thomas, Springfield, Illinois.
159. Taylor, H. L., Henschel, A., Brozek, J., and Keys, A. (1949). *J. Appl. Physiol.* 2, 223-239.
160. Tooshi, A. (1971). Paper presented to the American College of Sports Medicine, Toronto, Canada.
161. Wallin, C. C., and Schendel, J. S. (1969). *Res. Quart.* 40, 600-606.
162. Walter, C. E. (1953). *Res. Quart.* 24, 102-111.
163. Wessel, J. A., Small, D. A., Van Huss, W. D., Heusner, W. W., and Cederquist, D. C. (1966). *J. Geront.* 21, 168-181.
164. Williams, M. H., and Edwards, R. H. (1971). *Amer. Corr. Ther. J.* 25, 11-15.
165. Wilmore, J. H., and Haskell, W. (1971). *Amer. J. Clin. Nutr.* 24, 1186-1192.
166. Wilmore, J. H., Royce, J., Girandola, R. N., Katch, F. I., and Katch, V. L., (1970). *Med. Sci. Sports* 2, 7-14.

167. Wilmore, J. H., and Sigerseth, P. O. (1967). *J. Appl. Physiol.* **22**, 923–928.
168. Wyndham, C. H. (1967). *Can. Med. Ass. J.* **96**, 736–742.
169. Yeager, S. A., and Brynteson, P. (1970). *Res. Quart.* **41**, 589–592.
170. (1972). "Heart Facts, 1972." American Heart Association, New York.
171. (1971). "Physician's Handbook for Evaluation of Cardiovascular and Physical Fitness." Tennessee Heart Ass. Phys. Exercise Committee (B. D. Erb, Chm.), Nashville, Tennessee.
172. (1967). "The Scandinavian Committee on ECG Classification." *Acta Med. Scand. Suppl.* **481**.

Biomechanical and Neuromuscular Aspects of Running

Stanley L. James[1]

CENTER OF RESEARCH FOR HUMAN PERFORMANCE AND DEPARTMENT OF ATHLETICS,
UNIVERSITY OF OREGON, EUGENE, OREGON, AND UNIVERSITY OF
OREGON MEDICAL SCHOOL, PORTLAND, OREGON

and

Clifford E. Brubaker

CENTER OF RESEARCH FOR HUMAN PERFORMANCE, SCHOOL OF HEALTH, PHYSICAL
EDUCATION AND RECREATION, UNIVERSITY OF OREGON, EUGENE, OREGON

I. Introduction

The bipedal running gait of man is mechanically unique among terrestrial mammals. Man's adaptation to an upright posture has resulted in several disadvantages. Among the more dramatic changes are decreased stability and speed compared to some quadrupeds.

While running is, perhaps, of secondary importance to man as a means of locomotion, success in athletic endeavors is often dependent on one's ability to run. Running is also generally recognized as the most efficient method for developing cardiovascular endurance.

---

[1] Present address: Orthopedic and Fracture Clinic, P. C., 750 East 11th Avenue, Eugene, Oregon 97401.

The fact that running is a universal skill has resulted in the failure of many to appreciate the complexity of this act. The neuromuscular events that accompany even simple movements are staggering in their complexity. Although profound work has been done, the elucidation of many of the mechanisms which are essential to movement continues to be a challenge to neurophysiologists.

The mechanics of locomotion are also extremely complex. Bernstein (3) has reported that all human motion can be represented adequately by four harmonics, which indicates that the upper limits of human movement have at least some component velocity which is four times greater and acceleration which is 16 times greater than the basic component or period of the motion. Our own observations have indicated that 99% of the motion of the joints of the lower extremities of subjects running at a moderate pace can be described in three harmonics.

The difficulties in describing the mechanics of running quantitatively stem from the fact that virtually all the body parts are in motion simultaneously and, in the case of kinetic analysis, from the fact that precise determinations of the distribution of mass have been impossible.

II. Neuromuscular Aspects of Running

The neuromuscular events specific to human bipedal locomotion in general, and running in particular, are not unique. There is no evidence to indicate that natural locomotor behavior of humans is generated by mechanisms that are significantly different from those of other higher mammals. The phylogenetically unique bipedal gait of man would seem to require only differences in the sequence of neuronal transmission to produce a symmetrical running pattern as opposed to the asymmetric gait of the running quadruped. Evidence from clinical studies and research on animals with cortical lesions seems to indicate that there is some degree of inverse relationship between phylogenetic hierarchy and restoration of motor function following lesions in the motor areas of the cortex and pyramidal tracts. This would empirically suggest a greater level of involvement of cortical structures in the motor control of higher animals (14).

While this discussion is specifically directed to neuromuscular involvement in running, there is a relative paucity of specific information on this subject. Subsequent sections will be devoted to describing the functional mechanisms which regulate movement and to defining the anatomical structures involved. It is the purpose of this discussion to correlate these mechanisms to neuromuscular control of running.

A. Central Control of Movement

Patterned muscular activity is initiated and controlled through a hierarchical system of neural circuits which is somewhat analogous to a corporate bureaucracy in terms of organization and relegation of function at various levels. This similarity is limited, however, since the efficiency and precision of the nervous system are unparalleled in manmade control systems. The executive or highest level of control is responsible for decisions to initiate voluntary movement. Such activities are generally limited to the desire to accomplish some form of behavior, such as moving from one point to another, which incidentally involves locomotion. The urgency of the desire to move would presumably determine whether one walks or runs. It seems evident, however, that only the notion and the urgency of movement are decided at a conscious level. The detailed act of locomotion is controlled at subconscious levels of the nervous system. The nature of this process has been described by Adrian (1) who stated, ". . . the mind orders a particular movement but leaves its execution to the lower levels of the nervous system."

The execution of a patterned movement involves, in descending order, the central nervous system, peripheral neurons, muscles, and a system of bony levers upon which the muscles can exert force. Malfunction at any level can effectively eliminate the possibility of movement. Although the muscles, and the peripheral nerves which innervate them, are necessary to movement, it is evident that central mechanisms represent the essence of movement. Both nerve and muscle fibers exhibit a characteristic "all or none" response and, therefore, function in response to transmission from higher centers. It is the timing and distribution of impulses which cause the muscles to contract in an appropriate sequence to produce controlled movement. The formulation of such patterned neural transmission is dependent to some degree upon peripheral information to describe the attitude and position of body segments and length and tension of muscles. The process by which this information is used to modify efferent neural transmission to produce these movements, has been a topic of interest and discussion for nearly a century and has yet to be completely resolved.

Bernstein (3) posed certain minimum requirements for a self-regulated system to control movement. According to Bernstein, such a system must include an *effector*, a *control element*, a *receptor*, a *comparator*, an *encoding device*, and a *regulator*. Precise anatomical analogs of this system are evident for some elements but are necessarily vague for others. Two of the definite anatomical components necessary for movement according to this scheme are the muscles and proprioceptors which fulfill the respective roles of the effector and receptor elements. The anatomical delineation of a control element is less precise, but it is definitely of central origin. The specific designation of the remaining functions is speculative to some extent. The comparing, encoding, and regulating elements undoubtedly involve interconnections among cortex, basal ganglion, cerebellum, brain stem, and spinal cord. The functions of these structures in the control of movement are substantial and constitute the central feature of what has been described as the integrative action of the nervous system.

Houk and Henneman (*30*) have described a rather precise system for the control of voluntary movement. This system is illustrated in Fig. 1 with various subsystems presented in block form. The operation of the overall system depends on the presence of an independent signal which is generated as a result of a desire to move and a feedback signal which indicates the positions at joints which will participate in the movement. Although some important central structures are not included in this diagram, it serves to illustrate a hierarchical involvement in the control of movement. It is possible, from Fig. 1, to distinguish four levels of integration in the control of voluntary movement. Integrative activity occurs in respective order in the cerebral cortex, the descending pathways, the segmental levels of the spinal cord (as indicated by the positional control system), and in the ascending pathways which complete the feedback loop from the joint receptors (and other receptor mechanisms).

The notion of integrative activity at various levels of the nervous system is generally appreciated, and the idea of cortical information being transmitted downstream along the descending tracts is reasonably straightforward. However, a description of the mechanisms which

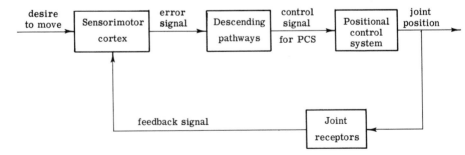

Fig. 1. A basic system to control voluntary movement. Reproduced from J. Houk, and E. Henneman (1968). *In* "Medical Physiology" (V. B. Mountcastle, ed.). Mosby, St. Louis, Missouri.

exercise control over skeletal muscles at the segmental level seems appropriate at this point.

Houk and Henneman (30) have used the term "positional control system" to describe the mechanisms by which length and tension are regulated for the muscles acting on a joint. They have pointed out that separate systems are necessary to control muscles acting in different planes of movement at a joint and that a single system is operative for two joints when it exercises control over biarticular muscles. For illustrative purposes, as in Fig. 1, the positional control system is considered to represent all length and tension control systems associated with a desired movement. In a complex movement such as running, this would include an enormous number of these subsystems.

The length-control system is based on excitation or inhibition of the alpha and gamma motor neurons which innervate paired antagonist muscles and their spindles which must shorten or lengthen to produce coordinated movements at the appropriate joints. Excitation can occur independently through either the alpha or gamma motor neurons. However, there is strong evidence to indicate that muscular contraction is mediated by means of simultaneous alpha and gamma activation.

A measure of control is exercised over muscles in opposition to a desired movement by means of afferent projections from the muscle spindles. Paired antagonist muscles have reciprocal innervations via spinal interneurons. These interneurons or internuncial cells are activated by afferent fibers from the muscle spindle and have an inhibitory effect on motor neurons of antagonist muscles.

The second component of the positional control system, the tension control system, is composed of a muscle and its Golgi tendon organ, which is geometrically "in series" with the muscle. The tendon organ is sensitive to tension and generates impulses which activate interneurons which have an inhibitory effect on the motor neurons innervating the muscle. The inhibitory effect of the interneuron biases the control signal which impinges on the motor neuron, resulting in the generation of an "error signal" to the muscle in a manner similar to the effect of muscle spindles on antagonist muscles.

The two systems operate in a complementary fashion to monitor and, to some extent, regulate the state of contraction in paired muscles. Although Houk and Henneman (30) have limited their definition of the positional control system to paired antagonist muscles, the influence of muscle spindles and tendon organs of a positional control system extends to synergist muscles about the joint and probably to muscles controlling joints in other extremities involved in a movement. The fact that the afferent fibers from the muscle spindles and tendon organs synapse on interneurons indicates the potential influence of these receptors on a large number of muscles. This concept will be discussed more fully in Section II,B.

The precision with which complex movements can be reproduced suggests that a central information storage exists which serves as a basis for voluntary movements. Hoyle (*31*) proposed a model to describe movement patterns in invertebrates by means of "motor tapes." According to this system, the initiation of instinctive behavior patterns would depend on either internal cues or some form of afferent input. However, after the appropriate "motor tape" is selected the behavior would be stereotyped and independent of feedback. Hoyle proposed a second model based on afferent or "sensory tapes" which contain stored proprioceptive data which could be compared with actual proprioception to generate specific motor commands. He suggested that the latter model would be more difficult to accept as a viable system for control of motor patterns. There is evidence to indicate that elements of both models are necessary to describe the control of movement in some invertebrate nervous systems (*12*).

The controversy over the control of movement has generally been concerned with the degree to which movement is affected by peripheral feedback. This subject has been reviewed recently by Delong (*12*), who pointed out that the control of movement is specific to different species and that there are examples of systems which are completely under central control. The amount of feedback evident in the regulation of movement appears to be directly related to phylogenetic hierarchy. In his review Delong discussed studies which lent support to three types of central patterning in the control of movement. The first type discussed was central patterning with automaticity, which can be described as a reverberating circuit in which control is mediated by means of rhythmic discharges from pacemaker neurons. This type of patterning is not thought to depend on any type of feedback. The second type of patterning was identified as central patterning with triggered movements. This form of control would seem to be exemplified by Hoyle's (*31*) motor tape model when "triggered" by afferent cues. Delong also discussed central patterning dependent on peripheral feedback. The earlier description of Houk's and Henneman's voluntary control system would serve to illustrate central control subject to feedback.

While the existing evidence of central patterning of higher mammals is mostly limited to behavioral research, there can be little serious doubt that complex movement patterns are subject to some form of centrally programmed control (*38*).

Egger and Wyman (*20*) have presented evidence which challenges the existence of an autonomous central patterning of movements. They found that the "reflex stepping" demonstrated by Sherrington (56) on de-afferented cats did not occur when both of an animal's hind limbs were stimulated simultaneously at identical frequencies. This lack of stepping activity was contrasted with a rhythmic stepping action when the two limbs were stimulated simultaneously at different frequencies. They found that a rhythmic alternate "stepping" response occurred at a rate of one step a second by each limb when the frequencies of the two stim-ulators differed by 1 Hz. They concluded that the occasional "stepping" observed by Sherrington may have been due to a frequency difference of his stimulators and that his demonstration may no longer be accept-able as evidence of an autonomous central rhythmicity. Although these findings would appear to discredit Sherrington's experiment, they do not preclude the probability of centrally programmed locomotor patterns. The quantitative and qualitative delineation of control mechanisms for mammalian locomotion (and other movement patterns) has suffered from the inability of investigators to completely isolate systems for study. Findings from such attempts have been subject to predictable criticisms.

Support for central programming in locomotion of cats has been pro-vided by Engberg and Lundberg (21). They found that the contraction of extensor muscles as indicated by electromyographic recordings pre-ceded contact of the foot with the supporting surface. They accepted this as evidence that feedback from the muscle spindles was not involved in initiating this extensor action and suggested that extensor and flexor ac-tivity was controlled by a central program.

The appearance of movements in infants resembling basic locomotor patterns would seem consistent with central patterning. Although such movement patterns exist, it is clear that the development of basic loco-motor movements, such as walking and later running, evolves in an orderly fashion and requires learning. The ability to improve movement patterns indicates a degree of plasticity in the central patterning of the nervous system as peripheral tracts and feedback loops are not subject to change under normal circumstances. This is important from a develop-mental standpoint as modification in movement patterns are necessary during periods of rapid growth. While a degree of plasticity in central patterning can be implied from an empirical standpoint, the extent of movement possible for any individual is limited by anatomical restric-tions and peripheral neural organization.

It has been observed that control of motion in running develops earlier in the proximal segments of the lower extremities of children than in their distal segment (3). Such an observation parallels the rather obvious lag in the development of control of hand movements with respect to gross limb movements of the more proximal segments of the upper extremity. Recent experiments (*37,52*) have revealed a considerably greater number of monosynaptic connections from pyramidal tract neurons of segmental motor neurons innervating the muscles that control the distal segments of a primate (baboon) than for a carnivore (cat). As will be discussed later, the greater number of pyramidal tract neurons synapse on interneurons and therefore, can potentially influence large numbers of muscles. This arrangement is advantageous in terms of coordinated actions of muscles and groups of muscles. However, such a system lacks the specific control of individual muscles necessary to produce fine movements or movements which require opposition of segments which normally act in concert. The latter acts are more readily accomplished by direct innervation of muscles as provided by monosynaptic connections. In terms of human locomotion, the movements involved at the ankle joint in placing the foot are more intricate than the basically reciprocal movements at the more proximal joints. The intricacy of finger manipulation as compared to upper extremity motion in more proximal segments illustrates this point more dramatically.

It is also interesting to consider movement patterns in terms of permanence. It is to be expected that inherent movement patterns such as running and walking will not be forgotten, but it is well known that such learned activities as swimming (various strokes) and cycling are retained indefinitely. This feature of the nervous system is two-edged. When a motor pattern has become habitual it yields to change rather grudgingly. It is obvious, however, that the advantages accruing to the ability to perform consistently with minimum concentration outweigh the disadvantage encountered when attempting to alter a movement pattern.

A comprehensive review of the central control of movement is not possible in the present treatment. For an extensive review of this subject the reader is referred to a report of the Neurosciences Research Program Work Session: "Central Control of Movement" (E. V. Ewarts, E. Bizzi, R. E. Burke, M. Delong, and W. T. Thach, Jr., eds.), *Neurosci. Res. Progr. Bull.* **9.**

B. NEURAL STRUCTURES

The localization of functions in the cerebral cortex has been the subject of extensive investigation. The results of these efforts have revealed the existence of discrete motor and sensory areas of the cortex. Although the concept of such a dichotomy has not been completely accepted by neurophysiologists due to the presence of sensory fibers in the motor cortex and similarly, motor fibers in the sensory cortex, it has considerable utility as a model. Precise electrical stimulation in the precentral or motor area can elicit specific behavioral responses. However, these responses may be significantly affected by other cortical areas and subcortical structures (2).

The efferent projections of the cerebral cortex extend over two tracts which have been designated as pyramidal and extrapyramidal tracts. The pyramidal system neurons descend as corticobulbar and corticospinal fibers. The corticospinal neurons form three tracts at the level of the medulla, with three-fourths of the fibers distributed into lateral tracts which decussate and descend bilaterally. The remaining fibers do not cross and descend bilaterally as lateral fibers or ventral corticospinal fibers. Approximately 80% of the corticospinal fibers terminate on interneurons with the remaining fibers ending in monosynaptic connections with segmental motor neurons (2). The greatest densities of monosynaptic connections from the corticospinal tracts have been observed in primates to be on alpha motor neurons innervating the more distal muscles of the limbs (50,52).

The significance of innervation of motor neurons at the segmental level via interneurons or by monosynaptic connections was mentioned earlier but bears repeating. The mechanism of dispersing cortical influence to a large number of motor neurons through interneurons provides a coordinating or integrative function essential to patterned movement. On the other hand, monosynaptic innervation provides for that precise manipulative control which is a distinguishing characteristic of man and the higher primates. The loss of pyramidal function, as in the case of cortical lesions, results in impaired function characterized by loss of fine motor control and decreased voluntary movement. The former is evident in the manifestation of cerebrovascular damage, in which upper extremity paralysis, particularly of the hand, predominates. Although some locomotor function may be restored eventually, it is present at a diminished level (2).

The extrapyramidal system collectively includes all efferent projections of the cerebral cortex which are not included in the pyramidal tracts. The projections of the extrapyramidal system terminate in the intermediate nuclei of the basal ganglia, brainstem reticular formation, and a number of additional subcortical structures. The interconnections of these various structures are extensive. The spinal projections of this extracorticospinal system are distributed via the rubrospinal, vestibulospinal, tectospinal, and reticulospinal tracts. It is apparent that extrapyramidal innervation can provide a measure of motor function exclusive of pyramidal innervation. However, such function is limited and deliberate in nature. The control functions of the extrapyramidal systems are apparent following pyramidal section and appear to be more substantial in the more primitive mammalian nervous systems. Evidence for a partial explanation of this observation was provided by Lund and Pompeiano (41), who found that monosynaptic connections to alpha motor neurons in the cat were from vestibulospinal tract neurons.

The effects of the reticular formation on muscular activity were demonstrated by Rhines and Magoun (43,54). In these classical studies with decerebrate preparations, they discovered that weak electrical stimulation in specific areas of the reticular formation could either facilitate or inhibit muscular activity. The significance of this structure on muscular activity is apparent from the relatively greater number of fibers in the reticulospinal tract as compared to the other extrapyramidal projections. While considerable reticulopetal influences have been attributed to the reticular formation, equally important is the integrative action of this structure in processing afferent transmission. This structure has the capacity to reject, modify, and integrate all sensory input to the brain (25). It is this process which allows the nervous system to function in the midst of a constant afferent bombardment. With the aid of this selective filtering action of the reticular formation, the nervous system is able to establish priorities and execute complex patterns of behavior.

The cerebellum receives afferent input similar to the reticular formation and has extensive interconnections with other supraspinal structures as well as direct spinocerebellar input. The efferent cerebellar influences are mediated in two stages. In the first stage impulses are transmitted from the cerebellar cortex to the intracerebellar nucleus by Purkinje cells. In the second stage fibers from the intracerebellar nuclei innervate the brainstem and thalamus. The projections of the extrapyramidal tracts from the reticular system were mentioned earlier; however, the cerebellar projections to the thalamus are relayed to the cerebral cortex. In addition, a number of Purkinje axons directly innervate Deiter's nucleus, which sends fibers directly to the spinal cord which end monosynaptically on motor neurons (34).

The cerebellum has long been recognized as a coordinating center for reflex and voluntary movement. Much of this control is affected by the damping of motor output from the cerebral cortex. The integrative function of the cerebellum is evident from observations of patients with cerebellar lesions. Such lesions are characterized by loss of coordination, poor equilibrium, and decreased tonus (55).

Although integration has been shown to be largely a supraspinal function, the spinal cord performs extensive motor and sensory integrative roles in voluntary and reflex movement which are mediated at segmental levels of the spinal cord through feedback loops facilitated by extensive reciprocal innervation of receptor organs and muscles. The multiple synaptic connections of interneurons with motor neurons at various segmental levels provide a control network capable of distributing impulses to the muscles in a temporal sequence that can produce coordinated locomotor movements. The basic elements of this system include the muscle spindle, Golgi tendon organ, and joint receptors. The latter category includes Pacinian corpuscles, Ruffini spray endings, and free nerve endings.

Segmental control was discussed earlier in terms of a "positional control system"; however, a more specific discussion of the elements of this system seems in order. The muscle spindle which functions as a length measuring device is arranged in parallel with extrafusal muscle fibers. Impulses are transmitted from the muscle spindle to the spinal cord, where dispersion occurs as a result of synapses on interneurons. In addition, the spindle afferents synapse with the alpha motor neurons to the extrafusal muscle. The spindles are innervated by gamma efferent neurons. Although a feedback system exists which would theoretically permit activation of alpha motor neurons by way of the gamma motor neurons, the bulk of evidence indicates that this does not occur. Several investigators have shown that muscular contraction occurs as a result of alpha and gamma coactivation (27,50,64). Recent evidence confirms that alpha and gamma activation in the spinal cord occur simultaneously (64). The importance of this coactivation has been described by Granit (27), who pointed out that the length detecting function of the spindle would be lost if alpha activation preceded gamma activation.

In contrast to the muscle spindle, the tendon organ is arranged "in series" with extra-fusal muscle and responds to tension. Afferent volleys from the tendon organ are transmitted to the cord where its dispersed effect is generally opposite to that of the muscle spindle as it has an inhibitory influence on the agonist muscle.

The Pacinian corpuscle, which is the third component of what Gardner (26) has referred to as the proprioceptive triad, provides information to describe the position of a joint. The Pacinian corpuscle provides information principally to describe movement, while other joint receptors indicate position. The perception of movement appears to be considerably more precise than the determination of position.

Although these kinesthetic receptors provide adequate information to control movement, it is apparent that visual input is used extensively to determine position and provide information necessary for precise regulation of movement.

C. LIMITING NEUROMUSCULAR FACTORS IN RUNNING

The basic considerations in running are speed, endurance, and efficiency. The last-mentioned is, of course, related to both speed and endurance. Although speed and endurance can be improved through training, it can be stated with confidence that genetic potential is the most important determinant of success for champion athletes. Much of the effort expended in the subdiscipline of exercise physiology has been devoted to determining the differences between champion athletes and the so-called "normal" population. It is important to distinguish that which is genetic from that which is developmental in considering factors which are limiting in human performance. Increased strength and endurance can be developed by appropriate changes in the muscular and cardiovascular systems and homeostatic equilibria. These topics are, however, covered extensively in other contributions to this volume and, therefore, will not be discussed here.

The activation of a neuron results from a summation of electrical activity to a threshold level. The classical model of neuronal activation is characterized by the summation of excitatory and inhibitory postsynaptic potentials which results in the generation of a spike potential at the initial segment if the threshold level is exceeded. The primary firing area of the neuron is the axon hillock. More recently, a secondary firing area in the dendritic region has been suggested. It is possible that small spike potentials in the dendrites increase to mature action potentials at confluences of dendrites (27).

The tension generated in a muscle contraction is determined by the number of motor units that are activated simultaneously. It is evident, then, that the number of motor neurons which receive sufficiently greater excitatory stimulation than inhibitory stimulation will determine the strength with which the muscle contracts. As indicated earlier, supraspinal centers exert a tonic inhibitory influence on motor neurons. A decrease in this inhibitory level allows for facilitated transmission, which can result in a greater expression of strength. Evidence to support this point was presented by Ikai and Steinhaus (33), who found that the expression of maximum voluntary strength could be increased when subjects were under the influence of posthypnotic suggestion or following an unexpected loud noise. They concluded that this phenomenon was due to a process of disinhibition.

Two early studies would appear to offer evidence of a relationship between such factors as reaction time, running speed, and running event. Westerlund and Tuttle (65) found that reaction time was fastest for sprinters, and slowest for distance runners, with middle distance runners in between. Lautenbach and Tuttle (*39*) found similar results for differences in reflex time. In both studies, high correlations were found for the variables of reaction time and reflex time with sprinting speed.

Slater-Hammel (*59*) attempted to determine if there was a neuromuscular factor which limited the rate of leg movement in sprinting. He found the stride rates of sprinting subjects to be considerably lower than their pedaling frequencies in maximum attempts on a stationary bicycle. He concluded that leg movements were not limited by a neuromuscular mechanism but rather by the load imposed on the muscles.

An increase in the efficiency of leg movements would appear to be a contributing factor to both speed and endurance. The degree to which efficiency can be effectively improved is, of course, related to a number of factors. What may appear to be inefficient movement is often secondary to a structural feature which may or may not be compatible with modification in movement patterns. Muscular characteristics can be quite influential in running; however, within genetic limitations, the muscular factors associated with running are affected principally by specific training.

D. Summary of Neuromuscular Events in Running

On the basis of present evidence it is quite reasonable to assume that there is a central program for running which can be activated by cortical action as a result of a desire to move. Although it is not possible to describe the precise mechanism, it is apparent that the basic pattern can be modulated according to immediate needs by afferent input. This could be conceived as a supraspinal operation which, through an integrative process, results in a patterned transmission of impulses to the spinal cord. The spinal cord would then provide a secondary integration, in which impulses are distributed in a synchronous fashion at segmental levels. The influence of the reciprocity of innervations of paired muscles about joints as well as with muscles at other joints and in other extremities, contributes to an orderly and coordinated pattern of movement.

III. Biomechanics of Running

A. Physical Characteristics

Inherited and developmental factors are responsible for the particular running form of an individual. No two people run precisely the same way because of variations in anatomic structure, anthropometric proportions, muscular strength, posture, training, and even mental attitude. Certainly there are inherited physiological and anatomic characteristics which are particularly advantageous but even with these, running is not a natural skill but one which must be learned.

Clarke (8) has shown that certain developmental and nondevelopmental traits of longitudinal significance are identifiable from elementary through high school levels of athletic competition. Good athletes displayed many common characteristics, but not all shared the same ones and those lacking in one trait compensated by superiority in another. Successful competitors were generally superior in maturity, body size, physique type, muscular strength and endurance, muscular power, social adjustment, and peer status. Longitudinal profile patterns differentiated among athletes who were outstanding at 12 years but not at 15, those not outstanding at 12 or at 15 years, and those who maintained excellence throughout. The four tests with greatest longitudinal significance in track and field were the 60 yard shuttle run, standing broad jump, Roger's Strength Index, and the physical fitness index, with only the standing broad jump being significant at all ages.

Tanner (63) studied the physiques of athletes who had met the qualifying standards for the 1960 Olympic Games. Data from anthropometric measurements, photogrammetric photographs, and X rays were analyzed. Significant differences in body size, shape, and structure among competitors in different events were noted. Sprinters were found to be generally small, muscular men with short legs, the middle distance runners were large, long-legged, fairly heavily muscled, and the long distance runners were small, short-legged and not very muscular. Tanner pointed out that not everyone had all the physical characteristics ideal for a particular event but some, through training, were able to compete successfully in an event for which they did not seem physically suited. The physiological and mechanical requirements of each event were discussed in relation to physique.

Malina et al. (44) studied the physiques of female track and field athletes. They found women sprinters to be short-legged and muscular, whereas distance runners were small, with narrow shoulders and hips and light muscles. In general, their findings were similar to Tanner's except for distance runners, where women were found to be relatively long-legged compared to their short-legged male counterparts. They concluded that gradients in size, physique, and body composition between events agreed with those reported for male athletes. Other studies have also reported the physical characteristics of distance runners (9–11,53).

B. Age and Sex

Running and walking are such familiar means of locomotion that we seldom consider them to be learned skills. Bernstein (*3*) has found no clear cut difference between running and walking up to age two. From two to five the earliest mechanical similarities to running first appear and between five years of age and puberty the evolution of walking and running patterns parallel each other until the adult form ensues at about puberty. Typical mechanical characteristics of the running gait first appear in the proximal lower extremity segments, and as the child grows, migrate to more distal segments. Bernstein felt that this is related to the greater degree of neuromuscular development necessary to coordinate the more distal segments. Beyond puberty, the basic gait pattern for running is established by physical and developmental determinants.

In general, women do not have the speed or endurance that men have. This is undoubtedly related to many factors, both physiological and structural. The relatively wider pelvis in women has been postulated to be a significant factor. Mechanically, a wider pelvis requires greater pelvic shift to keep the center of gravity over the weight bearing foot. Additional adjustment by the postural muscles is necessary and this contributes to inefficiency. Sills (*57*) has observed that females of a more masculine body build can run better than women with a more feminine build. Oyster and Wooten (*48*) conducted a study to determine the relationship of several anthropometric measures to the sprinting velocity of college women. They found the bitrochanteric diameter to exert a slightly negative effect on the ability to run rapidly. Other measurements, such as the obliquity of the femur and lateral hip displacement during single leg stance, showed little or no relationship to sprinting ability.

C. Segmental Body Analysis

Accurate determination of segmental centers of gravity presents a difficult problem. Although many data are available, they have limited applicability. The work of Braune and Fischer (*4*) has been utilized for years in kinetic gait analysis but the data were based on the study of a small number of frozen cadavers. They located the body's center of gravity just anterior to the second sacral vertebra but, unfortunately, it does not remain in this position when the body is in motion. It shifts position even with breathing, and with some body positions becomes extracorporeal. More recently, Dempster (*13*) and Drillis and Contini (*16*) have presented quite comprehensive data but still with limited applicability for analysis of a specific subject because of variations in age, sex, and physical stature. Bernstein (3) devised a method for determining the mass and center of gravity of limbs in living subjects by "planimetric measurements of volumes and volume moments of the limbs of the body and to the weighing of subjects in numerous, carefully determined, controlled positions on special twin support scales." Although this type of technique may be reasonably accurate, it can be very laborious. Duggar (17) made a comprehensive review of the literature concerning locations of centers of gravity of the human body and its segments. Data from several sources were compared along with a discussion of methods, limitations, and applicability. He concluded that, although the various techniques for determining the center of gravity have their limitations, they can provide useful data. Application of such data must be made with regard for (a) the accuracy required, (b) anthropometric characteristics of the population under consideration, and (c) equipment and body positions anticipated. Petak (49) has reported a method being developed for measuring body segment parameters using gamma radiation. The mass distribution of a human limb is determined by measuring its absorption of gamma radiation, which is proportional to the total mass of material through which the ray has passed. Data are fed directly into a computer which can quickly determine the center of gravity and moments of inertia. This approach to segmental analysis appears most promising.

D. KINEMATICS AND KINETICS

The mechanics of the running gait may be discussed in terms of kinematics, the geometry of motion, and kinetics, which deal with forces producing motion. The kinetics have not been as precisely defined as the kinematics due to the inability of investigators to accurately determine masses and centers of gravity of body segments. As a result, uniform values have been used which generally preclude sophisticated kinetic comparisons.

Running is a form of locomotion with an alternate support and airborne phase. The airborne phase is the characteristic which most differentiates running from walking. Each lower extremity has a cyclical motion divided into a support and recovery phase. Slocum and James (60) further divided the support and recovery phases into three periods each. The three periods in the support phase are *foot strike, midsupport,* and *take-off.* Functions of the support extremity are (a) to absorb the impact of foot strike, (b) support the body's weight, (c) maintain forward motion, and (d) accelerate the body's center of gravity against internal and external resistances. At foot strike (Fig. 2a), the initial impact is absorbed by the foot, ankle, and knee joints reenforced by appropriate musculotendinous units. When maintaining constant velocity, foot contact is slightly ahead of the body and ideally at zero velocity in relation to the ground. This minimizes the braking action from ground reaction; however, a small degree of braking action is present due to forward inclination of the extremity at foot strike. The body then passes over the foot by a combination of active hip extension and the body's inertia (Fig. 2b). The segmental articulation of the lower extremity and the mobile lumbar spine–pelvic unit function as a stable, adjustable strut to assure that the body's center of gravity follows a smooth undulating path in the sagittal plane, with the low point occurring during midsupport and the high point just after take-off. This necessitates relative shortening of the extremity during midsupport and relative lengthening during take-off. Relative shortening is accomplished by downward pelvic tilt, knee flexion, and ankle dorsiflexion. Relative lengthening is a function of upward pelvic tilt, posterior pelvic rotation, hip extension, knee extension, and ankle plantar flexion. During take-off (Fig. 2c), a powerful extensor thrust is created which initiates in the stronger, slower muscles of the lumbar spine–pelvic unit and migrates to the distal, but faster and weaker, muscles of the leg and foot. This sequential muscular activity provides a summation of forces (18) whose resultant propels the body into its airborne trajectory.

The recovery phase requires that the extremity's direction be reversed twice and consequently it consumes the greater amount of time and energy. The efficiency with which the recovery phase can be performed is a major factor in determining maximum speed. Efficiency is greatly influenced by the lower extremity's inertia and the power available to accelerate and decelerate it. As speed increases, time for the support phase decreases and a point is eventually reached when the recovery extremity cannot be brought forward rapidly enough for the next succeeding foot strike without creating an excessive braking action. The recovery phase consists of three periods, which are *follow through, forward swing,* and *foot descent.* Follow through (Fig. 2d) begins immediately after "toe off." The thigh is decelerated and the knee begins to flex either passively, due to a relative difference in the rate of deceleration of the thigh and leg, or by active muscular contraction of the hamstrings or possibly the gastrocnemius. With active hip flexion, the thigh swings forward, transferring angular momentum to the lighter leg and foot segment enhancing knee flexion. The foot passes backward and upward in an arc, attains its maximum trailing position, and continues to swing upward and forward behind the thigh. The forward swing period (Fig. 2e) begins with forward motion of the foot rather than the thigh because the path of the foot more closely coincides with the path followed by the extremity's common

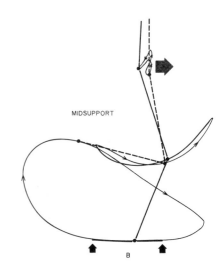

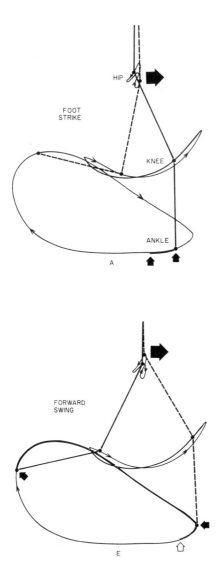

Fig. 2. Diagrammatic illustration of the relative positions of a subject's lower extremities while running on a treadmill at 12 m.p.h. The path of the hip, knee, and ankle are labeled in (a). The heavy dark line along the path of the ankle depicts the approximate duration of each period through the support and recovery phases. The right extremity is represented by a solid line connecting the three joints and the left extremity by a dotted line. The figures are as follows: (a) right foot strike and early left forward swing; (b) right midsupport and left forward swing; (c) start of right take-off (heel rise) with left forward swing; (d) start of right follow through (toe off) and late left forward swing; (e) simultaneous onset of right forward swing and left foot descent (with the subject airborne). A step would be completed at the subsequent left foot strike.

center of gravity. The amount of knee flexion increases with greater speed. This effectively reduces the extremity's moment of inertia about the hip and facilitates rapid forward swing with minimal muscular exertion. The vigorous forward swing of the recovery extremity increases ground reaction of the support extremity and enhances forward thrust. The thigh terminates its forward swing coincident with toe off of the op-

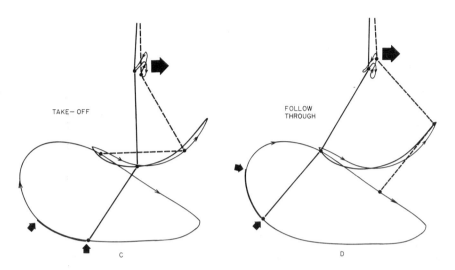

TAKE—OFF

FOLLOW
THROUGH

C

D

posite extremity and then reverses direction. Meanwhile the quadriceps
have already initiated active knee extension, which is enhanced by transfer of angular momentum from the rearward swinging thigh. A moment
later, the leg and foot are decelerated and their forward motion arrested
by vigorous hamstring activity. The foot descent (Fig. 2e) period is
entered and the foot accelerates toward the running surface, attaining a
velocity equal but opposite to that of the center of gravity at foot strike
and a stride is completed. Throughout the running cycle, the lower extremities are temporally 180 deg out of phase.

The reciprocal action of the lower extremities creates moments about
the body's center of gravity which must be counteracted. This is accomplished by rotation of the upper body and a reciprocal action of the arms.
The arms swing synchronously with their respective contralateral extremities and the trunk rotates away from the support extremity. Forward
translation of the center of gravity occurs with optimal vertical and
transverse displacement.

Slocum and Bowerman (61) have indicated that the trunk should be
nearly erect in running. This position favors mobility of the lumbar
spine–pelvic unit and requires less effort in maintaining postural equilibrium. Excessive forward lean reduces mobility of the lumbar spine–pelvic
unit, reduces hip flexion relative to the running surface, prevents maximum forward placement of the recovery foot, places excessive stress on
the foot at foot strike, and requires additional effort from the postural
muscles to maintain balance.

Kinetic analysis of walking has provided considerable data gathered
through the use of accelerometers, electrogoniometers, force plates, various

photographic techniques and electromyography. Many of these techniques are also applicable to running gait analysis but some have definite limitations.

In 1865 E. J. Marey (*46*) gave a detailed description of running utilizing the chronophotographic technique, an antecedent of the movie camera. Data for Fenn's (*22,23*) classic works on running in 1929 and 1930 were collected using a movie camera at 120 frames per second. Since then, cinematographic analysis in biomechanical investigation of gait has become commonplace (see Atwater, this volume, p. 217; Adrian, this volume, p. 339). High speed cameras are now available and analysis of data from the film is greatly facilitated by the use of motion analyzers. Three dimensional photographic analysis by using two cameras simultaneously from different angles is currently being utilized for motion analysis and seems promising for running gait studies (*28*). Plagenhoef (*51*) has formulated computer programs for obtaining kinetic data on human movement recorded by means of cinematography. The first program computes body segment angular velocities and angular accelerations, and the second program determines joint forces, moments of force, total body centers of gravity, and the contribution of each body segment to the whole motion. Present data for segmental analysis impose obvious limitations already discussed. Cavagna *et al.* (*5*) initially determined the displacement of the center of gravity and mechanical work in running using a triple accelerometer and motion pictures at 32 frames per second, but found that it was difficult to position the accelerometer so that consistent results could be obtained. They subsequently resorted to the use of high speed cinematography and made calculations according to the method of Fischer (*24*) and Fenn (*22*).

Sinning and Forsyth (*58*) have used one plane electrogoniometers to measure step length, frequency, and angular displacement of the hip, knee, and ankle at different running velocities. Johnston and Smidt (*35*) developed an electrogoniometer capable of measuring motion about three primary axes at the hip; Kettelkamp *et al.* (*36*) adapted it to the knee for walking, but the mass of the instrument precludes its use in running. Unfortunately, techniques requiring instruments to be attached to the limb in running are hampered by difficulty in securing them adequately to the rapidly moving extremity so that reliable readings can be taken; also, they may alter the stride (see Adrian, this volume).

Fenn (*23*) used a force plate to record the horizontal forces of the foot during support and found a slight, initial backward force which momentarily checked the runner's forward velocity at foot strike. However, some recordings, particularly those of the better runners, were not inconsistent with zero velocity of the foot at contact. He attributed the initial braking action to the fact that foot strike occurred slightly ahead of the body's center of gravity due to forward inclination of the extremity. The forces at foot strike resolved into a vertical and horizontal component. The average loss of forward velocity at foot strike was 13 cm/sec. The disadvantage of using a force plate is that the runner may modify his gait slightly to strike the plate and only one step at a time can be analyzed. Cavagna *et al.* (*6*) have used a force plate to study the mechanics of sprinting. Their data indicated a progressive reduction, with increasing speed, of the efficiency by which the positive work furnished by the muscles is transformed into a kinetic energy increase of the body. They concluded that the speed in sprint running is limited by (a) the deceleration of the body at each step, (b) air resistance, and (c) reduction of the duration of the push. Based on data from this study and earlier work (*7*), they felt that a significant portion of the power output at high speed was sustained by mechanical energy stored in the "series elastic elements" during stretching of the contracted muscles (negative work) and released immediately afterward in the positive work phase.

Dillman (*15*) conducted a kinetic analysis of the lower extremity during the recovery phase. His study revealed muscular torque patterns, the sequence of dominant muscular group activity, types of muscular contraction (concentric or eccentric), and ranges of segmental motion where effective muscular torques were applied. Body segment parameters for the subjects were estimated from average values determined in previous studies. The largest torques were developed about the hip, torques about the knee were somewhat less, and torques about the ankle were almost negligible. A greater percentage of time for effective torque application at the hip was devoted to concentric contraction and, conversely, eccentric contraction at the knee. The sequence of muscle group activity during recovery was initially the hip flexors, followed by the knee extensors and ankle plantar flexors.

The pattern of muscular contraction about both the hip and knee was eccentric, concentric, ballistic (period of negligible muscular activity), eccentric, and concentric. This sequence coincides nicely with kinematic analysis of the recovery phase. The initial eccentric contraction of the hip flexors decelerates the thigh during follow through. The flexors are put on a slight stretch which enhances their forceful concentric contraction to initiate forward swing of the thigh. Subsequently, an eccentric contraction of the hip extensors decelerates the thigh and a final concentric contraction at the termination of the recovery phase reverses the motion of the thigh and the hip extends.

The initial eccentric contraction of the knee extensors controls the amount of knee flexion during follow through and the first portion of forward swing. About midway through forward swing, a concentric contraction of the knee extensors initiates extension to swing the leg and foot forward. The knee flexors contract eccentrically to decelerate the leg and foot at the end of forward swing and then contract concentrically to flex the knee slightly during foot descent in preparation for foot strike.

Ballistic motion is defined as movement of a segment secondary to its momentum and in the absence of muscular activity. Hubbard (*32*) felt ballistic motion prevailed during the recovery phase. He proposed that isometric contractions at the moment the limb segment reversed directions imparted sufficient momentum to the segment to carry it through the necessary range of motion without additional muscular activity. Dillman's (*15*) work corroborates this theory in some respects in that he felt there was a period of ballistic motion, although of shorter duration, and that perhaps isometric contraction occurred between each eccentric and concentric phase when limb segments reversed direction. Whether or not a ballistic motion occurs in the true sense of the word is problematic. MacConaill and Basmajian (*42*) state that ballistic motion occurs only with "very violent activity" and that one prime mover is always active while a bone is moving at a joint, unless gravity can take its place. The final answer awaits the application of electromyographic analysis to running.

Our own attempts to describe and compare the running gaits of individuals have been based on mechanical analysis of motion of segments and joint centers of the extremities. Bernstein (*3*) conducted a number of investigations on human motion utilizing Fourier analysis and concluded that human motion can be described by four harmonics. Our attempts to determine functions to fit the paths of motion of joint centers with polynomials can only be described as unsuccessful. Subsequent attempts to describe these motions by means of Fourier analysis were made in collaboration with members of the Physics Department of the University of Oregon.[2] In these investigations the first seven harmonics were computed for the motion of the joint centers of running subjects. The original data were then plotted and successive harmonics were superimposed. The first order harmonic in each case was an ellipse. The addition of higher order harmonics resulted in successive perturbations until the resultant pattern included or very closely approximated all the original datum points. This was accomplished in each case with the addition of the fourth order harmonic. On the basis of these observations, we have concluded that, due to the error of measurement, the approximation of

---

[2] Professor J. L. Powell, and J. Nosler, Systems Engineer, Department of Physics, University of Oregon, Eugene, Oregon.

the path of motion by Fourier analysis more closely approaches the real movement than our actual data.

Our results are generally in agreement with Bernstein's conclusion with respect to the extent of motion. The distribution of the first seven harmonics of the motion of the head and the hip, knee, and ankle joints for a middle distance runner running on a treadmill at 9 m.p.h. are presented in Table I. The numbers in Table I can be considered the percentage of the motion contributed by the harmonic order. These "percentages" were determined from coefficients of the function for the X and Y components and normalizing them to 100 for the first seven harmonic orders.

The paths of motion of the joint centers of the hip, knee, and ankle joint represented in Fig. 2 and the harmonic distributions in Table I were determined from the same data. When viewing Fig. 2, it is not particularly difficult to see that the component of the motion for the ankle joint would be elliptical; however, some imagination is helpful in visualizing the ellipse of best fit for the first harmonic of motion at the knee and hip joints.

The data for the computations reflected in Table I were collected from high speed motion picture film and digitized by hand using a reticule. The "percentages" of 1.91 and 1.55 for the X component of the fifth harmonic for the head and knee are the result of incorrect coordinates. The contributions of all harmonics after the fourth order are undoubtedly due to errors in the data. If the latter are disregarded, it becomes evident that more than 99 "percent" of the motion was described by the first three harmonics. These results, and those of Bernstein, are quite reasonable when one considers that while velocity is directly proportional to the harmonic order, acceleration is directly proportional to the square

TABLE I

THE DISTRIBUTION OF HARMONIC ORDERS FOR THE HEAD AND JOINT CENTERS OF THE LOWER EXTREMITY DURING RUNNING

	Distribution of harmonics (%)							
	Head		Hip		Knee		Ankle	
Harmonic order	X	Y	X	Y	X	Y	X	Y
1	54.95	18.17	96.03	31.25	80.50	7.59	98.58	97.57
2	39.75	78.02	3.47	60.05	12.02	89.45	1.19	2.19
3	2.11	2.96	0.45	8.01	0.48	0.71	0.21	0.18
4	0.85	0.55	0.03	0.15	0.89	0.59	0.01	0.00
5	1.91	0.05	0.01	0.20	1.55	0.05	0.00	0.01
6	0.02	0.11	0.00	0.06	0.07	0.09	0.00	0.04
7	0.09	0.08	0.00	0.09	0.47	0.13	0.00	0.00

of the harmonic order. This would mean that the motion described by the fourth harmonic would have accelerations 16 times greater than the first harmonic. The presence of higher order harmonics would indicate extreme accelerations. Subsequent efforts at data collection and processing were made utilizing stroboscopic and on-line computerized procedures. Some preliminary work, with accomplished runners serving as subjects, has provided information which may cast some doubt on the precision with which a skilled runner executes successive strides. Further work is under-way to determine if the extent of an individual's variability is great enough to preclude quantitative comparisons among individuals.

IV. Pathological Factors Affecting Running Gait

A track athlete with certain desirable, basic physical and structural characteristics, along with appropriate training, has the potential for ex-ceptional performance. As previously indicated, inherited traits vary from one individual to the next and the athlete may not be able to com-pensate for some of the less desirable ones. The skeleton determines the mechanical relationship of muscle to joints and the various body seg-ments must be coordinated to produce a smooth, forward translation of the center of gravity. Any alteration in function of one part, whether inherited or acquired, will necessitate compensatory changes throughout. These changes may affect overall mechanical efficiency sufficiently to eliminate an individual from competitive status. Coaching and training can improve certain postural and technical discrepancies but little can be done for significant anatomic variations detrimental to running.

Foot problems are quite common to runners and are related to struc-tural abnormalities, overuse, and faulty technique. The foot usually strikes the running surface in a mildly inverted position so that the axes of the talonavicular and calcaneocuboid joints are in divergent planes to provide stabilization of the midtarsal joints (45). During mid-support, the foot everts and additional support to the longitudinal arch system is provided by the intrinsic and extrinsic muscles of the foot and the plantar fascia. The universal jointlike action of the ankle, subtalar, and midtarsal joints provides mobility so that the foot may adapt to the running surface (67). During take-off the foot inverts to stabilize the midtarsal joints when maximum thrust is exerted against the ground. The most common problems associated with the foot are stress fractures of the second, third, and fourth metatarsals, plantar fascial strains, and strains of the longitudinal arch and transverse metatarsal arch. Fatigue or stress fractures quite commonly occur with repetitive overuse, particularly associated with running on the ball of the foot, running on hard surfaces, and with prolonged, strenuous effort by unconditioned athletes. The plantar fascia, which arises from the calcaneus and inserts into the proximal phalanx of each toe distally, helps maintain the height of the longitudinal arch of the foot when the heel is off the ground (29). Considerable stress is placed on the plantar fascia at take-off, and a strain may occur from overuse, particularly with a high arched foot (pes cavus), or by overloading the forefoot due to faulty techniques. Longitudinal arch strain is a result of dynamic depression of the arch when the foot everts in midsupport (62). The intrinsic musculature reinforces the arch with assistance from the extrinsic plantar flexors. These structures, as well as ligaments of the long arch, may react to overload from repetitive stress. Flat feet (pes planus) may contribute to longitudinal arch strain because in this condition the forefoot is excessively pronated and stability of the midtarsal joints is diminished. The intrinsic and extrinsic muscles must contract sooner during the support phase to support the arch, and early fatigue ensues. Metatarsal arch strain is a result of spreading the foot and straining the intermetatarsal ligaments. This is likely to occur with a high arched foot, running on the toes excessively, or forward lean which places an increased load on the metatarsal heads.

Rotational deformities of the lower extremities are caused by tibial torsion, femoral torsion, femoral neck anteversion or retroversion, and flat feet. Severe flat feet create an internal rotation of the entire lower extremity with internal rotation of the hips, forward tipping of the pelvis, increased lumbar lordosis with reduced hip flexion, and diminished lumbar spine–pelvic unit mobility. Regardless of rotational abnormalities, the hip abductor mechanism is usually positioned to provide optimum mechanical advantage for the abductors, and any deviation from this diminishes the efficiency of the abductor mechanism during the support phase (47). An attempt to correct rotation so that the individual runs with his feet straight ahead alters the abductor mechanism and, in addition, may place a torsional stress on ligamentous structures at the knee. In essence, the gait may appear improved, but actually is less efficient. A painful condition from chronic, torsional stress of the knee ligaments sometimes occurs. Rotational deviations may also create malalignment of the quadriceps mechanism, resulting in excessive wear of the patella and joint surfaces.

Moderate genu valgum (knock knees) and genu varum (bow legs) are tolerated well. Excessive genu valgum creates increased stresses on the medial capsular structures of the knee and excessive lateral joint wear. If the foot is placed along the line of progression, excessive lateral trunk shift will be required to keep the body over the support foot by an additional effort of the postural muscles. Severe genu varum places increased stress on the lateral capsular structures and medial joint surfaces. Again, excessive trunk shift is required to keep the center of gravity over the support foot.

A normal, mobile, lumbar spine–pelvic unit is necessary to initiate forces for lower extremity motion and it relatively lengthens the lower extremity by making the effective length of the extremity extend from the lumbar spine to the foot, rather than just from the hip to the foot. Limitation of motion in the lumbar spine–pelvic unit may result from scoliosis, epiphysitis, habitual lumbar lordosis, dorsal kyphosis, spondylolisthesis, degenerative disc disease, and spinal fusion. Reduced lumbar spine–pelvic mobility seriously hampers running form.

Musculotendinous injuries commonly involve the hamstrings and quadriceps. They are often the result of intrinsic overload involving the contractile elements. Quadriceps strains are most likely to occur during take-off, particularly in sprinting when there is a vigorous contraction of the quadriceps during acceleration. A rupture within the substance of the muscles or avulsion from the patella can occur. Hamstring strains are most prone to occur at the termination of forward swing when they are contracting vigorously to simultaneously extend the hip and decelerate the forward swinging leg and foot in preparation for reversal of direction. Muscle fatigue with incomplete relaxation between contractions and perhaps disturbances in neuromuscular coordination quite likely play an additional role in musculotendinous injuries.

There does appear to be increased vulnerability to injury in athletes over 30 years of age. Tendonitis, fatigue fracture, musculotendinous strains, ligament sprains, and low back pain are quite common. Levinthal (40) attributes this to residual effects of previous injuries, slowing of reflexes, decreased "elasticity" of connective tissue, and the inability of certain tissues to restore themselves after injury.

References

1. Adrian, E. D. (1947). "The Physical Background of Perception." Oxford Univ. Press, London and New York.
2. Bard, P. (1968). *In* "Medical Physiology" (V. B. Mountcastle, ed.) pp. 1790–1807. Mosby, St. Louis, Missouri.
3. Bernstein, N. (1967). "The Co-ordination and Regulation of Movements." Pergamon, Oxford.
4. Braune, W., and Fischer, O. (1889). *Abh. Math.-Phys. Kl. Saechs. Ges. Wiss.* **15**, 561–572.
5. Cavagna, G. A., Margaria, R., and Arcelli, E. (1965). *Encycl. Cinematog.* **5**, 309–319.

6. Cavagna, G. A., Komarek, L., and Mazzoleni, S. (1971). *J. Physiol. (London)* **217**, 709–721.
7. Cavagna, G. A., Saibene, F. A., and Margaria, R. (1964). *J. Appl. Physiol.* **19**, 249–256.
8. Clarke, H. H. (1966). *Proc. 8th Nat. Con. Med. Aspects Sports*, pp. 49–57.
9. Costill, D. L. (1967). *J. Sports Med. Phy. Fitness* **7**, 61–66.
10. Cureton, T. K. (1951). "Physical Fitness of Champion Athletes." Univ. of Illinois Press, Urbana, Illinois.
11. Currens, J. H., and White, P. D. (1961). *New Engl. J. Med.* **265**, 788–793.
12. Delong, M. (1971). *Neurosciences Res. Progr. Bull.* **9**, 10–30.
13. Dempster, W. (1955). *WADC Tech. Rep. No. 55–159*.
14. Denny-Brown, D. (1966). "The Cerebral Control of Movement." Thomas, Springfield, Illinois.
15. Dillman, C. J. (1970). *In* "Biomechanics II" (J. M. Cooper, ed.), pp. 132–165. Athletic Institute, Chicago, Illinois.
16. Drillis, R., and Contini, R. (1966). *Tech. Rep. No. 1166.03*. Clearing House for Federal and Technical Information, Springfield, Va.
17. Duggar, B. C. (1962). *Human Factor* **4**, 131–148.
18. Dyson, G. H. G. (1967). "The Mechanics of Athletics." Univ. of London Press, London.
19. Eccles, J. C. (1964). "The Physiology of Synapses." Springer-Verlag, Berlin and New York.
20. Egger, M. D., and Wyman, R. J. (1969). *J. Physiol. (London)* **202**, 501–516.
21. Engberg, I., and Lundberg, A. (1969). *Acta Physiol. Scand.* **75**, 614–630.
22. Fenn, W. O. (1929). *Amer. J. Physiol.* **92**, 583–611.
23. Fenn, W. O. (1930). *Amer. J. Physiol.* **23**, 433–462.
24. Fischer, O. (1911). *Tigerstedts Handb. Physiol. Meth. II* **1**, 118–208.
25. French, J. D. (1960). *In* "Handbook of Physiology," Section I, Vol. 2: Neurophysiology (J. Field, H. W. Magoun, and J. Hall, eds.), pp. 1281–1305. Amer. Physiol. Soc., Washington, D. C.
26. Gardner, E. (1963). "Fundamentals of Neurology." Saunders, Philadelphia, Pennsylvania.
27. Granit, R. (1970). "The Basis of Motor Control." Academic Press, New York.
28. Gutewort, W. (1971). *In* "Human Body Motions" (J. Vredenbregt and J. Wartenweiler, eds.). Univ. Press, Baltimore, Maryland.
29. Hicks, J. H. (1954). *J. Anat.* **88**, 25–31.
30. Houk, J., and Henneman, E. (1967). *Brain Res.* **5**, 433–451.
31. Hoyle, G. (1964). *In* "Neural Theory and Modeling" (R. F. Reiss, ed.), pp. 346–376. Stanford Univ. Press, Stanford, California.
32. Hubbard, A. W. (1939). *Res. Quart.* **20**, 28–38.
33. Ikai, M., and Steinhaus, A. H. (1961). *J. Appl. Physiol.* **16**, 157–163.
34. Ito, M. (1967). *In* "Neurophysiological Basis of Normal and Abnormal Motor Activities" (M. D. Yahr and D. P. Purpura, eds.), pp. 119–140. Hewlett, New York.
35. Johnston, R. C., and Smidt, G. L. (1969). *J. Bone Joint Surg.* **51-A**, 1083–1094.
36. Kettlekamp, D. B., Johnston, R. C., Smidt, G. L., Chao, E. Y. S., and Walker, M. (1970). *J. Bone Joint Surg.* **52-A**, 775–790.
37. Koeze, T. H., Phillips, C. G., and Sheridan, J. D. (1968). *J. Physiol. (London)* **195**, 419–449.
38. Konorski, J. (1967). "Integrative Activity of the Brain." Univ. of Chicago Press, Chicago, Illinois.

39. Lautenbach, R., and Tuttle, W. W. (1932). *Res. Quart.* **3**, 138–143.
40. Levinthal, D. H. (1960). *Postgrad. Med.* **28**, 121–129.
41. Lund, S., and Pompeiano, O. (1968). *Acta Physiol. Scand.* **73**, 1–21.
42. MacConaill, M. A., and Basmajian, J. V. (1969). "Muscles and Movements." Williams & Wilkins, Baltimore, Maryland.
43. Magoun, H. W., and Rhines, R. (1946). *J. Neurophysiol.* **9**, 165–171.
44. Malina, R. M., Harper, A. B., Avent, H. H., and Campbell, D. E. (1971). *Med. Sci. Sports* **3**, 32–38.
45. Mann, R., and Inman, V. T. (1964). *J. Bone Joint Surg.* **46-A**, 469–481.
46. Marey, E. J. (1865). "Development de la method gratique par l'emploi de la photographie." Paris.
47. Merchant, A. C. (1965). *J. Bone Joint Surg.* **47-A**, 462–476.
48. Oyster, N., and Wooten, E. P. (1971). *Med. Sci. Sports* **3**, 130–134.
49. Petak, K. L. (1970). *In* "Biomechanics" (J. M. Cooper, ed.), pp. 201–205. Athletic Institute, Chicago, Illinois.
50. Phillips, C. G. (1969). *Proc. Roy. Soc. Ser. B* **173**, 141–174.
51. Plagenhoef, S. (1968). *J. Biomech.* **13**, 221–234.
52. Preston, J. B., Shende, M. C., and Uemura, K. (1967). *In* "Neurophysiological Basis of Normal and Abnormal Motor Activities" (M. D. Yahr and D. P. Purpura, ed.), pp. 61–72.
53. Pugh, L. G. C. E., Corbett, J. L., and Johnson, R. H. (1967). *J. Appl. Physiol.* **23**, 347–352.
54. Rhines, R., and Magoun, H. W. (1964). *J. Neurophysiol.* **9**, 219–229.
55. Ruch, T. C. (1965). *In* "Physiology and Biophysics" (T. C. Ruch and H. D. Patton, eds.), pp. 280–301. Saunders, Philadelphia, Pennsylvania.
56. Sherrington, C. S. (1913). *J. Physiol. (London)* **47**, 196–214.
57. Sills, F. D. (1960). *In* "Science and Medicine of Exercise and Sports" (W. R. Johnson, ed.), p. 51. Harper, New York.
58. Sinning, W. E., and Forsyth, H. L. (1970). *Med. Sci. Sports* **2**, 28–34.
59. Slater-Hammel, A. T. (1941). *Res. Quart.* **12**, 745–746.
60. Slocum, D. B., and James, S. L. (1968). *J. Amer. Med. Ass.* **205**, 720–728.
61. Slocum, D. B., and Bowerman, W. (1962). *Clin. Orthop.* **23**, 39–45.
62. Slocum, D. B. (1960). *Instruct. Lect. Amer. Acad. Orthopaed. Surg.* **17**, pp. 359–367.
63. Tanner, J. M. (1964). "The Physique of the Olympic Athlete." Allen & Ulwin, London.
64. Vallbo, A. B. (1971). *J. Physiol. (London)* **318**, 405–431.
65. Westerlund, J. H., and Tuttle, W. W. (1931). *Res. Quart.* **2**, 95–100.
66. Woodbury, W. J. (1965). *In* "Physiology and Biophysics" (T. C. Ruch and H. D. Patton, eds.), pp. 26–58. Saunders, Philadelphia, Pennsylvania.
67. Wright, D. G., Desai, S. M., and Henderson, W. H. (1964). *J. Bone Joint Surg.* **46-A**, 361–464.

Cinematographic Analyses of Human Movement

Anne E. Atwater

DEPARTMENT OF PHYSICAL EDUCATION FOR WOMEN,
THE UNIVERSITY OF ARIZONA, TUCSON, ARIZONA

I. Introduction

During the past quarter century, cinematography, in particular, high speed photography, has become increasingly useful as a technique for studying human movement (*48,123*). The motion picture camera has made it possible to record transient, rapid movements so that they may be preserved and viewed later at slower speeds. Qualitative and quantitative analyses of such films have revealed many details of motor skills that previously had not been observed or described accurately.

Numerous motor skills have been subjected to cinematographic analysis with the purpose usually being to identify the motion characteristics of skillful performers (*44*). Investigations of the movement patterns of unskilled subjects or of subjects with movement disabilities also have been conducted and, in several instances, the differences in the patterns of performers at various levels of skill have been identified (*220*). For the most part, these studies of motor skills have been confined to an analysis of temporal and kinematic aspects of the movement and only occasionally have encompassed kinetic factors.

The cinematographic analyses of human movement to be reviewed in this paper have been categorized according to the type and purpose of the motion that was studied. Motor skills having similar purposes or goals and similar joint actions or movement patterns will be discussed within the same category. The classification scheme used in this paper is a modification of that originally proposed by Glassow (*94*) and of those found in several current kinesiology publications (*25,44,220*). Only the motor skills or patterns for which there exists sufficient material obtained from cinematographic analyses are included in this review.

II. The Body Moving and Supporting Itself

The capability of man to move his entire body or its parts from one place to another or to maintain any desired position is essential to participation in sport, dance, and exercise activities, and to the quality and enjoyment of life itself. Movement of the entire body over a changing base of support occurs in locomotor activities, whereas, in maintaining a position, the base of support is not changed. The point of contact between the body and the supporting surface need not be the feet, but may, instead, be the hands, head, or other body segment.

The types of human movement to be dealt with in this category are a variety of locomotor forms and skills in which the body is supported by, or suspended from, the arms.

A. LOCOMOTION ON AND FROM LAND

All of the locomotor forms discussed within this section require a push against the supporting surface with one or both feet. The height, range, and duration of the flight phase are determined by the forcefulness and direction of this push, as reflected by the initial velocity and projection angle of the body's center of gravity. The method of landing in these activities varies considerably, depending on the landing surface and on whether or not the locomotor pattern is a single or a repeated projection of the body.

1. Walk (Gait)

The detailed components of walking have been studied by relatively few investigators even though this locomotor form is one of the most universal of all human activities. Limited by lack of devices for making objective measurements, studies of gait prior to the mid-nineteenth century were primarily observational. During the latter part of the nineteenth century, however, Muybridge (*159*) developed photographic methods of recording serial displacements of the body in locomotion.

These techniques were perfected and applied to the study of human gait by Marey in France and by Braune and Fischer in Germany (*156*).

One of the most comprehensive kinematic gait studies during the twentieth century was conducted by Eberhart and associates (*66*) at the University of California, Berkeley. In a series of related investigations, clear identification was made of the excursions of the lower extremities and pelvis under various conditions of walking, such as speed and inclination of the walking surface.

Within the past decade, walking patterns of normal men have been analyzed extensively by Murray and associates (*154–158*). Employing the technique of interrupted-light photography, the investigators recorded the displacements occurring during walking, with the goal of providing ranges of normal values and standards against which measurements of abnormal gait could be compared. It was concluded that, for normal men from 20 to 65 years of age, there were striking similarities within and between subjects in the speed and timing aspects of the walking cycle, in stride dimensions, and in sagittal displacements of the trunk and extremities during free-cadence walking. Only in the transverse rotations of the pelvis and thorax was there wide variation among the subjects, suggesting that these actions may not be obligatory elements of normal gait (*156*).

Normal arm swing patterns in the sagittal plane also were studied by Murray *et al.* (*158*). The amplitude of shoulder and elbow sagittal rotation was significantly greater for fast speed walking (136 steps/min) than for free speed walking (114 steps/min). Another characteristic of the normal arm swing was the close temporal relationship between the upper and lower limb movements. The shoulder and elbow were found to be in maximum flexion at the time of contralateral heel strike and in maximum extension at the time of ipsilateral heel strike.

In support of Murray's observations of consistency in most aspects of the walking pattern over repeated trials of the same subject, Williams (*225*) concluded that normal gait was not changed significantly by the presence of spectators. Fatigue, however, did produce a significant increase in stride length and in the speed of arm action for the 22 college males filmed in this study.

2. Running

Running has been described as a natural extension of the basic skill of walking, the distinguishing feature being that running has a flight phase with no support from either leg, while walking has no airborne phase and even has a brief period when both feet are in contact with the ground (*44,220*). Several aspects of running have been studied in cinematographic analyses, and these factors serve as the topic headings in the following discussion.

a. Temporal Phases of the Stride. In a temporal analysis of running, Slocum and James (*196*) identified the basic unit of the movement pattern as a full stride, or a cycle of motion, starting when one foot strikes the ground and continuing until the same foot again strikes the ground. Each cycle has a phase of unilateral weight bearing or support and a phase of forward recovery when the extremity does not bear weight. The forward recovery phase has been observed to last approximately three times as long as the period of support at moderate running speeds (*60,196*). During the phase of forward recovery there are two periods when the body is airborne; one, just after take-off, and the second, following take-off from the weight bearing phase of the opposite leg. On the basis of their analysis of a number of sprinters, Slocum and James reported that the elapsed time of the support phase of a cycle was equal to or slightly less than that of the airborne period, regardless of running velocity. Other investigators have concluded that the proportionate duration of the support phase decreased as running velocity increased in preschool boys (*37*), in elementary school boys and girls (*16,61*), and in college men and women (*160,162,206,207*).

b. Support Phase. Evidence from cinematographic analyses suggests that variations in the part of the foot that first contacts the ground may accompany alterations in running velocity. At low speeds, initial contact is made with the heel or the whole foot, while at faster speeds, first contact is made with the lateral border of the ball of the foot (*65,95,196,220*). However, Fenn (*76*) reported that the foot landed "flat" on some occasions, even in sprinters running at maximum velocity.

The greater the horizontal distance that the support foot strikes the ground ahead of the body's center of gravity, the greater would be the potential retarding effect upon the desired movement of the body in running. Several investigators have verified that the center of gravity moves more nearly over the foot at landing in the strides of accomplished or fast runners than it does in runners of relatively inferior ability or slower speed (*54,61,65,76*). In fact, Fortney (*82*) observed that, immediately prior to foot contact with the ground, the heel had already started to move backward with reference to the knee even though it moved forward at this time with reference to a fixed point in space.

Joint actions of the extremity in contact with the ground during the support phase have been studied in several cinematographic analyses (*37,44,61,75,76,196*). There is general agreement among these researchers that the knee continues to flex and the ankle dorsiflexes immediately, though for a very brief period of time, after the foot contacts the ground. As the center of gravity moves ahead of the supporting foot and as the supporting thigh inclines forward from the vertical, ankle plantar flexion and knee extension occur and hip extension continues, resulting in an upward and forward propulsive thrust applied to the center of gravity. Slocum and James (196) have emphasized that the lumbar spine rather than the hip joint is the pivotal point of the lower extremity lever system action during the support phase.

In studies of preschool boys (37) and elementary school girls (61), an increase in the velocity of extending the supporting leg at take-off was observed as subjects grew older and improved in running speed. A greater angle of knee extension (5) and location of the total body farther ahead of the supporting foot at take-off (37,61) also were found to be characteristics of faster runners. Thus, the amount of extension and forward inclination of the supporting leg at take-off appears to be directly associated with running velocity.

c. *Forward Recovery Phase.* Two aspects of the swinging limb action during the forward recovery phase have been identified which clearly distinguish between good and poor runners. Analyses of running in children and adults have revealed that faster runners tend to flex the knee more and to bring the heel closer to the buttock as the swinging limb moves forward (5,37,61,82). A second characteristic of faster runners is the high knee lift which brings the swinging thigh close to the horizontal in front of the body as the opposite weight bearing foot leaves the ground (37,54,61,76,77,82,196). The angle of the thigh below a horizontal line through the hip joint becomes smaller in value as the thigh is raised closer to the horizontal. For example, Osterhoudt (162) found that for 16 intercollegiate male runners the mean angle of thigh elevation with the horizontal at a running velocity of 11 ft/sec was 60 deg, whereas at 16 and 21 ft/sec the mean angle decreased to 47 and 36 deg, respectively. In an analysis of running patterns in 28 college women, Teeple (207) reported the following mean values of thigh inclination to the horizontal at specified running velocities: 59 deg at 12.5 ft/sec, 49 deg at 17 ft/sec, and 38 deg at 22 ft/sec. Not only is the thigh of the recovery leg moved forward through a greater range in faster runners, but it also is brought forward more rapidly, as determined by Clouse (37) in an analysis of running in preschool boys, and by Fortney (82) and Glassow et al. (95), who studied elementary school children.

d. *Stride Length and Rate.* Since running speed can be defined logically as a product of the length and frequency of stride, several investigators have sought supporting evidence on this topic from films of runners at different age and proficiency levels. A positive relationship between stride length and running velocity has been observed in pre-school boys (*37*), elementary school boys and girls (*16,61,95*), college women (*5,207*), and in adult male athletes (*32,54,60,76,160,162,181, 196,206*). From high speed motion pictures taken of six highly skilled runners as they ran at maximum velocity (i.e., 25.72 to 30.02 ft/sec), Dillman (*60*) found that stride lengths from right foot take-off to left foot take-off were all greater than 6.3 ft, with two runners exceeding 6.5 ft.

Generally, stride rate also has been reported to increase with speed of running (*32,65,76,118,160,162,207*). Cavagna and associates (*32*) noted that the frequency of strides appeared to be much higher during the brief period of initial forward acceleration than during the sustained run. While a linear relationship between stride rate and running speed has been observed up to velocities of approximately 20 ft/sec (excluding the starting period), increases in velocity beyond this point have been attributed primarily to greater stride frequency rather than to greater step length (*76,118,162*). Stride rates of the six adult male runners studied by Dillman (*60*) ranged from 3.71 to 4.54 steps/sec, whereas Dyson (*65*) stated that the striding cadence of top-class competitors ranged from 4.50 to 5.00 steps/sec.

e. Vertical Movements of the Center of Gravity. The path of the body's center of gravity during running has been described as a wave-like oscillating curve (*16,37,131*). With increases in age and running speed, the magnitude of body rise, or vertical displacement of the center of gravity, becomes less, while the horizontal displacement increases (*16,181*). Both Fenn (*76*) and Beck (*16*) found that the center of gravity moved upward as the leg extended during the support phase and reached its maximum vertical height at or just following take-off. The center of gravity then moved in a downward and forward direction, reaching its low point just after the supporting foot made contact with the ground. Fenn (*76*) measured the total rise of the center of gravity while the foot was in contact with the ground as approximately 6 cm in adult male sprinters.

f. Trunk Position. Much of the literature on running reflects the belief that a forward trunk lean is an aid to the forceful forward projection of the body. Slocum and Bowerman (*195*), writing together and with others (*20,196*), have provided pictorial evidence and logical reasons that refute the forward-lean theory. They state that, after the acceleration phase of the start, good runners keep the trunk essentially erect regardless of the distance of the run. Dyson (*65*) has suggested that there may be an illusion of forward lean in sprinting due to the extremely inclined position of the propulsive leg at the moment it thrusts the body into flight. Measurements of the forward trunk lean of several top male and female sprinters were reported by Wickstrom (*220*) to range from 12 to 20 deg, with a tendency to be nearer the lower figure. An average body angle for three milers studied by Ehrhart (*69*) was found to be 15 deg from the vertical. Taylor (*206*) observed that the mean trunk inclination from the vertical for 30 varsity track team members running on a treadmill was 10 deg, with a standard deviation of 3.5 deg.

g. Arm Action. The arm action in running was observed by Wickstrom (*220*), who reported that the hand swings almost chin high and slightly toward the midline of the body on the forward swing and the elbow reaches nearly as high as the shoulder on the back swing. A difference of approximately 6 in. in the height of the path of the hand during forward and backward swings was measured by Altfillisch (*4*). According to his findings, the wrist followed a path below the hip line on the backward swing and above it on the forward swing. The change in wrist height thus reflects the increase in elbow extension during the backward swing, followed by an increase in elbow flexion during the forward swing (*220*).

3. Sprint Start

The effect of variations in the distance between starting blocks and the distance between the front block and the starting line was investigated by Gagnon (*85*) in a film study of four sprinters. It was concluded that better performances in the times at 2.5 and 6 yards from the starting line were achieved when a short footspacing and a short foot–hand-spacing were used. Location of the center of gravity in the set position closer to the starting line was the factor most closely related to the achievement of the fastest time to cover 6 yards. Both Gagnon (*85*) and Desrochers (*55*) observed that footspacing differences affected the length and time of the first stride, but not of subsequent strides.

4. Standing Long Jump

The purpose of the standing long jump is to project the body into the air in such a way that the greatest horizontal distance is traversed from a standing start. This distance is made up of three components: the distance of the center of gravity ahead of the toes at take-off, the horizontal distance through which the center of gravity is projected during flight, and the distance that the heels reach beyond the center of gravity at landing (44). Cinematographic analyses dealing with aspects of the take-off, flight, and landing phases of the standing long jump will be reviewed in this section.

a. *Preparatory and Take-off Phases.* In a partial longitudinal study of 47 boys ranging from 14 months in age to fifth grade students, Hellebrandt *et al.* (114) described the emergence and maturation of the standing long jump pattern as determined from analysis of high speed motion picture film frames. Some of the immature motion characteristics identified by Hellebrandt *et al.* in preschool boys also were observed by Zimmerman (232,233) in unskilled jumpers of college age. Both Felton (74) and Zimmerman (233) found that the total range of movement at the metatarsophalangeal, ankle, knee, and hip joints from deepest crouch until take-off was greater for good than for poor college women performers.

Roy (185) studied the standing long jump in average performers age 7, 10, 13, and 16 years. These boys exhibited strong similarities in joint and segment maximum angular velocity and acceleration both within and between groups. It was reported that shoulder joint maximal acceleration was usually attained 0.35 sec prior to take-off, while the other joints' peak accelerations were reached in descending order in such a way that the ankle and metatarsophalangeal joints were the last two to impart final velocity to the body. Roy concluded that there was virtually no age trend in angular kinematic measures and that the trend in linear kinematic measures was primarily accounted for by increase in body mass. Thus, on the basis of this study, the jumping pattern may be viewed as essentially well established by the beginning of school age.

At take-off in the standing long jump, good performers of kindergarten age (107), elementary school age (95,227), and college age (74,233) have been observed to incline the leg, thigh, and trunk segments farther forward, and to extend the knees more completely than poor jumpers at these ages. Reports of the initial velocity of projection of the center of gravity at take-off ranged from 6 ft/sec in kindergarten children (107) and 5.9 ft/sec in nonskilled college women (74), to 12.9 ft/sec for average male performers at 16 years of age (185). Jumpers having the longest distance scores also were found to have a lower angle of projection of the center of gravity than did poorer performers (74,107,227). This projection angle approached 21 deg for skilled college women (74).

b. *Flight Phase.* Clayton (35) studied the flight phase of the standing long jump performed by children from 6 through 12 years of age, and concluded that the older and more proficient subjects had a tendency to flex at the hip joint earlier in the mid-air phase of the jump than did younger children. Zimmerman (*232*) reported that the most highly skilled women performers of college age reached and tended to hold a greater amount of hip flexion and knee extension than poorly skilled jumpers while in the air.

c. Landing Phase. In a 5 year longitudinal study of motor development in elementary school boys and girls, Glassow *et al.* (*95*) found that children with better jumping distance scores had a tendency for the trunk and thigh to be closer to the horizontal at landing. This same conclusion also was drawn by other investigators (*74,107,233*). Felton (*74*) added that college women who jumped the greatest distance landed with the heels 5.56 in. ahead of the center of gravity, while the heels of the poorest jumpers were 3.60 in. ahead of the center of gravity.

d. Arm Swing. The mature arm swing pattern, as identified from films of proficient jumpers (*44,114,232,233*), consists of swinging the almost fully extended arms downward from a position of hyperextension behind and above the trunk. The arms pass the vertical as the knees reach their deepest flexion prior to take-off. The swing continues forward and upward as the legs extend, and the arms reach their highest point overhead at the time of take-off. However, as mentioned in Section II,A,4,a, peak acceleration of the armswing occurs just prior to take-off. In very young or immature jumpers, the arms tend to retract at take-off, or to be abducted in the frontal plane to aid as stabilizers (*114*). Zimmerman (*232*) observed that unskilled jumpers of college age had limited arm movements and continued to swing their arms sideward as they prepared for landing rather than to reach forward with the arms as in mature landing form.

5. Vertical Jump

Cinematographic analyses in which the vertical jump and the standing long jump have been compared report that the same joint actions are used in the propulsive phase of both jumps, namely, hip and knee extension, ankle plantar flexion, and shoulder flexion (*67,97,227*). However, in a study of 29 male and female university students, Eckert (*67*) found that the angular velocity and range of movement at the hip joint were greater in the long jump than in the vertical jump, while the velocity and range at the knee and ankle joints were greater in the vertical jump than in the standing long jump.

Wilson (*227*) analyzed the changes in form in the jump and reach version of the vertical jump performed by children ages 4 through 12 and noted the following improvements which accompanied increases in age and skill: a small progressive increase in crouch, more effective arm lift, greater leg extension at take-off and in flight, and greater extension of the trunk at the peak of the reach. Observations by Wickstrom (*220*) indicated that, if the vertical jump did not require purposeful reaching with the arm, less mature arm and leg action was seen in the jumping pattern of children.

Skilled and nonskilled college women performing the vertical jump have been compared in cinematographic analyses. Couper (*47*) reported that the skilled jumpers had a more erect trunk at the low point of the crouch, greater vertical velocity of projection, and greater backward inclination of the trunk at the high point of the jump than did the nonskilled jumpers. However, Graves (*99*) did not discover any movement factors which differentiated between skilled and unskilled groups of college women. The five best vertical jumpers of 806 junior and senior high school boys were filmed and studied by Haldeman (*106*). A similar pattern of movement was observed in all jumpers, with variations in such details as the amount of hip flexion and trunk lean during the preparatory crouch, and the movement of the nonreaching arm.

Cinematographic techniques have been used to investigate the force, velocity, and power aspects of the vertical jump. Gerrish (*93*) obtained power values as high as 5.9 hp during a vertical jump executed by an adult. The highest vertical velocity was 10.5 ft/sec, and a maximum force of 330 lb was developed. From an analysis of the vertical jump performed by 30 adult males, Barlow (*12*) concluded that typical measurements of proficiency in this skill did not represent power. Instead, body weight was determined to be the most influential factor affecting the development of power, whereas factors of time and center of gravity displacement were not significantly related to power.

6. High Jump

The mechanics of take-off in the straddle style of high jumping have been analyzed in skilled performers. Gombac (*98*), who filmed over 60 jumps of three Yugoslav high jumpers and also recorded ground pressure under the take-off foot, divided the take-off into three phases. The shortest phase, lasting about 0.020 to 0.024 sec, occurred as the heel hit the ground and resulted in the greatest vertical pressure (over 159 lb) recorded at any time during the take-off. The ground pressure dropped sharply as the foot was lowered toward the ground. The second phase, beginning when the whole foot was in contact with the ground, lasted from 0.10 to 0.12 sec, which Gombac stated was considerably longer than with the world's best jumpers. During this phase, the vertical pressure first increased rapidly and then decreased as the knee reached its point of greatest flexion. The upward drive, or leg extension, during the third phase of the take-off lasted about 0.125 to 0.150 sec and produced a vertical pressure which was large, but still some 45 lb below what it was at the moment of placing the heel on the ground.

The straddle high jump of John Thomas was analyzed by Ward (216). Action of the lead leg during the final step was described as the most outstanding feature of this jumper's style. Vertical linear momentum established by this leg contributed one-third of his total vertical linear momentum at take-off. Hay (112,113) compared the impulses exerted at take-off in the straddle and the western-roll styles of high jumping and found a significant difference (P = 0.05) in the resultant vertical impulses between the two styles. Since the western-roll jumpers obtained greater vertical impulses than the straddle style jumpers, the former may be judged to have a more efficient take-off, but Hay cautioned that this conclusion applied only to relatively low jumping heights. Peiniger (167), in an analysis of two good and two fair women high jumpers, indicated that the biomechanical factors selected for study did not clearly differentiate between good and fair jumpers. Instead, the physical characteristic of height of the jumper was more directly related to a good jump than were mechanical factors.

7. Diving

The majority of cinematographic analyses dealing with diving skills can be grouped according to the type of dive under investigation. Two broad categories of dives will be considered in this section, namely, springboard dives and racing dives. Only one analysis of a standing front dive, which fit into neither category, was located (125).

a. Springboard Dives. In 1936, Lanoue (136) performed one of the earliest and most comprehensive analyses of springboard diving. Cinematographic procedures were used in the descriptive phase of this investigation to study divers of championship caliber. From his observations of the films projected in slow motion, Lanoue concluded that all divers initiated rotation about the transverse axis before leaving the board. Lanoue (136,137) also described the mechanics of twisting dives and indicated that more twists could be performed by a diver pushing off from the diving board than by a diver allowed to free-fall in a pike position. Later support for Lanoue's observations was provided by Winter (228), who found that twisting was initiated from the board in dives where the body could not move from a pike to a layout position, and by Leigh and Bangerter (142), who reported that twisting was initiated on the springboard for forward and backward twisting dives. The kinematics of the full twisting forward one-and-one-half somersault also were analyzed by McCormick (*149*).

Films of seven different dives of a 1 m diving champion were studied by Lafler (*133*) in 1943, and these same films were analyzed by Groves (*102*) in 1949. Lafler found that the amount of forward lean at take-off varied with the amount of turning. For example, the greatest amount of lean from the vertical was 27 deg in the two-and-one-half somersault, but was only about half as much (14 deg) in the jackknife dive. Groves (*102,103*) supported and elaborated upon Lafler's observations, using a board with spring scales attached at the corners to determine the location of the center of gravity of three subjects in 13 characteristic diving positions observed from the films. More recently, cinematographic analyses of dives in the forward, backward, and reverse groups have been conducted (*50,80,105*).

A computer simulation model of the airborne phase of nontwisting dives in the pike and layout positions was developed and validated by Miller (*152*). Cinematographic techniques, including a three-dimensional film analysis method, were employed to obtain, from the films of six adult male divers performing selected forward dives, the displacement and velocity data necessary for the simulation model. The experimental data collected from the films were compared with the simulated results and the correspondence between the two was judged as acceptable.

b. Racing Dives. The arm and leg actions during the propulsion phase of the racing dive are similar, in many respects, to the actions that occur in the standing long jump (*44*). However, in the racing dive, the projection force is directed almost entirely horizontally. Pelchat (*168*) compared, through cinematography, the biomechanics of the free style and breast stroke swimming starts. All but one of the ten varsity male swimmers used the circular backswing of the arms. No differences were found in the mechanics of the two swimming starts, except for the angle of body position at water entry, which was greater for the breast stroke than for the free style start. The mechanical aspects of four styles of competitive back stroke starts were analyzed by Scheuchenzuber (*190*) in 1970. It was determined that the starting style accepted for Olympic and A.A.U. competition produced a significantly slower completion time to a point 4 m from the starting wall than did the standard N.C.A.A. start or either experimental standing start (20 or 30 in. hand-grips).

8. Pole Vault

The motor skill of pole vaulting generally can be classified as a locomotor skill, although use of a flexible pole makes the major contribution in projecting the vaulter over the crossbar. Based on analyses of pole vaulting with fiberglass and nonfiberglass poles, Ganslen (86,87) has contended that, irrespective of the height of the vault or what type of pole is used, the mechanical principles of vaulting are the same and only the timing is different. Pikulsky (169) studied motion pictures of 24 successful college vaulters and found that the fiberglass pole allowed faster take-off velocities when compared with take-off velocities reported in previous studies of nonfiberglass pole vaulting. A strong positive relationship between the amount of pole bend and the height of the vault also was reported in this investigation.

Hay (110,111) conducted an analysis of the factors influencing pole bend and reported significant positive correlations ($P < 0.05$) between the magnitude of pole bend and the following factors: the angle of take-off, the horizontal velocity at take-off, and the horizontal distance between the vaulter's top hand and his supporting foot at take-off. From a cinematographic study of the energy transformations during three phases of pole vaulting with a fiberglass pole, Dillman (59) concluded that this type of pole provided an effective means of converting kinetic energy to potential energy. Other investigations of pole vaulting with a fiberglass pole (14,153,200) have examined the relationships between selected performance variables and the vaulting height achieved.

9. Other Locomotor Skills

For certain locomotor skills, cinematographic analyses are not numerous and, therefore, will not be reviewed. Such is the case for hurdling (1), the running long jump (31), and the triple jump (65,197).

B. LOCOMOTION IN WATER

It appears that the most extensive application of cinematographic techniques in analyzing swimming skills has been made by Counsilman (46). Using underwater movies to examine the path of the swimmer's hand in relation to his body, Counsilman observed that this path was not a straight line but resembled an inverted question mark for the crawl stroke, and a double "S" pattern for the butterfly stroke. Recently, the path of the hand in relation to still water rather than to a fixed point on the body was examined by Brown and Counsilman (27). An analysis of this path and of the angle that the hand's direction of motion made with the body's direction of motion in the breast stroke, butterfly stroke, and crawl led these investigators to conclude that outstanding swimmers used primarily sculling motions (and hydrodynamic lift) rather than paddling motions (and drag force) in propelling themselves. Side and front view film tracings showing the path of the crawl stroke arm and leg action relative to still water and to a fixed point on the body also have been prepared by Plagenhoef (*172*).

An analysis of the butterfly swimming stroke by DeVries (*58*) revealed that the highest velocity of the body occurred toward the completion of the arm stroke, and the lowest velocity occurred in the last part of the arm recovery. Cinematography also was employed to study the arm action (*193*) and the kick (*45*) of the butterfly stroke. The flutter kick, side stroke kick, and breast stroke kick were analyzed by Collins (*41*) from films of 25 advanced swimmers, and the joint actions which contributed to greater speed or power were identified for each type of kick. Chadwick (*33*) studied underwater films of the breast stroke performed by ten swimmers of varying ability and described the selected strength, flexibility, and anthropometric variables that were found to be related to swimming speed.

In synchronized swimming, sculling is a necessary and a frequently used skill. Vanderbeck (*212*) analyzed motion pictures of experienced swimmers performing head-first, arms-at-the-sides sculling in an attempt to identify common elements in the patterns of motion among the 19 subjects. With two minor variations, a sequence-of-motion pattern involving actions at the shoulder and elbow joints was found to be common to all subjects even though there was wide variation among subjects in the range of motion at these two joints. Underwater films of selected synchronized swimming stunts were studied by Lent (*143*), and a sequential description of movements and body positions in each stunt was prepared and illustrated with stick figures.

C. ARM SUPPORTED SKILLS

In many gymnastic skills the body is supported by one or both hands for varying lengths of time as the body is rotated in a vertical or a horizontal plane around the support. Several types of tumbling and apparatus skills, most requiring two hands to support the body, will be reviewed within this section.

1. Tumbling

The methods of cinematography and electromyography were employed by Duck (*63*) to record four front handsprings by each of seven highly proficient gymnasts. Findings indicated that the rapid knee extension and ankle plantar flexion in the take-off leg, and hip extension in the swing leg, contributed a major portion of the force-producing rotary movement around the axis formed by the hands on the floor. The hands were placed on the floor an average distance of 27.1 in. in front of the take-off foot. Holmes (*120*) analyzed films of expert, average, and poor performers executing the backward handspring. The experts were shown to have more backward lean at take-off, greater height of projection, greater horizontal velocity during the initial flight phase, and a more upright landing than the average or poor performers. In an analysis of both the forward and backward handsprings, Fortier (*81*) investigated the initial velocity of projection, body angle at take-off, distance and time of flight, and the path of the center of gravity.

The performance of skilled and unskilled subjects in the round-off was studied by Wilson (*226*). Skilled performers were found to have a greater forward trunk lean from the vertical at take-off, a more erect trunk at landing, and a faster completion time for the stunt than did the unskilled performers. In an analysis of the double backward somersault, Austin (*10*) reported that the preceding round-off and back handspring permitted the translation of horizontal energy to vertical to the extent that the body rose 32 to 39 in. above the level of take-off. Compared with the single backward somersault, the tuck was started sooner, was tighter, and was held longer in the double backward somersault. Two twisting stunts, the full twisting front dive (*141*) and the double twisting backward somersault (*224*), also have been subjected to cinematographic analysis.

2. Long Horse Vaulting

Guerrera (*104*) filmed 26 superior collegiate and amateur gymnasts performing the handspring and swan vaults under competitive conditions. The mechanics of these two vaults were quantified and related to scores awarded by the judges. Higher-scoring handspring vaults were characterized by shorter contact times with the springboard, greater take-off velocities, and shorter contact times with the long horse. Higher-scoring swan vaults were observed to have a greater range of angular movement of the center of gravity on the springboard, a larger take-off velocity, a higher angle of the legs above the horizontal at initial contact with the long horse, and a greater amount of time to attain the highest position of the center of gravity during free flight.

A descriptive analysis of the Yamashita vault over the long horse was made by Vanis (*213*) from films of six gymnasts. By comparing excellent, good, and fair performers, he derived a set of "most desirable practices" as aids to teaching. Based on a cinematographic analysis of the front handspring vaults executed by six women gymnasts, Ferriter (*78*) described the movement characteristics associated with performers in the excellent, good, and fair categories. In excellent performance, the gymnast leaned into the take-off, remained on the horse for the shortest time, and covered a greater horizontal distance during flight after contact with the horse than during flight prior to contact with the horse.

3. Parallel Bars

A comparative kinematic analysis of the early drop and late drop felge handstand (peach hand) was conducted by Lascari (*140*). The early drop style, in which the arms were straighter at regrasp than during the late drop style, was found to be the superior technique because of the greater vertical impulse generated. The continuous rapid kipping action, timed to achieve large, simultaneous force values of trunk and lower limbs as the body began to rise, appeared to be the reason for the greater effectiveness of the early drop. However, peak vertical force of 650 lb was measured toward the bottom of the early drop, which resulted in a more severe strain on the grasp than was caused by the peak vertical force of 480 lb produced in the late drop. In Plagenhoef's (*170*) analysis of the peach to a handstand, the performer was less skilled than the gymnast in Lascari's study, and performed the stunt with extremely flexed elbows upon regrasp.

Grossfeld (*101*) studied films of the underbar somersault (felge handstand) on the parallel bars and observed that the height achieved at regrasp was directly proportional to the skill level of the five gymnasts who performed the event. The best performer in this investigation regrasped the bar with the elbows flexed at 89 deg rather than fully extended as in top caliber performers. Grossfeld concluded that the greater hip extension resulting from acutely flexed hips produced the best performances. Other parallel bar skills for which cinematographic analyses have been conducted include the forward somersault (*201*), the Stutzkehre (*11*), and the glide kip mount for women on the uneven parallel bars (*122*).

4. Still Rings

Dusenbury (*64*) analyzed motion pictures of the forward and reverse giant swings on still rings as performed by gymnasts with varied body types. The conclusion was reached that the reverse giant swing produced 35% less maximum vertical force on the hands than the forward giant swing, and was, therefore, termed the easier of the two skills. The straight arm backward giant swing on still rings was investigated by Peek (*166*). The paths of the shoulder, hip, ankle, and center of gravity of the entire body were plotted and served as the basis for a descriptive analysis of the movement characteristics of the outstanding performers. This same type of descriptive analysis was carried out by Pataky (*164*) in his study of the backward lever pull to an iron cross on the still rings.

5. Horizontal Bar

Cinematographic analyses of the back giant swing on the horizontal bar have been conducted by Cureton (*48*) and by Schaefer (*189*). Both investigators found that the center of gravity was farthest from the bar on the downswing and that successful performers attained their greatest speed in the 45 deg sector before swinging under the bar. At this point of greatest speed, a centrifugal force of 789.3 lb was developed, which, according to Cureton, would have the tendency to pull the hands away from the bar if the performer did not possess sufficient grip strength. During the latter portion of the upswing, the center of gravity moved in toward the bar and the center of rotation shifted from the hands to the shoulders. By thus shortening the radius of rotation, enough angular velocity was maintained to enable the performer to complete the circle. Harris (*109*) studied the upstart (kip) on the horizontal bar executed by subjects of excellent, medium, and poor ability. The film analysis revealed the critical timing point when the body straightened forcefully from the pike and the center of gravity rose toward the bar. Cinematographic analyses of the arched kip and of other selected skills performed on the horizontal bar by expert gymnasts also have been conducted by George (*91,92*).

6. Side Horse

Several investigators have analyzed motion pictures of gymnasts performing leg circles on the side horse (*18,139,174,188*). The best performers studied by Blievernicht (*18*) and by Sarver (*188*) showed greater body extension throughout the double leg circle. They also had less rise and fall of body parts, maintained a more circular pattern with the feet, and kept the legs higher throughout the circle than did the less skilled performers (*188*). Sarver reported that a single double leg circle required an average of 1.03 sec to complete, this time being divided equally between the forward and backward halves, and that simultaneous hand contact with the horse lasted for no longer than 27% of the circle.

III. Moving External Objects

The primary purpose of many motor skills used in athletics and in team and individual sports is to move an external object away from or toward the body. A variety of different movement patterns may be employed to accomplish this purpose. The object may be projected or moved with a throw, a strike, a push, or a pull. While a throw can be made with an overarm, a sidearm, or an underhand pattern, so also may a strike be made with these patterns. In the following section, cinematographic analyses of many of these movement patterns and motor skills will be reviewed.

A. Throwing

Bunn (*28*) has stated that throwing is probably second only to running as a common element in a wide range of sports. Film studies of throwing skills have investigated not only the movement characteristics of expert performers, but also the differences between skilled and unskilled subjects and the developmental aspects of the throwing pattern.

1. Baseball and Softball Overarm and Sidearm Throws

The overarm pattern is generally employed when great speed is desired in a throw. In a cinematographic study of speeds of pitched balls, Kenny (*127*) found that the overarm fast ball was delivered with greater velocity than the sidearm or underhand fast ball, and the overarm curve ball was slower than the overarm fast ball but faster than the sidearm or underhand curve ball. Ball velocity also has been one of the "product" measures most frequently used as a criterion to reflect the extent of proficiency and maturation in the "process" or movement pattern of throwing (*44*). Several investigators who have conducted film analyses of the overarm throw observed that initial ball velocity increased as subjects advanced in age (*70,95,194,222*), or as they received throwing instruction (*26*). Other researchers, in their preparation to undertake comparative cinematographic analyses of throwing, have selected subjects at distinctly different levels of skill based on their maximal initial ball velocity achieved at release (*9,21,57,194*).

Perhaps the most extensive and definitive study of developmental form in the overarm throw was completed by Wild (*222,223*) in 1937. Based on an analysis of motion pictures of the throwing form in a selected cross section of normal boys and girls ranging from 2 to 12 years of age, four distinct stages of throwing development were identified. The mature form, or stage four, was achieved by the majority of boys 6½ years of age and up in Wild's study, but was rarely attained by girls of that age. Across the four stages, the outstanding trends disclosed were a change from movements in the sagittal plane to movements largely in the horizontal plane, and progression from an unchanging base of support to a step forward with the foot opposite the throwing arm. Another cross-sectional study of throwing skills in children ages 4½ through 10½ was conducted by Jones (126), whereas longitudinal cinematographic analyses of the overarm throw in elementary school children over a period of 4 to 6 years were carried out by Ekern (70), Glassow et al. (95), and Singer (194). Some of the key developmental trends observed by these investigators will be described in the subsequent discussion of the overarm throwing motion.

Several studies of the movement characteristics of performers at different levels of skill have revealed that the better (faster) throwers expanded the range of the backswing or preparatory movements and tended to turn approximately 90 deg from the direction of the throw before stepping forward onto the opposite foot (9,26,70,95,194,222). Poorly skilled (slower) throwers exhibited a smaller range of trunk rotation during the backswing. The length of the forward stride also has been shown to be considerably longer in better throwers than in the less skilled (9,26, 57,70,95,194,222). Average stride lengths have been reported as 3.87 ft in skilled adult baseball players (9), 2.65 ft in sixth grade boys (95), 2.30 ft in college women of average throwing skill (9), and 0.40 ft in first grade girls (95).

Accompanying or even slightly preceding the step is the action of forward trunk rotation occurring primarily at the hip joint of the leading leg (44). The increased angular range and velocity of this joint action in better throwers has been noted by several researchers (9,21,26,126,194, 222). As the trunk rotates forward, the upper arm maintains a position in line with the shoulders and the elbow remains in approximately 90 deg of flexion (9,145). During this period of forward trunk rotation, the shoulder of the throwing arm has been observed to undergo considerable lateral rotation, thus permitting the forearm, hand, and ball to lag briefly in a position behind the elbow (9,73,128,205). King and associates (128) have described some consequences of this position of extreme valgus strain at the elbow in their clinical and cinematographic analysis of the act of pitching.

In a three-dimensional film analysis of skilled male throwers, Atwater (9) reported that the resultant velocity of the ball in the hand increased from less than 20 ft/sec at the point where it lagged behind the body less than 0.10 sec before release, to a velocity ranging from 111 to 122 ft/sec at release. Joint actions observed to be occurring during this rapid increase in ball velocity were the continuing, but decelerating, forward trunk rotation, extremely fast elbow extension, shoulder medial rotation, and radio-ulnar pronation (9). Several investigators have found the elbow to be more fully extended and the ball farther from the head at release in skilled throwers than in less skilled performers (*9,21,70,95,222*). While wrist flexion has been identified by some (*40,146,178*) as an important action contributing to ball velocity, the validity of this finding recently has been questioned (*9,205*). Further analysis is needed of the arm and hand actions just prior to release using motion picture cameras capable of higher frame rates and smaller shutter openings than have typically been employed in the past.

The trunk position at release in an overarm throw is one of lateral inclination to the side away from the throwing arm (*9,40,95,145*). Films taken from behind the performer have been used by Lindner (*145*) to support the concept of "freedom of lateral deviation in throwing" ("Wurfseitenfreiheit") which was seen during the final phase before release in a baseball pitch and in several other overarm throwing skills. The shoulders and the entire arm were observed to form almost a straight line at release, with the degree to which this line was slanted from the horizontal being dependent primarily upon the amount of lateral trunk lean (*9,145*). Forward inclination of the trunk at the hip joint also has been described as characteristic of the release position in skilled throwers (*70,146*).

Comparisons between the overarm and sidearm throws performed by adult men and women have been the subject of two cinematographic analyses (*8,40*). Both investigators concluded that the range of movement of the acting joints and the sequence and timing of these actions were impressively similar for both throws.

2. Underhand Throw

The most outstanding characteristic of the underhand throwing pattern is the joint action of shoulder flexion, usually with the elbow joint extended (*44*). At least three cinematographic analyses have been carried out in which both the underhand and overarm throws were examined. Bowne (*21,22*) reported that, in high school girls categorized on the basis of ball velocity as skilled, average, or poor performers, there was no significant relationship between underhand throwing velocity and either moment arm measures or structure–length variables. College women representing expert, average, and poor levels of underhand and overarm throwing skill were studied by Deutsch (*57*). Synchronized film records and electromyograph records served as the basis for this graphic and descriptive analysis.

In an investigation of several unilateral and bilateral throwing skills used by children ages 4½ to 10½ years, Jones (*126*) identified the joint actions of trunk rotation, shoulder flexion, and wrist flexion as being fundamental to the underhand throw. These same joint actions were observed to occur in the underhand pitch, with shoulder flexion contributing the largest percentage of linear velocity to the ball at release (44). Verwey (214) indicated that the radius for shoulder action was shortened at the beginning of the delivery in a windmill style softball pitch, but was lengthened during the latter part of the circle to achieve greatest linear velocity of the hand at release.

The underhand pattern, in conjunction with several approach steps, also is used in the delivery of a bowling ball. In this skill, as in the softball pitch, shoulder flexion has been found to contribute the majority of the velocity to the ball at release (44). Widule (221) analyzed films of men and women bowlers of high and average skill to determine differences in anthropometric, strength, and performance characteristics that might account for the differences in the bowling league averages of these groups of bowlers. Skilled bowlers were observed to make better postural adjustments during the backswing which determined an optimum ball height and an optimum range of forward swing. The skilled bowlers did not differ from the average bowlers in strength or length of body levers.

3. Football Forward Pass and Javelin Throw

The movement pattern in the football pass is very similar to that used in an overarm baseball throw (44,220). However, the larger size of the football and the necessity of releasing it without wobble, result in arm actions that are somewhat more restricted in range than those in a baseball throw (28,220). Heydman (116) investigated differences between the short (25 yard) and the long (50 yard) forward pass performed by a nationally recognized varsity quarterback. For the long pass, the subject consistently demonstrated a greater angle of release, a longer supporting base, and a greater amount of shoulder rotation, upper arm abduction, and shoulder elevation. Films of four outstanding quarterbacks photographed under game conditions were analyzed by Carlson (30) to determine the fundamental body movements used in executing the drop-back, roll-out, and jump passes. Very few differences among these three passes were found.

The javelin throw involves a slight modification of the run, coupled with an overarm throw. Joint actions occurring during this event have been described in a cinematographic study by Lamb (135). From an analysis of overhead and rear view films of the javelin throw, Lindner (145) concluded that the throwing arm performs a flinging motion beside the body and not directly above the shoulder as the javelin is released. The angle of release used by four highly skilled performers to achieve their best distance was found, by Dolan (*62*), to be close to 30 deg. An optimum release angle of 28 to 30 deg for the aerodynamically designed modern javelin also was recommended by Kuznetsov (*132*).

4. Discus and Hammer Throws

Both the discus and the hammer throws can be classified as sidearm patterns, with the preparatory turns, trunk rotation, and arm movement occurring essentially in a horizontal plane. In a cinematographic study of the discus throw, Whitmore (*219*) presented a descriptive analysis of the actions used by five successful performers. Bunn (*28*) has reported some details of a film study in which it was observed that the discus arm trailed the line of the shoulders at all times prior to release. The arm was 11 deg behind the shoulder line at the start of the throw and as much as 60 deg behind as the forward foot was planted following the spin. Rotation of the hips and upper trunk then was followed by a change in the shoulder joint angle, bringing the arm to a position slightly in advance of the shoulder line at release.

The skill of hammer throwing requires that some preliminary swings and several body turns or whirls be performed to progressively increase the hammer speed up until the point of release (*28,65*). Velocity curves for the hammer head during throws using two, three, and four turns have been recorded from film by Lapp (*138*). The hammer velocity at release was 49.7 ft/sec for two turns, and 51 and 48 ft/sec for three and four turns, respectively. Thus, three turns would appear to be optimal. The velocity curves also showed that there was a gradual, but not constant, increase in the velocity of the hammer during the turns, with the greatest increase coming between the final step and the point of release.

B. STRIKING

Striking skills can take place in a variety of planes and with various implements. Among the implements used to strike an object are body parts, including the hand, the head, and the foot, and special pieces of equipment, such as the bat, the racket, and the club. Overarm, sidearm, underhand, and leg swinging movement patterns are the means employed to accomplish the purpose of projecting the object.

1. Baseball Batting

During the baseball swing the movement of the body and the bat occurs primarily in the horizontal plane. While the body rotates through approximately 90 deg, the bat moves through an arc of almost 180 deg (*176*). The sequence of actions generally observed to occur in skilled performers during batting commences with the stride and is followed rapidly by hip rotation, extension of the rear elbow, and wrist action (42,43,202,220). The leading arm tends to be straighter in good than in poor hitters early in the forward swing of the bat (23), with the elbow angle stabilizing in the range of 168 to 177 deg (79). Higher skilled batters were reported to have greater angular velocity of wrist action just prior to ball contact than less skilled performers (43). Swimley (202) noted that the "wrist roll" did not occur until after the ball had left contact with the bat.

In the professional batters photographed by Hubbard and Seng (124), the start of the stride was found to be geared to release of the ball. Ball velocities of the pitches thrown to these players ranged from 80 to 130 ft/sec. The investigators also observed that the finish of the stride preceded the start of the swing by approximately 0.042 sec (124,192). Regardless of ball speed, the swing appeared to have relatively uniform duration since it was started later for slower pitches. Race (179,180), in a study of films of 17 Class A Eastern League hitters, reported no relationship between either length or velocity of the stride and batting or slugging average. The stride length and position of the forward foot were constant for any given player, regardless of the type of pitch, in the major league batters photographed by Breen (23).

In several studies, the position of the head during the baseball swing has been examined (23,124,161,177,180,192). Breen (23) and Race (180) reported that professional batters made small vertical and lateral adjustments in head position during both the stance and the swing. However, the close-up, front view films taken of major league players by Hubbard and Seng (124) revealed that the visual tracking of the ball during the swing was accomplished with the head essentially fixed and the eyes moving. Evidence provided in this analysis also showed that tracking of the ball with eye movements was not continued by many batters during the latter portion of the ball's flight toward the plate or at contact.

Additional analyses of batting include a description of the changes occurring in this striking skill at successive ages as observed from films of preschool children ranging in age from 21 to 60 months (220), and a combined cinematographic and electromyographic study of the batting swing in experienced and inexperienced performers (129,130).

2. Golf

Cinematographic analyses of the movement pattern used in the golf swing have been undertaken by several investigators (38,44,88,89,100,144, 163,172). During the backswing, most golfers rotate the hips about 30 to 40 deg from ball address, with the shoulders rotating about 90 deg around the spinal axis (172). All 20 professional golfers studied by

Plagenhoef (*172*) started the shift of weight onto the front foot before the club had reached the top of the backswing. The pelvic and spinal rotation accompanying the weight shift moves the arms and club downward until the left arm has reached the horizontal before shoulder joint action noticeably changes the arm position relative to the shoulder line (*44,172*). As the hands approach waist level, wrist action rapidly increases the angle between club and forearms. After impact, the "roll" of the forearms produces a crossing of the wrists (*172*).

Identifiable variations have been observed in certain aspects of the golf swing among highly skilled performers. Motion picture measurements of 20 touring professionals revealed that the width of the stance varied as much as 10 in. (*172*). Clemence (*36*) reported that the width of the stance was not correlated with the momentum of the clubhead before or after impact. Variations also existed in the body and club positions at the top of the backswing among professional golfers. At this point in the swing, the club moved as far back as 40 deg below the horizontal in one subject, reached a point parallel to the ground in the majority of subjects, or stopped as early as 40 deg above the horizontal in another subject (*172*). The stroke performed by these subjects was the drive.

The path of the clubhead during the backswing and the downswing has been traced from high speed film by Cochran and Stobbs (*38*). In the front view diagrams, the backswing path of hands and club was always behind (outside) the downswing path for skilled golfers. The illustrations prepared from film taken behind and in line with the ball flight path showed that good golfers did swing the clubhead in an inclined plane, but the backswing was not necessarily in the same plane as the downswing nor were these planes the same for all good golfers. Danforth (*49*) also has analyzed the path of the clubhead and attempted to relate this path to various types of deviation in the resulting drive.

Far more similarities than differences have been found between golf swings with irons and those with woods (*24,88,100,151*). However, McIntyre and Snyder (*151*) observed that 20 professional golfers used a flatter downswing with the driver than they did with the 8-iron. The five skilled women golfers filmed by Brennan (*24*) showed that, with the driver, the pelvis had rotated 7.2 deg farther at contact than with the 7-iron. Since clubhead velocities with woods have been reported to exceed the clubhead velocities with irons (*24,44,151*), it may be concluded that the major difference between these full swings is the length of the club rather than the pattern of joint actions employed.

The position of the body at impact was described by Plagenhoef (*172*) as being dissimilar to the position of address due to the leg and trunk action. Most golfers had their hips turned open toward the line of ball flight more than the upper trunk was turned at impact. Not only was the head position shown to be farther behind the ball at impact than at address (*38*), but the head was observed to move at least 1.27 in. on each swing of professional golfers (*150*). Cochran and Stobbs (*38*) determined from film measurements that the "hub" for the swing, or central pivot point, was the center of the upper chest rather than the head.

Cinematography also has been used to study the following aspects of golf: the relationship between hip joint flexibility and success in golf (*134*), the changes in the movement pattern of the golf drive as a result of instruction (*165*), the performance of the short chip shot (*230*), and the performance of the putting stroke (*72*).

3. Tennis and Badminton

Striking skills used in tennis and badminton generally can be classified as sidearm and overarm patterns. Only the long and short serves in badminton, which have been contrasted to one another in a film study by Tetreault (*208*), fit best into the category of underhand patterns.

The tennis and badminton forehand and backhand strokes are similar in that the racket is moved essentially in the horizontal plane. However, wrist action has been found to make the greatest contribution to racket velocity in both of these badminton strokes (*13,175*), whereas the wrist joint remains relatively firm in the tennis drives (*171*). The joint action making early and major contributions to the forward movement of the tennis racket in the forehand and backhand drives of good tennis players has been identified as forward rotation of the pelvis at the hip joint of the leading leg (*44,117,119*). Analysis of factors influencing the direction of ball flight in the tennis forehand drive revealed that, not only were there differences in the racket angle at contact, but balls hit to the right were contacted approximately opposite the right shoulder while balls hit to the left were contacted before the oncoming ball reached the left shoulder (*19,90*).

Cinematographic analyses of the tennis serve have been conducted by Holcomb (*119*), Plagenhoef (*171,172*), and Woods (*229*). Not only the tennis serve but also the tennis smash and the badminton clear and smash all employ an overarm type of movement (*25,44*). Although the similarities among these four striking patterns and the overarm throw have been given much emphasis, Adrian and Enberg (*3*) suggested that the differences in performance of similar overarm patterns might be as important as the similarities, especially at the highly skilled level. From high speed films of three skilled college women, these investigators observed that the subject who was most proficient in all three sports showed greater intra-individual differences in the contact or release position than did the other two subjects. In the latter two subjects, the position at contact more closely resembled the contact position in their best sport.

4. Kicking Skills

Cooper and Glassow (44) have described the kicking pattern as a variation of running, in which the force is applied with the swinging limb rather than with the supporting limb. The existence of a basic pattern of movements common to all types of kicks has been recognized by several investigators (44,96,172,184,220). In this pattern, the position in which the supporting foot is placed relative to the ball is determined mainly by the desired elevation in the ball trajectory for that kick (220). Rotation of the pelvis at the supporting hip then occurs, its magnitude being related directly to the length of the last approach step and the angle of the approach (172,184). The thigh of the kicking leg is brought forward by this hip rotation and also by hip flexion in the kicking leg. Knee flexion reduces the angle between the thigh and lower leg to approximately 90 deg as the thigh swings forward, and it is not until the thigh decelerates and almost stops flexing just before impact that knee extension begins and rapidly accelerates (44,172,184). At the time of impact, knee extension is the major joint action contributing to ball velocity (17,44,184).

Motion pictures of one performer executing the football toe kick as well as using the instep kick on a soccer ball and a football from both the side and straight approaches were analyzed by Plagenhoef (172). The angled approach was found to produce a greater ball velocity than did the straight approach. However, the greatest foot velocity just before impact did not always result in the greatest ball velocity, since ball velocity was dependent upon both the foot velocity and the firmness of the foot at impact. In addition to determining ball and foot velocities in different types of kicks, Plagenhoef presented a descriptive analysis and comparison of selected movement aspects in these kicks.

Cinematographic analyses of the following kicking skills performed by adults have provided qualitative and quantitative information regarding the movement pattern essentials: the soccer style place kick in football (51,71,183), the instep kick of a soccer ball (29,184,187), the football place kick and kickoff (17,199), the football punt (44,96,172,184,198,220), and the soccer cross kick (172). From films of preschool children, developmental changes in the skill of punting (220) and in the skill of kicking a stationary ball from a starting position directly behind the ball (53) have been recorded.

5. Other Striking Skills

For certain striking skills, cinematographic analyses were not of sufficient number to warrant a detailed review. These striking skills include the field hockey pass (39) and drive (231), the volleyball spike (52) and forearm bump pass (173), selected handball strokes (121), and two techniques of heading a soccer ball (148).

C. PUSHING AND PULLING

In general, during the preparatory phase of pushing skills, the acting body segments are moved toward each other, and in the force-producing phase they are moved away from each other. The direction of these movements is reversed in the two phases of pulling skills (44). Lifting actions used to raise heavy weights include a pushing pattern in the lower extremities and a pull followed by a push in the upper extremities as the weight is raised above shoulder level.

1. Basketball Shooting

The basketball shooting style used by most expert performers consists of a pushing pattern in one upper limb. Relative changes in the relationship between the segments of the shooting arm during the field goal shot (68) and the jump shot (108,191,203,204) have been analyzed from motion picture films. Joint actions used to project the ball were reported to be shoulder flexion, elbow extension, and wrist flexion. The best performer of the four professional basketball players studied by Szymanski (203,204) kept his shoulder, elbow, and wrist in the same plane as the center of the basket as revealed by the front view camera. Other subjects who positioned the elbow joint either toward the inside or outside of the plane joining the shoulder and center of the basket had greater angular deviations of the shot.

2. Shot Put

The sequence of movements in putting the shot can be described by dividing the action into three phases: the glide, the trunk rotation, and the arm thrust. Aspects of these actions and their effect on the velocity of the shot have been analyzed from films of skilled performers (34,44, 65,83,84). The path of the shot from starting point until release was plotted by Dyson (65) and by Francis (83,84) for skilled putters. Those subjects who achieved the greatest velocity of the shot at release tended to increase this velocity gradually and smoothly during the glide, or first phase of this skill.

Greatest acceleration of the shot occurred, for most subjects, as the supporting foot came to rest at the end of the glide and the trunk rotation and final step onto the front foot began (65,84). At the start of the second phase, however, some performers were observed to dip markedly toward the center of the circle, which resulted in a decrease in the velocity of the shot before the final thrust and a lower release velocity. During the last portion of forward trunk rotation the arm thrust, consisting of shoulder horizontal adduction and flexion, elbow extension, and wrist flexion gave final impetus to the shot (44). The mean height of release for the eight outstanding shot-putters studied by Francis (84) was reported to be 6 in. above the 6 ft average height of these subjects.

3. Fencing

The upper limb action of the foil arm in many fencing moves can be considered to be a pushing action (44). Mastropaolo (147) analyzed motion pictures of European champion fencers and concluded that performances from each of five variations in the classical on-guard were superior, for certain fundamentals of fencing, to performances from the classical on-guard position.

4. Weight Lifting

Cinematographic techniques have been used to analyze the two hand snatch (6) and the clean and jerk (217) events in weight lifting. The five proficient subjects performing the clean and jerk were found by Whitcomb (217) to have in common numerous aspects of the general movement pattern. However, definite differences among the lifters were observed on specific factors selected for measurement, such as barbell path, barbell and lifter velocity, joint angles, and foot and hand positioning.

IV. Stopping Moving Objects

Many motor skills performed by man require the ability to stop a moving object. In some skills this object may be an external one, such as a ball, or it may be the performer's own body, as when he lands from a jump. Although the joint actions in the movement pattern vary with the situation, they are generally ones that allow the momentum of the moving object to be decreased gradually.

Cinematographic analyses of movement patterns within this category are relatively limited in number. Some studies have been conducted on the skill of catching, but the specific analysis of the landing or falling aspects of an activity was rarely the primary focus of any investigation.

The fundamental skill of catching can be considered to include the stopping and controlling of any moving ball, whether it is rolling, bouncing, or aerial (*220*). In a film study of children 2 through 6 years of age, Deach (*53*) observed that one of the first developmental stages in attempts to catch a softly tossed aerial ball was a fear reaction. Indications of this reaction included turning the head to one side to avert the eyes and head from the line of ball flight, closing the eyes, and bending the trunk backward slightly. At this stage, the ball frequently rebounded from the child's chest or from the outstretched, rigid arms. Subsequent stages in catching behavior were characterized by scooping the ball toward the chest, and finally, by using the hands to grasp and control the ball (*220*).

A cinematographic analysis of the arm and hand positions used by 7 and 9 year old boys to catch balls 3 in. and 10 in. in diameter was conducted by Victors (*215*). While considerable variability was found to exist among and within the subjects, it was concluded that the grasping pattern and the hand position immediately prior to contact most clearly differentiated successful from unsuccessful performances. Catching was more successful when both hands contacted the ball simultaneously and when closure was simultaneous with both hands. The hand position observed most frequently in successful catchers was with the fingers forward and the palms up. A vicelike position with the palm of the top hand facing forward and the palm of the bottom hand facing upward also was used often and successfully by these subjects. Although some components in catching behavior were reported to differ as ball size varied, the distinction between successful and unsuccessful catches was not otherwise related to the variable of ball size.

V. Additional Cinematographic Studies

Several cinematographic analyses have been conducted on skills and motor patterns that either cannot easily be categorized according to the movement classification scheme employed in this paper, or contain elements within the performance that fit into more than one category of the scheme. Therefore, these analyses will be mentioned here and grouped, where possible, according to the activity or sport in which the skill occurs.

Within the sport of judo, the external mechanics of eight judo throws were examined by Uchida (*210*), while a kinetic analysis of the back breakfall and force of impact was carried out by Deusinger (*56*). Cinematographic techniques have been used to analyze several basic wrestling moves: the double leg takedown (*2*), the double leg drop, switch, and sit-out (*15*), two methods of "riding" to control an opponent from behind (*209*), and selected leg maneuvers (*211*).

Study of motion picture films also has enabled investigators to obtain descriptive and quantitative information regarding the performance of the parallel skiing turn downhill on steep and low slopes (*7*), the lacrosse cradle (*186*), the center snap in the football punt formation (*115*), and selected techniques in horseback riding (*182,218*).

VI. Concluding Statement

The cinematographic approach to the study of human motion has revealed information that can be of value to teachers, performers, coaches, clinicians, and to scientists from many fields who are interested in how man moves. While a common method of investigation was employed by all researchers whose studies were reviewed in this paper, the variety in the types of motor skills examined was great. For some skills, however, only one or two film analyses have been conducted, while for many other motor patterns not reported here, research incorporating cinematographic techniques has been virtually nonexistent. Surely, with the continual improvement of equipment and procedures for filming and for analysis of films, the number and the quality of cinematographic analyses of motor skills will increase in the years to come.

References

1. Abbot, R. R. (1943). A Cinematographic Analysis of the Technique of Hurdling. Unpublished Master's Thesis, Univ. of Illinois, Urbana, Illinois.
2. Adler, C. E. (1970). A Comparison of Beginning and Experienced Wrestlers Using the Double Leg Takedown Through Cinematographical Analysis. Unpublished Master's Thesis, Brigham Young Univ., Provo, Utah.
3. Adrian, M. J., and Enberg, M. L. (1971). *In* "Kinesiology Review 1971" (C. Widule, ed.), pp. 1–9. AAHPER, Washington, D. C.
4. Altfillisch, J. (1947). A Mechanical Analysis of Starting and Running. Unpublished Master's Thesis, Univ. of Iowa, Iowa City, Iowa.
5. Anderson, N. M., and Randall, F. C. (1931). An Experimental Study of Factors Which Influence Speed in Running. Unpublished Master's Thesis, Univ. of Wisconsin, Madison, Wisconsin.
6. Arsenault, A. S. (1957). A Mechanical Analysis of the Two Weight Lifting Methods of Two Hands Snatching. Unpublished Master's Thesis, Springfield College, Springfield, Massachusetts.

7. Artus, M. A. (1967). A Comparative Study of the Mechanics of a Parallel Skiing Turn Downhill Between Two Different Angles of Slopes Through Cinematographical Analysis. Master's Thesis, Smith College, Northampton, Massachusetts. (Univ. of Oregon Microcard, PE 993.)

8. Atwater, A. E., and Roberts, E. M. (1968). In "Research Abstracts," p. 81. AAHPER, Washington, D. C.

9. Atwater, A. E. (1970). Movement Characteristics of the Overarm Throw: A Kinematic Analysis of Men and Women Performers. Doctoral Dissertation, Univ. of Wisconsin, Madison, Wisconsin. (Univ. of Oregon Microcard, PE 1235.)

10. Austin, J. M. (1959). Cinematographic Analysis of the Double Backward Somersault. Unpublished Master's Thesis, Univ. of Illinois, Urbana, Illinois.

11. Bare, F. L. (1959). A Cinematographic Analysis of the Stutzkehre on the Parallel Bars. Unpublished Master's Thesis, Univ. of Illinois, Urbana, Illinois.

12. Barlow, D. A. (1970). Relationship Between Power and Selected Variables in the Vertical Jump. Unpublished Master's Thesis, Pennsylvania State Univ., University Park, Pennsylvania.

13. Barth, D. A. (1961). A Cinematographic Analysis of the Badminton Backhand Stroke. Master's Thesis, Univ. of Illinois, Urbana, Illinois. (Univ. of Oregon Microcard, PE 559.)

14. Bartholomaus, S. K. (1967). A Mechanical Analysis of Selected Differentials Between Maximal- and Submaximal-Ability Pole Vaulters. Master's Thesis, Washington State Univ., Pullman, Washington. (Univ. of Oregon Microcard, PE 996.)

15. Bartkowiak, D. S. (1959). A Cinematographical Analysis of Three Basic Wrestling Moves. Unpublished Master's Thesis, Univ. of Wisconsin, Madison, Wisconsin.

16. Beck, M. C. (1966). The Path of the Center of Gravity During Running in Boys Grades One to Six. Doctoral Dissertation, Univ. of Wisconsin, Madison, Wisconsin. (Univ. of Oregon Microcard, PE 733.)

17. Becker, J. W. (1963). The Mechanical Analysis of a Football Place Kick. Master's Thesis, Univ. of Wisconsin, Madison, Wisconsin. (Univ. of Oregon Microcard, PE 661.)

18. Blievernicht, D. L. (1964). Side Horse Double Leg Circles: A Cinematographic Analysis. Master's Thesis, Univ. of Wisconsin, Madison, Wisconsin. (Univ. of Oregon Microcard, PE 662.)

19. Blievernicht, J. G. (1968). Res. Quart. 39, 776–778.

20. Bowerman, B., and Brown, G. S. (1971). Sports Illus. (Aug. 2) 35, 22–29.

21. Bowne, M. E. (1956). The Relationship of Selected Measures of Acting Body Levers to Ball Throwing Velocities. Unpublished Doctoral Dissertation, Univ. of Wisconsin, Madison, Wisconsin.

22. Bowne, M. E. (1960). Res. Quart. 31, 392–402.

23. Breen, J. R. (1967). J. Health, Phys. Educ., Recreation 38, 36–39. April.

24. Brennan, L. J. (1968). A Comparative Analysis of the Golf Drive and Seven-Iron Shot with Emphasis on Pelvic and Spinal Rotation. Master's Thesis, Univ. of Wisconsin, Madison, Wisconsin. (Univ. of Oregon Microcard, PE 922.)

25. Broer, M. R. (1966). "Efficiency of Human Movement," 2nd ed. Saunders, Philadelphia, Pennsylvania.

26. Brophy, K. J. (1948). A Kinesiological Study of the Improvement in Motor

Skill. Unpublished Doctoral Dissertation, Univ. of Wisconsin, Madison, Wisconsin.

27. Brown, R. M., and Counsilman, J. E. (1971). *In* "Proceedings of C. I. C. Symposium on Biomechanics" (J. Cooper, ed.), pp. 179–188. Athletic Inst., Chicago, Illinois.
28. Bunn, J. W. (1960). "Scientific Principles of Coaching." Prentice-Hall, Englewood Cliffs, New Jersey.
29. Burdan, P. (1955). A Cinematographical Analysis of Three Basic Kicks used in Soccer. Master's Thesis, Pennsylvania State Univ., University Park, Pennsylvania. (Univ. of Oregon Microcard, PE 312.)
30. Carlson, R. E. (1962). Analysis of the Forward Pass. Master's Thesis, Washington State Univ., Pullman, Washington. (Univ. of Oregon Microcard, PE 585.)
31. Carter, V. A. (1969). *New Zealand J. Phys. Educ.* **2**, 42–50. November.
32. Cavagna, G. A., Margaria, R., and Arcelli, E. (1965). *Res. Film* **5**, 309–319.
33. Chadwick, A. W. (1967). A Cinematographical Analysis of Ten Breaststroke Swimmers, Including Certain Strength and Anthropometric Measures. Unpublished Master's Thesis, Michigan State Univ., East Lansing, Michigan.
34. Cheffers, J. T. F. (1970). A Cinematographical Comparison of Seven Aspects of Two Shot Put Actions. Unpublished Master's Thesis, Temple Univ., Philadelphia, Pennsylvania.
35. Clayton, I. A. (1936). A Study of the Evidence of Motor Age Based on Technique of Standing Broad Jump. Unpublished Master's Thesis, Univ. of Wisconsin, Madison, Wisconsin.
36. Clemence, W. J. (1968). A Cinematographical Study of the Variation in Momentum When Swinging Varying Clubhead Weights. Doctoral Dissertation, Univ. of Arkansas, Fayetteville, Arkansas. (Univ. of Oregon Microcard, PE 1239.)
37. Clouse, F. C. (1959). A Kinematic Analysis of the Development of the Running Pattern of PreSchool Boys. Doctoral Dissertation, Univ. of Wisconsin, Madison, Wisconsin. (Univ. of Oregon Microcard, PE 776.)
38. Cochran, A., and Stobbs, J. (1968). "The Search for the Perfect Swing." Lippincott, New York.
39. Cohen, J. S. (1969). The Field Hockey Pass: A Cinematographic Analysis. Master's Thesis, Univ. of Wisconsin, Madison, Wisconsin. (Univ. of Oregon Microcard, PE 1061.)
40. Collins, P. A. (1960). Body Mechanics of the Overarm and Sidearm Throws. Master's Thesis, Univ. of Wisconsin, Madison, Wisconsin. (Univ. of Oregon Microcard, PE 508.)
41. Collins, P. A. (1968). A Film Analysis of Selected Swimming Stroke Kicks. Doctoral Dissertation, Univ. of Iowa, Iowa City, Iowa. (Univ. of Oregon Microcard, PE 1124.)
42. Conard, R. M. (1951). A Mechanical Analysis of the Skill of Batting. Unpublished Master's Thesis, Univ. of Wisconsin, Madison, Wisconsin.
43. Conard, R. M. (1965). A Cinematographical Analysis of the Major Sequential Movement Patterns of Skilled, Semi-Skilled, and Non-Skilled Baseball Batters. Doctoral Dissertation, Temple Univ., Philadelphia, Pennsylvania. (Univ. of Oregon Microcard, PE 1003.)
44. Cooper, J. M., and Glassow, R. B. (1972). "Kinesiology," 3rd ed. Mosby, St. Louis, Missouri.
45. Counsilman, J. E. (1948). A Cinematographic and Mechanical Analysis of the

Butterfly Breaststroke. Unpublished Master's Thesis, Univ. of Illinois, Urbana, Illinois.

46. Counsilman, J. E. (1968). "The Science of Swimming." Prentice-Hall, Englewood Cliffs, New Jersey.

47. Couper, M. E. (1965). An Analysis of the Transfer of Horizontal Momentum to a Vertical Jump. Master's Thesis, Smith College, Northampton, Massachusetts. (Univ. of Oregon Microcard, PE 742.)

48. Cureton, T. K. (1939). *Res. Quart.* **10,** 3–24.

49. Danforth, S. P. (1964). Cinematographic Analysis of Clubhead Withdrawal in Golf. Unpublished Master's Thesis, Univ. of California, Los Angeles, California.

50. Darda, G. E. (1972). A Method of Determining the Relative Contributions of the Diver and Springboard to the Vertical Ascent of the Forward Three and One-Half Somersaults Tuck. Unpublished Doctoral Dissertation, Univ. of Wisconsin, Madison, Wisconsin.

51. Davies, M. H. (1969). A Cinematographic Analysis Comparing Two Selected Styles of Place Kicking. Unpublished Master's Thesis, Sacramento State College, Sacramento, California.

52. Davis, D. L. (1968). A Cinematographic Comparison of a Volleyball Spike Performed With and Without Ankle Weights. Unpublished Master's Thesis, Univ. of Massachusetts, Amherst, Massachusetts.

53. Deach, D. (1950). Genetic Development of Motor Skills in Children Two Through Six Years of Age. Unpublished Doctoral Dissertation, Univ. of Michigan, Ann Arbor, Michigan.

54. Deshon, D. E., and Nelson, R. C. (1964). *Res. Quart.* **35,** 451–455.

55. Desrochers, R. A. (1963). A Cinematographical Study on the Effects of Four Different Footspacings on the Starting Time of Trained Sprinters. Unpublished Master's Thesis, Univ. of Maryland, College Park, Maryland.

56. Deusinger, R. H. (1968). A Kinetic Analysis of the Back Breakfall and Force of Impact in Judo. Unpublished Master's Thesis, Univ. of Massachusetts, Amherst, Massachusetts.

57. Deutsch, H. M. (1969). A Comparison of Women's Throwing Patterns. Doctoral Dissertation, Univ. of Illinois, Urbana, Illinois. (Univ. of Oregon Microcard, PE 1296.)

58. deVries, H. A. (1959). *Res. Quart.* **30,** 413–422.

59. Dillman, C. J. (1966). Energy Transformations During the Pole Vault With a Fiberglass Pole. Master's Thesis, Pennsylvania State Univ., University Park, Pennsylvania. (Univ. of Oregon Microcard, PH 196.)

60. Dillman, C. J. (1970). Muscular Torque Patterns of the Leg During the Recovery Phase of Sprint Running. Unpublished Doctoral Dissertation, Pennsylvania State Univ., University Park, Pennsylvania.

61. Dittmer, J. A. (1962). A Kinematic Analysis of the Development of the Running Pattern of Grade School Girls and Certain Factors which Distinguish Good from Poor Performance at the Observed Ages. Master's Thesis, Univ. of Wisconsin, Madison, Wisconsin. (Univ. of Oregon Microcard, PE 614.)

62. Dolan, J. L. (1969). A Cinematographical Analysis of Selected Javelin Throwers. Unpublished Master's Thesis, Pennsylvania State Univ., University Park, Pennsylvania.

63. Duck, T. A. (1970). An Electrogoniometric Study of the Front Hand Spring. Unpublished Master's Thesis, Springfield College, Springfield, Massachusetts.

64. Dusenbury, J. (1968). A Kinetic Comparison of Forward and Reverse Giant

Swings on Still Rings as Performed by Gymnasts with Varying Body Types. Unpublished Master's Thesis, Univ. of Massachusetts, Amherst, Massachusetts.
65. Dyson, G. H. G. (1971). "The Mechanics of Athletics," 5th ed. Univ. of London Press, London.
66. Eberhart, H. D., Inman, V. T., Saunders, J. B. DeC. M., Levens, A. S., Bresler, B., and McCowan, T. D. (1947). Fundamental Studies of Human Locomotion and Other Information Relating to the Design of Artificial Limbs. A Report to the National Research Council, Committee on Artificial Limbs. Univ. of California, Berkeley, California.
67. Eckert, H. M. (1968). *Res. Quart.* **39,** 937–942.
68. Edwards, J. H. (1958). A Cinematographical Study of Field Goal Shooting Characteristics as Indicated by Successful College Basketball Teams. Unpublished Master's Thesis, Univ. of Maryland, College Park, Maryland.
69. Ehrhart, R. R. (1957). A Cinematographic Analysis of the One Mile Run. Unpublished Master's Thesis, Univ. of Illinois, Urbana, Illinois.
70. Ekern, S. R. (1969). An Analysis of Selected Measures of the Overarm Throwing Patterns of Elementary School Boys and Girls. Doctoral Dissertation, Univ. of Wisconsin, Madison, Wisconsin. (Univ. of Oregon Microcard, PE 1128.)
71. Fairey, M. (1966). A Kinesiological Analysis of the Soccer Style Placekick in Football Through the Use of Cinematography. Unpublished Master's Thesis, Univ. of Maryland, College Park, Maryland.
72. Fako, P. (1952). A Mechanical Analysis of the Golf Putt. Unpublished Master's Thesis, Springfield College, Springfield, Massachusetts.
73. Fanning, W. J. (1961). A Cinematographic and Mechanical Analysis and Comparative Study of the Catcher's Throw. Unpublished Master's Thesis, Univ. of Illinois, Urbana, Illinois.
74. Felton, E. A. (1960). A Kinesiological Comparison of Good and Poor Performers in the Standing Broad Jump. Master's Thesis, Univ. of Wisconsin, Madison, Wisconsin. (Univ. of Oregon Microcard, PE 510.)
75. Fenn, W. O. (1930). *Amer. J. Physiol.* **92,** 583–611.
76. Fenn, W. O. (1930). *Amer. J. Physiol.* **93,** 433–462.
77. Fenn, W. O. (1931). *Sci. Mon.* **32,** 346–354.
78. Ferriter, K. J. (1964). A Cinematographic Analysis of Front Handspring Vaults of Women Gymnasts. Unpublished Master's Thesis, Univ. of Illinois, Urbana, Illinois.
79. Finley, R. (1961). Kinesiological Analysis of Human Motion. Unpublished Doctoral Dissertation, Springfield College, Springfield, Massachusetts.
80. Flanagan, J. J. (1961). A Descriptive and Mechanical Analysis of the First Three Dives in the Reverse Group. Master's Thesis, Florida State Univ., Tallahassee, Florida. (Univ. of Oregon Microcard, PE 617.)
81. Fortier, F. J. (1969). A Cinematographical and Mechanical Analysis of the Forward Handspring, the Backward Handspring, and the Forward Somersault. Unpublished Master's Thesis, McNeese State College, Lake Charles, Louisiana.
82. Fortney, V. (1963). The Swinging Limb in Running of Boys Ages Seven Through Eleven. Master's Thesis, Univ. of Wisconsin, Madison, Wisconsin. (Univ. of Oregon Microcard, PE 648.)
83. Francis, S. (1941). Mechanical Analysis of the Acceleration and Velocity Involved in the Technique of Putting the Shot. Unpublished Master's Thesis, Univ. of Iowa, Iowa City, Iowa.
84. Francis, S. (1948). *Athletic J.* **28,** 34–50. January.

85. Gagnon, M. (1969). The Biomechanics of the Sprint Start. Master's Thesis, Pennsylvania State Univ., University Park, Pennsylvania. (Univ. of Oregon Microcard, PE 1250.)
86. Ganslen, R. V. (1940). A Mechanical Analysis of the Pole Vault. Unpublished Master's Thesis, Springfield College, Springfield, Massachusetts.
87. Ganslen, R. V. (1965). "Mechanics of the Pole Vault," 6th ed. John Swift, St. Louis, Missouri.
88. Garrison, L. E. (1963). Electromyographic-Cinematographic Study of Muscular Activity During the Golf Swing. Doctoral Dissertation, Florida State Univ., Tallahassee, Florida. (Univ. of Oregon Microcard, PE 618.)
89. Gearon, J. (1970). A Comparison of the Golf Drive of Saunders and Weiskopf. Unpublished Master's Thesis, Univ. of Massachusetts, Amherst, Massachusetts.
90. Gelner, J. (1965). Accuracy in the Tennis Forehand Drive—A Cinematographic Analysis. Master's Thesis, Univ. of Wisconsin, Madison, Wisconsin. (Univ. of Oregon Microcard, PE 747.)
91. George, G. S. (1967). A Cinematographic and Mechanical Analysis of the Arched Kip on the Horizontal Bar. Unpublished Master's Thesis, Springfield College, Springfield, Massachusetts.
92. George, G. S. (1970). A Cinematographic and Comparative Analysis of National Class Gymnasts Performing Selected Skills on the Horizontal Bar. Unpublished Doctoral Dissertation, Louisiana State Univ., Baton Rouge, Louisiana.
93. Gerrish, P. H. (1934). A Dynamic Analysis of the Standing Vertical Jump. Unpublished Doctoral Dissertation, Columbia Univ., New York.
94. Glassow, R. B. (1932). "Fundamentals of Physical Education." Lea & Febiger, Philadelphia, Pennsylvania.
95. Glassow, R. B., Halverson, L. E., and Rarick, G. L. (1965). Improvement of Motor Development and Physical Fitness in Elementary School Children. Cooperative Research Project No. 696, Univ. of Wisconsin, Madison, Wisconsin. (Univ. of Oregon Microcard, PE 708.)
96. Glassow, R. B., and Mortimer, E. M. (1971). In "Selected Soccer and Speedball Articles," 3rd ed., pp. 29–34. AAHPER, Washington, D. C.
97. Glencross, D. J. (1964). New Zealand J. Phys. Educ. 3, 29–37. July.
98. Gombac, R. (1971). In "Biomechanics II, Medicine and Sport," Vol. 6 (J. Vredenbregt and J. Wartenweiler, eds.), pp. 232–235. Karger, New York.
99. Graves, S. A. (1964). A Cinematographical Analysis of the Vertical Jump. Unpublished Master's Thesis, Smith College, Northampton, Massachusetts.
100. Griffiths, A. M. (1970). A Cinematographic Analysis of Selected Golf Strokes. Unpublished Doctoral Dissertation, Univ. of Iowa, Iowa City, Iowa.
101. Grossfeld, A. I. (1962). The Underbar Somersault on the Parallel Bars. Master's Thesis, Univ. of Illinois, Urbana, Illinois. (Univ. of Oregon Microcard, PE 620.)
102. Groves, W. H. (1949). A Study in the Mechanical Analysis of Diving. Unpublished Master's Thesis, State Univ. of Iowa, Iowa City, Iowa.
103. Groves, W. H. (1950). Res. Quart. 21, 132–144.
104. Guerrera, D. H. (1968). A Cinematographical and Mechanical Analysis of Selected Long Horse Vaults. Master's Thesis, Pennsylvania State Univ., University Park, Pennsylvania. (Univ. of Oregon Microcard, PE 1132.)
105. Hairbedian, T. M. (1969). Selected Factors Affecting the Success of the Forward Three and One-Half and Backward Two and One-Half Somersault Dives. Unpublished Doctoral Dissertation, Univ. of Missouri, Columbia, Missouri.

106. Haldeman, N. D. (1958). A Cinematographical Analysis of the Standing High Jump as Related to the Basketball Jump-Ball Situation. Unpublished Master's Thesis, Pennsylvania State Univ., University Park, Pennsylvania.

107. Halverson, L. E. (1958). A Comparison of Performance of Kindergarten Children in the Take-Off Phase of the Standing Broad Jump. Doctoral Dissertation, Univ. of Wisconsin, Madison, Wisconsin. (Univ. of Oregon Microcard, PE 750.)

108. Hamilton, P. A. (1970). A Mechanical Analysis and Comparison of Two Jump Shots Performed by a Female Basketball Player. Unpublished Master's Thesis, Univ. of Massachusetts, Amherst, Massachusetts.

109. Harris, R. B. (1939). A Cinematographical Study of the Upstart on the High Horizontal Bar. Unpublished Master's Thesis, Springfield College, Springfield, Massachusetts.

110. Hay, J. G. (1965). Pole Vaulting: A Mechanical Analysis of Factors Influencing Pole-Bend. Master's Thesis, Univ. of Iowa, Iowa City, Iowa. (Univ. of Oregon Microcard, PE 782.)

111. Hay, J. G. (1967). *Res. Quart.* 38, 34–40.

112. Hay, J. G. (1967). An Investigation of Mechanical Efficiency in Two Styles of High Jumping. Doctoral Dissertation, Univ. of Iowa, Iowa City, Iowa. (Univ. of Oregon Microcard, PE 1134.)

113. Hay, J. G. (1968). *Res. Quart.* 39, 983–992.

114. Hellebrandt, F. A., Rarick, G. L., Glassow, R. B., and Carns, M. L. (1961). *Amer. J. Phys. Med.* 40, 14–25.

115. Henrici, R. C. (1967). A Cinematographical Analysis of the Center Snap in the Punt Formation. Master's Thesis, Univ. of Wisconsin, Madison, Wisconsin. (Univ. of Oregon Microcard, PE 895.)

116. Heydman, A. W. (1970). A Mechanical Analysis of the Forward Pass. Unpublished Master's Thesis, North Texas State Univ., Denton, Texas.

117. Hobart, D. J. (1967). A Cinematographical Analysis of the Tennis Backhand Using Three Different Levels of Skill. Unpublished Master's Thesis, Univ. of Maryland, College Park, Maryland.

118. Högberg, P. (1952). *Arbeitsphysiologie* 14, 431–436.

119. Holcomb, D. L. (1962). A Cinematographical Analysis of the Forehand, Backhand, and American Twist Serve Tennis Strokes. Unpublished Master's Thesis, Florida State Univ., Tallahassee, Florida.

120. Holmes, H. Z. (1968). A Cinematographic Analysis of the Backward Handspring. Unpublished Master's Thesis, Univ. of Illinois, Urbana, Illinois.

121. Holt, L. E. (1963). A Comparative Study of Selected Handball Techniques. Unpublished Master's Thesis, Springfield College, Springfield, Massachusetts.

122. Hough, J. E. (1970). A Film Analysis of the Glide Kip. Unpublished Master's Thesis, Univ. of Tennessee, Knoxville, Tennessee.

123. Hubbard, A. W. (1959). *In* "Research Methods in Health, Physical Education, and Recreation" (M. G. Scott, ed.), 2nd ed., pp. 128–147. AAHPER, Washington, D. C.

124. Hubbard, A. W., and Seng, C. N. (1954). *Res. Quart.* 25, 42–57.

125. Jones, C. L. (1970). Cinematographic Analysis of Two Techniques of Performing a Standing Front Dive. Unpublished Master's Thesis, Southern Illinois Univ., Carbondale, Illinois.

126. Jones, F. G. (1951). A Descriptive and Mechanical Analysis of Throwing

Skills of Children. Unpublished Master's Thesis, Univ. of Wisconsin, Madison, Wisconsin.

127. Kenny, J. O. (1938). A Study of Relative Speeds of Different Types of Pitched Balls. Unpublished Master's Thesis, Univ. of Iowa, Iowa City, Iowa.

128. King, J. W., Brelsford, H. J., and Tullos, H. S. (1969). *Clin. Orthop.* **67**, 116–123.

129. Kitzman, E. W. (1962). Baseball: Electromyographic Study of Batting-Swing. Doctoral Dissertation, State Univ. of Iowa, Iowa City, Iowa. (Univ. of Oregon Microcard, PE 627.)

130. Kitzman, E. W. (1964). *Res. Quart.* **35**, 166–178.

131. Knoll, W., and Morenz, W. (1932). *Arbeitsphysiologie* **5**, 227–238.

132. Kuznetsov, V. L. (1960). *Track Tech.* **2**, 46–52. December.

133. Lafler, J. (1943). A Mechanical Analysis of Diving Techniques. Unpublished Master's Thesis, State Univ. of Iowa, Iowa City, Iowa.

134. Lamaster, M. A. (1960). Flexibility of the Hip Joint and its Relationship to Success in Golf. Unpublished Master's Thesis, Univ. of Wisconsin, Madison, Wisconsin.

135. Lamb, W. H. (1968). A Cinematographical Analysis of the Javelin Throw. Unpublished Master's Thesis, Univ. of Kansas, Lawrence, Kansas.

136. Lanoue, F. R. (1936). Mechanics of Fancy Diving. Unpublished Master's Thesis, Springfield College, Springfield, Massachusetts.

137. Lanoue, F. R. (1940). *Res. Quart.* **11**, 102–109.

138. Lapp, V. (1938). A Motion Picture Analysis of the Technique of the Throw of National Champions. Unpublished Master's Thesis, Univ. of Iowa, Iowa City, Iowa.

139. Lascari, A. T. (1967). *Gymnast* **2**, 13–14, February.

140. Lascari, A. T. (1970). The Felge Handstand—A Comparative Kinetic Analysis of a Gymnastics Skill. Doctoral Dissertation, Univ. of Wisconsin, Madison, Wisconsin. (Univ. of Oregon Microcard, PE 1309.)

141. Lashuk, M. (1967). A Cinematographic Study of the Full Twisting Front Dive in Gymnastics. Unpublished Master's Thesis, Southern Illinois Univ., Carbondale, Illinois.

142. Leigh, L. Y., and Bangerter, B. L. (1967). *In* "Research Abstracts," p. 65. AAHPER, Washington, D. C.

143. Lent, J. I. (1960). An Analysis of Selected Synchronized Swimming Stunts. Unpublished Master's Thesis, State Univ. of Iowa, Iowa City, Iowa.

144. Lesh, L. M. (1968). A Kinematic and Kinetic Comparison of Varying Golf Drive Distances of a Woman State Champion. Unpublished Master's Thesis, Univ. of Massachusetts, Amherst, Massachusetts.

145. Lindner, E. (1971). *In* "Biomechanics II, Medicine and Sport," Vol. 6 (J. Vredenbregt and J. Wartenweiler, eds.), pp. 240–245. Karger, New York.

146. Lyon, W. R. (1961). A Cinematographical Analysis of the Overhand Baseball Throw. Master's Thesis, Univ. of Wisconsin, Madison, Wisconsin. (Univ. of Oregon Microcard, PE 552.)

147. Mastropaolo, J. A. (1958). An Analysis of the Fundamentals of Fencing. Unpublished Doctoral Dissertation, State Univ. of Iowa, Iowa City, Iowa.

148. Mawdsley, H. P. (1969). A Kinematic and Kinetic Analysis of the Technique of Heading in Soccer. Unpublished Master's Thesis, Univ. of Massachusetts, Amherst, Massachusetts.

149. McCormick, G. P. (1954). A Kinesiological Study of Four Divers Executing the Full Twisting Forward One and One-Half Somersault. Unpublished Master's Thesis, Univ. of Southern California, Los Angeles, California.

150. McIntyre, N., and Snyder, R. (1962). *Golf Dig.* **12**, 86–90. December.
151. McIntyre, N., and Snyder, R. (1964). *Golf Dig.* **14**, 48–51. March.
152. Miller, D. I. (1970). A Computer Simulation Model of the Airborne Phase of Diving. Unpublished Doctoral Dissertation, Pennsylvania State Univ., University Park, Pennsylvania.
153. Morris, R. H. (1958). A Cinematographic Study of the Pole Plant and Take-Off of Successful Pole Vaulters. Unpublished Master's Thesis, Univ. of Southern California, Los Angeles, California.
154. Murray, M. P. (1967). *Amer. J. Phys. Med.* **46**, 290–333.
155. Murray, M. P., and Clarkson, B. H. (1966). *J. Amer. Phys. Therapy Ass.* **46**, 585–599.
156. Murray, M. P., Drought, A. B., and Kory, R. C. (1964). *J. Bone Joint Surg., Amer. Vol.* **46**, 335–360.
157. Murray, M. P., Kory, R. C., Clarkson, B. H., and Sepic, S. B. (1966). *Amer. J. Phys. Med.* **45**, 8–24.
158. Murray, M. P., Sepic, S. B., and Barnard, E. J. (1967). *Physical Therapy* **47**, 272–284.
159. Muybridge, E. (1955). "The Human Figure in Motion." Dover, New York.
160. Nelson, R. C., and Osterhoudt, R. G. (1971). *In* "Biomechanics II, Medicine and Sport," Vol. 6 (J. Vredenbregt and J. Wartenweiler, eds.), pp. 220–224. Karger, New York.
161. Nieman, R. J. (1960). A Cinematographical Analysis of Baseball Batting. Unpublished Master's Thesis, Univ. of Wisconsin, Madison, Wisconsin.
162. Osterhoudt, R. G. (1969). A Cinematographic Analysis of Selected Aspects of the Running Stride of Experienced Track Athletes at Various Speeds and on Different Slopes. Unpublished Master's Thesis, Pennsylvania State Univ., University Park, Pennsylvania.
163. Parchman, L. L. (1970). Cinematographical and Mechanical Analysis of the Golf Swing of Female Golfers. Unpublished Doctoral Dissertation, Louisiana State Univ., Baton Rouge, Louisiana.
164. Pataky, R. L. (1969). A Cinematographic and Mechanical Analysis of the Backward Lever Pull to Iron Cross on the Still Rings. Unpublished Master's Thesis, Springfield College, Springfield, Massachusetts.
165. Peaseley, H. V. (1932). Experimental Study of Kinesiological Factors Influencing the Learning of the Golf Drive. Unpublished Master's Thesis, Univ. of Wisconsin, Madison, Wisconsin.
166. Peek, R. W. (1968). A Cinematographic and Mechanical Analysis of the Straight Arm Backward Giant Swing on the Still Rings. Master's Thesis, Springfield College, Springfield, Massachusetts. (Univ. of Oregon Microcard, PE 1090.)
167. Peiniger, M. (1969). A Cinematographical Analysis of Women High Jumpers. Unpublished Master's Thesis, Pennsylvania State Univ., University Park, Pennsylvania.
168. Pelchat, C. (1971). A Biomechanical Analysis of Selected Racing Starts in Swimming. Unpublished Master's Thesis, Pennsylvania State Univ., University Park, Pennsylvania.
169. Pikulsky, T. (1964). A Cinematographical and Mechanical Analysis of Pole Vaulting with the Fiberglass Pole. Unpublished Master's Thesis, Univ. of Maryland, College Park, Maryland.
170. Plagenhoef, S. (1969). *Mod. Gymnast* **11**, 19, February.
171. Plagenhoef, S. (1970). "Fundamentals of Tennis." Prentice-Hall, Englewood Cliffs, New Jersey.

172. Plagenhoef, S. (1971). "Patterns of Human Motion: A Cinematographic Analysis." Prentice-Hall, Englewood Cliffs, New Jersey.
173. Plunkett, F. J. (1969). Performance Characteristics in the Volleyball Bump Pass: A Cinematographic Analysis of Four Skilled Women Performers. Master's Thesis, Univ. of Wisconsin, Madison, Wisconsin. (Univ. of Oregon Microcard, PE 1094.)
174. Polacek, J. J. (1970). A Cinematographical Analysis of Loop Circles on Side Horse. Unpublished Master's Thesis, Illinois State Univ., Normal, Illinois.
175. Poole, J. R. (1970). A Cinematographic Analysis of the Upper Extremity Movements of World Class Players Executing Two Basic Badminton Strokes. Unpublished Doctoral Dissertation, Louisiana State Univ., Baton Rouge, Louisiana.
176. Puck, E. (1948). Mechanical Analysis of Batting in Baseball. Unpublished Master's Thesis, Univ. of Iowa, Iowa City, Iowa.
177. Puck, P. E. (1964). Cinematographical Analysis of Effective Batting Performance. Unpublished Master's Thesis, Illinois State Univ., Normal, Illinois.
178. Quandt, H. H. (1964). A Cinematographical Analysis of the Palm Ball Pitch Compared to the Fast Ball Pitch in Baseball. Master's Thesis, Univ. of Wisconsin, Madison, Wisconsin. (Univ. of Oregon Microcard, PE 689.)
179. Race, D. E. (1960). A Cinematographic and Mechanical Analysis of the External Movements Involved in Hitting a Baseball Effectively. Unpublished Master's Thesis, Springfield College, Springfield, Massachusetts.
180. Race, D. E. (1961). Res. Quart. 32, 394–404.
181. Rapp, K. (1963). Running Velocity: Body-Rise and Stride Length. Unpublished Master's Thesis, Univ. of Iowa, Iowa City, Iowa.
182. Re Qua, J. (1939). A Study of Essential Elements to be Used in Testing Riding Techniques. Unpublished Master's Thesis, Univ. of Wisconsin, Madison, Wisconsin.
183. Rexroad, M. R. (1968). A Cinematographical Analysis of the Soccer-Style Football Place-Kick. Unpublished Master's Thesis, Univ. of Tennessee, Knoxville, Tennessee.
184. Roberts, E. M., and Metcalfe, A. (1968). In "Biomechanics I, Medicine and Sport," Vol. 2 (J. Wartenweiler, E. Jokl, and M. Hebbelinck, eds.), pp. 315–319. Karger, New York.
185. Roy, B. G. (1971). Kinematics and Kinetics of the Standing Long Jump in Seven, Ten, Thirteen and Sixteen Year Old Boys. Doctoral Dissertation, Univ. of Wisconsin, Madison, Wisconsin. (Univ. of Oregon Microcard, PE 1323.)
186. Rozzi, L. M. (1969). A Cinematographic Analysis of the Lacrosse Cradle. Unpublished Master's Thesis, Univ. of North Carolina at Greensboro, North Carolina.
187. Russo, T. M. (1970). A Kinematic and Kinetic Analysis of the Soccer Instep Kick. Unpublished Master's Thesis, Univ. of Massachusetts, Amherst, Massachusetts.
188. Sarver, R. E. (1962). A Cinematographical Analysis of the Double Leg Circle on the Side Horse. Master's Thesis, Washington State Univ., Pullman, Washington. (Univ. of Oregon Microcard, PE 604.)
189. Schaefer, J. E. (1956). A Cinematographical Analysis of the Regular Giant Circle on the Horizontal Bar. Unpublished Master's Thesis, Univ. of Wisconsin, Madison, Wisconsin.
190. Scheuchenzuber, H. J. (1970). A Biomechanical Analysis of Four Backstroke Starts. Unpublished Master's Thesis, Pennsylvania State Univ., University Park, Pennsylvania.

191. Scolnick, A. (1968). An Electrogoniometric and Cinematographic Analysis of the Arm Action of Expert Basketball Jump Shooters. Doctoral Dissertation, Springfield College, Springfield, Massachusetts. (Univ. of Oregon Microcard, PE 905.)

192. Seng, C. N. (1952). Visual Movements of Batters in Baseball. Unpublished Master's Thesis, Univ. of Illinois, Urbana, Illinois.

193. Shea, J. (1970). A Cinematographic Study of Two Methods of Performing the Propulsive Hand-Arm Phase of the Butterfly Stroke. Unpublished Master's Thesis, Springfield College, Springfield, Massachusetts.

194. Singer, F. (1961). Comparison of the Development of the Overarm Throwing Patterns of Good and Poor Performers (Girls). Master's Thesis, Univ. of Wisconsin, Madison, Wisconsin. (Univ. of Oregon Microcard, PE 576.)

195. Slocum, D. B., and Bowerman, W. (1962). *Clin. Orthop.* **23**, 39–45.

196. Slocum, D. B., and James, S. L. (1968). *J. Amer. Med. Ass.* **205**, 721–728.

197. Smith, R. L. (1967). A Cinemagraphical Analysis of the Triple Jump. Master's Thesis, Univ. of Kansas, Lawrence, Kansas. (Univ. of Oregon Microcard, PE 984.)

198. Smith, W. H. (1949). A Cinematographic Analysis of Football Punting. Unpublished Master's Thesis, Univ. of Illinois, Urbana, Illinois.

199. Stalwick, D. W. (1967). A Cinematographic Analysis of the Football Kickoff. Unpublished Master's Thesis, Univ. of California, Los Angeles, California.

200. Steben, R. E. (1970). *Res. Quart.* **41**, 95–104.

201. Sullivan, R. M. (1955). The Forward Somersault on the Parallel Bars. Unpublished Master's Thesis, Univ. of Illinois, Urbana, Illinois.

202. Swimley, P. S. (1964). A Cinematographic Analysis of Two Selected Baseball Swings. Master's Thesis, Sacramento State College, Sacramento, California. (Univ. of Oregon Microcard, PE 1286.)

203. Szymanski, F. A. (1966). A Cinematographical Analysis of the Mechanics of the Jump Shot as Performed by Professional Basketball Players. Unpublished Master's Thesis, Univ. of Maryland, College Park, Maryland.

204. Szymanski, F. A. (1967). *Scholastic Coach* **37**, 8–9, 59–60. October.

205. Tarbell, T. (1971). *In* "Proceedings of C. I. C. Symposium on Biomechanics" (J. Cooper, ed.), pp. 71–81. Athletic Inst., Chicago, Illinois.

206. Taylor, P. R. (1971). The Relationship Among Mechanical Characteristics, Running Efficiency, and Performance of Varsity Track Men. Unpublished Doctoral Dissertation, Indiana Univ., Bloomington, Indiana.

207. Teeple, J. B. (1968). A Biomechanical Analysis of Running Patterns of College Women. Master's Thesis, Pennsylvania State Univ., University Park, Pennsylvania. (Univ. of Oregon Microcard, PE 1163.)

208. Tetreault, E. H. (1964). A Mechanical Analysis of Two Badminton Serves. Unpublished Master's Thesis, Springfield College, Springfield, Massachusetts.

209. Turner, B. J. (1959). A Cinematographic Analysis of a Wrestling Technique— Control of Opponent from Behind. Unpublished Master's Thesis, Univ. of Illinois, Urbana, Illinois.

210. Uchida, G. S. (1967). The External Mechanics of Eight Judo Throws. Unpublished Master's Thesis, San Jose State College, San Jose, California.

211. Valentine, J. C. (1961). Mechanical Analysis of Selected Leg Maneuvers in Wrestling. Master's Thesis, State Univ. of Iowa, Iowa City, Iowa. (Univ. of Oregon Microcard, PE 528.)

212. Vanderbeck, E. R. (1967). A Cinematographic Study of Sculling Patterns. Unpublished Master's Thesis. Illinois State Univ., Normal, Illinois.
213. Vanis, G. J. (1965). A Cinematographic Analysis of the Yamashita Vault Over the Long Horse. Unpublished Master's Thesis, Univ. of Illinois, Urbana, Illinois.
214. Verwey, P. T. (1957). A Cinematographical Analysis of Two Types of Softball Pitch. Unpublished Master's Thesis, Univ. of Wisconsin, Madison, Wisconsin.
215. Victors, E. E. (1961). A Cinematographical Analysis of Catching Behavior of a Selected Group of Seven- and Nine-Year-Old Boys. Doctoral Dissertation, Univ. of Wisconsin, Madison, Wisconsin. (Univ. of Oregon Microcard, PE 579.)
216. Ward, E. B. (1968). A Cinematographical Analysis of the Straddle High Jump. Master's Thesis, Univ. of Western Ontario, London, Ontario. (Univ. of Oregon Microcard, PE 1111.)
217. Whitcomb, B. M. (1969). A Cinematographical Analysis of the Clean and Jerk Lift Used in Olympic Weightlifting. Unpublished Master's Thesis, Univ. of Maryland, College Park, Maryland.
218. White, D. M. (1940). The Development of a Specific Method of Teaching the Technique of Keeping the Seat at the Canter and Evidence of the Effectiveness of This Method. Unpublished Master's Thesis, Univ. of Wisconsin, Madison, Wisconsin.
219. Whitmore, W. W. (1958). A Cinematographical Analysis of the Discus Throw. Unpublished Master's Thesis, Univ. of Wisconsin, Madison, Wisconsin.
220. Wickstrom, R. L. (1970). "Fundamental Motor Patterns." Lea & Febiger, Philadelphia, Pennsylvania.
221. Widule, C. J. (1966). A Study of Anthropometric, Strength, and Performance Characteristics of Men and Women League Bowlers. Doctoral Dissertation, Univ. of Wisconsin, Madison, Wisconsin. (Univ. of Oregon Microcard, PE 841.)
222. Wild, M. R. (1937). The Behavior Pattern of Throwing and Some Observations Concerning its Course of Development in Children. Doctoral Dissertation, Univ. of Wisconsin, Madison, Wisconsin. (Univ. of Oregon Microcard, PE 769.)
223. Wild, M. R. (1938). *Res. Quart.* 9, 20–24.
224. Wiley, J. F. (1964). A Cinematographic and Mechanical Analysis of the Backward Somersault with a Double Twist in Tumbling. Unpublished Master's Thesis, Sacramento State College, Sacramento, California.
225. Williams, I. D. (1967). Consistency of Walking. Unpublished Master's Thesis, Univ. of Illinois, Urbana, Illinois.
226. Wilson, G. G. (1959). A Cinematographic Analysis of the Round-off. Unpublished Master's Thesis, Univ. of Illinois, Urbana, Illinois.
227. Wilson, M. (1945). Development of Jumping Skill in Children. Unpublished Doctoral Dissertation, Univ. of Iowa, Iowa City, Iowa.
228. Winter, F. W. (1966). A Photographic Analysis of Selected Twisting Dives. Unpublished Master's Thesis, Springfield College, Springfield, Massachusetts.
229. Woods, R. B. (1965). A Cinematographic Analysis of the Differences Between Good Servers in Tennis and Poor Servers. Unpublished Master's Thesis, Univ. of Massachusetts, Amherst, Massachusetts.
230. Wrigglesworth, F. (1964). A Cinematographical Analysis of the Short Chip Shot in Golf. Master's Thesis, Univ. of Wisconsin, Madison, Wisconsin. (Univ. of Oregon Microcard, PE 698.)
231. Zerbe, A. J. (1970). A Cinematographic Analysis of Two Hand Positions in Field Hockey Drives for Novice and Advanced Players. Unpublished Doctoral Dissertation, Temple Univ., Philadelphia, Pennsylvania.

232. Zimmerman, H. M. (1951). Characteristic Likenesses and Differences Between Skilled and Non-Skilled Performance of the Standing Broad Jump. Unpublished Doctoral Dissertation, Univ. of Wisconsin, Madison, Wisconsin.
233. Zimmerman, H. M. (1956). *Res. Quart.* **27,** 352–362.

Electromyographic Analyses of Basic Movement Patterns

John V. Basmajian

REGIONAL REHABILITATION RESEARCH AND TRAINING CENTER,
EMORY UNIVERSITY, ATLANTA, GEORGIA

I. Structural and Functional Bases of Electromyography

In the past two decades electromyography, in conjunction with related techniques, has greatly expanded our knowledge of kinesiology. Although an obvious approach to the study of muscular function, EMG was overshadowed by EEG and ECG until the 1950's, and in the years between the two world wars it remained a novelty. Toward the end of World War II, with a marked improvement in electronic apparatus, kinesiologists and clinical scientists made increasing use of EMG.

The first significant EMG study was conducted on the movements of the human shoulder region by Inman, Saunders, and Abbott (*30*). During the 1950's and 60's the use of electromyography for kinesiological studies became widespread. Frequent but scattered reports became commonplace in the literature; yet most were clinical. Because of the many different fields of biology in which EMG is employed, the kinesiologic studies are reported in a multitude of different journals, making the job of keeping up with the literature difficult. Several books with localized interest have been published and one book offers a review up to the year 1967 (5).

A. MOTOR UNIT AND MOTOR UNIT POTENTIALS

Each impulse descending a nerve axon causes all the muscle fibers it supplies to contract (1). The number of muscle fibers per axon, i.e., the number in a "motor unit," varies widely. Generally, muscles controlling tiny movements and adjustments (such as those attached to the tiny ossicles of the middle ear and to the eyeball and the larynx) have the smallest number of muscle fibers per motor unit. On the other hand, large, coarse-acting muscles, e.g., those in the limbs, have many more fibers per motor unit. Quadriceps femoris has motor units containing about 2000 muscle fibers per nerve axon (5).

Individual muscles of the body consist of many hundreds of such motor units and it is their summated activity that develops the tension in the whole muscle. The motor units twitch repetitively and asynchronously. This randomized activity causes the smooth tension of the whole muscle.

The amount of work produced by a single motor unit is quite small, being insufficient to produce any observable movement of a joint spanned by the muscle of which it is a part. Even in the case of small joints, such as those of the thumb, at least two or three motors units are needed to give a visible movement. Under normal conditions, small motor units are recruited early, and, as the force is automatically or consciously increased, larger and larger motor units are recruited, while all the motor units also increase their frequency of twitching (28). There is no single, set frequency; individual motor units can fire very slowly and will increase their frequency of response on demand. Further, the normal recruitment pattern of a phasic contraction is not necessarily duplicated in reflex contractions (26) and it can be overcome with the artificial feedback techniques described as single motor unit training later in this review.

The motor unit potential that results from each of its twitches has a brief duration (with a median of 9 msec) and a total amplitude measured in microvolts or millivolts (5). Recorded by conventional intramuscular techniques, most are sharp triphasic or biphasic spikes; from fine-wire electrodes, the potentials are much more complex and individually recognizable. Surface electrodes give potentials which are generally smaller and rounder. Generally, the larger the motor-unit potential involved, the larger is the motor unit that produced it. However, distance from the electrodes, the type of electrodes and equipment used (and many other factors) influence the final size and shape of the potential.

B. TECHNIQUE

Electromyographic techniques are considered fully in the article by Adrian (this volume, p. 339). Here we only need to note the chief elements from which data are derived.

1. Electrodes

There are a multitude of special electrodes. For obvious reasons, surface electrodes which have a global pick-up have been used widely by physical educators and others. Fine-wire intramuscular electrodes are now being used in many kinesiology laboratories (5).

2. Apparatus

Electromyographs are high-gain amplifiers with a preference for frequencies from about 10 to about 1000 Hz. Ideally, the recording device should either be photographic or employ electromagnetic tape recording. In recent years, multitrack FM tape recorders have provided a relatively cheap method of storing EMG signals, especially for subsequent computer analysis (39).

3. Telemetering of EMG

As with any electric signal, EMG potentials can be transmitted by FM radio (12). Single-channel telemetering of EMG is simple; multichannel EMG telemetry is more difficult but will be quite common by the mid-1970's. A substitute for telemetering is the tape recording of the signals by means of a pack carried by the subject (13).

II. Muscle Tone and Fatigue

A. TONUS

EMG shows conclusively the complete relaxation of normal human striated muscle at rest, i.e., a normal human being can voluntarily abolish neuromuscular activity. Thus, tone of a muscle is determined both by the passive elasticity or turgor of muscular (and fibrous) tissues and by the active (though not continuous) contraction of muscle in response to neural stimuli. At complete rest, a muscle has not lost its tone even though there is no measurable myoelectric activity in it.

Even with multiple electrodes, normal muscle at complete rest never shows any sign of neuromuscular activity, i.e., no alpha motor neuron discharge is present, although it appears during a stretch that is rapid enough to initiate a reflex response (*45*). "Complete rest" requires some qualification, because a normal person does not completely relax all his muscles at once. Reacting to multiple internal and external stimuli, various groups of muscles show rising and falling amounts of activity.

B. Fatigue

Fatigue is a complex of numerous phenomena. The fatigue of strenuous effort is probably quite different from the weariness felt after a long day's routine sedentary work. Undoubtedly, the following types exist: emotional fatigue, central nervous system fatigue, "general" fatigue, and peripheral neuromuscular fatigue of special kinds. Various investigations in my laboratory have shown postural fatigue to be largely due to painful strain not on muscles (which often have been quite quiescent), but on ligaments, capsules, and other inert structures (*5,17*). This has led to the concept that *muscles are spared when ligaments suffice*. This concept is important not only in understanding the sources of postural fatigue in man but it also underlies another important principle in man's posture: *there should be a minimal expenditure of energy consistent with the ends to be achieved*.

MacConaill and I (*38*) proposed two laws which express the operation of this principle:

(a) *Law of Minimal Spurt Action*. No more muscle fibers are brought into action than are both necessary and sufficient to stabilize or move a bone against gravity and/or other resistant forces, and none are used insofar as gravity can supply the motive force for movement.

(b) *Law of Minimal Shunt Action*. Only such muscle fibers are used as are necessary and sufficient to ensure that the transarticular force directed toward a joint is equal to the weight of the stabilized or moving part, together with such additional centripetal force as may be required because of the velocity of that part when it is in motion.

EMG has clearly demonstrated these two laws to be valid. Especially dramatic is the biomechanics of the shoulder (glenohumeral) joint, where studies showed that the whole weight of an unloaded arm is counteracted by the upper part of its capsule alone, no muscles being normally required. In this area, a strong ligament (the coracohumeral) appears to reinforce the action of the joint capsule in preventing the head of the humerus from sliding downwards on the inclined plane formed by the glenoid cavity or shoulder socket. With moderate or heavy loads, a muscle adhering to the capsule (the supraspinatus) is brought into action to reinforce the original tension in the capsule.

Everyone knows that carrying a heavy weight (say, a suitcase) can become a painful experience. While it had been assumed that the reactive component which becomes fatigued and exhibits pain is muscular, in fact, the fatigue is chiefly ligamentous. This points up the importance of the inert structures. We have recently found (17) that the fatigue of hanging by the hands is governed by the same principle.

Another example of the Minimal Principle is that of arch support in the human foot. Generations of surgeons have stressed the importance of the muscular tie-beams in the plantigrade foot. Yet EMG studies have repeatedly pointed to the fundamental importance of plantar ligaments. Indeed, even very heavy loads do not recruit muscular activity in the leg and foot.

The character of the electrical activity during voluntary exercise is a reflection of the EMG, or vice versa. A number of authors have described various phenomena that occur with the progressive fatigue of continuous activity. These include synchronization of potentials, an augmentation of the amplitude and duration of potentials, and an increase in polyphasic potentials (5).

III. Coordination of Muscle Function

Although the cerebral cortex does not order a muscle to contract but orders movements of a joint, under certain circumstances the movement is the result of contraction in only one or two muscles. For example, pronation of the forearm (turning the hand into the palm-down position) is usually produced by one muscle alone (pronator quadratus), unless added resistance is offered to the movement; then more muscles are called upon. My colleagues and I have found this to be true in elbow flexion too, where brachialis (not biceps) often suffices (5). On the other hand, there are complex movements (such as rotation of the scapula on the chest wall during elevation of the limb) which obviously call upon groups of cooperating muscles to produce the basic movement pattern.

A. ANTAGONISTS

Sherrington's "reciprocal inhibition" for free movements without stress (44) rules that generally a so-called antagonist relaxes completely; but there is one exception, the burst of activity at the end of a whiplike motion of a hinge joint. The term antagonist should be replaced by the companion word synergist. The activity of muscles in the position of antagonists during a free movement can be willed by a subject. It may also be a sign of nervous abnormality (e.g., the spasticity of paraplegia), or, in the case of fine movements requiring training, a sign of ineptitude. The athlete's continued drill to perfect a skilled movement exhibits a large element of progressively more successful repression of undesired contractions (*5*).

B. Conscious Control and Feedback Training of Single Motor Units

The recently developed EMG feedback technique, motor-unit training, offers a useful approach to studies of the conscious control over spinal motoneurons, of the neurophysiological processes underlying proprioception and feedback, and of many related psychophysiological phenomena. It is based on the auditory and visual display to human subjects of individual myoelectric potentials recorded from fine-wire intramuscular electrodes. The cues provide the subject with an awareness of the twitching of individual motor units. They learn in a few minutes to control this activity and can give many bizarre responses with only the artificial feedback cues as a guide (*4*).

The best performers can learn to maintain the activity of specific motor-unit potentials in the absence of either one or both of the visual and auditory feedbacks. That is, the monitors are gradually turned off and, after a "weaning" period, the subject must try to maintain or recall a well-learned unit without the artificial "proprioception" provided earlier.

Any skeletal muscle may be selected. The ones my colleagues and I have used most often are the abductor pollicis brevis, abductor digiti minimi, tibialis anterior, biceps brachii and brachialis, and the extensors of the arm and forearm. But we have also successfully trained motor units in back muscles, shoulder and neck muscles, tongue muscles, etc. (*5*).

1. Effects of Previous Training and Skills

Our earliest studies, even though they included hundreds of subjects, failed to reveal any correlation between the ability of subjects to isolate and train individual motor units and such variables as sex, age, academic record, athletic ability, handedness, and general personality traits (*6*). The purpose of a recent study was to discover whether in fact there are any differences in the performance between subjects with special manual skills and those without, using the time required for training of motor units in one of the hand muscles as the criterion (42). The training time of most of the manually skilled subjects was above the median, although one might expect the opposite. Henderson (27) has suggested that the constant repetition of a specific motor skill increases the probability of its correct recurrence by the learning and consolidation of an optimal anticipatory tension. Perhaps this involves an increase in the background activity of the gamma motoneurons regulating the sensitivity of the muscle spindles of the muscles involved in performing that skill. Wilkins (52) postulated that the acquisition of a new motor skill leads to the learning of a certain "position memory" for it. If anticipatory tensions and/or position memory are learned, whether they are integrated at the cerebral level, at the spinal level, or both, these or some other cerebral or spinal mechanisms may be acting temporarily to block the initial learning of new skills. In a sense, perhaps some neuromuscular pathways acquire a habit of responding in certain ways, and it is not until that habit is broken that a new skill can be learned.

2. Effects of Handedness

When subjects were studied on two occasions using a different hand each time, Powers (41) found that they always isolated a unit more quickly in the second hand. Isolation was twice as rapid when the second hand was the preferred hand; it was almost five times as rapid when the second hand was the nonpreferred one. The time required to train a subject to control a previously isolated unit was shortened significantly only when the preferred hand was the second hand.

3. Effect of Competitive Nerve Stimulation

Contrary to expectation, the superimposing of a massive contraction in a muscle by electrical stimulation of its motor nerve does not significantly alter the regular conscious firing of a motor unit in that muscle (43).

4. Local Factors

Moving a neighboring joint while a motor unit is firing is a distracting influence but most subjects can maintain motor unit control in spite of the distraction (10,15,50). In order to maintain or recall a motor unit at different positions, the subject must keep the motor unit active during the performance of the movements; therefore, preliminary training is undeniably necessary.

IV. Electromyographic Kinesiology

A. VERTEBRAL COLUMN

Most human subjects require very slight activity or intermittent reflex activity of the intrinsic muscles of the back, according to a growing list of authors [see Reference (*5*) for a review]. During forward flexion there is marked activity until flexion is extreme, at which time the ligamentous structures assume the load and the muscles become silent. In the extreme-flexed position of the back, the erector spinae remained relaxed in the initial stages of heavy weight-lifting (*20*).

The force of gravity is counteracted by one set of muscles only, most often the back muscles, but in 20 to 25% of the cases, the abdominal muscles (*2*). The line of gravity passes very close to the axis of movement of the fourth lumbar vertebra and does not intersect with the curves of the spine as often postulated. Klausen (*36*), investigating the effect of changes in the curve of the spine, the line of gravity in relation to the fourth lumbar vertebra and ankle joints and the activity of the muscles of the trunk, concluded that the short, deep intrinsic muscles of the back must play an important role in stabilizing the individual intervertebral joints. The long intrinsic muscles and the abdominal muscles stabilize the spine as a whole. Donisch and I (*16*) found in a recent study that in the deep layers of the back muscles, studied in 25 healthy human subjects with bipolar fine wire electrodes, activity was registered simultaneously in sitting and standing, and during movements while in these positions. The muscle group displayed different patterns of activity at the thoracic level when compared to the lumbar level. Variations in the pattern of activity during flexion, extension, and axial rotation suggest that the transversospinal muscles adjust the motion between individual vertebrae. The experimental evidence confirms the anatomical hypothesis that the multifidi are stabilizers rather than prime movers of the whole vertebral column.

Placing a load high on the back automatically causes the trunk to lean slightly forward. The increased pull of gravity is counteracted by an increased activity in the lower back muscles. A load placed low on the back reduces the activity of the back muscles (*14*). There is increased activity when a load is held in front of the thighs. Thus, the position of the load—either back or front—either aids the muscles or reflexly calls upon their activity to prevent forward imbalance.

While some investigators believe that the vertebral part of the psoas major (a large hip-flexor which lies on the side of the vertebral column) acts on the spine, we found that this muscle shows only some slight activity during standing (7). Even strong attempts to increase the natural lumbar lordosis (the hollow of the back)—said to be a function of psoas in man—recruits little or no activity in the muscle.

B. General Studies of Gait

Multifactorial studies of gait are so difficult and time-consuming that there has been a very slow development. Only recently, equipment has improved to the point where EMG gives especially useful results. Some of this work is now appearing in the medical clinical literature and is too specialized for inclusion here.

In walking there is a very fine sequence of activity in various groups of muscles in the lower limb. As the heel strikes the ground the hamstrings and pretibial muscles reach their peak of activity. Thereafter, the quadriceps, the large muscle mass which extends the knee, increases in activity as the torso is carried forward over the limb, apparently to maintain stability of the knee. [See References (5) and (38) for a complete review of gait, with references to original works.]

During the stance phase the stabilizing function of the ankle plantar-flexors at the knee is most important (46). The period of activity in the calf muscles and of knee extension and dorsiflexion of the foot correspond. Only at the end of plantar-flexion of the ankle does plantar-flexion of the foot occur. Knee extension occurs after quadriceps activity ceases; this is related to the fact that full extension of the knee never occurs during walking in the way that it does in standing.

Knee extension in the stance phase is brought about by the force of the plantar-flexors of the ankle resisting the dorsiflexion of the ankle; this dorsiflexion is in turn the resultant of extrinsic forces—kinetic forces, gravity, and the reaction of the floor. Because the resultant of extrinsic forces proves to be dominant, increased dorsiflexion of the foot continues until heel-off begins. The restraining function of the ankle plantar-flexors in decelerating forward rotation of the tibia on the talus proves to be the key to their stabilizing action.

A movement of the torso and hip region that shifts their position over the feet initiates the movements of each foot during walking. Movements initiated in the trunk lead automatically to changes in the position of the leg and foot. Soleus stabilizes and adjusts the tibia on the talus. Apparently the movements of the ankle during walking occur as a reaction to muscular forces far removed from the foot. Inertial forces also play an important role throughout the lower limb.

A number of events occur during walking which will be catalogued here for easy reference:

1. Contraction of the triceps surae corresponds to the first hump of

the vertical accelerogram. However, it begins before the heel lifts off the ground and stops before the great toe leaves the ground.

2. Dorsiflexion of the foot begins at the time of maximum acceleration of the lower leg. Tibialis anterior is usually biphasic in activity, but sometimes it is active for a short time after the foot is flat on the ground.

3. Contraction of iliopsoas occurs simultaneously with that of gluteus maximus of the opposite side. Gluteus maximus shows activity at the end of the swing and at the beginning of the supporting phase. This is contrary to the general belief that its activity is not needed for ordinary walking. Perhaps gluteus maximus contracts to prevent or to control flexion at the hip joint.

4. Gluteus medius and gluteus minimus are active at the time that one would predict, i.e., during the supporting phase; however, some subjects show activity in the swing phase too. In the supporting phase, activity occurs early, in the calf muscles, hamstrings, and gluteus maximus, but ceases toward the end.

5. Quadriceps femoris contracts as extension of the knee is being completed, not during the earlier part of extension when the action is probably a passive swing. Quadriceps continues to act during the early part of the supporting phase (when the knee is flexed and the center of gravity falls behind it). Quadriceps activity occurs at the end of the supporting phase to fix the knee in extension, probably counteracting the tendency toward flexion imparted by gastrocnemius.

6. The hamstrings contract at the end of flexion and during the early extension of the thigh, apparently to prevent flexion of the thigh before the heel is on the ground and to assist the movement of the body over the supporting phase; this may prevent hip flexion. In the swing phase, the hamstrings are inactive (even though knee flexion occurs).

C. Lower Limb

1. Iliopsoas

All textbooks agree that the muscle is obviously a flexor of the hip and probably has influence on the lumbar vertebrae. It shows some slight activity during relaxed standing (7). As one would expect, action potentials are recorded during flexion of the hip in almost the whole range. The amount of activity varies directly with the effort or resistance. Iliopsoas is quite active during extreme abduction of the hip and during lateral rotation. It is not a medial rotator. The only lumbar movement which consistently recruits psoas is a deliberate increase in lumbar lordosis while standing erect, but this is not dramatic (7).

2. The Glutei and Tensor Fasciae Latae

Gluteus maximus is active only when heavy or moderate efforts are made in the movements classically ascribed to this muscle. It is active during extension of the thigh at the hip joint, abduction against heavy resistance with the thigh flexed to 90 deg and adduction against resistance that holds the thigh abducted. Lateral rotation (but not the opposite) also produces activity in gluteus maximus (51). While the whole muscle is engaged in extension and lateral rotation, only its upper part is abducent. As an abductor, gluteus maximus is a reserve source of power (35). It is not an important postural muscle even during forward swaying. In bending forward it exhibits moderate activity. When straightening up from the toe-touching position it shows considerable activity throughout the movement.

The gluteus maximus is not a postural abductor muscle even when the subject is standing on one foot (as are the medius and minimus), but when the center of gravity of the whole body is grossly shifted, activity of gluteus maximus occurs (33). In positions where one leg sustains most of the weight, the ipsilateral muscle is active in its upper or "abducent" part; apparently this is to prevent a drooping of the opposite side.

During standing, rotation of the trunk activates the muscle that is contralateral to the direction of rotation (i.e., corresponding to lateral rotation of the thigh). Forward bending at the hip joint and trunk recruits gluteus maximus, apparently to fix the pelvis. Complete paralysis of gluteus maximus in no way disturbs ordinary walking even though the muscle shows phasic activity.

The marked activity in the abductors when the subject stands on one foot is in sharp contrast with their quiescence during relaxed standing (24).

Duchenne clearly stated that the power of tensor fasciae latae as a rotator (in response to faradic stimulation) is weak; EMG findings agree with this (24). During bicycling, the muscle is active as the hip is being flexed (29).

3. Adductors of the Hip Joint

Forming an enormous mass on the medial side of the upper thigh, the adductors must have considerable importance. In spite of this, their exact function was a matter of guesswork until recently. The response of the adductors appears to be related to a postural response. Rather than being called upon as prime movers, they are facilitated through reflexes of the gait pattern. They are activated during movements of the knee, especially against resistance. But during movements of the hip, the role of the adductors is localized to their upper parts.

During free adduction, the adductor longus is always active, while magnus is almost always silent unless resistance is offered. Both muscles are active during medial rotation but not during lateral rotation of the hip, settling a classic argument that usually supported the opposite view (*24*). The upper fibers of adductor magnus show the greatest activity (*24*). During flexion of the thigh, the main activity occurs in the adductor longus (*22,24*), while the magnus is often completely silent (*24*). While standing in a relaxed natural posture, both muscles are inactive. However, weak activity sometimes appears when standing on one foot (*24*). The considerable activity in the adductors appears to be related to a stabilizing function of the hip joint (*22,24*).

4. Hamstrings

The three hamstrings, biceps femoris, semimembranosus, and semitendinosus, act on both hip joint and knee joint. The first is active in ordinary extension of the hip joint (in contrast to gluteus maximus which acts only against resistance) and in flexion and lateral rotation of the tibia at the knee. Biceps is active also in lateral rotation of the extended hip and in adduction against resistance of the abducted hip (*5,32*).

The semimembranosus and semitendinosus are active in extension and also during medial rotation of the hip, in adduction against the resistance of the abducted hip, and in flexion and medial rotation of the tibia at the knee joint. The hamstrings are quiescent in ordinary standing, but in flexion at the hip and in leaning forward they are quite active as supporters against gravity. Although both heads of biceps femoris act synchronously during a free-moving test of flexion, the short head acts during the swing phase of walking while the long head acts as a stabilizer when the foot is on the ground. In general, the hamstrings are usually active during the transition from the swing phase to the stance phase.

5. Gracilis and Sartorius

Though belonging to the adductor mass, the gracilis crosses and therefore acts on both hip and knee. It is active in flexion of the hip with the knee extended but is inactive if the knee is allowed to flex simultaneously. It adducts and rotates the femur medially (*34*). During flexion of the hip joint, gracilis is most active during the first part of flexion, both in free "basic movements" and during walking and cycling.

In walking on a horizontal level and on a staircase its activity occurs during the swing phase. At the knee it is a flexor and medial rotator of the tibia, although in medial rotation and in relaxed standing its activity appears to be slight.

Sartorius is active during flexion of the thigh (regardless of whether the knee is straight or bent), during lateral rotation of the femur or abduction of the thigh, and during flexion of the knee joint or medial rotation of the tibia. Both sartorius and gracilis may play a role in the fine postural adjustments of the hip and knee.

6. Quadriceps Femoris

The vasti, of course, are powerful extensors of the knee joint, but generally they are quiescent during relaxed standing (32). During the movement of rising from the sitting to the standing position and vice versa, the activity in the three heads is not synchronized and equal. The vastus medialis is retarded and is not as active as the other two. In erect standing the activity in the three heads falls rapidly. The three heads apparently act in different ways in various phases of movement (8). During resisted extension of the knee, the various parts of quadriceps come into action at different phases of the movement (8).

7. Leg Muscles

Gastrocnemius is active only intermittently in most persons during relaxed standing (5); very few women show no activity with high heels. The tibialis anterior and the peroneus longus (and, as we shall see, the intrinsic muscle of the foot) play no important active role in the normal static support of the long arches of the foot. Whatever postural activity there is in human legs during standing is intermittent.

Along with the peroneus longus, peroneus brevis acts only intermittently as a postural muscle, becoming very active in leaning forward and silent when leaning backward. Peroneal activity is pronounced during the propulsive phase of normal walking, and the activity of the two muscles is synchronous. Their discreteness suggests that each has its own special additional function(s).

The tibialis anterior has been a favored object of attention, and so it is commonly accepted that peak EMG activity occurs in it at heel-strike of the stance phase. Movies show the foot to be inverted and dorsiflexed at this time (22).

Notwithstanding the above, there has been no general agreement as to the function of tibialis anterior at heel-strike. Without offering direct evidence, some suggest only that it counteracts forces applied to the heel by the ground, while others propose that the tibialis anterior decelerates the foot at heel-strike and lowers it to the ground by gradual lengthening (eccentric contraction). Perhaps the clinical condition known as "drop-foot" due to paralysis of the tibialis anterior forces this conclusion.

During the more central moments of the stance phase (full-foot, midstance, and heel-off) modern techniques reveal no tibialis anterior activity in "normal" subjects. Our flatfooted subjects and those of Battye and Joseph (*12*) are like the "normals" except for extended activity into full-foot. Curiously, the movies of our flatfooted subjects show the foot staying inverted during full-foot, maintaining inversion in order to distribute the body weight along its lateral border.

A peak of EMG activity that occurs at toe-off of the stance phase is apparently related to dorsiflexion of the ankle, presumably to permit the toes to clear the floor. This peak of activity tapers to a slight-to-moderate level of activity during acceleration of the swing phase. Conversely, prior activity in deceleration of the swing phase builds up to a peak of activity at heel-strike. Thus, the pattern of activity of tibialis anterior is biphasic. Apparently, tibialis anterior is in part responsible for dorsiflexion during acceleration and for inversion of the foot during deceleration of the swing phase.

Although earlier workers believed that there is a slight fall in the activity of tibialis anterior at midswing, there is, in fact, a period of electrical *silence* at mid-swing. The explanation emerges from our movies which show the foot everting at the end of "acceleration" and remaining everted through mid-swing. This allows for adequate clearance, while the inactivity of the invertor fits the concept of reciprocal inhibition of antagonists. We conclude that the brief period of electrical silence of tibialis anterior is essential.

The pattern of activity of tibialis anterior suggests that it does not lend itself to direct support of the arches during walking. At heel-strike, when the muscle shows its greatest activity, the pressure of body weight is negligible. Conversely, during maximum weight bearing at midstance when all the body weight is balanced on one foot, the tibialis anterior is silent. When the activity resumes at toe-off, the weight bearing of the involved foot is minimal.

During ordinary walking tibialis posterior shows activity at midstance of the stance phase (*22*). The movies show the foot remaining inverted throughout full-foot and turning to a neutral position (between inversion and eversion) just before midstance. First, the fourth and fifth metatarsal heads make contact; then, as the foot everts increasingly toward neutral, more of the ball of the foot makes contact at midstance until the entire contact area of the foot is applied. Although the tibialis posterior is an invertor in non-weight bearing movements of the foot, its role at "midstance" appears to be a restraining one, to prevent the foot from everting past the neutral position.

In human cadaveric preparations, the tibialis posterior distributes body weight among the heads of the metatarsals (31). In living subjects, a lateral torque on the tibia results in an increase or shift of body weight onto all but the first metatarsal head; a medial torque has the opposite effect. By inverting the instep of the foot, the tibialis posterior increases the proportion of body weight borne by the lateral side of the foot. Sutherland (46) concluded that the plantar flexors, including the tibialis posterior, have a restraining function, to control or decelerate medial rotation of the leg and thigh observed at midstance; by controlling the eversion of the foot at midstance, the tibialis posterior provides an appropriate placement of the foot.

By maintaining inversion, the foot is supported in order to keep the body weight on the lateral border of the sole. The foot must be inverted to accomplish lateral weight bearing in the early "moments" of the stance phase.

Although tibialis posterior is often considered to be a plantar flexor of the ankle, during level walking with an accustomed foot position it shows nil activity at heel-off (when plantar flexion of the ankle takes place to raise the heel). This is not to deny that tibialis posterior may be a plantar flexor of the ankle when more powerful contractions are needed.

At midstance, when the entire body weight is concentrated on one foot, flexor hallucis longus shows its greatest activity. Flexing the big toe apparently positions and stabilizes it during midstance. During heel-off, our movies show the big toe hyperextended. There is a slight activity during heel-off which may be related to preventing overextension and so giving a better balance. In contrast, the "normal" subjects show negligible activity. Consequently, one may conclude that the flexor hallucis longus is not needed in most "normal" subjects to play this role.

The pattern of activity of the peroneus longus confirms the findings of many who have suggested that the peroneus longus helps to stabilize the leg and foot during midstance. Our movies and electromyograms show how the peroneus longus and tibialis posterior, working in concert, control the shift from inversion during full-foot to neutral at midstance. We found that eversion of the foot and medial rotation of the lower limb occur together. One may conclude that the peroneus longus is in part responsible for returning the foot to, and maintaining it in, a neutral position at midstance.

8. Foot Muscles

The abductor hallucis and flexor digitorum brevis become active at midstance and continue through to toe-off in "normal" subjects; in flatfooted subjects most show activity from heel-strike to toe-off. The most controversial function of the muscles that traverse the foot is the support of the arches. Electromyography shows that these muscles provide movements of the joints of the foot, propulsion of body, and stability of joints during walking, but are not required for static arch support except where they attempt (with limited success) to support the arches (*38*).

D. Upper Limb

1. Movements of the Shoulder Joint

The joint may be flexed, extended, abducted, adducted, and rotated (medially or laterally). Any movements that elevate the arm above the level of the shoulder involve extensive scapular and clavicular movements as well. Indeed, it is probable that most movements of the humerus call for some concomitant movement of the glenoid cavity even before the horizontal plane is reached. The chief muscles that act upon the shoulder (glenohumeral) joint are the deltoid, the pectorales, the latissimus dorsi, teres major, and the four rotator cuff muscles—subscapularis, supraspinatus, infraspinatus, and teres minor.

The obvious activity in the deltoid increases progressively during *abduction* and becomes greatest between 90 deg and 180 deg of elevation; the activity of supraspinatus increases progressively, too—it is not simply an initiator of abduction as was formerly taught (*5,30*). Complete experimental paralysis of supraspinatus in man simply reduces the force of abduction and power of endurance. In abduction, supraspinatus plays only a quantitative and not a specialized role. No part of pectoralis major is active during abduction. The role of biceps brachii in abduction seems to be confined to a contribution in maintaining this position while the arm is laterally rotated and the forearm supine. When the arm is medially rotated and the forearm prone, biceps does not contribute to abduction.

In *flexion*, the clavicular head of pectoralis major along with the anterior fibers of deltoid are the chief flexors; the former reaches its maximum activity at 115 deg of flexion. Both heads of biceps brachii are active in flexion of the shoulder joint, the long head being the more active.

Subscapularis, infraspinatus, and teres minor form a functional group which acts as the second or inferior group of the force couple during abduction of the humerus. They act continuously during both abduction and flexion. In abduction, activity in infraspinatus and teres minor rises linearly, while activity in subscapularis reaches a peak or plateau beyond the 90 deg angle and then falls off.

Pectoralis major and latissimus dorsi produce *adduction*. The posterior fibers of deltoid are also very active, perhaps to resist the medial rotation that the main adductors would produce if unresisted.

2. Muscles of the Shoulder Joint

The classic article in the literature on the kinesiology of the shoulder region is that of Inman, Saunders, and Abbott (*30*). Their findings have, in general, withstood the test of time and few of their conclusions have been contradicted by subsequent investigators.

One point of controversy has been the function of the teres major muscle, which, they reported, never showed activity during motion, having a purely static function. But others, using surface electrodes, denied this, reporting that teres major was indeed active during active motion of the arm. My colleague, Dr. H. L. Broome, and I found in a recent study that the teres major had no electrical activity in motions without resistance. But against active resistance, it consistently showed electrical activity during medial rotation, adduction, and extension in both the static and the dynamic exercises. The latissimus dorsi had similar activity during both static tension and resisted motion; without resistance, in five of the seven acceptable subjects, latissimus dorsi had activity during medial rotation, adduction, and extension. If it is resisted, teres major is always active. If added resistance is lacking, free movement of the shoulder joint in all its directions does not recruit the teres major although it usually recruits its close relation, latissimus dorsi.

The three parts of deltoid are active in all movements of the arm. In flexion and medial rotation, the anterior part is more active than the posterior; in extension and lateral rotation, the posterior is the more active; and, in abduction, the middle part is the most active. While one part of the deltoid is acting as the prime mover, the other parts may be stabilizing the joint in the glenoid cavity. The posterior part has its principal action in extension, but the action is inconstant and slight in abduction and elevation of the arm. Its participation in lateral rotation is minimal, being practically absent. It also becomes active during heavy downward pulls on the humerus as part of a locking mechanism at the shoulder joint.

3. Swinging of the Arm during Gait

In normal persons, the posterior and middle parts of deltoid begin to show activity slightly before the arm starts its backward swing, and this continues throughout the backward swing. The upper part of the latissimus dorsi acts from the onset of the backward swing until the arm reaches the line of the body (18). While the teres major is reported to act in concert (18), the amount of resistance to the motion was no specified. During forward swing of the arm, activity is confined to some of the medial rotators; the main flexors are strikingly silent. Apart from brief silent periods in the extreme positions of swing, trapezius is active in both phases to maintain elevation of the shoulder. Similar activity occurs in supraspinatus; this obviously is related to the prevention of downward dislocation, mentioned earlier.

4. The Elbow Joint

The biceps brachii, the brachialis, and the brachioradialis are primarily concerned with flexion. A variety of theories have obscured the role played by each during flexion and other movements of the elbow. Actually, in the movements produced by the flexors there is a fine interplay among them and a wide range of response from person to person. Thus, there is not unanimity of action. For example, the brachialis is generally markedly active during quick flexion of the supine forearm, but occasionally it is completely inactive (9).

There is an irregular selection in the sequence of appearance and disappearance of activity in these muscles. Any one may function first or last in an unpredictable fashion, i.e., there is no set pattern. In the same way, the activity ceases in the muscles in an unpredictable order. Moreover, the muscles that show the greatest activity in individual subjects only occasionally begin first and end last.

The long head of the biceps generally shows more activity than the short head during slow flexion of the forearm, during supination of the forearm against resistance, and during flexion of the shoulder joint (although there is little difference between the activity of the two heads during isometric contraction and during extension of the elbow).

The biceps is generally active during flexion of the supine forearm under all conditions and during flexion of the semiprone forearm when a load of approximately 1 kg is lifted. However, with the forearm prone, in the majority of instances the biceps plays little if any role in flexion, in maintenance of elbow flexion, and in antagonistic action during extension, even with a load. If the forearm is in supination, the biceps acts during flexion when there is only slight resistance, but in a position of complete pronation it does not act until the resistance is approximately 2 kg.

The biceps is usually described as a supinator of the forearm. However, no activity occurs in the muscle during supination of the extended forearm through the whole range of movement except when resistance to supination is given. Apparently because of the tendency of the biceps to flex the forearm, it is reflexly inhibited during ordinary supination; thus, position of the forearm is maintained while the supinator does the supinating. On the other hand, when supination is resisted, the biceps comes into strong action; usually the previously extended forearm is partly flexed as well during supination against resistance.

The brachialis has been generally and erroneously considered to be a muscle of speed rather than one of power because of its short leverage. Yet it is a flexor of the supine, semiprone, and prone forearm in both slow and quick flexion, and either with or without an added weight, apparently because the line of its pull does not change with pronation or supination.

Maintenance of specific flexed postures of the elbow, i.e., isometric contraction, and the movement of slow extension (when the flexors must act as antigravity muscles) both generally bring the brachialis into activity in all positions of the forearm. This is not the case with the other two flexor muscles. Thus, we have dubbed the brachialis the "workhorse" among the flexor muscles of the elbow (9).

A short burst of activity is generally seen in all the muscles during quick extension. This activity can hardly be considered antagonistic in the usual sense. Rather, it may provide a protective function for the joint.

In the past, the brachioradialis has been described as a flexor, acting to its best advantage in the semiprone position of the forearm. Almost never does the brachioradialis play an appreciable role during maintenance of elbow flexion and during slow flexion and extension when the movement is carried out without a weight. When a weight is lifted during flexion, the brachioradialis is generally moderately active in the semiprone or prone position of the forearm and is slightly active in the supine position. There is no comparable increase in activity with the addition of weight during maintenance of flexion and during slow extension.

During both quick flexion and quick extension, the brachioradialis is quite active in all three positions of the forearm. It follows that the muscle is recruited for occasions when speedy movement is required and when weight is to be lifted, especially in the semiprone and the prone positions. In the latter position, the biceps usually does not come into prominent action. More important, the activity of the brachioradialis in speedy movements is related to its function as a shunt muscle (*5,9,38*).

The brachioradialis neither supinates nor pronates the extended forearm. When these movements are performed against resistance, brachioradialis acts only as an accessory muscle, or as a synergist (*9*).

While the biceps, brachialis, and brachioradialis differ in their flexor activity in the three positions of the forearm (prone, semiprone, and supine), all three act maximally when a weight is lifted during flexion of the semiprone forearm. The semiprone position of the forearm is the natural position of the forearm, the position of rest and the position of greatest advantage for most functions of the upper limb.

Pronator teres contributes to elbow flexion only when resistance is offered to the movement. It shows no activity during unresisted flexion whether the forearm is prone, semiprone, or supine.

The long head of triceps is surprisingly quiescent during active extension of the elbow, regardless of the position of either the subject or his limb (*48*). The medial head, however, is always active and appears to be the prime extensor of the elbow; meanwhile, the lateral head shows some activity as well. Against resistance, the lateral and long heads are recruited. Therefore, we might compare the medial head of triceps to the brachialis, which we noted above to be the workhorse of the elbow flexors; it is the workhorse of the extensors. The lateral and long heads are reserves for extension. The long head is less involved than the lateral one, probably owing to the lack of fixation of the scapular origin and the necessity of adducting the shoulder with the forearm either flexed or extended. Too strong a contribution from the long head would tend to give extension during adduction of the arm.

The *anconeus* should be regarded as an integral part of triceps with which it acts in extension (*25*). Its other debated functions are insignificant except, perhaps, that of stabilization of the elbow and superior radio-ulnar joints.

5. The Forearm and Hand

Both pronator quadratus and pronator teres are active during pronation, the consistent prime pronating muscle being the pronator quadratus (*11*). This is true irrespective of the positions of the forearm in space or the angulation of the elbow joint. In general, the pronator teres is called in as a reinforcing pronator whenever the action of pronation is rapid. Similar reinforcement occurs during pronation against resistance. Whether pronation is fast or slow, the activity in the pronator quadratus is markedly greater than that in the pronator teres. Regardless of whether the pronating action is carried out swiftly or slowly, the angle of the elbow joint has no bearing on the amount of activity of the pronator teres. During slow supination there is no activity whatsoever in either of the pronators—though some have suggested that the deeper layer of the pronator quadratus acts as a supinator. The flexor carpi radialis, brachioradialis, and extensor carpi ulnaris have no pronating function.

Brachioradialis (known for years as "supinator longus") is not a true supinator. Slow unresisted supination, whatever the position of the forearm, is brought about by the independent action of the supinator alone. Similarly, fast supination in the extended position requires only the supinator, but fast unresisted supination with the elbow flexed is assisted by the action of the biceps. All movements of forceful supination against resistance require the cooperation of the biceps during resisted supination, especially when the elbow is flexed (49). Both supinator muscles are completely relaxed during pronation (slow, fast, or resisted). This is similar to our findings for pronation, where complete relaxation of the pronator quadratus and the pronator teres during supination is the rule.

The "hold" or static position of supination depends on activity in supinator for the maintenance of the supine posture. Against added resistance, however, the biceps always becomes active. The movement of supination is initiated, and mostly maintained, by the supinator; it is assisted by the biceps only as needed to overcome added resistance.

Of the two radial extensors of the wrist, the extensor carpi radialis brevis is much more active during pure extension than the longus whether the movement is slow or fast (47). Actually, except with fast extension, the longus is essentially inactive. However, the roles of the two muscles are completely reversed during prehension or fist-making; now the longus is very active as a synergist. The two muscles are both quite active during abduction of the wrist, as one would guess from their positions.

During simple extension of the wrist there is a reciprocal innervation between extensors and flexors (3). Extensores carpi radialis (longus et brevis) and extensor carpi ulnaris, as well as the extensor digitorum, work synchronously; none seems to be the prime mover. During forced extreme flexion of the wrist, there is a reactive co-contraction of the extensor carpi ulnaris, apparently to stabilize the wrist joint or because ulnar deviation is a regular concomitant; activity does not occur in the extensor digitorum and extensores carpi radiales.

There are six flexors in the forearm arranged in three layers, and the deeper the layer the more distal the insertions of its muscles. In general, the three in the superficial layer, flexor carpi radialis, palmaris longus, and flexor carpi ulnaris, all flex the wrist, although the flexor palmaris longus is not very powerful. The flexor carpi radialis is not an important abductor of the wrist; for that matter, the wrist can be abducted very little from "neutral." But the flexor carpi ulnaris is an important adductor, acting in concert with the extensor carpi ulnaris. All the muscles of the wrist are quite important for their synergistic use in stabilizing the wrist so that the fingers and fist work to best advantage.

During flexion of the wrist, the flexores carpi radialis, ulnaris, and superficialis act synchronously—none is the sole prime mover (*3*). Flexor digitorum profundus plays no role. Two possible muscles in the antagonist position (the radial extensors of the wrist and the extensors of the fingers) are passive, even in extreme flexion of the wrist, but the extensor carpi ulnaris shows marked activity either as an antagonist or because of ulnar deviation.

In abduction and adduction, the appropriate flexors and extensors act reciprocally as one might expect, the antagonist muscles relaxing. Extensor digitorum contracts during abduction (radial abduction), but this contraction is not limited to the radial part of the muscle, and the flexor digitorum superficialis may be active too. Apparently this type of activity has a synergistic function. Similarly, there is antagonist activity in the flexors when the wrist is extended and the metacarpophalangeal joints hyperextended (*3*).

6. The Fingers

When all the fingers are moving simultaneously, the activity of the "antagonist" muscles conforms to the principle of reciprocal inhibition (*36*). When only the little finger or ring finger is moved while the others are kept bent, the flexor is active during both movements. If a single finger moves, the "antagonist" must remain active to immobilize the other fingers. However, if the other fingers are held immobile by an observer, there is no activity in the antagonist muscle.

The lumbricals of the hand are important only in extension of the interphalangeal joints. It is now generally accepted that the importance of lumbrical–interosseus extension at the interphalangeal joints is in the prevention of hyperextension of the proximal phalanx by the extensor digitorum (*37*). This preventive action allows a more efficient pull on the dorsal expansion which extends the interphalangeal joints. These muscles are capable of bringing about the rotations necessary to bring them into their close-packed position, which is that of full extension.

Metacarpophalangeal flexion is performed by a lumbrical only when the interphalangeal joints are extended. A lumbrical has no effect on rotation or radial deviation of its finger during opposition with the thumb. The extensor digitorum begins or increases its activity with the inception of interphalangeal (IP) joint extension regardless of the position of the metacarpophalangeal (MP) joints, and even with moderate effort. During extension or hyperextension of the MP joint, extensor digitorum alone is active. Flexor digitorum superficialis is active during flexion of the middle phalanx (proximal IP joint), and it is active in flexion of the MP joint providing the next distal joint is stabilized. Surprisingly, the superficialis is active during rapid, forceful IP extension regardless of the position of the MP joint (37).

The interossei act as MP flexors only when their other action of IP extension does not conflict (37). Therefore, they act best and most strongly when combined MP flexion–IP extension is performed. During all IP extension, the intrinsic muscles of the hand contract regardless of MP posture. The long tendons of the fingers provide the gross motion of opening and closing of the fist at all the joints simultaneously. However, the intrinsic muscles perform their major function during any departure from this simple total opening or closing movement. Thus, they are the primary IP extensors while the MP joints are flexing.

Neither the interossei nor the lumbricals of one finger act during closing of the full hand, suggesting that in this total movement they are not synergists. The activity of the long extensors and flexors occurs in special sequences. Extensor digitorum acts during MP extension—in both the movement and the "hold" position. But it is also active in many flexion movements of that joint, apparently acting as a brake. The flexor profundus is the most consistently active flexor of the finger. Joined by the flexor superficialis, the profundus may act as a secondary flexor of the wrist joint also. The superficialis has its maximal action when the hand is being closed or held closed without flexion of the distal IP joint.

7. The Thumb

Each of the thenar muscles is involved to some extent in most of the gross movements of the thumb. The abductor pollicis brevis contracts strongly during opposition and flexion of the thumb as well as in abduction. The opponens shows strong activity in abduction and flexion of the metacarpal, as it does in opposition. The flexor pollicis brevis shows considerable activity in opposition as well as in flexion and in adduction. The adductor pollicis (which is, of course, not properly a thenar muscle) is active in adduction and opposition, and to a slight extent in flexion of the thumb.

During extension produced by the extensors only the opponens pollicis and abductor pollicis brevis show reciprocal activity (21). During abduction, the same two muscles show marked activity on the average, whereas the activity of the flexor pollicis brevis is slight. During flexion, the mean activity of the flexor pollicis brevis is moderate to marked, but the opponens pollicis is only slightly active and the abductor pollicis brevis is essentially inactive.

The occurrence of equal levels of activity in both the abductor pollicis brevis and the opponens pollicis during extension and abduction of the thumb cannot be rationalized on the basis of their insertions. These are such that these muscles would be expected to move the thumb in opposite directions, especially during extension and to a lesser extent during abduction. Stabilization of the part in order to produce a smooth, even movement results from the significant activities of these muscles.

Not all thenar muscles are active during extension and flexion of the thumb. During flexion, the abductor pollicis brevis exhibits negligible activity; the opponens pollicis, slight activity on the average, and the flexor pollicis, moderate-to-marked activity. Indeed, in the position of flexion, most subjects have little activity in both the opponens and abductor while the flexor is significantly active.

In one other position there is coincident activity and inactivity in the thenar muscles. During firm pinch between the thumb and the side of the flexed index finger, only negligible activity is recorded from the abductor pollicis brevis (21). Yet the opponens pollicis and, in particular, the flexor pollicis brevis are significantly active.

8. The Little Finger

During extension of the little finger, all three hypothenar muscles are rather inactive on the average. During abduction, although the abductor digiti minimi fulfills the function indicated by its name and is the dominant muscle with strong activity, the other hypothenar muscles are also significantly active. During flexion, considerable activity occurs in all three hypothenar muscles (21).

The abductor digiti minimi is very active during flexion of the little finger at the metacarpophalangeal joint. (The participation of this muscle in this position of the finger is also obvious by palpation.) Part of the explanation for this activity depends on the insertion of the muscle into the ulnar side of the base of the proximal phalanx. The abductor digiti minimi is also significantly active when the thumb is held opposed to either the ring or little finger (21). Some of this activity is possibly associated with the small degree of flexion at the fifth metacarpophalangeal joint that is required when the thumb and little finger are opposed. Yet such flexion is obviously not required during opposition of the thumb and ring finger. Some of the activity of the abductor digiti minimi, then, may be to provide stability, and simple abduction of the little finger may be the least important function of the abductor of this finger.

V. A Final Word

Electromyographic kinesiology has now reached a new level of productivity and significance. Along with modern biomechanics, it promises to place a strong substrate of scientific information beneath the theory and practice of neuromuscular performance. Without such a base, no new progress can be expected. In the decade ahead, scientific studies of kinesiology and biomechanics will take their rightful place alongside exercise physiology as fundamentals in the research and training of physical education. Indeed, as exercise physiology has begun to lose its glamour, these newer approaches to human performance have captured an increasing interest.

References

1. Adrian, E. D., and Bronk, D. W. (1929). *J. Physiol. (London)* **67**, 119–151.
2. Asmussen, E., and Klausen, K. (1962). *Clin. Orthop.* **25**, 55–63.
3. Bäckdahl, M., and Carlsöö, S. (1961). *Acta Morphol. Neer.-Scand.* **4**, 136–144.
4. Basmajian, J. V. (1963). *Science* **141**, 440–441.
5. Basmajian, J. V. (1967). "Muscles Alive: Their Functions Revealed by Electromyography," 2nd ed. Williams & Wilkins, Baltimore, Maryland.
6. Basmajian, J. V., Baeza, M., and Fabrigar, C. (1965). *J. New Drugs* **5**, 78–85.
7. Basmajian, J. V., and Greenlaw, R. K. (1968). *Anat. Rec.* **160**, 310.
8. Basmajian, J. V., Harden, T. P., and Regenos, E. M. (1972). *Anat. Rec.* **172**, 15–19.
9. Basmajian, J. V., and Latif, A. (1957). *J. Bone Joint Surg., Amer. Vol.* **39**, 1106–1118.
10. Basmajian, J. V., and Simard, T. G. (1967). *Amer. J. Phys. Med.* **46**, 1427–1449.
11. Basmajian, J. V., and Travill, A. A. (1961). *Anat. Rec.* **139**, 45–49.
12. Battye, C. K., and Joseph, J. (1966). *Med. Biol. Eng.* **4**, 125–135.
13. Brandell, B. R. (1971). *4th Int. Congr. EMG, Brussels* (abstr.), pp. 9–10.
14. Carlsöö, S. (1964). *Acta Orthop. Scand.* **34**, 299–309.
15. Carlsöö, S., and Edfeldt, Å. (1963). *Scand. J. Psychol.* **4**, 231–235.
16. Donisch, E. W., and Basmajian, J. V. (1972). *Amer. J. Anat.* **133**, 25–36.
17. Elkus, R., and Basmajian, J. V. (1973). *Amer. J. Phys. Med.* (In press.)
18. Fernandez-Ballesteros, M. L., Buchthal, F., and Rosenfalck, P. (1964). *Acta Physiol. Scand.* **63**, 296–310.
19. Fischer, F. J., and Houtz, S. J. (1968). *Amer. J. Phys. Med.* **47**, 182–192.
20. Floyd, W. F., and Silver, P. H. S. (1955). *J. Physiol. (London)* **129**, 184–203.
21. Forrest, W. J., and Basmajian, J. V. (1965). *J. Bone Joint Surg., Amer. Vol.* **47**, 1585–1594.
22. Gray, E. G., and Basmajian, J. V. (1968). *Anat. Rec.* **161**, 1–16.
23. Green, D. L., and Morris, J. M. (1970). *Amer. J. Phys. Med.* **49**, 223–240.
24. Greenlaw, R. K., and Basmajian, J. V. (1968). Unpublished studies.
25. Griffin, W. R., and Basmajian, J. V. (1971). Unpublished study.

26. Grimby, L., and Hannerz, J. (1968). *J. Neurol., Neurosurg., Psychiat.* **31,** 565–573.
27. Henderson, R. L. (1952). *J. Exp. Psychol.* **44,** 238–241.
28. Henneman, E., Somjen, G., and Carpenter, D. O. (1965). *J. Neurophysiol.* **28,** 599–620.
29. Houtz, S. J., and Fischer, F. J. (1959). *J. Appl. Physiol.* **16,** 597–605.
30. Inman, V. T., Saunders, J. B. DeC. M., and Abbott, L. C. (1944). *J. Bone Joint Surg.* **26,** 1–30.
31. Jones, R. L. (1941). *Amer. J. Anat.* **68,** 1–39.
32. Joseph, J., and Nightingale, A. (1956). *J. Physiol. (London)* **132,** 465–468.
33. Joseph, J., and Williams, P. L. (1955). *J. Physiol. (London)* **127,** 617–625.
34. Jonsson, B., and Steen, B. (1966). *Acta Morphol. Neer.-Scand.* **5,** 269–276.
35. Karlsson, E., and Jonsson, B. (1965). *Acta Morphol. Neer.-Scand.* **6,** 161–169.
36. Klausen, K. (1965). *Acta Physiol. Scand.* **65,** 176–190.
37. Long, C. (1968). *J. Bone Joint Surg., Amer. Vol.* **50,** 973–984.
38. MacConaill, M. A., and Basmajian, J. V. (1969). "Muscles and Movements: A Basis for Human Kinesiology." Williams & Wilkins, Baltimore, Maryland.
39. Milner, M., Basmajian, J. V., and Quanbury, A. O. (1971). *Amer. J. Phys. Med.* **50,** 235–258.
40. Person, R. S., and Roshtchina, N. A. (1958). *J. Physiol. USSR* **94,** 455–462.
41. Powers, W. R. (1969). Conscious Control of Single Motor Units in the Preferred and Non-Preferred Hand. Ph.D. Thesis, Queen's University, Kingston, Canada.
42. Scully, H. E., and Basmajian, J. V. (1969a). *Psychophysiology* **5,** 625–632.
43. Scully, H. E., and Basmajian, J. V. (1969b). *Arch. Phys. Med.* **50,** 32–33.
44. Sherrington, C. S. (1929). *Proc. Roy. Soc. Ser. B* **105,** 332–362.
45. Stolov, W. C. (1966). *Arch. Phys. Med.* **47,** 156–168.
46. Sutherland, D. H. (1966). *J. Bone Joint Surg., Amer. Vol.* **48,** 66–71.
47. Tournay, A., and Paillard, J. (1953). *Rev. Neurol.* **89,** 277–279.
48. Travill, A. A. (1962). *Anat. Rec.* **144,** 373–376.
49. Travill, A. A., and Basmajian, J. V. (1961). *Anat. Rec.* **139,** 557–560.
50. Wagman, I. H., Pierce, D. S., and Burger, R. E. (1965). *Nature (London)* **207,** 957–958.
51. Wheatley, M. D., and Jahnke, W. D. (1951). *Arch. Phys. Med.* **32,** 508–515.
52. Wilkins, B. R. (1964). *J. Theor. Biol.* **7,** 374–387.

Technological Advances in Sports Medicine and in the Reduction of Sports Injuries

Allan J. Ryan

DEPARTMENTS OF PHYSICAL EDUCATION AND REHABILITATION MEDICINE,
UNIVERSITY OF WISCONSIN–MADISON, MADISON, WISCONSIN

I. Introduction

The past 25 years have seen greater advances in the technology of sports medicine, broadly conceived, than in the entire preceding period of its recorded history. Thus, the selection of specific topics for the purpose of writing this review was difficult due to limitations of space. Advances in the study of nutrition of persons exercising could make a chapter by themselves and are not dealt with here at all. Many developments in sports safety and protective equipment are not documented in the scientific literature and were, therefore, omitted. Some selectivity was necessary in the interests of brevity and some topics are treated with less elaboration than might be desired. If this impels the reader to refer to the original sources referenced, and to look even beyond them, the purpose of this review will have been largely achieved.

II. The Individual and His Internal Environment

A. DIAGNOSTIC MEASURES

1. Physical Signs

The most striking advance in the areas of history recording, physical examination, and the use of diagnostic laboratory tests has been the development of computer-based systems for multiphasic screening of the apparently healthy individual. A variety of such systems is currently operative, as described by Clark (*34*), Collen (*36*), Kanner (*86*), Grossman *et al.* (*64*), and in two staff-written articles in *Medical World News* (*47a,128a*). In a typical system the examinee answers one or more questionnaires relating to his medical history, his present state of health, and perhaps his emotional state. He passes through a series of examinations and tests in one or more locations in the testing area, where he is seen by one or more technicians or physicians, provides a urine sample for analysis and has blood drawn to be analyzed for a number of different factors. Results are often provided before he leaves the examination area. The greatest advantages lie in the thoroughness of the procedure, and the saving of time. These examinations are expensive, however, even though the net cost is much less than if all these procedures were done separately. They have received only limited application so far in the examination and qualification of athletes. With increasing demand for such examinations and little or no increase in the personnel available to perform them, the adoption of these systems may become a necessity.

In the area of body composition, Tipton and Tcheng (*179*) have developed a method for predicting the safe limits of weight loss for high school wrestlers. Their work was based on the earlier estimations of lean body weight from skeletal measurements by Behnke (*15*) and studies by Hall *et al.* (*68*) of the relationships of ideal body weight, anthropometric measurements, and physical tests in boys and girls. This method offers a rational approach to settling the difficult problems posed by starvation and dehydration in young wrestlers anxious to wrestle at many pounds below their natural weights.

The history of, or physical signs of, heart disease have been frequent causes for exclusion of candidates for sports teams. Feinstein *et al.* (*49*) found in a 21-year follow-up of 216 young patients who had had acute rheumatic fever that about the same percentage became worse, better, or were unchanged, regardless of whether they were subjected to physical restriction or not; adverse psychosocial reactions were eight times more frequent in those who were restricted. Hyman (*81*) stated that many young persons were excluded from sports unnecessarily because of findings of heart murmurs, mild hypertension, and irregular rhythms. The criterion should be the functional capacity of the heart, even though it may show some evidences of disease. He recommended the calculation of a cardiopulmonary index before, immediately after, and 5 min after a brief bout of exercise. The formula for the index is

$$\frac{VC + MBH + MEP + \text{age}}{SP + DP + PR} = CPI$$

where VC is vital capacity in units of 100 cc, MBH is maximum breath holding time in seconds, MEP is maximum expiratory pressure in min Hg, age is given in years, and SP, DP, and PR are systolic and diastolic blood pressures and pulse rate, respectively.

Rose (155) described a rapid screening electrocardiographic technique for athletes, using a chair in which copper electrodes contacted both arms and legs to record standard leads I and a V_F in a period of about 30 sec. In a population of 1219 asymptomatic college sports candidates, ten abnormal tracings were found. Confirmation of these abnormal tracings by a 12-lead electrocardiogram showed three with the Wolff–Parkinson–White syndrome, two with complete right bundle–branch block, two with incomplete right bundle–branch block, one with myocardial ischemia, and two with atrioventricular block or nodal rhythm.

Allman (5) and many others have recommended careful preparticipation evaluation of the musculoskeletal system of the prospective athlete with particular regard to the muscle strength in the lower extremities and the stability of the knee. Abbott and Kress (1) found that lack of balance in muscle strength in the lower extremities of West Point cadets, whether or not there was a definite history of previous knee injury, had a high predictive value for the occurrence of knee injury in basic training, field exercises, and sports. Muscle strengthening exercises reduced the occurrence of knee injury among susceptible cadets dramatically.

Nicholas (134) described five tests to divide professional football players into those with "loose" or "tight" joints. He theorized that the "loose" player is more susceptible to knee injury. This theory was supported by Linder (113) but not by Morehouse (126) and Marshall (114), who found no relationship between "loose" or "tight" joints and the occurrence of knee injuries. Ryan (157) pointed out that the situation at the ankle joint differs from that at the knee joint where there are powerful muscles that cross, or whose tendons cross, the joint. The only powerful muscles whose tendons cross the ankle joint are the soleus and gastrocnemius, whose combined tendon (Achilles) crosses so far posterior to the center of the joint that it does not contribute substantially to its lateral stability. The tightness and strength of the ligaments of the ankle are therefore critical in the prevention of sprains of that joint. These ligaments should be protected in sports such as football, where the ankle may be subjected to unusual strains, by wrapping or taping as a means of minimizing or preventing ankle sprains.

Michele (118) described a "spring" sign to detect injury to a meniscus of the knee, elicited by attempting to force the knee into hyperextension. In the presence of meniscal injury the knee will resist this action tending to return forcibly to partial flexion. Cary (31) described a test for the presence of a small effusion in the knee joint by massaging upward and inward on the joint with the knee extended, and then producing a sudden compression of the suprapatellar pouch from the lateral aspect of the knee. A positive reaction is the appearance of a sudden bulge on the medial aspect of the pouch. Slocum and Larson (165) described the pathogenesis of rotary instability of the knee, and a test to detect its presence with the knee flexed to 90 deg and the foot and leg rotated inward 30 deg and then outward 15 deg. Instability is most marked with outward rotation.

Shaffer (162) has suggested that junior high school athletes be evaluated for their physical maturity by measuring the strength of their hand grips with a hand dynamometer.

Lampi (103) has described a simple eyelid test to determine whether an individual has suffered a concussion. A finger is held 6 in. in front of one eye and the patient focuses on it while the examiner closes his opposite eyelid and presses on it gently. The closed eye is then passively opened. If the individual has suffered a concussion, the fixating eye will close partially or completely and tension will be felt in the eyelid muscle of the passively opened eye.

2. Laboratory Measurements

Dunea and Freedman (44) have discussed the significance of proteinuria from both qualitative and quantitative standpoints. The weight of evidence favors increased permeability as the cause, but tubular mechanisms may be involved. Intermittent or orthostatic proteinuria may be found in young athletes and is usually associated with a normal life expectancy. Constant asymptomatic proteinuria, especially in excess of 300 mg per 24 hr period, is indicative of kidney disease. Robinson (152) has reviewed the definition, determination, and significance of orthostatic proteinuria. He states that those patients in whom kidney pathology cannot be found by any other means have an excellent prognosis for life.

Forty-five years after Barach (11) had reported finding microscopic evidence of hematuria in oarsmen and marathon runners, Boone et al. (19) described the presence of red cells in the urine of football players, who apparently had no kidney disease, after practice and games. Gardner (56) described an "athletic pseudonephritis" which included the presence in the urine of albumin and casts, as well as red cells, 49 years following Collier's (37) description of albuminuria in athletes. Kurtz et al. (101) detected similar findings in football players, cross-country runners, and basketball players.

Alyea and Parish (7) found similar postexercise changes in urines of rowers, swimmers, and lacrosse players. Amelar and Solomon (8) and

Kleiman (95) found pseudonephritis following competition in boxing, wrestling, and ice hockey. Additionally, Kleiman found evidence in some patients of a true renal deformity characterized by pericalyceal and peripelvic changes, which he described as "athlete's kidney." Perlman et al. (146) examined the urine of 499 males aged 10 through 69 following an exercise test on a treadmill. All had a negative pretest for proteinuria, but 53 showed protein after the test. The percentage was highest between the ages of 20 and 40. They concluded that increased blood pressure during exercise played some part, but the precise mechanism could not be clearly defined. Kachadorian et al. (85), however, after studying the occurrence of increased protein excretion and increased presence of casts in 41 of 52 cross-country runners following a 20 km run, concluded that glomerular filtration was decreased during exercise, and that decreased tubular reabsorption with temporary damage to the tubules was responsible for both the increased numbers of casts and content of protein.

Stahl (172) reported five cases of myoglobinuria following recent exhaustive exercise in otherwise healthy university students aged 20 to 21. He concluded that it was due to the release of myoglobin from the breakdown of muscle fibers. Howenstine (77) reported the occurrence of exertion-induced myoglobinuria and hemoglobinuria in Marine recruits. These episodes resulted from excessive repetitions of squat jumps, and did not recur when the exercise was repeated at a normal level. Smith (167) treated eight naval aviation officer candidates for rhabdomyolysis and myoglobinuria following very strenuous exercise, and examined 38 other officer candidates with a mean age of 22.7 years before and after training. He concluded that although myoglobinuria occurred most often in the untrained person subjected to intensive heavy work, an individual susceptibility factor seemed to be involved.

3. Radiologic Techniques

The diagnosis of injuries to the elbow joint has been improved somewhat as the result of the description by Newman (133) of the "fat pad" sign. The fat pad, lying behind the humerus at the elbow, is not normally visualized by X rays taken in the lateral position. When it can be seen, it indicates that an injury has occurred to one of the bones around the elbow requiring urgent attention. Such an injury may be a stress fracture or one not otherwise easily visualized. Rogers and MacEwan (153) have described a similar sign to help determine the presence of an injury to the bones just below the elbow joint. In this case, a fat pad lying just over the upper end of the radius may reveal the presence of a stress fracture when it is pushed up and away from the bone.

Diagnosis of injuries to soft tissues around the shoulder has been greatly facilitated by using arthrography as first described by Kernwein *et al.* (*91*), and later amplified by Kernwein (*90*). An opaque, but readily absorbable, dye is injected directly into the shoulder joint, and films are taken with the arm in different positions and from different angles. Tears in the capsule, injuries to tendons and bursa, and osteochondral fractures may all be readily identified. These observations have been extended by the report of Killoran *et al.* (*92*) who added 200 studies to the 200 of Kernwein. In many of these cases, serious and extensive tears of the rotator cuff and other structures were disclosed in the absence of significant clinical or conventional X-ray findings.

Arthrography of the wrist for the diagnosis of ganglia, and as an aid in their more effective removal (recurrence rate of only 6%), has been described by Nelson *et al.* (*130*). These cystlike swellings arise frequently in athletes following injuries to the hand and wrist.

The knee joint is the site of many serious and disabling injuries sustained in sports. Early surgical treatment has resulted in a more rapid return to competition and a decrease in chronic disability for those undergoing surgery. The indications for surgery and for the types of surgical procedures to be used have been clarified by the use of arthrography. Freiberger and Killoran (*53*) described the injection of air in addition to contrast material using multiple films with horizontal rather than vertical beams to diagnose meniscal injuries in the knee. They amplified their observations in collaboration with Nicholas *et al.* (*136*) in 1970 by reporting a 97.5% accuracy of diagnosis of meniscal tear in 225 consecutive knee operations. Similar success has been reported by Olson (*138*), Leclerc *et al.* (*108*), and Butt and McIntyre (*28*).

Better diagnosis of the extent and severity of ankle sprains, a very common sports injury, has been made possible by the use of another technique. Laurin (*104*) described the use of a hinged platform by which the angle of "talar tilt" could be objectively measured under local anesthesia in the injured ankle. The two ankles are examined by conventional exposures and the difference in the degree of tilt indicates the extent of injury. Contrast arthrography, using air and dye, for the same purpose has been described by Percy (*145*) and Olson (*139*), who indicate a high degree of accuracy in diagnosis.

An addition to the ordinary intravenous pyelogram to diagnose the extent of injury to a kidney has been suggested by Morse and Smith (*128*). Visualization of urine that has escaped from a damaged kidney is very difficult with the average 20 cc dose of contrast medium ordinarily given intravenously to a child. With an infusion of dilute sodium diatrizoate given in a dosage of 2 cc per pound of the child's body weight over a period of 5 min, superior visualization not only of the kidney itself, but of any extrarenal spill, is obtained, allowing an early decision to be made regarding the necessity for surgery.

There is even greater need for the prompt and accurate diagnosis of splenic injury, since anything more than a minor insult may lead to extensive hemorrhaging, which can be controlled only by splenectomy. Stein (173) has described an improvement on the technique of percutaneous transfemoral arteriography. The intra-arterial injection of epinephrine at the time that the dye is also injected enhances the detail of the films taken because of the contraction of unaffected intrasplenic arteries. The use of a scintiscan with radioactive chromium (^{51}Cr) to establish a diagnosis of ruptured spleen is described by Jackson and Albright (82) and with technetium sulfur colloid by O'Mara et al. (140). Although a useful adjunct, scintiscanning does not reliably detect defects smaller than 1.5 cm, and a filling defect on a scan is a nonspecific finding.

4. Endoscopy

Arthroscopy of the knee has been described by Casscells (32) as a means of improving the accuracy of the diagnosis of internal derangements. Through a small incision made under local anesthesia on one side of the knee, a small lighted telescope instrument is inserted into the joint for direct visual inspection of the menisci, cartilage, and cruciate ligaments. Biopsies may also be taken through the instrument. Casscells finds it helpful in studying the gliding action of the patella on the femur to determine whether this function is normal or not.

B. THERAPEUTIC MEASURES

1. Nonsurgical

From the standpoint of medical conditions which commonly affect sportsmen, there have been significant advances in six major areas in recent years: (a) more accurate identification and control measures for certain infectious diseases; (b) an improved means of eradicating chronic fungal disease of the skin and nails; (c) the control of noninfectious acute and chronic inflammatory conditions; (d) better understanding and control of the diarrhea of travelers; (e) the control of epistaxis; and (f) a more definitive differential diagnosis of shin splints and related conditions.

a. The Identification and Control of Infectious Diseases. The number of antibiotics available continues to multiply almost monthly. Organisms known to be resistant to the broad spectrum antibiotics most commonly used can now be attacked by newly developed ones. It can now be said that, generally, bacterial diseases can be well controlled, even though those caused by viruses are still elusive. On the other hand, the development of safe and effective vaccines for diseases such as roseola, mumps, and rubella, gives promise of better control of this type of infection (*176*).

Epidemics of skin infections among members of teams are becoming rare, and can be quickly controlled when identified (*64*). The herpes simplex infections which have been such a plague to wrestlers can now be cleared up promptly by photodynamic inactivation (*50*), using proflavine or neutral red dye with two exposures to fluorescent light for 15 min, 4 hr apart.

Infectious mononucleosis is not as yet controlled, although a potential vaccine has been developed and tested clinically (*170*). This disease is much better understood, however, as the result of recent investigations which have clarified its viral etiology and the fact that it confers a life-long immunity. Treatment of the more seriously ill patient with corticosteroids was first described by Bender and Houghton (*17*). A rapid slide test for the identification of mononucleosis was described by Hoff and Bauer (*74*), and, in 1967, Lee and Davidsohn (*109*) introduced a 2-min spot test on paper with an accuracy of almost 100%. Dalrymple (*42*) reported that 24 of 30 college health services banned students from sports participation during the active phase of the disease because of the danger of splenic rupture. Twenty college health services utilized disappearance of a palpable spleen as an important criterion in deciding on the return to sports activity.

b. Chronic Fungal Disease. Epidermophytosis (athlete's foot) and other fungal infections of the skin have responded at the acute stage to the local administration of undecylenic acid and tolnaftate (*151*). In the chronic stage, especially where the toenails have been involved, and seriously deformed, there was no reliable cure until the introduction of griseofulvin as an oral agent to eradicate these conditions (*174*).

c. Acute and Chronic Inflammations. Acute and chronic strain causing inflammation of ligaments, tendons, and bursas can now be controlled in large measure by the oral administration of phenbutazone and oxyphenbutazone, or the local injection of any of the many soluble preparations of the corticosteroids (*94*). Precautions must be taken to follow the white blood count with the long-term administration of either of the oral agents (*71*). Repeated injections of the corticosteroids are not advisable if a response is not obtained to the first two or three injections, since there is a tendency to delay the healing response, and undesirable systemic side effects may occur (*22*).

d. The Diarrhea of Travelers. The studies of Sakazaki *et al.* (*158*), Ozawa *et al.* (*142*), Gorbach (*62*), DuPont *et al.* (*45*), and Etkin and

Gorbach (48) are summarized in an editorial (47a) which indicates that, under certain conditions, strains of *Escherichia coli* which are not ordinarily pathogenic may become so, and that this transformation is undoubtedly responsible for the great majority of cases of traveler's diarrhea. Kean (88) had already described the use of phthalylsulfathiazole (2 gm daily) or neomycin sulfate (1 gm daily) as a reliable prophylaxis. Nicholas et al. (137) showed that the former medication could be given to runners without impairing their performances.

Moore et al. (124) and Babb et al. (10) have also described intestinal infection with *Giardia lamblia* as a cause of traveler's diarrhea in epidemic form at a ski resort, and as seen in a number of individual cases. Treatment with quinacrine hydrochloride (300 mg daily for 5 to 7 days) is effective.

A related, although not exactly similar circumstance, was the outbreak of water-borne hepatitis in members and coaches of a football squad described by Morse et al. (127).

e. Nosebleeds. These may occur spontaneously or as the result of trauma in athletes in many sports. The use of isobutyl cyanoacrylate as a local spray to control epistaxis has been described by Dutisch and Frable (46). Berkstein (18) describes the control of epistaxis with one application of a nasal spray of aminocaproic acid.

f. Shin Splints. The shin splint syndrome was defined restrictively by Slocum (164). He provided a comprehensive differential diagnosis, and stated that the most important principle in treatment was rest. Leach (106) has suggested that those runners who develop shin splints show a greater angle of hip adduction of the lower extremities than a control group of runners. He attributes this chiefly to abnormal action, and mechanical compensation due to running curves at high speed.

2. Surgical

Fractures of the facial bones are common in sports, and all are potentially deforming. Fractures of the orbital floor are particularly troublesome, because if there has been a "blowout" with entrapment of the orbital structures, permanent impairment of vision may result. Converse et al. (39), Hoffman et al. (75), and Leare (107) have described the diagnosis of ocular complications and repair of the floor through a lower eyelid or transantral approach with the use of bone grafts or alloplastic implants.

The treatment of first degree sprains of the acromioclavicular joint has always been conservative, utilizing a sling for support of the arm, with or without adhesive strapping over the end of the clavicle. The correct treatment of second degree sprain continues to be a matter of dispute. There is a greater tendency now to operate on this injury and to repair the torn acromioclavicular ligaments at an early date. For late cases, where supportive therapy has not yielded good results, the distal end of the clavicle may be resected and sometimes combined with a transplantation of the coracoid process into the outer third of the clavicle to give a dynamic stabilization (43). Ahstrom (6) has described a surgical repair of a third degree (complete) acromioclavicular separation, removing the articular cartilage, repairing the torn ligaments if possible, suturing a segment of the tendon of the short head of the biceps to the clavicle (in the manner of Vargas), and fixing the joint temporarily with a heavy threaded wire.

Neviaser (131) demonstrated that the diagnosis of rupture of the rotator cuff of the shoulder could be made when an arthrogram of the glenohumeral joint was performed. With the arm in about 100 deg of abduction, dye flows into the subdeltoid bursa. He has since reported (132) that in chronic rupture there is frequently a normal range of motion, including abduction, the "droparm" test is negative, and pain is the predominant symptom. He described a repair using a portion of the tendon of the long head of the biceps, opened out to close the defect in the cuff, and has obtained excellent functional results.

The cause of the symptomatic condition commonly known as "tennis elbow" has been variously described as being due to a radiohumeral bursitis (141), inflammation of a synovial protrusion from the radiohumeral joint (181), fraying of the orbicular ligament of the radial head (171), calcareous tendinitis at the lateral epicondyle of the humerous (79), hyalin degeneration of the orbicular ligament (20), chondromalacia of the capitellum or radial head (21), traumatic synovitis of the redundant synovial pouch surrounding the radial head (120), neuritis of the posterior interosseous nerve (87), traumata to the radiohumeral synovial fringe (3,125), and a number of other less likely possibilities.

Osgood (141) recommended excision of the radiohumeral bursa, Trethowan (181), excision of the synovial fringe from the joint, and Hughes (79), excision of tissue beneath the origin of the wrist extensors. Bosworth (20) performed resection of the orbicular ligament, Kaplan (87) advised denervation of the radiohumeral joint, and Garden (55), tenotomy of the extensor carpi radialis brevis. Friedlander et al. (54) treated ten involved elbows by section of the common extensor origin and resection of the orbicular ligament following their failure to respond to more conservative treatment. All, except two, became asymptomatic.

One of the most frequent causes of low back pain in athletes is spondylolysis of a lumbar vertebra (183). It is finally being accepted that this is more commonly a traumatic than a congenital defect, especially when it is found unilaterally. A very simple direct surgical approach to the problem has been advocated by Collis (*38*), who excises the fibrous tissue and bony fragments which form a false joint without performing a spinal fusion, the traditional method of dealing with intractable pain from this cause. Barash *et al.* (*12*) have described a relationship between tight hamstring muscles and spondylolisthesis in ten patients. Treatment by laminectomy and spinal fusion resulted in complete remission of symptoms.

Injuries to the knee are common causes of serious and lasting disabilities among athletes. The combination of three injuries (to the anterior cruciate, medial collateral ligaments, and the medial meniscus), which has become known as the "triad of O'Donoghue," presents a constant challenge to the sports surgeon. The most recent contribution to the prevention of instability following this injury is "The Five-in-one Reconstruction for Antero-medial Instability" of Nicholas (*135*). This procedure includes: promixal posterior advancement of the loose medial collateral ligament to the femoral condyle with barbed staple fixation; menisectomy or debridement of the posterior medial corner of the knee; mobilization with distal and anterior transposition of the posterior capsule over the transferred medial collateral ligament; advancement of the trailing edge of the vastus medialis posteriorly to the posterior capsule; and pes anserinus transfer. Forty three of 52 patients were able to return to sports activities in follow-up periods ranging from 1 to 8 years.

Some surgeons do not repair a torn anterior cruciate ligament because they feel that when the tear exists alone it does not cause instability of the knee and because the failure rate for this procedure has been high in the past. Jones (*84*), however, has described a technique of repair in which he uses an excised central portion of patella with intact patellar ligament to fasten into the intercondylar notch of the femur, and he has been successful in 60 cases. Sikand and LeRoy (*163*) have reported using his technique with success in 21 knee operations. Stewart and Winslow (*175*) have had success in repairing 34 out of 41 cases of fresh isolated anterior cruciate ligament tear using a primary repair. They have also operated on 37 old untreated cruciate tears and obtained good results in 28 cases.

Smillie (*166*) has pointed out that surgery should not be delayed when a diagnosis of a tear of the medial meniscus can be made, since the anterior cruciate ligament and articular cartilage of the knee may be damaged in the course of continuing to use the knee. Frankel and Burstein (*52*) have analyzed the biomechanical forces which lead to the destruction of articular cartilage in a knee whose normal pattern of motion was altered by meniscal or ligamentous injury. Powers (*147*) has warned, however, about an apparently much higher rate of misdiagnosis (23% false positive and 25% false negative) in exploratory arthrotomies in women as compared to men (from 4 to 13% false positive), and recommended more careful preoperative evaluation.

Balancing the necessity for early surgery is the discouraging fact that the end result is not always normal, pain-free knee function. Huckell (*78*) found in a 10-year follow-up period that only 76 of 134 postmenisectomy patients, who did not have other diseases at the time of surgery, had satisfactory results. Only 44 had comparatively normal knees following surgery. Jackson (*83*), in a 5–40 year follow-up of 577 knees following menisectomy, reported that degenerative changes were noted on X-ray examination in 23%, as compared to only 5% in the patient's unoperated knee which served as the control. Tapper and Hoover (*178*) found satisfactory clinical results in 145 out of 213 knees followed for 10 to 30 years after surgery, but the knee was considered normal in only 82 cases. Becton and Young (*13*) described 57 cases of cyst of the semilunar cartilage treated surgically and recommended removal of the entire meniscus with the cyst.

The anterior compartment syndrome has been described by many authors who discuss the differential diagnosis between this condition and shin splints. Leach et al. (*105*) stressed the importance of early fasciotomy to prevent permanent disability. Meiers (*117*) has indicated that permanent damage may occur in as little as 24 hr from the onset of symptoms.

Early weight-bearing on tibial fractures has been practiced in U. S. Army Hospitals recently as the result of experiences in the Vietnam war. Brown and Urban (*25*) described their experience in treating 63 compound tibial fractures in 60 patients with minimal shortening and delayed union. Burgess (*26*) reported on the treatment of 47 patients with a patella-bearing short leg cast and early weight-bearing with no non-union and a maximum length loss of 1.25 cm. Sarmiento (*159*) has described the use of a short leg articulated cast-brace for tibial fractures which leaves the knee and ankle free. Mooney et al. (*123*) have applied a similar principle to the treatment of fractures of the distal femur, using a cast which takes the weight chiefly on the soft tissues of the thigh and whose metal brace is hinged at the knee. Leidholt et al. (*112*) reported 63 tibial fractures in persons over 17 years of age (35 due to ski injuries) treated by weight-bearing casts above the knee with good functional results. Full weight-bearing was not achieved, however, until 12 to 17 weeks, depending on the character and stability of the fracture.

Surgical repair of severely sprained ankles has not usually been performed unless a frank dislocation or significant diastasis of the ankle mortise is demonstrated at the time of the initial injury. Most sprains are still treated by plaster casts, adhesive strapping, or no support at all, depending on the severity of the sprain and particular prejudice of the person providing treatment. Broström (23) explored and repaired 105 sprained ankles when the arthrogram revealed extra-articular leakage of the contrast medium. He found ligamentous tears in 99 patients, and 90 with complete rupture of the anterior talofibular ligament. Clark et al. (33) treated 24 patients with severe ankle sprains, operating on 12 and immobilizing 12 in plaster. Results were excellent in nine in each group, but surgery prolonged morbidity.

Stonham (177) described the use of tenodesis of the short peroneal tendon through the lateral malleolus to stabilize recurrent subluxation in the ankle joint. Laing (102) described the treatment of 30 similar cases using the same tendon, but passing through the lateral malleolus and os calcis and back to the lateral malleolus. There was only one failure in this series.

3. Assistive Devices

The multiplicity of knee braces which have been available bear testimony to their inefficacy. The most recent development is the derotation brace of Nicholas (135). This brace is made to fit the measurements of each person who wears one, and is designed principally to prevent the rotary instability of the knee which is such a common sequel to knee injuries, even when they are treated by definitive surgery.

The air splint for fractures was probably first used by Curry (41). In the past 10 years its use has become almost universal. Clear polyvinyl plastic or neoprene-coated nylon fabric are the materials commonly used. Ashton (9) and Ginsberg et al. (60) have issued warnings about the possibly serious consequences of inflation at pressures in excess of 30 mm Hg. Gardner (57) and others (144) have discounted the possibility of this occurring if mouth inflation is employed, and have denied the likelihood of impairment of blood flow even at 40 mm Hg.

4. Physical Therapy

The three principal modes of therapy currently employed in the treatment of sports injuries are the application of heat and cold, active and resistive exercise, and passive exercise including stretching. Although there are virtually no recent developments in the latter, many changes have been advocated and adopted in the first two.

a. External Application of Heat and Cold. Abramson *et al.* (*2*) have summarized the effects of topical application of wet heat. Skin temperatures rose 6.4°C, subcutaneous temperatures 5.4°C, and muscle temperatures 1.8°C when wet heat was applied for 30 min. The average total excess blood flow over control values was four times that obtained by short-wave diathermy, one-third more than that obtained by iontophoresis for the same time, and five times that obtained by ultrasound for 20 min. Muscle temperature increases were also greater than those obtained with iontophoresis and only slightly less than those obtained that diathermy and ultrasound. Lehmann *et al.* (*111*) reported that the application of microwaves at a frequency of 900 MHz is the best method of distributing therapeutic heat to deep tissues. Lehmann *et al.* (*110*) reported on experiments in heating deep structures of the knee joint with ultrasound. The highest temperatures were found in the meniscus and the superficial bone above, with the next highest in the capsular tissue. Short-wave diathermy at 27.12 MHz, using a helical induction coil applicator, was also reported by Lehmann *et al.* (*110*) to be an effective method for heating musculature. Brown (*24*) cautioned about the potential dangers in the use of diathermy and ultrasound, and recommended topical wet heat as much safer in most hands.

The local application of cold in the immediate posttraumatic treatment of sports injuries is now almost universally applied. The use of cold for the extended treatment of these injuries had its start with the publication of a report by Grant (*63*), which described his experience in the treatment of injuries at the Brooke Army Medical Center over a period of 2½ years. He designated the technique of massage of the affected area with ice to produce relief of pain and allow increased range of motion as cryokinetics, but it is generally known today as "ice massage." Its use has rivaled the popularity of heat, but it may be used alternatively by those who wish to continue applying deep heat to muscles. A double-walled neoprene boot which allows the circulation of an alcohol–water coolant mixture was developed by Mitchell *et al.* (*121*) and has been used in the immediate treatment of ankle and knee injuries in football players to reduce pain and minimize swelling.

b. Muscle Retraining by Exercise. The principles of isokinetic exercise were described by Hislop and Perrine (*72*), who developed a machine to produce this continuously accommodating resistive exercise. The most important development embodied in the new apparatus is a means of maintaining constant speed through the range of motion. The clinical use of the isokinetic device has been described by Coplin (*40*).

C. Preventive Measures

1. Protective Equipment

Although there have been many advances in the development of new and improved protective equipment in recent years, there is relatively little published research in this area. The innovations which have characterized these developments have originated for the most part in the laboratories of the manufacturers. They have resulted primarily from suggestions made by coaches, trainers, and athletes. Field testing without controls has been the principal means of justifying the equipment for both the manufacturer and the public.

Research reports regarding the need for and evaluation of protective equipment have been largely limited to head protection, especially in American football and ice hockey. There are also a few clinical studies relating the nature and placement of cleats on the football shoe to the occurrence of ankle and knee injuries.

a. Helmets. The beginning of reported research on the protective qualities of football helmets appears to be the report of Eastwood (47) to the Board of Trustees of the American Football Coaches Association on December 31, 1956. He refers to studies by Dr. Charles Lombard of the Division of Mine Safety Appliances of Protection, Inc. on "Football Helmet Design," which outline the protective and other qualities which should be embodied in the helmet and suggest an ideal structure. The statement is made that, "It is believed impossible to provide a sling suspension system that will provide for both the resilient energy alternation and the energy absorption without making the helmet shell extremely rigid by an abnormally heavy increase in weight." The work of Dr. Edward Dye at the Cornell Aeronautical Laboratory, Inc. is also referred to. The requirements for a satisfactory helmet are described, along with a suggested method for testing. A key statement is that, "In general, it [football helmet] should be constructed of a hard, stiff, and tough shell with a smooth exterior supported from the head by a suspension system of padding, straps, webbing or a combination of such to prevent relative movement of the helmet and head and to keep any part of the shell from "bottoming" on the head under any impact blow which could be received in the game of football."

The studies of Montoye at Michigan State University in testing football helmets, the studies at the Ohio State University Research Foundation on crash helmets, and the studies of Gurdjian and associates at Wayne State University College of Medicine on heat tolerance to impact in automobile crashes were also referred to. It is quite apparent that the majority of these researchers had other major goals, and that their interest in football headgear was secondary. A proposed program of research for the next 3 years was recommended by Dr. Eastwood but never implemented.

Schneider *et al.* (*161*) attempted to identify a common factor in the occurrence of 14 fatal injuries to the head and spinal cord in American football during the 1954 season and several injuries and deaths which occurred in 1960. In three detailed case reports, they blamed the forward projection of the face guard from the helmet and its unyielding character as being responsible for throwing the head into hyperextension on the neck, causing the posterior rim of the helmet to be driven against the spine, causing injury to the spinal cord at that level. They recommended shortening the back of the helmet and eliminating or modifying the face guard.

In the Proceedings of the National Conference on Head Protection for Athletes, held on May 19, 1962, Gurdjian *et al.* (*66*) summarized their studies on human head tolerance to impact and concluded that, "Individual design of the helmet for each sport is mandatory if maximum protection is to be obtained." Kovacic (*96*) summarized his conclusions in helmet design based on laboratory and field testing. He stated that, "A close fitting helmet is essential . . . a hard shell is a necessity . . . the more rigid the better . . . there should be a nonresilient liner . . . there should be a slow rebound type material next to the head." Miller (*119*) described studies in which the g forces sustained by a football player's head were measured by an accelerometer placed in the helmet. One player received a peak force of 316 g's. Montoye (*122*) described the testing of 13 different models of helmets on a metal head form. Although differences were noted in the potential ability of these helmets to decelerate the head safely, it was not possible to state any rank order of superiority. Rachun (*148*) reported on the design of the Cornell football helmet, which was designed by Dye. Reid (*149*) reported on his first experiments in telemetering the impact forces on the helmet of a football player from the field of play.

The first report on football helmet testing from the Snell Memorial Foundation and the University of California at Davis was made by Snively *et al.* (*169*) in 1959. In testing 11 helmets they found none that produced satisfactory deceleration to severe impacts from every angle. Based on their experience with testing and constructing crash helmets for automobile racing, they proposed a prototype helmet with a fiberglass shell with a nonresilient plastic liner and an inner layer of soft, slow-rebound plastic foam. Further studies on a similar type of helmet were reported by Fenner (*51*) in 1964, who described his favorable experience with the use of this helmet for a high school football team. The work of the Snell Memorial Foundation in testing and designing helmets eventually resulted in the publication of their "Standard for Protective Headgear" (*168*) in 1970. This standard was accepted, with slight modification, by the manufacturers of football helmets as a basis for testing of helmets until very recently. This standard has been questioned because it is based on the use of a metal head form under conditions which are quite dissimilar to those found on the football field.

In 1962, Gurdjian *et al.* (*66*) amplified their observations on protection of the head and neck in sports. They reported that linear skull fractures could be produced in cadavers by energies of 4.6 to 6.9 kg·m, which impart an average acceleration of 112 *g* and increase the intracranial pressure by 1450 mm Hg. These figures provide one basis for football helmet construction. The same group, from Wayne State University, reported on experiments with animals and human cadaver heads with and without helmet protection in 1964 (*65*). They established a term, "protective index," which they defined as "a ratio of the impact velocity with helmet on to velocity without helmet for the same effective acceleration." In both animals and cadavers the helmet increased the protective index substantially. A further report (*73*) was published in 1970, describing the extension of studies of impact on the human and animal heads, with and without helmets. They concluded that for blows delivered to the occiput of monkey's heads, the ratio of force to head weight was the best single index of the degree of concussion.

Alley (*4*) reported on a comparison of head injuries in 19,413 high school football players in Southern California in the fall season of 1961 and compared the head injuries with those reported in high school players in Wisconsin, Minnesota, and Michigan in 1948. In 1961, almost all players were wearing hard shell plastic helmets and all were wearing face guards, as opposed to few with plastic headgear and face guards in 1948. There was a reduction of 57% in the 13 year period.

Schneider and Antine (*160*) reported in 1965 that football players wearing six different headgear and face mask combinations suffered from narrowing of their visual fields laterally and inferiorly. They recommended modifications of helmet and facemask design to decrease these "blind" areas to a minimum in the interests of self-protection for the player. Rontal and Rontal (*154*), however, after studying the occurrence of facial fractures in 20 universities over a 10 year period, advocated that all players wear the full cage face mask, and that the chin strap be enlarged and additionally padded to protect against mandibular injury. They felt that the players could adjust to the visual field impairment which would result from the full-cage mask.

Kindt *et al.* (*93*) in 1971 described a new technique for comparing the impact absorption characteristics of football helmets. The head and neck are simulated by using a plastic headform and a flexible metallic rod attached to a sled. Impacts were delivered to the occiput to simulate the severe concussion which might produce brain damage and to the vertex to simulate the force which might produce a fractured cervical vertebra. They found considerable differences in effectiveness for the various helmets tested.

Reid *et al.* (*150*) summarized their work on brain tolerance to impact in football in 1971. Their studies have shown that the magnitude of the force applied to the helmet, as measured by a telemetered signal from the player on the field, is of secondary importance in measuring the tolerance of the brain to impact. A combination of the duration and magnitude of the accelerations applied to the brain are more reliable measurements of its response. The maximum tolerance of the living human brain to accelerations appears to be in the range of 188 to 230g, with a time duration of 310 to 400 msec.

Hughes and Hendrix (*80*) reported in 1968 on telemetering the EEG from a football player during ten games in the fall season of 1966. The dominant frequency of the background was found to be constantly changing according to moment to moment changes in the environmental conditions. Relatively high frequencies were seen during conditions of great anxiety and anticipation. Theta rhythms appeared rarely, and only briefly, after severe injuries.

Mattmiller (*115*) reported in 1969 on the use of a special headgear for touch football. The headgear was composed of Plastisol foam stitched together with nylon and with many perforations for ventilation. The helmet was well accepted by the players. The occurrence of head injuries in 1965, when no headgear was used, was compared with 1966 and 1967, when some players wore the new headgear, and 1968, when all players wore it. There was a significant decrease in serious head injuries from 1965 to 1968.

Bellow *et al.* (*16*) reported in 1970 on an investigation into the evaluation of ice hockey helmets. They tested ten hockey helmets with a new testing apparatus and technique, using a wooden headform suspended by a cable and a striker with a wooden impactor. The general shape of the acceleration–time curve, the peak acceleration, and the area under the acceleration–time curve were studied. It was shown that it was not adequate to evaluate helmets on the basis of their response to peak acceleration alone, but only when all three factors are considered. The experimental results showed differences in protection within the same helmet, depending on the area impacted.

Kraus et al. (97) reported on the use of a special helmet to reduce head injuries in college intramural ice hockey. A flexible vinyl foam helmet, stitched with nylon strips, was used by 100% of all intramural ice hockey players at the University of Minnesota during the 1969 season. The occurrence of all head injuries was compared with the 1968 season, when no helmets were worn. During the control season, the head injury rate was 8.3 per 100 games, compared to 3.8 per 100 games for the experimental season.

b. *Shoe Cleats.* Hanley (69) reported in 1963, as the result of his observations on the field and the study of films of football games over a 4-year period, that the rear cleats of the football shoe were implicated in knee injuries. He found that 77% of knee injuries occurred when the foot was flat on the ground, allowing fixation of the foot by both the long cleats in front and the heel cleats. He introduced a flat $\frac{7}{8}$ in. rubber heel and shortened the front cleats on the shoes of his players to $\frac{1}{2}$ in. During the next four seasons the Bowdoin college team had no serious injuries. Other colleges and high school teams began using heels and short front cleats, and in 1966 Hanley (70) reported that of 1089 players on 75 teams wearing heels and short cleats, 103 suffered knee injuries, while among 4441 players wearing regular football shoes, 239 suffered knee injuries.

Nedwidek (129) in 1966 described a study of 288 high school football players on eight teams. The players were divided into three groups by random sampling. One group (A) wore shoes with oblong cleats on the heel set in a "V" shape and regular front cleats. The second group (B) wore short soccer-type cleats on both sole and heel, and the third group (C) wore conventional cleats on both sole and heel. In group A there were three knee injuries, with one being severe; in group B, seven, with two severe; and in group C, 13, with six being severe.

Kress (98) reported in 1966 on the use of cleatless heels at the West Point Military Academy in intramural football over a 2-year period. Ninety-nine cadets wearing cleatless heels suffered five knee injuries (5.5%), with none of them requiring hospitalization. Among 323 cadets who wore conventional football shoes, there were 27 knee injuries (8.3%) and three cadets required knee surgery.

Rowe (156) studied 1325 high school football players from 44 schools during one season of play. The players were about equally divided between those wearing high- and those wearing low-cut shoes, and also between those wearing disc heels and those wearing cleated heels. Ten percent of the players wore soccer cleats. The highest injury rate for combined knee and ankle sites, adjusted for game exposures, was 166 per 100,000 hr, sustained by those wearing low shoes and heel cleats. The lowest was 83 per 100,000 hr for those wearing soccer cleats. Those wearing low-cut shoes and disc heels were injured at the rate of 103 per 100,000 hr.

The New York State Public High School Athletic Association (*29*) studied an average of 17,800 high school football players for two seasons of play. Their data showed a reduction in ankle and knee injuries for those players using disc or flat heels and/or short cleats on their football shoes.

Gibbs (*59*) studied knee injuries on Harvard freshman football players from 1960 through 1969. From 1967 through 1969, a heel bar was used on the football shoes in place of cleats. From 1963 through 1966 (three seasons), 58 knee injuries were sustained, but from 1967 through 1969 there were only ten.

Cameron and Davis (*30*) developed a swivel with four short cleats to replace the front cleats of the football shoe. They studied the use of this shoe, which also had a heel bar, on 466 high school players and compared the occurrence of knee and ankle injuries in one season of play with that in players who wore full-cleated shoes (2055), front cleats and a heel plate (52), and soccer shoes (266). Those wearing full-cleated shoes suffered 7.88% knee and 8.46% ankle injuries, compared to 5.77% and 7.69% for the heel group, 5.27% and 5.64% for the soccer shoe group, and 2.14% and 3.00% for the swivel cleat group.

Torg (*180*) reported in 1971 on knee injuries among 34 Philadelphia High School football teams over a 3-year period. In 18 Public League teams in 1968, when all players wore conventional cleats, there were 51 knee injuries in 155 games. Twenty-nine of these were classified "severe," of which 11 were treated surgically and 13 were thought to require surgery eventually. In 1969, when players wore shoes with molded soles and soccer cleats, there were 24 knee injuries, of which seven were "severe" and four required surgery. In 1970, with 177 games, there were only 30 knee injuries with nine "severe," of which seven required surgery. In 16 Catholic League teams, knee injuries decreased from 40 "severe" and 32 knee injuries requiring surgery in 1969 with conventional cleats to eight "severe" and four requiring surgery in 1970 with soccer cleats.

2. Artificial Turf

The first installation of artificial turf for sports use was in the Astrodome in Houston in 1964. Its purpose was not the improvement of playing conditions, but simply the fact that grass could not be grown under the light filtered through the glass dome. The second installation did not occur until 1966, and in 1967 there were only two more. The number of installations for stadiums catering primarily to baseball and football by the three companies in the field reached 95 by 1971.

During the first part of this period, attitudes towards the safety of these installations compared to natural grass surfaces were conditioned by a 1967 survey report of knee and ankle injuries sustained in college football. A comparison between injuries sustained on artificial turf and natural grass was reported to be very favorable to the artificial turf (89). This impression was reinforced by a subsequent physician's report on the experience of a university football team which had played for two seasons on the artificial turf and had had a remarkably low occurrence of knee injuries (184).

The first unfavorable reports of injuries experienced with artificial turf appeared in March, 1970 (182), where Brashear and Allman reported that brush burns occurred, which require protection of the exposed legs and forearms, and Nicholas reported on the occurrence of foot sprains which seemed to be related to softer-soled shoes used on the artificial turf. Then in November of the same year, Behling (14) reported that from the 1967 through the 1969 football season in the Pacific Eight Conference, "the severity of knee injuries incurred on artificial turf, as opposed to grass, may be slightly less as judged by the decrease in percentage of players treated surgically." In the same publication, however, Kretzler (99) reported that in his experience with high school football players during the same period, knee injuries sustained on artificial turf were "no less severe than on grass." Actually, 13 of the 39 knee injuries sustained on artificial turf in 1967–1969 required surgery. The following year, Garrick (58) reported, in a study of 228 high school games played on natural grass and artificial turf in 1970, that the rate of serious injuries per game was 0.76 on the synthetic as compared to 0.52 on the natural grass.

The most recent report by Kretzler (100) covers a four-season study of injuries occurring in 14 high school teams, playing 176 games on artificial turf and 47 on grass fields. The incidence of knee injuries on the artificial turf was 0.312 per game and on grass 0.298; of ankle injuries, the incidences were 0.170 and 0.149, respectively. He pointed out that the variations in condition of artificial surfaces were minimal compared to those found in grass fields.

The build-up of heat on and over artificial turf has been a major complaint of professional baseball players especially. Blistering of feet, requiring the wearing of insulating insoles, has been a problem. Buskirk *et al.* (*27*) reported that their investigations of the microclimate over artificial turf indicated that wide extremes could occur in the differences from ambient air temperatures, depending on many circumstances. On one day with air temperature at 71°F, temperature on natural grass was 90°F, and on the artificial turf practice field 140°F. Over a 28 day period of 12 hr observations during the daytime, the natural grass was 28°F cooler on the average than the artificial turf. Temperature in a central shoe cleat applied to the artificial turf reached the turf temperature of 125°F on one day in 15 min, and at the sock–sole interface, with a player's foot in the shoe, reached 107°F in 5 min. Air movement from the sides of the artificial turf tends to make the periphery colder than the center of the field.

Howard *et al.* (*76*) have reported on experiments in which thermocouples were installed at the surface of a field of artificial turf, at the turf–pad interface, and 4 in. below the surface of the asphalt base. Thermocouples were also installed 1 in. and 4 in. below the surface of an immediately adjacent field of Tifton bermuda grass. Air temperatures were also measured with wet and dry bulb thermometers 18 and 60 in. above both grass and artificial surfaces. Nearly continuous recording was made between August 27, 1970 and September 14, 1970. A light breeze was blowing across both fields most of the time. Cloudiness was variable.

At midday, 18-in. air temperatures were 2° to 4°F higher than the 60-in. air temperatures for both surfaces. Air temperatures above the synthetic surface were often 2° to 3°F higher than the corresponding air temperatures above grass. Surface temperatures of the artificial turf during periods of peak incoming radiation were considerably higher than those of grass. On one occasion, when grass temperature reached 110°F, surface temperature of the artificial turf reached 150°F. Wetting the synthetic material produced rapid and prolonged lowering of surface temperatures. Effective air temperatures, as calculated by using the temperature–humidity index and the wet-bulb-globe temperature index, were 2° to 3°F higher for the synthetic than the grass surface.

Patrick and Barton (*143*) studied air temperatures and humidity over the artificial turf in a football stadium and over grass in a nearby practice field between July 26 and August 5, 1971. Air temperatures were taken at elevations of 0, 15, and 54 in. A sling psychrometer was used to measure the wet-bulb temperature at 15 and 54 in. Although the average daily temperature at 0 in. elevation averaged 4.9°F higher on the artificial turf during the entire period, the peak difference was 16°F one day at 3:00 P.M. At 54 in. elevation the average difference was only 0.4°F and the greatest difference at 54 in. was only 8°F. The relative humidity was 2.5% lower on the average at 15 in. elevation, and 3.0% lower at 54 in., over the artificial turf than the grass surface. At a hearing before the Subcommittee on Commerce and Finance of the Committee on Interstate and Foreign Commerce of The House of Representatives of the Ninety-Second Congress on the subject of the Consumer Product Safety Act, Clarke (*35*) stated that the research which had been conducted up to that time by the three companies which had submitted evidence regarding their studies of their products was inadequate in terms of characterizing the effects of vigorous activities on these surfaces. The properties of friction, hardness, abrasiveness, and heat build-up had not been adequately dealt with. There was no systematic surveillance of the actual injury experience after installation. There was little evidence of postinstallation retesting to determine whether there was any change in the properties of the surface. He concluded that it was not possible to determine from the data reviewed and the opinions which had been presented whether synthetic turf was more or less hazardous for sport participation than natural turf. Similar conclusions were reached by McGuire and Taner (*116*), in their "Evaluation of Synthetic Turf Safety Test Programs" for the National Bureau of Standards.

References

1. Abbott, H. G., and Kress, J. B. (1969). *Arch. Phys. Med. Rehabil.* **50**, 326–333.
2. Abramson, D. E., Mitchell, R. E., Tack, S., Jr., Bell, Y., and Zayas, A. M. (1961). *Arch. Phys. Med. Rehabil.* **42**, 305–318.
3. Allen, J. C., Bell, H., and Shearman, C. H. (1947). *Med. J. Aust. Tal.* **1**, 48–51.
4. Alley, R. H., Jr. (1964). *J. Amer. Med. Ass.* **188**, 418–422.
5. Allman, F. L., Jr. (1964). *Proc. 5th Nat. Conf. Med. Aspects Sports, Chicago* pp. 64–70.
6. Ahstrom, J. P. (1971). *J. Amer. Med. Ass.* **217**(6), 785–789.
7. Alyea, E. P., and Parish, J. H., Jr. (1958). *J. Amer. Med. Ass.* **167**(7), 807–813.
8. Amelar, R. D., and Soloman, C. (1954). *J. Urol.* **72**, 145.
9. Ashton, H. (1966). *Brit. Med. J.* **2**, 1427–1430.
10. Babb, R. R., Peck, O. C., and Vescia, F. G. (1971). *J. Amer. Med. Ass.* **217**(10), 1359–1361.
11. Barach, J. H. (1910). *Arch. Intern. Med.* **5**, 382–405.
12. Barash, H. L., Galante, J. O., Lambert, C. N., and Ray, R. D. (1970). *J. Bone Joint Surg., Amer. Vol.* **52**, 1319–1328.
13. Becton, J. L., and Young, H. H. (1965). *Arch. Surg.* **90**, 708–712.
14. Behling, F. L. (1970). *Med. Trib.* Nov. 16.
15. Behnke, A. R. (1959). *Human Biol.* **31**, 295–315.
16. Bellow, D. G., Mendryk, S., and Schneider, V. (1970). *Med. Sci. Sports* **2**, 43–49.
17. Bender, C. E., and Houghton, B. C. (1953). *Northwest Med.* **52**, 922–925.

18. Berkstein, A. (1971). *Arch. Otolaryngol.* **93**, 456–457.
19. Boone, A. W., Haltiwanger, E., and Chambers, R. L. (1955). *J. Amer. Med. Ass.* **158**(17), 1516–1517.
20. Bosworth, D. M. (1955). *J. Bone Joint Surg., Amer. Vol.* **37**, 527–533.
21. Bosworth, D. M. (1965). *J. Bone Joint Surg., Amer. Vol.* **47**, 1533–1536.
22. Brewer, B. J. (1969). *In* "American Academy of Orthopedic Surgeons Symposium on Sport Medicine," pp. 97–100. Mosby, St. Louis.
23. Broström, L. (1964). *Acta Clin. Scand.* **128**, 483–495.
24. Brown, A. M. (1971). *Med. Trib.* Jan. 20.
25. Brown, P. W., and Urban, J. G. (1968). *J. Amer. Med. Ass.* **203**(8), 39–44.
26. Burgess, E. M. (1968). *Med. Trib.* Dec. 19.
27. Buskirk, E. R., McLaughlin, E. R., and Loomis, J. L. (1971). *J. Health, Phys. Educ. Rec.* **42**, 29–30.
28. Butt, W. P., and McIntyre, J. L. (1969). *Radiology* **92**, 487–499.
29. Callahan, W. T., Crowley, F. J., and Hafner, J. K. (1969). "A Statewide Study Designed to Determine Methods of Reducing Injury in Interscholastic Football Competition by Equipment Modification." N. Y. State Public High School Athletic Ass., Albany.
30. Cameron, B. M., and Davis, O. (1970). "The Swivel Football Shoe: A Controlled Study." Cameron Athletic Corp., Houston.
31. Cary, G. R. (1966). *J. La. State Med. Soc.* **118**, 147–149.
32. Casscells, S. W. (1971). *Med. Trib.* Jan. 6, p. 20.
33. Clark, B. L., Derby, A. C., and Power, G. R. I. (1965). *Can. J. Surg.* **8**, 358–363.
34. Clark, T. W. (1966). *J. Amer. Med. Ass.* **195**, 30–31.
35. Clarke, K. C. (1971). House of Representatives, 92nd Congress, Serial 92–59, Committee on Interstate and Foreign Commerce. pp. 294–297.
36. Collen, M. F. (1966). *J. Amer. Med. Ass.* **195**(10), 142–145.
37. Collier, W. (1907). *Brit. Med. J.* **1**, 4–6
38. Collis, J. S. (1971). *Med. World News* Dec. 24, p. 17.
39. Converse, J. M., Smith, B., Obear, M. F., and Wood-Smith, D. (1967). *Plast. Reconstr. Surg.* **39**, 20–36.
40. Coplin, T. H. (1971). *J. NATA* **6**, 3.
41. Curry, G. J. (1944). *J. Amer. Med. Ass.* **125**, 966–968.
42. Dalrymple, W. (1965). *Med. Trib.* July 12.
43. Dewar, F. P., and Barrington, T. W. (1965). *J. Bone Joint Surg., Brit. Vol.* **47**, 32–35.
44. Dunea, G., and Freedman, P. (1968). *J. Amer. Med. Ass.* **203**(11), 171–172.
45. DuPont, H. L., Fornal, S. B., and Hornick, R. B. (1971). *New Engl. J. Med.* **285**, 1–9.
46. Dutisch, L. L., Jr., and Frable, M. A. (1971). *Surg. Gynecol. Obstet.* **133**, 699–670.
47. Eastwood, F. R. (1956). Confidential Report on Present Research on Football Helmets and Future Study Needs to the Board of Trustees of the American Football Coaches Association, December 31.
47a. Editorial (1970). *J. Amer. Med. Ass.* **218**, 248.
48. Etkin, S., and Gorbach, S. L. (1971). *J. Lab. Clin. Med.* **78**, 81–87.
49. Feinstein, A. R., Taube, H., Cavilieri, R., Schultz, S. C., and Kryle, L. (1962). *J. Amer. Med. Ass.* **180**(12), 1028–1031.
50. Felber, T. D., Wallis, C., Smith, E. B., Melnick, J. L., and Knox, J. M. (1972). *Med. Trib.* Jan. 12.

51. Fenner, H. A., Jr. (1964). *GP* **30**(4), 106–113.
52. Frankel, V. H., and Burstein, A. H. (1970). "Orthopedic Biomechanics," p. 188. Lea & Febiger, Philadelphia, Pennsylvania.
53. Freiberger, R. H., and Killoran, P. J. (1965). *Med. World News* Feb. 19.
54. Friedlander, H. L., Reid, R. L., and Cape, R. F. (1967). *Clin. Orthop.* **51**, 109–116.
55. Garden, R. S. (1961). *J. Bone Joint Surg., Brit. Vol.* **43**, 100–106.
56. Gardner, K. D., Jr. (1956). *J. Amer. Med. Ass.* **161**(17), 1613–1617.
57. Gardner, W. J. (1967). *J. Amer. Med. Ass.* **201**(8), 149.
58. Garrick, J. G. (1971). *Med. World News* May 28, pp. 18–19.
59. Gibbs, R. W. (1969). Presented at the Annual American College Health Association Meeting at Oklahoma City, April 23.
60. Ginsberg, M., Miller, J. M., and McElfatrick, G. C. (1967). *J. Amer. Med. Ass.* **200**(2), 180–181.
61. Glezen, W. P., Lindsay, R. L., DeWalt, J., and Dillar. H. C., Jr. (1972). *Lancet*, Feb. 5, pp. 301–303.
62. Gorbach, S. L. (1970). *New Engl. J. Med.* **283**, 44–45.
63. Grant, A. E. (1964). *Arch. Phys. Med.* **45**, 233–238.
64. Grossman, J. H., Barnett, G. O., McGuire, M. T., and Swedlow, D. B. (1971). *J. Amer. Med. Ass.* **215**, 1286–1291.
65. Gurdjian, E. S., Hodgson, V. R., Hardy, W. G., Patrick, L. M., and Lissner, H. R. (1964). *J. Trauma* **4**, 309–324.
66. Gurdjian, E. S., Lissner, H. R., and Patrick, L. M. (1962). *Proc. Nat. Conf. Head Protection Athletes* pp. 1–15.
67. Gurdjian, E. S., Lissner, H. R., and Patrick, L. M. (1962). *J. Amer. Med. Ass.* **182**, 509–512.
68. Hall, D. M., Cain, R. L., and Tipton, C. M. (1965). "Keeping Fit: A 23 Year Study of Evaluation of Physical Fitness Tests. Cooperative Extension Service," pp. 1–37. Univ. of Illinois, Urbana, Illinois.
69. Hanley, D. F. (1963). *Med. Trib.* Nov. 11.
70. Hanley, D. F. (1966). "Results of Knee and Ankle Injury Survey for Fall 1965 Season," p. 1. Bowdoin College, Brunswick, Maine.
71. Hartl, W. (1965). *Seminars Hematol.* **2**, 313.
72. Hislop, H. J., and Perrine, J. J. (1967). *J. Amer. Phys. Ther. Ass.* **47**, 116.
73. Hodgson, V. R., Gurdjian, E. S., and Thomas, L. M. (1970). "Football Injuries," pp. 61–79. National Academy of Sciences, Washington, D. C.
74. Hoff, G., and Bauer, S. (1965). *J. Amer. Med. Ass.* **194**(4), 119–121.
75. Hoffman, S., Weiner, D. L., and Barsky, A. (1967). *Arch. Surg.* **94**, 403–412.
76. Howard, M. K., Koon, J. L., and Rochester, E. W. (1971). *J. Nat. Athlete Trainer's Ass.* **6**, 157–159.
77. Howenstine, J. A. (1960). *J. Amer. Med. Ass.* **173**(5), 493–499.
78. Huckell, J. R. (1965). *Can. J. Surg.* **8**, 254–260.
79. Hughes, E. S. R. (1950). *J. Bone Joint Surg., Brit. Vol.* **32**, 30–34.
80. Hughes, J. R., and Hendrix, D. E. (1968). *Electroencephalogr. Clin. Neurophysiol.* **24**, 183–186.
81. Hyman, A. S. (1964). *Texas J. Med.* **60**, 571–576.
82. Jackson, G. L., and Albright, D. (1968). *J. Amer. Med. Ass.* **204**, 930–931.
83. Jackson, J. P. (1968). *Brit. Med. J.* **2**, 525–527.
84. Jones, J. C. (1970). *Surg. Advan.* **1**, 4.

85. Kachadorian, W. A., Johnson, R. E., Buffington, R. E., Lawler, L., Serbin, J. J., and Woodall, T. (1970). *Med. Sci. Sports* **2**, 142–145.
86. Kanner, I. F. (1971). *J. Amer. Med. Ass.* **215**(8), 1281–1285.
87. Kaplan, E. (1959). *J. Bone Joint Surg.* **41**, 147–151.
88. Kean, B. H. (1963). *Ann. Intern. Med.* **59**, 605.
89. Kelly, R. E. (1968). "Survey of Football Knee and Ankle Injuries, 1967." Monsanto Co., St. Louis, Missouri.
90. Kernwein, G. A. (1955). *J. Amer. Med. Ass.* **194**(10), 1081–1085.
91. Kernwein, G. A., Roseberg, B., and Sneed, W. R., Jr. (1957). *J. Bone Joint Surg., Amer. Vol.* **39**, 1267–1279.
92. Killoran, P. J., Marcove, R. C., and Freiberger, R. H. (1968). *Amer. J. Roentgenol.* **103**, 658–668.
93. Kindt, G. W., Schneider, R. C., and Robinson, J. L. (1971). *Med. Sci. Sports* **3**, 203–209.
94. King, J. W., Brelsford, H. J., and Tullos, H. S. (1969). *In* "American Academy of Orthopedic Surgeons Symposium on Sports Medicine," pp. 75–86. Mosby, St. Louis, Missouri.
95. Kleiman, A. H. (1960). *J. Urol.* **83**, 312–329.
96. Kovacic, C. R. (1962). *Proc. Nat. Conf. Head Protection Athletes* pp. 29–30.
97. Kraus, J. F., Anderson, B. D., and Mueller, C. E. (1970). *Med. Sci. Sports* **2**, 162–164.
98. Kress, J. B. (1966). *Med. Trib.* May 2.
99. Kretzler, H. H. (1970). *Med. Trib.* Nov. 16.
100. Kretzler, H. H. (1972). *Med. Trib.* April 26.
101. Kurtz, C. F., Wesemann, M. M., Ruffalo, P., and Gray, W. J. (1957). *J. Indiana Med. Ass.* **50**, 1348–1353.
102. Laing, P. G. (1971). *Med. Trib.* Aug. 11.
103. Lampi, O. (1967). *Med. World News* Nov. 17.
104. Laurin, C. A. (1967). *Med. World News* Oct. 20, pp. 50–51.
105. Leach, R. E., Zohn, D. A., and Stryker, W. S. (1963). *Med. Trib.* Aug. 5.
106. Leach, W. F. (1971). *Med. Trib.* Aug. 25.
107. Leare, C. R., Jr. (1972). *Amer. Fam. Prac.* **5**, 102–106.
108. Leclerc, J., Aube, L., and Dionne, G. (1968). *Can. J. Surg.* **11**, 466–472.
109. Lee, C. L., and Davidsohn, I. (1967). *J. Amer. Med. Ass.* **202**(2), 21.
110. Lehmann, J. F., DeLateur, B. J., Warren, C. G., and Stonebridge, J. B. (1968). *Arch. Phys. Med.* **49**, 28–30.
111. Lehmann, J. F., Silverman, D. R., Baum, B. A., Kirk, N. L., and Johnston, V. C. (1966). *Arch. Phys. Med.* **47**, 291–299.
112. Leidholt, J. D., Clayton, M. L., and Gamble, W. E. (1970). *Med. Trib.* March 23.
113. Linder, F. T. (1971). *Med. Trib.* Sept. 1.
114. Marshall, W. A. (1970). Doctoral Dissertation, Univ. of Wisconsin, Madison, Wisconsin.
115. Mattmiller, E. D. (1969). *J. Amer. Coll. Health. Ass.* **18**, 162–164.
116. McGuire, B. J., and Taner, S. D. (1972). Evaluation of Synthetic Turf Safety Test Programs. Technical Report to Subcommittee on Commerce and Finance of the Interstate and Foreign Commerce Committee of the House of Representatives. U. S. Dept. of Commerce, Nat. Bur. Standards, Washington, D. C.
117. Meiers, H. G. (1971). *Deut. Med. Wochenschr.* **96**, 1357–1359.
118. Michele, A. A. (1961). *New York J. Med.* **61**, 1534–1536.

119. Miller, F. L. (1962). *Proc. Nat. Conf. Head Protection Athletes* pp. 31–33.
120. Mills, G. P. (1937). *Brit. Med. J.* **2**, 212–213.
121. Mitchell, J. W., Myers, G. E., and Galvez, T. (1969). *Univ. Wisc. Hosp. News Rev.* 8(10), 2.
122. Montoye, H. J. (1962). *Proc. Nat. Conf. Head Protection Athletes* pp. 34–37.
123. Mooney, V., Nickel, V. L., and Snelson, R. (1970). *Med. World News* Feb. 20.
124. Moore, G. T., Cross, W. M., McGuire, D., Mollohan, C. S., Gleason, N. N., Healy, G. R., and Newton, L. H. (1969). *New Engl. J. Med.* **281**, 402–407.
125. Moore, M., Jr. (1952). *Arch. Surg.* **64**, 501–505.
126. Morehouse, C. A. (1971). Presented at the Thirteenth National Conference on the Medical Aspects of Sports, New Orleans, November 28.
127. Morse, L. J., Bryan, J. A., Hurley, J. P., Murphy, J. F., O'Brien, T. F., and Wacker, W. E. C. (1972). *J. Amer. Med. Ass.* **219**(6), 706–708.
128. Morse, T. S., and Smith, J. P. (1968). *Med. World News* Dec. 6, p. 42.
128a. Multiphasic Testing. (1971). *Med. World News* Oct. 15, pp. 51–62.
128b. Multiphasic Screening Cut Down to Size. (1966). *Med. World News* Sept. 6, pp. 60–61.
129. Nedwidek, R. A. (1966). *Med. Trib.* Dec. 21.
130. Nelson, C. L., Sawmiller, S., and Phalen, G. S. (1971). *Surg. Advan.* **2**, 1–6.
131. Neviaser, J. S. (1954). *Clin. Orthop.* 92–98.
132. Neviaser, J. S. (1971). *Arch. Surg.* **102**, 483–485.
133. Newman, M. (1958). *Kaiser Found. Med. Bull.* **6**, 380–381.
134. Nicholas, J. A. (1970). *J. Amer. Ass.* **212**(13), 2236–2239.
135. Nicholas, J. A. (1972). *Med. World News* Feb. 18.
136. Nicholas, J. A., Freiberger, R. H., and Killoran, P. J. (1970). *J. Bone Joint Surg., Amer. Vol.* **52**, 203–220.
137. Nicholas, W. C., Kollias, J., Buskirk, E. R., and Tershak, M. J. (1968). *J. Amer. Med. Ass.* **205**, 757–761.
138. Olson, R. W. (1967). *Amer. J. Roentgenol.* **101**, 897–914.
139. Olson, R. W. (1969). *Radiology* **92**, 1439–1446.
140. O'Mara, R. E., Hall, R. C., and Danbroski, D. L. (1970) *Surg. Gynecol. Obstet.* **131**, 1077–1084.
141. Osgood, R. (1922). *Arch. Surg.* **4**, 420–433.
142. Ozawa, H., Nakamura, A., and Sakazaki, R. (1968). *Jap. J. Med. Sci. Biol.* **21**, 333–349.
143. Patrick, C., and Barton, B. (1972). *J. Nat. Athlete-Trainer's Ass.* **7**, 47–48.
144. Paul, W. D., ed. (1967). *Phys. Ther. Bull.* (Iowa Chapter, Arthritis Rheumatism Found., Des Moines, Iowa) **5**, 2.
145. Percy, E. C. (1968). *Med. World News* Nov. 25, p. 8.
146. Perlman, L. V., Cunningham, D. A., Montoye, H., and Chiang, B. (1970). *Med. Sci. Sports* **2**, 20–23.
147. Powers, J. A. (1969). *J. Amer. Med. Ass.* **208**, 663–664.
148. Rachun, A. (1962). *Proc. Nat. Conf. Head Protection Athletes* pp. 38–39.
149. Reid, S. E. (1962). *Proc. Nat. Conf. Head Protection Athletes* pp. 40–43.
150. Reid, S. E., Tarkington, J. A., Epstein, H. M., and O'Dea, T. J. (1971). *Surg. Gynecol. Obstet.* **133**, 929–936.
151. Robinson, H. M., and Raskin, J. (1965). *Arch. Dermatol.* **9**, 372.
152. Robinson, R. R. (1971). *Kidney* **4**, 1–5
153. Rogers, S. L., and MacEwan, D. W. (1969). *Radiology* **92**, 954–958.
154. Rontal, E., and Rontal, M. (1971). *J. Sports Med. Phys. Fit.* **11**, 241–245.

155. Rose, K. D. (1969). *J. Amer. Med. Ass.* **208**(12), 2319–2324.
156. Rowe, M. L. (1969). *Med. Sports* **9**, 3.
157. Ryan, A. J. (1971). Presented at the Thirteenth National Conference on the Medical Aspects of Sports, New Orleans, November 28.
158. Sakazaki, R., Tamura, K., and Saito, M. (1967). *Jap. J. Med. Sci. Biol.* **20**, 387–389.
159. Sarmiento, A. (1969). *J. Amer. Med. Ass.* **207**, 23.
160. Schneider, R. C., and Antine, B. E. (1965). *J. Amer. Med. Ass.* **192**, 616–618.
161. Schneider, R. C., Reifel, E., Crisler, H. O., and Oosterbaan, B. G. (1961). *J. Amer. Med. Ass.* **177**, 361–367.
162. Shaffer, T. E. (1971). *Med. Trib.* Oct. 6.
163. Sikand, S. D., and LeRoy, J. B. (1967). *Med. Trib.* Aug. 21.
164. Slocum, D. B. (1967). *Amer. J. Surg.* **114**, 875–881.
165. Slocum, D. B., and Larson, R. L. (1968). *J. Bone Joint Surg., Amer. Vol. 50*, **2**, 211–225.
166. Smillie, I. (1967). *Med. Trib.* **1**(28), 2.
167. Smith, R. F. (1968). *Arch. Intern. Med.* **121**, 313–319.
168. Snively, G. G. (1970). Standard for Protective Headgear. p. 8. Snell Memorial Found., San Francisco.
169. Snively, G. G., Kovacic, C., and Chichester, C. O. (1959). *Proc. 1st Nat. Conf. Med. Aspects Sports, Chicago* pp. 69–75.
170. Springer, G. F., Seifert, M. H., Adye, J. C., and Eyquem, A. (1972). *Med. World News* Feb. 11.
171. Stack, J. K. (1949). *Surg. Clin. N. Amer.* **29**, 155–162.
172. Stahl, W. C. (1957). *J. Amer. Med. Mass.* **164**, 1458–1460.
173. Stein, H. L. (1969). *Radiology* **93**, 367–372.
174. Steinberg, T. H., Newcomer, V. D., Reisner, R. M., Haver, R. S., and Sorenson, L. J. (1959). *Curr. Ther. Res.* **1**, 1.
175. Stewart, M. J., and Winslow, J. E., Jr. (1967). *Med. Trib.* July 12.
176. Stokes, J., Jr., Weibel, R. E., Villarejos, V. M., Arguedas, J. A., Buynak, E. B., and Hilleman, M. R. (1971). *J. Amer. Med. Ass.* **218**, 57–61.
177. Stonham, F. V. (1960). *Med. J. Aust.* **1**, 44–45.
178. Tapper, E. M., and Hoover, N. W. (1969). *J. Bone Joint Surg., Amer. Vol.* **51**, 517–603.
179. Tipton, C. M., and Tcheng, T. K. (1970). *J. Amer. Med. Ass.* **214**, 1269–1274.
180. Torg, J. S. (1971). *J. Amer. Med. Ass.* **218**, 1504–1506.
181. Trethowan, W. H. (1929). *Brit. Med. J.* **2**, 1218–1219.
182. Tribune Sports Report (1970). *Med. Trib.* March 5.
183. Turner, R. H., and Bianco, A. J., Jr. (1971). *J. Bone and Joint Surg., Amer. Vol.* **53**, 1298–1306.
184. Whitehurst, J. R. (1968). *J. Amer. Coll. Health Ass.* **17**, 136–137.

Physiological Assessment of Maximal Performance

Francis J. Nagle

DEPARTMENTS OF PHYSIOLOGY AND PHYSICAL EDUCATION,
UNIVERSITY OF WISCONSIN, MADISON, WISCONSIN

I. Introduction

Maximal performance may assume a myriad of forms but all forms include energy output, neuromuscular functions involving strength and technique, and psychological factors, including motivation and tactics (*10*).

Many individuals today have a great interest in maximal performance and for the competitive sportsman the interest is readily appreciated. However, even to the nonexerciser and the increasing number of noncompetitive exercise enthusiasts, maximal performance has meaning for assessing capability for occupational demands and in evaluating the efficacy of various physical training procedures.

Since this review is concerned with the physiological assessment of maximal performance, the text will focus on energy output (aerobic and anaerobic metabolism) as the primary factor in maximal performance. Strength and its physiological correlates are treated by Clarke (this volume, p. 73).

Muscle contraction and ultimately human movement depends on the splitting of high-energy adenosine triphosphate (ATP) stored in skeletal muscle.

(1) $ATP \rightarrow$ energy for contraction $+ ADP +$ heat $+$ inorganic phosphate. ATP is quickly regenerated from another high-energy compound found in muscle, viz. creatine phosphate (CP);

(2) $CP + ADP \rightarrow ATP +$ creatine. The energy store of ATP and CP is replenished by the aerobic oxidation of foodstuffs;

(3) Foodstuffs $+ O_2 \rightarrow ATP + CO_2 + H_2O +$ heat. ATP is also generated by the anaerobic oxidation of glucose or glycogen (glycolysis);

(4) Glucose or glycogen $\xrightarrow{\text{ATP}}$ pyruvic acid $\rightleftharpoons$ lactic acid.

It has been demonstrated empirically (*49,86*) and shown experimentally (*91*) that man is capable of a running power output approximating 1.3 to 1.6 hp (10.4 to 12.8 liters O_2/min) over 5 to 6 sec of time. Virtually the total energy for such performances is derived from ATP and CP from the muscle stores (*94*). Since these stores are quite limited and only regenerated through time-dependent processes of aerobic and anaerobic metabolism, the power output curve (Fig. 1) decreases exponentially with time. In maximal running efforts of 30 sec duration, the power output decreases to 0.7–0.8 hp (5.6 to 6.4 liters O_2/min) (Fig. 1) and continues to decline dramatically until aerobic synthesis of ATP begins to keep pace with the rate at which it is being utilized. The intensity of the running at which such a balance is struck may range from a 5-min to a 12-min mile pace, depending on the state of training of an individual. Some marathon runners, for example, may maintain a 5-min mile pace over a 2½ hr period (*33,34*), while some untrained, male adults may have difficulty maintaining a 12-min mile pace for a few minutes at a time. It is readily apparent, then, that the caliber of maximal human performance, defined as a rhythmic, large muscle activity of the nature of running or cycling, is dependent on

(1) the level of high-energy phosphate stores (ATP, CP), and

(2) the ability to resupply the stores through aerobic and anaerobic mechanisms.

It is conventional to express man's anaerobic contribution to physical performance in units of oxygen taken up after exercise in excess of the

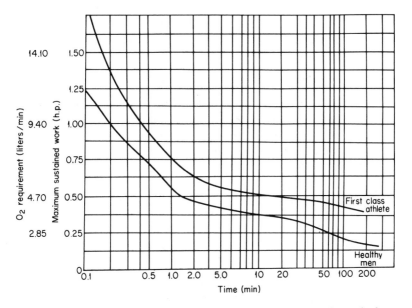

Fig. 1. Semilog plot of energy requirement in horsepower and O_2 equivalents on the ordinate and time of performance on the abscissa. [Adapted from Fletcher (*49*).]

rest requirement (*60,95*). This is identified as the O_2 debt or O_2 repayment since it contributes to the restoration of normal resting levels of ATP, CP, body O_2 stores, and lactic acid (LA) formed during exercise. LA is formed from pyruvic acid in the process of glycolysis which supplies limited ATP. Classical theory holds that LA is formed only when the O_2 supply is inadequate, which limits the aerobic machinery in accommodating pyruvic acid directly for aerobic synthesis of ATP (*67,95*). There is accumulating evidence that LA levels may increase in response to factors other than an O_2 deficit in working muscle. Keul *et al.* (*80*) showed that at identical venous O_2 tensions in cardiac and skeletal muscle the cardiac muscle utilizes LA for substrate, while skeletal muscle is producing LA. This would suggest a relative deficiency in aerobic metabolism machinery in skeletal muscle since it is functioning more anaerobically (producing LA) despite identical cardiac and skeletal muscle O_2 tensions. It has also been demonstrated that LA levels are higher in untrained than trained humans working at identical percentages of maximal aerobic power or at identical loads (*62,145*). This suggests a greater dependence in the untrained on glycolytic energy production with resulting LA accumulation. It should be understood that this difference is apparent when exercising well within aerobic power limits. A theoretical explanation for this has been proposed by Holloszy (*70*), who attributes the higher LA values in the untrained to higher skeletal muscle concentrations of ADP, which in turn stimulate glycolytic activity. The point to be stressed is that the relationship of LA accumulation to O_2 deficit, debt, or repayment is by no means clear-cut.

The aerobic contribution to physical performance is measured by the O_2 utilized by the body during activity. The capacities of the anaerobic and aerobic metabolic mechanisms would therefore be identified with the maximum O_2 debt or repayment, expressed in liters, and the maximal O_2 uptake, expressed in liters per minute, respectively. The latter measure is an expression of human power (energy per unit time).

II. Anaerobic Capacity

Hermansen (60) showed that the magnitude of the O_2 repayment after exercise rises with increased work intensity and also depends on the duration of the work period. Repayments were observed to increase in magnitude with maximal performance in swims of 100, 200, and 400 meters. Maximal repayments were observed in events requiring from 1 to 3 min in time for their completion as the aerobic contribution to the total energy demand approaches 50%. As the duration of the maximal effort exceeds 1 to 3 min, aerobic metabolism contributes proportionately more energy (50 to 95%) to the performance and anaerobic mechanisms proportionately less (50 to 5%) (10).

There is considerable discrepancy in the literature regarding the magnitude of the maximal O_2 repayments (120,67,93,60,113), the reported values varying from 4 to 5 liters up to 20 to 22 liters of O_2. Numerous factors contribute to the difficulty of quantifying the O_2 repayment, such as (1) duration of measurement time, (2) determination of the metabolic baseline, (3) elevation of body temperature after work with its calorigenic effect, and (4) elevated O_2 demands of respiratory muscles and the heart (10,84,135,79). Hermansen (60) was able to show significant differences in O_2 repayment capacity among athletes (100 and 200 meter swimmers and 400 and 800 meter runners), trained individuals (physical education students) and untrained subjects. The athletes exhibited the highest anaerobic capacities and the untrained subjects the lowest.

Numerous studies (36,77,82,112) have shown that training may increase both the anaerobic and aerobic capacity simultaneously. Margaria *et al.* (93) estimated that the anaerobic capacity in liters may equal or slightly exceed the maximal O_2 consumption in liters per minute (MAP), which implies the existence of a direct, positive relationship between the two. While this is probably an acceptable generalization for the population at large, it must be recognized that training for specific power events, such as the 200 and 400 meter runs, and endurance events, such as the marathon, tends to obscure the relationship, as Volkov et al. (132) and Margaria et al. (91) have strikingly shown. Volkov et al. (132) showed a low, positive correlation between sprint performance and maximum aerobic power (MAP) and similar low correlations between distance performances and maximal anaerobic capacity. However, the sample studied consisted of sportsmen trained for diverse running and swimming events and constituted homogeneous groupings.

Margaria et al. (91) attempted to quantify the maximal rate of anaerobic energy release using a short burst of running activity, i.e., running up a staircase at maximal speed, with a time duration of approximately 5 sec. By determining the vertical component of the speed and assuming a mechanical efficiency of 0.25 the maximal rate of energy release was calculated. For 20–30 year olds a mean value of 50 kcal/kg/hr was observed. Wide individual variability was found, indicative of differences in training states. Costill et al. (35) applied a similar procedure in an assessment of anaerobic power of college football players.

III. Aerobic Power

Unlike the measurement of the anaerobic capacity, the quantitation of aerobic power in human performance is quite straightforward. By indirect calorimetry (109,54), the amount of O_2 transferred from the lung alveoli to the blood is measured. This is indicative of the rate of utilization of O_2 in oxidizing foodstuffs in the tissues. Since this utilization of O_2 increases proportionately with the intensity of work, man's MAP must be directly related to the capacity to do work (124). This certainly holds for work performances exceeding 2 to 3 min, where the aerobic contribution to the work energy exceeds 50% and approaches 100% of the total energy costs (10). Since most human effort in sport, occupation, and recreation involves an appreciable time commitment, minutes to hours, the MAP must play a role in regulating the intensity with which these efforts are pursued (98,24,10).

The practical significance of the assessment of MAP is identified by I. Åstrand (3) in its application to (1) occupational settings to determine man's adaptability to job demands, (2) the clinic, in the diagnosis of disease and evaluation of rehabilitative procedures, (3) sports and domestic work for evaluating preparedness, and (4) in physiological studies in assessing metabolic changes with age, nutrition, etc.

Physiologically, the MAP assessment is indicative of the functional

Francis J. Nagle

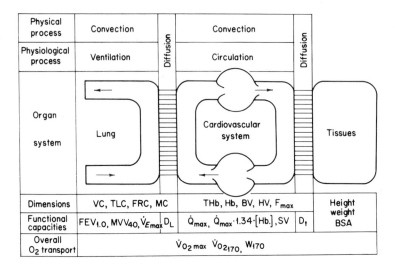

Fig. 2. Illustration of the O_2 transport system. VC = vital capacity, TLC = total lung capacity, FRC = functional residual capacity, MC = pulmonary midcapacity, THb = total hemoglobin, Hb = hemoglobin concentration, BV = blood volume, HV = heart volume, F_{max} = maximal heart rate, $FEV_{1.0}$ = forced expiratory volume in 1 sec, MVV = maximal ventilatory volume, estimated at 40 breaths/min, $\dot{V}_{E\,max}$ = minute ventilation during $\dot{V}_{O_2}$ determination, D_L = diffusing capacity of lungs, $\dot{Q}_{max}$ = maximal cardiac output, SV = stroke volume during $\dot{Q}_{max}$ determination, D_t = diffusing capacity of tissues, $\dot{V}_{O_2\,max}$ = maximal O_2 uptake, $\dot{V}_{O_2170}$ and W_{170} = O_2 uptake and rate of work at heart rate of 170. [From Holmgren (72).]

state of the respiratory, circulatory, and metabolic systems. This is comprehensively illustrated in Fig. 2, from Holmgren (72), where maximal oxygen uptake ($\dot{V}_{O_2\,max}$) is shown to depend on the convection functions of the pulmonary and cardiovascular systems and the diffusion functions of the lung to blood and the blood to active tissue. The greater the capacity of the dimensional and functional factors of these systems the higher the MAP. Considering only the cardiovascular system in O_2 transport, its contribution is strikingly summarized in the Fick equation where $\dot{V}_{O_2}$ = heart rate × stroke volume × arteriovenous O_2 difference (117).

A. CHARACTERISTICS OF THE O_2 RESPONSE CURVE

With the onset of work, the O_2 uptake response increases exponentially (67,124,58,28,41), with a half-time reaction of approximately 30 sec (111,28). At work loads requiring the maximal aerobic power, Robinson (111) found 90 to 98% of the required $\dot{V}_{O_2}$ was attained in the second minute of exercise. Åstrand and Saltin (11) confirmed Robinson's observations but indicated that at submaximal aerobic demands, steady state $\dot{V}_{O_2}$ values are not attained by the second minute of work. However,

Nagle et al. (101) found that over light to moderate work loads on the treadmill, bicycle, and a step device, steady state $\dot{V}_{O_2}$ values were attained by the second minute.

The kinetics of the O_2 response in work appear unrelated to the O_2 requirement since, regardless of work load, approximately 70% of the requirement is met in the first minute of work and 90 to 100% in the second minute (28). Such observations would appear consonant with the hypothesis that the lag in $\dot{V}_{O_2}$ at the onset of work depends on the development of a need for O_2 in active muscle and does not reflect on the adaptability of the cardiovascular system to transport O_2 (121,75,70).

B. MAXIMAL AEROBIC POWER VALUES

The highest values recorded for MAP have been measured on male cross-country skiers (mean: 82.0 ml/kg/min, $n = 5$) and middle- and long-distance runners (mean: 78.0 ml/kg/min, $n = 3$) (118). The highest value recorded on a male cross-country skier was 85.1 ml/kg/min. Female cross-country skiers averaged 61.8 ml/kg/min in aerobic power with the highest reported value 66.3 ml/kg/min. The same investigators (118) reported that a MAP value of 74.0 ml/kg/min had been observed for a Russian female cross-country skier. MAP values measured on various types of competitive sportsmen are reported by Åstrand and Rodahl (10).

Adult population norms for MAP based on observations of Scandinavian males and females (3) are shown in Table I. Balke and Ware (19), using heart rate and blood pressure as criteria for the attainment of MAP, made assessments on 523 healthy, male U. S. military and nonmilitary personnel between the ages of 19 and 66 years. A distribution of treadmill performances and MAP values expressed as multiples of the resting metabolic rate (assumed to be 3.5 ml/kg/min) is given in Fig. 3 (16). The mean maximal performance time was 15 min to a 15% treadmill grade. The standard deviation was 2.8 min. The required energy expenditure for this mean performance is ten times rest ($10 \times 3.5 = 35$ ml/kg/min), with a standard deviation of two times rest (MAP > 28.0 and <42.0 ml/kg/min). On the basis of these data, Balke and Ware (19) devised the performance ratings shown in Table II (16). Individuals exhibiting aerobic power of 12 times the rest level (MAP = 42.0 ml/kg/min) are fully one standard deviation above the mean for normal individuals and this is cited by Balke (16) as a desirable goal for normal, male adults in aerobic power training.

C. EFFECTS OF AGE AND TRAINING ON MAXIMAL AEROBIC POWER

Before puberty there is no significant difference in MAP, expressed in liters per minute, between boys and girls (4,139). However, for adult

Francis J. Nagle

TABLE I
EVALUATION OF THE AEROBIC WORK CAPACITY IN THE VARIOUS AGE
GROUPS FOR FEMALES AND MALES[a,b]

| Age group (years) | Aerobic work capacity, $\dot{V}_{O_2}$ (liters/min and ml/kg/min) | | | | | |
	Low	Fair	Average	Good	High	n
Females						
20–29	≦1.69	1.70–1.99	2.00–2.49	2.50–2.79	2.80≧	8
	≦28	29–34	35–43	44–48	49≧	
30–39	≦1.59	1.60–1.89	1.90–2.39	2.40–2.69	2.70≧	12
	≦27	28–33	34–41	42–47	48≧	
40–49	≦1.49	1.50–1.79	1.80–2.29	2.30–2.59	2.60≧	8
	≦25	26–31	32–40	41–45	46≧	
50–65	≦1.29	1.30–1.59	1.60–2.09	2.10–2.39	2.40≧	16
	≦21	22–28	29–36	37–41	42≧	
Males						
20–29	≦2.79	2.80–3.09	3.10–3.69	3.70–3.99	4.00≧	4
	≦38	39–43	44–51	52–56	57≧	
30–39	≦2.49	2.50–2.79	2.80–3.39	3.40–3.69	3.70≧	13
	≦34	35–39	40–47	48–51	52≧	
40–49	≦2.19	2.20–2.49	2.50–3.09	3.10–3.39	3.40≧	9
	≦30	31–35	36–43	44–47	48≧	
50–59	≦1.89	1.90–2.19	2.20–2.79	2.80–3.09	3.10≧	66
	≦25	26–31	32–39	40–43	44≧	
60–69	≦1.59	1.60–1.89	1.90–2.49	2.50–2.79	2.80≧	8
	≦21	22–26	27–35	36–39	40≧	

[a] Adapted from Åstrand (*3*).
[b] The aerobic work capacity, $\dot{V}_{O_2}$ ml/kg, was calculated with a "normal" body weight chosen as 58 and 72 kg for females and males, respectively. These figures for weight were taken from W. S. Spector, ed. ("Handbook of Biological Data," p. 180, Saunders, Philadelphia, Pennsylvania, 1956), and represent the averages for a white woman and man between 25 and 35 years of age.

women the MAP in liters per minute is only 70 to 75% that of men (*5*). This difference is reduced if corrections are made for body weight or fat free weight (*5*). In both sexes there is a peak in MAP (liters per minute) at 18 to 20 years (*4,96a*). Drinkwater and Horvath (*44*) found that MAP (liters per minute) increased with age for girls between 12 and 18 years. However, when MAP was expressed in milliliters per kilogram of body weight a trend towards reversing the relationship between age and MAP was found.

With increasing age over the adult years, there is a gradual decline in MAP (*111,8,1,69*). At 65 years the MAP is about 70% that of the 25-year-old individual (*4*). Aging is also marked by a greater variability

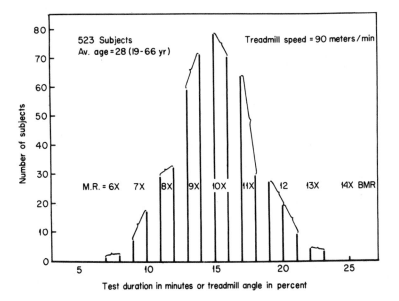

Fig. 3. Distribution of the work capacity of 523 male individuals determined by the Work Capacity Test as time (or percent angle) until a pulse of "180" is reached. The metabolic requirements of the maximum loads are indicated as approximate multiples of the rest metabolic rate (MR). [From Balke (*16*).]

TABLE II

EVALUATION OF PHYSICAL PERFORMANCE CAPACITY BY THE WORK CAPACITY
TEST, RELATING THE CRITICAL TEST TIME (OR PERCENT OF GRADE),
THE METABOLIC COSTS, AND THE EMPIRICAL RATING (BASED
ON PERFORMANCES OF 523 HEALTHY MALES)[a]

Minute or per-cent angle	O₂ intake at "180" (ml/kg/min)	Metabolic requirements in multiples of BMR	Performance rating
−8	−25	−6×	pathologic
9–10	25–28	7×	very poor
11–12	28–31	8×	poor
13–14	31–35	9×	fair
15–16	35–38	10×	average
17–18	38–42	11×	good
19–21	42–47	12×	very good
22–23	47–52	13–14×	superior
24+	52+	14×+	excellent

[a] From Balke (*16*).

in MAP due to body weight changes and to differences in training states (*1*).

Studies have shown that training increases MAP from 7 to 33% depending on the frequency, period, and intensity of training as well as the initial training state (*112,82,130,46,119*). Saltin *et al.* (*119*) showed that 20 days of bed rest decreased MAP by 31%, a trend that was dramatically reversed by subsequent training. However, Klissouras (*81*) has suggested that the human capacity for increasing MAP is quite limited, since he accounted for 93.4% of the interindividual variability in MAP as due to differences in genetic characteristics.

D. Factors Influencing the Measurement of Maximal Aerobic Power

The magnitude of the measured MAP is influenced by such factors as the muscle mass involved, body position, body weight, and rhythms of movement (*27,12,63,76*). Åstrand and Saltin (*12*) demonstrated that supine cycling resulted in MAP values 15% lower than those attained in cycling while sitting. MAP measured in cycling with the arms reached only 66 to 70% of levels attained in leg cycling (*12,128*). The same investigators reported that combined work with the arms and legs resulted in MAP levels no higher than those attained with the legs alone. It would appear that the ceiling for $\dot{V}_{O_2}$ is independent of the mass of muscle employed in the exercise as soon as it exceeds a certain amount (*12*).

Correlations of MAP with body weight, fat free weight, and active tissue yielded values of 0.63, 0.85, and 0.91, respectively (*27*). The same investigators reported that the ideal reference for MAP for an assessment of cardiovascular fitness might well be the muscle mass involved. Consideration of the MAP as a test of physical performance, on the other hand, is better related to the unit of weight, since the ratio $\dot{V}_{O_2}/kg$ of body weight provides a measure of the immediately available oxidative energy which can be supplied to move a kilogram of body weight from one point to another. Changes in body weight and fat free weight have been shown to markedly affect MAP (*127,134*).

E. The Work Form and the Measurement of Maximal Aerobic Power

Conventional procedures for imposing an exercise or work stress in a laboratory setting include the use of a treadmill, bicycle ergometer, and some form of stepping device. The aerobic responses to gradually increased work loads on the three instruments are illustrated in Fig. 4. It will be observed that the $\dot{V}_{O_2}$ responses increase in an approximately

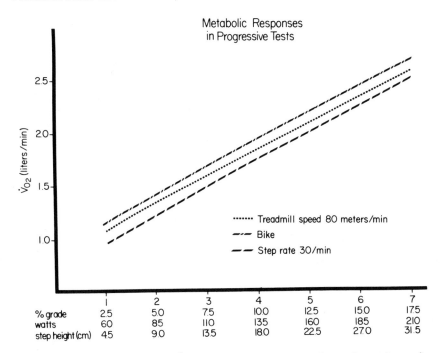

Fig. 4. Aerobic requirements ($\dot{V}_{O_2}$) for walking, cycling, and stepping at increasing work loads. [From Nagle *et al.* (*101*).]

direct proportion to the increased loads. When the speed in walking on a treadmill is changed (Fig. 5), the $\dot{V}_{O_2}$ response is curvilinear (*92,107,22*). On the other hand, the $\dot{V}_{O_2}$ response to running at increasing speed, bicycle loading, and stepping rate and height follows a straight line (*10,92, 90,102*). The curvilinearity of the $\dot{V}_{O_2}$ response to walking at increasing speeds is minimized by the narrow range of speeds normally used in exercise testing (2–3.8 mph) and rectilinearity of the response within this range may be assumed without appreciable error. Assuming the rectilinearity of the V_{O_2} response to increasing work, various equations have been formulated for predicting walking, running, cycling, and stepping energy requirements (*15,17,92,90,59,107,22,140,5,102,76*).

Rowell (*115*) has pointed out that MAP expresses the functional capacities of physiological systems to transport O_2 so the measurement must be independent of the nature of the test and the subject's skill in performing it. The three work forms, cycling, walking, and stepping, are familiar tasks to most people. Walking and stepping are distinguished from cycling in that the former two work forms are weight-bearing and the latter one non-weight-bearing. The advantages of the use of one or another of these instruments is discussed by numerous investigators (*10,*

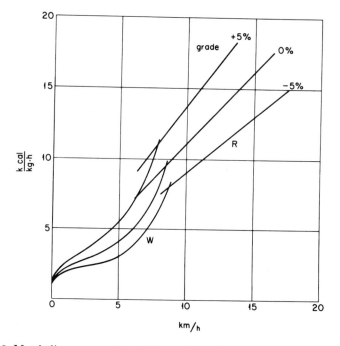

Fig. 5. Metabolic responses to walking and running on a treadmill at increasing speeds and grades. [From Margaria *et al.* (*92*).]

122,20,133,142,42). Åstrand and Rodahl (*10*) state that differences in efficiency among individuals in cycling may amount to 6%. Other studies have shown that cycling efficiency does not change over a range of work loads, while that for step and treadmill work does, mechanical efficiency being lower at light and heavy loads (*122*). It has been observed that differences in efficiency in walking are negligible (*92,107*), while those for running may amount to 6 to 8% (*92,5*).

Roberts and Alspaugh (*110*) recently reported that subjects who trained on a bicycle improved their PWC_{150}, whereas no improvement was observed in PWC_{150} for the same subjects tested on a treadmill. Subjects trained on a treadmill, on the other hand, improved their PWC_{150} on both treadmill and bicycle tests. The investigators concluded that bicycle training is more specific in its effects than treadmill training and that this fact has implications for maximal performance testing.

In assessing MAP, Kasch *et al.* (*78*) have shown that a comparison of step and treadmill procedures yielded an $r = 0.95$. The work was done with a step of constant height (30.4 cm), as the step rate was adjusted upward. They reported MAP values as high as 58 ml/kg/min, necessitating step rates of 60 per minute. Obviously, a step rate of one per second on a 30.4 cm bench would offer some difficulty in manipulation. The step procedure, then, appears to have mechanical limitations in testing individuals with very high aerobic power whether the step height, step rate, or both, are altered (102). For submaximal work, where use is made of prediction formulas for assessments of MAP, a step procedure may well be the method of choice for reasons of economy, space, maintenance, and simplicity (122).

Åstrand and Saltin (12) found that MAP was not significantly greater when measured running uphill on a treadmill than when cycling, the difference being 5% greater in uphill running. Hermansen and Saltin (63) reported that MAP in running uphill (3 deg treadmill slope) exceeded that in cycling by 8%. This agreed with observations of Glassford (56), Chase et al. (29), Hermansen et al. (61), Wyndham et al. (142), and Miyamura and Honda (100). Chase et al. (29) indicated that cycling work underestimated MAP measured on a treadmill by 4 to 23%. Åstrand (4) and Hermansen and Saltin (63) suggested that such differences are due to testing techniques and procedures, and explained that the work position on the cycle, pedal frequency, motivation, and stimulation of subjects are critical. The importance of a cycle pedal frequency greater than 60 rpm and a treadmill incline greater than 1% in assessing MAP have also been cited (63). In measuring MAP, at least with preadolescents, if not adolescents and some adults, the treadmill is the method of choice (10). This is apparently based on muscle power limitations of small individuals in adapting to bicycle ergometer loads. It has been reported that in cycling, the contraction portion of the contraction–relaxation cycle is prolonged and that the peak loads are approximately twice the load settings (68). Such a factor would contribute to a mechanical impairment of muscle blood flow (63,61,48) to an already limited muscle mass. Given such conditions, the tension demands per unit of muscle are extreme and motivation becomes an increasingly important factor in the MAP assessment (63,61,10). This consideration may also partially explain the underestimates of MAP reported by Chase et al. (29) in comparing cycling and treadmill work. In longitudinal studies where weight loss may be a factor, preference may be given to a bicycle test in measuring MAP since the activity is non-weight-bearing, a factor that facilitates data comparisons (10).

F. Methods of Measuring Maximal Aerobic Power

Any test of MAP should meet the following requirements: (1) the work must involve large muscle groups, (2) the work must be measurable and reproducible, (3) test conditions should be such that the results are comparable and repeatable, (4) the test must be well tolerated by healthy individuals, and (5) the mechanical efficiency required should be as uniform as possible in the population tested (*10*).

Widespread use has been made of a short treadmill run test at a speed of 7 mph for a 3 min duration (*130,129,99,29*). Initially the grade is set at zero and increments of 2½% are used for subsequent 3 min bouts of work until MAP is observed. If, in consecutive 3 min bouts, with 10 min rest periods intervening, the O_2 uptake does not increase by more than 150 ml/min, the measurement is accepted as maximum. In establishing this discontinuous test procedure, only 7 of 115 subjects failed to reach MAP by this method (*129*). Expired air collections for measurement of CO_2 and O_2 are made from 1.75 to 2.75 min into the work bouts. Repeated trials with this test ($n = 15$), using a slightly modified criterion for the attainment of MAP, revealed means of 3.06 ± 0.046 and 3.07 ± 0.44 liters O_2/min (*99*). Other investigators have found that repeated determinations of MAP on the same subject reveal a standard deviation of 3% (*6,129*).

Costill and Fox (*34*) and Costill (*33*) used a continuous running test with trained runners to assess MAP. A constant speed of 240 meters/min (8.9 mph) was used and the grade was increased from zero in increments of 2% every 2 min. This test was continued until the runner indicated he could not continue. Minute-by-minute gas collections were begun when the heart rate measured from the ECG tracing attained 155 beats/min. In the final 3 min of the runs, a leveling of the O_2 uptake occurred and the highest of these values was taken as the maximum. In measuring MAP by both procedures described above (*129,34*), the test was preceded by 10 min of warming up by means of walking or running on a treadmill.

Rather than doing serial measurements at increasing loads in assessing MAP, which may be very time consuming, a procedure has been adopted whereby MAP is first estimated from submaximal exercise heart rates (*3*). Besides the benefit of warm-up from such submaximal exercise, an estimate of MAP is derived so that treadmill or bicycle loads may be set that will directly elicit the estimated maximal $\dot{V}_{O_2}$ response (*118,63*). Table III shows the initial treadmill work loadings for subjects varying in MAP (*63*).

The work loads for treadmill running and for cycling may be set from running and cycling $\dot{V}_{O_2}$ prediction equations (*92,17,59,6*). If the subsequently measured values for $\dot{V}_{O_2}$ at the selected loads are less than the predicted requirements, one may be assured that MAP was attained, assuming the duration of the effort was sufficient at the load predicted to elicit MAP (*63,101*). It should be borne in mind that MAP can be assessed with an effort of less than maximum intensity, defined by Karls-

TABLE III
Treadmill Speed and Grade Settings for Subjects Differing in Predicted MAP[a]

$\dot{V}_{O_2 max}$ predicted from submax HR (ml/kg/min)	km/hr	miles/hr	Percent grade
<40	10	6.2	5.25
40–50	12.5	7.8	5.25
55–75	15	9.3	5.25
>75			
Skiers	15	9.3	7.00
Cross-country runners	17.5	10.2	5.25
Track runners	20	12.5	2.67

[a] Adapted from Hermansen and Saltin (63).

son et al. (77) as a running effort inducing exhaustion in 4 min. Using this criterion for maximal effort in treadmill running, the investigators found that the treadmill speed could be reduced by 3 km/hr and the work time extended well beyond 4 min before a reduction in $\dot{V}_{O_2}$ was observed. This factor could also account for MAP differences in treadmill and cycle work cited above, for the bicycle work MAP determination probably necessitates an effort more closely approaching maximum intensity.

Running tests for assessment of MAP have limitations. One is that the procedures are not conducive to extensive physiological monitoring, such as auscultatory blood pressure monitoring and blood sampling for metabolites. A second disadvantage resides with the limited population capable of adapting to a stress of this nature. For such reasons a continuous or discontinuous bicycle ergometer or treadmill walking test has had popular use (97,3,139,26,1,65,83,74,20,101,136,143,25,87). The criterion used for the attainment of maximal performance is MAP (with a leveling of $\dot{V}_{O_2}$ in the terminal minutes of work) or the workload attained at exhaustion. Because of motivational considerations in maximal effort, additional factors have been monitored to confirm the attainment of MAP. These have included blood lactate concentrations of 90 to 100 mg % as a criterion of maximal effort (3), and the blood pressure–heart rate relationship as a criterion of cardiovascular decompensation in maximal effort (13,19). Such criteria for confirming the attainment of MAP have been questioned by Rowell (115) and Wyndham (141). Both investigators question the value of a "MAP indicator" such as blood lactate or heart rate level, since interindividual differences for both of these factors in work are very large, due to age, sex, state of training, and the nature of the work form (10,62,115).

Discontinuous treadmill walking and cycling tests are usually performed for 2 to 6 min, with a rest interval intervening. For bicycle tests, a pedal frequency of 50–60 rpm is used, although the need for a 60 rpm frequency for measuring MAP has been emphasized (*63*). Increments of work loads of 150 to 300 kilopond meters per minute with each bout of work are usually applied. Typical of a discontinuous test is the Bruce Multistage Test (*25*). In this test the treadmill speeds and grades are increased in four stages. Work bouts at O_2 requirements of 1.1, 2.2, 3.0, and 3.5 liters/min are continued for 3 min except for the last bout which is continued to exhaustion. As previously indicated, a 5 min duration of effort has been recommended for $\dot{V}_{O_2}$ steady state determinations in submaximal work (*10*). It has been well documented, however, that in maximal work 3 to 4 min of effort is sufficient for assessment of MAP (*111,130,129*).

In continuous treadmill walk and cycle tests, work increments are applied every 1 to 2 min (*26,139,101,136*) until performance limitations and/or MAP is attained. Normally treadmill speed and cycling pedal frequency are maintained constant, while the treadmill grade (1 to 2½% increments) and cycle work load (150 to 300 kilopond meters per minute increment) are increased. Maksud and Coutts (*88*) showed no differences in MAP determinations between continuous and discontinuous test applications.

Wahlund (*133*) stated that working capacity, for practical use, should be defined as the maximum work intensity consistent with steady state. It is in terms of this concept of a *functional* maximal work capacity that the test of Physical Work Capacity (PWC) to a heart rate of 170 beats/min (PWC$_{170}$) was designed (*125,133*). It is implied then that the attainment of a heart rate of 170 beats/min marks a physiological state that can be endured for an extended period of time. The measured $\dot{V}_{O_2}$ attendant to this state would represent a functional peak $\dot{V}_{O_2}$ and not absolute MAP. The PWC$_{170}$ test has been found to correlate well with MAP $r = 0.88$ (*40*).

It was from a similar base that the Balke Progressive Treadmill Test was designed (*13,14,19*). The nature of the test permits measurement of cardiopulmonary function over a wide range of performances from minimal muscular activity up to critical work loads within a period of time which is adequate for physiological adaptation (*13*). Here the criterion for maximal aerobic effort is the attainment of a heart rate near 180 beats/min with a simultaneous decrease in pulse pressure, signaling imminent cardiovascular decompensation. This would not necessarily occur simultaneously with the attainment of MAP, as the investigators clearly state (*19*). Obviously, age and sex variability in maximal heart rates presents some limitations to the application of this procedure.

Balke (17) reported that given adequate motivation and some sense of pace in running, an individual would run at a pace at which he would attain and maintain a heart rate of 180 beats/min over the duration of a 15 min run. This run pace would also induce the attainment of the functional maximal aerobic power. Such is the rationale behind Balke's (17) field test of maximal aerobic performance (functional maximum) of 15 min duration and Cooper's (32) 12 min duration test. These will be discussed in more detail below. The point to be made here is that it is highly unlikely that an absolute maximum O_2 uptake level could be maintained over a 12- or 15-min, best-effort run, as it has been shown that 3000 and 5000 meter runners performing well within a 15 min interval do so at something less than 100% of MAP (approximately 90 to 95% MAP) (38,34,33). Applying the criteria of the Balke Treadmill Test (13,19) to young male adults with maximal heart rates of 190 to 195 beats/min, the functional MAP assessment should then be 5 to 10% less than that measured by the procedures of Taylor et al. (130) or Costill and Fox (34).

Laboratory performance tests utilizing the element of progressive loading are widely used in evaluating patient populations (104,103,105,25,106, 146,57,30,52). Such procedures are not only amenable to measurement of MAP, but monitoring of the ECG, blood pressure, and other physiological factors. Such monitoring is essential in evaluating patients "at risk" to disease states and invaluable for clinical diagnosis and evaluation of training procedures used in rehabilitation programs. A refinement of progressive test procedures has established work increments for cycling, walking, and stepping that approximate metabolic stresses in single increments of the resting metabolic rate, assumed to be 3.5 ml O_2/kg/min (101). This allows for an interchange of work stress instruments and observations of the ECG and other physiological parameters at known, small increments in metabolic demands up to maximal levels. Such a refinement in test procedures facilitates data interpretation and data comparisons and reflects a sound, cautious approach to evaluative exercise testing, an essential in dealing with "high risk" populations.

G. PREDICTIONS OF MAXIMAL AEROBIC POWER FROM SUBMAXIMAL WORK TESTS

Measurement of MAP requires laboratory facilities and sophisticated equipment. In addition, judgments must be made about subjecting older, debilitated, or ill individuals to severe exercise stresses. To circumvent such problems, attempts have been made to predict MAP from heart rate (HR) determinations made during submaximal exercise (9,146,90,

2,65,142,144). I. Åstrand (*3*) identified the specific criteria that must be met when using the Åstrand Rhyming nomogram for MAP prediction, which would hold for similar procedures. These criteria are: (1) that the heart rate during submaximal work increases rectilinearly with O_2 uptake, (2) that a submaximal HR not lower than 125 beats/min be used for prediction, (3) that the maximal heart rate is 195 beats/min, (4) that the mechanical efficiency is 23%. Since the maximal HR decreases with age (*111*), a correction factor must be applied (*3*). When this is done the standard error of the method is about 10% for well-trained and 15% for less well-trained individuals. This method has been reported to over- and underestimate measured MAP values (*116,29*). It has also been pointed out by Taylor *et al.* (*131*) that the pulse rate–work rate curve is displaced to the left by such factors as temperature, meals, time of day, and fatigue which would cause an underestimation of MAP. Other observations have shown that the HR–$\dot{V}_{O_2}$ curve is not strictly linear (*143*), so extrapolation to a maximal HR from a submaximal HR would not be appropriate. Wyndham *et al.* (*144*) calculate the MAP from three submaximal $\dot{V}_{O_2}$ and HR values, fitting straight lines by a least squares technique.

Other HR extrapolation procedures have been proposed by Asmussen and Hemmingsen (*2*) and Margaria *et al.* (*90*) in which two heart rate determinations at rest and during submaximal exercise are used to establish the slope of the HR–$\dot{V}_{O_2}$ line. In both procedures adjustments are made for the maximal heart rate based on age differences.

Use has been made of the Åstrand Rhyming nomogram (*9*), whereby heart rates at two submaximal stepping loads were used to predict MAP. Discrepancies between measured and predicted values amounted to 8 to 9% (*114*). A detailed analysis and discussion of HR prediction procedures is given by Davies (*39*).

Issekutz and Rodahl (*74*) and Issekutz *et al.* (*73*) have proposed the use of submaximal observations of the respiratory quotient (RQ) in predicting MAP. They observed that the maximal O_2 uptake occurred when the RQ increased to 1.15 from an assumed metabolic RQ of 0.75, a change of 0.40 units. MAP is then predicted from the equation

$$\dot{V}_{O_2\,max} = 2 \frac{\log 0.4 - \log 0.08}{\log RQ - \log 0.08} \times \text{work load} \times \frac{1}{1000} + 0.320,$$

where log 0.08 represents the unit change in RQ from rest (0.83) to work (0.75) and RQ represents the RQ observed in submaximal work; 0.320 is taken as the rest metabolic rate in liters per minute. However, it has been observed that RQ in maximal work may vary greatly and cannot be assumed to be 1.15 (*116,23*).

Attempts have also been made to use the ventilation response in submaximal exercise to predict energy expenditure, but not necessarily MAP (89,50). Girandola et al. (55) found high correlations between $\dot{V}_{O_2}$ and minute ventilation in heavy bicycle exercise.

Mastropaolo (96) found that multiple regression analysis, in which such factors as submaximal exercise blood pressure, respiratory exchange ratio (RER), heart rate, and ventilation were considered, was a better predictor of MAP than any single factor such as heart rate or RER. Recently, Hermiston and Faulkner (64) used a stepwise regression to calculate MAP from data secured during submaximal walking on a treadmill. Most accurate predictions from physically active men were derived from an equation that included the subject's age, fat free weight, heart rate, fraction of expired CO_2, and tidal volume at submaximal work, in addition to the change in RER.

Falls et al. (47) and Drake et al. (43) have attempted to predict MAP from items of the AAHPER fitness test battery. The former group found a multiple correlation of 0.76 between MAP expressed per kilogram of body weight and AAHPER test scores. Drake et al. (43) concluded that the fitness test battery was not a good predictor of MAP.

H. Predictions of Maximal Aerobic Power from Running Tests

Balke (17) measured the functional MAP of eight trained male adults. Subsequently, each subject ran for a duration of 1, 5, 12, 20, and 30 min on different days, attempting to cover the greatest possible distance on each run. For each of the runs, the average velocity was calculated and, in turn, expressed in terms of the O_2 requirement. Henry (59), Margaria et al. (92), Åstrand (6), and Balke (17) have shown the relationship of speed in running to O_2 requirement to be rectilinear, at least between speeds of 130 and 290 meters/min.

It was observed that the calculated estimates of O_2 requirements for running 12 min slightly exceeded the treadmill-measured, functional MAP values, while the estimates of the O_2 requirements for running 20 min fell below the measured MAP values. This indicated that only in runs of a duration between 12 and 20 min did individuals settle down to a run pace which reflected their aerobic work capacity.

Cooper (32) measured MAP with the procedure of Taylor et al. (129) on 115 Air Force officers. The same subjects performed a 12 min run covering as great a distance as possible. A correlation of 0.897 was observed between performance and MAP, which was highly significant. Balke (17) and Ribisl and Kachadorian (108) found that MAP was highly related to performance time on a 2 mile run. The latter investigators calculated an $r = 0.85$ and $r = 0.86$ for young and middle-aged

males, respectively. Recently, Wiley and Shaver (*137*) measured the
MAP and 2 mile run time in untrained adults (18–25 years). They reported a significant correlation between MAP and 2 mile run time ($r =$
0.47), which is much lower than that reported by Cooper (*32*) and Ribisl
and Kachadorian (*108*). Since the experimental group was classified as
"untrained," the subjects of Wiley and Shaver constituted a homogeneous
group and this factor undoubtedly contributed to the lower correlation
observed between MAP and 2 mile run performances.

I. Equipment, Supplies, and Techniques in Maximal Performance Assessments

1. Gas Exchange

Direct measurement of MAP necessitates the use of gas exchange
equipment including mouthpiece, breathing valve, tubing, collection bags,
and gas meters, or spirometers. It is most important that the total dead
space of the collection system components be minimal. To minimize
resistance to breathing at very high work loads it is suggested that the
mouthpiece inner area be at least 400 mm², the inner diameter of tubes,
valves, and stopcocks be at least 28 mm and the inner diameter of the
tubing be 33 mm and kept as short as possible (*7*).

Arrangements of equipment for gas collections may take many forms,
depending on the experimental protocol. A recently designed gas collecting system is described in a report by Daniels (*37*). Measurement of
gas exchange during actual running performance is made possible with
this system.

Standard equipment for O_2 and CO_2 gas analysis must include a volumetric analyzer of the Haldane, Scholander, or Lloyd–Gallenkamp type.
The volumetric analysis is essential for O_2 and CO_2 measurements of
gases used for calibrating electronic analyzers if the volumetric analyzer
is not used to measure unknown gas samples directly. Various types of
electronic hardware for gas analyses are available commercially. For
guidance on such equipment, the essential supplies, techniques, and calculations used, the reader is referred to Consolazio *et al.* (*31*) and Shephard (*123*).

2. Blood Pressure

Monitoring of blood pressure by auscultation can be readily accomplished in cycling, walking, and stepping tests. This is especially
expedient in dealing with a patient population and important to the
assessment of cardiac function (*126,71*). A bracelet-type microphone
(Becton-Dickinson) is applied over the brachial artery and attached to

a stethoscope. The cuff and manometer are standard equipment (Baumanometer). When care is taken to avoid extraneous noises from the tapping of adjacent tubes and from microphone and cuff contact, clear (Korotkov) sounds may be detected (18). Cardiac frequency may also be counted by the sounds if ECG monitoring is not available.

3. Electrocardiogram

Numerous procedures for monitoring the ECG during exercise have been described in the literature (85,53,3,21). Aside from the use of the stress ECG in the diagnosis of heart disease and evaluating cardiac function, it is effectively used for monitoring the heart rate during exercise tests.

4. Blood Sampling

The procedure used depends, of course, on the protocol pursued. For brief exercise tests, simple venipuncture may be the method of choice. Where serial sampling is necessary some type of indwelling catheter or needle is the preferred procedure. Forster et al. (51) described a procedure in which a 21-gauge, thin-wall vein needle (Travenol Laboratories, Morton Grove, Illinois) was inserted and maintained in a superficial, dorsal hand vein. Simultaneous sampling from this site and from arterial blood showed slight, but constant and consistent differences in P_{O_2}, P_{CO_2}, pH, and lactate in blood taken from the two sites. This allows for accurate correction of venous to arterial acid–base values. It was necessary to heat the hand on which vein sampling was done, but the technique is amenable to the most difficult exercise conditions.

IV. Summary

Maximal performance is dependent on energy stores and rapid resynthesis of these stores through aerobic and anaerobic processes. Maximal human power is shown to decrease exponentially with time with progressively greater dependency on aerobic energy mechanisms and less on anaerobic mechanisms for the sustenance of effort. The practical significance of the maximal aerobic power assessment is cited, first as a measure of respiratory, circulatory, and muscle tissue function, secondly as a measure of preparedness for sport and occupation, and thirdly as a diagnostic tool in disease and an evaluative tool in rehabilitation medicine.

Maximal aerobic power is affected by age, training, sex, and genetic endowment and its measurement influenced by the work form used.

Methods were discussed for measuring peak maximal aerobic power and functional maximal power, a distinction made by Wahlund (*133*) and Balke and Ware (*19*). Procedures for indirect measurement of MAP were also elucidated along with details on gas exchange measurement equipment and procedures for ECG, blood pressure, and blood assessments.

References

1. Andersen, K. L., and Hermansen, L. (1965). *J. Appl. Physiol.* **20**, 432–436.
2. Asmussen, E., and Hemmingsen, L. (1958). *Scand. J. Clin. Lab. Invest.* **10**, 67–71.
3. Åstrand, I. (1960). *Acta Physiol. Scand.* **49**, Suppl. 169.
4. Åstrand, I. (1967). *In* "Physiology of Muscular Exercise" (C. Chapman, ed.), Monograph No. 15, pp. 202–210. Amer. Heart Ass., New York.
5. Åstrand, P.-O. (1956). *Physiol. Rev.* **36**, 307–335.
6. Åstrand, P.-O. (1952). "Experimental Studies of Physical Working Capacity in Relation to Sex and Age." Munksgaard, Copenhagen.
7. Åstrand, P.-O. (1967). *Can. Med. Ass. J.* **96**, 732–734.
8. Åstrand, P.-O., and Christensen, E. H. (1964). *In* "Oxygen in the Animal Organism" (F. Dickens and E. Neil, eds.), p. 295. Pergamon, New York.
9. Åstrand, P.-O., and Rhyming, I. (1954). *J. Appl. Physiol.* **7**, 218–221.
10. Åstrand, P.-O., and Rodahl, K. (1970). "Textbook of Work Physiology." McGraw-Hill, New York.
11. Åstrand, P.-O., and Saltin, B. (1961). *J. Appl. Physiol.* **16**, 971–976.
12. Åstrand, P.-O., and Saltin, B. (1961). *J. Appl. Physiol.* **16**, 977–981.
13. Balke, B. (1952). Report No. 1, School of Aviation Medicine, Randolph Field, Texas.
14. Balke, B. (1954). *Arbeitsphysiologie* **15**, 311–323.
15. Balke, B. (1960). *In* "Medical Physics" (O. Glasser, ed.), pp. 50–52. Yearbook, Chicago, Illinois.
16. Balke, B. (1961). *In* "Performance Capacity" (H. Spector, J. Brozek, and M. Peterson, eds.), pp. 13–19. Nat. Res. Council, Washington, D. C.
17. Balke, B. (1963). CARI Bull. 63–6, Federal Aviation Agency, Oklahoma City, Oklahoma.
18. Balke, B. (1970). "Advanced Exercise Procedures for Evaluation of the Cardiovascular System." Burdick Corp., Milton, Wisconsin.
19. Balke, B., and Ware, R. W. (1959). *Armed Forces Med. J.* **10**, 657–688.
20. Binkhorst, R. A., and Van Leuwen, P. (1963). *Int. Z. Angew. Physiol.* **19**, 459–467.
21. Blomqvist, G. (1965). *Acta Med. Scand.* **178**, Suppl. 440.
22. Bobbert, A. C. (1960). *J. Appl. Physiol.* **15**, 1015–1021.
23. Bouhuys, A., Pool, J., Binkhorst, R. A., and Van Leuwen, P. (1966). *J. Appl. Physiol.* **21**, 1040–1046.
24. Brouha, L. (1960). "Physiology in Industry." Pergamon, London.
25. Bruce, R. A., Blackmon, J. R., Jones, J. W., and Straight, G. (1963). *Pediatrics* **32**, Suppl., pp. 742–756.

26. Buskirk, E., Kollias, R. J., Akers, F. R., Prokop, E. J., and Reategui, E. P. (1967). *J. Appl. Physiol.* **23**, 259–266.
27. Buskirk, E., and Taylor, H. L. (1957). *J. Appl. Physiol.* **11**, 72–78.
28. Cerretelli, P., Sikand, R., and Fahri, C. E. (1966). *J. Appl. Physiol.* **21**, 1345–1350.
29. Chase, G. A., Grove, C., and Rowell, L. B. (1966). *Aerospace Med.* **37**, 1232–1238.
30. Clausen, J. P., Larsen, O. A., and Trap-Jensen, J. (1969). *Circulation* **40**, 143–154.
31. Consolazio, C. F., Johnson, R. E., and Pecora, C. J. (1963). "Physiological Measurements of Metabolic Functions in Man." McGraw-Hill, New York.
32. Cooper, K. (1968). *J. Amer. Med. Ass.* **203**, 135–138.
33. Costill, D. L. (1970). *J. Appl. Physiol.* **28**, 251–255.
34. Costill, D. L., and Fox, E. L. (1969). *Med. Sci. Sports* **1**, 81–86.
35. Costill, D. L., Hoffman, W. M., Kehoe, F., Miller, S. J., and Myers, W. C. (1968). *J. Sports Med. Phys. Fitness* **8**, 103–106.
36. Cunningham, D. A., and Faulkner, J. A. (1969). *Med. Sci. Sports* **1**, 65–69.
37. Daniels, J. (1971). *J. Appl. Physiol.* **31**, 164–167.
38. Daniels, J., and Oldridge, N. (1970). *Med. Sci. Sports* **2**, 107–112.
39. Davies, C. T. M. (1968). *J. Appl. Physiol.* **24**, 700–706.
40. deVries, H. A., and Klafs, C. E. (1965). *J. Sports Med. Phys. Fitness* **5**, 207–214.
41. di Prampero, P. E., Davies, C. T. M., Cerretelli, P., and Margaria, R. (1970). *J. Appl. Physiol.* **29**, 547–551.
42. Doroschuk, E. V. (1969). *In* "Exercise and Fitness 1969" (B. Don Franks, ed.), pp. 243–254. Athletic Inst., Chicago, Illinois.
43. Drake, V., Jones, G., Brown, J. R., and Shephard, R. J. (1968). *Can. Med. Ass. J.* **99**, 844–848.
44. Drinkwater, B. L., and Horvath, S. M. (1971). *Med. Sci. Sports* **3**, 56–62.
45. Ekblom, B. (1970). *Acta Physiol. Scand.* **78**, 145–158.
46. Ekblom, B., Åstrand, P.-O., Saltin, B., Stenberg, J., and Wallström, B. (1968). *J. Appl. Physiol.* **24**, 518–528.
47. Falls, H. B., Ismail, A. H., and MacLeod, D. F. (1966). *Res. Quart.* **37**, 192–201.
48. Faulkner, J. A., Roberts, D. E., Elk, R. L., and Conway, J. (1971). *J. Appl. Physiol.* **30**, 457–461.
49. Fletcher, J. B. (1964). *In* "Bioastronautics Data Book," NASA-SP-3006 (P. Webb, ed.), pp. 167–190. Webb Associates, Yellow Springs, Ohio.
50. Ford, A. B., and Hellerstein, H. K. (1959). *J. Appl. Physiol.* **14**, 891–893.
51. Forster, H. V., Dempsey, J. A., Thomson, J., Vidruk, E., and Do Pico, G. A. (1972). *J. Appl. Physiol.* **32**, 134–137.
52. Frick, M. H., and Katila, M. (1968). *Circulation* **37**, 192–202.
53. Friedman, A. H., Abarquez, R. F., Reicel, F., Datta, A., and LaDue, J. S. (1961). *J. Amer. Geriat. Soc.* **9**, 477–490.
54. Gemmill, C. L., and Brobeck, J. R. (1968). *In* "Medical Physiology" (V. B. Mountcastle, ed.), pp. 473–497. Mosby, St. Louis, Missouri.
55. Girandola, R. N., Katch, F. I., and Henry, F. M. (1971). *Res. Quart.* **42**, 362–373.
56. Glassford, R. G. (1965). *J. Appl. Physiol.* **20**, 509–513.
57. Hagerup, L., and Schnohr, P. (1971). *In* "Coronary Heart Disease and Physical Fitness" (O. A. Larsen and R. O. Malborg, eds.), pp. 219–223. Univ. Park Press, Baltimore, Maryland.
58. Henry, F. (1951). *J. Appl. Physiol.* **3**, 427–438.

59. Henry, F. (1953). *Res. Quart.* **24**, 169–175.
60. Hermansen, L. (1969). *Med. Sci. Sports* **1**, 32–38.
61. Hermansen, L., Ekblom, B., and Saltin, B. (1970). *J. Appl. Physiol.* **29**, 82–86.
62. Hermansen, L., Hultman, E., and Saltin, B. (1967). *Acta Physiol. Scand.* **71**, 129–139.
63. Hermansen, L., and Saltin, B. (1969). *J. Appl. Physiol.* **26**, 31–37.
64. Hermiston, R. T., and Faulkner, J. A. (1971). *J. Appl. Physiol.* **30**, 833–838.
65. Hettinger, T. L., Birkhead, N. C., Horvath, S. M., and Issekutz, B. (1961). *J. Appl. Physiol.* **16**, 153–156.
66. Hill, A. V. (1925). *Sci. Mon.* **25**, 409–428.
67. Hill, A. V., Long, C. N. H., and Lupton, H. (1924). *Proc. Roy. Soc. Ser. B* **97**, 84–137.
68. Hoes, M. J. A. J. M., Binkhorst, R. A., Smeekes-Kuyl, A., and Vissers, A. C. A. (1968). *Int. Z. Angew. Physiol.* **26**, 33–42.
69. Hollmann, W. (1963). "Höchst- und Dauerleistungtähigkeit des Sportlers." Barth, Munich.
70. Holloszy, J. O. (1971). *In* "Coronary Heart Disease and Physical Fitness" (O. A. Larsen and R. O. Malmborg, eds.), pp. 147–151. Univ. Park Press, Baltimore, Maryland.
71. Holmberg, S., Paulin, S., Prerovsky, I., and Varnauskas, E. (1967). *Amer. J. Cardiol.* **19**, 486–491.
72. Holmgren, A. (1967). *Can. Med. Ass. J.* **96**, 697–702.
73. Issekutz, B., Birkhead, N. C., and Rodahl, K. (1962). *J. Appl. Physiol.* **17**, 47–50.
74. Issekutz, B., Jr., and Rodahl, K. (1961). *J. Appl. Physiol.* **16**, 606–610.
75. Kaijser, L. (1970). *Acta Physiol. Scand. Suppl.* **346**.
76. Kamon, E., and Pandolf, K. B. (1972). *J. Appl. Physiol.* **32**, 467–473.
77. Karlsson, J., Åstrand, P.-O., and Ekblom, B. (1967). *J. Appl. Physiol.* **22**, 1061–1065.
78. Kasch, F. W., Phillips, W. H., Ross, W. D., Carter, J. E. L., and Boyer, J. L. (1966). *J. Appl. Physiol.* **21**, 1387–1388.
79. Katch, F. I., Girandola, R. N., and Henry, F. M. (1972). *Med. Sci. Sports* **4**, 71–76.
80. Keul, J., Doll, E., and Keppler, D. (1967). *Experientia* **23**, 974–979.
81. Klissouras, V. (1971). *J. Appl. Physiol.* **31**, 338–344.
82. Knehr, C. A., Dill, D. B., and Neufeld, W. (1942). *Amer. J. Physiol.* **136**, 148–156.
83. Knuttgen, H. G. (1967). *J. Appl. Physiol.* **22**, 655–658.
84. Knuttgen, H. G. (1970). *J. Appl. Physiol.* **29**, 651–657.
85. Lindeman, R., Kyriacapoulos, J., and Conrad, L. (1962). *Amer. Heart J.* **65**, 24–31.
86. Lloyd, B. B. (1967). *In* "Physiology of Muscular Exercise" (C. Chapman, ed.), Monograph No. 15, pp. 218–226. Amer. Heart Ass., New York.
87. Luft, U., Cardus, C., Lim, T., and Anderson, E. (1963). *Ann. N. Y. Acad. Sci.* **110**, 795–808.
88. Maksud, M. G., and Coutts, K. D. (1971). *Med. Sci. Sports* **3**, 63–65.
89. Malhotra, M. S., Ramaswamy, S. S., Ray, S., and Shrivastav, T. N. (1962). *J. Appl. Physiol.* **17**, 775–777.
90. Margaria, R., Aghemo, P., and Rovelli, E. (1965). *J. Appl. Physiol.* **20**, 1070–1073.

91. Margaria, R., Aghemo, P., and Rovelli, E. (1966). *J. Appl. Physiol.* **21,** 1662–1666.
92. Margaria, R., Cerretelli, P., Aghemo, P., and Sassi, G. (1963). *J. Appl. Physiol.* **18,** 367–370.
93. Margaria, R., Cerretelli, P., di Prampero, P. E., Massari, C., and Torelli, G. (1963). *J. Appl. Physiol.* **18,** 371–377.
94. Margaria, R., di Prampero, P. E., Aghemo, P., Derevenco, P., and Mariani, M. (1971). *J. Appl. Physiol.* **30,** 885–889.
95. Margaria, R., Edwards, E. T., and Dill, D. B. (1933). *Amer. J. Physiol.* **106,** 689–715.
96. Mastropaolo, J. A. (1970). *Med. Sci. Sports* **2,** 124–127.
96a. Matsui, H., Miyashita, M., Miura, M., Kobayashi, K., Hoshikawa, T., and Kamei, S. (1972). *Med. Sci. Sports* **4,** 29–32.
97. Michael, E. D., Jr., and Horvath, S. M. (1965). *J. Appl. Physiol.* **20,** 263–266.
98. Michael, E. D., Jr., Hutton, K. E., and Horvath, S. M. (1961). *J. Appl. Physiol.* **16,** 997–1000.
99. Mitchell, J. H., Sproule, B. J., and Chapman, C. B. (1958). *J. Clin. Invest.* **37,** 538–547.
100. Miyamura, M., and Honda, Y. (1972). *J. Appl. Physiol.* **32,** 185–188.
101. Nagle, F., Balke, B., Baptista, G., Alleyia, J., and Howley, E. (1971). *Med. Sci. Sports* **3,** 149–154.
102. Nagle, F., Balke, B., and Naughton, J. P. (1965). *J. Appl. Physiol.* **20,** 745–748.
103. Naughton, J., Balke, B., and Nagle, F. (1964). *Amer. J. Cardiol.* **14,** 837–843.
104. Naughton, J., Sevelius, G., and Balke, B. (1963). *J. Sports Med. Phys. Fitness* **3,** 201–207.
105. Naughton, J., Shanbour, K., Armstrong, R., McCoy, T., and Lategola, M. (1966). *Arch. Intern. Med.* **117,** 541–545.
106. Newman, E. V. (1969). *Trans. Amer. Clin. Clim. Ass.* **81,** 130–142.
107. Passmore, R., and Durnin, J. V. G. A. (1955). *Physiol. Rev.* **35,** 801–840.
108. Ribisl, P. M., and Kachadorian, W. A. (1969). *J. Sports Med. Phy. Fitness* **9,** 17–22.
109. Ricci, B. (1967). "Physiological Basis of Human Performance." Lea & Febiger, Philadelphia, Pennsylvania.
110. Roberts, J. A., and Alspaugh, J. W. (1972). *Med. Sci. Sports* **4,** 6–10.
111. Robinson, S. (1938). *Arbeitsphysiologie* **10,** 251–323.
112. Robinson, S., and Harmon, P. M. (1941). *Amer. J. Physiol.* **132,** 757–769.
113. Robinson, S., Mountjoy, R. J., and Bullard, R. W. (1958). *J. Appl. Physiol.* **12,** 197–201.
114. Rode, A., and Shephard, R. J. (1971). *J. Appl. Physiol.* **31,** 519–526.
115. Rowell, L. B. (1967). *Can. Med. Ass. J.* **97,** 736.
116. Rowell, L. B., Taylor, H. L., and Wang, Y. (1964). *J. Appl. Physiol.* **19,** 919–927.
117. Saltin, B. (1964). *Acta Physiol. Scand.* **62,** Suppl. 230.
118. Saltin, B., and Åstrand, P.-O. (1967). *J. Appl. Physiol.* **23,** 353–358.
119. Saltin, B., Blomqvist, G., Mitchell, J. H., Johnson, R. L., Jr., Wildenthal, K., and Chapman, C. (1968). *In* "Response to Exercise after Bedrest and after Training," Monograph No. 23, pp. 1–78. Amer. Heart Ass., New York.
120. Sargent, R. M. (1926). *Proc. Roy. Soc. Ser. B* **100,** 10–22.
121. Schneider, E. G., Robinson, S. M., and Newton, J. C. (1968). *J. Appl. Physiol.* **25,** 58–62.

122. Shephard, R. J. (1966). *Intern. Z. Angew. Physiol.* **23**, 219–230.
123. Shephard, R. J. (1969). "Endurance Fitness." Univ. of Toronto Press, Toronto.
124. Simonsen, E., and Enzer, N. (1942). *Medicine* **21**, 345–419.
125. Sjöstrand, T. (1947). *Acta Med. Scand.* **196**, Suppl. 687.
126. Sonnenblick, E. H. (1971). *In* "Coronary Heart Disease and Physical Fitness" (O. A. Larsen and R. O. Malmborg, eds.), pp. 90–92. Univ. Park Press, Baltimore, Maryland.
127. Sprynarova, S., and Parizkova, J. (1965). *J. Appl. Physiol.* **20**, 934–937.
128. Stenberg, J., Åstrand, P.-O., Ekblom, B., Royce, J., and Saltin, B. (1967). *J. Appl. Physiol.* **22**, 61–70.
129. Taylor, H. L., Buskirk, E., and Henschel, A. (1955). *J. Appl. Physiol.* **8**, 73–80.
130. Taylor, H. L., Henschel, A., Brozek, J., and Keys, A. (1949). *J. Appl. Physiol.* **2**, 223–239.
131. Taylor, H. L., Wang, Y., Rowell, L. B., and Blomquist, G. (1963). *Pediatrics* **32**, Suppl., pp. 703–722.
132. Volkov, N. I., Gordon, S. M., Cheremisinov, V. N., and Shirkovets, Y. A. (1966). *Proc. World Congr. Sports Med., Hanover, Germany.*
133. Wahlund, H. (1948). *Acta Med. Scand.* **1**, Suppl. 215.
134. Welch, B. E., Riendeau, R. P., Cuisp, C. E., and Isenstein, R. S. (1958). *J. Appl. Physiol.* **12**, 395–398.
135. Welch, H. G., Faulkner, J. A., Barclay, J. K., and Brooks, G. A. (1970). *Med. Sci. Sports* **2**, 15–19.
136. Wells, J. G., Balke, B., and VanFossan, D. D. (1957). *J. Appl. Physiol.* **10**, 51–55.
137. Wiley, J. F., and Shaver, L. G. (1972). *Res. Quart.* **43**, 89–93.
138. Williams, C. G., Wyndham, C. H., Kok, R., and von Rahden, M. J. E. (1967). *Int. Z. Angew. Physiol.* **24**, 18–23.
139. Wilmore, J. H., and Sigerseth, P. O. (1967). *J. Appl. Physiol.* **22**, 923–928.
140. Workman, J. M., and Armstrong, B. W. (1964). *J. Appl. Physiol.* **19**, 150–151.
141. Wyndham, C. H. (1967). *Can. Med. Ass. J.* **96**, 736–742.
142. Wyndham, C. H., Strydom, N. B., Leary, W. P., and Williams, C. G. (1966). *Int. Z. Angew. Physiol.* **22**, 285–310.
143. Wyndham, C. H., Strydom, N. B., Martiz, J. S., Morrison, J. F., Peter, J., and Poteiger, Z. V. (1959). *J. Appl. Physiol.* **14**, 927–936.
144. Wyndham, C. H., Strydom, N. B., Morrison, J. F., Peter, J., Williams, C. G., Bredell, G. A. G., and Joffe, A. (1963). *J. Appl. Physiol.* **18**, 361–366.
145. Wyndham, C. H., Strydom, N. B., van Rensburg, A. J., and Benade, A. J. S. (1969). *S. Afr. Med. J.* **43**, 996–1002.
146. Wyndham, C. H., and Ward, J. S. (1957). *Circulation* **16**, 384–393.

Cinematographic, Electromyographic, and Electrogoniometric Techniques for Analyzing Human Movements

Marlene Adrian

DEPARTMENT OF PHYSICAL EDUCATION,
WASHINGTON STATE UNIVERSITY,
PULLMAN, WASHINGTON

I. Introduction

Research in the area of biomechanics or kinesiology (the kinetics and kinematics of movement of living beings) is conducted by means of a variety of instrumentation systems which can be categorized into four major types: mechanical, electrical, optical, and acoustical. The mechanical types incorporate springs, levers, and pneumatic chambers to record characteristics of motion. These mechanical types are no longer commonly used, having largely been replaced by electrical systems. For example, strain gages and load cells generally are more reliable than springs for measuring forces produced by movements. Furthermore, electrical systems provide greater stability in the recording devices and allow more flexibility in the type of output than is possible with mechanical systems. The major electrical systems include electromyography, electrogoniometry, and force recording instrumentation.

The optical systems, involving lights, tripods, and cameras of numerous types, are not only used for research but also for the teaching of sports skills. Systems designed for research, however, tend to utilize electrical subsystems for power supplies, timing and synchronizing devices, and triggering switches.

The last category, acoustical systems, is least used in physical education or sports sciences research. This may be due to the lack of knowledge of the components, difficulty in interpreting the signals, or because of the expense of the systems. Radar, sonar, and ultrasound have future potential for use in the analysis of sports movements. Here, too, electrical subsystems must be utilized for operation of the acoustical system.

Within each category, the instruments described in the literature range from investigator-made types to highly sophisticated and automated commercial ones. But each is constructed to provide the researcher with a system which will enable him to collect data concerning the movement of man.

In order to provide the reader with a fundamental understanding of the three most commonly used systems (cinematography, electromyography, and electrogoniometry), the basic components of each system are shown in Fig. 1. As depicted, all instrumentation systems consist of inputs, modifier processes, and outputs. There are many types of compo-

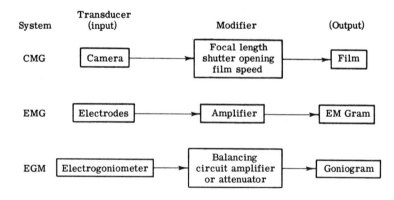

Fig. 1. Schematic of cinematography (CMG), electromyography (EMG), and electrogoniometry (EGM) systems.

nents available to fill these tasks. Careful selection of the best components with respect to precision, accuracy, rangeability, and sensitivity must be made by the investigator. The intent of this article is to review these three instrumentation systems and to determine the status of the instrumentation and their suitability for research in physical education and sports sciences. First, a brief description will be given of the purposes of these three systems.

Historically, with respect to these three techniques, the analysis of human movement was first conducted by means of cinematography (64). Experimentation with serial photography began in the 1860's and was directly linked to the study of movement by Marey and Muybridge. Motion pictures and roll type film were marketed just before the turn of the twentieth century and as early as the 1930's cinematographic instrumentation systems were being used by physical educators to study the kinematics of movement (29).

Cinematography enables the researcher to view the movements of the total body and to relate the body to three-dimensional space and external objects. The position of body parts, estimated segmental centers of mass, and gravitational line, as well as displacement, velocity, and acceleration vectors can be determined. Kinetics of the movement can be measured indirectly through cinematography since $F = ma$ and $T = I\alpha$, where F = force, m = mass, a = acceleration, T = torque, I = moment of inertia, and α = angular acceleration. However, individual muscle action can only be surmised by this method. This estimation can be done by viewing the change in form of the muscle or in contour of the body part, by assuming the movement to be caused by those muscles lying in the plane of movement or by calculating moments about joints. The inadequacy of these approaches led physical educators to look elsewhere for a means of studying muscle function.

In 1791, Luigi Galvani reported his classical frog muscle experiments. He discovered that an electrical stimulus will cause contraction of the muscle and that an electrical current will be produced when the contraction occurs. Although this might be considered the forerunner of electromyography, emphasis shifted from the study of skeletal muscle to the study of heart muscle and the brain and the development of electrocardiography and electroencephalography (20). Not until the twentieth century, through the adaptation of Einthoven's string galvonometer in electrocardiography, was any substantial progress made in electromyography. As late as 1925 the status of electromyography was such that the electromyogram was described as contributing only a small amount of knowledge, raising more questions than giving answers, and having questionable value to practical medicine (1). Electromyography, however, did provide an additional and very simple method of investigating diseases of the muscles and nervous system.

In the 1930's, modern high speed, high sensitivity recording systems brought forth greater reliability of the electromyogram. World War II brought a marked increase in neuromuscular disorders. Research using electromyography increased in volume in order to find solutions to the rehabilitation problems of these neuropathological cases. Electromyography therefore was being used to diagnose diseases of the nervous system and to contribute to the body of knowledge about the organization of normal voluntary movement and the disorganization of movement under certain pathological situations (20).

In conjunction with this greater use of electromyography by neurologists, persons in other professions began to use the device. Basic kinesiological evaluations were made by Bierman and Yamshon as early as 1948 (20). In that same year, Slater-Hammel (119) studied the action potentials of muscles involved during the execution of the golf stroke. This was the first evidence of the use of electromyography for the analysis of sports skills.

Of necessity, cinematography was combined with electromyography (53), since the sequencing, duration, and relative amount of muscle action potentials are the only data which can be obtained from the electromyogram. Without an event marker, film, or some other device such as the electrogoniometer, the electromyogram offers little information concerning the temporal aspects of muscle contraction with respect to the movement pattern.

Electrogoniometry, therefore, has become an important adjunct of electromyography. This, however, was not the main purpose for which electrogoniometry was developed. In the late fifties, Karpovich and Karpovich (73) were conducting foot gear research for the United States Army and needed a more convenient method of obtaining data. He developed electrogoniometry to provide some of the same data obtained from cinematography but in a less time consuming and tedious manner. The use of this device has spread around the world in a relatively short period of time, with research being reported primarily in the areas of sports sciences and rehabilitation (2,7). Some persons from countries outside the United States have called the technique "electrogoniographic" (81). Regardless of the term used, the data output remains the same: angular displacement, velocity and acceleration, and sequencing of rotations about the joints.

As separate units, each of the three systems described has proven to be valuable in providing data on how movement occurs. There has been an increase in the use of multiple systems as more research instruments have become available to researchers. Complementary and supplementary data can be derived from using two or more systems in conjunction with each other.

Combining the electromyographic and electrogoniometric systems is done easily since both outputs may be produced on the same recorder. Cinematographic instrumentation, however, requires a synchronization subsystem to allow it to be combined with the other two systems. Cinematographic, electromyographic, and electrogoniometric systems also are being used with systems employing the strain gage, accelerometer, natograph, photoelectric cell, roentgenogram, laser beam, stress coat, and other means of collecting data. These latter systems will not be discussed except as they relate to an evaluation of the electromyographic, electrogoniometric, and cinematographic systems.

II. Cinematography

A. GLIDING CYCLOGRAMS

The recording of human movement on film for quantified analysis has been done by means of gliding cyclograms, interrupted light photography (chronophotography), and motion pictures (*38,39*). Although the two former methods are mostly used in time/motion and clinical studies, they are described only briefly as they are basic to more recent advances in high speed photography. Gliding cyclograms were developed independently by Bernstein and Drillis to record repetitive or overlapping motion (*39*). The film was transported across the film aperture at a constant rate appropriate to the movement being recorded. Light reflecting tape affixed to the subject was illuminated with a photo-flood light, or miniature light bulbs were affixed to the subject in order to expose the film in a 35 mm camera with the shutter open. A rotating interrupter disk provided the temporal measure by interrupting the light reaching the film as frequently as 100 times per second or as infrequently as 25 times per second. The advantages of the disk method over light flashing methods were that overlap of light on consecutive pictures was eliminated and there was no chance of a subject flicker effect (*39*). However, the continuously recording camera, whether 35 mm or 16 mm, needs to possess both accuracy of the film transport mechanism and linearity of film movement across the shutter opening in order to provide valid data (*23*).

B. INTERRUPTED LIGHT PHOTOGRAPHY

If movement is not of an overlapping type, interrupted light photography will decrease the amount of time for data reduction required with gliding cyclograms and provide the entire movement on a 4 × 5 in. plate which may be enlarged. This method has been effectively used by Murray *et al.* (*92–94*) for investigations of gait. Their equipment consisted of a Speed Graphic camera with an Ascor Speedlight modified to flash 20 times per second. The light was sufficient to illuminate reflective targets on the body but not the body itself. A single flash from an Ultrablitz unit illuminated the total body at one instant during the movement being filmed in order to identify the targets. Scotchlite tape and reflective fabric were used as targets. An overhead mirror in the film frame provided information in another plane without the use of a second camera. This simple and inexpensive cinematographic system provided an abundance of kinematic data. Seven displacement patterns, sagittal rotation of the pelvis, hip, knee, and ankle and vertical, lateral, and forward movement of the trunk were graphed according to mean values for subgroups of the population sample. Transverse rotation of the pelvis and thorax was determined through the use of the overhead mirror and plastic rods projecting from the body (*94*).

The major disadvantages of this photographic system were the need to film in semidarkness and the low filming rate, 20 images per second. Waterland (*128*) successfully used a similar system to film jumping movements. Because of the low filming rate, however, certain important parts of high speed movement were not always exposed on the film. This limitation has been alleviated by the technological advances in electronic flash equipment. Multiflash photography, short flashes of less than 1 sec, has been developed by increasing the frequency of capacitor discharge, damping the circuit oscillations, and/or quenching the afterglow in the light discharge (*23*).

Since interrupted light photography has been used most extensively for small object photography with still backgrounds, it presents problems when attempting to use it with human movement analysis. Cross lighting to eliminate the background from being overexposed, draping unwanted objects with black velvet, or following the subject with a spotlight are methods that have been used. For example, to obtain the tracing of a golf club the golfer was covered with black velvet to provide a clear image of the club (*42*, p. 215).

Nelson *et al.* (*96*) blackened the test apparatus and background and covered the arm of the subject with a black stocking. A narrow white line on an aluminum bar attached to the limb was photographed at stroboscopic frequencies between 100 and 150 per second. Their findings confirmed that stroboscopy is an accurate method for calculating velocity and acceleration. However, overlapping of images would have occurred if the limb movement had consisted of flexion and extension movements. The problem encountered with such overlapping of movements has been solved by Jones and O'Connell (66,67), who placed a rotating transport filter disk in front of the shutter opening to color code the sequence of movement.

Light traces from flashing and nonflashing miniature bulbs attached to swimmers and runners have been utilized to view the path of joints and distal ends of limb segments (27,107). The flashing lights enabled the researcher to evaluate the temporal and spatial characteristics of the movement more accurately than with the nonflashing lights. In addition, the Super 8 mm camera was shown to be satisfactory for research of this type (27).

C. Motion Picture Filming

In contrast to the complexity of the previously described methods, motion picture filming is a relatively simple technique. Until recently most of the cinematographic systems used for sports filming consisted of a single 16 mm camera operating at 64 frames/sec with black and white film. This presented the largest film size, was inexpensive, and allowed filming to be accomplished under a wide range of lighting conditions. Standard filming procedures included placement of an object of known length in the photographic field in order to later convert projected size to actual size (122). The Bolex, Bell & Howell, Cine-Kodak, and Beaulieu cameras have been used in research where no more than 64 frames/sec were needed. At higher operating speeds the LoCam and HiCam cameras have provided the means to obtain impact data and fast movements (97). Ketlinski (75), however, has questioned whether the additional information obtained with the higher speeds justifies the increase in cost due to the greater amount of film used.

D. Correction of Distortion

One of the problems encountered with motion picture filming is the distortion due to parallax and perspective errors. The simplest technique for the correction of these errors continues to be the placing of cameras at right angles to the plane of movement. If the lens is not close to the person, movements within a plane are recorded with negligible angular or linear distortion. Scolnick (112) found no appreciable distortion during the basketball jump shot with one camera only 25 ft from the subject. Dillman (36) filmed a runner in a field of 22 ft at a distance of 73 ft without needing an angle or linear correction factor. Plagenhoef (106) lists correction factors with respect to angular distortion for different lenses at different distances. When movement essentially is in one plane, correction is so slight, being less than that which could occur through measurement of the data, that one might question whether or not it is necessary to apply a correction formula. For example, 0.0001 would be eliminated from any formula which required it to be subtracted from a three digit integer. Although angle and linear perspective errors exist in filming situations they can be eliminated from research investigations by prior testing of distances and field size, and by attaching projections to the body (*84*).

Doolittle (*37*) discusses the need for correcting perspective error when a grid or length standard is behind the object being filmed. The effect of a distance of 4 ft between object and grid was evaluated under conditions of 46 and 96 ft camera distances. A general formula was determined to correct for perspective errors under all conditions. An additional and greater error, however, was caused by calculating a scale factor. DeVries and Lersten (*35*) developed a specific formula for measuring the displacement values of swimming 5 ft in front of a grid. Shvartz (*114*) eliminated the need for these mathematical corrections by using a dichroic mirror to project a grid in the photographic plane.

The value of a grid, whether behind or superimposed on the subject, is questionable in measuring motion. Point by point displacement calculated from a scale factor will provide all the information needed without going through the extra step of converting to the grid. With the use of x–y coordinate readers or computerized tablets the grid becomes valueless. Shvartz stated that the grid was used only as an estimation of distance. Levens *et al.* (*85*) studied gait with three 35 mm cameras set at right angles to each other operating at 48 frames/sec 25 ft from the subject. Correction was made for possible perspective and parallax errors and was later found to be unnecessary because values obtained directly from the motion picture frames were not significantly different from computed values.

E. Timing Devices

Although the trend is toward electrically driven, high speed cameras with built-in timers, research continues to be conducted with spring-wound cameras. Calibration of the speed of operation of these cameras, as well as the more sophisticated ones, has been and is of major concern to researchers. The speed of the camera, and the time between frames, may be determined by several methods. The method of dropping a ball during the filming and computing the speed of the camera from the formula $t = (2ad)^{1/2}$ (*31*), where t = time, a = acceleration, and d = distance, is no longer considered desirable for research. It is more time consuming to determine the speed of the camera this way than from timing devices. Furthermore, it allows only one calculation unless a series of balls are dropped, thus increasing the complexity of the procedure. When dropping a single ball the assumption is made that the filming rate remains the same for the entire filming. With spring-wound cameras this is probably not true, since all cameras show a change in speed at the beginning and end of operation. Therefore, a stopwatch or chronoscope is used to determine how many frames are needed before constant speed is obtained and how many frames are obtained after releasing the drive mechanism.

Several decades ago clocks of 2 ft diameter were available commercially. The convenience of these and the fact that a continuous timing between frames was available made this single face clock common in research of sports. This clock operated at ⅓ rotations/sec and represented less than 1 deg of change per frame when the camera operated at 64 frames/sec.

Timing devices rotating at 6⅔ and 1 rotations/sec have been reported in the literature (3,12). These provide a greater angular displacement of the clock hand between each frame than with the ⅓ rotations/sec clock. However, use of reliable drafting tools and repeated measurements still is obligatory if accurate calculations are to be obtained. Both the speed and the size of the timing device contribute to the accuracy of measurements, as does the operating speed of the camera. Clocks with two hands and rotating cones marked as timing devices indicate further attempts to increase the accuracy in determining the time interval between frames (122). Other methods found in the literature include the use of the dichroic mirror (30) and prism or beam splitter (99), which allows a clock or grid image to be superimposed upon the film and to be placed on two camera views at the same time. A digital timing device developed by Walton (126) eliminates the measurement errors of the investigator and provides accuracy to 0.001 sec. Four rows of ten neon bulbs are displayed to indicate time up to 10 sec cycles with tenths, hundredths, and thousandths subdivisions. A Colpitts oscillator assures reliability over short term and long term usage. Two or more of these devices may be coupled together for use with simultaneous recordings from two or more cameras.

A signal generator attached to a camera will provide a pulsating signal which causes a mark on the film at intervals of 1, 0.1, or 0.01 sec. This is probably the most convenient timing device for a single camera but it does not directly provide an indication of time elapsed for each frame.

In summary, researchers generally apply the following criteria in selecting their timing devices: (1) large enough to be seen clearly, (2) great enough change from frame to frame to be measured accurately,

(3) constant speed of rotation or sequencing, (4) quickly translatable into actual frame time intervals, and (5) availability.

F. THREE-DIMENSIONAL PHOTOGRAPHY

The link from one-plane photography to triplane photography has already been described with respect to the camera and mirror used by Murray and Clarkson (*92*). Biplanar data from two motion picture cameras were obtained by Hay (*60*) and Scolnick (*112*) of pole vaulting and basketball shooting, respectively. Both researchers obtained more quantitative data from one camera than the other. During pole vaulting a side camera was operated at 128 frames/sec for the purpose of obtaining velocities, distance between hands, and maximum pole bend, whereas the front camera, operating at 24 frames/sec, provided data in determining lateral deviation of the body from the vertical. The side camera during basketball filming provided data to calculate angular velocities while the front camera was used to determine spatial relationships between body segments.

Duquet *et al.* (*41*) presented a graphical system for calculating actual positions in space, angles, displacements, linear and angular velocities, and accelerations from two cameras. Stereophotography as used by Ayoub and Ayoub (*13*) and Dubovik (*40*) and described in detail by Cimerman and Tomašegović (*26*) and Burton (*23*) also enables one to obtain triplanar data from two cameras.

In a study of throwing patterns, Atwater (*12*) used three cameras which were synchronized with a rotating cone timing device to obtain displacement and velocity data. Anderson (*11*) describes a method for processing cinematographic analysis of human motion in three dimensions.

G. ANALYSIS TECHNIQUES

Until recent years the methods for analyzing films consisted of still frame projection on a wall, projection via mirrors to a table top, and projection in film readers. The data analysis was primarily in the form of displacement and velocity graphs, stick figures, and contourograms (*33,49,120*). Because of the recent desire of investigators to engage in triplane photography, to obtain first and second derivatives of motion, to compute centers of mass and moments of force, and to obtain data from larger samples, computerized readers (*104,95,110*) and graphic tablets (*82*) have become basic equipment for film analysis. However, the use of this equipment and these methods of analysis (*52,54–56*) is still in its infancy, as evidenced by the amount of research focused upon the description and validation of techniques. For example, Noble and Kelley (98) tested the accuracy of their calculations of motion parameters by filming the helical path of a rolling ball. Displacement data correlated 0.99 on repeated measurements by the investigators, thereby ruling out lack of investigator reliability. Comparison of obtained data from three cameras with mathematically derived data showed acceptable findings for point position, displacement, elapsed time, and velocity. The greatest error was 6% of the criterion values. Acceleration values, however, showed a mean error of 35%. This large error is a function of the error introduced into the displacement data. Widule and Gossard (130) present methods of eliminating the random error found in the displacement data through smoothing techniques but caution investigators about introducing error by these methods.

It would appear that different smoothing techniques would be applicable for different samples and the different movement patterns being analyzed. For example, a smoothing technique used to calculate the velocity of a ballistic type movement might "smooth out" important changes in velocity occurring in slow precision-type movements but be valid for the ballistic type movement.

The complexity of the data derived from cinematography requires a greater knowledge of mathematics and mechanics on the part of the investigators than in the past. In addition, a knowledge of computer programming has become necessary in order to get data output in a reasonable amount of time. Hopper and Kane (63) described a rather lengthy method of calculating the center of mass of a body with the aid of paper and pencil and a projected image, whereas Garrett et al. (48), by means of a computer program, determined the same information in a matter of minutes. Computer programs have been reported by many investigators (36,47,48,62,106) for the purposes of enabling others to benefit from their experience. The programs include methods of calculating angles, accelerations and velocities, moments of force, moments of inertia of segments, and kinetic energy of the body. Motion picture films also have served as criteria for testing computer data modeling and simulation techniques (46,108,129). If the trend toward more automatization of film analysis continues, virtually all cinematography systems will include computer hardware and software components.

H. MULTISYSTEMS

A combination of a force recording and cinematographic system incorporated by Murray et al. (95) demonstrated the validity of calculating the vertical supportive force from film. A subject, marked with targets at the segmental centers of mass, was photographed at 32 frames/sec while performing on a force platform consisting of three superimposed platforms. The subject performed ascending, descending, and jumping movements. Vertical supportive force, moment of force, center of pressure, and line of gravity were determined for each frame. The values of the calculated supportive forces closely approximated the measured force patterns. The small differences occurred at the peak and valley of the magnitude.

Another innovation in cinematography was introduced by Dal Monte (*32*). An optical system was mounted on a dolly powered by an electric propulsion engine. The optical system consisted of an underwater motion picture camera, television, and a periscopic system of mirrors to view and record underwater swimming. The operator moved the dolly coincident with the swimmer's speed.

III. Electromyography

The instrumentation system for recording action potentials from the muscles has changed extensively—from nonlocomotor copper screened cells (faradic cages) to the telemetering of swimmers (*77*); from a limited number of large electrode types to a diversity of sizes, shapes, and designs; single channel to multichannel recording; and from ink-writing recorders to on-line computerized output.

Excellent reviews of electromyography (EMG) instrumentation exist in the literature (*16,17,34,55,59,100,103,115*). All concur on proper preparation of subject, selection of electrodes, selection of amplifiers and recorders, and the inadequacies of quantification methods for interpreting the electromyogram. O'Connell and Gardner (*99*) give details concerning all procedures for conducting EMG research.

A. Preparation of Subject

The subject is prepared for electrode attachment by cleaning the skin with alcohol or acetone, abrading the skin to reduce skin resistance, and thoroughly saturating the skin with electrode paste. The mode of attachment of electrodes will depend upon the type selected. However, all electrodes must be securely fixed so that no movement of the electrode over the body is possible. A variety of adhesives, including spray types, are being used. No one substance is recommended over any other. In addition, plastic varnish and rubber cement are used to form a protective coating over electrodes affixed to swimmers.

B. Types of Electrodes

Ideally, electrodes should introduce no potential or resistance into the circuit. Since no such electrodes of this capability exist, high impedance input amplifiers are used to render the electrode resistance negligible, and identical paired electrodes are used in order to balance potential build-ups.

Electrodes may be purchased or built by the investigator and are either of the surface adhering or inserted type. Since surface electrodes have more global pickup capabilities than do inserted types, the latter are useful in studies of single motor unit functioning (15,115,116) and for small and/or deep muscles. Surface electrodes are typically silver disks with a shallow cup-type shape. Their size ranges from a few millimeters to almost 25 mm in diameter. Small silver rods set in a plastic bar provide a means of recording from small muscles with surface type electrodes and still maintaining a secure anchoring to the skin. Also, suction type electrodes are being used to provide better anchoring for recording during sports movements. Inserted type electrodes are embedded into the muscle primarily by means of a small hypodermic needle which is withdrawn after insertion. Although glass, platinum, tinned copper, silver, and stainless steel wires are used, Basmajian (16) recommends bipolar electrodes made from nylon or polyurethane-insulated Karma alloy wire. He further states, however, that a "good electromyographer employs the whole range" (16, p. 110) of the available electrodes, including those that have special applications. For example, fine wires, 25 μ in diameter, inserted into the gastrocnemius, break more often during 2 min of walking than do 50 μ diameter wires (69).

C. Evaluation of Positioning of Electrodes

Placement of electrodes is done through stimulation of the muscle to find a motor point or stimulation through the wire electrode to confirm that the wire is in the desired muscle. Roentgenograms may also be obtained to determine where the wire electrode is embedded.

Jonsson and Rudgren (70) investigated the location of intramuscular electrodes by injecting carbon dioxide gas through the electrode. Since the gas stays within the muscle fascia for approximately 10 to 15 min, radiographs can be obtained to determine in which muscle or tissue the electrode is embedded. Their findings showed placement of electrodes outside the peronius longus and brevis muscles (the desired sites) in nine out of 37 instances. In seven cases it was not possible to locate the electrodes. Since proper insertion was a problem in superficial muscles, Jonsson (68), in order to prevent improper insertion of the needle in studying the erector spinae muscles, used TV fluoroscopy to determine when the insertion depth was adequate and at the desired site. Despite these precautions, valid EMG activity was recorded in only 56 of 71 cases. Correct initial positioning of wire electrodes does not alleviate the problem of wires being displaced or short circuited during the experiment. The wires shift both in the muscle and in the subcutaneous tissue after the first few contractions and even after as many as 50 contractions.

Komi and Buskirk (80) studied the reproducibility of EMG records from inserted and surface electrodes. Their findings showed good intra- and inter-day reliability for surface electrodes, but not for the wire inserted electrodes. The latter had average reliability coefficients of 0.15 to 0.85 on the first two test days as compared to a range of 0.83 to 0.92 for the surface electrodes. Later test day average coefficients were not higher than 0.44 for the inserted electrodes and not lower than 0.60 for the surface type.

Zuniga et al. (133) investigated the effect of skin electrode position on averaged electromyographic potentials. Monopolar and bipolar elec- trodes were positioned longitudinally, transversely, and circumferentially on the arm and forearm. Although amplitude changes were noted, the electromyogram–tension relationship remained parabolic. When the electrode position was connected with respect to the maximum EMG amplitude possible from each site, the respective curves were nearly identical.

D. Interpretation of the Electromyogram

Initially, the electromyographic output must be evaluated to differen- tiate action potentials from artifacts. Descriptions of interference pat- terns or noise are presented by Waterland and Shambes (129) and by O'Connell (100) so that investigators will not misinterpret such arti- facts as muscle activity. Since research publications include a typical record, or only tabulations from an analysis of the recordings, readers cannot determine the extent of noise in the output. There is a high prob- ability of artifact output when surface electrodes are used to record fast movements which cause the muscles to move asynchronously with respect to skin movement or which include impact type movement.

The literature includes a wealth of information concerning methods for interpreting and quantifying the electromyogram, the most common method being a gross quantification of the amplitude of the spike. By inspection, or by actual measurement, the electromyogram is assessed as showing no activity, slight, moderate, or marked activity (16). Although this type of interpretation was satisfactory for identification of muscle activity of a golf swing (24) and scissors exercise on a pommel horse (71), other investigators of sports skills developed a more sophisticated method of quantification. Oglesby (101), Lewillie (87), and Barthels and Adrian (14) evaluated the muscle activity in gymnastics and swimming skills with respect to a percentage of the EMG obtained during a maximal isometric contraction. Although values greater than 100% were obtained for some of the dynamic skills, this method was found to be an effective means of comparing inter- and intra-subject recordings. Researchers in sports sciences need such an approach, whereas clinical kinesiologists may not.

In attempting to investigate frequency and duration of spikes along with the amplitude by means of mean voltage, root mean square, and volts per second, integration systems were developed. Different methods of integration are reported in literature, and are obtained by electronic integrators summing the area under the spike, resistance–capacitance integrators, and voltage comparator reset integrators. Early descriptions of integration systems did not completely describe the circuitry. Descriptions now are included in the literature so that the reader can determine the type of circuitry system used, the method of integration, and evaluate the time delay of the averaging process (32,83,111,113).

Although the trend is toward greater use of integration techniques and Lewillie (86) indicates that integration techniques give a more precise analysis of the EMG, researchers are skeptical of recording only integrated EMG. Dual recording of integrated and nonintegrated EMG from the same muscle is commonly done to check the integrated record for noise.

E. SYNCHRONIZATION OF ELECTROMYOGRAPHY WITH OTHER SYSTEMS

Electromyography has been combined with force recording, motion picture, interrupted light photography, and electrogoniometric systems (48,61,78). Researchers are interested in relationships between strength, force, $\dot{V}_{O_2}$ as compared to angle of limb and EMG records (21,24,28, 83,88,89,90). These investigators indicated diversity and sophistication of instrumentation. Manually triggering an event marker and superimposing the EMG record on film or videotape have been reported in the literature (45,53,99,101). However, these are not as reliable a method or as satisfactory to interpret as are those incorporating synchronizing units. A microswitch (24), impulse generator (19), synchronizing light

(*21,71*), and photoelectric cell (*90*) have been used in synchronizing film with electromyograms. Bevan (*19*) describes such a device which is both simple and inexpensive to construct. This device has been tested on a Paillard Bolex spring-wound 16 mm camera operating between 32 and 64 frames/sec and connected with a pen oscillograph operating at 6 cm/sec. The synchronizer is attached to the camera and sends an impulse to the oscillograph for each closure of the camera switch. Although proven effective and valid for the instrumentation for which it was designed, it may not be valid at faster speeds of camera operation or slower oscillograph recording speeds.

One of the more comprehensive combinations of film and EMG was done by Broer and Houtz (*22*). Overhand, underhand, sidearm, and one-foot jump patterns were filmed and correlated with EMG from a series of surface electrodes attached in sets of seven pairs to muscles of the legs, arms, and trunk. The data are questionable, however, since electrode sites were determined by palpation, quantitative data were not given concerning the consistency of the performance, a pen writing oscillograph with a paper speed of 25 mm/sec was used, and the investigators gave no comments concerning the amount of artifact encountered. Furthermore, photographs other than those obtained during testing were substituted for publication purposes.

F. Telemetry

The possibilities for telemetering action potentials of the muscle are vast since EKG and EEG telemetry systems are in use for a variety of applications. For example, long distance FM telephone transmission of fetal electrocardiograms has proved effective over a distance of 265 miles (*60*). Young and Naylor (*132*) compared direct and telemetered EEG records from a two-way system and found the records to be nearly identical in frequency and amplitude. The transmitter not only stimulated the brain with a variety of intensities and durations but, in addition, transmitted the EEG response of the animal. Although both of these systems could transmit action potentials from muscles, neither has been put to this use. The reason for this may be that EMG recordings of several muscles are desirable for most biomechanics research.

Three investigations have been reported in which muscle action potentials have been telemetered. Moore *et al.* (*91*) telemetered EMG while simultaneously recording electrogoniometry by conventional means. A complete description of a telemetry system for recording action potentials during walking was given by Battye and Joseph (*18*). A frequency modulated transmitter was attached to the trunk of the subject and an audio amplifier and loudspeaker were used to receive the signals by ear. Lewillie (*86*) used a smaller transmitter for simultaneously recording action potentials from two muscles. An antenna was supported by a balloon to assist in the transmission. Only in this last investigation does it appear that telemetry was necessary for the success of the experiment.

IV. Electrogoniometry

The diversity of the components in electrogoniometric systems is contingent not only upon the instrumentation available to the investigator but upon the species and joint to be studied.

A. DESIGN AND VALIDITY OF ELECTROGONIOMETRY

More than a dozen types of electrogoniometers (elgons) have been reported in the literature since the first elgon was developed to measure pronation and supination of the human foot during barefoot walking (*74*). This first electrogoniometer consisted of a sliding mechanism and potentiometer fastened to the rear of the foot and lower leg. It was validated through the use of photographs and anatomical knowledge. The success of this research led to the concept of the universal electrogoniometer, a basic design which could be used to record changes in angles at the ankle, knee, hip, and elbow joints. This elgon consisted of two brass shafts attached to the knob and housing of a potentiometer. These shafts were secured by snap fasteners to a chassis strapped to a body segment. The lengths of the chassis and shafts were determined by the joint to be studied. Calibration of these elgons was done by matching a scale representing the changes in electrical resistance, and thereby current, to the known angles on a protractor. The validity of the elgon had to be established while the elgon was attached to the subject.

Extensive testing of the first universal elgon, attached to the elbow and knee joints, was conducted to establish validity, reliability, and objectivity (*72*). Selected elbow angles were measured by the use of steel rods attached to the arm. These measurements were compared with elbow angle measurements obtained with the elgon. The average difference between the two methods for 16 subjects was ±1 deg, with the greatest difference occurring at or near complete extension of the limb. Although the greatest single difference was almost 4 deg, the correlation coefficient between the two sets of data was 0.99. Since all tests were made with the subjects sitting with their arms supported on a table during flexion and extension movements there was no testing of validity of this elgon when forearm rotation occurred. Later research determined the shaft length necessary to prevent forearm rotation from affecting the elgon output. The forearm shaft must be no longer than a third of the length of the forearm (*109*).

Duplicate steel rod tests made with knee angle measurements produced similar results, but slightly larger differences than with the elbow tests. Additional comparisons were made with manual goniometers. The elgon showed the highest objectivity and appeared to measure more accurately the "true angle" (*72*) of the joint. Since there is no fixed axis of rotation at the knee, but an instant axis in time, further research was conducted with a center finder and roentgenographic observations to determine migration of the axis of rotation. Tracings from the center finder were obtained when the tibia moved, femur moved, and when both bones moved. Although the evidence supports the use of electrogoniometers for analyzing changes in joint angles, the behavior of the bones must be identified when studying a particular movement.

Additional investigation of the validity of electrogoniometry and the instant centers of knee motion was conducted by Kettelkamp *et al.* (*76*). A triaxial electrogoniometer with one potentiometer oriented in each of the three planes of motion was evaluated during normal walking. A correction factor never exceeded 2 deg, and the largest was coincidental with large amounts of internal and external rotation. Deliberate malalignment of the potentiometer provided evidence that an error of as much as 12.7 mm would not significantly affect the validity of the data. Further validity was substantiated by comparison with values obtained by investigators using photometric methods with skeletal pins or skin markers during walking. Reliability and objectivity were also found to be satisfactory. This same triaxial electrogoniometer was used initially to measure hip motion during walking (*25*). Since this model was large and bulky, having been built with materials used in braces, its size may negate its use in measurement of movement during sports skills. Another triaxial elgon was used to study forearm rotation during softball pitching. It is not known how much the inertia of the equipment influenced the data because the validity of the system during movement was not ascertained (*131*).

Since there are no criteria to validate the response of the elgon during high speed movement, substitute or pseudovalidity measures have been used. Comparison of pre- and post-test walking patterns are made in order to assure proper placement and lack of slippage of the elgon and reliability of the goniograms. Comparisons with film data taken simultaneously were thought to provide further substantiation of validity; however, the use of electrogoniometry has usually been done in lieu of cinematography, which was inadequate for the solution of the problem. Therefore, cinematography is not an acceptable criterion for validating electrogoniometry.

If the basic principles of mechanics are applied in the design stage, the assumption can be made that the elgon will provide accurate measures. The use of electrogoniometers to study the gaits of horses (121), jumping (79), running (118), basketball shooting (112), and sports movements in general (50) has indicated the following design characteristics. The elgons should be essentially without mass, should have a minimum of moving parts producing minimal friction, and must fit the subject. These requirements are met in a variety of ways, such as by the use of miniature potentiometers and lightweight plastics. The latter materials have the further advantage that when combined with electromyography the plastics are less apt to interfere with the EMG signal than would metal parts. At this time there is only one manufacturer of electrogoniometers producing a lightweight type suitable for use with all movements including sports skills (2). Elgons which are constructed by the investigator need to be carefully evaluated in terms of the above design requirements. The major concern once the elgon has been selected or designed and constructed is the reliability of the investigator in attaching the elgon to the subject.

Elgons may be used singly or in linked systems. Thomas and Long (123) devised a complex finger electrogoniometer with a double four-bar linkage consisting of two parallelograms. This electrogoniometer was designed to track the movements of two joints, the metacarpalphalangeal and the proximal interphalangeal. The complexity of this elgon was due primarily to the linking of two joints in one system and may not be necessary for recording movements in one plane or with two separate elgons. Other linked elgons have been used by Olson and Waterland (102) and Adrian et al. (9).

In seeking to control motion and because the computer is available, researchers have developed space linkage systems to be used in place of electrogoniometers (77). Motion of two body parts involves six degrees of freedom, rotation and translation components. Although this system is potentially more accurate than the planar type, it may not be feasible to develop. Data reduction by computer is mandatory; furthermore, a linkage system has greater potential for restricting motion and for having more "play" in the system than planar types. This is true especially for motions which are difficult to define beforehand. The accuracy may be worth the time in orthotics but may be more than is necessary for sports analysis.

B. CIRCUITRY

The second phase of the electrogoniometric system is the circuitry. There are two circuits commonly in use: the Wheatstone bridge and the double bucking circuit. The former is an easily obtained item but may not be satisfactory if the bridge cannot be balanced with precision. The latter provides an inexpensive circuit which may be easier to balance (10). Both circuits provide repeatable data from calibration procedures with a protractor.

Since the elgon signal may need to be attenuated rather than amplified, and since the signal is not affected noticeably by noise, many types of recorders have been used. The inertial lag of pen writing recorders and the low rate of speed of paper are limitations which can be offset by use of mirror galvanometric type oscillographs, oscilloscopes, magnetic tape recorders, or by direct input into an analog computer. Repeatability of values obtained from clockwise or counterclockwise and fast or slow movements may be affected by the type of recorder used. Data from reported research in which ink writing oscillographs are used must be interpreted with caution if a rapid change in direction of movement occurs. Pen reversal response time as well as small interval measurement techniques need to be evaluated. Most of the literature shows usage of oscilloscope or Honeywell Visicorders. Despite this, only displacement and velocity are the common parameters being investigated.

C. DUAL SYSTEMS

Singh and Ashton (117) investigated the effect of hip angle on back lift strength as measured by a dynamometer. Continuous and synchronous recordings were obtained for the angle at the hip as measured by an electrogoniometer and the amount of force exerted on the load cell. Scolnick (112) combined electrogoniometry with cinematography to supplement data unavailable from the film. Forearm pronation and supination and wrist flexion and extension were obtained simultaneously with goniograms obtained from an elgon measuring flexion and extension at the elbow. These were synchronized with film data by measuring the angle changes at the elbow as seen on the film and comparing these with the appropriate goniograms.

Several investigators have combined electrogoniometry with electromyography (8). Olson and Waterland (102) synchronized the EMG, EGM, and photography data with a photo event marker. Moore *et al.*

etry of electrogoniometers. Such a system does exist (4), but the desir-
transmitter does not exist.

D. TELEMETRY

To the author's knowledge, no research has been reported using telemetry of electrogoniometers. Such a system does exist (4), but the desir-
ability of multichannel recording has hindered its applications.

References

1. Adrian, E. D. (1925). *Lancet* 1, 1229–1233.
2. Adrian, M. (1971). "Selected Topics on Biomechanics," pp. 85–90. Athletic Inst., Chicago, Illinois.
3. Adrian, M. J., and Enberg, M. L. (1971). *Kinesiology Review*, pp. 1–9. AAHPER, Washington, D. C.
4. Adrian, M. J., and Karpovich, G. P. (1967). Paper for Laboratory Equipment Demonstration—Discussion Meeting, Res. Sect., Amer. Ass. Health, Phys. Educ. Recreation Nat. Conv., Las Vegas.
5. Adrian, M. J., and Karpovich, P. V. (1964). *Res. Quart.* 35, 398–402, 442.
6. Adrian, M. J., and Karpovich, P. V. (1966). *Res. Quart.* 37, 168–175.
7. Adrian, M. J., and Karpovich, P. V. (1965). *Med. Sport* 5, 645–652.
8. Adrian, M. J., and Oglesby, B. (1971). *In* "Biomechanics II" (J. Vredenbregt and J. Wartenweiler, eds.), Karger, Basel.
9. Adrian, M. J., Roy, W. E., and Karpovich, P. V. (1966). *Amer. J. Vet. Res.* 27, 90–95.
10. Adrian, M. J., Tipton, C. M., and Karpovich, P. V. (1965). "Electrogoniometry Manual." Springfield College, Springfield, Massachusetts.
11. Anderson, C. C. (1970). Unpublished Master's Thesis, Univ. of Wisconsin, Madison, Wisconsin.
12. Atwater, A. E. (1970). Doctoral Dissertation, Univ. of Wisconsin, Madison, Wisconsin.
13. Ayoub, M. S., and Ayoub, M. M. (1972). *Human Factors* 12, 523–535.
14. Barthels, K. M., and Adrian, M. J. (1970). *Proc. 1st Int. Symp. Biomech. Swimming, Waterpolo, Diving*, pp. 105–118.
15. Basmajian, J. V. (1968). *Amer. J. Phys. Med.* 46, 480–486.
16. Basmajian, J. V. (1971). "Selected Topics on Biomechanics," pp. 109–118. Athletic Inst., Chicago, Illinois.
17. Basmajian, J. V. (1968). *In* "Biomechanics I" (J. Wartenweiler *et al.*, eds.), pp. 110–112. Karger, Basel.
18. Battye, C. K., and Joseph, J. (1966). *Med. Biol. Eng.* 4, 125–135.
19. Bevan, R. J. (1972). *Res. Quart.* 43, 105–112.
20. Bierman, W., and Yamsho, L. (1948). *Arch. Phys. Med.* 29, 206–211.
21. Brandell, B. R. (1971). *Arch. Phys. Med. Rehabil.* 51, 278–285.
22. Broer, M. R., and Houtz, S. J. (1967). "Patterns of Muscular Activity in Selected Sport Skills." Thomas, Springfield, Illinois.
23. Burton, A. L. (1971). "Cinematographic Techniques in Biology and Medicine." Academic Press, New York.

24. Carlsöö, S. (1967). *J. Sports Med. Phys. Fitness* **7**, 76–77.
25. Chao, E. Y. S., Rim, K., Smidt, G. L., and Johnston, R. C. (1970). *J. Biomech.* **3**, 459–471.
26. Cimerman, V. J., and Tomašegović, Z. (1970). "Atlas of Photogrammetric Instruments." Elsevier, Amsterdam.
27. Clarys, J. P., and Lewillie, L. (1970). *Proc. 1st Int. Symp. Biomech. Swimming, Waterpolo, Diving,* pp. 249–255.
28. Close, J. R., and Kidd, C. C. (1969). *J. Bone Joint Surg.* **51**, 1601–1620.
29. Cooper, J. M., and Glassow, R. B. (1972). "Kinesiology." Mosby, St. Louis, Missouri.
30. Cooper, J. M., and Sorani, R. (1965). *Res. Quart.* **36**, 210–211.
31. Cureton, T. K. (1939). *Res. Quart.* **10**, 3–24.
32. Dal Monte, A. (1970). *Proc. 1st Int. Symp. Biomech. Swimming, Waterpolo, Diving,* pp. 73–80.
33. Debrunner, H. U. (1971). *In* "Biomechanics II" (J. Vredenbregt and J. Wartenweiler, eds.), pp. 304–307. Karger, Basel.
34. Deutch, H. (1971). *In* "Selected Topics on Biomechanics," pp. 119–128. Athletic Inst., Chicago, Illinois.
35. deVries, H. A. (1959). *Res. Quart.* **30**, 413–422.
36. Dillman, C. J. (1971). "Selected Topics on Biomechanics," pp. 137–168. Athletic Inst., Chicago, Illinois.
37. Doolittle, T. L. (1971). *Kinesiology Review,* pp. 32–38, AAHPER, Washington, D. C.
38. Drillis, R. (1958). *Ann. N. Y. Acad. Sci.* **74**, 86–109.
39. Drillis, R. J. (1959). *Human Factors* **1**, 1–11.
40. Dubovik, A. S. (1968). "Photographic Recording of High-Speed Processes." Pergamon, Oxford.
41. Duquet, W., Borms, J., and Hebbelinck, M. (1971). *3rd Int. Seminar Biomech., Rome.*
42. Edgerton, H. E. (1970). "Electronic Flash, Strobe." McGraw-Hill, New York.
43. Finley, F. R., and Karpovich, P. V. (1964). *Res. Quart.* **35**, 379–384.
44. Flint, M. M. (1968). *In* "Biomechanics I" (J. Wartenweiler *et al.*, eds.), pp. 132–137. Karger, Basel.
45. Flint, M. M., and Gudgell, J. (1965). *Res. Quart.* **36**, 29–37.
46. Garrett, G. E., and Reed, W. S. (1971). *In* "Selected Topics on Biomechanics," pp. 195–200. Athletic Inst., Chicago, Illinois.
47. Garrett, G. E., and Widule, C. J. (1971). *Kinesiology Review* pp. 49–54, AAHPER, Washington, D. C.
48. Garrett, R. E., Widule, C. J., and Garrett, G. E. (1968). *Kinesiology Review* pp. 1–4, AAHPER, Washington, D. C.
49. Glassow, R., and Hubbard, A. W. (1952). "Photographical and Cinematographical Research Methods Applied to Health, Physical Education, Recreation." AAHPER, Washington, D. C.
50. Gollnick, P. D., and Karpovich, P. V. (1964). *Res. Quart.* **35**, 357–369.
51. Gollnick, P. D., Tipton, C. M., and Karpovich, P. V. (1964). *Res. Quart.* **35**, 370–378.
52. Gombac, R. (1968). *In* "Biomechanics I" (J. Wartenweiler *et al.*, eds.), pp. 37–41. Karger, Basel.
53. Gray, E. G., and Basmajian, J. V. (1968). *Anat. Record* **161**, 1–16.

54. Groh, H., and Baumann, W. (1968). *In* "Biomechanics I" (J. Wartenweiler *et al.*, eds.), pp. 23–32. Karger, Basel.

55. Guld, C., Rosenfalck, A., and Willison, R. G. (1970). *Electroenceph. Clin. Neurophysiol.* **28**, 399–413.

56. Gutewort, W. (1968). *In* "Biomechanics I" (J. Wartenweiler *et al.*, eds.), pp. 53–60. Karger, Basel.

57. Gutewort, W. (1971). *In* "Biomechanics II" (J. Vredenbregt and J. Wartenweiler, eds.), pp. 290–298. Karger, Basel.

58. Hagan, W. K. (1963). *Amer. J. Med. Electron.* April June, 147–151.

59. Hall, E. A. (1970). *Phys. Therapy* **50**, 651–659.

60. Hay, J. G. (1967). *Res. Quart.* **38**, 34–40.

61. Hebbelinck, M., and Borms, J. (1968). *In* "Biomechanics I" (J. Wartenweiler *et al.*, eds.), pp. 324–326. Karger, Basel.

62. Hoffman, S. J., and Worsham, K. (1971). *Kinesiology Review* pp. 55–59, AAHPER, Washington, D. C.

63. Hopper, B. J., and Kane, J. E. (1968). *In* "Biomechanics I" (J. Wartenweiler *et al.*, eds.), pp. 42–44. Karger, Basel.

64. Hubbard, A. W. (1957). *In* "Research Methods in Health, Physical Education and Recreation" (M. B. Scott, ed.), AAHPER, Washington, D. C.

65. Johnston, R. D., and Smidt, G. L. (1969). *J. Bone Joint Surg.* **51**, 1083–1094.

66. Jones, F. P., and O'Connell, D. N. (1958). *J. Psychol.* **45**, 237–251.

67. Jones, F. P., and O'Connell, D. (1958). *Science* **127**, 1119.

68. Jonsson, B. (1971). *In* "Biomechanics II" (J. Vredenbregt and J. Wartenweiler, eds.), Karger, Basel.

69. Jonsson, B. (1968). *In* "Biomechanics I" (J. Wartenweiler *et al.*, eds.), pp. 123–127.

70. Jonsson, B., and Rundgren, A. (1971). *Electromyography* **1**, 93–103.

71. Kamon, E. (1966). *J. Sports Med. Phys. Fitness* **6**, 223–234.

72. Karpovich, P. V., Herden, E. L., and Asa, M. M. (1960). *U. S. Armed Forces Med. J.* **11**, 424–450.

73. Karpovich, P. V., and Karpovich, G. P. (1959). *Fed. Proc.* **18**. p. 79.

74. Karpovich, P. V., and Wilklow, L. B. (1959). *U. S. Armed Forces Med. J.* **10**, 885–903.

75. Ketlinski, R. (1971). *In* "Selected Topics on Biomechanics" pp. 59–62. Athletic Inst., Chicago, Illinois.

76. Kettelkamp, D. B., Johnson, R. J., Smidt, G. L., Chao, E. Y. S., and Walker, M. (1970). *J. Bone Joint Surg.* **52**, 775–790.

77. Kinzel, G., and Hillberry, B. M. (1971). *In* "Selected Topics on Biomechanics," pp. 223–232. Athletic Inst., Chicago, Illinois.

78. Kitzman, E. W. (1964). *Res. Quart.* **35**, 166–178.

79. Klissouras, V., and Karpovich, P. V. (1967). *Res. Quart.* **38**, 41–48.

80. Komi, P. V., and Buskirk, E. R. (1970). *Electromyography* **4**, 357–365.

81. Koniar, M. (1968). *In* "Biomechanics I" (J. Wartenweiler *et al.*, eds.), pp. 61–66. Karger, Basel.

82. Kreighbaum, E., and Adrian, M. (1971). *3rd Int. Seminar Biomech., Rome.*

83. Kuroda, E. V., and Milsum, J. H. (1970). *J. Appl. Physiol.* **29**, 358–367.

84. Lamaster, M. A., and Mortimer, E. M. (1964). Paper presented at AAHPER Convention, Washington D. C., 1964.

85. Levens, A. S., Inman, V. T., and Blosser, J. A. (1948). *J. Bone Joint Surg.* **30**, 859–874.

86. Lewillie, L. (1971). *In* "Biomechanics II" (J. Vredenbregt and J. Wartenweiler, eds.), pp. 253–259. Karger, Basel.
87. Lewillie, L. (1970). *Proc. 1st Int. Symp. Biomech. Swimming, Waterpolo Diving* pp. 155–159.
88. Lloyd, A. J. (1971). *J. Appl. Physiol.* pp. 713–719.
89. Long, C., II, Conrad, P. W., Hall, E. A., and Furler, S. L. (1970). *J. Bone Joint Surg.* 52, 853–867.
90. Marks, M., and Hirschberg, G. G. (1958). *Ann. N. Y. Acad. Sci.* 74, 59–77.
91. Moore, M. L., Farrand, S., and Thornton, W. (1963). *J. Amer. Phys. Therapy Ass.* 43, 787.
92. Murray, M. P., and Clarkson, B. H. (1966). *J. Amer. Phys. Therapy* 46, 585–589.
93. Murray, M. P., and Clarkson, B. H. (1966). *J. Amer. Phys. Therapy* 46, 590–600.
94. Murray, M. P., Drought, A. B., and Kory, R. C. (1964). *J. Bone Joint Surg.* 46, 335–360.
95. Murray, M. P., Seireg, A., and Scholz, R. C. (1967). *J. Appl. Physiol.* 23, 831–838.
96. Nelson, R. C., Petak, K. L., and Pechar, G. S. (1969). *Res. Quart.* 40, 424–426.
97. Nilsson, N. R., and Hogberg, L. (eds.) (1968). "High-Speed Photography." Wiley, New York.
98. Noble, M. L., and Kelley, D. L. (1969). *Res. Quart.* 40, 643–645.
99. O'Connell, A. L. (1968). *In* "Biomechanics I" (J. Wartenweiler *et al.*, ed.), pp. 128–131. Karger, Basel.
100. O'Connell, A. L., and Gardner, E. B. (1963). *Res. Quart.* 34, 166–184.
101. Oglesby, B. F. (1969). Thesis, Washington State Univ.
102. Olson, J. K., and Waterland, J. C. (1967). *Percept. Motor Skills* 24, 339–349.
103. Pearson, R. B. (1964). "Handbook on Clinical Electromyography." Meditron, El Monte, California.
104. Petak, K. L. (1971). *In* "Selected Topics on Biomechanics," pp. 201–206. Athletic Inst., Chicago, Illinois.
105. Pinelli, P., Buchthal, F., and Thiebaut, F. (eds.) (1961). "Progress in Electromyography." Elsevier, Amsterdam.
106. Plagenhoef, S. C. (1968). *J. Biomech.* 1, 221–234.
107. Prior, T., and Cooper, J. M. (1968). *Res. Quart.* 39, 815–817.
108. Reed, W. S., and Garrett, R. E. (1971). *Kinesiology Review* pp. 60–65, AAHPER Washington, D. C.
109. Ringer, L. B., and Adrian, M. J. (1969). Abstracts of Research Papers, AAHPER Convention.
110. Roberts, E. (1971). *In* "Selected Topics on Biomechanics," pp. 41–50. Athletic Inst., Chicago, Illinois.
111. Sato, M., and Tsuruma, S. (1967). *Annu. Rep. Phys. Educ.* 1, 7–28.
112. Scolnick, A. (1966). Doctoral dissertation, Springfield College, Springfield, Massachusetts.
113. Scott, R. N. (1967). *Med. Biol. Eng.* 5, 303–305.
114. Shvartz, E. (1967). *Res. Quart.* 38, 300–304.
115. Simard, T. G. (1971). *Electromyography* 1, 83–91.
116. Simard, T. G., and Basmajian, J. V. (1967). *Arch. Phys. Med. Rehabil.* 48, 12–19.
117. Singh, M., and Ashton, T. E. J. (1970). *Res. Quart.* 41, 562–568.
118. Sinning, W. E., and Forsyth, H. L. (1970). *Med. Sci. Sports* 2, 28–34.
119. Slater-Hammel, A. T. (1949). *Res. Quart.* 20, 95–104.
120. Steben, R. E. (1970). *Res. Quart.* 41, 95–104.

121. Taylor, B. M., Tipton, C. M., Adrian, M. J., and Karpovich, P. V. (1966). *Amer. J. Vet. Res.* **27**, 85–89.
122. Taylor, P. R. (1971). *In* "Selected Topics on Biomechanics" (J. M. Cooper, ed.), pp. 51–58. Athletic Inst., Chicago, Illinois.
123. Thomas, D. H., and Long, C., II (1964). *Amer. J. Med. Electron.* pp. 96–100.
124. Tipton, C. M., and Karpovich, P. V. (1964). *J. Ass. Phys. Mental Rehabil.* **18**, 90–94, 108.
125. Tipton, C. M., and Karpovich, P. V. (1965). *Arch. Phys. Med.* pp. 267–272.
126. Walton, J. S. (1970). *Res. Quart.* **41**, 213–216.
127. Walton, J. S. (1970). Unpublished Master's Thesis, Michigan State Univ., East Lansing, Michigan.
128. Waterland, J. C. (1967). *Quest May* pp. 15–25.
129. Waterland, J. C., and Shambes, G. M. (1969). *Phys. Therapy, J. Amer. Phys. Therapy Ass.* **49**, 1351–1356.
130. Widule, C. J., and Gossard, D. C. (1971). *Res. Quart.* **42**, 103–111.
131. Wolter, C. (1965). MS Thesis, Univ. of Wisconsin, Madison, Wisconsin.
132. Young, J., and Naylor, W. S. (1964). *Amer. J. Med. Electron.* Jan–March, pp. 28–33.
133. Zuniga, E. N., Truong, X. T., and Simons, D. G. (1971). *Arch. Phys. Med. Rehabil.* **51**, 264–272.

Sampling Theory and Procedures

Robert W. Schutz

SCHOOL OF PHYSICAL EDUCATION AND RECREATION,
THE UNIVERSITY OF BRITISH COLUMBIA, VANCOUVER, CANADA

I. Introduction

"Sampling is the science that guides quantitative studies of content, behavior, performance, materials, and causes of differences" (*20*, p. 23)

The process of sampling as defined by Deming in the above quotation is instrumental, absolutely necessary in fact, in any type of scientific investigative procedure. Its importance as a major tool in all types of research has been acknowledged for a long time, as shown in some of the early texts on statistics (*6,80*) and statistical meetings (*38*). However, it was not until the 1930s, with the publication of two statistical works of classical status, that sampling theory gained acceptance as a mathematically sound method in quantitative analysis. Jerzy Neyman's 1934 paper (*57*), considered to be a landmark in the development of modern sampling theory and practice, marked the beginning of the probability sampling era. Neyman placed sample surveys within the realm of random experiments and presented the first formal discussion on stratification and optimization in sampling designs. His introduction of the Gauss–Markov Theorem to sampling in order to obtain unbiased, minimum variance estimators, initiated considerable further research by mathematical statisticians in the area of estimation. Sir Ronald Fisher, whose classical works have strongly influenced all areas of applied and theoretical statistics, gave credence to the process of randomization in his 1937 text (*28*). He showed that only by random selection and assignment could the methods of statistical inference be applied in an experimental situation.

The purpose of this review is to present a broad overview of the current knowledge about sampling procedures, both theoretical and practical, as developed since the publication of Neyman's and Fisher's original works. Only very minor emphasis will be placed on procedures derived from Bayesian theory and cost functions, as these methods have their greatest utility in the fields of business, economics, and engineering. Sampling theory relative to Bayesian theory can be found in the works of Ericson (*25*), Solomon and Zacks (*69*), and Zacks (*81*), and comprehensive explanations of the role of cost functions in sampling are given in many sample survey texts (*11,19,20,35*).

II. Sampling Theory

A. Sampling and Statistical Inference

The basic relationship between statistical inference and sampling is obvious, for statistical inference implies the drawing of inferences from a sample to the population which it represents. *Random* sampling, when performed according to certain specified procedures, permits the use of statistical probability theory in drawing inferences regarding some attribute in a designated population. Without randomization *statistical* inference is invalid and any inferences made must be done so on the basis of logic, not probability. However, although the use of randomization ensures external validity in that the results can be generalized to the defined population from which the sample was drawn, it is not a sufficient condition for ecological validity. This latter type of validity pertains to the generalizability of experimental results from the highly controlled artificial laboratory condition to the practical, natural field situation (*54*). It would be interesting to know how many assumptions have been made regarding the U. S. population in general from statistical probability theory used on a *volunteer* sample of *college freshmen* tested under *laboratory conditions.*

The explicit formulas for the expected value of a statistic and, equally important, for its sampling variation, were derived under the assumption of randomization. Most investigators, although aware of this assumption, find it almost impossible to use truly random samples and thus resort to partially random or even "convenient" samples. Recent restrictions imposed by university administrations and government granting agencies regarding the use of human subjects have added to this difficulty. The problem facing the investigator then is one of degree—to what extent is statistical inference valid under varying levels of nonrandomization?

The basic assumption of random sampling, as given in virtually every text and paper on sampling, is that each unit (subject) in the population has an equal probability of being selected in the sample on each draw. This implies an infinite population, or else sampling with replacement after each draw. Under these assumptions the sample mean $\bar{X}$ is an unbiased estimator of μ, the population mean, and the sample distribution of $\bar{X}$ is normal with a standard deviation of

$$\text{S.E.} = S/\sqrt{n}, \qquad (1)$$

where S.E. is the standard error of the mean, S is the unbiased sample standard deviation, and n is the sample size. This standard error can then be used to establish confidence limits in order to provide a quantitative indicator of the accuracy of $\bar{X}$ as an estimator of μ.[1] Under certain violations of this sampling procedure, statistical inference is still valid, but it requires modifications, usually in Eq. (1). Many articles and texts (*11, 19,20,29,35,46,47,61,62,72*) give the modifications necessary under variations in the sampling design. These modifications are discussed in Section III of this article, in conjunction with the sampling procedures of these designs. A number of articles have been published on special aspects of nonrandomization and are discussed below.

---

[1] It should be noted that statistical inference permits one to make a rigorous statement regarding the probability of obtaining a statistic as large as the *sample* statistic obtained (under a specified null hypotheses), but it provides no basis whatsoever for making a probability statement regarding a true population value.

Burstein (*8*) has shown that although the normal distribution is often utilized when making inferences about a proportion (*p*), this is valid only when the population is infinite, *n* is large, and *p* is not near 0.0 or 1.0. The correct distribution, the binomial, is seldom used because of the laborious work required and/or the unreliable process of interpolating the binomial tables. The hypergeometric distribution, which is the correct one when the population is finite and for all values of *p*, is comprehensively tabled by Burstein.

Misuse of the traditional statistical procedures is the criticism of Simmons and Bean who state that ". . . much classical analysis is inappropriate when applied to data from complex surveys . . ." (*67*, p. 603). The authors determine the reduction in sampling variation due to various estimation procedures and show that the actual increase in variability due to clustering and stratification is far more than is usually assumed.

Edgington (*24*) claims that even when subjects are randomly selected the population defined is usually so specific that it is of limited value. The only statistical inference which is valid in this case then concerns the effects of different treatments on these particular subjects (providing the subjects were randomly assigned to treatments). Thus the inference being made, namely that the difference between two groups is not randomization error, is based on the probability that most top performers are in one treatment group. Edgington shows that the usual parametric tests are not appropriate in this case, and that nonparametric "randomization tests" (a combinatorial type procedure) are capable of providing exact probability statements.

B. Error Variance

The degree to which a sample statistic deviates from the parameter it estimates is a function of both sampling error (statistical error) and nonsampling error (nonstatistical error). Although the term "nonsampling" may seem to imply that discussion of this topic is irrelevant in an article on sampling theory, it is necessary to include this factor, since its components are often blamed for contributing to the sampling variance of an estimator. Hansen and Tepping (*36*) express the error variance of a statistic (the mean) as

$$E(\bar{X} - \mu)^2 = \sigma_{\bar{x}}^2 + \sigma_e^2 + \sigma_{\bar{x}}\sigma_e + \sigma_b^2, \qquad (2)$$

where $\sigma_{\bar{x}}^2$ is the sampling variance, σ_e^2 is the nonsampling error variance, $\sigma_{\bar{x}}\sigma_e$ is the covariance of sampling and nonsampling errors, and σ_b^2 is the bias. The covariance term is usually very small and consequently presumed to be zero. The bias term, which is often quite large, is difficult to estimate and usually is a result of measurement errors. The two sources of error relevant to this review, statistical and nonstatistical errors, are discussed below.

1. Sampling Variance

The sampling variance of a statistic, which is a direct reflection of the extent to which the sample fails to represent the population, is quantitatively represented by the error variance or the standard error as given in Eq. (1). In a complete census or experiment involving the total population of interest, this term is obviously zero. When sampling from a finite population the formula of Eq. (1) overestimates the true sampling variance, thus necessitating the following correction:

$$\text{S.E.} = (1 - n/N)^{1/2}(S/\sqrt{n}), \tag{3}$$

when N is the size of the population. As N becomes large (in the thousands) the effect of this correction factor becomes negligible in most experimental situations. In sample surveys however, when the size of the sample may be proportionately large, failure to use Eq. (3) may result in a considerable overestimation of the error variance. Further adjustments to Eq. (1), which are required with variations in the sampling design, are given in Section III in conjunction with the discussion of these designs.

A procedure for reducing sampling error resulting from extreme scores or "wild shots" has been suggested by Tukey (74). The sample is "trimmed" by removing equal numbers of the lowest and highest observations and treating the remaining data as a simple random sample. This procedure will certainly correct for any overestimation of the error estimate, but it can also cause gross underestimation when carried to the extreme. Unfortunately Tukey offers no rules for determining the cut-off point between a "wild shot" and an expected extreme score. Another adjustment procedure of this type is "Winsorizing," in which an extreme score is corrected by replacing it with the value of the nearest score "not seriously suspect" (74). However, like the trimming method, this procedure is based on logical decisions and thus should be done only by investigators who are thoroughly familiar with the type and distribution of data in the population being sampled.

It is generally agreed that the theory of sampling errors has been well researched; the important problems have been identified and solved, techniques for attacking new problems have been established, and the presently available knowledge in the area of sample designs and sampling procedures is such that only minor error should result from sampling (36,71,76). However, the state of the theory of nonsampling errors has not progressed nearly as well as the more mathematical theory of statistical error, and researchers are now turning their efforts in this direction.

2. Nonsampling Errors

Methods for minimizing various types of nonsampling errors are discussed in most sampling texts and also in a number of papers (*5,22,36,60, 71,76*). Following is a list of the most common types of errors (which are related to sampling), as indicated by a summary of these publications.

a. Inaccurately Defined Population. This may result from the population not being enumerated and thus making true random sampling impossible, or from failure to set precise physical boundaries on the area being sampled. The results of this error are biased estimates of means, variances, and strata sizes.

b. Incorrect Use of Random Numbers. Subjective randomization by an experimenter is not a guarantee of randomness—only intelligent use of tables of random numbers can provide this, and, unfortunately, even some tables of random numbers may have a systematic bias in them (*71*). Subjective randomization can be a very appealing method due to its inherent convenience. For example, adjusting the laboratory to 60°F for testing in the morning and then raising it to 75°F for the afternoon testing requires a minimum amount of change and adjustment time. However, using subjects who are available in the morning for the 60°F condition and those who are available only in the afternoon for the 75°F condition is a serious violation of randomization. There are many factors which relate to and/or cause the time availability of subjects, some of which may be related to the experimental variables (e.g., team athletes may not be available in the late afternoon).

c. Measurement Errors. Although not actually related to sampling, this factor is included, as careless, invalid, and unreliable measurement procedures in both experiments and in surveys are often the major source of nonsampling error variance.

d. Failure to Account for the Dynamic Nature of the Universe. This error is most relevant to studies in the behavioral sciences in which the environment is constantly changing. Social customs change, attitudes are altered, individuals change in age, fitness, and skill, etc. Any inferences to a population then must be made to the population as it existed at the time of measurement, not at the time of publication of the findings a few years later.

e. Missing Data. The presence of attrition, nonresponses, and refusals will seriously affect the population to which inferences can be made. The numerous methods which have been suggested for dealing with this common problem are discussed in Section III,C.

Although many of the nonsampling errors listed above can be minimized by paying attention to careful research procedures, it is not possible to eliminate them all—nor is it possible to get a statistical estimate of the error variance due to them. The method of interpenetrating replicate subsamples, consisting of drawing two or more independent samples and processing them independently, can be used to provide a check on nonsampling errors (10,60).

C. SAMPLE SIZE

The determination of the size of a sample, although only one aspect of the total concept of sampling theory, has received so much attention by investigators that it warrants a section devoted solely to its discussion. With the present emphasis being placed by authors and editors on statistical significance, the sample size is indeed a very important factor. However, it must be recognized that although the remainder of this section deals with the statistical aspects of sample size, this should not be construed as implying that meeting the requirements of power and type I error guarantee that the sample is a truly representative one. Well-planned sampling designs as presented in Section III are necessary to meet this criterion.

1. Practical versus Statistical Significance

In recent years tests of significance, when used as decision making tools in scientific research, have come under more than the usual amount of criticism (30,31,48,56,68,79). The primary objections to the use of such tests are: (1) that researchers make indiscriminate use of these tests without due regard to their appropriateness under the specific design and sampling procedures utilized, and (2) that the conclusions and research decisions made are often based solely on the results of the statistical test applied. This second criticism, which is basically a condemnation of the practice of using statistical significance to claim practical or substantive significance, can be eliminated by utilizing the statistical theory of sample size determination.

One must admit that the latter criticism is a justifiable one and can be directed to researchers in the area of sport and physical activity as well as numerous other areas of study. A brief survey of the October and December 1971 issues of *Research Quarterly*, in which 16 of the 18 studies using significance tests reported statistically significant results, indicates the strong emphasis researchers and editors place on attaining a probability value below the traditional 0.05 level. It is highly unlikely that 89% of all research conducted yields significant findings, nor that those which do report statistical significance are superior when judged on the basis of theoretical rationale, experimental design, and interpretation of results. It appears that many studies are deemed valuable primarily on the basis of the level of significance attained. This may be a suitable criterion (one of a number of criteria) for judging the value of a research study if in fact statistical significance reflects practical significance. If this is the case then the statistical test is a useful and powerful tool in making a research decision. A suggested solution to the problem of the indiscriminate use of significance tests has been to put less emphasis on the results of these tests and more on the use of abstract concepts and deductive theories (*56*).

Although a statistically significant result is not necessarily scientifically significant, it is possible to exercise control over the probability of rejecting a null hypothesis so that a meaningful decision can be made on the basis of the outcome of the significance test. It has been shown that the appropriate selection of both sample size and the probability of a type I error can assist a researcher in designing a statistical test in which a statistically significant result will, with a high degree of probability, reflect a practically significant result (*12,13,32,44,49,64*). Consequently, careful determination of sample size is a primary requisite for scientific research.

2. Determination of Sample Size

The well worn adage, "The larger the n, the better," is gradually coming into disfavor, on both practical and statistical grounds. It has been pointed out many times, especially in the field of sample surveys (*10,19,20,35,72*), that a small, carefully planned sample will provide more accurate results than a very large sample or even a complete census. This is primarily due to the greater feasibility of using only highly trained personnel and high quality measuring instruments with a small sample. On statistical grounds, too large a sample can destroy the delicate balance between statistical and practical significance.

a. Differences among Means. In applying a test of significance to research findings there are a number of factors influencing the outcome of this test. These are (1) the level of significance (α), (2) the sample size (n), (3) the error variance (σ_e^2) as estimated by the within-cell sample variability, and (4) the true magnitude of the difference in the population (Δ), referred to as the "non-nullity" (44,64) or the "effect size" (12,13), and related to σ_e^2 as in Eq. (4).

$$\Delta = (\Delta_1 - \Delta_2)/\sigma_e. \tag{4}$$

Two other parameters commonly associated with hypotheses tests, beta (β), the probability of committing a type II error, and power (P), the probability of rejecting the null hypothesis when it is false ($P = 1.0 - \beta$), are completely dependent on these four factors. Two special values of Δ which are of importance in determining sample size are Δ_1, the trivial non-nullity, which reflects the largest value of Δ the researcher considers too small to be important, and Δ_2, the important non-nullity, which reflects the smallest value of Δ the researcher considers to be practically meaningful. What is required is a sample size which will give a suitably high power at Δ_2 and, at the same time, provide a suitably low power at Δ_1. Since the error mean square tends to increase less rapidly than the between mean square when the sample size is increased, one increases the likelihood of obtaining statistical significance by increasing the sample size. This increased likelihood is a direct result of the inverse relationship between the variance ratio test statistic (F) and the estimate σ_e^2; thus the smaller the estimate, the larger the value of F.

Most investigators then, bound by tradition to an α level of 0.05 or 0.01 and a null hypothesis which states that two means are exactly the same (H_0: $\mu_1 - \mu_2 = 0$), are using a test of significance which is a function of both the true difference and the sampling procedures utilized. This is perfectly acceptable if the sampling procedures are adequate, but can be disastrous if they are not. If one draws the sample randomly from a defined population but does not consider the consequences of an incorrect choice of sample size, either of two undesirable situations may result. In the first case, the sample size may be too small and the power of the test is low for all but very large non-nullities. Although the researcher has results which are large enough to be practically significant, the statistical test outcome leads to an incorrect conclusion, namely that the hypothesized effect does not exist in the population. In the second situation, the sample size may be too large and the power of the test (for a set α of 0.05, say) is very high even for trivially small differences. This may result in small differences which are not considered practically significant showing up as statistically significant.

Numerous procedures have been suggested for determining the appropriate sample size. The most common one, found in many statistical texts, is based on confidence intervals with a specified power and α

level for a specific Δ_2 value. Such methods provide adequate approximations for n, but they fail to account for a Δ_1 level and thus do not protect against the possibility of statistical significance being claimed for
a difference which is not practically significant (*44,64*). Furthermore,
the assumption of a normal distribution when utilizing this procedure
is appropriate only for two means and for large n. The correct distribution on which to base calculations involving rejection of the null
hypothesis, such as power functions, is the noncentral F distribution
(*26,44,64*). Power function charts, such as those developed by Feldt
and Mahmoud (*26*), are based on the noncentral F and may be used
for ANOVA designs, but fail to incorporate the concept of trivial non-
nullity into the calculations. Still other procedures vary slightly but
have the same basic weaknesses (*12,13,49,58*). A rather different approach is taken by Friedman (*30*), who proposes a *post hoc* type of
power determination which estimates the magnitude of an experimental
effect based on the sample size used.

A procedure developed by Kroeker and Walster (*44*) eliminates the
above disadvantages by allowing the researcher to specify *both* the coordinates (Δ_1, P_1) and (Δ_2, P_2) and then solve for α and n simultaneously. The coordinate (Δ_i, P_i) describes the power (P_i) desired for
detecting a difference as small as Δ_i. Thus, by rationally choosing his
sample size, the researcher can be fairly confident that if a substantial
difference between the populations of interest does exist it will be
detected, and if a trivial difference exists the null hypothesis will not
be rejected. The methodology for using this technique, with examples
and reference to the necessary computer programs, has been given by
Schutz (*64*).

A few special situations warrant mention in this rather general discussion of sample size. It has been assumed in the above comments
that the sample size is always a constant, independent of the data or
experimental procedures once they are initiated. However, occasionally
n becomes a random variable due to dropouts, nonresponses, or through
the use of a sequential sampling procedure. Durbin (*23*) provides suggestions for treating data based on a random n resulting from experimental procedures, and Anscombe (*3*) considers both fixed and random
sample size in sequential sampling. Another situation requiring special
treatment concerns the adjustments necessary when dealing with small
samples. As rather small samples are frequently encountered in experimental studies, especially in the area of exercise physiology, this topic
is treated separately in Section IV,B. The extreme case of small samples,
the single-subject study, is recognized as an acceptable procedure in a
case study situation (see Section III,G), but is rarely approved of in
an experimental study. An opposite point of view is taken by Shine and

Bower (66), who cite a number of researchers advocating the use of precisely controlled single-subject experiments as "the most fruitful experimental approach." Although most single-subject studies use only descriptive statistics, Shine and Bower attempt to show how a two-way ANOVA (trials by conditions) can be applicable in certain situations. A technique is proposed to overcome the lack of a suitable error term due to the trials factor being a fixed variable rather than random as in the typical subject by conditions design. Dukes (22) provides further support for the "$n = 1$" case by citing numerous single-subject studies which were instrumental in advancing psychological theory. Despite these two publications supporting single-subject experiments, such procedures should be considered only as a last resort and any inferences or generalizations to a larger population of subjects must be made on a logical, and not statistical, basis.

b. Estimating Other Statistics. Although the large majority of surveys and experiments are primarily concerned with making inferences regarding some estimate of central tendency, in certain situations it is desirable to examine the data with other statistics. In these cases, methods for the determination of sample size must be adjusted accordingly. Thompson and Endriss (73) provide equations and tables for computing the sample size required to estimate standard deviations within certain limits of accuracy. The same topic is treated in greater depth by Graybill and Morrison (32), who also provide a more complete set of tables for selecting the most appropriate sample size. McHugh (51) describes the use of Fisher's z transformation to obtain a value of the sample size required to estimate a validity coefficient with a set precision and α level. The procedure could of course be applied to any correlation coefficient estimation problem, and could easily be adapted to a multiple correlation situation by making the necessary adjustment in the formula for the standard deviation of z. One other statistic which occasionally requires estimation is p, the proportion in a binomial population. Methods for calculating the required sample size for a specified α level and degree of accuracy are available in both mathematical and tabular form (43,56a).

III. Sampling Designs

There are two general components to a sampling design: (1) a selection process describing the rules and operations which determine the members of the population to be included in the sample, and (2) an estimation process for computing the sample statistics and their associated error variance which estimate the population parameters (41).

Each of the sampling plans described below is analyzed according to these two components, and evaluated in terms of its advantages and disadvantages relative to other plans.

A. SIMPLE RANDOM SAMPLING

1. Selection Procedures

Simple random sampling, or probability sampling as it is sometimes called, implies that all elements in the population have equal chances of being selected and the probability of selecting an element is constant at any draw (*71*). The most commonly used technique is to define and enumerate the whole population and then select the sample with the aid of a table of random numbers. Theoretically, each unit selected should be returned to the population and if it is drawn again it is treated as a new unit. However, in most experimental studies this is not advisable due to the contamination of the subject by the testing procedure. Once tested, it is unlikely that a subject is representative of the population originally defined.

Frequently there are no natural boundaries for defining the units (such as classrooms, cities, academic departments) or it is not possible to enumerate the total population. Procedures for dealing with these two problems can be found in articles by Jacobs (*37*) and Turk and Smith (*75*), respectively.

2. Estimation Procedures

Simple random sampling provides unbiased estimates of means and variances, with the degree of error being expressed by the standard error of the mean according to Eq. (1).

3. Advantages and Disadvantages

The primary advantage of simple random sampling is that in comparison to nonrandom samples it provides unbiased estimates and permits statistical inferences to be made to the population. The process of enumerating the total population and then using random numbers for selecting is an advantage in that it is conceptually simple but it is also a major disadvantage in that it can be extremely laborious.

B. STRATIFIED SAMPLING

1. Selection Procedures

In many instances the dependent variable of interest (x) may be related to some concomitant variable (y) for which information is readily available. The population can then be partitioned into sections or strata on the basis of the y values, and a simple random sampling plan used within each stratum. An alternate procedure of using previously established or natural strata is equally satisfactory providing the natural boundaries provide strata which are related to x. That is, the variability of x within each stratum should be less than the total population variance of x. The size of the sample drawn from each stratum (n_i) is usually proportional to the size of the stratum (N_i). Consequently, if a sample of size n was required from a population of size N, then the number of elements from stratum i would be

$$n_i = n(N_i/N). \tag{5}$$

As stratification is almost an automatic procedure in any type of survey, detailed descriptions of the many various forms of stratified sampling are presented in most sampling texts.

Deming (20) suggests that when measures on y are not available it is possible to use stratification after selection by using the sample data to estimate proportions for stratification. However, he claims it is better to draw a fairly large random sample first, obtain estimates of y, form strata, and then subsample from the larger sample. This procedure, introduced by Neyman (57), is termed double sampling.

2. Estimation Procedures

If unbiased estimates of the mean $(\bar{X}_i)$ and variance (S_i^2) are calculated for each stratum separately then the population mean and variance can be estimated by weighting in proportion to stratum size $(11,19,35,62)$.

$$\bar{X} = \Sigma(n_i/n)\bar{X}_i, \tag{6}$$
$$S^2 = \Sigma(n_i/n)^2 S_i^2. \tag{7}$$

Both these estimates are unbiased and thus allow for accurate confidence interval estimation based on the following standard error formula:

$$S_{\bar{x}}^2 = (1/n)(S^2 - S_{\bar{x}_i}^2), \tag{8}$$

where $S_{\bar{x}_i}^2$ is the variance of the $\bar{X}_i$ about $\bar{X}$ (53). When the stratification is based on some variable y on which measures can also be obtained, then

$$S_{\bar{x}}^2 = (1/n)(S^2 - S^2 r_{xy}^2), \tag{9}$$

which clearly shows that the increased precision due to stratification is related to the linear relationship between x and y (as r_{xy} approaches

1.0, $S_{\bar{x}}^2$ approaches zero, and as r_{xy} converges to zero, $S_{\bar{x}}^2$ is equal to the error variance obtained in a simple random sample).

3. Advantages and Disadvantages

The major advantage of stratification is that it provides a more precise estimate of the population mean (a smaller standard error) than could be obtained with a completely random sample of the same total size. It has been shown that the error variance can be reduced by stratification even with a sample size half that of a simple random sample (*16*). Stratification has the additional advantage that the strata can be chosen to cover important areas or classifications which are of importance by themselves (smokers, nonsmokers, age levels, etc.). The disadvantages, which are minimal compared to the advantages, are the additional labor required to identify the strata and make the adjustments in the statistical analyses, and the loss in precision in estimating the variance when the strata sample sizes are small (*62*).

C. CLUSTER SAMPLING

1. Selection Procedures

In many populations of interest it is not practically possible to list all the individual elements, and thus random selection of a single unit is not feasible. Consequently, groups of elements, labeled and enumerated in the population, are used as sampling units. This process, referred to as "cluster sampling," or "area sampling" when the clusters are geographical areas (*55*), should be conducted in precisely the same manner as that for simple random sampling, i.e., enumerate all the clusters in the population, select a certain number (determined *a priori* on statistical grounds) with the aid of random number tables, and then treat each cluster as a single sampling unit. Although all units in the population are usually given equal probabilities of being drawn, occasionally it is desirable to sample with "probability proportional to size" (*34,35,39,62,71*). This procedure is particularly important when the clusters are of varying sizes (e.g., classes) and stratification procedures cannot account for this variability. The term is self-explanatory in that one unit twice the size of another has twice the probability of being included in the sample.

The technique of cluster sampling has been used extensively in educational research due to the availability of convenient clusters in the form of classes and schools. However in many studies the researchers have utilized all the units in the cluster—a procedure which, depending on the homogeneity within clusters, may result in a considerable loss of efficiency as compared to simple random sampling (71). Butcher (9) has shown that a sample of a very few large intact schools may result in an error variance as much as 100 times larger than in a simple random sample of the same size. The determination of the optimum size and number of clusters is a rather involved process (11,35,62,63) and should not be done on the basis of convenience. In general, for a set number of units, greater precision can be attained by distributing the units over a large number of clusters than by selecting a few clusters and sampling all units in them.

2. Estimation Procedures

If the clusters are chosen with equal probabilities, but are of different size, then serious biases can result in estimating μ and σ^2 unless these factors are taken into account. An unbiased estimate of μ, which requires knowledge of the average cluster size in the *population* ($\bar{N}$), can be calculated as follows (62,63):

$$\bar{X} = \sum \frac{n_i \bar{X}_i}{k\bar{N}}, \tag{9}$$

where k is the number of clusters sampled. Using $\bar{n}$ instead of $\bar{N}$, where $\bar{n}$ is the average cluster size in the *sample*, the statistic $\bar{X}$ will be slightly biased when the number of clusters sampled is small. An unbiased estimate of the error variance is provided by the formula

$$S_{\bar{x}}^2 = S^2/k, \tag{10}$$

where S^2 is the variance of the cluster means about the grand mean. When necessary, the finite population correction factor must be applied (see Section II,A); however, for the error variance term, which is based on k observations, the correction term is $1 - (k/K)$, where K is the number of clusters in the population.

In general, if the clusters are drawn with equal probability, all estimates of μ and σ^2 will be biased to the extent that the clusters are of unequal size. If enumeration of the total population is possible and clusters can be sampled with probability proportional to size, unbiased estimates of μ and σ^2 are available.

3. Advantages and Disadvantages

The primary advantage of cluster sampling is its efficiency in terms of the time and effort required to test a certain number of individuals or objects. The disadvantages are its lack of precision (57), the possibility of obtaining biased estimators (*62,63*), and the difficulty in attaining independence among the units (*9*).

D. Systematic Sampling

1. Selection Procedures

In systematic sampling it is necessary to have a complete enumeration, or listing, of the population. The first unit is randomly chosen from among the first *n* elements and then every *n*th element after that is sampled. The size of *n* depends on the required sample size and the size of the population. It is a useful procedure for sampling from an electorate list, telephone book, or student directory.

2. Estimation Procedures

In situations where the listing of the population is virtually random, such as an alphabetical ordering, systematic sampling may be considered equivalent to simple random sampling (*71*). Estimation procedures then follow those for the simple random design as given in Section III,A. In other situations such as population lists, which have a certain order in space and time, the data may exhibit linear trends or periodic fluctuations (*16*). In these cases the precision depends on the nature of the log correlations and may be more or less precise than simple random sampling.

3. Advantages and Disadvantages

As in many designs, the major advantage of this procedure is its convenience and ease of administration. Furthermore, Sampford claims that the mean of a systematic sample provides a more precise estimate of μ than does a simple random sample of the same size (*63*). The primary disadvantage of this sampling procedure is that variance estimates are impossible without knowledge of the properties of the population. Also, it has been shown that systematic sampling is less accurate than stratified sampling when dealing with a linear trend (*35*).

E. Multi-Stage Sampling

Multi-stage sampling, although frequently dealt with as one of the basic sampling designs, may be regarded as a generalized master plan, with stratified, cluster, and systematic methods all being considered special cases (*62*). In all these methods, some type of initial selection is performed as the first stage (selection of strata, clusters, or a random integer between 1 and *n*), and then a more detailed sampling plan, often simple random sampling, is performed on the strata or clusters as the second stage. Because multi-stage sampling is not a unique method it is discussed here in generalities only, with no reference to estimation procedures.

Two basic methods are utilized in multi-stage sampling: (1) sampling with probability proportional to size at the first stage, and (2) sampling with probability proportional size at the second or third stage (10). An example of the first method is the random selection of classes within proportionally selected schools. When all schools are listed and the number of classes in each school is noted, a certain number of schools are then randomly selected with probability proportional to the number of classes followed by random selection of students within classes. The process could be taken one step further by proportional selection of classes followed by random selection of students within classes. Sampling with probability proportional to size at the second stage can be done by enumerating schools and then randomly choosing n schools, noting the number of classes in each of the selected schools. The required number of classes is then chosen such that it is prorated over the n schools in proportion to their number of classes.

Many combinations of cluster, random, and stratified sampling methods are possible in more complex multi-stage plans. Examples of these plans are available in the literature (9,11,14,15,29,62,71).

F. Sequential Sampling

1. Selective Procedures

Sequential sampling (acceptance sampling) is a fairly recently developed method and one which is used rather infrequently in fields other than business and engineering. It can, however, be a very useful sampling technique when the groups to be compared are not identifiable in advance. The selection process requires that elements are randomly sampled from the population, one at a time, and measured immediately. If the value (x) of the dependent variable (number of defectives, differences between means, etc.) becomes greater than a certain prespecified value r, then the null hypothesis is rejected and sampling terminated. If, after drawing a set number (n) of elements, the dependent variable statistic is less than some specified value (a), sampling is terminated and the null hypothesis is not rejected. When $a < x < r$ after n units have been sampled, another n units are drawn sequentially with the same stopping rules. Various modifications of this basic plan are discussed by Deming (20) and Sampford (63), and methods for determining the parameters a, r, and n are given by Anscombe (3), Mace (49), and Sedransk (65).

2. Estimation Procedures

In a sequential sampling plan where it is desired to estimate μ such that the confidence level is at most of width d, then sampling is continued until the following inequality is met (for some value α):

$$(S/\sqrt{n})t_{n-1;\alpha} < \tfrac{1}{2}d. \tag{11}$$

This is based on the standard confidence interval equation with S, an unbiased estimate of σ, and $t_{n-1;\alpha}$ the value of Student's distribution with $n - 1$ d.f. and level of significance α. However, because of the random n inherent in any sequential sampling procedure, the true probability that μ lies between $\bar{X} \pm \frac{1}{2}\,d$ is not α but slightly larger (3). The extent of this bias depends on d and n, with the true probability approaching α as d decreases and n increases. Anscombe (3) has shown that this bias, which is quite small for large n, can be reduced considerably by sampling until Eq. (11) is satisfied and then taking one more value.

3. Advantages and Disadvantages

The major advantage of sequential sampling is in the area of industrial sampling inspection where the purposes are to reject or accept a batch of materials instead of to make estimates regarding population values. It can be used advantageously in estimating the differences between two groups in a population where the cost of testing each individual is high. In this case the disadvantage of having to recalculate the various statistics after each draw would be more than compensated for by testing the minimum number of subjects.

G. SINGLE-SUBJECT STUDIES

1. Selection Procedures

The manner of selecting the one individual required for an idiographic study depends on the nature of the study. In a case study the objective is usually to acquire detailed descriptive characteristics about one particular person who has a distinct problem or uniqueness which needs investigation. The results are used primarily to assist in making recommendations concerning the behavior of that specific individual. Consequently, there is usually no selection process per se in a case study, but instead an individual exhibiting some unique characteristics is brought to the attention of a researcher and subsequently investigated.

In the experimental-type single-subject study as advocated by Dukes (22) and Shine and Bower (66), it is desirable to be able to make logical inferences from the single subject to a general population. The representative subject necessary for this study can best be chosen by purposive selection rather than by a random process. Randomization will only provide a high probability of representativeness with relatively large samples, whereas purposive selection can provide a subject who is very like the average on certain observable traits. Such a subject could still be an extreme case on certain nonobservable characteristics which may have a strong relationship with the dependent variables.

2. Estimation Procedures

As mentioned above, inferences are usually not attempted in a case study—the population of interest is the sample of one. A large number of observations on the one individual make inferences possible to the general behavior of that person. If a number of similar cases come under investigation then the results may be pooled and inferences drawn concerning the population of persons exhibiting the same characteristics as those individuals involved in the case studies.

If it is desired to make inferences to some population from the data of a single subject, then obviously no estimates of degree of precision or error variance can be made. Thus, any inferences must be logical and not statistical. Dukes (22) suggests that if the interindividual variance is known to be very low (as is the case with some physiological variables), then valid inferences can be made from the single-subject case. Shine and Bower (66) propose an inferential statistical process for a single-subject design, but the inferences are restricted to the population of responses of that subject.

3. Advantages and Disadvantages

The advantages of the single-subject study are that it allows for a detailed description of the characteristics of a unique individual, and it provides a method of investigating some phenomenon for which multisampling is impossible or extremely costly. The disadvantages are the extreme limitations with regard to making any inferences to a defined population.

H. Miscellaneous Sampling Designs

There exists a considerable number of sampling designs which are used rather infrequently but are of value in certain situations. The following list, by no means an exhaustive one, describes the basic characteristics of some of these designs.

1. Volunteer Samples

Although volunteer sampling is not a classified design, the process of using volunteers is so common in research involving human subjects that a discussion of this technique is necessary. Many researchers who use volunteers restrict the population on which they draw inferences to the set of all volunteers; however, this is usually done as a formality only and the actual interpretation by the writer and/or reader of the research report does not take this into account. Furthermore, such a procedure is acceptable only when the subjects used are randomly sampled from a much larger list of volunteers. Lasagna and von Felsinger (45), using 56 college volunteers in a drug experiment, administered the Rorschach test in conjunction with an interview in an attempt to examine the "normality" of a volunteer sample. They found the volunteers to be unusually high in self-esteem and 25 of the 56 subjects were classified as being seriously maladjusted. Brower (7) randomly selected 59 subjects from a population of 135 volunteers and compared them with a conscripted group from the same college (the latter group was not composed of the nonvolunteers, but was from a different, but similar, population). Performance on a motor maze task showed the volunteers to perform significantly better. Brower attributes this superior performance to the higher incentive level inherent in volunteer groups. In general, volunteers seem to possess a number of distinguishing characteristics when compared with nonvolunteers. Specifically, volunteers ". . . tend to be brighter, better educated, occupy higher status positions, possess higher approval need, are less authoritarian, more sociable, younger, more arousal-seeking, more unconventional, and more frequently firstborn than nonvolunteers" (54). Evidence on the extent to which volunteers differ from nonvolunteers in motor performance is limited, but it would be rather presumptuous to assume that they provide valid estimates of general population values.

2. Convenience Samples

A convenience sample is usually a group of subjects who are available at the right time and over whom the experimenter possesses some authority. First year college classes frequently fall into this classification. Abel (1) used five dependent variables of known population values to compare convenience samples of psychology classes with systematic samples from a registrar's list. Results showed "extreme bias" on all variables in the convenience samples as compared to "limited bias" in the systematic samples. Deming (20), who labels such samples "chunks," states that they are acceptable only for such purposes as pilot projects and test runs on equipment. Obviously, the absence of any type of random selection negates the correct use of inferential statistics.

3. Matched Samples

Matched sampling requires the selection of pairs of subjects who are equated with respect to certain measured traits. The more traits on which subjects are paired, the better the matching but the more difficult it becomes to acquire a suitable sample size. Complicating the problem of matching on a number of traits is the required assumption that there must be no interactions between the independent variables and the matching variables in their relationship to the dependent variable (2).

The precision gained by matching can be indicated by the standard error of the difference formula

$$S_D^2 = S_{\bar{x}_1}^2 + S_{\bar{x}_2}^2 - 2r_{12}S_{\bar{x}_1}S_{\bar{x}_2}, \qquad (12)$$

where r_{12} is the interpair correlation on the experimental variable (53). Thus, a value of 0.50 for r_{12} will increase the precision of the experiment to the same extent that doubling n would. If two groups are to be constructed by matching on a single variable y, and if the value r_{xy} is known, then the expected precision to be gained by matching is indicated by

$$S_D^2 = (S_{\bar{x}_1}^2 + S_{\bar{x}_2}^2)(1 - r_{xy}^2). \qquad (13)$$

This relationship is exact only when the matching is such that the distribution of y is identical for each group (a process requiring a *very* large initial population). As Eq. (13) shows, if r_{xy} is near zero then no advantage has been gained by matching—but a considerable amount of time and effort has been wasted.

4. Judgment Samples

Judgment, or purposive sampling, involves the selection of representative units by an individual knowledgable in the subject area under investigation. Blane (5) cites a frequent procedure used in clinical medicine in which a third party, not directly involved in the research, is asked to select representative subjects. Blane conducted a careful follow-up study of a program requiring referrals of alcoholics who were admitted to emergency wards. Results showed that the alcoholics referred possessed certain distinguishing characteristics and were not at all a representative sample of the alcoholics admitted to emergency wards.

It has been suggested by Deming (20) that when the size of the sample is less than ten, a judgment sample may be preferable to a random sample because of the large possibility of random errors in a probability sample of small size. Further support for the use of purposive sampling is given by Stephan (70) who shows that although such a method lacks randomization and is therefore biased, this should not negate its usefulness. He suggests that further research into the nature of the bias in purposive samples is required.

5. Quota Sampling

Quota sampling, which Deming (*20*) classifies as a type of judgment sample, was developed for use in surveys as a means of correcting for the problem of nonresponses. A fixed number of individuals are tested in each of a certain number of categories (male–female, high–low income, etc.), the number in each category being based on prior information. It is sometimes left up to the investigator's discretion as to what houses or people he should test, the only stipulation being that testing must continue until the quota is reached (*15*).

6. Rotation Sampling

Rotation samples are used in continuing studies in which it is desirable to examine change over periods of time and simultaneously obtain estimates for individual time periods (*78*). With certain testing procedures, repeated testing of the same individuals results in invalid and unreliable data after three or four exposures to the interview or measurement equipment. Subjects either become bored and disinterested in the study or else become too knowledgable and skilled in using the measurement instrument. The sampling procedure involves retaining some sampling units (say two-thirds or three-quarters of the units) and replacing the others following each testing period. The effect of this rotation is a systematic bias, often due to high values obtained from samples appearing for the first time. Cochran (*11*) provides methods for estimating the error variances required for testing the status and change statistics associated with rotation sampling.

7. Item Sampling

Item sampling refers to the process of administering parts of a questionnaire to a large number of subjects for the purpose of establishing norms. It has been shown by Lord (*47*) that better estimates of the norm's distribution may be possible by administering, say, only ten items of a 50 item test to each of 500 individuals rather than giving the total test to only 100 individuals. Items from the total test are randomly sampled, to form a number of nonoverlapping subtests which exhaust the total item population. These subtests are then randomly assigned to the groups of examinees (five groups of 100 examinees each in the above example). Further discussions on item sampling are given by Devries (*21*) and Webster (*77*).

IV. Problem Situations in Sampling

A. INCOMPLETE SAMPLES

One of the most frequent problems facing investigators concerns the analysis and/or resampling of studies with missing data. Whether the investigations are descriptive or experimental, the presence of errors, attrition, nonresponses, and refusals results in data with missing observations for some subjects on some variables. Methods for handling incomplete data, although numerous, may be dichotomized according to the type of investigation—experimental studies in which observations are lost due to error and attrition, and surveys in which "not-at-home" and refusals bias the results.

1. Missing Observations

Kosobud (42) suggests that the best procedure in correcting for missing observations is to assign a replacement value on the basis of other information available on the subject. This multiple regression type of approach is claimed to be superior to assigning a mean value or omitting that subject from the analysis. Although Kosobud states that the multiple regression estimation approach tends to bias some analyses in that it inflates the correlation coefficients, Guertin (33) claims that the use of this method is superior because of the higher correlation coefficients obtained. However, Guertin suggests that the extra labor of calculating multiple regression is not worth the slight improvement in accuracy of estimation, and either replacement of missing values by the group mean or omitting the subject from the calculations is a suitable alternative. The suggestion of dropping subjects with incomplete data must be seriously questioned, for if the cause of the missing observation is related in any way to the treatment effects, serious biases may result. When it is expected that such a relationship may exist, subjects with missing data must be dropped from the study, randomly selected new subjects used as replacements, and the complete experiment repeated on these individuals.

A useful technique for replacing a single missing observation in an ANOVA design is to insert a variable, say x, into the missing cell (28). The error variance will then take the form

$$SS_E = A - 2Bx + Cx^2, \tag{14}$$

where A, B, and C are numerical values. The error variance can then be minimized by setting x equal to B/C in Eq. (14). This value can now be inserted in the missing data cell and the sum of squares due to main effects and interactions calculated.

2. Nonresponses in Surveys

Procedures for handling refusals and "not-at-homes" in survey sampling are well documented (*11,15,19,20,35,59,71*). The problem of incomplete data is often a serious one, with the percentage nonresponse in mail surveys averaging between 10 and 25%, depending on the length of the questionnaire (*15*). To obtain a precision equivalent to that possible with 100% returns, an increase in sample size of two to five times is necessary when the expected nonresponse is even as low as 5 to 10% (*11*).

The most commonly advocated procedure for dealing with incomplete survey data is to enumerate all nonrespondents and then randomly sample a proportion of them (10 to 20%). This sample group is then approached with follow-ups and, if necessary, by interviews, until 100% return is obtained. The data analysis for this subsample is performed separately and then weighted according to the total number of nonrespondents before being combined with the data from the initial replies (*35*).

B. SMALL SAMPLE BEHAVIOR OF CERTAIN STATISTICS

Occasionally the high cost of testing or the severity of the demands on subjects necessitates the use of small samples and the associated loss in power. An excellent paper by McCullough *et al.* (*50*) provides methods for testing differences between means for small sample size. Two types of statistics are proposed: one based on prior knowledge of unequal variances, the other suitable for situations in which no prior information concerning variances is available. Power tables are provided for sample sizes ranging from four to ten.

Arnold has proposed an experimental rather than statistical procedure for dealing with small sample sizes (*4*). A method is suggested by which the population is dimensioned, and a typology is developed to use as a sort of stratified population plan. One case is then sampled from each cell of the typology, with the subsequent data analysis not requiring the properties and assumptions of large number studies.

C. SAMPLING EXTREME GROUPS

In studies investigating the relationship between a status variable y (attitude, personality, fitness, etc.), and an experimentally elicited dependent variable x (a performance or learning score), it is often desirable to use subjects who lie at the extremes of the status variable distribution. It is assumed that if in fact a relationship does exist, a test on the difference between means will be more powerful if the two groups are far apart with respect to the status variable then if they are the two halves of the same distribution. The sampling procedure requires the random sampling and status evaluation of a large group, with the top and bottom 10 to 30% being designated as the "high" and "low" subgroups. The experiment is then performed on these subgroups.

The problem relative to sampling extreme groups concerns the choice of the percentile cutoff points which define the subgroups. These percentiles have ranged from five to fifty in various psychological studies (27). The smaller the percentile, the greater the difference between the y means and, assuming a nonzero r_{xy}, the greater the difference between the x means. However, a low percentile results in small sample sizes and probably greater within-group variability, thus reducing power. Feldt (27) provides the mathematical relationships among r_{xy}, the optimal percentile point, and the within-group variance and total population variance of y. Subsequent analyses showed that maximum power can be achieved when the percent in each extreme group is approximately 25. In some studies the status variable has been researched to the extent that cutoff points can be determined a priori on the basis of operational definitions of "high fitness," "low anxiety," etc.

D. Pooling Samples

Occasionally, an investigator may have data from a number of independent samples which have undergone the same experiment or answered the same questionnaire. Pooling these samples, which provides a larger total n and consequently gives a more powerful statistical test, may be done in either of two ways: the raw data may be pooled and new statistics calculated, or the individual sample statistics may be averaged. The first procedure is a weighted method in that it gives more weight to the larger sample, whereas the second method weights all samples equally. Dalrymple-Alford (18) suggests that, if one assumes that all samples come from the same population, the weighted pooling procedure is to be recommended. However, he states that this is not the only correct method (a claim made by some statisticians), as the unweighted technique is appropriate when there is reason to believe that the samples come from different populations. A weighted method would seriously affect an estimate of the total population mean in that it would bias the value of $\bar{X}$ in the direction of the larger samples.

V. Summary

It has been shown that the theory and practice of sampling is a well researched and documented topic. Many different sampling designs are now available which enable a researcher to attain maximum precision in terms of estimating population parameters and at the same time minimize the sampling costs. Each design, providing it involves some type of randomization procedure, is associated with unique mathematical formulas for estimating these parameters and determining the error variance of the estimates. This review has also shown the important relationship between sample size and error variance, and reference is made to the available charts, tables, and formulas available for determining the optimal sample size. A few problem situations which arise rather frequently in studies in the area of sport and physical activity were examined, and methods for reducing the severity of the problems were presented.

In conclusion, there are well documented sampling procedures available for any type of research situation that might be encountered. It is now up to the individual researchers to make use of this information so that studies may be conducted with maximum efficiency and minimum error.

References

1. Abel, W. H. (1967). Ph.D. Dissertation, Univ. of Kentucky, Lexington, Kentucky.
2. Althauser, R. P., and Rubin, D. (1970). *Amer. J. Sociol.* **76**, 325–346.
3. Anscombe, F. J. (1954). *Biometrics* **10**, 89–100.
4. Arnold, D. O. (1970). *Amer. Sociol.* **5**, 147–150.
5. Blane, H. T. (1963). *Psychol. Rep.* **13**, 133–134.
6. Bowley, A. L. (1926). "Elements of Statistics." Scribner, New York.
7. Brower, D. (1948). *J. Gen. Psychol.* **39**, 145–147.
8. Burstein, H. (1971). "Attribute Sampling." McGraw-Hill, New York.
9. Butcher, H. J. (1966). "Sampling in Educational Research." Manchester Univ. Press, Manchester, England.
10. Cochran, W. G., Mosteller, F., and Tukey, J. W. (1954). *J. Amer. Statist. Ass.* **49**, 13–35.
11. Cochran, W. G. (1963). "Sampling Techniques." Wiley, New York.
12. Cohen, J. (1969). "Statistical Power Analysis for the Behavioral Sciences." Academic Press, New York.
13. Cohen, J. (1970). *Educ. Psychol. Meas.* **30**, 811–831.
14. Collier, R. O., Jr., and Elam, S. M. (Eds.) (1961). "Research Design and Analyses." Phi Delta Kappa, Bloomington, Indiana.
15. Conway, F. (1967). "Sampling." Allen and Unwin Ltd., London.

16. Cumbee, F. Z., and Harris, C. W. (1969). *In* "Research Methods in Health Physical Education and Recreation" (M. G. Scott, ed.), pp. 71–98. AAHPER, Washington, D. C.
17. Dalenius, T. (1969). *In* "New Developments in Survey Sampling" (N. L. Johnson and H. Smith, eds.), pp. 325–349. Wiley, New York.
18. Dalrymple-Alford, E. (1964). *Percept. Motor Skills* **19**, 741–742.
19. Deming, W. E. (1950). "Some Theory of Sampling." Wiley, New York.
20. Deming, W. E. (1960). "Sample Design in Business Research." Wiley, New York.
21. Devries, A. G. (1966). *Psychol. Rep.* **18**, 843–850.
22. Dukes, W. F. (1965). *Psychol. Bull.* **64**, 74–79.
23. Durbin, J. (1969). *In* "New Developments in Survey Sampling" (N. L. Johnson and H. Smith, eds.), pp. 629–651. Wiley, New York.
24. Edgington, E. S. (1966). *Psychol. Bull.* **66**, 485–487.
25. Ericson, W. A. (1969). *J. Roy. Statist. Soc. B* **31**, 195–233.
26. Feldt, L. S., and Mahmoud, M. W. (1958). *Psychometrika* **23**, 201–209.
27. Feldt, L. S. (1961). *Psychometrika* **26**, 307–316.
28. Fisher, R. A. (1937). "The Design of Experiments." Hafner, New York.
29. Frankel, M. R. (1971). "Inference From Survey Samples." Litho Crafters, Ann Arbor, Michigan.
30. Friedman, H. (1968). *Psychol. Bull.* **70**, 245–251.
31. Gold, D. (1969). *Amer. Sociol.* **4**, 42–46.
32. Graybill, F. A., and Morrison, R. D. (1960). *Biometrics* **16**, 636–641.
33. Guertin, W. H. (1968). *Psychol. Rep.* **22**, 896.
34. Hansen, M. H., and Hurwitz, W. N. (1946). *J. Amer. Statist. Ass.* **41**, 517–529.
35. Hansen, M. H., Hurwitz, W. N., and Madow, W. G. (1953). "Sample Survey Methods and Theory," Vols. I, II. Wiley, New York.
36. Hansen, M. H., and Tepping, B. J. (1969). *In* "New Developments in Survey Sampling" (N. L. Johnson and H. Smith, eds.), pp. 1–26. Wiley, New York.
37. Jacobs, P. (1969). *Sankhya B* **31**, 113–116.
38. Jensen, A. (1926). *Bull. Int. Statist. Inst.* **22**, 359–379.
39. Jessen, R. J. (1969). *J. Amer. Statist. Ass.* **64**, 175–193.
40. Johnson, N. L., and Smith, H. (Eds.) (1969). "New Developments in Survey Sampling." Wiley, New York.
41. Kish, L. (1961). *In* "Research Design and Analysis" (R. O. Collier and S. M. Elam, eds.), pp. 45–63. Phi Delta Kappa, Bloomington, Indiana.
42. Kosobud, R. (1963). *Econometrica* **31**, 562–563.
43. Krejcie, R. V., and Morgan, D. W. (1960). *Educ. Psychol. Meas.* **30**, 607–610.
44. Kroeker, L. P., and Walster, G. W. (1969). Paper presented at AERA Convention, Los Angeles, California.
45. Lasagna, L., and von Felsinger, J. M. (1954). *Science* **120**, 359–361.
46. Lord, F. M. (1959). *J. Exp. Educ.* **27**, 247–263.
47. Lord, F. M. (1962). *Educ. Psychol. Meas.* **22**, 259–267.
48. Lykken, D. T. (1968). *Psychol. Bull.* **70**, 151–159.
49. Mace, A. E. (1964). "Sample-Size Determination." Reinhold, New York.
50. McCullogh, R. S., Gurland, J., and Rosenberg, L. (1960). *Biometrika* **47**, 345–353.
51. McHugh, R. B. (1957). *Educ. Psychol. Meas.* **17**, 136–141.
52. McHugh, R. B. (1961). *Amer. Statist.* **15**, 14–17.
53. McNemar, Q. (1940). *Psychol. Bull.* **37**, 331–365.
54. Morgan, W. P. (1972). *In* "Ergogenic Aids and Muscular Performance" (W. P. Morgan, ed.), Academic Press, New York.

55. Monroe, J., and Finkner, A. L. (1959). "Handbook of Area Sampling." Chilton, Philadelphia, Pennsylvania.
56. Morrison, D. E., and Henkel, R. E. (1969). *Amer. Sociol.* **4**, 131–139.
56a. NEA (1960). *NEA Res. Bull.* **38**, 99.
57. Neyman, J. (1934). *J. Roy. Statist. Soc.* **97**, 558–606.
58. Overall, J. E., and Dalal, S. N. (1968). *Percept. Motor Skills* **27**, 363–367.
59. Politz, A., and Simmons, W. (1949). *J. Amer. Statist. Ass.* **44**, 9–31.
60. Rao, R. J. (1970). *Math. Spectrum* **3**, 57–61.
61. Raj, D. (1968). "Sampling Theory." McGraw-Hill, New York.
62. Sampford, M. R. (1962). "An Introduction to Sampling Theory." Oliver & Boyd, Edinburgh.
63. Sampford, M. R. (1962). *Biometrika* **49**, 27–40.
64. Schutz, R. W. (1970). Paper presented at AAHPER National Convention, Seattle, Washington.
65. Sedransk, J. (1966). *Biometrika* **53**, 85–97.
66. Shine, L. C., and Bower, S. M. (1971). *Educ. Psychol. Meas.* **31**, 105–113.
67. Simmons, W. R., and Bean, J. A. (1969). *In* "New Developments in Survey Sampling" (N. L. Johnson and H. Smith, eds.), pp. 601–628. Wiley, New York.
68. Skipper, J. K., Guenther, A. L., and Nass, G. (1967). *Amer. Sociol.* **2**, 16–18.
69. Solomon, H., and Zacks, S. (1970). *J. Amer. Statist. Ass.* **65**, 653–677.
70. Stephan, F. F. (1959). *Estadistica* **17**, 691–695.
71. Sukhatme, P. V. (1959). *Estadistica* **17**, 652–679.
72. Sukhatme, P. V., and Sukhatme, B. V. (1970). "Sampling Theory of Surveys with Applications." Asia Publ. House, Bombay.
73. Thompson, W. A., and Endriss, J. (1961). *Amer. Statist.* **15**, 22–23.
74. Tukey, J. W. (1962). *Ann. Math. Statist.* **33**, 1–67.
75. Turk, H., and Smith, J. (1968). *Sociol. Soc. Res.* **53**, 78–87.
76. Wasson, C. R. (1963). *Harvard Bus. Rev.* **41**, 109–114.
77. Webster, H. (1962). *Educ. Psychol. Meas.* **22**, 321–324.
78. Williams, W. H. (1970). *Publ. Opin. Quart.* **33**, 593–602.
79. Winch, R. F., and Campbell, D. T. (1969). *Amer. Sociol.* **4**, 140–143.
80. Yule, G. U. (1929). "An Introduction to the Theory of Statistics." Griffin, London.
81. Zacks, S. (1970). *Technometrics* **12**, 119–130.

Analysis of Change

Charles O. Dotson

DEPARTMENT OF PHYSICAL EDUCATION,
UNIVERSITY OF MARYLAND,
COLLEGE PARK, MARYLAND

I. The Central Problems of Change Measurement

A survey of the professional literature reveals that a substantial proportion deals with measuring and conceptualizing change. Yet careful study reveals that sophistication of procedures is seriously lacking in many papers. It is further noted that there is lack of agreement as to what are satisfactory procedures for defining change concepts (*37,31,11*).

It can be said that researchers have not been deterred by this lack of sophistication or agreement on procedures, but have plunged into the study of change, applying almost every standard analysis tool available to them at the time. In retrospect, the application of standard experiment design techniques to change measurement has been shown to differ little from their familiar use in individual difference studies on time-invariant data. Change measurement, however, and its subsequent analysis make greater demands on dependable scaling concepts and on clear recognition of assumptions than is usually required in individual difference studies.

The analyses of change can be summarized as involving parameters or characteristics of the set of measurements related to: (a) individual scores, (b) the central tendency, (c) the standard deviation or higher moments, (d) the correlations among scores, and (e) the form of the univariate and multivariate distributions (*11*).

Each of these parameters interacts with the other four to give 2^5 combinations or sets of parameters related to change measurement. This paper attempts to summarize the methodological contributions to the study of change but can by no means consider in detail the status of our knowledge with respect to all of the 2^5 areas. A long-term interest (by the author's standards) in some of the modes of describing change motivated the discussion which follows.

Certain special cases within the areas enumerated may be mentioned to show the complexity of the change measurement problems. Lord (*42*) studied a system of change, "the dynamic equilibrium process," possessing the unique properties where moments of the distribution may remain constant over a period of time while individual scores systematically change. This occurs because of the well-known but paradoxical regression effect which produces a predictive true score change in individuals, independent of error or any treatment effect. Existence of the dynamic equilibrium process would generally imply that the correlations also change, thereby creating a confounded situation (no pun intended) which is difficult to resolve.

As noted above, analysis of individual differences involving time-variant data differs in only a few minor points from the application of standard statistical tools to time-invariant data. Sophistication of concepts, however, has not yet progressed to the point of clearly indicating whether, for example, the inferences we wish to make in the analyses of mean or group changes can be made as well from the statistical treatment of separate "before" and "after" measures as they can from, say, the analyses of differences directly. There are those who believe that the decisive approach is the employment of devices to eliminate correlation between absolute base line measures and difference or final measures (*42,19,61*). Others argue that this approach is usually unwise because it tends to mask effects and relationships that we should be interested in discovering (*11*).

Methods of study related to changes in the standard deviation and higher moments have generally been lacking except insofar as they may be incidental to the study of other problem areas defined previously under (a)–(e). Mention will be made at appropriate places in the following sections when the second and higher moments merit special consideration. For example, the effect of change upon group heterogeneity will be discussed in the regression analysis section.

Attempts to correlate various variables with change have led to considerable controversy (42). This controversy exists with respect to both the univariate and multivariate techniques for assessing relationships with change. To be sure, controversy exists even between those who advocate handling change in a single dimension and advocates of the so-called less restrictive methods of conceptualizing change along multidimensional lines. It is not the purpose of this paper to resolve the controversy, but hopefully some light can be shed on the appropriateness of each argument.

Most considerations of change measurement techniques have been taken with little regard to noncentral distributional problems. This is true with both univariate and multivariate distributions, although more advances have probably been made with the latter [see, e.g., Pillai (48)–(50)]. Thus, within the controversial issues, justifications for a given method of analysis are entirely heuristic, and, therefore, its application in any particular problem has to be justified by the operating characteristics for that situation with no "good" properties being guaranteed in advance by the method itself.

II. Regression Analysis and the Measurement of Change

A. Errors of Measurement

An individual possessing a value t of a specified characteristic may be observed, when appraising this characteristic with some measuring device, to have the value $t + e_x$. An algebraic expression for this observed score concept gives

$$x = t + e_x. \tag{1}$$

The observed value x is seen from Eq. (1) to be fallible, due to the fact that it differs from t, the true value of the characteristic measured, by the quantity e_x, generally defined as an error of measurement. As a simple example, we note that an individual with a true $\dot{V}_{O_2 \max}$ of 4.00 liters may be observed to have the quantity 4.10 liters, giving an error of measurement of $+0.10$ liters. We note also that a second determination may yield the quantity 3.80, giving an error of measurement of -0.20 liters. If we assume that the individual's true $\dot{V}_{O_2 \max}$ did not change for the intervening period, then the errors of measurement reported are due in part to the measuring device(s) and in part to the conditions surrounding the measurement.

Under the assumption of no true score change, the mean value of many replicated measurements on the same individual will ordinarily approach a limit as the number of replications increases. That is,

$$\text{Limit}_{n \to \infty} \bar{x} = c, \tag{2}$$

where n is the number of measurements used to calculate $\bar{x}$ and c is a constant. If $c = t$, then the expected value of the error of measurement $E(e_x)$ for any individual is zero and the errors are called unbiased. Thus, in effect, replicated measurements average out errors of measurement. If $c \neq t$ and t is assumed to remain unchanged during the period of assessment, then the errors of measurement are biased and either the measuring instrument is not measuring properly or conditions surrounding the measurement have changed. In either case, biased measures must be remedied before further analysis can be performed.

In addition to the requirement of unbiased errors, reliable measures require that (a) e_x be unbiased across the range of x values in the population of individuals, (b) the e_x's are independently distributed across individuals and test occasions, and (c) the e_x's are independent of true score values.

These observations call attention to the fact that we are interested in observed scores only insofar as they allow us to make inferences about true scores. In practice we argue that the observed scores will place individuals in the same order as the true scores, i.e., the functional relationship between observed and true scores is monotonic. This assumption generally holds for analyses of time-invariant data but often can be questioned for change data. Consequently, the issue of establishing a rational and defensible scaling system for change measurements (to be discussed below) becomes vital (*11,4,43*).

Two important problems involving errors of measurement should be discussed here. First, when several replications of a single or similar test(s) are available on each individual, the question arises as to which assessment or function of assessments to use as a criterion measure, and, second, what effect do errors of measurement have on change scores?

Several authors (*37,31,5,59*) in the exercise and sport sciences have concerned themselves with the problem of selecting a criterion measure. In general, their papers considered only the univariate case and centered around the controversy of selecting the "best" or "average" individual score. Kroll (*37*) employed reliability theory to shed considerable light on the subject. He suggested that if the variances of e_x across trials are random and uncorrelated then the mean of all assessments is justified as the criterion measure. On the other hand, if a significant trend effect across trials exists ". . . then the investigator is faced with several and mostly unpleasant alternatives" (37, p. 417). Kroll concluded that the researcher should search for a measurement schedule free of systematic error variance. The intent of this approach is clear, i.e., to avoid the difficulty of subjectively selecting a single criterion measure. It behooves workers in the field, however, not to cling to rule-of-thumb procedures. Rather they should explore the possibilities within their area of interest, if need be, without errors of measurement assumptions, and establish laws about what actually happens typically (11). Some isolated attempts at this have been undertaken with exercise and sport science data ($38,52,6$). In addition, many physiological responses of interest to the psychologist have previously been shown to reliably fluctuate with time, and these fluctuations have been shown to correlate with measures on other variables of interest ($12,13,24,18$). Generally, this would suggest the application of multivariate techniques as a first approach with the view to establishing relevant hypotheses to be tested later. To be sure, researchers of both time-invariant and change measurement problems must be prepared to recognize that certain interaction and emergent effects may go undetected unless we are equipped, in theories and in techniques, to handle measures simultaneously on many variables (11).

Relative to the second problem, it is widely recognized that errors of measurement introduce more serious and complex problems in change scores than is the case with time-invariant data. The problem occurs as a purely algebraic consequence of error terms from two fallible measures appearing in the difference expression used to define observed change. That is, if x and y represent the initial and final measures, respectively, and observed change is defined as

$$g = y - x, \tag{3}$$

then, from Eq. (1) and the usual formula for variances, we get

$$V(g) = V(t_y) + V(t_x) - 2\,\mathrm{COV}(t_y,t_x) + V(e_y) + V(e_x). \tag{4}$$

Thus, the variance of observed change is influenced by two independent error variances, one associated with the initial measure and one with the final measure. It is this double error effect which has led many psychometrists to propose working with a difference score from which the initial score has been partialled out ($42,61,44$). As statistical procedures, these are clear in intent, but the researcher is warned that such procedures are poor substitutes for placing greater emphasis on experimental error reduction in the measures making up change scores. We are not at liberty to relax time-invariant analysis requirements when change score analyses are involved just because greater errors of measurement are expected, e.g., accepting lower zero-order and partial correlation coefficients as evidence of an association between a third variable and change.

B. Estimating Change

Once a criterion measure has been selected some subtle issues still remain for change measurement which are not present or as great in ordinary individual difference research. The problem of estimating change has been extensively discussed in the realm of psychology by a number of authors (*43,41,42,44,7,10,29,32,39,46,55,57*) and very thoroughly reviewed by Cattell (*11*). He points out that there are five possibilities:

(a) Take raw score differences of initial and final measures. Change = $y_i - x_i$.

(b) Take standard score difference for separately standardized initial and final measures. Change = $Z_{y_i} - Z_{x_i}$.

(c) Take standard score difference for jointly standardized initial and final measures. Change = $Z'_{y_i} - Z'_{x_i}$.

(d) Subtract the regression estimate of the initial measure from the observed final measure using regression of initial on final measures. Change = $y_i - \bar{y}_i b_{y \cdot x}(x - \bar{x})$.

(e) Take the joint mean of each individual's initial and final measures and define his change on each occasion from that.

Cattell (*11*) suggests that each has advantages and disadvantages which are only briefly reviewed here. In general, defining change as the raw score difference is the most desirable approach of the five because change relationships with other variables are more likely to be detected provided equal units across the change scale exist. The latter assumption may be difficult to make and, in addition, in exploratory work utilizing the factor analytic technique we are reminded that we do not yet know enough about the rotation problems for nonstandardized measures (nonnormalized, in factor analysis terminology). Jointly standardizing initial and final measures before calculating differences is advanced as a useful approach when little is known about the units of the change scale, because it keeps absolute and change scores in the same scale metric. Cattell (*11*) points out that calculations (b) and (d) have the disadvantage of throwing away whatever correlation does and should exist between initial level and the rate of change in the measured trait. Method (e) may prove useful in certain exploratory studies when other criterion measures are difficult to justify but any device ". . . which makes gain independent of the conceived absolute score of the individual is suspect" (*11*, p. 374).

Previous mention has been made of the assumption of a monotonic relationship between observed and true change. If we assume the measuring device(s) is (are) measuring the same thing on both occasions, then the question of equal units across the full range of the interval scale arises. If we could assume that the measuring devices are true ratio scales, no problem exists, but we often can claim little beyond ordinal properties. Thus, while single-occasion scores will provide a monotonic function between observed and true scores, the difference measure may become quite erratic even in the ranking of individuals. It is not surprising, then, that equal units across the change score has been made the subject of serious debate. Proponents of most scale transformations have justified their respective approaches on the intuitive presence of either an upper- or lower-bound effect or the operation of a "homeostatic" process (30,39,45). The former is suggested to occur in learning experiments and physical performance assessments where movements away from the mean produce a compression effect on the score scale due to psychological, physiological, or artificial limits. The latter has plagued physiologists with such variables as blood pressure, where it is intuitively suggested that an upward shift of an individual's value already upwardly deviant is more important than a similar shift from the mean.

General scale transformations suggested to adjust for the compression effect include the logarithmic, square root, and reciprocal transformation. Few general scale transformations have been proposed for the "homeostatic" process. One example is Hooke's law describing tension on a stretched spring. In any case, the basis for suggested scale transformations rests on the notion that the initial level of the individual should enter into evaluation of the observed change. Such base level corrections should be judged with caution unless a priori theory and/or experience has demonstrated that they are experimentally sound and not artificially imposed. The reader is advised to guard against the indiscriminate selection of a scale transformation for some immediate seeming gain at the expense of masking underlying effects and interactions. Lacking adequate theory and experience to serve as a guide, it is suggested that the appropriate scale of measurement be determined only after the experimental data have been partially analyzed with equal units assumed. In this instance, the author would permit the concession of correcting the data to a normal distribution. The pervasiveness and importance of a normality transformation (for it may succumb to the same pitfalls outlined above) lie in its convenient mathematical properties leading directly to much of the theory of statistics available as a basis for practice. But, more importantly, two joint, normally distributed variables are statistically independent when a zero correlation coefficient exists, while one can claim only a failure to demonstrate existence of a linear relationship using nonnormal variables (9). The reader is referred to several excellent and readable summaries on scale transformations presented in articles included in the bibliography (*47,58,60,11*).

C. THE REGRESSION EFFECT

The dynamic equilibrium phenomenon produced by a regression effect demonstrates that initial measures will regress toward the general mean of the final measure, i.e., initially high or low scores are expected to show losses and gains, respectively, following a period of time (*36*). An example will serve to illustrate some of the problems confounded by the regression effect.

Suppose we consider the isometric wrist flexor strength of a group of individuals. Figure 1 represents a scatterplot showing the initial and final strength scores for (say) a 6 week period with no experimental conditions imposed. Suppose, further, that the initial mean strength is equal to the final mean strength, e.g., $\bar{X} = \bar{Y} = 80$. This requirement need not exist for the regression effect to operate and what follows holds equally well when a mean change between initial and final measures exists.

Regression lines representing change scores of -30 to $+30$ are given in Fig. 1, and the ellipse drawn is assumed to enclose all cases in the scatterplot. We note also that line $g = 0$ divides the group between "gainers" and "losers."

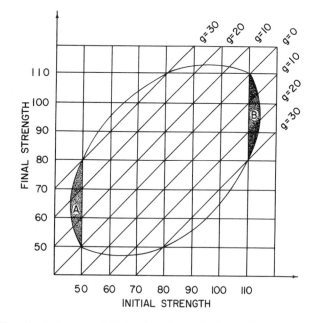

Fig. 1. Hypothetical scatterplot showing change in isometric wrist flexor strength.

The regression effect is best seen by considering the shaded areas (A) and (B) bounded by the ellipse, $x = 110$ and $x = 50$. All individuals with initial scores of $x > 110$ lost strength during the period, whereas all individuals with initial scores of $x < 50$ gained in strength. These gains and losses are not due to measurement error, treatment effect, or a statistical artifact of some sort. They are, rather, true score changes which may actually exist in such a set of data (36).

The regression effect can be expected to operate to either suppress or inflate treatment effects, depending upon the position of initial scores about the population mean exhibited by subjects permitted in the sample. In our example, if only subjects with initial strength scores greater than 80 are included in an experimental study, a suppressive effect will tend to operate on scores reflecting the experimental treatment effect. Suppose this sample were selected (as might be the case if only physical education majors were permitted in the sample) and we arbitrarily subdivided the subjects into three groups, labeling them high, medium, and low. Clearly, the effectiveness of any factorial design to reveal an interaction effect between the strength level factor and other variables of interest is greatly reduced because only the suppressive effect is operating. The problem with this arbitrary classification of subjects is that equal proportions of "gainers" and "losers" were not included in the sample, permitting the regression effect to reveal itself. Not infrequently, this kind of arbitrary classification of subjects is employed in exercise and sport science research.

Change, under arbitrary classification of subjects, may be estimated by determining the scatterplot between initial and final measures assessed with no intervening treatment. This "no-treatment effect" scatterplot may be estimated empirically or suggested from some theoretical model. The scatterplot describing change due to a treatment effect may then be compared with the "no-treatment effect" scatterplot, with any difference logically interpreted as representing a true treatment effect. Lord (41) provides an excellent discussion of the regression effect, including additional methods for its control in change measurement research.

D. RELIABILITY ESTIMATES FOR CHANGE SCORES

It was noted in Section I that the difference between two fallible measures is generally much more fallible than either. The possibility, then, of assessing experimental treatment effects based upon difference scores of near-zero reliability exists. This is true even though the reliability of the initial and final measures taken separately may be quite acceptable for a single-occasion assessment. The reason for this seeming paradox is the quite easily shown fact that the unreliability has two sources: unreliability in initial and final scores and a positive correlation between the initial and final measures. That is, if $r_{xx'}$ and $r_{yy'}$ are the correlations between experimentally independent replicated measurements for the initial and final measures, respectively, and r_{xy} is the test–retest correlation, then the reliability of the measured change is

$$r_{gg'} = \frac{s_y^2 r_{yy'} - 2s_y s_x r_{xy} + s_x^2 r_{xx'}}{s_y^2 - 2s_y s_x r_{xy} + s_x^2}. \tag{5}$$

As an example, consider a situation where x and y have reliabilities of 0.80 and correlate 0.70 with each other. Assuming their variances to be the same (for the sake of convenience), the reliability of the measured change will be 0.33, a fairly typical result. Suppose we assume that $r_{xx'} = r_{yy'}$ and $s_y = s_x$. Then Eq. (5) may be simplified, for purposes of illustration, to

$$r_{gg'} = \frac{r_{yy'} - r_{xy}}{1 - r_{xy}}. \tag{6}$$

Equation (6) clearly shows that improvement in the reliability of the measured change is limited by the attainment of greater reliability in the initial and final measures but greatly inhanced by a reduction in the test–retest correlation r_{xy}. For example, increasing the initial and final measures' reliability to a realistic upper limit of 0.90 for most exercise and sport science measures will also increase r_{xy} to about 0.80 but the reliability of the measured change to only 0.50. On the other hand, leaving $r_{xx'}$ and $r_{yy'}$ at 0.80 while reducing the test–retest correlation to zero will increase $r_{gg'}$ to 0.80. The latter approach, the reader will readily note, is most often produced when the ordering of subjects is changed from initial to final measures. But if r_{xy} is low, we may rightly question whether the two tests measure the same thing. Given that they no longer measure the same thing, then it appears meaningless to talk about change. Clearly, the reliability of measured change presents an unreliability–invalidity dilemma. High reliability is desired, but to what extent is validity of change affected?

The dilemma is not something we can sweep under the rug for it presents itself all the way along the spectrum of change measurement applications—from classroom examinations to scientific research. For example, scores on an initial test of tennis skills may reflect individual differences in prior experience with tennis while scores on a post-test for the same battery may reflect learning ability. A $\dot{V}_{O_2 \max}$ test assessed on a bicycle ergometer may initially reflect (or be limited by) muscular endurance of the lower extremities, whereas the final measure, following a running program, may reflect overall cardiovascular endurance. These examples very likely would result in high reliability for the measured change but low validity as an indication of a single trait change.

The difficulty suggested by the examples above can be resolved, or at least solutions can be suggested, by distinguishing between the meaningfulness of average changes and the meaningfulness of individual differences in change. Certainly, large average tennis skill and $\dot{V}_{O_2 max}$ changes are of interest in and of themselves. The fact that average change has been demonstrated in each example is meaningful. It is only when we attempt to explain why individuals changed that the above measures become meaningless. That is, no answer is provided by the change scores alone to the question: change in what?

Thus, in the latter example, the relation between effectiveness of training the circulorespiratory system and various modes of exercise is limited by the relationship between localized muscular endurance and physical working capacity. The change score alone, therefore, does not permit an adequate comparison among the modes of exercise, and renders any generalizations explaining change useless. As a final remark, if the researcher notes that considerable differences exist between the standard errors of measurement for the initial and final measures based on separate reliability determinations, then he should suspect either that (a) the relationship between initial scores and true gain is curvilinear, (b) difference metrics exist between initial and final measures, or (c) the unreliability–invalidity dilemma. Bereiter (4), Lord (43), and McNemar (46) have discussed these problems in detail and the interested reader is referred to their articles for further details.

E. The Effect of Change on Group Heterogeneity

While discussing reliability of change we assumed that the variances of initial and final measures were equal. It seems reasonable to investigate the validity of this assumption. Our simple mathematical model assumes that true change is given by

$$t_g = t_y - t_x. \tag{7}$$

Rewriting Eq. (7) gives the true final measure in terms of the functional equation

$$t_y = t_g + t_x, \tag{8}$$

and from the usual formula for variances we get

$$V(t_y) = V(t_g) + V(t_x) + 2\,\text{COV}(t_g, t_x). \tag{9}$$

Thus,

$$V(t_y) > V(t_x), \tag{10}$$

indicating that group heterogeneity increased with the passage of time, unless

$$V(t_g) = 0 \quad \text{and} \quad \text{COV}(t_g, t_x) = 0, \tag{11}$$

in which case no change occurred; or

$$V(t_g) < -2\,\text{COV}(t_g, t_x), \tag{12}$$

indicating that a sizable negative correlation exists between true gain and true initial scores. If we substitute the value of $V(t_g)$ from Eq. (9) in Eq. (12), we get

$$V(t_y) < V(t_x). \tag{13}$$

In addition, if

$$V(t_g) = -2\,\text{COV}(t_g, t_x), \tag{14}$$

then

$$V(t_y) = V(t_x), \tag{15}$$

and the dynamic equilibrium process accounts for the nonzero value for $\text{COV}(t_g, t_x)$ (*41*). In general, conditions producing a sizable negative correlation between initial scores and observed gain and/or the dynamic equilibrium process can be expected to occur, leaving us with a more realistic assumption.

$$V(t_y) \leq V(t_x). \tag{16}$$

Finally, it is because of this likely negative correlation that many writers have suggested partialling out the initial measure from the final measure and using the residual as the real measure of change (*42,61*).

F. Correlations of Other Variables with Change

Once we have demonstrated that change has occurred it becomes logical to ask what accounts for the individual changes. The correlation of change with other variables, however, seems to run into quite a bit of either statistical or logical difficulties. Thus, a number of methods have been suggested, including: (a) simple zero-order correlations between true change and initial scores, (b) partialling out the initial scores from the final, leaving zero correlation between the two, (c) partialling out the initial scores from the observed change, (d) eliminating the correlation between the mean of the initial and final scores and obtaining the "corrected" difference score based on the joint mean, and (e) using part correlations (similar to partials except that the denominator carries only one of the error terms), permitting, say, the variance of the final scores to be eliminated from the difference score before correlating it with the initial scores.

Advocates of one or more of these correlational procedures to identify relationships between change and a third variable point out several convincing reasons for their use. First, there is the likely spurious negative correlation between initial scores and observed change produced by the sharing of errors (with different signs) which might advantageously be removed. Second, it is pointed out that change scores, by definition, must assume that initial and final scores have the same metric, which often is violated by homeostatic or bounding effects. Finally, it is suggested that the unreliability–invalidity dilemma produced by the testing instrument failing to measure the same thing across the full range of scores might be resolved by partialling out the initial scores from the relationship between the final standing and a third variable.

As statistical procedures, all have been shown to be quite useful in a number of situations. The major drawbacks to these methods rest on two grounds. First, the inherent difficulties associated with change scores are not to be avoided by statistical acrobatics but through better development of measuring instruments and in other ways to reduce errors of measurement in the experimental situation itself. Second, the appropriateness of these *ad hoc* adjustments to a mathematical model with desirable statistical properties has been insufficiently examined. For example, the distributional problems for coefficients corrected for spurious correlations have been examined only on an empirical basis (25). In addition, little is known about the operating characteristics advanced for them.

Naturally, if an investigator has *a priori* hypotheses in mind that are suggested from well formulated theory and experience, then it is worthwhile to test these hypotheses. Within this context, one of the partial correlational methods given above may be suggested. Exactly what that method will and will not do, however, should be well understood. Cattell (11) and Lord (42,43) present excellent summaries of opposing views on the correlational problem and the latter (42) provides computational formulas for their derivation.

III. Univariate Designs for the Analysis of Change

In general, the ingredients for a well designed experiment (which connotes selecting the appropriate statistical analysis) start with a well defined problem. Familiarity with the subject matter, then, is absolutely essential, so that the investigator may choose elements of the problem considered important and relevant. That is, relevant hypotheses must be formulated that theory suggests will provide explanations of already known facts and in addition give predictions of observations that can be verified. The next step calls for the design satisfying the basic requirements of inference space, randomization, and replication. The latter two terms are familiar requirements of experiment designs and will not be elaborated upon here. They will, however, be important in the discussion which follows. Inference space is commonly referred to as the population of interest, but the former term seems more explicit. That is, inferences can be made only to that population represented by the sample, but, more importantly, only when the correct error terms used as a basis for testing hypotheses reflect the peculiarities of the population. This implies that inference is broad only to the extent that it contains in its error a reflection of the variability of sampled experimental units. For example, in a criterion measure of strength, three sources of error (and their interaction if nonzero) important to the inference space are those due to subjects, trials, and days (37).

Determination of the proper experiment design depends upon the inferences the researcher desires and the randomization procedures available to him. In the case of change data, the researcher must have available an initial score (x) and a final score (y) from which observed change can be derived, or at least the final score (y), under assurance that all subjects or groups of subjects were initially equal. Within this context, three basic designs present themselves for the univariate case. These are factorial experiments for (a) nonrepeated measures, (b) repeated measures, and (c) designs involving the use of covariance(s). In most instances it is to be noted that the appropriate design for the analysis of change will include combinations of all three, depending upon the extent and number of sampling stages. Each is discussed separately to point out its applicability in different situations.

A. Factorial Experiments—Nonrepeated Measures

Nonrepeated measures designs are characterized by the fact that each experimental unit is exposed to only one combination of treatments (in the factorial sense) and observed only on one occasion. The basic designs included under this type are the completely randomized (CR), nested factorial (NF), and split-plot (SP) designs. All other nonrepeated measures designs are special cases of one of these three.

Application of the nonrepeated measures designs to change measurement may be employed in a number of situations: (1) when initial scores are nonassessable, e.g., when assessment of initial scores is likely to produce a contaminating effect on either the treatments or the final scores,

(2) when change is observed over an extended period of time, producing different metrics for the initial and final test instrument(s), (3) when randomized groups included in the study possess equal initial means, and (4) when change across time is desired but scores on a single set of experimental units cannot be obtained over the total time interval. It should be noted that, generally, greater efficiency in design exists when initial and final scores are available. These examples, however, indicate that sometimes this is not possible.

The most perplexing problem in experimental research, for both time-invariant and change studies, is recognizing the appropriate design. In the case of the CR, NF, and SP designs this is particularly critical since incorrect F ratios may be used for hypothesis testing, leading to large Type II errors. More importantly, estimates of appropriate error terms used to formulate correct F ratios may not be possible, depending upon the design. Obviously, if hypotheses of interest cannot be tested the study must be redesigned.

The method of randomization employed in assigning levels of factors to experimental units completely determines the appropriate design for analysis. The CR design, by definition, requires that no restrictions be placed on the randomization procedures. Restrictions, however, do exist for the NF design, where certain levels of one factor are not or cannot be observed in combination with the levels of a second factor, and in the SP design, where a single level of one factor is assigned at random to a group of experimental units while levels of a second factor are assigned at random to experimental units within each group. In the NF design, generally (but not always) a combination of experimental treatments and modes of classification constitutes the factorial experiment. The modes of classification are included primarily to isolate differences among experimental units from experimental error. The SP design is appropriate when intact classes are used.

Anderson (1) has proposed including a random component called a "restriction error" into the linear statistical model corresponding to every restriction on randomization introduced in the design. The real power of such restriction errors is that they force the experimenter not only to recognize the restrictions on randomization he has imposed on his design (usually to save time and/or money) but also to see their effect on the overall analysis of the experiment.

B. Factorial Experiments—Repeated Measures

Considerable efficiency in design of change experiments is provided by repeated measures designs. In this type of experiment, time is usually the repeated measures factor, in view of the fact that scores for each experimental unit are assessed repeatedly on the criterion measure over time. The efficiency results from the control placed on the likely source of variability due to differences in experimental units. This is particularly true in the exercise and sport sciences, where the experimental units are frequently people.

Repeated measures designs have wide applicability in the analyses of change. Not only is it quite useful in the analysis of trends with respect to time but also as a means of estimating reliability coefficients for criterion measures. The latter is particularly important with respect to observed change scores, since, it will be recalled, usual correlational approaches for estimating reliability provide coefficients reflecting only one source of error at a time. Kroll (*36*) used a repeated measures design to aid in the selection of a criterion measure useful in the study of strength changes and also shed considerable light on the controversy of selecting the "best" or "average" scores among multiple trials.

A multivariate normal distribution underlies the repeated measures design. Thus its appropriateness as a univariate technique depends upon the very special case when the population variance–covariance matrix for the repeated measures factor is of the form:

$$\begin{bmatrix} \sigma^2 & \rho\sigma^2 & \cdots & \rho\sigma^2 \\ \rho\sigma^2 & \sigma^2 & \cdots & \rho\sigma^2 \\ \vdots & & & \\ \rho\sigma^2 & \rho\sigma^2 & \cdots & \sigma^2 \end{bmatrix},$$

where σ^2 is the population variance for each level and ρ is the product–moment correlation between pairs of measurements on the same experimental unit. Thus, the assumptions underlying the repeated measures design are the usual ones for any analysis of variance plus the requirement that ρ is constant between every pair of levels for the repeated measures factor. In the event $\rho \neq$ constant, the univariate F test is inappropriate, and a multivariate analysis should be performed. It has been assumed by many individuals that partitioning a source of variation attributable to subjects handles the problem of unequal correlations, but the reader is warned that this is not true (*26*). Some approximate F tests have been suggested (*8,27,28*), but exact power comparisons for more appropriate multivariate test criteria have suggested that these approximations are at best conservative (*49*).

Once change has been demonstrated it becomes of interest to describe how that change occurs with respect to time. The whole field of motor learning, for example, is concerned with identifying response curves describing the acquisition of a task, "transfer" learning rates for "whole versus part" practice, or other practice variables (*17*).

Trend analysis based on successive observations of an individual on the criterion measure over time permits such functional relationships to be established.

Many different curves may be found to fit a given set of experimental data. It is preferred that the researcher have some functional relationship in mind suggested by theory or experience. However, a kth order polynomial equation of the form

$$Y = B_0 + B_1 x + B_2 x^2 + \cdots + B_k X^k + e \qquad (17)$$

may be employed to estimate the true functional relationship, in the absence of theoretical suggestions, under the assumption that the derived polynomial is a power series expansion of the true function. Within this context, use of orthogonal polynomials greatly simplifies fitting the curve to experimental data, since each polynomial component $(B_i, i = 1, \ldots, k)$ can be independently estimated. Thus, successive components can be added to the equation from linear to higher order polynomials until an adequate description of the trend defined by the experimental data is found.

Orthogonal polynomial components are more easily applied when levels of the repeated measures factor are equally spaced over time and an equal number of observations per level exists. This is because coefficients needed to estimate the B's have been extensively tabulated previously and need not be derived when the levels are equally spaced. Thus, equal spacing of factor levels is not a requirement to use orthogonal polynomials, only to use the tabled values. If equal spacing is not possible (and there may be strong reasons why it should not be), then orthogonal polynomials may still be used, provided one is willing to solve a series of simultaneous equations to obtain the necessary coefficients (40).

Unless the time interval is relatively short, equal spacing of factor levels may result in the polynomial equation poorly describing the trend when the true function is exponential (a common occurrence in motor learning and certain physiological problems). Thus, if an exponential relationship is suspected, geometric rather than equal spacing should be followed by equally spacing the natural logarithm of the repeated measures factor. Similar results may occur for other functional forms thought to describe the trend and thus dictate factor level spacing other than equal time intervals. The reader is referred to Li (40) and Finney (21) for additional details.

The analysis of trends using the repeated measures devices must be done with caution. It has been advised that the researcher have a priori functions in mind, suggested by theory, as hypothesized explanations for the trends analyzed. Short of this, significant functional equations suggested by the analysis should be accepted only if plausible *ad hoc* reasons exist for not discounting them. Hypotheses that are formulated from or modified by the observations are always suspect, and it is one of the elementary notions of statistical tests that probability statements cannot be made about statistical tests suggested by the data to which they are applied (*35*).

Special attention should be given to the possible presence of nonadditive sequence effects associated with the criterion measure, such as learning or "carry-over" effects. Such effects may be controlled in time-invariant studies involving repeated measures by counterbalancing the order of treatment combinations, but no such control exists for time-variant data.

An additional problem is the distinction between learning and performance or, as Cattell suggested, "our capacity to distinguish change in a trait from changes in states" (*11*, p. 356). Dunham (*20*) has suggested an approach which involves crossing over the experimental treatment(s) between experimental and control groups. His suggestion that the analysis is a factorial design is incorrect, however, since a restriction on the ordering of treatments to groups exists, requiring the use of the crossover design (*15,21*).

Finally, the testing of trends can be easily contaminated if one has different numbers of cases at different points in time, suffers some selection when the same experimental units are carried on through a time series, or the regression effect operates.

Excellent presentations on repeated measures are given by Winer (*60*), and Gaito and Wiley (*26*). The reader is referred to these references for additional details and computational procedures.

C. ANALYSIS OF COVARIANCE

Preferred procedures in the analysis of mean change require either experimental or statistical control of initial differences among experimental groups arising from sampling fluctuations. Experimental control includes classifying experimental units into homogeneous groups, maintaining uniform conditions under which the experiment is run, and increasing the accuracy of measurement. Statistical control involves the use of the analysis of covariance (ANOCOV) and is effective when one or more concomitant variables (hereafter called covariates), known to cause extraneous variations in the criterion measure, are available.

Measurements on the covariates are made for the purpose of adjusting measurements on the criterion measure. There are many ways in which this may be done. The ANOCOV makes use of a regression analysis to adjust the criterion measure for the linear effects of the covariates. In essence, this is a technique that removes that part of an observed treatment effect which can be attributed to a linear association with other variables. This serves to reduce the experimental error, and the amount of reduction depends upon the linear correlation between the criterion measure and the covariate(s).

The use of a single covariate provides a reduction in the experimental error that is equal to the reduction achieved from classifying experimental units into homogeneous groups, provided the relationship between the criterion measure and the covariate is linear. If the relationship is not linear, however, the classification scheme will generally provide greater reduction in the experimental error, since the nonlinear part of the relationship will still be included in the experimental error for the ANOCOV.

The usual assumptions for an analysis of variance are required for ANOCOV, and in addition it is assumed that no interaction exists between treatments and covariate. Under these assumptions, means for the criterion measure are adjusted as follows:

$$\text{adj } \bar{y}_i = \bar{y}_i - B(\bar{x}_i - \bar{x}), \tag{18}$$

where B is the regression coefficient for y on x. If an interaction exists between treatments and covariate, then the adjustment becomes

$$\text{adj } \bar{y}_i = \bar{y}_i - B^l(\bar{x}_i - \bar{x}) - I. \tag{19}$$

Then the adjustment process removes more than an error component from the criterion; it also removes part of the treatment effect.

It is also necessary that the covariate not be affected by the treatments for a valid ANOCOV. Examples in the exercise and sport sciences include physical conditioning studies, where initial maximal assessments on the criterion measures may change initial status and produce spurious effects in groups assigned no treatment or exercise modes involving low intensities, and motor learning experiments, where ability traits are assessed as reference variables to clarify learning sequences for various practice schedules. The latter example draws attention to the fact that the factorial structure of skill being learned (the criterion measure) may have changed during the experiment and the reference variables are no longer important. This problem is discussed further in Section IV. In order to reduce the possibility that the covariate has been affected by treatments, Cox suggests that we (a) make the covariate observations before assignment of treatments, or, if this is impossible, (b) make the covariate observation after assignment of treatments, but before the treatments have a chance to affect the covariate; and if this, too, is impossible, (c) be sure on the basis of knowledge of the nature of the covariate that it is not affected by treatments (*16*). An excellent summary of the wide variety of uses and underlying problems for the ANOCOV is given by Cochran (*14*) in a special issue of *Biometrics* devoted entirely to this topic.

IV. Multivariate Techniques for the Analysis of Change

Multivariate analysis is a class of statistical procedures concerned with the analysis of multiple variates assessed on a number of individuals. The basic distinction between multivariate and univariate analysis is that the multiple variates are analyzed simultaneously in the former but in at least one subset only one variable is analyzed at a time in the latter. For example, the multiple regression technique is actually a univariate analysis, since only one dependent variable is analyzed at a time. The multivariate counterpart to the multiple regression technique is the canonical correlation analysis which identifies the relationship between a p-set and a q-set of variates in a $(p + q)$-variate population. Other generalized statistical analyses from the univariate case include (a) discriminant function analysis, which is an extension of the familiar t-test, (b) multivariate analysis of variance, which is an extension of (a) to multiple groups, (c) comparisons of variance–covariance matrices, which is an extension of the chi-square test for homogeneity of variances, (d) partial canonical correlation analysis, which considers q dependent variables, and (e) factor analysis, which has no true univariate counterpart.

One or more of the multivariate techniques should be utilized in the place of its corresponding univariate approach when the criterion measure is of necessity multivariate. The decision to be made, then, is whether the phenomenon under investigation can be adequately described with one, or more than one, variable. Of course, if an *a priori* function of several variables can be derived, then the phenomenon may still be multivariate but permit the investigator to utilize univariate techniques, since the derived function operates as a single variable. For example, linear compounds have been derived to describe such phenomena as physical fitness (*33*), intelligence (*56*), motor ability (*3*), and some special subareas as circulorespiratory capacity (*2*), body density (*2*), heat balance (*2*), and the class of sport skill tests. It was previously warned, however, that such analysis may mask certain interactions and emergent effects within the phenomenon.

Aside from the nature of the phenomenon, multivariate techniques may be utilized in the study of change when (a) the variance–covariance matrix for repeated measures has unequal variances and covariances, (b) little is known about the time-variant behavior of the phenomenon, including appropriate criterion measures and independent variables likely to affect change, and (c) the criterion measure is suspected to measure different points on the interval scale.

Trend analyses by the univariate and multivariate approaches have the same objective, namely, to describe the mean "time curves" for the criterion measure over a specified time interval (7). An intermediate step in either analysis requires computation of the linear compound

$$Z = a_1y_1 + a_2y_2 + \cdots + a_ky_k, \tag{20}$$

where y_i is the criterion measure for the ith time interval and a_i is its partial regression weight. When the sampling variance–covariance matrix exhibits equal variances and covariance $a_i = \text{constant} \ (i = 1, 2, \ldots, k)$, Eq. (20) is easily obtained. This favorable condition permits the univariate trend analysis to be run. When unequal variances and covariances exist, the partial regression weights are not equal and must be provided by the investigator or estimated by multivariate analysis. The latter condition is most likely to occur in motor learning experiments because of the differential change in correlations between practice trials. The reader is refered to Gaito and Wiley (26) and Bock (7) for additional details and computational procedures.

When little is known about the time-variant behavior of a phenomenon, an exploratory study can be conducted to investigate a number of variables thought to give significant information or explain variability within the phenomenon. A study of this nature is performed for the purpose of isolating relevant variables describing the phenomenon, to formulate hypotheses for later testing, and to derive functional compounds among the relevant variables suggested to adequately describe the phenomenon under study. In each case the methods of multivariate analysis can be effectively employed. Relevant variables can be isolated when the phenomenon is not too complex through canonical correlation, or factor analysis when complex causation is suspected. Fruitful hypotheses may be suggested from any of the methods but particularly so through factor analysis. Thanks to the methods of Fisher (22), all multivariate analysis techniques provide linear compounds for the set of variables analyzed as a byproduct of the analysis.

As a general rule, experimenters should know their experimental material well enough to isolate the five or six relevant variables. In many cases experimenters are prone to say that a large number of variables influences the change phenomenon, but this is almost always in error. Multivariate techniques can generally bear this out, but it is always time consuming and costly. In addition, the techniques can yield erratic results by sometimes showing significance and sometimes not, depending upon the set and subsets of variables used. For example, combining several variables in a discriminant function analysis may yield nonsignificant discrimination among groups because of the presence of only a few nonsignificant variables. Similar results may occur in canonical correlation analysis where significant relationships between a given set of dependent and independent variables shift to nonsignificance as additional variables are added, even though the canonical correlations themselves increase. What to make of these and similar situations depends upon the investigator's knowledge of the phenomenon leading to his ability to attach, e.g., physiological, psychological, or social significance to the linear compounds derived.

When the criterion measure is suspected to measure different things, depending on the level along the interval scale, the problem of interpreting change becomes difficult but also offers the investigator a challenging area for research. The isolation of ability traits and environmental factors which explain change is an important phase of change measurement research. The fact that the criterion measure changes connotations makes the latter difficult but suggests that underlying contributions of the basic ability traits change as a function of time. This is, of course, valuable information in its own right and provides an added dimension to change measurements.

Study of this dimension in, e.g., motor learning, is required to provide an in-depth analysis of the learning process as well as to contribute significantly to the development of appropriate practice schemes and maximized predictive powers of test batteries useful as criterion measures along the learning curve. Studies of this type are rare in the professional literature (*17*). Yet in the area of psychology, it has been demonstrated empirically since the early work of Spearman (*54*) that the variable weights for estimating the factors of intelligence change appreciably with intelligence level. Fleishman and Hempel (*23*) and Tucker (*57*) have also shown that the factor composition of a particular learning performance changes as higher levels are reached on the learning curve.

Figure 2 provides a graphic illustration of the fact that learning curves have "thickness" as well as length. The graph describes the factor structure change of a complex coordination test as a function of practice and skill acquisition isolated by Fleishman and Hempel (*23*). Generalizations from the graph include the notion that the number of

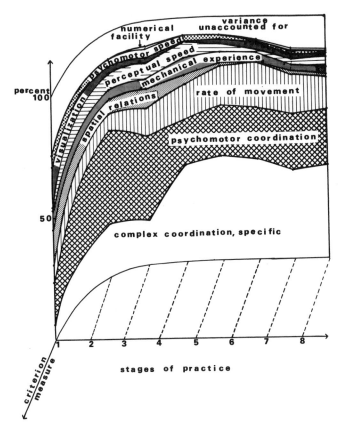

Fig. 2. Factor structure change of a complex coordination test as a function of practice and skill acquisition (factor names adopted from Fleishman and Hempel (*23*)).

factors contributing to performance decreases and the nature of the factors shifts from "nonmotor" to "motor," including a factor specific to the task, as learning increases.

The factor structure changes can be isolated using factor analysis techniques, while the multivariate analysis of variance and canonical correlation methods will permit the development of appropriate practice schemes and test batteries, respectively.

The matter of significance tests for multivariate hypotheses needs special note. Unlike the univariate analyses leading to the t, F, or chi-square statistic, multivariate problems yield multiple statistics that appear useful as a significance test criterion. Until recently, tabled values for these statistics have not been available, resulting in the use of approximation methods depending on F and chi-square distributions.

Recent power comparisons (*48,49*) among exact statistics cast serious doubt on the usefulness of the approximation methods as more than crude tests of significance. Even though exact significance tests are now possible, one commonly finds researchers drawing conclusions about change measurements on the basis of these approximation methods.

V. In Retrospect

Exercise and sport scientists have been slow to formulate appropriate models for the analyses of change. The models discussed in this paper have been borrowed primarily from the area of psychology, where psychometrists have largely been responsible for their formulation. Wide use of these methods in exercise and sport science research, however, has been limited, since much of their theoretical basis is steeped in psychological test nomenclature (*37*). In addition, application of change analysis methods often has been made with little regard to their underlying assumptions.

It was noted that many of the theoretical considerations justifying available methods rest mainly on heuristic grounds. In view of this, most methodological developments have emphasized the measurement and conceptualization of change, with distributional problems only occasionally receiving consideration. Some important distributional problems not adequately answered at present include (a) the effect of certain scale transformations upon the invariant properties of suggested test statistics, (b) the usability of test statistics in the sense of availability of large or small sample distributions of the statistics involved, and (c) the operating characteristics of the test statistics, such as their unbiasedness against all relevant alternate hypotheses, or something stronger, namely, a power which is a monotonically increasing function of each deviation alternate hypothesis (*51*).

Some important models for the analyses of change have not found their way into the exercise and sport science literature. Among these are included Cattell's (*11*) "five concepts" model for the study of change in (a) traits, (b) levels on temporary states, (c) the environment or environmental relations of the person or group, (d) tendency to change, i.e., as lability or instability, and (e) a characteristic configurational sequence or process. It appears that this model might fruitfully be employed to investigate such exercise and sport science problems as distinguishing between performance fluctuations and learning, and the effect of certain social motives and maturational processes on performance.

Other models noticeably absent include the analysis of repeated measures by stochastic processes and the differential calculus. The former is a method of time-series analysis in which performance fluctuation is treated as an inherent characteristic of the measure rather than assuming it is largely due to error, as in experiment designs. Thus, its use within Cattell's model above might permit the motor learning theorist, exercise physiologist, or sport psychologist to establish more inclusive mathematical models describing change. An excellent communication on stochastic processes is given by Schutz (53).

Differential calculus is the main tool utilized to study change in the so-called pure sciences. Its use in the social sciences has been limited, due to an inadequate description of social phenomena in mathematical terms. Its use could, however, aid the study of performance and learning through the isolation of oscillations and fluctuations of the experimental material which naturally occur.

References

1. Anderson, V. L. (1970). "Restriction Errors for Linear Models (An Aid to Develop Models for Designed Experiments)," Mimeograph Ser. No. 210, Dept. of Statistics, Purdue Univ., Lafayette, Indiana.
2. Åstrand, P.-O., and Rodahl, K. R. (1970). "Textbook of Work Physiology." McGraw-Hill, New York.
3. Barrow, H. M. (1954). *Res. Quart.* **25**, 253–260.
4. Bereiter, C. (1963). *In* "Problems in Measuring Change" (C. W. Harris, ed.), pp. 3–20. Univ. of Wisconsin Press, Madison, Wisconsin.
5. Berger, R. A., and Sweney, A. B. (1965). *Res. Quart.* **36**, 368–370.
6. Blair, S., and Vincent, M. L. (1971). *Res. Quart.* **42**, 7–13.
7. Bock, R. D. (1963). *In* "Problems in Measuring Change" (C. W. Harris, ed.), pp. 85–103. Univ. of Wisconsin Press, Madison, Wisconsin.
8. Box, G. E. P. (1954). *Ann. Math. Statist.* **25**, 484–498.
9. Brunk, H. D. (1960). "An Introduction to Mathematical Statistics." Ginn, Boston, Massachusetts.
10. Campbell, D. T. (1963). *In* "Problems in Measuring Change" (C. W. Harris, ed.), pp. 212–242. Univ. of Wisconsin Press, Madison, Wisconsin.
11. Cattell, T. B. (1966). *In* "Handbook of Multivariate Experimental Psychology" (T. B. Cattell, ed.), pp. 355–402. Rand McNally, Chicago, Illinois.
12. Cattell, T. B. (1943). *Amer. J. Psychol.* **56**, 195–216.
13. Cattell, T. B. (1957). "Personality and Motivation Structure and Measurement." World Book, Yonkers-on-Hudson, New York.
14. Cochran, W. G. (1957). *Biometrics* **44**, 261–281.
15. Cochran, W. G., and Cox, G. M. (1957). "Experimental Designs." Wiley, New York.
16. Cox, D. R. (1958). "Planning of Experiments." Wiley, New York.
17. Cratty, B. J. (1967). "Movement Behavior and Motor Learning." Lea & Febiger, Philadelphia, Pennsylvania.

18. Doust, L. (1960). *J. Nerv. Ment. Dis.* **123**, 471–491.
19. DuBois, P. H., and Manning, W. H. (1961). Methods of Research in Technical Training, Tech. Rep. No. 3, ONR No. Nonr 816(02). Washington Univ., St. Louis, Missouri.
20. Dunham, P. (1971). *Res. Quart.* **42**, 334–337.
21. Finney, D. J. (1960). "An Introduction to the Theory of Experimental Design." Univ. of Chicago Press, Chicago, Illinois.
22. Fisher, R. A. (1936). *Ann. Eugen. London* **1**, 179–190.
23. Fleishman, E. A., and Hempel, W. E. (1954). *Psychometrika* **19**, 239–252.
24. Flugel, J. C. (1929). *Brit. J. Psychol.* **4**, Monogr. Suppl. 13.
25. Forsyth, E., and Feldt, M. (1969). *Educ. Psychol. Meas.* **29**, 137–160.
26. Gaito, J., and Wiley, D. E. (1963). *In* "Problems in Measuring Change" (C. W. Harris, ed.), pp. 60–84. Univ. of Wisconsin Press, Madison, Wisconsin.
27. Geisser, S., and Greenhouse, S. W. (1958). *Ann. Math. Statist.* **29**, 885–891.
28. Greenhouse, S. W., and Geisser, S. (1959). *Psychometrika* **24**, 95–112.
29. Gullidsen, H. (1950). "Theory of Mental Tests." Wiley, New York.
30. Haggard, A. (1949). *J. Exp. Psychol.* **39**, 389–392.
31. Henry, F. M. (1967). *Res. Quart.* **38**, 317–320.
32. Humphreys, L. G. (1960). *Psychometrika* **25**, 313–323.
33. Ismail, A. H., Falls, H. B., and MacLeod, D. F. (1965). *J. Appl. Physiol.* **20**, 991–999.
34. Katch, F. I. (1971). *Res. Quart.* **42**, 280–285.
35. Kempthrone, O. (1952). "The Design and Analysis of Experiments." Wiley, New York.
36. Kroll, W. (1966). *Res. Quart.* **37**, 62–65.
37. Kroll, W. (1967). *Res. Quart.* **38**, 412–419. ·
38. Kroll, W. (1970). *Res. Quart.* **41**, 155–163.
39. Lacey, J. I., and Lacey, B. C. (1958). *Amer. J. Psychol.* **71**, 50–73.
40. Li, J. C. R. (1964). "Statistical Inference II (Multiple Regression)." Edwards, Ann Arbor, Michigan.
41. Lord, F. M. (1956). *Educ. Psychol. Meas.* **16**, 421–437.
42. Lord, F. M. (1963). *In* "Problems in Measuring Change" (C. W. Harris, ed.), pp. 21–38. Univ. of Wisconsin Press, Madison, Wisconsin.
43. Lord, F. M. (1967). *In* "Problems in Human Assessment" (D. N. Jackson and S. Messick, eds.), pp. 258–266. McGraw-Hill, New York.
44. Manning, W. H., and DuBois, P. H. (1962). *Psychol. Rep* **3**, Monogr. Suppl. V18.
45. McCloy, C. H., and Young, N. D. (1954). "Tests and Measurements in Health and Physical Education.' Appleton-Century-Crofts, New York.
46. McNemar, Q. (1958). *Educ. Psychol. Meas.* **18**, 47–55.
47. Olds, E. G., Mattson, T. B., and Odeh, R. E. (1956). "Notes on the Use of Transformations in the Analysis of Variance." WADC Tech. Rep. 56-308, Wright Air Development Center, Ohio.
48. Pillai, K. C. S., and Al-Ani, S. (1967). "On Some Distribution Problems Concerning Characteristics Roots and Vectors in Multivariate Analysis," Mimeograph Ser. No. 123, Dept. of Statistics, Purdue Univ., Lafayette, Indiana.
49. Pillai, K. C. S., and Al-Ani, S. (1967). "On the Distributions of Some Functions of the Roots of a Covariance Matrix," Mimeograph Ser. No. 125, Dept. of Statistics, Purdue Univ., Lafayette, Indiana.
50. Pillai, K. C. S., and Jayachandran, K. (1968). *Biometrika* **55**, 353–378.
51. Roy, S. N. (1957). "Some Aspects of Multivariate Analysis." Wiley, New York.

52. Ryan, E. D. (1961). *Res. Quart.* **32**, 83–87.
53. Schutz, R. W. (1970). *Res. Quart.* **41**, 205–213.
54. Spearman, C. J. (1937). *Educ. Psychol.* **28**, 629–631.
55. Thurstone, L. L. (1931). *J. Soc. Psychol.* **2**, 230–235.
56. Thurstone, L. L. (1948). "Primary Mental Abilities," Psychometric Lab. Res. Rep. No. 50, Univ. of Chicago, Chicago, Illinois.
57. Tucker, L. R. (1960). "Determination of Generalized Learning Curves by Factor Analysis," Tech. Rep. Educ. Testing Service, Princeton, New Jersey.
58. Tukey, J. W. (1949). *Biometrics* **5**, 232–242.
59. Whitley, J. D., and Smith, L. E. (1963). *Res. Quart.* **34**, 248–249.
60. Winer, B. (1962). "Statistical Principles in Experimental Design." McGraw-Hill, New York.
61. Woodrow, H. (1938). *J. Educ. Psychol.* **29**, 215–230.

Author Index

Numbers in parentheses are reference numbers and indicate that an author's work is referred to although his name is not cited in the text. Numbers in italics show the page on which the complete reference is listed.

A

Abarquez, R. F., 333(53), *335*
Abbot, R. R., 229(1), *246*
Abbott, H. G., 287, *307*
Abbott, L. C., 259, 274(30), 275, *284*
Abel, W. H., 384, *390*
Abramson, D. E., 298, *307*
Ackerman, K. J., 84(75), *100*
Adamek, J. A., 59(59), 61(59), *70*
Adams, F. H., 126(2), 134, *150*
Adams, R. D., 94(1), *98*
Adams, W. C., 143, *150*
Adler, C. E., *246*
Adrian, E. D., 191, *214*, 260(1), *283*, 341 (1), *359*
Adrian, M. J., 131(73), 137, *152*, 241, *246*, 342(2, 7), 347(3), 348(82), 353, 356 (109), 357(2), 358(8, 10), *359*, *361*, *362*, *363*
Adye, J. C., 292(170), *312*
Aghemo, P., 314(91, 94), 317(91), 323 (90, 92), 324(92), 326(92), 329(90), 330(90), 331(92), *336*, *337*
Ahlborg, B., 65(1), *68*
Ahrens, R. A., 106, 114(40), *120*, *121*
Ahstrom, J. P., 294, *307*
Akers, F. R., 327(26), 328(26), *335*
Al-Ani, S., 395(48, 49), 408(49), 416(48, 49), *418*
Albright, D., 291, *309*
Aldinger, E. E., 106, 111(24), *121*
Allen, C. L., 126(71), 133(10, 70), 139 (10), *150*, *152*
Allen, J. C., 294(3), *307*
Alley, R. H., Jr., 301, *307*
Alleyia, J., 319(101), 323(101), 326(101), 327(101), 328(101), 329(101), *337*
Allman, F. L., Jr., 287, *307*
Alspaugh, J. W., 166(131), *186*, 324, *337*

Altfillisch, J., 223, *246*
Althauser, R. P., 385(2), *390*
Alyea, E. P., 288, *307*
Amano, K., 128(53), *152*
Amarasingham, C. R., 3(43), *41*
Amelar, R. D., 288, *307*
Andersen, K. L., 126, 127(40), 129(40), 130, 131(40), *150*, *151*, 320(1), 322 (1), 327(1), *334*
Anderson, B. D., 303(97), *310*
Anderson, C. C., 348, *359*
Anderson, E., 327(87), *336*
Anderson, J. T., 115(15), 119(15), *120*
Anderson, N. M., 221(5), 222(5), *246*
Anderson, V. L., 407, *417*
Andres, R., 25(1), *39*
Anscombe, F. J., 374, 381, 382, *390*
Antel, J., 126(26), 127(26), *151*
Antine, B. E., 301, *312*
Arcelli, E., 208(5), *214*, 222(32), *248*
Archibald, L. D., 131(79), *152*
Arcos, J. C., 61, *68*
Arguedas, J. A., 292(176), *312*
Argus, M. F., 61(2), *68*
Armstrong, B. W., 323(140), *338*
Armstrong, R., 329(105), *337*
Armstrong, R. B., 2(51), 3(51, 53, 55), 4(2, 54), 38(51), *39*, *41*
Arnold, D. O., 388(4), *390*
Arnold, H., 7(3), *39*
Arsenault, A. S., 244(6), *246*
Artus, M. A., 246(7), *247*
Asa, M. M., 97, *101*, 355(72), 356(72), *361*
Ashton, H., 297, *307*
Ashton, T. E. J., 358, *362*
Asmussen, E., 18, 20(5), 35, *39*, 266(2), *283*, 330, *334*

421

C

Cader, G., 25(1), *39*

Cain, D. F., 6(19), *40*

Cain, R. L., 286(68), *309*

Callahan, W. T., 304(29), *308*

Calvin, S., 84, *99*

Cameron, B. M., 304, *308*

Campbell, D. E., 167(18), 172(22), 180 (108), *183, 186,* 202(44), *216*

Campbell, D. T., 371(79), *392,* 398(10), *417*

Campbell, R. L., 84(22), 85, *99*

Campney, H. K., 166(19), *183*

Canary, J. J., 118(4), *120*

Cape, R. F., 294(54), *309*

Capen, E. K., 76, 88, *99*

Cardus, C., 327(87), *336*

Carlson, F. D., 6(20), *40*

Carlson, L. A., 20, *40,* 55(34), *69*

Carlson, L. D., 50(26), *69*

Carlson, R. E., 237, *248*

Carlsöö, S., 265(15), 266(16), 279(3), 280 (3), *283,* 353(24), *360*

Carlsten, A., 25(22), *40*

Carns, M. L., 224(114), 225(114), *252*

Carpenter, D. O., 20(62), *41,* 260(28), *284*

Carrow, R., 59(23), 60(23), 61(23), *69*

Carrow, R. E., 96, *99*

Carter, J. E. L., 110, 119(19), *121,* 173, 178, 179, *183,* 324(78), *336*

Carter, V. A., 229(31), *248*

Cary, G. R., 287, *308*

Casner, S. W., 172, *183*

Casscells, S. W., 291, *308*

Cassel, J. C., 155(79), *185*

Cattell, T. B., 393(11), 394(11), 396(11), 397(11, 12, 13), 398, 400(11), 405, 410, 416, *417*

Cavagna, G. A., 208, 209, *214, 215,* 222, *248*

Cavilieri, R., 286(49), *308*

Cederquist, D. C., 111(52), 114(52), *122,* 136(80), *152,* 179(163), *187*

Cernak, V., 134(66), *152*

Cerretelli, P., 5(107), 6(107), 11(93), 19 (94), 25(94), 32(23), 34, *40, 42, 43,* 64(82), *71,* 316(93), 318(28, 41), 319 (28), 323(92), 324(92), 326(92), 331 (92), *335, 337*

Chadwick, A. W., 230, *248*

Chamberlain, D. A., 117(66), *122*

Chambers, R. L., 288(19), *308*

Chance, B., 63(11, 12, 13), *68*

Chao, E. Y. S., 208(36), *215,* 356(25, 76), *360, 361*

Chapler, C. K., 62(14), *68*

Chapman, C. B., 46(91), 47(91), 48(91), 66(91), *71,* 158(141), 164(141), 165 (141), 168(141), 175(141), *187,* 322 (119), 326(99), *337*

Chapman, E. C., 147, *151*

Chase, G. A., 325, 326(29), 330(29), *335*

Cheffers, J. T. F., 243(34), *248*

Chepinoga, O. P., 37(24), *40*

Cheremisinov, V. N., 317(132), *338*

Chiang, B., 289(146), *311*

Chichester, C. O., 300(169), *312*

Christensen, E. H., 48(15), 53(15), 65 (16), *68, 69,* 166(24), 180, 181(23), *183,* 320(8), *334*

Christensen, J. H., 106(63), 111(63), *122*

Chui, E. F., 80, 84(26), 85, 87, *99*

Cillo, A. R., 167(12), *183*

Cimerman, V. J., 348, *360*

Clark, B. L., 297, *308*

Clark, T. W., 286, *308*

Clarke, D. H., 76(30), 78(28), 86(29, 30), 87, 89, *99, 102*

Clarke, H. H., 73(32, 33, 34), 93, *99,* 202, *215*

Clarke, K. C., 307, *308*

Clarkson, B. H., 219(155, 157), *254,* 344 (92, 93), 348, *362*

Clarys, J. P., 345(27), *360*

Clausen, J. P., 48(17), 50(17, 18), *69,* 329(30), *335*

Clayton, I. A., 224, *248*

Clayton, M. L., 296(112), *310*

Cleland, T., 145, *151*

Clemence, W. J., 240, *248*

Close, J. R., 353(28), *360*

Clouse, F. C., 220(37), 221, 222(37), *248*

427

Subject Index

A

Acclimatization, to heat, 144–145
Accommodating resistance exercise, *see* Isokinetic exercise
Acid–base balance, 31–34
  maximal work, changes during, 31–34
Activities
  archery, 167
  badminton, 167
  basketball, 164, 167
  bicycling, 157, 166
  bowling, 167
  calisthenics, 166
  dancing, 167
  football, 167
  golf, 166, 167
  handball, 167
  rope skipping, 167
  running, 157, 166, 167
  skiing, 157, 166
  soccer, 164, 167
  swimming, 157, 166
  tennis, 167
  weight lifting, 167
  wrestling, 167
Adenylate charge, 10
  glycolysis, regulation of, 10
Adipose tissue
  cellularity, 112–113
  changes with weight loss, 114
  methods of assessment, 112–113
ADP, 63–64
  ATP synthesis, 63, 314, 316
Adrenodemedullectomy, 10
  glycolysis, effect on, 10
Aerobic, type of training, 181
Aerobic capacity, *see also* Oxygen uptake, maximal
  alterations with training, 46–48, 53, 65–68, 139–141, 158–165, 168–170, 174–178, 179–182, 322
  assessment of, 322–329
  in athletes, 319
  factors influencing the measurement of, 322

in females, 126–130, 133–141, 319–320
  influence of body composition on, 127, 130, 134, 320
  prediction of, 329–332
  variations with age, 133–136, 319–320
  variations with sex, 319–320
Aerobic power, *see* Aerobic capacity; Oxygen uptake, maximal
Age
  importance in exercise prescription, 156, 157, 167, 174–177
  physiological variations with, 132–136, 140–141, 159, 174–177, 180
Altitude, and physical performance in women, 147–148
AMP, 3′,5′-cyclic, 7–10
  electrical stimulation and, 7
  glycolysis, regulation of, 9–10
Amplifiers, electromyographic, 261
Anaerobic, type of training, 181
Anaerobic capacity
  maximal valves, 316
  measurement of, 317
  trained vs. untrained, 316–317
Appetite
  effect of exercise on, 104–107
  stimulation, 104
  suppression, 106
Athletes
  female, 136–139, 164, 179–180
  male, 156, 164, 165, 166, 170, 176, 182
ATP
  enzyme regulation, role in, 7–10
  muscle content in, 4–6, 48
  muscular contraction and, 1–2, 4–7, 13, 19, 21–22, 26–29, 314–316
  synthesis, 52, 63, 314–316
  training and, 39

B

Bedrest, *see also* Detraining
  changes in work capacity with, 164–165
Beta adrenergic blockade, 10–11
  anaerobic metabolism and, 10–11
Biomechanics, 339–343